WHEN HELL CAME TO
SHARPSBURG

The Battle of Antietam and Its Impact
on the Civilians Who Called It Home

Steven Cowie

SB

Savas Beatie
California

Library of Congress Cataloging-in-Publication Data

Names: Cowie, Steven, author.
Title: When Hell Came to Sharpsburg: The Battle of Antietam and Its Impact on the Civilians Who Called it Home / Steven Cowie.
Other titles: Battle of Antietam and Its Impact on the Civilians Who Called it Home
Description: El Dorado Hills, CA: Savas Beatie, [2022] | Includes bibliographical references and index. | Summary: "When Hell Came to Sharpsburg: The Battle of Antietam and its Impact on the Civilians Who Called it Home investigates how Antietam wreaked emotional, physical, and financial havoc on the people of Sharpsburg, Maryland. Author Steven Cowie explores the savage struggle and explains how soldiers stripped the community of resources and spread diseases. Cowie also examines the civilians' struggle to recover from their unexpected and often devastating losses"— Provided by publisher.
Identifiers: LCCN 2022006590 | ISBN 9781611215908 (hardcover) | ISBN 9781611215915 (ebook)
Subjects: LCSH: Antietam, Battle of, Md., 1862. | Maryland—History—Civil War, 1861-1865 | United States—History—Civil War, 1861-1865—Social aspects. | Sharpsburg (Md.)—History—19th century.
Classification: LCC E474.65 .C69 2022 | DDC 973.7/336—dc23/eng/20220210
LC record available at https://lccn.loc.gov/2022006590

First Edition, First Printing

Savas Beatie
989 Governor Drive, Suite 102
El Dorado Hills, CA 95762
916-941-6896 / sales@savasbeatie.com

Savas Beatie titles are available at special discounts for bulk purchases in the United States. Contact us for more details.

Proudly published, printed, and warehoused in the United States of America.

For Alexandra

Contents

Photographs have been placed throughout the book
for the convenience of the reader.

Foreword

Antietam is personal to me.

My mother, you see, was born a Poffenberger. You will visit with Poffenbergers in these pages. Every chapter, in fact, reveals Poffenberger stories. You will experience their war with war. These are my uncles, my aunts, my cousins. Distant family, indeed; and distanced in time. But I am a Poffenberger.

Antietam is in my genes.

Aficionados who share study of the Civil War often gather at Civil War Round Table meetings and inquire: Did you have an ancestor in the war? The query resonates as if a current event, though nearly 160 years has passed since civil war erupted.

My response perplexes people. "Kind of," I'll say. "What does that mean?" retorts the inquisitor. "My ancestors didn't fight the war. Instead, *they hosted it*."

This is a book about those who hosted the Civil War. The guests were not invited. Rather, they were invaders. All Union and Confederate soldiers at Antietam were unwelcome intruders. In fairness, the two most powerful armies in North America did not target the residents of the Antietam Valley. Happenstance forced their tectonic collision. The ensuing earthquake killed and wounded more American soldiers than any single day in American history. The quake's aftershocks, however, reverberated across generations.

Often we forget that a battlefield, first and foremost, is someone's home. Every battle is juxtaposition over a livelihood. Armies arrive, fight, and depart. Battle days are finite. But a battlefield forges itself into the permanent heart of the land and sears into the souls of its caretakers. Too often, we extract the civilians. Our focus on military matters fails to appreciate that not all casualties wear uniforms. We memorialize our battlefields, but we subdue the memories of the hosts.

Steven Cowie resurrects the memory of Antietam's resident guardians.

Steve's recitation of Antietam's citizens will make you shudder. You will feel their burden; you will sense their tragedy. You will experience their devastation; you will share their losses. You will curse in frustration; you will scream in anger. You will shake in their disarray; you will quake in their disharmony.

Cowie captivates your conscience. His untold tales and graphic descriptions are powerfully presented—so much so that you transcend into a Sharpsburg resident. You meld into one with them. The war will violate you. Shatter your peace; break you into pieces. It steals your fortune; robs your dreams. War kidnaps your property and your life; and your government will hold you as ransom.

"We have been invaded—our fences burned—our wheat crops obliterated from the face of the earth—our stock driven off—our farms and houses pillaged," proclaimed the area's leading newspaper. "Many of us are ruined. We are naked in property as we were in the flesh when we were born into the world. Cannot the Government make some provision for us?"

The government's response—or lack thereof—forms the basis for much of Cowie's investigation. The United States Army, and eventually the U.S. Congress, recognized that private property had been appropriated or destroyed on behalf of the Union war effort. Provisions for payment were ordered or legislated—but only if supported with mandated paperwork. Fortunately for historians, the government excels at manufacturing paperwork. Skid loads of Civil War-era documents are housed at the National Archives (NARA) in Washington, D.C., including civilian claims for war damages and their requested compensation.

Antietam Valley residents impart a trove within this massive war claims collection. Existence of their claims has been known for decades, but historians have largely ignored it due to difficult accessibility, no digitized or microfilmed copies, and endless transcription of nineteenth-century scribbles. Mr. Cowie cast these obstacles aside. Motivated by the untapped potential within this reservoir of war claims, the author embarked on a multi-year exploration in the secluded vaults of NARA, sacrificing daylight for enlightenment scouring nearly 200 war claims.

The result is a study unmatched. *When Hell Came to Sharpsburg* is the most comprehensive compendium and scholarly dissertation on the Civil War's effect upon Antietam's citizenry.

This does not diminish the fine Antietam civilian studies of Kathleen Ernst's *Too Afraid to Cry* (2007) or Ted Alexander's essay "Destruction, Disease and Death" from the special Antietam issue of the journal *Civil War Regiments* (1998). Both are significant contributions to Civil War social history, and both established new understandings of epic struggles of survival in Antietam's aftermath. Cowie builds upon their foundational work, masterfully weaving details of everyday life into a holistic quilt that rips and shreds into everyday misery.

It is this formulation that differentiates Cowie's scholarship. His study examines the effects of war as an *ecosystem of expansive horrors*. In other words, everything bad makes everything worse. His approach is Newtonian, i.e., every action generates a reaction. It is hard to examine everything, and historians often resort to cherry-picking evidence. Cowie rejects this temptation. His ecosystem is holistic. His narrative interweaves interdependence between life and land. He integrates relationships between natural resources and health and disease. The author intersects social and political intercourse with the dynamics of government action and inaction. He explains economics as agricultural practices (so familiar to these characters and so foreign to us) that define life and death financial decisions. Cowie combines all into a comprehensive web that personalizes the civilian drama and trauma of Antietam.

Fence rails—yes, simple fence rails—present a sample of Cowie's ecosystem approach. What's important, you ask, about fence rails? First, nothing is or was more ubiquitous upon Antietam's landscape than fencing. Fences defined property boundaries and kept livestock within, and livestock without. Fences protected yards, gardens, fields, and orchards. Fences bordered turnpikes, roads, lanes, and walkways. Thousands of rails, nay tens of thousands, crisscrossed Antietam's hills and dales.

No rail existed independent of the ecosystem that created it. Consider the production process. First the forest, followed by the farmer as logger, transport to the sawmill, rail-splitting, return transport to the farm, and finally construction. During a time when the average American earned $1.00 a day in wages, one fence panel cost $1.50. This is understandable considering the labor, time, and brute mechanics required to generate one rail.

What happens, as a farmer, if your fences disappear? It is life-altering. Livestock is not constrained. Crop fields and orchards are not secured. Fields cannot be planted, and yards and gardens are left unenclosed. Roadways are less distinguishable. Your existence changes dramatically. "[F]arms which one month ago were in a high state of culture, are now to be seen without a sign of cultivation," recorded one Antietam witness. "[E]verywhere with rails and fences almost entirely burned for wood."

Accounts of narrative nature are familiar, but Cowie's ecosystem model goes beyond quotations. Cowie quantifies the loss. The author methodically examined 75 war claims, searching diligently for fence rails and fence posts devoured as firewood by the voracious U.S. army occupation. Cowie added the results: *615,885 rails and posts destroyed.* Having problems relating? Try this: stretched rail tip to rail tip, that is enough fencing to drive from Washington, D.C. to Wichita, Kansas!

Surely the government would compensate the loyal farmers of Sharpsburg for such incomprehensible loss. Western Maryland was, after all, strong Union country. Allegiance to the boys in blue permeated almost every household. Losses of such magnitude—caused by the 41-day post-battle Sharpsburg-area occupation by three corps of the Army of the Potomac—certainly demanded recompense. Certainly.

*   *   *

Antietam boasts uniqueness amongst battlefields on Northern soil. The U.S. army remained stationed there after the battle ended. Not so at Gettysburg (1863) and Monocacy (1864), where the contesting armies abandoned those battlefields (except for medical personnel and wounded) soon after the fighting ended. For six weeks in the fall of 1862, however, Sharpsburg swelled into the second largest city in Maryland—temporary public housing for nearly 45,000 Union soldiers. The region imploded.

Water proved problematic for this occupation city. Its existence determined existence. Every spring, every well, every cistern on every farm, and every lot in town became a target for thirsty soldiers. Alarmed civilians, aware that a severe summer drought constrained their supply and endangered subterranean reservoirs, locked or removed pump handles to prevent bleeding wells dry. Worse than water scarcity was water pollution.

Cowie's ecosystem model is especially effective here. He begins with geology. Strange to encounter a geology lesson in a Civil War book, but this is the brilliance of Cowie's analysis. Citing scientific studies in interesting fashion (Cowie excels at melding science with history), the author explains the phenomenon of Karst—soluble limestone with its myriad of ground surface openings, unstable uprisings, and underground cavities. Upon this, he superimposes rainfall that drains human feces, human urine, and decomposing human bodies (near 6,000) *into the drinking water.* This will make you ill.

If not, Cowie further explains the effect of the equine population on the liquid of life. Nearly 33,000 horses and mules occupy the Antietam Valley with the Army of the Potomac. Cowie details how each creature produces an average of 31 pounds of feces and 2.4 gallons of urine *daily.* Much of this ends up leaching into the drinking water. The result is rampant disease. Diarrhea and dysentery sicken hundreds of soldiers and civilians. Worst of all, typhoid fever runs rampant. The Antietam Valley becomes "a gigantic petri dish."

A pest we have all gone to war against—the common housefly—helps spread the disease. Cowie observes that the housefly's "habit of walking, feeding, and breeding on manure, human excrement, garbage, and carrion makes it an ideal disease vector." Consider this the next time a fly lands on your outdoor barbecue.

Overriding this putrid environment, literally, was the air. Since the germ had not yet been discovered by medical science, common belief held that foul air was a principal contributor to pervasive sickness. The stench of so many half-buried dead men and rotting horse carcasses, even a month after they fell, permeated every pore of the living. "We couldn't eat a good meal," recalled resident Alex Davis, "and we had to shut the house up just as tight as we could at night to keep out that odor." Davis recoiled: "We couldn't stand it, and the first thing in the morning when I rolled out of bed I'd have to take a drink of whiskey. If I didn't I'd throw up before I got my clothes all on."

Throwing up, unfortunately, debilitated and dehydrated hundreds of soldiers and civilians. Who was treating these infirm? We have heard of the heroics of Clara Barton at Antietam, but what of Dr. Augustin A. Biggs?

Mr. Cowie discovered a treasure of Dr. Biggs's ledgers and daybooks preserved within the remarkable history collection of the Western Maryland Room of the Washington County Free Library. Obtained by my father, John C. Frye, curator there for 52 years, the Biggs artifacts documented the local doctor's day-by-day appointments and cases as he tended to Sharpsburg's civilian trauma.

Cowie is indefatigable in tracking Biggs and his patients, so much so that you feel like you are walking and observing astride Biggs during his urgent house calls. Particularly impressive is the author's statistical analysis comparing Biggs's patients before and after Antietam. Cowie proves a direct connection between diseases caused by the Antietam battle and the subsequent weeks-long occupation. Through careful examination of Biggs's meticulous notations, Cowie discovers not only the types of resident ailments, but also Dr. Biggs's treatments. Most fascinating is that the doctor's patient load doubles after Antietam—from 7.20 patients a day before the battle to 15.94 patients a day by the last week of October. Precision analysis by Cowie of this genre permeates the pages of *When Hell Came to Sharpsburg*.

I do not like statistics. How can you have .94 of a patient? I assiduously avoided a 400-level statistics class so that I could graduate. Historians and statistics is proverbial right-brain left-brain warfare. I do, however, admire Mr. Cowie for his deliberation of and patience with statistics. His indomitable calculations of thousands upon thousands of numbers within the Sharpsburg-area war claims form the foundation for his ecosystem model.

Cowie employs stats to humanize the aftermath of Antietam. This seems counterintuitive. Numbers are cold, harsh, and rational. Frightened humans solicit our warmth, compassion, and charity. But Cowie's additions and multiplications reveal the enormity of the Antietam disaster by converting numbers into emotional connections. When Dunker farmer and pacifist Samuel Mumma drags 55 dead horses from near his burned house and barn into the East Woods to torch the carcasses, you feel the man's strain and drain. When Henry Rohrback, near Burnside Bridge, spies U.S. soldiers swiping 400 bushels of his apples "from as fine as orchard loaded with fruit as I ever saw," you see his tears. When Joseph Poffenberger helplessly watches his seven cattle, 15 sheep, and 20 swine "all taken by the troops," you share his pain. "He was so distressed he could not eat."

These represent individual losses. Most powerful, though, are the collective losses. Through brilliant detective-like evidence gathering, Cowie compares war claim damages against the 1860 Agricultural Schedule for the Sharpsburg District. This yields impressive data. For example, during the U.S. occupation the army slaughtered 954 swine (war claims total), which is 45% of the total 2,117 pigs enumerated in the 1860 schedule. The author uses similar comparatives for wheat, corn, hay, straw, sheep, chickens, cattle, horses, potatoes, butter, fruit, and cured meats. If the army could eat it or use it, it disappeared.

Army officers knew their quartermasters were confiscating from Antietam Valley residents. When Joseph Poffenberger "made complaint about the taking" to Gen. George Meade (who had launched attacks from Poffenberger's farm and then occupied it), Meade instructed the distraught landowner "to make out a bill of all the property taken and that the Government would compensate him for it." Meade was right and the government did pay—*in 1899*!

Antietam-area war claims are both blessing and curse. For historians like Cowie and for aficionados like us, they are a blessing that provide exhaustive details into everyday life in the Antietam Valley. They are a curse, however, that tortured nineteenth-century Sharpsburg residents, some for more than 50 years. Their claims, in essence, became chains.

Cowie excels at explaining the complex and convoluted war claims process, making sense of a system that reeked of nonsense. No damage caused by battle, for example, could be included in a claim. Samuel Mumma's house and barn were burned on the day of the main battle and were thus excluded from compensation. Congress eliminated settlements "for the occupation of or injury to real estate . . . [and] the consumption, appropriation, or destruction of or damage to personal property." Does anything remain for the petitioner? What about pillaging?

Congress discovered this loophole, and barred claims "for damages or for losses sustained by thefts or depredations committed by troops."

Should an aggrieved civilian find some category not exempt from petition, the law required him or her to: 1) Obtain a certificate from a U.S. officer vouching for your loss; and 2) Prove your loyalty to the United States. The first requirement proved a difficult hurdle. Many officers were killed in battle or hard to track down during the postwar period. Proof of loyalty was less strenuous, but still onerous. At least two witnesses needed to affirm an applicant's allegiance with an affidavit before the local justice of the peace. Even with this, a single personal enemy could sabotage your loyalty, or the U.S. officers investigating the claim could suspect, and thus deny, your loyalty—if you were a Democrat.

Your blood will boil as Cowie leads you through claims and outcomes. You will feel the emotions of the claimants—frustration, anger, desperation, despondency. The government you supported will abandon you, or at best, minimize you. For many Antietam Valley residents, perpetual debt became life's lifeline. For too many others, bankruptcy ruined them.

"The county will not recover from the effects of this heart-rending disaster for years to come," lamented a local newspaper. "[P]robably not in our day and generation." Steve Cowie's work proves the editor correct.

War is a human tornado.

Dennis E. Frye
Burnside's Headquarters
Raleigh Showman's "Antietam Farm"

I dedicate this Foreword to my mother,
Janice Marie Poffenberger Frye.

"Ravages of War"

On Monday, September 15, 1862, approximately 125,000 troops descended upon the Antietam Valley, along with cannon, supply wagons, and horse-drawn ambulances. Previously, the farmers and residents had led a quiet, uneventful life. That was all about to change.

On the evening of Tuesday, September 16, and all day Wednesday, September 17, the Army of Northern Virginia and the Army of the Potomac clashed on the hills of Sharpsburg and along Antietam Creek. It was the 75th anniversary of the signing of the Constitution, and now the fate of the nation hung in the balance. By the end of the day, 23,000 young Americans had been killed, wounded, or were missing/captured. It was and remains the bloodiest single day in American history. President Lincoln used the strategic victory to issue the Emancipation Proclamation.

Many books have been written on the battle, and rightfully so. In the volume you now hold, Steven Cowie brings to life the story of the farmers and villagers who were eyewitnesses and experienced their own horrific 9/11. *When Hell Came to Sharpsburg* tells what it was like for the Millers, Poffenbergers, Mummas, Pipers, Rohrbacks, and others. Cowie gleaned the material from scores of primary sources and extensively researched the landowners.

In "you are there" moments, we see tents and campfires dotting the landscape, fences disappear as fuel for campfires, and hogs, cattle, and chickens consumed as supplemental rations for hungry soldiers. We read of the anxiety of the civilians, the barking of excited dogs, and the crying of fearful children. Overnight their world changed. Suddenly, the barns, houses, churches, and nearly every other building became a hospital. Blood drips from the floorboards of ambulances onto the floors of homes and barns. Those who lived through the trauma of those September days carried the memories to their graves. They experienced and lived with the true ravages of war long after the armies were done with them.

Steven Cowie brings these events to life in a moving, dramatic manner. This book is another must-have for those who seek to learn about the days of old and remember the years of past generations.

John W. Schildt
Sharpsburg, Maryland
Author of *Drums Along the Antietam*

Acknowledgments

This project took fifteen years to complete, and I am grateful to many people who helped along the way. To anyone I have forgotten to acknowledge, thank you, and please accept my sincere apologies.

First, I would like to recognize Kathleen Ernst, whose book, *Too Afraid to Cry: Maryland Civilians in the Antietam Campaign*, inspired me to learn more about the people of Sharpsburg during the Civil War.

I respectfully acknowledge many authors, park rangers, and licensed guides who educated me during countless tours of the Antietam National Battlefield, South Mountain, and regional towns impacted by the 1862 Maryland Campaign.

My appreciation also goes to local members of the community and descendants of Sharpsburg's 1862 residents for their assistance with my research: Jo Ann Abell, Joanne and Paul Breitenbach, Lou and Regina Clark, Troy and Emily Cool, Linda Irvin-Craig, Jodi Knode-Decker, Robert Eschbach, Mark Fedorka, Kim Grove, Jim Hade, Christine Leddon, Erin Moshier, Sandy and Brian O'Neil, the late Earl Roulette, Cindy Spong, Don Stoops, Marcia Swain, Chris Vincent, and Betsy Webb.

I extend my gratitude to the staff at various repositories for their help in locating sources archived in special collections: Diana Bachman, Joseph Berger, Katie Blum, Meredith Gozo, Frances Marshall, Morgan Swan, and employees at the Maryland State Archives.

Thanks, also, to many persons who took the time to answer my research inquiries: Emilie Amt, John Banks, Jeff Brown, Jim Buchanan, Dr. John Coski, Anna Cueto, Kimberly Gabriel, Dr. Jonathan S. Jones, Julie Mueller, Dr. Michael T. Osterholm, Kevin Pawlak, Paula Reed, Jeff Semler, Ron Stonelake, Keven Walker, Edie Wallace, Ian Workman, Adam Zimmerli, and members of Brian Downey's former forum, Talk Antietam.

I received valuable advice and assistance from numerous people to whom I am tremendously thankful: Michael Arant, Alan Axelrod, the late Doug Bast, Ed

Beeler, Reverend Delancy Catlett, Susie Cramer, Jane Custer, Joseph Davis, Dr. Lisa Tendrich Frank, Sylvia Frye, Daria Gasparini, Sue Gemeny, Cindy Harkcom, Melody Jackson, Shannon Leidig, Skye Loyd, John Nelson, Leon Reed, Terry Reimer, and J. Scott Shipe. Special thanks go to Brad Toole, who shared his extensive research on Sharpsburg's town lots. I am immensely grateful to Wayne Wolf for proofreading the manuscript and Hal Jespersen for creating maps for this project.

I wish to express my sincere appreciation to Elizabeth Howe and John Frye at the Western Maryland Room, and Stephanie Gray and the late Ted Alexander at the Antietam National Battlefield's library. All enthusiastically provided books, manuscripts, and vertical files during my visits to the repositories.

I am deeply indebted to the archivists at the National Archives in Washington, D.C., namely Deanne Blanton, Robert Ellis, Danielle Ireland, and Trevor Plante, for helping me unearth a trove of war claims and congressional cases relating to the battle of Antietam.

I would like to thank several esteemed historians for taking time from their busy schedules to read my manuscript and provide advance praise: Joan E. Cashin, Thomas G. Clemens, D. Scott Hartwig, and James M. McPherson. Alexander B. Rossino corrected several errors and kindly offered constructive advice. Special gratitude is owed to Dennis E. Frye for scrutinizing my manuscript, making valuable suggestions, and generously offering to write the foreword.

A huge thanks to Vernell and Tim Doyle for supporting my research from the very beginning, as well as providing leads, materials, and photographs, and accommodating me at their guest home in Sharpsburg. I have also greatly benefited from the wisdom and advice of John W. Schildt, who shared a wealth of information on local farmsteads, accompanied me on tours of private properties near the Antietam battlefield, and encouraged me to write this book.

To Theodore P. Savas of Savas Beatie: I am incredibly grateful for your dedication to this project, and it is a true honor to be associated with such a class-act publisher. Without your support, my research would not have seen the light of day. I would also like to thank the staff at Savas Beatie—Veronica Kane, Lee Merideth, Sarah Keeney, Sarah Closson, Lisa Murphy, and Donna Endacott—for their dedication and work in producing and marketing my book.

Last, I thank my parents, siblings, and friends for their love and encouragement, and express heartfelt gratitude to my wife and daughters for allowing me to dedicate so many years to this passion project.

List of Abbreviations

ANB: Antietam National Battlefield

ANBL: Antietam National Battlefield Library

BA: Clifton Johnson, *Battleground Adventures: The Stories of Dwellers on the Scenes of Conflict in Some of the Most Notable Battles of the Civil War* (New York, 1915).

BOA: Oliver T. Reilly, *The Battlefield of Antietam* (Hagerstown, MD, 1906).

C & O: Chesapeake and Ohio Canal

CWSS: Civil War Soldiers and Sailors System database, National Park Service

HEPL: Harris-Elmore Public Library, Grace Luebke Local History Room, Elmore, OH

HFTL: *Herald of Freedom and Torch Light*

HTL: *Herald and Torch Light*

HWC: Thomas J. C. Williams, *A History of Washington County, Maryland: From the Earliest Settlements to the Present Time, Including a History of Hagerstown*, 2 vols. (Baltimore, 1906).

HWM: J. Thomas Scharf, *History of Western Maryland: Being a History of Frederick, Montgomery, Carroll, Washington, Allegany, and Garrett Counties From the Earliest Period to the Present Day; Including Biographical Sketches of Their Representative Men*, 2 vols. (Philadelphia, 1882)

LC: Library of Congress

MHT: Maryland Historic Trust

NA: National Archives and Records Administration, Washington, D.C.

NYHSM: New York Historical Society Museum & Library, Digital Collections

NYPL: New York Public Library

OR: *The War of the Rebellion: A Compilation of Official Records of the Union and Confederate Armies*, 128 vols. (Washington, DC, 1880–1901).

PPT: Samuel H. Williamson, "Purchasing Power Today of a U.S. Dollar Transaction in the Past," MeasuringWorth.com

RG: Record Group

SHS: Sharpsburg Historical Society

TATC: Kathleen A. Ernst, *Too Afraid to Cry: Maryland Civilians in the Antietam Campaign* (Mechanicsburg, PA, 2007)

UMLA: Upper Midwest Literary Archives, Elmer L. Andersen Library, University of Minnesota, Minneapolis, MN

USAMHI: United States Army Military History Institute

WCC: Samuel Webster Piper, *Washington County Cemeteries—Samuel Piper and the DAR*

WHILBR: Western Maryland Historic Library

WMR: John Clinton Frye Western Maryland Room

List of Maps

Overview of the 1862 Maryland Campaign

Overview of the Battle of Antietam

Wide View of the Sharpsburg Vicinity

1862 Sharpsburg Area Landowners (Northwest)

1862 Sharpsburg Area Landowners (Southwest) 1862 Sharpsburg Area Landowners (Northeast)

1862 Sharpsburg Area Landowners (Southeast)

1862 Sharpsburg Village Lots

Sharpsburg Village Lot Owners: September 1862

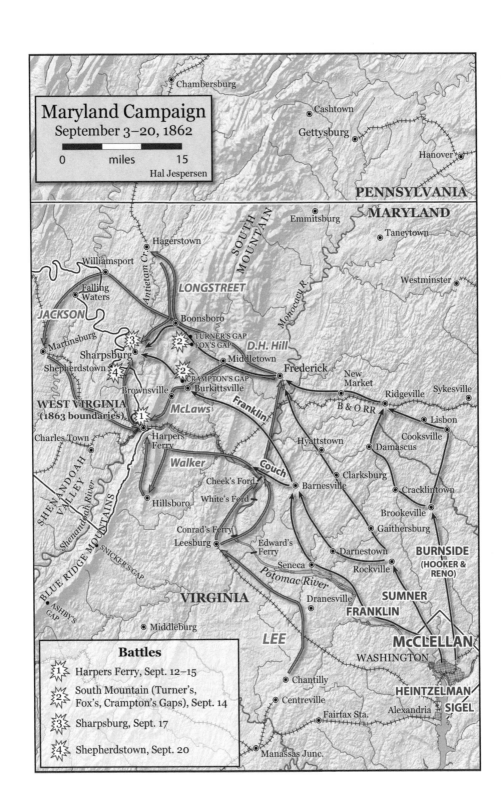

Maryland Campaign
September 3–20, 1862

0   miles   15

Hal Jespersen

PENNSYLVANIA

MARYLAND

Chambersburg

Cashtown

Gettysburg

Hanover

Emmitsburg

Taneytown

Westminster

SOUTH MOUNTAIN

Hagerstown

LONGSTREET

Williamsport

Antietam Cr

Falling Waters

JACKSON

Boonsboro

TURNER'S GAP
FOX'S GAP

D.H. Hill

Frederick

New Market

Ridgeville

Sykesville

Martinsburg

Sharpsburg

Middletown

B & O RR

Lisbon

Shepherdstown

CRAMPTON'S GAP

Cooksville

Burkittsville

Brownsville

McLaws

Franklin

Hyattstown

Damascus

WEST VIRGINIA
(1863 boundaries)

Charles Town

Harpers Ferry

Clarksburg

Cracklintown

Walker

Barnesville

Brookeville

Cheek's Ford

Gaithersburg

Hillsboro

White's Ford

SHENANDOAH VALLEY

Conrad's Ferry

Darnestown

BURNSIDE
(HOOKER & RENO)

Shenandoah River

Leesburg

Edward's Ferry

Seneca

Rockville

SUMNER

BLUE RIDGE MOUNTAINS

SNICKER'S GAP

Potomac River

Dranesville

FRANKLIN

ASHBY'S GAP

VIRGINIA

McCLELLAN

Middleburg

LEE

WASHINGTON

HEINTZELMAN

Chantilly

Centreville

SIGEL

Fairfax Sta.

Alexandria

Manassas Junc.

Battles

1. Harpers Ferry, Sept. 12–15

2. South Mountain (Turner's, Fox's, Crampton's Gaps), Sept. 14

3. Sharpsburg, Sept. 17

4. Shepherdstown, Sept. 20

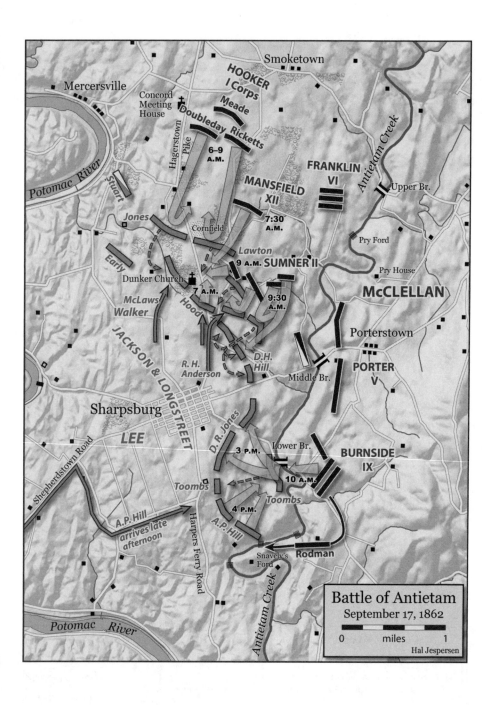

Battle of Antietam
September 17, 1862

0   miles   1

Hal Jespersen

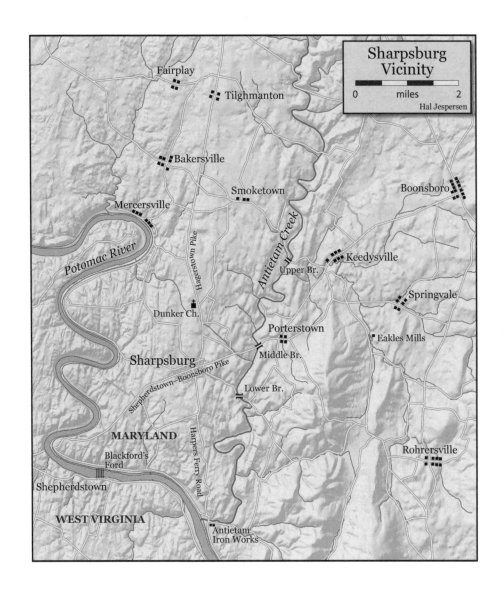

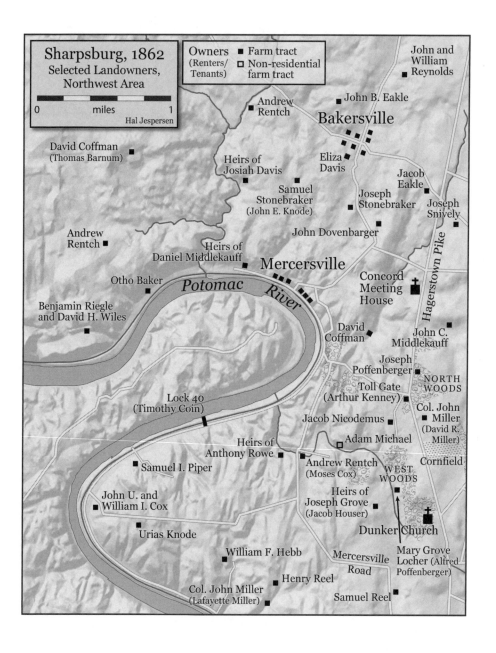

Sharpsburg, 1862
Selected Landowners, Northwest Area

Owners (Renters/Tenants) ■ Farm tract □ Non-residential farm tract

0 — miles — 1

Hal Jespersen

John and William Reynolds

David Coffman (Thomas Barnum)

Andrew Rentch

John B. Eakle

Bakersville

Heirs of Josiah Davis

Eliza Davis

Jacob Eakle

Samuel Stonebraker (John E. Knode)

Joseph Stonebraker

Joseph Snively

John Dovenbarger

Andrew Rentch

Heirs of Daniel Middlekauff

Mercersville

Concord Meeting House

Hagerstown Pike

Otho Baker

Potomac River

David Coffman

John C. Middlekauff

Benjamin Riegle and David H. Wiles

Joseph Poffenberger

NORTH WOODS

Toll Gate (Arthur Kenney)

Col. John Miller (David R. Miller)

Lock 40 (Timothy Coin)

Jacob Nicodemus

Adam Michael

Cornfield

Heirs of Anthony Rowe

Andrew Rentch (Moses Cox)

WEST WOODS

Samuel I. Piper

Heirs of Joseph Grove (Jacob Houser)

John U. and William I. Cox

Dunker Church

Urias Knode

William F. Hebb

Mercersville Road

Mary Grove Locher (Alfred Poffenberger)

Henry Reel

Col. John Miller (Lafayette Miller)

Samuel Reel

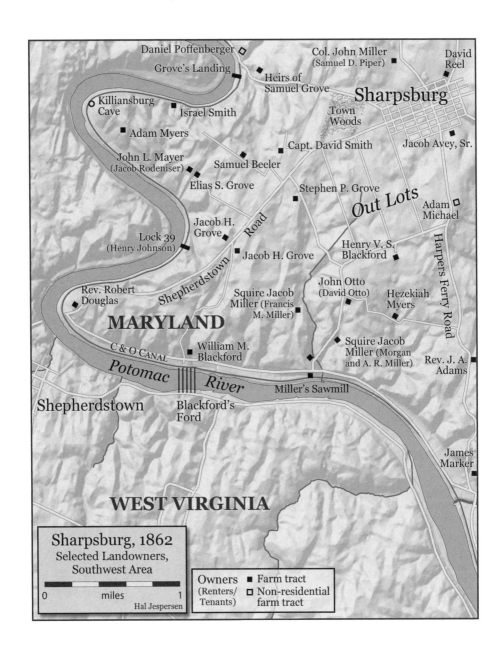

Daniel Poffenberger

Grove's Landing

Col. John Miller
(Samuel D. Piper)

David
Reel

Killiansburg
Cave

Israel Smith

Heirs of
Samuel Grove

Sharpsburg

Town
Woods

Adam Myers

Capt. David Smith

Jacob Avey, Sr.

John L. Mayer
(Jacob Rodeniser)

Samuel Beeler

Elias S. Grove

Stephen P. Grove

Out Lots

Adam
Michael

Jacob H.
Grove

Road

Lock 39
(Henry Johnson)

Jacob H. Grove

Henry V. S.
Blackford

Shepherdstown

Harpers Ferry Road

Rev. Robert
Douglas

John Otto
(David Otto)

Hezekiah
Myers

Squire Jacob
Miller (Francis
M. Miller)

MARYLAND

C & O CANAL

William M.
Blackford

Squire Jacob
Miller (Morgan
and A. R. Miller)

Rev. J. A.
Adams

Potomac River

Shepherdstown

Blackford's
Ford

Miller's Sawmill

James
Marker

WEST VIRGINIA

Sharpsburg, 1862
Selected Landowners,
Southwest Area

| 0 | miles | 1 |

Hal Jespersen

Owners
(Renters/
Tenants)

■ Farm tract
□ Non-residential
farm tract

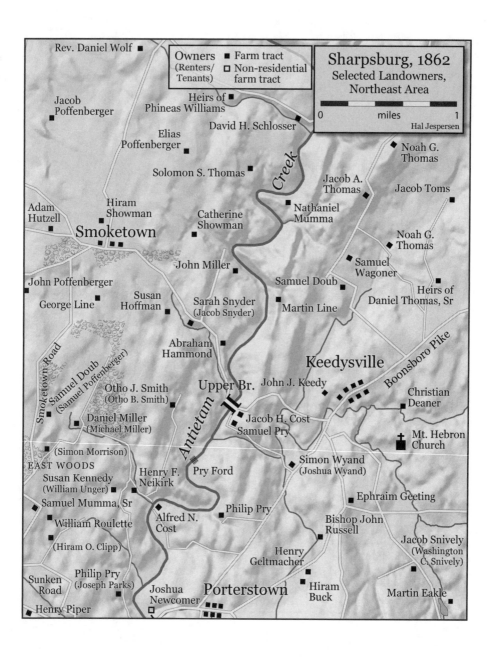

Rev. Daniel Wolf ■

Owners
(Renters/Tenants)
■ Farm tract
□ Non-residential farm tract

Sharpsburg, 1862
Selected Landowners,
Northeast Area

0   miles   1

Hal Jespersen

Jacob Poffenberger

Heirs of
Phineas Williams ■

David H. Schlosser

Noah G. Thomas ◆

Elias Poffenberger ■

Solomon S. Thomas ■

Jacob A. Thomas ■

Jacob Toms ■

Adam Hutzell ■

Hiram Showman

Catherine Showman ■

Nathaniel Mumma ■

Noah G. Thomas ◆

Smoketown

John Miller ■

Samuel Wagoner ■

John Poffenberger ■

Samuel Doub ■

Heirs of Daniel Thomas, Sr ■

George Line ■

Susan Hoffman ■

Sarah Snyder (Jacob Snyder) ■

Martin Line ■

Abraham Hammond ■

Keedysville

Samuel Doub (Samuel Poffenberger)

Otho J. Smith (Otho B. Smith) ■

Upper Br.

John J. Keedy ◆

Boonsboro Pike

Christian Deaner ■

Daniel Miller (Michael Miller) ■

Jacob H. Cost ■
Samuel Pry ■

Mt. Hebron Church ✝ ◼

(Simon Morrison)

EAST WOODS

Susan Kennedy (William Unger) ■

Henry F. Neikirk ■

Pry Ford

Simon Wyand (Joshua Wyand) ◆

Samuel Mumma, Sr ■

Ephraim Geeting ■

William Roulette ■

Alfred N. Cost ■

Philip Pry ■

Bishop John Russell ■

Jacob Snively (Washington C. Snively) ■

(Hiram O. Clipp) ■

Henry Geltmacher ■

Sunken Road ■

Philip Pry (Joseph Parks) ■

Joshua Newcomer □

Porterstown ■

Hiram Buck ■

Martin Eakle ■

Henry Piper ■

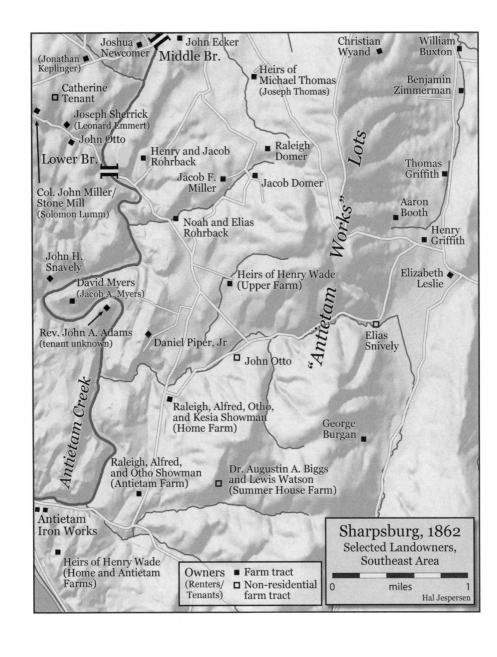

Joshua Newcomer
(Jonathan Keplinger)
John Ecker
Middle Br.
Christian Wyand
William Buxton

Catherine Tenant
Heirs of Michael Thomas (Joseph Thomas)
Benjamin Zimmerman

Joseph Sherrick (Leonard Emmert)
John Otto

Lower Br.
Henry and Jacob Rohrback
Raleigh Domer
"Antietam Works" Lots
Thomas Griffith

Jacob F. Miller
Jacob Domer
Aaron Booth

Col. John Miller/ Stone Mill (Solomon Lumm)
Noah and Elias Rohrback
Henry Griffith

John H. Snavely
David Myers (Jacob A. Myers)
Heirs of Henry Wade (Upper Farm)
Elizabeth Leslie

Rev. John A. Adams (tenant unknown)
Daniel Piper, Jr
"Antietam Works"
Elias Snively

John Otto

Antietam Creek
Raleigh, Alfred, Otho, and Kesia Showman (Home Farm)
George Burgan

Raleigh, Alfred, and Otho Showman (Antietam Farm)
Dr. Augustin A. Biggs and Lewis Watson (Summer House Farm)

Antietam Iron Works

Heirs of Henry Wade (Home and Antietam Farms)

Sharpsburg, 1862
Selected Landowners, Southeast Area

Owners (Renters/ Tenants)
■ Farm tract
□ Non-residential farm tract

0   miles   1
Hal Jespersen

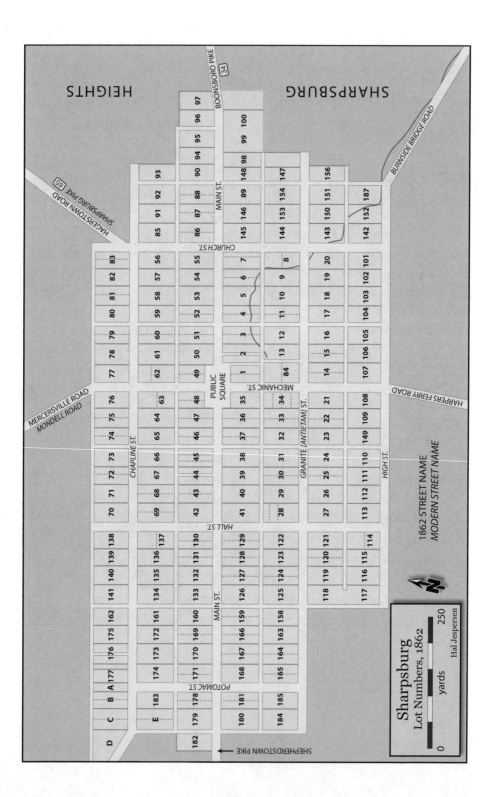

Sharpsburg
Lot Numbers, 1862

Hal Jespersen

yards
0   250

1862 STREET NAME
MODERN STREET NAME

Sharpsburg Village Lot Owners: September 1862

Based on the author's research of land records, equity cases, wills, war claims, census records, and other primary sources

1P	Margaret and David Souders
1P	Susan Kuhn owned, wife of Jeremiah Kuhn
1P	James H. Grove
2W	William M. Cronise
2E	Heirs of William Rohrback
3W	Heirs of William Rohrback | Vacant lot
3E	Captain David Smith owned | Jacob and Julia Baker may have occupied
4W	Abraham Smith
4E	Heirs of Hannah Kretzer owned | Henry Rohrer and wife Mary possibly occupied
5	John and Susan Kretzer
6W	Sarah Hedrick owned | Rhinehart Line and wife possibly occupied
6E	Henry and Sarah Bamford
7	Squire Jacob Miller, primary residence
8	James Marker
9	James Marker
10	Margaret Early
11W	Benjamin Wagoner
11E	John and Delana Davis owned | Franklin Kretzer may have occupied
12	Elizabeth and Harriet Good
13	Elizabeth Hammond | Site of Sharpsburg's Big Spring
14	Lavinia Irvin owned, wife of Jacob Irvin
15W	John and Eliza Benner owned | Occupant unknown
15E	Benjamin Wagoner
16	Benjamin F. Rohrback | Vacant lot
17	Unconfirmed | Later known as the "School House lot"
18	Joseph Alfred Seiss
19	Eliza Simons
20	Magdalene Jones | "Spring House lot"

21	John Shay
22	Samuel Boyer owned | Occupant unknown
23	Heirs of Elizabeth Hine
24	Eliza Myers owned, wife of Jacob Myers
25W	Aaron Fry
25E	Ann Wilhelm
26	Rebecca Benner and the heirs of Elizabeth Hine | Vacant lot
27	Widow Margaret Highbarger
28N	Trustees of the Methodist Episcopal Church
28 Mid	Trustees of the Methodist Episcopal Church
28S	Jacob Lopp
29	Margaret Santman
30	James and Sarah Clayton
31	Margaret Shackelford
32	Col. John Miller | Vacant lot
33W	Col. John Miller | Vacant lot
33E	Col. John Miller | Vacant lot
34N	John and Eliza Benner, primary residence
34N2	Magdalene Jones
34S2	John Hill
34S	John Hill
35	Jacob H. Grove, primary residence
36W	Col. John Miller
36E	Col. John Miller
37W	Catherine Tenant
37E	Col. John Miller, primary residence
38	Peter Beeler
39	Elizabeth Russell
40	Samuel Show
41	Samuel Show
42	Robert Shafer owned | Rev. Mortimer Shuford and wife possibly occupied

43W	Unconfirmed | Likely owned by the heirs of David Highbarger
43E	Solomon Renner, primary residence
44W	Captain David Smith, primary residence
44E	Heirs of George Smith owned | Elizabeth Blackford possibly occupied
45W	Methodist Episcopal Church
45 Mid	Mary Jane and Barney Houser
45E	Mary Jane and Barney Houser
46	Mary Ground
47W	Catherine Knode
47E	Dr. Augustin A. Biggs, primary residence
48W	Benjamin F. Cronise
48E	Ellen Mantz, granddaughter of Kesia Showman
49W	Leah Keedy owned | Elias U. Knode occupied | Site of the Maryland Hotel
49E	Hilliard and Eliza Hebb
50W	John and Louisa Emmert owned | Henry Smith occupied
50E	Harvey Kile owned | Occupant unknown
51W	Harvey Kile owned | Occupant unknown
51E	Nancy Zentmyer
52W	Heirs of John Kretzer, Sr. | Mary Kretzer possibly occupied
52E	Heirs of Col. Jacob Rohrback
53	Heirs of Samuel and Lavenia Grove
54	John Hamilton Smith, father of John P. Smith
55	Adam Michael, primary residence
56	John and Mary Grice | Vacant lot
57W	Heirs of John Glass | Vacant lot
57E	John and Mary Grice | Vacant lot
58	Heirs of John Glass
59	Heirs of Col. Jacob Rohrback | Occupant unknown
60W	Heirs of John Kretzer, Sr. owned | Noah Kretzer may have occupied
60E	Heirs of William Harris
61	German Reformed Church Cemetery
62N	Estate of Norman Robinson | Occupant unknown

62S	Estate of Norman Robinson | Occupant unknown
63N	Judge David Smith, primary residence
63S	Nancy Miller
64	Judge David Smith | Vacant lot
65	Dr. A. A. Biggs | Vacant lot
66	Captain David Smith | Vacant lot
67	Captain David Smith | Vacant lot
68W	Solomon Renner | Occupant unknown
68E	Solomon Renner | Vacant lot
69N	John and Mary Bowers
69S	William M. Hill
70	David Spong | Vacant lot
71	David Spong | Vacant lot
72W	Martha and Robert Wood
72E	Owner unconfirmed | Eva Piper possibly occupied
73	Elizabeth and Samuel Bender AKA Painter
74	Elizabeth and Samuel Bender AKA Painter
75	Heirs of Col. Jacob Rohrback owned | Occupant unknown
76	Judge David Smith
77	James Marker owned | Occupant unknown
78	James Marker | Vacant lot
79W	James Marker | Vacant lot
79E	James Marker owned | Martin L. Fry and wife possibly occupied
80	William Gloss
81W	John and Susanna Bender
81E	Heirs of Christian Bender
82	Heirs of John Glass
83W	Sarah Stiffler owned | Van S. Brashears possibly occupied
83E	Sarah Stiffler owned | Fonrose Bowers possibly occupied
84N	Heirs of Richard Moore
84S	John Hill
85	Squire Jacob Miller

86W	Raleigh Showman owned | Occupant unknown
86E	John and Delana Davis
87W	Jacob and Priscilla Bowers
87E	Perry and Sophia Roderick owned | Occupant unknown
88W	Orlando Stephens possibly owned | Occupant unknown
88E	Mary Hill Bash and Dr. A. A. Biggs co-owned | Occupied by Anna and Joseph Emory Smith
89	Heirs of Daniel Piper | Vacant lot
90	Heirs of Peter Marrow
91	Squire Jacob Miller
92	Squire Jacob Miller
93	Squire Jacob Miller
94W	Nancy Miller owned | Noah Putman occupied
94E	Nancy Miller
95	Jointly owned by Hannah, Nancy, and Polly Benner
96	Susan Kennedy | Vacant Lot
97	Jacob Benner
98	Lutheran Church
99	Susan Kennedy
100	Susan Kennedy
101	Samuel and Cassey Craig
102	Unconfirmed | Later owned by Hilary and Christina Watson
103	Samuel and Cassey Craig
104	Samuel and Cassey Craig
105	Elizabeth and John L. Highbarger | Vacant lot
106	Elizabeth and John L. Highbarger | Vacant lot
107	Elizabeth and John L. Highbarger
108	Margaret Smith Earlougher
109	Margaret Smith Earlougher
110	Rebecca Benner and the heirs of Elizabeth Hine | Vacant lot
111	Rebecca Benner and the heirs of Elizabeth Hine | Vacant lot
112	Rebecca Benner and the heirs of Elizabeth Hine | Vacant lot

113	Rebecca Benner and the heirs of Elizabeth Hine
114N	Jacob H. Grove owned | Jacob Lakin and wife possibly occupied
114S	Mary Moore
115	James Marker | Vacant lot
116	James Marker | Vacant lot
117	James Marker | Vacant lot
118	Catherine Rohrback owned | Occupant unknown
119	Elizabeth Russell
120W	Jacob Lopp
120E	Heirs of Samuel Beckley owned | Charles W. Porter possibly occupied
121	Susan Jackson
122	Jacob Hewett
123	Benjamin Cookerly
124W	Solomon Boyer owned | Occupant unknown
124E	Jacob Myers
125	Solomon Boyer | Vacant lot
126	Michael and Mary Himes owned | David Pennel possibly occupied
127W	Samuel Highbarger
127E	Abner Highbarger
128W	Abner Highbarger
128E	Sarah and Samuel Swain
129	John Zimmerman
130W	Heirs of Susan Cline
130E	Rev. Jacob Highbarger
131W	Rev. John A. Adams | Vacant lot
131E	Margaret Reynolds owned | Occupant unknown
132	St. Paul's Protestant Episcopal Church
133	William Ecton
134	Daniel Poffenberger owned | Martin Himes possibly occupied
135	Rev. John A. Adams | Vacant lot
136	John and Eliza Benner owned | John T. Swain possibly occupied

137N	Heirs of Henry McCoy owned | Mary McCoy occupied
137S	Methodist Episcopal Church Cemetery
138	David Spong
139W	Daniel L. Grove owned | Stephen P. Grove was a mortgagee
139E	Andrew and Amelia Snyder
140W	Unconfirmed
140E	Daniel L. Grove owned | Stephen P. Grove was a mortgagee
141	Henry Craig
142	Magdalene Jones owned | Eli Hiatt possibly occupied
143	Samuel Benner
144	Jacob Avey, Jr.
145	Heirs of Daniel Piper | Rev. Christian Startzman possibly occupied
146	John and Mary Grice, primary residence
147	Unconfirmed
148	Heirs of Daniel Piper | Vacant lot
149	William Gloss | Vacant lot
150	Magdalene Jones | Vacant lot
151	Heirs of Col. Jacob Rohrback | Vacant lot
152	Col. John Miller | "Mill Race lot"
153	George Peterman
154	Heirs of Daniel Piper
156	Susan Kennedy
158	Col. John Miller owned | Ellenora and Robert Wilson possibly occupied
159W	Margaret Reynolds
159E	William Brashears
160	Daniel Poffenberger
161	John Zimmerman
162	Mary and Daniel Himes
163	Heirs of Nancy Carter
164W	Heirs of Nancy Carter
164E	Heirs of Nancy Carter

165W	Samuel Mumma, Sr. owned | Occupant unknown
165E	Unconfirmed | Likely owned by the heirs of Emanuel Rollins
166W	Elizabeth Weaver Rye
166E	James Marker owned | Occupant unknown
167W	Joanna Kidwiler
167E	Elizabeth and John L. Highbarger | Vacant lot
168	Daniel Poffenberger
169W	George Swain
169E	Daniel Poffenberger | Vacant lot
170	Andrew & Amelia Snyder
171	Jointly owned by brothers David and Jacob Knode
172	Heirs of John Weaver
173	Rosanna Mumma Thomas and husband Jonathan Thomas
174	Israel Fry
175	Joseph Bowers
176W	Catherine Chapline | Vacant lot
176E	Joseph, Catherine, and Daniel Bowers
177	Catherine Chapline | Vacant lot
178W	Samuel and Julia Ann Ward
178E	Adam Michael
179W	Sarah Mose
179E	Sarah Mose
180	Jacob Benner
181W	Sarah Himes
181E	Samuel Nichols
182	Heirs of John Mumma
183	Henry Boyd owned | Mahala Bowers possibly occupied
184	John Otto | Vacant lot
185	John Otto owned | James A. Seaman possibly occupied
187	Sarah McGrath AKA McGraw
A	Catherine Chapline

BW	Likely owned by the heirs of Samuel Grove
BE	Likely owned by the heirs of Samuel Grove
CW	Likely owned by the heirs of Samuel Grove
CE	Likely owned by the heirs of Samuel Grove
D	Likely owned by the heirs of Samuel Grove
EW	Edwin T. B. Renner

Chapter 1

Something of the Terrible:
The Gathering of the Armies

Cannon fire shook the earth as villagers fled their homes. Buildings burned. Dogs howled. Birds darted through the smoky sky, shifting direction with each explosion. "In the street there was the greatest confusion," remembered one witness. "Dead and wounded men and horses lay about in every direction . . . waggons and ambulances overturned in the hurry and anxiety of everybody to get out of the village, where cannon-balls whizzed incessantly through the air, and pieces of bursting shells, splinters of wood, and scattered fragments of brick were whirled about in the dense cloud of powdersmoke that enveloped all things."[1]

"We hadn't gone only a couple of houses," recalled a villager, "when a shell busted right over our heads. So we took back to the cellar in a hurry. The way they was shootin' and goin' on we might have been killed befo' we was out of town."[2]

Elizabeth Miller Blackford, 50 and widowed, studied the terrifying scene from her village home while wrestling with a gut-wrenching decision. Stay to protect her property or flee the missiles plunging into town?

---

1 Heros von Borcke, *Memoirs of the Confederate War for Independence*, 3 vols. (Philadelphia, 1867), 1:227-228; Several sources describe artillery shells exploding in Sharpsburg village on Sep. 16, 1862. These include Joseph L. Harsh, *Taken at the Flood: Robert E. Lee and the Confederate Strategy in the Maryland Campaign of 1862* (Kent, Ohio, 1999), 336. See also D. Scott Hartwig, *To Antietam Creek: The Maryland Campaign of September 1862* (Baltimore, 2012), 600, and William Miller Owen, *In Camp and Battle with the Washington Artillery* (Boston, 1885), 141. Further details of the Sep. 16 bombardment appear later in Chapter One.

2 Clifton Johnson, *Battleground Adventures: The Stories of Dwellers on the Scenes of Conflict in Some of the Most Notable Battles of the Civil War* (New York, 1915), 109-11. Hereafter cited as *BA*.

"I was standing in the window," Elizabeth remembered, "when a shell exploded in Mr[s] Russel's house between the roof and the ceiling [it] sent the shingles flying every direction . . . it was that, that unnerved me at the moment. I gave way and we left."

Elizabeth, her children, and a slave named Nan fled their village home, rushing west up Main Street. All was chaos. Ambulances rumbled past burning buildings, hauling mangled Confederates, their blood dripping onto the dusty street. A dead horse lay in the road "with his whole backbone split wide open." Elizabeth and her family ran for their lives, "going out the back way to Gerry Groves Town woods, with the shells flying over our heads and around us, we were in more danger than if we had staid home."[3]

It was September 16, 1862. For all the violence, the actual battle had yet to begin. The rural village of Sharpsburg, Maryland was just hours away from the bloodiest day in American military history, during which 100,000 soldiers would clash near a creek called Antietam.

*   *   *

Up to 1862, Sharpsburg had avoided the ravages of war. Historian Stephen W. Sears described it as "a quiet place, an entirely ordinary little rural community where the roads came together." Founded in 1763, Sharpsburg rested near the

---

3 Elizabeth Miller Blackford to Amelia Houser, February 8, 1863, "The Letters of the Jacob Miller Family of Sharpsburg, Washington County, Maryland," unpublished correspondence, 1851–1864, John Clinton Frye Western Maryland Room, Washington County Free Library, Hagerstown Maryland. Hereafter referred to as WMR. The Miller letter collection spans beyond 1864 but said correspondence does not relate to this study. "Nan" may have been a slave owned by Elizabeth's father, Squire Jacob Miller. After evacuating Sharpsburg village on Sep. 16, Elizabeth sheltered at her brother's farmhouse south of town. She noted there were "not many soldiers" on this farm on the 16th, "but the next day, Wednesday it was cro[w]ded with them going and coming;" Active Land Record Indices, 1776–1977, Washington County Circuit Court Land Records, Maryland State Archives, Annapolis, Maryland, liber IN 19 / folios 422-23. Land records are hereafter cited by liber and folio and encompass real estate purchases, mortgages, bills of sale, and deeds of manumission. Deed IN 19 / 422-23 associates Elizabeth R. Blackford with Lot 44E (131 West Main Street). Blackford may have rented this property in 1862. Records II / 623, II / 175, and WMCKK 3 / 170 show the Russell family's ownership of Lot 39 (128 West Main Street), located directly across West Main Street from Lot 44E. The 1860 Federal census for Sharpsburg lists Elizabeth Blackford in Dwelling #1571 next to Solomon Renner (who owned Lot 43E in 1862). The 1860 census places Elizabeth Russell and her daughter Lucinda in Dwelling #1698 near Colonel John Miller, who owned and occupied Lot 37E. Regarding "Gerry Groves Town woods," Jeremiah P. Grove and his siblings owned the Town Woods in 1862, which adjoined Sharpsburg village on the west.

Sharpsburg, Md., Principal Street. This 1862 view of Sharpsburg village, taken from the eastern edge of town, looks northwest down Main Street. Photograph by Alexander Gardner. *Library of Congress*

Potomac River, which bisected Federal Maryland and Confederate Virginia. Because Maryland was a Union state, U.S. forces picketed the river to watch for potential passage by the Rebel army. Maryland was also a slaveholding border state. Its eastern and southern sections had many Confederate sympathizers, while citizens in Western Maryland—which included Sharpsburg—predominantly favored the Union. As a result, Sharpsburg's initial military experiences were reasonably pleasant. When the 9th Regiment, New York State Militia, marched through town in July 1861, pro-Union villagers cheered the troops and showered them with American flags. One New Yorker recalled, "It is doubtful whether any regiment in the service ever marched under so many banners as did the Ninth on its departure from Sharpsburg."

Two months later, citizens embraced the 13th Massachusetts Infantry during its two-week encampment near town. "Relations with the people of Sharpsburg were very pleasant," wrote the regiment's historian, "and they did their best to prevent our departure."[4]

---

4 Stephen W. Sears, *Landscape Turned Red* (Boston, 2003), 167; Kathleen A. Ernst, *Too Afraid To Cry: Maryland Civilians in the Antietam Campaign* (Mechanicsburg, PA, 2007), 5-6. Hereafter

When the 12th Indiana Infantry occupied Sharpsburg during the winter of 1861–62, townsfolk welcomed the Hoosiers. Jacob H. Grove boarded the regiment's officers while Robert Leakins, an eleven-year-old African-American who lived in town, visited the camp "to hear the band play." When temperatures dropped, the Indianans leaned on the community for support, requesting timber from private woodlots for constructing military cabins. The troops "had our tinner here to make them sheet iron stoves which they used in the huts," remembered one townsman.[5]

As winter progressed, some soldiers sheltered along the Potomac River in Jacob C. Grove's warehouse and Squire Jacob Miller's sawmill complex. Others, exposed to the elements, asked citizens for firewood or felled trees at will—and without asking. Much of the wood was valuable oak reserved for market sale and building barns. Squire Jacob Miller, a prominent landowner, complained that the soldiers were "comitting great depradations" to the timber supply and "thining it out most retchidly." Destruction ceased when the 12th Indiana departed in March 1862. Yet, by this time, some residents no longer saw them as soldiers crusading to save the Union but as an unwelcome army of occupation.[6]

---

referred to as *TATC*; *Herald and Torch Light* [Hagerstown, MD], September 23, 1886. This newspaper is hereafter cited as *HTL*. It is not to be confused with its predecessor, the *Herald of Freedom and Torch Light*, which changed to the shorter title in 1863; George A. Hussey, *History of the Ninth Regiment N.Y.S.M.—N.G.S.N.Y. (Eighty-Third N.Y. Volunteers) 1845-1888* (New York, 1889), 55-56. The 9th New York State Militia was also known as the 83rd New York Infantry, and is not to be confused with the 9th New York Infantry; Charles E. Davis, Jr., *Three Years in the Army: The Story of the Thirteenth Massachusetts Volunteers* (Boston, 1894), 8; Because of Maryland's bitterly divided allegiances, the Federal government took severe measures to ensure that it remained in the Union. For further reading on this subject, see J. Thomas Scharf, *History of Western Maryland: Being a History of Frederick, Montgomery, Carroll, Washington, Allegany, and Garrett Counties From the Earliest Period to the Present Day; Including Biographical Sketches of Their Representative Men*, 2 vols. (Philadelphia, 1882), 1:194-211 (hereafter, *HWM*). See also Michael Powell, "Civil Liberties in Crisis," online article, Crossroads of War, http://www.crossroadsofwar.org/discover-the-story/civil-liberties-in-crisis/civil-liberties-in-crisis-full-story/.

5   Timothy R. Snyder, *Trembling in the Balance: The Chesapeake and Ohio Canal During the Civil War* (Boston, 2011), 45; Congressional case of the heirs of Samuel Grove, Record Group 123, Records of the U.S. Court of Claims, Congressional Jurisdiction Case Files, 1884-1943, National Archives and Records Administration, Washington, DC, Entry 22, Box 985, Case No. 9313. All congressional cases cited in this study, unless noted, are archived at the National Archives in Washington, DC. References to the National Archives and record groups appear hereafter, respectively, as *NA* and *RG*. All congressional cases archived in Record Group 123 are hereafter cited as claims, followed by case numbers. Testimony in the Groves' case stated that the 12th Indiana established headquarters "in the woods at the suburbs of town."

6   Quartermaster claim of Jacob C. Grove, Record Group 92, Office of the Claims of the Quartermaster General, Claims Branch 1861-1889, Quartermaster Stores (Act of July 4, 1864),

Despite suffering property damages from U.S. troops in 1861 and early 1862, Sharpsburg had avoided the scourge of war. Nevertheless, fears swirled that the Confederate army might cross the Potomac River one day. As one skittish Unionist put it, "Invasion by the Southern army was considered equivalent to destruction." Not only could a battle erupt near the town; Rebels might plunder personal property, force Maryland men into the Confederate ranks, or banish them to a Southern prison, none of which were "attractive prospects for quiet, Union-loving citizens."[7]

Not all Sharpsburg residents feared the Rebels. Many Southern sympathizers lived in the area, and more than a dozen stole across the Potomac to enlist in the Confederate army. Still, Sharpsburg was predominantly pro-Union, described by one historian as a "Unionist and Republican bastion." More than 130 Sharpsburg men fought for the United States. The district raised two companies of the 1st Maryland Infantry, Potomac Home Brigade, and sent other men into the 1st Maryland Cavalry, known initially as Cole's Cavalry.

Notwithstanding, the political divide strained relations in the Sharpsburg environs. Pro-Lincoln Republicans deemed Democrats as disloyal because they opposed the war. "In our community politics ran pretty high during the war," explained farmer David R. Miller, "and some persons called every man who voted the democratic ticket a rebel, but there were many democrats who were loyal and

---

National Archives and Records Administration, Washington, DC, Book G, Box 95, Claim G-1649. All quartermaster claims cited in this study, unless noted, were pulled at the National Archives in Washington, DC. Hereafter, quartermaster claims archived in Record Group 92 are cited as claims, followed by claim numbers; Jacob Miller to Amelia and Christian Houser, February 17, 1862, "The Letters of the Jacob Miller Family of Sharpsburg," WMR. Catherine Amelia Houser was Miller's daughter. She and her husband, Christian Houser, appear in the 1860 Federal census for Muscatine County, Bloomington, Iowa, Dwelling #547. Squire Jacob Miller, who resided on Lot 7 in Sharpsburg village, should not be confused with his nephew, Jacob F. Miller, who lived on a farm southeast of town in 1862. Early historians of the battle, John P. Smith and Oliver T. Reilly, identified Jacob Miller as "Squire Miller" or "Esquire Miller," and Miller's obituaries refer to him as "Jacob Miller, Esq.," and "Squire Miller." See *Herald and Torch Light*, December 15, 1875, and *Hagerstown Mail* [Hagerstown, MD], December 10, 1875; *Herald of Freedom and Torch Light* [Hagerstown, MD], November 27, 1861 (hereafter cited as *HFTL*); M. D. Gage, *From Vicksburg to Raleigh; Or a Complete History of the Twelfth Regiment Indiana Volunteer Infantry and the Campaigns of Grant and Sherman, with an Outline of the Great Rebellion* (Chicago, 1865), 20-21.

7 Lewis H. Steiner, *Report of Lewis H. Steiner, M.D., Inspector of the Sanitary Commission: Containing a Diary Kept During the Rebel Occupation of Frederick, Md. and An Account of the Operations of the U.S. Sanitary Commission During the Campaign in Maryland, September, 1862* (New York, 1862), 6. It is important to recognize that Steiner's fears of the Confederate army in September 1862 likely stemmed from Northern propaganda.

patriotic citizens." James Marker, an outspoken Democrat, "was not allowed to vote from 1862 until after the war on account of his disloyal sentiments." Adam Michael's family "were strong Democrats, and on some occasions the father and sons were stoned at the polls by some of the Republican elements of the town and not allowed to vote."[8]

Political tensions escalated as the war progressed. Secessionists hacked down the U.S. flag on Sharpsburg's public square, while Unionists torched the barns of Reverend Robert Douglas and John E. Knode. Douglas had two sons in the Southern army. Knode, a pro-Northern Whig, married into the Rebel Stonebraker family. After Knode's barn burned, his nephew, a Confederate soldier, quipped, "It cost something in those days to be joined to a Southern woman in wedlock."

Tragedy struck when unknown parties murdered Dewitt Clinton Rentch, a local Democrat. Debate swirled as to whether Rentch was shot "by Union soldiers as a rebel spy" or killed by pro-Northern roughs "in a drunken row." Sheriff E. M. Mobley "went with the states attorney to make an investigation, but nothing was done about it." Rentch's family seethed at the injustice. "Oh my I did not know I had so much gall in my nature until this war question was brought up," wrote Rentch's cousin. "I shudder now at my feelings . . . I hated my most intimate friends because they were in favor of the Union right or wrong."[9]

*   *   *

---

8 Dean Herrin, *Antietam Rising: The Civil War and Its Legacy in Sharpsburg, Maryland, 1860-1900* (Sharpsburg, MD, 2002), Antietam National Battlefield Library (hereafter, ANBL), 6-7; Ted Alexander, "Destruction, Disease, and Death: The Battle of Antietam and the Sharpsburg Civilians," ed. Mark A. Snell, in *Civil War Regiments, A Journal of the American Civil War* (Mason City, IA, 1998), vol. 6, no. 2, 150; Ernst, *TATC*, 19; Claim of Daniel Poffenberger (*RG* 123, Entry 22, No 1505). David R. Miller testified in Poffenberger's case; Claim of James Marker (*RG* 123, Entry 22, Box 232, No. 1292); Thomas J. C. Williams, *A History of Washington County, Maryland: From the Earliest Settlements to the Present Time, Including a History of Hagerstown*, 2 vols. (Hagerstown, MD, 1906), vol. 2, pt. 1, 734 (hereafter referred to as *HWC*).

9 Joseph R. Stonebraker, *A Rebel of '61* (New York, 1899), 41; *HFTL*, November 27, 1861, 2C; Robert Douglas to Fitz John Porter, October 24, 1862, M-345, Union Provost Marshals' File of Papers Relating to Individual Civilians, Microfilm Roll 0076, *RG* 109, *NA*; Undated "Letter from Millie" to Amelia Houser, "The Letters of the Jacob Miller Family of Sharpsburg, Washington County, Maryland," WMR. Savilla Miller, one of Squire Jacob Miller's daughters, may have written the letter; Ernst, *TATC*, 21-22; Claim of Andrew Rentch (*RG* 123, Entry 22, Box 537, Case No. 4235). Rentch's case contains details describing the shooting death of his son, Dewitt Clinton Rentch. The 1860 Federal census for Sharpsburg shows Andrew Rentch owning $100,000 in real estate. Rentch's claims case describes him as "the wealthiest farmer in Washington Co. Md."

When September 1862 arrived, farmers of both political parties focused on the fall harvest. They busily threshed grains and stuffed mountains of hay into barns while eyeing their nearly-ripe corn, potatoes, fruits, and vegetables. Pastures bloomed with second crops of clover. Freshly plowed fields awaited seeding with winter wheat. The community depended on all of these resources for subsistence, livestock feed, and annual income. In many respects, this was the worst possible time for disruption of farming.

Then came the shocking news that the Confederate Army of Northern Virginia had marched into Maryland.

General Robert E. Lee had good reasons for advancing north. The Confederacy recently seized the initiative in the war by repulsing the Union army from the Richmond peninsula and then crushing it at the Battle of Second Manassas (Bull Run). By entering Maryland, Lee could build on the momentum and bring the war out of Virginia. He also entertained the hope of "liberating" the slaveholding "Old Line State," which, as he and other Secessionists believed, the United States withheld from the Confederacy against the will of a majority of its people. Most important, Lee sought a decisive battle against the battered Yankees on ground of his choosing. Despite the advantages of fighting a defensive war on home territory, Lee knew the Confederacy could not win a long-term war of attrition against the industrial North. He needed a quick victory, now, while the Union was on the ropes.

The United States was indeed reeling. Routed at Second Manassas, Federal forces had retreated to the fortifications of Washington. Fall mid-term elections were looming, and if morale continued to decline, Northern voters might demand an end to the bloody war by granting independence to the Confederacy. Moreover, the American crisis was injuring the economies of England and France. If Rebel armies continued their military successes, these foreign powers might intervene on behalf of the South.[10]

In early September, Lee's Army of Northern Virginia (ANV) crossed the Potomac River into Maryland at White's Ford and other points, more than forty

10 Gary W. Gallagher, "Season of Opportunity," ed. Gary W. Gallagher, in *Antietam: Essays on the 1862 Maryland Campaign* (Kent, OH, 1989), 1-9; James M. McPherson, *Crossroads of Freedom: Antietam* (New York, 2002), 56-61, 91-95; Harsh, *Taken at the Flood*, 25-26, 46-50, 57-58; Alexander B. Rossino, *Their Maryland: The Army of Northern Virginia from the Potomac Crossing to Sharpsburg in September 1862* (El Dorado Hills, CA, 2011), 3-10; Many historians refer to Robert E. Lee's offensive as the 1862 Maryland Campaign. Although primary sources support the possibility of British-French intervention, evidence does not show that foreign affairs factored into Lee's strategy in September 1862.

miles southeast of Sharpsburg. Unfortunately for Lee, many Marylanders in the vicinity did not welcome the ANV as he had hoped, despite the large number of southern sympathizers living in Montgomery and Frederick counties. On the contrary, numerous civilians hurriedly packed valuables, withdrew savings from banks, and fled north. In Sharpsburg, however, there was no great panic. Most residents remained to thresh their grain crops and watch over their property. Lee's army seemed to pose no immediate threat.

When he entered Maryland, Lee expected U.S. military garrisons near Harpers Ferry to evacuate, but, to his surprise, they stayed put, threatening his supply and communication lines to the Shenandoah Valley. To address this threat, Lee sent Major General Thomas "Stonewall" Jackson and two thirds of the army to confront the enemy at Harpers Ferry. Lee then continued toward Hagerstown with the rest of the ANV, but ordered a division to guard the gaps of South Mountain and thereby prevent the enemy from attacking his divided army.

When news of Lee's incursion reached Washington, President Abraham Lincoln found himself forced to act fast. He reached out to Major General George B. McClellan, whom he had relieved as commander of the Army of the Potomac (AOP) a few weeks earlier. Lincoln restored McClellan to the AOP and gave the commander simple orders. Drive the Rebels out of Maryland.

Robert E. Lee assumed that his demoralized enemy would "take some time to prepare for the field," but he was wrong. McClellan was a brilliant organizer, who quickly restored the vigor of the Union's flagship force, rebuilt its crippled morale, and led his men into Maryland to locate the invaders. By mid-September, the Army of the Potomac caught up to the Army of Northern Virginia.[11]

*   *   *

Sunday, September 14, started peacefully at Sharpsburg. Rumors of the approaching armies, North and South, put the community on alert. Nonetheless, in

---

11 Hartwig, *To Antietam Creek*, 92-106; The forty-mile distance from Sharpsburg to White's Ford is based on historic roads; Scharf, HWM, 1:231-232; Ernst, *TATC*, 40-41; War claims, letters, and other sources reviewed for this study revealed no accounts of Sharpsburg civilian evacuations before Sep. 15, 1862. Most of Sharpsburg's evacuations took place on Sep. 15 and 16, and some people fled their homes on Sep. 17; Dennis E. Frye, *The Battle of Harpers Ferry: History and Battlefield Guide* (Harpers Ferry, WV, 2011); Hartwig, *To Antietam Creek*, 32-34, 43-47; Ethan S. Rafuse, *McClellan's War: The Failure of Moderation in the Struggle for the Union* (Indianapolis, 2005), 236-240, 267-269, 278-295; George McClellan commanded Washington's defenses at the time of his reinstatement to field command.

the absence of immediate threat, parishioners flocked to houses of worship, sang hymns, and sat through sermons—until the distant sound of cannon fire reached their ears.

The ominous harbingers of approaching battle wafted through open church windows as fighting erupted at South Mountain, seven miles east. Alarmed worshipers left their pews to study the distant heights, straining their eyes toward Fox's Gap, where advance units of the Union army attacked the Confederates. Then, suddenly, horsemen from the Southern army rumbled through Sharpsburg village.

"We were all up in the Lutheran Church at Sunday-school," recalled Maria "Teresa" Kretzer, "when the Rebel cavalry came dashing through the town. The whole assembly flocked out . . . we just imagined something was going to happen, and the children ran home from church in terror. There was no dinner eaten that day. The people were too frightened."[12]

At South Mountain, a civilian named John J. Keedy assisted Union forces. The fifty-nine-year-old farmer lived in Keedysville, a town he helped found, located three miles from Sharpsburg. Described as "intensely loyal" to the U.S., Keedy observed Confederate movements before the mountain battle and hatched a plan. He rode to the Rebel picket line at Turner's Gap and attempted "to pass through the Confederate lines on the plea that his wife was sick." The ruse reportedly worked. After riding through the gap, Keedy "penetrated into the Federal lines where he gave all the information possible to the Commanding General." Afterward, the farmer remained with the Federal army, serving as a guide during the Battle of South Mountain.[13]

It is unclear what information Keedy gave Gen. McClellan, but in the late afternoon of September 14, Federal forces attacked Turner's Gap and Crampton's Gap. Sharpsburg residents anxiously watched and listened past sunset, when the Union army captured both gaps.

As the evening passed, citizens waited in suspense to see what would happen next. As mentioned earlier, Stephen W. Sears described Sharpsburg as a place "where the roads came together." These arteries connected Sharpsburg to Boonsboro, Hagerstown, Shepherdstown, and Harpers Ferry. Along with roads,

---

12 Johnson, *BA*, 118; Ernst, *TATC*, 113.

13 Chapman Publishing Company, *Portrait and Biographical Record of the Sixth Congressional District, Maryland* (New York, 1898), 550; Claim of John J. Keedy (RG 123, Entry 22, Box 348, No. 2157). Three witnesses gave sworn testimony describing Keedy's actions on South Mountain.

though, Sharpsburg rested near a major crossing point of the Potomac River—Blackford's Ford—a shallow stretch that allowed persons, horses, and wagons to wade between Union Maryland and Confederate Virginia. From a military perspective, after Southern troops burned the Sharpsburg-Shepherdstown bridge in June 1861, it left Blackford's Ford as the only convenient crossing between the regional towns of Harpers Ferry and Williamsport.

When the fighting on South Mountain concluded on September 14, General Lee decided to retreat to Virginia via Blackford's Ford. Additionally, he chose to reunite his army and abort the Harpers Ferry operation. "The day has gone against us," Lee wrote to Major General Lafayette McLaws, "and this army will go by Sharpsburg and cross the river." After sending those orders to McLaws, Lee descended with his men toward Antietam Creek.[14]

*   *   *

The night was tense for Sharpsburg's townsfolk. Fourteen-hundred Union cavalrymen rode through the village that evening after escaping from Harpers Ferry. With mounted soldiers from both armies rushing through town the same day, residents feared an imminent clash. Teresa Kretzer recalled, "We couldn't help being fearful that we were in danger. We expected trouble that night, but all was quiet until the next day."[15]

---

14 Sears, *Landscape Turned Red*, 167; "WA-II-034 Blackford's Ford (Boteler's Ford, Packhorse Ford)," architectural survey file, Maryland Historic Trust, sec. 8, pp. 1-2, https://mht.maryland.gov/secure/medusa/PDF/Washington/WA-II-034.pdf. Maryland Historic Trust is hereafter cited as MHT; Harsh, *Taken at the Flood*, 287-289; Joseph L. Harsh, *Sounding the Shallows: A Confederate Companion for the Maryland Campaign of 1862* (Kent, Ohio, 2000), 181; before the settlement of Sharpsburg, Native Americans accessed the nearby ford to traverse the Potomac River. The crossing point went by the name Packhorse Ford in the early 1800s, and during the Civil War, locals and soldiers referred to it as Blackford's Ford, Boteler's Ford, and Shepherdstown Ford. The name Blackford's Ford stems from Colonel John Blackford (1771-1839), who owned a large amount of acreage southwest of Sharpsburg adjoining the Potomac River. In 1862, two of Col. Blackford's children—William M. Blackford and Helen Blackford Douglas (wife of Rev. Robert Douglas)—owned and resided upon this land. Another son, Henry V. S. Blackford, owned a farm north of Blackford's Ford near Sharpsburg village.

15 Dennis E. Frye, *Harpers Ferry Under Fire: A Border Town in the American Civil War* (Harpers Ferry, WV, 2012), 91-92; Donald C. Caughley, "The Cavalry Escape From Harpers Ferry, Part III," blog, *Crossed Sabers*, September 15, 2007, http://crossedsabers.blogspot.com/2007/09/; Oliver T. Reilly, *The Battlefield of Antietam* (Hagerstown, MD, 1906). Reilly's book is hereafter referred to as *BOA*. Reilly did not paginate his book, but readers can search the text at the

At sunrise on September 15, waking villagers beheld two brigades of Confederate infantry march through town. These were advance forces Lee had sent to secure Blackford's Ford for the army's retreat to Virginia. Brigadier General Robert Rodes halted his brigade southwest of town while Colonel Alfred Colquitt led his command to the ford. Citizens who feared Rebels early in the war now had hundreds in their backyard, but movements toward the river crossing suggested the soldiers would pass to Virginia.[16]

While Confederates secured the ford, General Lee halted east of Sharpsburg at a meadow overlooking Antietam Creek. He could see that the U.S. army was not far behind, but two deliveries arrived around this time to lift his spirits: a hot pot of coffee and a game-changing message from Stonewall Jackson predicting the imminent capture of Harpers Ferry. Lee had already ordered Jackson to abort the operation there, but capturing the garrison would net 12,500 prisoners and much-needed supplies for the ill-equipped Rebel army while adding to Union demoralization. Moreover, if the Confederates at Harpers Ferry could march to Sharpsburg after the capture, Lee might continue the Maryland Campaign, with his army reunited.

The view from Lee's meadow offered a commanding panorama. Sharpsburg lay to the west, fronted by a ridge running north to south. The rolling farmland provided hilltops for Lee's artillery and low ground to hide his outnumbered infantry. Making a stand on such topography might keep the enemy at bay until Jackson finished his mission. Even so, halting here carried the risk of trapping Lee against the Potomac River. There was no bridge to afford swift crossing, and Blackford's Ford provided a cumbersome passage to Virginia. If Lee suffered

---

HathiTrust Digital Library, https://catalog.hathitrust.org/Record/102359684; Johnson, *BA*, 119.

16 Hartwig, *To Antietam Creek*, 481, 747; Claim of Hezekiah Myers (*RG* 123, Entry 22, Box 234, Case No. 1301). Myers testified that Confederates encamped on the neighboring farm owned by Reverend John A. Adams. Benjamin F. Rohrback, a witness in Myers's case, testified that Myers's farm "was in possession of the rebel forces commanded by D. H. Hill Sept. 15, 16, 17, 18 until the morning of Friday the 19th Sept. 1862." Various battlefield maps depict "H. Myers" between the Miller's Sawmill and Harpers Ferry roads; Official report of Brigadier General Robert Rodes, in *The War of the Rebellion: A Compilation of Official Records of the Union and Confederate Armies*, 128 vols. (Washington, DC, 1880–1901), Series 1, Volume 19, Part 1, 1036. Hereafter cited as *OR*. All references are to Series 1 unless otherwise noted. Rodes reported, "On the 15th, after resting on the heights south of Sharpsburg long enough to get a scanty meal and to gather stragglers, we moved back through that place to the advanced position in the center of the line of battle before the town."

defeat on this ground, his army faced potential destruction. Ever the risk-taker, the Confederate commander chose to remain briefly at Sharpsburg.[17]

*   *   *

Residents of the Sharpsburg community stirred into early wakefulness on the morning of September 15. Collective anxiety disrupted regular business, and nervous citizens went door-to-door to learn the latest news. Farmhand Alexander W. "Alex" Davis remembered, "We expected there was goin' to be another battle, but we didn't know where or when it would be fought. Nobody was a-workin' . . . they was ridin' around to find out what was goin' to happen."

In the early morning, the head of the Confederate column manifested at Sharpsburg, crossing Antietam Creek over the Middle Bridge. Watching from a nearby hilltop was twenty-one-year-old Mary Ellen Piper, who lived with her parents on a nearby farm. "The principal part of them was then crossing into a field about half a mile from where I stood," she wrote shortly after the Confederate army's arrival. "In a short time, I perceived them throwing down our fence, and the whole column was entering. In a few minutes, the fences were all level with the ground and as far as the eye could see was one living mass of human beings."

Confederates besieged the Pipers' house, begging for breakfast. Mary Ellen's father, Henry Piper, "was opposed to the rebellion" and "anxious to see it suppressed." Yet, he also needed to protect his property and thus set aside his political leanings to accommodate the hungry Rebels. "They would come in six, eight, and ten at a time for breakfast," Mary Ellen recounted. "They would eat anything they could lay hands on. I believe we fed 200 in half a day."[18]

---

17 Hartwig, *To Antietam Creek*, 482, 518-519; Harsh, *Taken at the Flood*, 301-303, 426, 446; Sears, *Landscape Turned Red*, 168; Guided crossing of Blackford's Ford on September 20, 2008, with Dr. Thomas G. Clemens and Save Historic Antietam Foundation (SHAF). The author found the narrow, thigh-deep passage challenging to wade on account of slick rocks lining the bottom of the Potomac River. However, similar conditions may not have existed in 1862. According to historian Dennis E. Frye via email communications in Feb. 2022, "The Boteler mill dam upstream 400 yards impounded water, reduced flow, and made the ford much more manageable [in Sep. 1862]. In addition, the area was suffering from an extreme drought—the worst in recorded history according to local papers."

18 Johnson, *BA*, 96; E. P. to Sally Farran, October 4, 1862, cited in Daniel A. Masters, "Elizabeth Piper and the Battle of Antietam," blog, *Dan Masters' Civil War Chronicles*, September 29, 2017, https://dan-masters-civil-war.blogspot.com/2017/09/elizabeth-piper-and-battle-of-antietam.html. The October 4, 1862 letter originally ran in the Wilmington [OH] *Watchman*, October 23, 1862. Blogger Daniel A. Masters located and transcribed the letter. Masters

South of the Pipers, a similar scene occurred at the home of John and Catherine Otto. Hungry Confederates swarmed onto the farm. Hilary Watson, one of the Ottos' slaves, recalled, "The hill at our place was covered with 'em. They'd walk right into the house and say, 'Have you got anything to eat?' like they was half starved. We'd hardly fix up for a couple when a lot mo' would come in." Aided by the Ottos, Hilary and his mother Nancy struggled to feed many troops that morning.

"The white people and my mother was in the kitchen givin' 'em bread and bacon," explained Hilary. "Some sat down at table, and some would just take a chunk of food in their hands. They e't us out directly."[19]

*   *   *

As the morning progressed, Confederate artillery and infantry deployed across the fields of Susan Kennedy and Squire Jacob Miller on Sharpsburg Heights. Below the high ground, Rebels continued converging on the Piper farm. According to Mary Ellen Piper, "Our yard was so crowded that it was almost impossible to move." Among the masses was Confederate high command. "At 10 o'clock, Generals Longstreet, Lee, and Hill were on our porch," Mary Ellen remembered. "We inquired of them if there was any danger, and if they anticipated having a battle. They answered us they did not—that they intended only remaining an hour or two and passing on, although they admitted it was the most splendid position they could possibly have." When asked about the cannon surrounding their home,

---

identified "E. P." as Henry Piper's daughter, Elizabeth Piper, but evidence supports that a different daughter may have written the letter. The letter's context suggests that its writer lived in her parents' household on the battlefield. Elizabeth Piper, however, married Raleigh Showman nearly two years earlier, and the couple likely resided on Showman's farm located four miles south of the battlefield. Their son, David William, was two weeks shy of turning two in September 1862, yet the letter mentions no husband or child. On the contrary, Mary Ellen Piper, 21, testified in her father's claims case (*RG* 123, No. 445) that in 1862, "I resided with my father Henry Piper the claimant on his farm north of Sharpsburg." The Federal census for Sharpsburg, Dwelling #1737, lists three daughters (Elizabeth, Mary Ellen, and Susan) in their parents' household, but the Sep. 1860 census enumeration occurred three months before Elizabeth Piper's marriage to Raleigh Showman. The postwar marriage announcement of Mary Ellen Piper and David M. Smith, cited in the *Herald and Torch Light*, Nov. 1, 1865, identified Mary Ellen as "Ellie Piper." In the 1880 Federal census for Sharpsburg, Dwelling #16, Mary Ellen appears as "Ellen M. Smith." This evidence supports that the letter's author, "E. P.," was Mary Ellen Piper.

19 Johnson, *BA*, 105.

the generals assured them "it was merely to cover their retreat, and gave us every assurance if there was any danger whatever, they would give us warning in time."[20]

The Pipers offered the Confederate commanders a meal, including Major General James Longstreet and Brigadier General Daniel Harvey Hill. Mary Ellen and her sister Susan were supposedly "badly frightened [but] wanted to show their kindness to the officers" by offering some wine. Longstreet declined, fearing the Unionist family poisoned the beverage. Nonetheless, after Hill took a sip and showed no ill effect, Longstreet changed his tune. "Ladies," he asked, "I will thank you for a little bit of that wine."[21]

Hungry Confederates also sought meals in Sharpsburg village. Locals took note of the Rebels' ravenous appetites and poor appearance. The soldiers "nearly worried us to death asking for something to eat," recalled a townswoman. Others described the Rebels as "half famished" and "filthy and ragged . . . they would eat anything they could lay hands on." Dr. Augustin A. Biggs, the town's physician, described them as "barefooted, dirty, and filthy in the extreme . . . most of them indecently ragged and their person exposed." Additionally, Biggs noted, "I never saw a set of men reduced so far to the point of starvation."[22]

While some soldiers begged for meals, others took a tougher approach with the locals. Northwest of town, Confederate officers impressed citizens to point out additional river crossings to Virginia. Near Blackford's Ford, Rebel guards

---

20 "Jones's Division, Longstreet's Command," Antietam Battlefield Historical Tablet #368, Antietam on the Web, http://antietam.aotw.org/tablet.php?tablet_id=3680; Harsh, *Taken at the Flood*, 304-305; Washington County land records IN 18 / 57 and 84 / 586 show that Squire Miller's 30-acre tract spanned from Boonsboro Pike to Hagerstown Pike and adjoined Henry Piper's farm on the south. The parcel presently contains Mountain View Cemetery and Battleview Market. Sharpsburg Heights is also known as Cemetery Hill, based on the Lutheran graveyard's nearby location and postwar cemeteries established on the Jacob Miller and Susan Kennedy properties; E. P. to Sally Farran, October 4, 1862, *Dan Masters' Civil War Chronicles*.

21 Reilly, *BOA*. Reilly identified the Piper daughters as Mary Ellen and Susan. Some authors have assumed this account occurred on the evening of Sep. 16. The war claims testimonies of Jeremiah Summers and Mary Ellen Piper, combined with the "E. P." letter on Oct. 4, 1862, support that the Pipers evacuated their farm around 2:00 p.m. on Sep. 15 and returned on Sep. 19. The Oct. 4 letter noted that Confederate generals visited the home at 10:00 a.m. on Sep. 15. Thus, if the wine story is accurate, it likely occurred between 10:00 a.m. and 2:00 p.m. on Sep. 15.

22 Johnson, *BA*, 105, 119; E. P. to Sally Farran, October 4, 1862, *Dan Masters' Civil War Chronicles*; Augustin A. Biggs to Elijah Kalb, September 29, 1862. Biggs's letter first ran in the *Weekly Lancaster Gazette* (Lancaster, Ohio), October 16, 1862. Daniel A. Masters later transcribed it in "A Sharpsburg Resident's View of the Battle of Antietam, Maryland, September 17, 1862," *Maryland Historical Magazine*, Winter 2015, WMR.

confined the family of William M. Blackford inside their farmhouse "for several days." When Blackford demanded an explanation, sentries explained it was "for fear that I would give information to the Federal officers." In Keedysville, Frederick Wyand had just stocked his new store with goods. To his dismay, stragglers in Lee's army pried open the shutters with bayonets and ransacked his inventory.[23]

The mere presence of Confederates was sufficient to terrify some local citizens. Early on September 15, Samuel Ward, a machinist, rode to Captain David Smith's farm west of Sharpsburg village. Ward intended "to set a machine to thresh the wheat out of the barn," but soon after arriving, he observed Rebels deploying throughout the area. The sight drove him from Smith's farm—his threshing machine left behind. "I only stayed until breakfast was ready," Ward recounted, "and didn't stay to eat that."[24]

*   *   *

At noon, a courier from Harpers Ferry delivered Lee an update from Stonewall Jackson: "Through God's blessing, Harpers Ferry and its garrison are to be surrendered." Jackson planned to march his command to Sharpsburg, leaving Major General Ambrose Powell Hill's division to parole the 12,500 prisoners. This news may have elated Lee, but another message soon arrived informing him that the Federal army was approaching Antietam Creek.[25]

Shortly after noon, the United States II Corps, commanded by Major General Edwin V. Sumner, led the Army of the Potomac into the Sharpsburg area. After skirmishers drove Rebel pickets across the Middle Bridge, Major General Israel Richardson of II Corps ordered Federal artillery atop a nearby bluff, then instructed the Irish Brigade to form east of Antietam Creek.

---

23 Reilly, *BOA*. Confederate officers reportedly impressed John Hebb, Moses Cox, and Joe Hoffmaster to identify local fords; Claim of William M. Blackford (*RG* 123, Entry 22, Box 236, Case No. 1324); Harsh, *Taken at the Flood*, 325, 420; Reilly, *BOA*. In addition to Wyand's store, Reilly wrote that Confederates plundered another Keedysville shop owned by John Cost, emptying goods into wagons before "knocking the heads of the molasses and oil barrels in and running it over the floor." Some writers have connected the Cost account with Antietam, but Reilly cited no date, only noting that it occurred during a Confederate raid.

24 Claims of David Smith (*RG* 123, Entry 22, Box 1097, Cases 1244, 1262, and 10237). Captain David Smith's farm is located west of the present-day Antietam Station on Route 34. Smith's rank of captain stemmed from his service in the War of 1812.

25 Harsh, *Taken at the Flood*, 307, 324-325.

The same citizens who earlier watched the Confederate army cross the Middle Bridge now saw U.S. forces swarm into the area. Major General Joseph Hooker's I Corps (10,000 troops) followed II Corps (18,000) on the Boonsboro Pike. To the east, the XII Corps (8,000), commanded by Brigadier General Joseph K. F. Mansfield, followed Burnside's IX Corps (12,000 troops) down the Old Sharpsburg Road into Keedysville. Resident John J. Keedy guided part of the U.S. army past his Keedysville farm, where Maj. Gen. McClellan based AOP headquarters. Soon, "Artillery Cavalry am[m]unition Trains Hospital and Ambulance Trains and herd of Beef Cattle were quartered" on and near Keedy's farm.[26]

Union troops overran nearby properties. Families, who hours earlier went about their daily business, now hosted hundreds of uniformed men. The scene appeared surreal as soldiers moved in all directions, the lines of the contending armies slowly uncoiling across farms like giant serpents. A *New York Daily Tribune* correspondent imbibed the vast deployment. "We had arrived before their [Confederate] line of battle was complete," he wrote. "Columns were moving and deploying in all directions and positions—almost all on open ground, or ground covered only with growing corn. As a spectacle it was magnificent."

Across the creek, farmhand Alex Davis saw Confederate pickets arrive near his employer's farm. "None of 'em didn't offer to do me no harm," remembered Alex. "They asked me for some tobacker. I had a right good plug in my pocket, and I divided it up among 'em." The Rebels took a liking to the young farmhand. "An officer lent me his glasses," Alex recalled, "and I could see the Union army maneuvering over on the hills beyond the creek."

---

26 Hartwig, *To Antietam Creek*, 509-513, 644-645, 677-678; Additionally, Major General Fitz John Porter, commanding V Corps, arrived in Keedysville on Sep. 15 with 3,000 men from Brig. Gen. George Sykes's division. Porter's other two divisions did not reach the battlefield area until the 17th and 18th; Ezra A. Carman, *The Maryland Campaign of September 1862*, ed. Thomas G. Clemens, 3 vols. (El Dorado Hills, CA, 2012), 2:569-570; Harsh, *Taken at the Flood*, 348-349. Harsh's estimate for McClellan's strength is higher than the estimates of Hartwig and Carman; Thomas G. Clemens, *History of Keedysville*, video, October 1, 2018, https://www.youtube.com/watch?v=AxYX0vtUWhU; Thomas G. Clemens, "In Search of McClellan's Headquarters," *Civil War Times* (June 2016), 26-33; Thomas G. Clemens, email message to author, November 30, 2021. Dr. Clemens noted that the quartermaster general's returns on October 1, 1862, list the AOP's headquarters strength as 1,171 men, 120 wagons, six ambulances, and 983 horses (Rufus Ingalls's report, OR Series 1, vol. 19, pt. 1, 94-7). Clemens also clarified, "[T]echnically, the Army of the Potomac headquarters camp was in Keedysville [on John J. Keedy's farm], and McClellan established a 'command post' or 'field headquarters' at the Pry house on the evening of the 16th;" Claims of John J. Keedy (54-1488 and No. 2157).

General James Longstreet also studied the arriving Federals. "The number increased, and larger and larger grew the field of blue until it seemed to stretch as far as the eye could see, and from the tops of the mountains down to the edges of the stream gathered the great army of McClellan. It was an awe inspiring spectacle."[27]

Confederate artillery opened on the arriving enemy. Any local folk unaware of the armies' presence were now alerted spectacularly. Explosions rocked the countryside. The Pipers' farmhouse "was completely surrounded with cannon," which drew the attention of Union artillery. "[B]efore 2 o'clock I was startled to hear the report of the cannon of the Federal army," wrote Mary Ellen Piper. "The shell exploded about ten yards from the house and wounded two men. The next moment a messenger came directing us to leave the house instantly as it was in the range of the Federal army's guns. We took a few dresses on our arms, locked up the house, and started off."

The Pipers left "every thing as it was on the farm." Mary Ellen remembered that Jeremiah Summers, one of the Pipers' slaves, "took the horses and we all walked about a mile and a half when father said, if possible, we should walk on and they would go back for the buggy. They again reached the house though it was raining grape and shell in every direction." Henry Piper and Jeremiah returned with the horse-drawn carriage and drove the family three miles northwest to the farm of Henry's brother, Samuel I. Piper.[28]

Near the Nicodemus farm, Alex Davis continued mingling with Confederates as artillery thundered in the valley. The young farmhand found the experience sobering. "[W]hile I was layin' there talkin' to the pickets, a shell landed in a fence 'bout thirty yards from me. I'd never seen no battle nor no war, and I was scared." Having seen enough, Davis left the soldiers and prepared to evacuate.[29]

Fleeing one's home is a difficult decision. True, artillery shells could maim or kill occupants standing guard inside dwellings to protect their belongings, but

27 Hartwig, *To Antietam Creek*, 509-511; Johnson, *BA*, 96; James Longstreet, "The Invasion of Maryland," *The Century Illustrated Monthly Magazine* (London, 1886), May–October 1886, 312.

28 E. P. to Sally Farran, October 4, 1862, *Dan Masters' Civil War Chronicles*. Mary Ellen Piper's reference to her parents' farmhouse being "completely surrounded with cannon" likely refers to Confederate artillery crowning nearby ridges, given that the extant Piper dwelling sits on low ground; Hartwig, *To Antietam Creek*, 512-513; Claim of Henry Piper (*RG* 123, Entry 22, Box 100, No. 445). Piper deposed that his family left in the evening, while Jeremiah Summers testified they evacuated in the afternoon, corroborating Mary Ellen Piper's estimate of 2:00 p.m. The 1860 Federal slave schedule for Sharpsburg lists Henry Piper as owning six slaves.

29 Johnson, *BA*, 96.

evacuating a house carried risk as well. With thousands of soldiers in the area, break-ins were a genuine threat, despite orders against plundering civilian property. Jacob McGraw, a canal boatman who lived in the village, recalled, "The people was hidin' and g'tting' away as fast as they could. But we'd had word that any one who owned a good house had better stay and take care of it because in an army there's always fellows who will plunder houses left unprotected. So I stayed at home."

Some residents hid or buried valuables before fleeing their homes. Joseph Sherrick allegedly stashed $3,000 of gold "in the stone wall around his yard" and later recovered this fortune—valued at more than $84,000 in 2022 money. Jacob C. Grove, however, had secreted his money so well that he "forgot the hiding place and never did find it."[30]

The decision to evacuate tore at Samuel and Elizabeth Mumma. The couple had nine children, ripening crops, and a host of neighbors seeking refuge at their house. Yet, with batteries firing nearby, self-preservation took priority, and the Mummas decided to leave. Their son, Samuel, Jr., took horses from the stable, but there was little time to pack provisions. "Some clothing was gotten together," Samuel, Jr. recalled, "and the silverware packed in a basket ready to take but in our haste to get away, all was left behind." The Mummas and their neighbors trekked four miles north and "camped in a large church called the Manor Church, where many others were also congregated."[31]

30 Ibid., 114; Samuel Webster Piper, *Piper Family History*, unpaginated binders, courtesy of Lou and Regina Clark, Sharpsburg, Maryland. Samuel W. Piper, a grandson of Henry Piper, wrote, "Mr. & Mrs. Piper made hasty preparations for moving, burying the dishes in the ash piles;" Williams, HWC, vol. 2, 1:361; Ernst, *TATC*, 135; Reilly, *BOA*; Samuel H. Williamson, "Purchasing Power Today of a U.S. Dollar Transaction in the Past," MeasuringWorth, https://www.measuringworth.com/calculators/ppowerus/index2.php. Cited hereafter after as *PPT*. The Measuring Worth website uses seven different indexes to estimate relative worth over time. This Antietam study bases estimates on real prices from the year 1862, "measured as the relative cost of a (fixed over time) bundle of goods and services such as food, shelter, clothing, etc., that an average household would buy." Measuring Worth cites that, "in theory the size of this bundle does not change over time, but in practice, adjustments are made to its composition. This measure uses the CPI [Consumer Price Index]." For comparative purposes, one dollar in 1862 equates to roughly $28 in 2022 U.S. real prices.

31 The Mummas' evacuation is a synthesis of several sources: Jacob Miller to Amelia and Christian Houser, October 1862, *WMR*; Claim of Samuel Mumma, Sr. (*RG* 123, Entry 22, Box 82, No. 334); Reilly, *BOA*; Wilmer M. Mumma, *Antietam: The Aftermath* (Sharpsburg, MD, 1993), 23-26; Ernst, *TATC*, 119-120; J. Maurice Henry, *History of the Brethren Church in Maryland* (Elgin, ILL), 1936. 370-371. Jacob Miller wrote, "Susan Kenady went to the country for safety to Sam Mummas but soon found out that would not do. [T]hey all left." The Manor Church is located about one mile southeast of Tilghmanton. Reilly cited that the Mummas fled to Susan Hoffman's farm on the Keedysville-Bakersville road before trekking to the church;

*   *   *

Union artillery posed little threat to Sharpsburg village on the fifteenth, but the armies' presence spooked many townsfolk into evacuating. Seventeen-year-old John P. Smith lived on East Main Street and remembered that some of the "terror stricken" inhabitants "fled from the town to the country, carrying with them a few articles of clothing." Smith's father chose to remain in the cellar, while John, his mother, and siblings "fled to the farm of Harry Reel . . . just west of Sharpsburg."

On the west end of Main Street lived sixteen-year-old James Snyder and his parents, who were "intensely loyal to the Union cause." When Rebels arrived in Sharpsburg, the Snyders closed their shutters and locked their doors. James's father went to Killiansburg Cave on the river. James and his mother, meanwhile, fled south to Reverend John A. Adams's farm, where a "large number of refugees were already congregated, and the house and even the barns and stables [were] full of apprehensive and terrified people."

Dozens of villagers evacuated to Grove's Landing on the Potomac River. Presumably, many left town via Chapline Street and took the landing road to the river. Some carried little but the reins of a horse or the hand of a child. Their ages and gender varied, but in the dire moment, all shared one singular motive. War had visited their doorstep.[32]

The sporadic artillery fire on September 15 continued until nightfall. Across Antietam Creek, thousands of sleeping Yankees sprawled from Jacob H. Cost's farm near the Upper Bridge to Joseph Thomas's farm in Porterstown. In Keedysville, Gen. McClellan dined at Jeptha and Mary Taylor's stone mill, paying

---

Genealogical records show that Samuel and Elizabeth Mumma were the parents of 13 children in 1862. Three offspring from Samuel's first marriage—all adults in 1862—lived in different households. Another son, Samuel Mumma, Jr., testified in his father's claims case (No. 334) that he did not live with his parents in September 1862. He stated, "I was living about a mile away but was on the place [the Samuel Mumma, Sr. farmstead] every day." Thus, the displaced Mumma family in September 1862 included the couple and nine children.

32 John P. Smith, "No Civilian Died in the Great Battle of Antietam in '62," *Morning Herald* [Hagerstown, MD], January 25, 1951. John Philemon Smith, a son of John Hamilton Smith, later wrote manuscripts and articles about Sharpsburg's history. The *Morning Herald* in 1951 reprinted Smith's original, undated article; Alexander, "*Destruction, Disease, and Death*, 153;" Fred W. Cross, "A Sharpsburg Boy at Antietam," *The Daily Mail* [Hagerstown, MD], January 16, 1934, 10. Snyder told Cross, "[H]e and his mother went down to Parson Adams place a mile and a half from Sharpsburg on the road to Harpers Ferry;" Alfred R. Waud, *Sharpsburg citizens leaving for fear of the Rebels*, 1862, sketch, Library of Congress, https://www.loc.gov/item/2004660777/. Library of Congress is hereafter referred to as *LC*.

the couple "a two dollar and a half gold piece" for the meal. Afterward, he rode to his headquarters on John J. Keedy's farm.[33]

At Sharpsburg, Hilary Watson left the Otto farm and "went up to the village" to check on his enslaved wife, Christina Watson. She was a slave owned by Jacob H. Grove and lived with her master on Sharpsburg's public square, working as the family's cook. That night, Christina Watson may have prepared dinner for generals Lee and Longstreet, who boarded at the house.

Reaching the Grove home, Hilary Watson found that Christina "was skeered up a little but hadn't got into no trouble." After visiting, he bade his wife farewell and returned to his master's farm. En route, Watson found Rebels "sleepin' along

---

33 Hartwig, *To Antietam Creek*, 515; Carman, *The Maryland Campaign*, 1:411; Reilly, *BOA*. Reilly originally dated McClellan's dinner as Sep. 16. Later, in the *Shepherdstown* [WV] *Register*, March 15, 1934, he revised the account to Sep. 15.

Sharpsburg citizens leaving for fear of the Rebels. Dated September 15, 1862, Alfred R. Waud's sketch looks southeast down Snyder's Landing Road where it bends east into West Chapline Street. South Mountain is visible in the distance, along with St. Paul's Methodist Episcopal Church, the German Reformed Church, the Lutheran Church, and the irregular window pattern of Catherine Chapline's stone home at 229 West Chapline Street. *Library of Congress*

the edge of the road same as a lot of hogs might. I stumbled over some of 'em, but they didn't say anything."[34]

34 Johnson, *BA*, 106. Federal census records for Sharpsburg from 1870–1910 list Hilary and Christina Watson as a married couple. Census entries for 1880 and 1900 list Christina by her nickname, Tenie or Tiney, which some secondary sources have interpreted as "Teenie;" Owen, *In Camp and Battle with the Washington Artillery*, 139. Owen spent the night of Sep. 15 in Sharpsburg village "in a dwelling-house on the edge of town." He recalled that "Gens. Lee and Longstreet were in a house on the opposite side of the street;" Harsh, *Taken at the Flood*, 326; Carman, *The Maryland Campaign*, 2:15-16. Harsh wrote that Lee boarded at Jacob H. Grove's house on the 15th. Editor Clemens noted that Charles Venable "had Lee breakfasting in Sharpsburg on the morning of September 16, which confirms William Owen's statement that Lee stayed overnight in a house in town." Clemens cited Charles Venable, *Personal Reminiscences of the Confederate War* (University of Richmond, accession #2969-a, 1889), 66.

*   *   *

When the sun rose on September 16, fog cloaked the Antietam Valley. General Lee paced the misty fields of Sharpsburg Heights, awaiting the arrival of Stonewall Jackson's command from Harpers Ferry. Across Antietam Creek, George McClellan, blinded by the fog, wondered if the Confederate army had vanished in the night or swelled with reinforcements. Nearby, the Federal Reserve Artillery, twenty long-range guns, deployed along the ridge east of the creek. Many of Reserve's 20-pound Parrott guns and 3-inch ordnance rifles swung their barrels toward Sharpsburg, targeting Confederate cannon dotting the heights near the village.[35]

Southwest of Sharpsburg, Gen. Stonewall Jackson and a portion of his command splashed across Blackford's Ford, having completed their night march from Harpers Ferry. After meeting with Lee on Sharpsburg Heights, Jackson rode through town and stopped at Jacob H. Grove's house, where James Longstreet and Major General James Ewell Brown Stuart based their headquarters. The Groves, Southern sympathizers, invited Stonewall to breakfast. When Jackson declined and rejoined his troops, Julia Grove, a daughter in the household, sent a meal to the general. Touched by the gesture, Jackson scribbled a thank you note to the Confederate-sympathizing lass.[36]

East of the Groves lived the family of John Kretzer, staunch Unionists known for flying an American flag over Main Street. When Confederates occupied Sharpsburg, the Kretzers hid Old Glory in a "strong wooden box, and buried it in the ash pile behind a smokehouse." Soon, though, pro-South neighbors informed Rebel officers of the hidden U.S. flag. On the morning of September 16, Confederate troops confronted the Kretzers' adult daughter, Teresa. When soldiers demanded the flag, she told them no such thing was in the house. Not buying the story, the armed men threatened to search the home at gunpoint.

---

35 Harsh, *Sounding the Shallows*, 18-19; Hartwig, *To Antietam Creek*, 582-585, 598-599; Harsh, *Taken at the Flood*, 330-331; Carman, *The Maryland Campaign*, 2:22-23. McClellan ordered the deployment of long-range guns on the evening of Sep. 15, and these batteries took position on the morning of the 16th.

36 Hartwig, *To Antietam Creek*, 598-599; Harsh, *Taken at the Flood*, 334-335. Harsh wrote that Jackson's division arrived first (commanded by J. R. Jones), followed closely by Ewell's division (under Alexander Lawton). John G. Walker's division reportedly did not arrive on the 16th "until noon or shortly thereafter;" Harsh, *Sounding the Shallows*, 196-197; Henry Kyd Douglas, *I Rode With Stonewall, Being Chiefly the War Experiences of the Youngest Member of Jackson's Staff from the John Brown Raid to the Hanging of Mrs. Surratt* (Chapel Hill, N.C, 1940), 167.

Thinking fast, Teresa played with words: "I knew somebody would tell you about that flag, and rather than have it fall into your hands, I laid it in ashes." Assuming that the young woman burned the Yankee banner, the troops departed.[37]

*   *   *

The fog lifted between eight and nine that morning, uncloaking the contending armies. Batteries began sporadic cannonading, including several guns of the Federal Reserve Artillery—powerful cannon capable of firing deadly shells more than two miles. The town of Sharpsburg sat within this range, and many residents had not evacuated, risking their lives to guard personal possessions. Occupants of log and frame dwellings were especially vulnerable, as solid shots could smash through walls, while case shot and rifled shells might set houses ablaze.[38]

Confederates urged the civilians to evacuate. One resident, Maggie Grice Hoffmaster, remembered that a "short, stout man with curly hair" went door to door on Main Street, "telling all the people that they should vacate their homes." Another villager, Susan Lopp Santman, recalled that, on September 16, "an order was given to cease firing so that women and children could leave the town for places of refuge."[39]

Many villagers complied with the advice, and some fled to nearby stone homes. Teresa Kretzer remembered neighbors flocking to her parents' house. "Our basement was very large with thick stone walls," she recounted, "and they wanted to take refuge in it . . . there were women and children of all ages and some very old men." Sarah Cronise lived in a weather-boarded home west of the Kretzers. Ordered to evacuate, she escorted her three children to the increasingly crowded house. Susan Ward also fled to the Kretzers', bringing her newborn child, a girl

37 Johnson, *BA*, 123-124; Fred W. Cross, "Story of Flag Woman Saved at Antietam," *The Daily Mail* [Hagerstown, MD], April 9, 1931, 2; Fred W. Cross, "Story of Flag at Antietam," *The Daily Mail*, January 30, 1934; Fred W. Cross, "The Strong Stone House," *The Daily Mail*, March 22, 1934, 2. Maria "Teresa" Kretzer told her flag story on different occasions to Fred Cross and Clifton Johnson (*Battleground Adventures*), and the interviews reveal minor discrepancies. In Johnson's account, Kretzer described the soldiers' threats of searching her home and implied that she buried the flag by herself. In Cross's accounts, Kretzer did not mention the threats and stated that her father and one of Col. Jacob Rohrback's daughters buried the flag.

38 Hartwig, *To Antietam Creek*, 585, 598-599; Carman, *The Maryland Campaign*, 2:22-23; Harsh, *Taken at the Flood*, 335.

39 Reilly, *BOA*; "Aged Woman Tells of Giving Food to Antietam Soldiers," *Morning Herald* [Hagerstown, MD], July 10, 1937, 10C.

born one week earlier. Before long, the Kretzer home became a refuge for scores of villagers.[40]

*   *   *

Most civilians who fled town on the 16th sought refuge along the Potomac, sheltering in caves, lockhouses, and dwellings. Union artillery fire, remaining light throughout the morning, funneled many evacuees to the riverside havens of Grove's Landing and Killiansburg Cave.[41]

Grove's Landing was a small, commercial port on the C & O Canal. Several buildings stood in the vicinity, including a grain warehouse and a dwelling owned by Jacob C. Grove and his siblings. Evacuees quickly overcrowded the Grove house. Bud Shackelford and Susan Lopp Santman estimated that 150 to 200 people crammed inside the home, many of whom were children and teens. Shackelford recalled that bedding was scant, and thus he "slept on a piece of bark." The displaced children, he added, "had nothing to eat until someone thought of getting flour out of the ware house. Two barrels were rolled out and soon they were all eating short cakes."[42]

40 Johnson, *BA*, 123-124; Cross, "Story of Flag Woman Saved at Antietam;" Cross, "Story of Flag at Antietam;" Cross, "The Strong Stone House;" Reilly, *BOA*; Mumma, *Antietam: The Aftermath*, 43; Smith, "No Civilian Died." Smith's article named several villagers who sheltered in the Kretzer home. Census, land, and architectural records suggest that many of these persons lived on or near East Main Street.

41 Some civilians evacuated across the Potomac River to Virginia on September 15–16, 1862. See Ernst, *TATC*, 156-157. See also Virginia Mumma Hildebrand, "Mount Airy Has Its Moments of History," *Antietam Remembered*, unpublished manuscript, WMR, 83-85. See also Harry Warner, "Battle of Sharpsburg's Effect on Civilians," *The Daily Mail* [Hagerstown, MD], September 21, 1976.

42 Jacob C. Grove and his siblings—Jeremiah P., Laura L., William H., and Franklin L.—were also known as the heirs of Samuel Grove. Jacob C. Grove operated the Grove's Landing warehouses in Sep. 1862 but he did not own the landing's real estate until 1863. Land records IN 7 / 62-64 and IN 17 / 89 show that William and Rachel Loughridge owned the tract in Sep. 1862 (Grove and the Loughridges agreed to the sale in Jan. 1862, but the Washington County Circuit Court did not record the deed until Apr. 1863). Deed IN 17 / 89 mentions that the land contained "a brick warehouse and other buildings thereon;" William "Bud" Shackelford interview, January 24, 1934, "Civilian Reports," folder, ANBL; "Aged Woman Tells of Giving Food to Antietam Soldiers," *Morning Herald*, July 10, 1937, 10C. The Grove dwelling described by Shackelford and Santman may have been the Mount Pleasant house owned by the heirs of Samuel Grove or a tenant home on the property. See "WA-II-1143 Morgan Property (Portion of the Mt. Pleasant Estate of Captain Joseph Chapline)," architectural survey file, MHT. See also "WA-II-461 Part of Mt. Pleasant" and "WA-II-110 Mt. Pleasant Secondary Dwelling," MHT. The C & O Canal, 184.5 miles in length, ran along the Potomac River, from Georgetown in Washington, DC, to Cumberland, MD.

Killing's Cave on the Banks of the Potomac near Sharpsburg. Incorrectly dated July 3, 1863, the image shows civilians and Confederate stragglers sheltering in Killiansburg Cave in September 1862. Sketch by Frank H. Schell. *New York Public Library Digital Collections*

When the Grove house filled to capacity, evacuees needing shelter pressed southwestward along the canal towpath until they reached various caves. The largest formation was Killiansburg Cave, its entrance resembling the gaping mouth of a whale. The cavern's rocky floor, at a glance, might accommodate forty people. One villager, though, reckoned, "[S]eventy-five went to that cave." Others described it as "packed full of people" and "crowded with a variety of people of all classes." The occupants of Killiansburg Cave, safe from cannon fire, "collected food from area farms and slept on the ground."[43]

*   *   *

43 On-site visit to Killiansburg Cave, 2008; Ernst, *TATC*, 140; Johnson, *BA*, 120; Henry Marion Johnson, 1934 interview, "Civilian Reports" folder, ANBL; Elizabeth Miller Blackford to Amelia Houser, February 8, 1863, WMR; Roger Keller, *Roster of Civil War Soldiers from Washington County, Maryland* (Baltimore, MD, 1998), 46.

Around 11:00 a.m. on September 16, artillery in both armies erupted. Heavy pieces of the Washington Artillery on Sharpsburg Heights opened fire on Union batteries across Antietam Creek. Federal long-range guns instantly replied. Badly outgunned, the Washington Artillery dueled the powerful U.S. batteries for forty minutes, creating a continual, rolling thunder. One Confederate described the exchange as "one of the hottest artillery duels I have ever witnessed."[44]

Some Rebel personnel took cover behind Sharpsburg Heights. Among them was William M. Owen, who recalled that the enemy's batteries made "their shot whistle over our heads, and plunge into the town, setting fire to some houses."

In one home, a townsman and his family prepared "to sit down at the dinner table, when a solid shot crashed through the wall, and, falling on the table, spoiled the dinner and dishes, and . . . also our appetites." As villagers fled, straggling Rebels ducked into abandoned homes. A group of hungry Georgians entered a dwelling and "found a table with the meal all ready to sit down to, when the occupants were frightened away." As the soldiers began devouring the food, "a cannonball came crashing through the wall, knocked the legs off from under the table, and dropped it on the floor . . . That put an end to the feast."[45]

Private Randolph Shotwell of the 8th Virginia Infantry left Sharpsburg Heights to seek food. He found that "only a very few of the citizens had remained to face the bombardment which had already begun." He also observed, "[S]everal houses and stables were in flames from the bursting shells. The crackling flames and lurid volumes of smoke, joined to the rapid clatter of horse's hoofs, as couriers and aides de camp galloped up and down, gave a feverish aspect to the scene that was in singular contrast to the long rows of abandoned houses." As Shotwell hurried up Main Street to rejoin his command, he recalled that "quite a number of huge missiles fell near me, making a terrible sound as they crashed through the thin walls and hurtled among the tree-tops."[46]

As shells exploded in the town, General Lee left Jacob H. Grove's house and transferred his headquarters west of Sharpsburg's limits in the Town Woods. The

44 Harsh, *Taken at the Flood*, 335-336; Hartwig, *To Antietam Creek*, 600; W. H. Andrews, *Footprints of a Regiment: A Recollection of the 1st Georgia Regulars, 1861-1865* (Atlanta, 1992), 75.

45 Owen, *In Camp and Battle*, 141; Hartwig, *To Antietam Creek*, 600; J. L. Smith, *History of the Corn Exchange Regiment, 118th Pennsylvania Volunteers* (Philadelphia, 1888), 52; Andrews, *Footprints of a Regiment*, 75.

46 Randolph A. Shotwell, *The Papers of Randolph Abbott Shotwell*, 3 vols. (Raleigh, NC, 1929), 1:345-349.

Groves and their slaves remained inside their brick home, gawking at the commotion outdoors. Major Johann August Heinrich Heros von Borcke, a Prussian Confederate cavalry officer, also sheltered inside Jacob H. Grove's house on September 16. When shells exploded nearby, von Borcke urged the residents to shelter in the cellar.[47]

He remembered, "About noon the bombardment became really appalling." A Union shell "pierced the wall of the room a few feet above my head, covered me with the debris, and, exploding, scattered the furniture in every direction. At the same moment another missile, entering the upper part of the house, and passing directly through, burst in the courtyard, killing one of our horses, and rendering the others frantic with terror."

Von Borcke and his couriers fled outside "amid the blinding dust and smoke" and saddled up while artillery shells exploded around them. The heavy cannonading terrified the Grove residents. Christina Watson, joined by other slaves and members of the Grove family, "made a run for it," but didn't get far. Shortly after fleeing outside, a shell exploded overhead, driving them all back into the Groves' cellar, where they huddled for the rest of the day.[48]

---

47 Harsh, *Taken at the Flood*, 339; Hartwig, *To Antietam Creek*, 600; Owen, *In Camp and Battle*, 141. In Sep. 1862, the heirs of Samuel and Lavenia Grove owned the Town Woods, where General Lee established his headquarters; Von Borcke, *Memoirs*, 1:227-228. Von Borcke described the dwelling as "just opposite the principal church." The church closest to Jacob H. Grove's house, the German Reformed Church, was located around 300 feet west. Von Borcke identified one of the home's occupants as "Dr. G.," likely referring to Jacob H. Grove's son, Dr. Philip D. Grove. In Jacob H. Grove's claim (No. 1267), sworn testimony cites that Dr. Philip Grove lived with his parents in 1862 but enlisted in the Rebel army during or shortly after the Sep. 15–18 Confederate occupation of Sharpsburg.

48 Von Borcke, *Memoirs*, 1:227-228; Johnson, *BA*, 109-11. Johnson referred to his interview subject as the "slave woman at the tavern." Evidence supports that she was Christina Watson, the wife of Hilary Watson. In Johnson's *BA*, 104-106, he interviewed a "slave foreman" who identified himself as Hilary and cited his master's name as Otto. Similarly, in the claim of Solomon Lumm (*RG* 123, Entry 22, Box 83, No. 340), Hilary Watson identified himself as a former slave owned in 1862 by John Otto. Federal census records from 1870–1910 show Hilary and Christina Watson as a married couple, but their names do not appear in the 1860 census because of their status as slaves. In the preface of *BA*, Johnson wrote, "The material for the volume was gathered in 1913." The "slave woman at the tavern" told Johnson circa 1913, "I'm goin' on eighty-seven years old." Census entries from 1870– 1910 list Christina Watson's birth year between 1825 and 1827, and the 1900 census cites her birth as December 1826. Based on this data, she would have been 87 years old in 1913—the same age noted by Johnson. Sharpsburg's census listings for 1910 do not show any African American women close to Christina's age. The 1860 Federal slave schedule for Sharpsburg lists Jacob H. Grove owning nine slaves. The listing included three adult females aged between 20 and 40. Christina Watson was 34 years old in 1860. The "slave woman" told Johnson, "Our old boss was a Democrat."

Elizabeth Miller Blackford also risked her life by fleeing town during the artillery barrage. She initially planned to "remain at home and go in the Seller," but Confederate surgeons occupying her home "prevailed on us to leave." Elizabeth dreaded the thought of leaving her home and personal belongings "to the mercy of stranglers [strangers]." Still, when a missile struck the neighbor's house, Elizabeth, her children, and a slave fled west up Main Street, stopping near General Lee's headquarters in the Town Woods. Seeing the women and children in danger, Confederates offered them a ride. "[W]e went to Stephen Groves in an Ambulance from the woods," wrote Elizabeth, "passing through several Regiments, poor men marching in to battle, I left the girls and nan there, took John Frank and walked down to Frances we found Mr. Peter Beeler, and all his family there, not many soldiers."[49]

The artillery duel also forced farm families to evacuate. Southwest of town, the household of Jacob Avey, Sr., took flight. Nearby, the Ottos and their slaves fled "down country" for safety. Hilary Watson, one of the Ottos' slaves, returned to ensure they had locked the house. He found that "some one had broke a pane of glass in a window . . . he'd raised the window and crawled in." Watson confronted the burglar—a young Rebel lacking a weapon. "I was skeered," Hilary remembered, "but he was mo' skeered than I was . . . I could have mashed him, for

---

According to Jacob H. Grove's claim (*RG* 123, No. 1267), "during the war he [Grove] was a prominent Democrat." The woman's account of the artillery bombardment closely matches von Borcke's description of Jacob H. Grove's home on Sep. 16. She also stated that a shell struck the tavern, which "scattered brick." Jacob H. Grove's dwelling in 1862 was a brick house on Lot 35 on the southwest corner of the public square. The slave woman also stated, at the time of the 1862 battle, "I was the cook at Delaney's Tavern hyar in Sharpsburg." Delaney's Tavern was actually Delauney's Tavern, a postwar name for Lot 35. Land records cite that the lot passed from the Groves to Robert Delauney (WMCKK 6 / 29-30, 99 / 696, 105 / 120-121). Delauney operated a tavern on Lot 35 in 1913—the same year that Johnson interviewed the "slave woman." Williams in *A History of Washington County*, 2(1):781, wrote, "Robert Ferdinand de Launey, the popular proprietor of the Antietam Hotel . . . is the owner of the substantial brick building on the public square, once the headquarters of Gen. Robert E. Lee;" "WA-II-541 Grove-Delauney House," architectural survey file, MHT. The report identified Jacob H. Grove as a former owner of Lot 35 in Sharpsburg village and cited that Robert Delauney began operating the Antietam Hotel on Lot 35 in 1911.

49 Elizabeth Miller Blackford to Amelia Houser, February 1863, WMR. "Frances" was Elizabeth's older brother, Francis M. Miller, who lived near Miller's Sawmill. "John Frank" was Elizabeth's son. Squire Jacob Miller's sawmill, also known as Miller's Sawmill, was a milling complex located along the Potomac River, east of Blackford's Ford. For further reading, see "WA-II-381 Miller's Sawmill Vicinity," architectural survey file, MHT. See also Squire Miller's biography in Williams, HWC, vol. 2, 1:912-13.

I saw he had no revolver. He didn't say anything. He left. I reckon I was too big for him."[50]

*   *   *

In the East Woods, Confederate cavalry deployed near the farms of Daniel Miller and Samuel Poffenberger. Perhaps it was the artillery duel or the Rebels' proximity, but Miller evacuated with his family at noon on the 16th. Indeed, it was not easy for Daniel to up and leave, for he was 84 and ailing.[51]

Next door, Samuel Poffenberger watched Confederates occupy his farm. Worried that Rebels might steal his horses, the farmer sneaked the animals into his cellar and then evacuated with his wife to Keedysville. Poffenberger was not the only farmer who hid horses in his home. William Unger, a near neighbor, muffled his animals' hooves with grain sacks to prevent soldiers from detecting the equines in his cellar.[52]

---

50 Jonathan T. Trowbridge, *The South: A Tour of its Battlefields and Ruined Cities, a Journey Through the Desolated States, and Talks with the People* (Hartford, CT, 1866), 51. Evidence supports that Trowbridge interviewed a daughter of Jacob Avey, Sr., who stated that "she and her neighbors fled from their home on Tuesday before the battle, and did not return until Friday." The woman's home was located on modern-day Burnside Bridge Road "on a rising bank near the edge of the town." The farmhouse of Jacob Avey, Sr., located at the southeast edge of town on Burnside Bridge Road, also sits on a rising bank. The woman told Trowbridge that her father died one year after the battle, matching Jacob Avey, Sr.'s death in Dec. 1863. Trowbridge described the dwelling as stone, with an east-facing porch. The Maryland Historic Trust's architectural survey file for "WA-II-151 Avey-Stransky House" notes that Avey's brick and frame house faces east. This construction does not match Trowbridge's description, but the home includes a "hip-roofed front porch supported by stone piers;" Johnson, *BA*, 106-107. John Otto may have taken his family to a farm tenanted by his son, David Otto, situated southwest of town, near Miller's Sawmill.

51 Claim of Samuel Poffenberger (*RG* 92, Entry 812, Book F, Box 89, Claim F-1434). Michael Miller, a son of Daniel Miller, cultivated his father's farm in 1862. Michael testified "that when he, affiant, left his own place at noon, he could still see a few rebels on claimant's [Poffenberger's] farm." Jacob Miller to Amelia and Christian Houser, December 7, 1862, WMR. Miller wrote, "Uncle Daniel and Mike all left their homes . . . He [Daniel] was not well when he left home, the day before the big battle."

52 Harsh, *Taken at the Flood*, 354-355; Hartwig, *To Antietam Creek*, 613-615; Claim of Samuel Poffenberger (No. 4298). Poffenberger estimated that about "one hundred Confederates" occupied his farm on Sep. 16. Poffenberger's neighbor, tenant farmer Simon Morrison, deposed that he saw Rebels posted "on the extreme corner" of Poffenberger's farm; Williams, HWC, vol. 2, 1:927-28; Pat Schooley, "Kef-Poff Farm - Early 1800s farmhouse served as a hospital after Antietam." *The Daily Mail* [Hagerstown, MD], September 5, 1997. Samuel and Catherine Poffenberger evacuated to the farm of Catherine's father, Samuel Doub; Reilly, *BOA*. William Unger tenanted Susan Kennedy's farm in 1862, which adjoined Henry F. Neikirk.

*   *   *

During the artillery bombardment, McClellan prepared to attack Lee. First, he ordered IX Corps south to threaten the Confederate right flank. He then sent I Corps north toward the Confederate left.[53]

After a slow start, advance forces of I Corps crossed Antietam Creek. The main column crossed the Upper Bridge while the 3rd Pennsylvania Cavalry, a few hundred yards downstream, led Brigadier General Abner Doubleday's division across Pry's Ford. Reaching the western side of the creek, Doubleday halted to observe the fording. Nearby, Confederate videttes of the 9th Virginia Cavalry, hidden in a nearby cornfield, also watched the activity. The Southern troopers immediately sent word to General J. E. B. Stuart that the enemy was crossing. Next, they opened "a sharp fire" on Doubleday and his staff. The musketry spooked nearby residents. Samuel Pry and his family lived northeast of Pry's Ford and evacuated their home due to "the firing of the rebels." Doubleday, meanwhile, sent sharpshooters to drive off the Southern pickets, who fell back across the farms of Henry F. Neikirk and Susan Hoffman. Directly opposite Antietam Creek from the Neikirk farm, members of Alfred N. Cost's family went to their spring to fetch water, during which time "the women of this family were fired at by the rebel skirmishers."[54]

The artillery duel finally ended, and the outnumbered Rebel guns withdrew behind Sharpsburg Heights. Confederate General Daniel Harvey Hill described the lopsided artillery fight as a "melancholy farce," but the violent exchange terrified town residents and damaged several homes.

With Federal batteries no longer firing toward the town, Robert E. Lee returned to Jacob H. Grove's house and held a war council with Jackson and Longstreet. But then came a series of significant events. First, the Federal Reserve Artillery resumed firing at Sharpsburg Heights, the center of Lee's line. Next, two

---

53 Harsh, *Taken at the Flood*, 349-350; Hartwig, *To Antietam Creek*, 613.

54 Harsh, *Taken at the Flood*, 350-352, 354-355; Hartwig, *To Antietam Creek*, 607-608; Claim of Samuel Pry (*RG* 92, Entry 797, Book 95, Box 238, Claim 95-1691); Claims of Henry F. Neikirk (*RG* 92, Entry 812, Book H, Box 131, Claims H-4108 and H-4109). A quartermaster agent investigating the case reported that Neikirk's horses "may have been scared out by the rattle of Musketry when the rebel line" fell back; Claim of Susan Hoffman (*RG* 123, Entry 22, Box 235, No. 1318). Hoffman's son, Euromus Hoffman, testified, "There was no fighting done on this place unless some slight skirmishing;" *New York Times*, September 21, 1862. While not documented, bullets fired toward Alfred N. Cost's farm on Sep. 16 may have been stray fire from skirmishing on Henry F. Neikirk's farm.

messages arrived, informing Lee that the enemy was moving toward both Confederate flanks. The U.S. IX Corps, approaching the Lower Bridge, threatened to block passage to Virginia at Blackford's Ford. The Union I Corps, marching toward Lee's left, blocked the route north. With options for movement limited and the enemy threatening the Confederate center and both flanks, Robert E. Lee faced two choices: retreat to Virginia and lose the momentum he had gained or stay and fight. Lee chose to stand his ground. He began his preparations for a full-scale battle at Sharpsburg.[55]

After crossing Antietam Creek, the 3rd Pennsylvania Cavalry led nearly 10,000 men of I Corps toward Lee's left flank. The main column marched northwest along the Keedysville-Williamsport Road. Doubleday's division, advancing 100 yards west, slowly traversed the fenced farms of Dr. Otho J. Smith and Sarah Snyder.

About this time, a civilian rode forth and offered his assistance. Jacob Snyder was a son of Sarah Snyder. He rented his mother's farm on shares, receiving half the crops raised. He was also a Union man and saw the Yankees might benefit from a shortcut through his cornfield. General Hooker reportedly approved the idea, and Snyder guided U.S. soldiers through his 14-acre field, destroying most of the corn in the process. He continued leading the troops west until nearing George Line's farm, where Confederate pickets opened fire. Hooker discharged Snyder and sent the patriotic farmer home.[56]

Around five in the afternoon, Maj. Gen. McClellan established his observation post on the farm of Philip and Elizabeth Pry. Oral history holds that George Armstrong Custer, then an officer on McClellan's staff, notified the Prys they would soon have company—and that they did. Their home became "a beehive of activity" as couriers, aides, and signal corps personnel converged on the farm to establish McClellan's field headquarters. Messengers raced to and from the house while soldiers carried parlor chairs outside for the officers. Nevertheless, the Prys

---

55 Harsh, *Taken at the Flood*, 335-339, 343-344, 354-361; Harsh, *Sounding the Shallows*, 197-198; Hartwig, *To Antietam Creek*, 598-599; Lee may have decided to fight at Sharpsburg on Sep. 15 rather than the 16th. See Rossino, *Their Maryland*, 207-209. See also Hartwig, *To Antietam Creek*, 518-520.

56 Hartwig, *To Antietam Creek*, 605, 615-616; Harsh, *Taken at the Flood*, 350-352; Carman, *The Maryland Campaign*, 2:28-32; Claim of Jacob Snyder (RG 92, Entry 812, Book F, Box 92, Claim F-1537). Snyder sought compensation for corn destroyed by I Corps's march on Sep. 16. He swore under oath that he served as "a guide at the battle of Antietam for Genl. Hooker and he was discharged by him when he began the engagement on George Line's farm towards Duncan [Dunker] Church." The 1860 Federal census lists Snyder and his siblings in their mother's household. The Snyders lived on the Keedysville-Bakersville Road, adjoining Susan Hoffman on the south. See "WA-II-255 Snyder-Thomas Farmstead," architectural survey file, MHT.

had more significant concerns. They owned two farms within view of the house, both containing a bounty of valuable crops. Like most farmers in the community, the couple certainly worried their fall harvest might be damaged by a potential battle or consumed by famished soldiers.[57]

Hunger was chronic in the Confederate army, but it plagued Union soldiers as well. Logistical delays and road traffic following the Battle of South Mountain prevented commissary wagons from advancing. In consequence, many U.S. units lacked rations. To appease their hunger, Federal troops seized crops from farms east of Antietam Creek. An IX Corps regiment "was ordered to go into a Corn field & potato patch which was Close by & to supply from that." A XII Corps soldier picked wheat seeds from a nearby stack to make pudding. After he pointed out the grain to his comrades, the ravenous troops swarmed onto the farm, "and in less time than it takes to tell it, the stacks were so covered with hungry boys, it looked, in the distance, as if an immense flock of crows had lit on them."

For hungry soldiers in the I Corps, eating would have to wait. When U.S. forces approached the East Woods, Brigadier General John Bell Hood advanced his Confederate division to contest the enemy. Skirmishing exploded in the woods. Soon, artillery on both sides joined the fight, and Union long-range batteries fired into the West Woods, where Stonewall Jackson's forces arrived to support Hood.[58]

As skirmishing intensified, civilians near the West Woods fled toward the Potomac River. Samuel Reel took his horses up the Mercersville Road (now Mondell Road) to Moses Cox's farm, while his wife, Cerusha, escorted their children north to Mercersville. Next door to the Reels, Jacob and Harriet Houser were "ordered to vacate their buildings" due to the danger. Jacob opted to remain at home. Harriet, meanwhile, led her young boys toward the river. While evacuating, William Houser, nine years old in 1862, remembered "a shell hitting the fence near by." Finally reaching the Potomac, Harriet and her children stayed at Timothy and Eliza Coin's lockhouse on the C & O Canal.[59]

---

57 Hartwig, *To Antietam Creek*, 608; Harsh, *Taken at the Flood*, 350-352; John W. Schildt, *Drums Along the Antietam* (Parsons, West Virginia, 2004), 174-175; Ernst, *TATC*, 121-122.

58 Hartwig, *To Antietam Creek*, 604; Robert M. Green, *History of the One Hundred and Twenty-Fourth Regiment Pennsylvania Volunteers in the War of the Rebellion* (Philadelphia, 1907), 120; Harsh, *Taken at the Flood*, 359.

59 Claim of Samuel Reel (*RG* 123, Entry 22, Box 437, Case No. 3209). Cerusha Reel testified that she resided in Sep. 1862 "on the Mercersville road a little west and north of Sharpsburg about [one quarter] of a mile" and "was living with my sister in law in a little house on the same farm." Cerusha's brother, Jessie Price, also lived on the Reel farm in 1862. Cerusha was Samuel

Adjoining the Coins to the north was the riverside farm of Samuel I. Piper, where other displaced citizens gathered. John Francis, a teenage African American farmhand, arrived at Piper's farm after evacuating his residence. Jessie Price, another young farmhand, reached Samuel I. Piper's farm after fleeing his tenant house on Samuel Reel's farm. Jessie arrived at nightfall, finding "quite a number of families over there who had taken shelter out of range of battle." One can imagine the mood on the Potomac farm as nervous citizens listened to the din of gunfire in the East Woods.[60]

During the skirmish, two Union brigades commanded by Colonel Albert L. Magilton and Lieutenant Colonel Robert Anderson advanced toward the North Woods, crossing farms between Smoketown Road and Hagerstown Pike. However, fencing impeded their passage, prompting men from the pioneer corps to ax gaps in the barriers. A soldier from I Corps observed John C. Middlekauff and Joseph Poffenberger, owners of the farms, approach the pioneer corps to inspect damages to their fencing. Rather than complaining of "the wreck and ruin," the soldier recounted, Middlekauff and Poffenberger "aided us in demolishing their property as well as kindly encouraging us in our undertaking."[61]

As Federals marched onto Poffenberger's farm, Confederate guns on Jacob and Hannah Nicodemus's farm opened fire, hurling projectiles over the Nicodemus farmhouse. The blasts no doubt frightened the couple and their three children. Fortunately, U.S. pickets from the 10th Pennsylvania Reserves crept to

---

Reel's second wife, and the couple had two young children at the time of the battle. Claims testimony cites that Samuel Reel owned one slave in 1862. Reel's father, Jacob Reel, devised the slave to Samuel in his last will and testament, describing him as "My negro man named William Tyler" (Will liber D / folio 547, Maryland Register of Wills Records, 1629-1999, Washington County, Register of Wills Office, Hagerstown, MD). The 1860 Federal slave schedule for Sharpsburg lists Samuel Reel with one male slave, aged 60; Reilly, *BOA*. William Houser told Reilly that he evacuated to "Timothy Coin Lock, now known as Kerfoot's." Thomas Kerfoot worked at Lock 40 after the war, adjoining the Samuel I. Piper farm. In 1862, Timothy Coin occupied the Lock 40 lockhouse with his wife Eliza and their children. The Coins appear in Dwelling #534 in the 1860 Federal census for Sharpsburg.

60 Claim of Samuel D. Piper (*RG* 123, Entry 22, Box 100, No. 440). Samuel D. Piper was the son of Henry Piper and nephew of Samuel I. Piper. John Francis testified that he lived with Samuel D. Piper in Sep. 1862 and evacuated to Samuel I. Piper's farm on Sep. 16. Samuel D. Piper remained at home on the 16th.

61 Harsh, *Taken at the Flood*, 350-352, 358; Hartwig, *To Antietam Creek*, 613, 622, 624-628.

the house and "received this family within our lines." Dangerously close to Rebel cannon, the pickets quietly escorted the Nicodemus clan to safety.[62]

*   *   *

The fading light diminished fighting in the East Woods, and troops on both sides settled in for the night, preparing for what promised to be a colossal battle. The tiny community of Sharpsburg, less than 48 hours earlier a virgin to combat, was now the unwilling host to more than 100,000 soldiers, 500 cannon, and two generals intent on destroying one another.[63]

The stress on residents was already intense, though the main battle had yet to begin. Hundreds had been forced from their homes and into such wretched, crowded shelters as damp cellars, dank caves, and distant dwellings along the Potomac. Everyone had questions. When would the nightmare end? When could they return home? Moreover, would they have a home to which they might return?

This last question especially dogged those who had fled. These evacuees heard the day's roar of musketry and blasts of cannon. Some, unable to bear further suspense, sneaked through military lines and returned to their houses. Henry Piper testified, "I came back to my place on the morning of the 16th & found my property all safe. I then went away." Samuel Mumma, Jr. and a friend stole past Confederate pickets during the night of the 16th to gather clothing for their displaced families. To the boys' dismay, Southern soldiers had ransacked the Mummas' house, and "everything of value had been taken." So Samuel and his

---

62 Robert E. L. Krick, "Defending Lee's Flank," ed. Gary W. Gallagher, in *The Antietam Campaign* (Chapel Hill, NC, 1999), 199-200; A. J. Warner to John M. Gould, October 19, 1894, John M. Gould papers relating to the Battle of Antietam, Dartmouth University, Rauner Special Collections Library, Hanover, NH. Warner mentioned the Nicodemus family by name; Johnson, *BA*, 97. Alex Davis lived with Jacob and Hannah Nicodemus in 1862, based on his sworn war claim testimonies and interviews with Clifton Johnson and Fred W. Cross. In Johnson's interview for *Battleground Adventures*, Davis corroborated A. J. Warner's account by recalling that U.S. troops took "the [Nicodemus] children and the old man and old woman off the battlefield before day on Wednesday."

63 Carman, *The Maryland Campaign*, 2:600; Hartwig, *To Antietam Creek*, 674-680. Carman wrote, "In all, on both sides, Union and Confederate, there were engaged [at Antietam] 75,368 infantry, 9,611 artillery, and 8,328 cavalry, an aggregate of 93,307. The number of guns brought into action was 520." Regarding present-for-duty estimates on Sep. 16–17, Hartwig arrived at 72,727 for the AOP and 38,095 for the ANV—a combined total of 110,822. Hartwig based his Sep. 2 and Sep. 16–17 estimates on several sources, including John Owen Allen, "The Strengths of Union and Confederate Forces at Second Manassas," master's thesis, George Mason University, 1993.

friend left the farm but unfortunately didn't make it through the Rebel line. "General D. H. Hill and some other officers had me brought to them," remembered Samuel, "and questioned me as to whether I was a member of that family, and then asked me about the different roads to Antietam Creek." Despite being a "Union boy," Samuel told Hill the truth and was released.[64]

Next door to the Mummas, William Roulette returned home—but not in time to save his horses. Under cover of darkness, Union soldiers sneaked west of the creek and stole Roulette's bay mare and sorrel horse. Rebels near the farm did not see the thieves, but Roulette's neighbor did. Joseph Parks "was employed as a farmhand" on Philip Pry's Lower farm, which adjoined Roulette's land. Parks saw three Federal privates "drive two young horses into my employer's—Philip Pry's—stable, where they put bridles on them." Parks intervened, telling the soldiers the animals "belonged to Mr. William Roulette on the adjoining farm." The men replied that "they had to have the horses and intended to take them to their camp." The helpless farmhand watched the troops ride Roulette's equines "toward their camp about half a mile distant."[65]

Around 9:00 p.m., a light rain misted the area. Along the Potomac, displaced villagers squeezed inside the shallow depths of Killiansburg Cave, no longer to shelter against cannon fire but now to dodge the precipitation. Beyond physical discomfort, other concerns burdened the locals. Many residents had sons or husbands in the local Maryland Potomac Home Brigade, who surrendered to Stonewall Jackson's Confederates the day prior. Did these families know their sons were prisoners? Were they paroled? Wounded, killed, or safe?

Mary Douglas, Sarah McGraw, and Mary Ann Newcomer had sons in the Confederate army, some of whom were present at Sharpsburg. How did the impending battle strain the nerves of these mothers? One, we know, feared her

---

64 Claim of Henry Piper (No. 445); Mumma, *Antietam: The Aftermath*, 23-26; Claim of Samuel Mumma, Sr. (No. 334). Mumma's son, Samuel, Jr., testified, "I was back of the rebel lines" on the night of the 16th.

65 Keven M. Walker and K. C. Kirkman, *Antietam Farmsteads: A Guide to the Battlefield Landscape* (Sharpsburg, MD, 2010), 70-71; Richard Clem, "Farmer Cheers Federals at Antietam," *The Washington* [DC] *Times*, February 5, 2009, https://www.washingtontimes.com/news/2009/feb/5/witness-to-americas-bloodiest-day/; Claim of William Roulette (RG 92, Entry 812, Book L, Box 169, Claim L-832). Roulette's 179-acre farm spanned "to the bank of Antietam Creek," near Philip Pry's Lower farm, west of the creek, occupied by Joseph Parks. See land records IN 6 / 394 and IN 7 / 653. In Roulette's claim, Joseph Parks swore under oath, "[I]n September, 1862, I was employed as a farmhand on the farm of Philip Pry, adjoining the farm of William Roulette." See also "WA-II-331 Joseph Parks Farm (Log Farmhouse, Antietam Creek, Cunningham Farm)," architectural survey file, MHT.

soldier-boy might die in the looming fight. When stragglers entered her home earlier in the day, they found the lady "softly singing before the fire . . . apparently heedless of the shells which were passing over her house." Her son served in Stonewall Jackson's brigade, "whose death she apparently regarded as certain— something to which she had long since made up her mind."[66]

Tensions on September 16 likely exacerbated stress for those grieving. Mary McCoy, a sixty-seven-year-old widow, cared for a mentally disabled son while mourning the death of her other boy, killed a month earlier in a train accident. Hezekiah Myers, "crippled by a kick from a horse," grieved the death of his wife, Mary, who died four months earlier, leaving him with four young daughters.[67]

Reverend Mortimer and Lucinda Shuford lost two daughters to diphtheria a few weeks earlier. Now, the mourning couple huddled inside Killiansburg Cave as rain fell through the gloomy night. John Beeler, a Union corporal from Sharpsburg, suffered a mortal wound two weeks earlier and passed away on September 16. Did Samuel and Amanda Beeler know their son had died on this day? If so, how did the armies' presence at Sharpsburg amplify their shock and sorrow?[68]

The upheaval caused by military operations hit the disabled, pregnant, and elderly especially hard. Villagers in their seventies and eighties may have found the explosions and evacuations almost too much to bear. Henry V. S. Blackford, "a

---

66 The Confederate sons were Henry Kyd Douglas, John B. Douglas, Joseph McGraw, and John Clinton Newcomer; Napier Bartlett, *A Story of the War Including the Marches and Battles of the Washington Artillery* (New Orleans, 1874), 136-137.

67 Federal census listings for Sharpsburg from 1860–80 list Daniel McCoy as idiotic. He died in 1884 at Belleview Asylum. An announcement of Henry McCoy's death appears in the *HFTL*, August 13, 1862, 2C. Land records IN 8 / 570 and 82 / 256 support Mary McCoy's 1862 occupancy of Lot 137N; Claim of Hezekiah Myers (No. 1301). Myers testified that, at the time of the battle, "I remained quietly at home; I lost my wife about that time." Burial records cite that his wife, Mary E. Myers, died on May 9, 1862. Federal census listings for Sharpsburg from 1860-1870 list Hezekiah Myers with four daughters.

68 John Philemon Smith, "Reminiscences of Sharpsburg, Washington County, Maryland, From the Date of its Laying Out July 9, 1763 to the Present Time, July 9th, 1899," typescript, 1912, WMR, 76; Lucy Grayson Ditto, "Journal of Deaths in Sharpsburg," loose-leaf notebook, Sharpsburg Historical Society, Sharpsburg, Maryland; Julius H. Shuford, *A Historical Sketch of the Shuford Family* (North Carolina. 1902), 28-29; Scharf, *HWM*, 1:227; Corporal John C. Beeler of Sharpsburg served in Cole's U.S. Cavalry, Co. A, and received a mortal wound at Leesburg on September 2, 1862. His parents, Samuel and Amanda Beeler, lived west of Sharpsburg village near Captain David Smith. Beeler's headstone in Sharpsburg's Methodist Cemetery reads, "Son of Samuel & Amanda." He appears in the National Park Service's Civil War Soldiers and Sailors System database, https://www.nps.gov/civilwar/search-soldiers-detail.htm?soldierId=D43 EDA80-DC7A-DF11-BF36-B8AC6F5D926A (hereafter cited as *CWSS*).

cripple from childhood," remained home with his wife and children, dangerously close to the Confederate right flank.[69]

Barbara Piper Cost was nine months pregnant, forced to evacuate her home near the Upper Bridge while caring for two toddlers. Lydia Snavely, Elizabeth Line, and Mary Jane Mumma were six to eight months pregnant; all three remained home caring for other children while surrounded by military forces.

Sickly persons also suffered. Susan Ward's week-old daughter caught a fever in the Kretzers' chilly cellar. "It's a wonder we didn't all take our deaths of colds in that damp place," remembered Teresa Kretzer. In Killiansburg Cave, Martha Anna "Georgia" Buchanan suffered from an unspecified illness, which worsened in the cavern's cold, dank atmosphere. One villager in the cave "was afraid that Georgia would die there she was so much exasted."[70]

What were the fears of Sharpsburg's African-Americans on September 16? If Confederates routed the Northern army as they did in the recent battle at Second Manassas, would Rebels seize local slaves and sell them south? Would free blacks be enslaved?

It was a nightmarish possibility. Less than 48 hours earlier, Stonewall Jackson's soldiers had captured hundreds of African Americans at Harpers Ferry—runaways and contrabands who had found freedom in the Union garrison. The Rebels returned the prisoners to their Virginia masters and forced others south into slavery. If the news from Harpers Ferry traveled to Sharpsburg by September 16, how did it affect people of color? Could married slaves like Hilary and Christina Watson be seized, sold south, and separated? Were former slaves, now free citizens, at risk? Thomas Barnum toiled for his freedom, paying wages to his master

---

69 Federal census records, genealogical data, and war claims show that, in September 1862, Colonel John Miller, Squire Jacob Miller, Catherine Rohrback, and Elizabeth Russell were in their late 70s and early 80s; Claims of Henry V. S. Blackford (RG 92, Box 95, Book G, Claims G-1630, G-1648, and G-1654). Civilian Urias Knode testified that Henry V. S. Blackford "was a cripple from childhood & very little about" during the war.

70 Census and genealogical records show that Rolla Cost, Ella Snavely, Edward Line, and Mary Jane Mumma were born between Sep. 17–Dec. 31, 1862; Johnson, BA, 123-124; Elizabeth Miller Blackford to Amelia Houser, February 8, 1863, WMR. Martha Anna "Georgia" Buchanan was the daughter of Eleanor Miller and Dr. James Buchanan. John P. Smith wrote in the *Antietam Valley Record* [Keedysville, MD], September 12, 1895, "Among the number who sought refuge in this [Killiansburg] cave was Miss Georgianna Buchanan, daughter of Dr. James Buchanan."

Nancy Campbell, also known as Nancy Camel, was manumitted from slavery in 1859. In September 1862, she lived in the household of William and Margaret Roulette, working as a domestic servant. *ANB*

for sixteen years to manumit himself, his wife, and their children. Would a Confederate victory at Sharpsburg end their freedom?[71]

The tense evening unnerved citizens and soldiers alike. Near the East Woods, the "popping of musketry" and "occasional rapid volleys of pickets" frequently shattered the night's silence. Thousands of men slept on their arms without rations, exposed to the rain. On George Line's farm, XII Corps soldiers sprawled in wet cornfields and ploughed dirt sown with cow manure. Near the West Woods, Confederates in the 5th Virginia dozed on the soaked ground using stones as pillows. Then, in the wee hours of September 17, all became eerily still as a palpable foreboding hung heavy over the Valley of the Antietam. Brigadier General Alpheus S. Williams of XII Corps described the night as "so dark, so obscure, so mysterious, so uncertain." An Ohio soldier added, "Everything became terrifically quiet. For the quiet that precedes a great battle has something of the terrible in it."[72]

---

71 Frye, *Harpers Ferry Under Fire*, 75-77, 101-102. The number of African Americans seized by Jackson is unknown, but some sources list up to 2,000. See also Rossino, *Their Maryland*, 274-277; Arabella M. Wilson, *Disaster, Struggle, Triumph: The Adventures of 1000 "Boys in Blue"* (Albany, New York, 1870), 88; Hartwig, *To Antietam Creek*, 564-565; McPherson, *Crossroads of Freedom*, 114; *HTL*, April 18, 1895. To secure freedom for himself, his wife, and his children, Barnum paid a total of $1,100 to his master, Josiah Davis.

72 Miles Clayton Huyette, *The Maryland Campaign and the Battle of Antietam* (Buffalo, NY, 1915), 28; Sears, *Landscape Turned Red*, 177; Ezra E. Stickley, "The Battle of Sharpsburg," *Confederate Veteran*, Volume 22, Issue 2 (Nashville, TN, 1914), 66; Hartwig, *To Antietam Creek*, 642-644; Alfred Deane Richardson, *The Secret Service, the Field, the Dungeon, and the Escape* (Hartford, CT, 1865), 283-284; Alpheus Williams, *From The Cannon's Mouth: The Civil War Letters Of General Alpheus S. Williams*, ed. Milo M. Quaife (Detroit, 1959), 125; Thomas Francis Galwey, *The Valiant Hours: Narrative of "Captain Brevet," An Irish-American in the Army of the Potomac*, ed. W. S. Nye (Harrisburg, PA, 1961), 38.

Across the Potomac River at Shepherdstown, Charles Andrews, rector of the Trinity Church, penned a late-night letter to an acquaintance. "[A] great battle as we suppose [is] pending at Sharpsburg," wrote Andrews. "All is terrible suspense. You will know the result long before this reaches you."

Another Shepherdstown citizen, Mary Bedinger Mitchell, summed up the evening's mood. She wrote, "Whispers of a great battle to be fought the next day grew louder, and we shuddered at the prospect, for battles had come to mean to us, as they never had before, blood, wounds, and death."[73]

---

73 Thomas A. McGrath, *Shepherdstown: Last Clash of the Antietam Campaign, September 19-20, 1862* (Lynchburg, VA, 2012), 43. McGrath cited Charles Andrews to "Don," Sept. 17, 1862, Charles Andrews papers, Duke University; Mary B. Mitchell, "A Woman's Recollections of Antietam," *Battles and Leaders of the Civil War*, eds. Robert Underwood Johnson and Clarence Clough Buel, 4 vols. (New York, 1887), 2:686.

Chapter 2

A Savage, Continual Thunder:
The Battle of Antietam

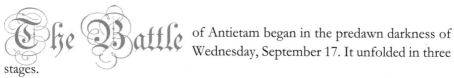 of Antietam began in the predawn darkness of Wednesday, September 17. It unfolded in three stages.

Phase 1 erupted north of Sharpsburg, where Gen. Joseph Hooker's I Corps attacked the Confederate left flank, defended by Stonewall Jackson. During the morning phase, roughly 24,000 Federals clashed with 20,000 Confederates on open, exposed ground in a concentrated area. Combat extended into the East and West Woods and stretched onto the farms of Colonel John Miller, Samuel Mumma, Sr., and Mary Grove Locher.

Artillery crews sprayed the massed troops with antipersonnel ordnance that included canister and spherical case, all intended to explode into destructive patterns. In addition, the guns fired both solid shot and more precise rifled shells. The volume and variety of projectiles inflicted staggering casualties on both armies. And errant shells, fired by the hundreds, hammered civilian properties on and near the battlefield, damaging structures, eviscerating livestock, and terrifying citizens.

At first light of the "moisty, misty morning," Confederate guns on Nicodemus Heights targeted I Corps on the Joseph Poffenberger and John C. Middlekauff farms. "The opposite hill seemed suddenly to become an active volcano, belching forth flame, smoke, and scoriae," recalled a Union artilleryman. Confederate missiles struck Joseph Poffenberger's house, "ripping up the roof, tossing the boards and shingles into the air." Another shell hit a threshing machine "and exploded in the center of the moving mass," killing three Union men and wounding eleven others. The Confederate bombardment terrified people and animals alike. A "cross bull" owned by Poffenberger's neighbor, "excited and maddened by the artillery fire . . . smashed through the barnyard gate, and with flaming eyes and waving tail charged . . . until he had reached the banks of Antietam creek." A U.S. soldier near Joseph Poffenberger's house donned his coat amid the explosions, only to find a terrified rabbit hiding in his sleeve.[1]

Adding to the chaos, artillery on other parts of the field opened fire, including Federal batteries east of Antietam Creek and Confederate cannon on Sharpsburg Heights and the Dunker Church plateau. In all, more than 500 artillery pieces took part in the battle.[2]

At one point during the morning's fighting, a newspaper correspondent rode to Joseph Poffenberger's farm and counted "thirty guns in position there pointing south-west." These were the massed cannon of the I Corps artillery, some of which targeted Nicodemus Heights to silence the Confederate guns. Federal artillery crews struggled to find their range, their longshots and shortfalls tearing up the Nicodemus property. One projectile tore through the main dwelling, while another blasted through the guesthouse walls. Eventually, the Federal counterbattery fire forced Confederate artillery to retire from the Nicodemus farm.[3]

A family near the West Woods evacuated amid the shell storm. Captain William W. Blackford, a Confederate staff officer, noticed a "handsome country house" situated between contending batteries. As the guns traded fire, shells screeched "clear over the top of the house," flushing out the terrified occupants. "Like a flock of birds they came streaming out," Blackford recalled, "hair streaming in the wind and children of all ages stretched out behind, and tumbling at every step over the clods of the ploughed field." Blackford rode to the evacuees and escorted them to safety.[4]

---

1 Carman, *The Maryland Campaign*, 2:113; Albert J. Monroe, *Battery D, First Rhode Island Light Artillery at the Battle of Antietam* (Providence, 1886), 13-14; Charles Carleton Coffin, *Following the Flag* (Boston, 1886), 165; Carman, *The Maryland Campaign*, 2:69; Fred W. Cross, "Alexander W. Davis, of Sharpsburg," *The Daily Mail* [Hagerstown, MD], March 13, 1934, 3. The bull allegedly belonged to David R. Miller; Walker and Kirkman, *Antietam Farmsteads*, 25.

2 Carman, *The Maryland Campaign,* 2:600; Curt Johnson and Richard C. Anderson, *Artillery Hell: The Employment of Artillery at Antietam* (College Station, TX), 1995. 39-40.

3 Charles Carleton Coffin, "Antietam Scenes," *Battles and Leaders of the Civil War*, 2:682-683; Johnson, *BA*, 99.

4 Claim of Alfred Poffenberger (*RG* 123, Entry 22, Box 234, No. 1308). The claim cited that Poffenberger "rented from Mrs. Locker of Penna.;" *Rochester* [NY] *Daily Union and Advertiser,*

The bloodiest combat took place on the 265-acre farm of Colonel John Miller. The colonel's son, David R. Miller, tenanted the farm in 1862. The property included a 30-acre cornfield, but after a few hours of savage fighting, Gen. Hooker reported, "every stalk of corn in the northern and greater part of the field was cut as closely as could have been done with a knife." In addition, the battle injured other parts of the Miller farm. Soldiers dismantled fencing, projectiles struck the dwelling house, and shells destroyed two outbuildings. Nevertheless, David R. Miller and his family escaped injury, having vacated their home before the battle.[5]

South of the Miller farm, the Dunker Church also suffered damage. Confederate artillery near the building drew fire from Union forces, which perforated the church "with bullets and solid shot in many places." When a Federal battery spotted Rebel sharpshooters inside the building, it "opened with spherical case" and fired "several well directed round shot which passed entirely through the [church] house." One soldier later observed that a shell "went entirely through" the building, leaving "a hole at either end through which a large man might crawl with ease." Federal fire inflicted scores of casualties near the church. The scene was one of bitterest dissonance, as corpses and dead horses lay helter-skelter on the sacred ground.[6]

*　　*　　*

September 26, 1862. Captain John A. Reynolds of the 1st New York Light Artillery, Battery L, described the damage to the cabin; William W. Blackford, *War Years with Jeb Stuart* (New York, 1945), 149-151. Blackford did not identify the fleeing civilians. Evidence rules out the families of Jacob Nicodemus, Jacob Houser, and Samuel Reel, who evacuated the day before the battle.

5 Claim of John Miller (*RG* 123, Entry 22, Box 358, No. 2227). Colonel John Miller claimed $25 in damages to "Farm Dwelling House by the shells" and $40 for "Damage to Two one story Blacksmith shop & granary." He referred to his farm as "Occupied as Tennant by David R. Miller." Corroborating this statement, David R. Miller testified that he "resided during the war on his father's farm" and "was a tenant of his father." Size estimates of Miller's 1862 cornfield range from 24 to 30 acres. Colonel John Miller served in the War of 1812. Battlefield maps and Ezra A. Carman's postwar manuscript refer to the property as the "D. R. Miller" farm. However, quartermaster claims, congressional case depositions, land records, agricultural schedules, and census listings reviewed in this study suggest that the tenant farmer identified himself as David R. Miller rather than D. R. Miller; Sears, *Landscape Turned Red,* 181; McPherson, *Crossroads of Freedom,* 118; Official report of Major General Joseph Hooker, November 8, 1862, *OR,* vol. 19, 1:218.

6 Johnson and Anderson, *Artillery Hell,* 118; Stephen H. Bogardus to the *Poughkeepsie* [NY] *Daily Eagle,* June 5, 1863, in *Dear Eagle: The Civil War Correspondence of Stephen H. Bogardus, Jr. to the Poughkeepsie Daily Eagle, Jr.* ed. Joel Craig (Wake Forest, 2004), 72.

While fighting raged across the Miller farm, Brigadier General Roswell S. Ripley's Confederates lay pinned near Samuel Mumma's farmhouse. Enduring a "severe enfilading fire," Ripley feared the situation would worsen if Federals seized the nearby dwelling house and turned it into a sniper's nest. To avoid this possibility, he ordered his men to burn the Mumma home. "A volunteer call was made as to who would go and do it," and several privates of the 3rd North Carolina came forward. Sergeant Major James F. Clark led them to the house as shells exploded nearby, wounding Clark in the process. One man "picked up a chunk of fire from where they had been cooking" and carried it to an open window. The North Carolina soldier glanced inside the home, saw a bed covered with a colorful quilt, and tossed the burning wood onto it. The flames quickly kindled and spread.

As fire consumed the farmhouse, a stray shell torpedoed the Mummas' barn. Charles Coffin, a correspondent for the *Boston Journal*, reported, "A shell bursts in the barn and sets it on fire. A black cloud rises. The flames burst forth." The fire from the house and barn spread to the outbuildings. The stately Mumma farmstead, home to a family of Dunker pacifists, was now a raging inferno, its smoke wafting over the battlefield and intermingling with clouds of gunpowder. "The dark pillar of cloud, the bright flames beneath," wrote Coffin, "the constant flashing of artillery, and the hillsides alive with thousands of troops, their banners waving, their bayonets gleaming, is a scene of terrible grandeur."[7]

Hooker's forces eventually gained the field, but John Bell Hood's Confederate counterattack reclaimed the ground—until Union reinforcements and artillery drove Hood's men into the West Woods. Back and forth the battle raged, leaving both sides battered with little ground gained on either side.

Scenes from the slugfest were horrific. One soldier found it "awful beyond description . . . dead men were literally piled upon and across each other." General Hooker observed, "[T]he slain lay in rows precisely as they had stood in their ranks a few moments before. It was never my fortune to witness a more bloody, dismal battle-field." Similarly, a Federal officer watched "an arm go 30 feet into the air and fall back again." A Union artilleryman saw a Confederate's "brains splattered over our gun where they were baked as quickly as if they had been dropped on a hot stove." Artillery discharges of canister—tin cans lacquered with beeswax and

---

7 Official report of Brigadier General Roswell S. Ripley, September 21, 1862, *OR*, vol. 19, 1:1032-1033; Mumma, *Antietam: the Aftermath*, 23-26. Mumma transcribed written correspondence from March 1906 between his paternal grandfather, Samuel Mumma, Jr., and Sgt. Major Clark of the 3rd North Carolina, regarding the burning of the Mumma house during the battle; Coffin, *Following the Flag*, 243.

packed with iron balls—fired outsized shotgun blasts that liquefied human beings into clouds of pink mist. Union general Alpheus Williams saw batteries blast "a tornado of cannister" into charging Confederates. When the smoke and dust lifted, "[N]o regiment and not a living man was to be seen."

Projectiles also killed army animals and civilian livestock. Captain William W. Blackford saw a horse emerge from the smoke "dragging something." Thinking the equine was pulling its fallen rider, Blackford "moved to intercept and stop the animal, but to my horror discovered that the horse was dragging his own entrails from the gaping wound of a cannonball, and after passing us a few yards the poor brute fell dead with a piercing scream."[8]

A brief "lull in the strife" lured newspaper correspondents to the north end of the field, where they viewed the carnage at close range. Frank H. Schell, a sketch artist for *Frank Leslie's Illustrated Newspaper*, observed a "feast of horrors" on David R. Miller's farm. "On the west side of the pike," Schell wrote, "were Miller's barn, haystacks, and mowing and threshing machines, in close communion with the open-mouthed cannon and other implements of destruction. The wheat was gathered in, the corn was destroyed, and the crop of corpses and misery was being industriously harvested in all directions."

North of the Miller farm, correspondent Charles Coffin found Arthur Kenney's toll house on the Hagerstown Pike "riddled with bullets." Across from Kenney was Joseph Poffenberger's farm, where Coffin saw "two horses killed by the cannon shot which smashed the head of one and tore open the neck of the other." Looking southwest, he studied human corpses in blue and gray uniforms, strewn "as thick as the withered leaves in autumn."[9]

*   *   *

8 Sears, *Landscape Turned Red*, 201, 211, 249; *OR*, vol. 19, 1:218; Thomas M Aldrich, *History of Battery A, First Regiment Rhode Island Light Artillery* (Providence, 1904), 143; Blackford, *War Years*, 150.

9 Frank H. Schell, "Sketching Under Fire at Antietam: A War Correspondent's Personal Account of His Experience During the Battle," *McClure's Magazine* (New York, 1904), vol. 22, November 1903 to April 1904, 427-428; Coffin, *Following the Flag*, 176; Charles Carleton Coffin, *The Boys of '61: Or, Four Years of Fighting* (Boston, 1896), 147; Claim of Joseph Poffenberger (*RG* 123, Entry 22, Box 233, No. 1300). Arthur Kenney testified that he "lived across the road" from Joseph Poffenberger in 1862. Federal census records list Kenney as "Gate Keeper on Turn Pike." His obituary in *The Daily Mail*, January 2, 1891, described him as "the well known old toll-gate keeper, for many years stationed at the Sharpsburg pike gate."

The first three hours of fighting inflicted 8,700 casualties, and the floodtide of wounded overwhelmed medical staff in both armies. Confederate forces seized farms west of the battlefield for use as field hospitals. Henry Reel owned one such property, located southwest of the Dunker Church. Displaced villagers, sheltering on Reel's farm, watched medical personnel haul wounded Confederates onto the farm. Civilian John P. Smith particularly remembered one soldier. "His entire abdomen had been torn and mangled by a piece of exploded shell," Smith recounted. "He uttered piercing and heart rendering cries, and besought those who stood by for God's sake to kill him and thus end his sufferings. Death however came to his relief in a short time and he was hastily buried in a shallow grave."

We can only imagine the shadow the intense scene cast over the life of John P. Smith, who was at the time but seventeen years old.[10]

The Federal medical department also commandeered homes as hospitals. In the rear of the I and XII Corps, ambulances hauled wounded to the farms of Samuel Poffenberger, Daniel Miller, Susan Hoffman, Catherine Showman, and George Line. A witness estimated that U.S. forces transported "thousands of wounded" to these farms. "Long lines of ambulances were coming down from the field. The surgeons were at work. It was not a pleasant sight to see many torn, mangled arms, legs, heads; men with their eyes shot out, their arms off at the shoulders, their legs broken and crushed by cannon shot."

Dr. James King took charge of the small, 572 square-foot farmhouse of George Line. To accommodate the wounded, King ordered Line "to take his things from his house" and "take his household furniture, bedding, carpets into one room for safe keeping." With no space left for the family, Line took his pregnant wife and two-year-old son to the farm of his father-in-law, Jacob Poffenberger, "which was out of reach of musketry and artillery fire."[11]

Near the North Woods, Clara Barton arrived with her volunteer staff to minister to the wounded. Barton quickly discovered that Union medical forces lacked supplies, having staged their wagons miles away to prevent capture by

---

10 Harsh, *Taken at the Flood*, 376; William H. Taylor, *De Quibus: Discourses and Essays* (Richmond, VA, 1908), 330; Kevin R. Pawlak, *Shepherdstown in the Civil War: One Vast Hospital* (Charleston, SC, 2015), 70-71; John P. Smith, "History of the Antietam Fight," Typescript, ANBL.

11 Coffin, *Following the Flag*, 235; Claims of George Line (RG 92, Book F, Box 86, Claims F-1186 and F-1187). Line's wife, Elizabeth Poffenberger Line, was the daughter of Jacob Poffenberger. In 1862, Jacob Poffenberger owned a tract east of Bakersville, adjoining Hiram Showman. The 1860 Federal census for Tilghmanton lists Jacob Poffenberger in Dwelling #1137, two dwellings removed from Hiram Showman.

Confederates. So desperate was the shortage, recalled Barton, that an army surgeon "showed me some poor fellows whose raw new wounds were actually dressed with those rough corn leaves."

Barton and her team aided the sufferers, despite their location within a dangerous range of bullets and shells. While giving a drink to a wounded soldier, a bullet pierced through Barton's dress and killed the man. Unscathed by the close call, she continued her work, despite shells crashing near the farm. When the fighting intensified, Barton recalled, "the tables jarred and rolled until we could hardly keep the men on them, and the roar was overwhelming."[12]

* * *

Despite the Union army suffering heavy losses in the morning phase, the Federal assaults weakened Stonewall Jackson's command. In an attempt to shatter Lee's left flank, Maj. Gen. Edwin Sumner led his first division of II Corps into the West Woods. However, in so doing, he failed to protect his left flank, and a Confederate counterattack routed the Northern troops.

During Sumner's attack, musketry and artillery damaged structures in and near the West Woods. Mary Grove Locher's cabin, rented to Alfred Poffenberger in 1862, was "literally riddled by balls." Federal ordnance struck the farm of Jacob and Harriet Houser, damaging the farmhouse, bake oven, and outbuildings. To seek shelter, several Confederates ran inside the Housers' dwelling. A shell, though,

---

12 "Antietam: Clara Barton and the International Red Cross Association," ANB. Transcribed from the Clara Barton Papers, Library of Congress, reel # 109, beginning at frame # 409, https://www.nps.gov/clba/learn/historyculture/antietam.htm. In 1862, Barton resided in Washington, DC; Schildt, *Drums Along the Antietam*, 150; William E. Barton, *The Life of Clara Barton in Two Volumes* (Boston, 1922), 1:200-202. Confederate artillery on Nicodemus Heights targeted I Corps forces on the Joseph Poffenberger and John C. Middlekauff farms. The house that Barton described, being "under the lee of a hill," may have been the John C. Middlekauff home. This farm sat below Joseph Poffenberger's high ground, where I Corps staged its artillery. The Maryland Historic Trust's architectural survey file for the John C. Middlekauff farm ("WA-II-281 Middlekauff-Poffenberger Farm") cites, "A hospital located here was shelled during the battle and later reestablished." Historians have long debated whether Clara Barton worked on the farm of John C. Middlekauff, Joseph Poffenberger, or Samuel Poffenberger. Evidence shows that other nurses, including Anna Holstein and Mary W. Lee, aided the wounded at multiple locations. Thus, it's possible that Clara Barton worked on more than one farm during and after the battle.

smashed through a wall and exploded, killing four soldiers. The blast spared Jacob Houser, who hid in his cellar.[13]

Union ordnance soared over Confederate batteries on the Samuel Reel and Jacob Houser farms, dropping on civilian properties farther west. John P. Smith, sheltering on Henry Reel's farm, recalled that "shot and shell . . . fell in the yard where we were staying." As a result, Smith and the other residents "were obliged, amid flying shot and shell, to retreat to the farm of William Cox, a mile further west."[14]

Despite its distance from the battle lines, the farm of brothers William I. and John U. Cox was not safe. Witnesses saw Confederates "on the place for a little [while] during the heat of the battle." The Rebel cavalry was "throwing down fences" and going "through the corn field . . . back and forth." Worse for the citizens, shells were falling in the vicinity.[15]

Adjoining the Cox brothers' place was Samuel I. Piper's farm, where dozens of evacuees sheltered. When errant shells exploded nearby, the panicked civilians splashed across the Potomac River.

"The Federal army began shelling a house just below where we were," Mary Ellen Piper remembered. "We were quite near the river and there was no other alternative; we were compelled to cross into Virginia." Mary Ellen's father, Henry Piper, recalled fording the Potomac during the battle with "a number of my neighbors with their families." Stray artillery rounds, too close for comfort, pinned the evacuees in the Virginia cliffs for several hours.[16]

---

13 Reily, *BOA*; Claim of Jacob Houser (*RG* 92, Book F, Box 80, Claim F-814). In 1862, Houser cultivated a farm "belonging to Joseph Grove's heirs," to whom he "paid a money rental of $325 per annum;" Claim of the heirs of Joseph Grove (*RG* 123, Entry 22, Box 957, No. 9057). The heirs owned the Houser farm in 1862 and filed a claim for various injuries to the property. Their petition included $50 for "Damage done to Dwelling House" and $10 for "Damage done to Bake Oven & out buildings;" Land records, war claims, agricultural schedules, and other primary sources spell the claimant's name as Houser. A variation, spelled as Hauser, appears in Antietam battlefield maps and Ezra A. Carman's study of the battle.

14 Smith, "History of the Antietam Fight;" Claim of Henry Reel (*RG* 92, Entry 843, Box 772, Book 304, Claim 328). Reel claimed $325 in damages to his house, barn and fencing. It's unclear what portion of the $325 relates to shell damages.

15 Claim of William I. Cox and John U. Cox (*RG* 92, Entry 812, Box 208, Book M, Claim M-901). The claim listed John W. Cox as the co-claimant. Genealogical records, however, suggest that John's middle name was Upton.

16 E. P. to Sally Farran, October 4, 1862, *Dan Masters' Civil War Chronicles*; Claim of Henry Piper (No. 445).

U.S. ordnance also struck the farm of David Reel, which adjoined the town of Sharpsburg. Reel's dwelling suffered damage by "cannon balls passing through" and his barn caught fire "from the bursting of shell." Reel's barn ignited so quickly that medical staff could not evacuate the wounded in time. Consequently, the fire reportedly incinerated Confederates trapped inside the structure.[17]

Samuel Reel's farm adjoined David Reel's property on the north. During Sumner's attack in the West Woods, grapeshot struck Captain Henry W. Addison of the 7th South Carolina. While "hobbling back to the rear," Addison came across "numbers of our wounded" sheltering inside a barn, which may have belonged to Samuel Reel. Addison stopped to visit injured comrades, but "the fire of the Federal Batteries on this point was terrific," forcing him to evacuate. Moments later, a shell struck the barn and ignited the dried grains inside. "I final[ly] got off some hundred of yards toward the Town," Addison remembered. "I looked back, and saw that the Barn or building had been fired, and suppose some of our wounded were burned to death."[18]

*   *   *

The first four hours of fighting saw more than 13,000 men killed, wounded, or missing, with no tactical advantage won by either army. And this was just the

17 Claim of David Reel (*RG* 123, Entry 22, Box 744, No. 6619). Reel claimed $500 for "One Barn destroyed by fire," along with $1,000 for the barn's contents. He also filed $100 for "Damage to House by cannon balls passing through." Reel's claim notes, "This property was all burned on the evening of the battle and was supposed to have been caught from the bursting of shell;" Reilly, *BOA*. Reilly reported that local youths, while inspecting the ruins of David Reel's barn, "found portions of bones of human beings in the ashes."

18 H. W. Addison to Ezra Carman, July 4, 1898, cited in Jim Buchanan, "H. W. Addison and the 7th South Carolina, Part 1," blog, *Walking the West Woods*, November 25, 2001, http://walkingthewestwoods.blogspot.com/2011/11/it-was-where-i-was-bloodiest-for-us-h w.html. Addison noticed the fire after walking "some hundred of yards toward the Town." He likely described Samuel Reel's barn, because David Reel's property adjoined the town. Claim of Samuel Reel (G-1923). Reel sought payment of "$1,500 for One barn destroyed by fire." His claim alleged, "On the 17th of September 1862 his barn &c. were burned during the progress of the battle of Antietam;" A. A. Biggs to Elijah Kalb, September 29, 1862, WMR; Samuel Michael to David Michael, November 27, 1862, [Adam] Michael Family Letters Collection, unpublished correspondence, 1859–1865, WMR. Samuel Michael wrote, "David Reel and Samuel Reel lost their barns—both burned down by the Yankee [shells];" *Herald of Freedom and Torch Light*, September 24, 1862, 2B. The newspaper mistakenly reported, "The barns of Samuel and Henry Reel were also destroyed by fire." Individual claims filed by brothers Samuel, Henry, and David Reel—who owned their own, separate farms in 1862—clarify that Samuel and David Reel each lost a barn to fire during the battle. Henry Reel's barn suffered damages but remained intact.

beginning of the battle. Observers studied the hellscape, where smoke from gunpowder and burning buildings drifted above the dead and dying. A *New York Times* correspondent reported, "Five different conflagrations have occurred on the field of barns and houses which were set on fire by exploding shell, or purposely fired by the enemy. While I write the whole heavens are lighted up by burning barns and wheat stacks. It is an immense conflagration."[19]

Federal artillery fire forced Confederate medical personnel to move their patients to safer distances. Soon, the area west of Sharpsburg became a vast, impromptu hospital. Ambulances hauled wounded to the farms of Capt. David Smith, John L. Mayer, Samuel Beeler, Elias S. Grove, Stephen P. Grove, Grove's Landing, and other properties in the vicinity. Given the safe distance from artillery fire, many families in this sector remained home on the 17th. Imagine their horror on seeing ambulances stream onto their properties, disgorging hundreds of pitifully wounded men into homes, barns, and outbuildings.

Men, women, and children sheltering at Grove's Landing watched Confederates haul their wounded into the grain warehouse. Teenager William "Bud" Shackelford remembered seeing the warehouse doors "torn off and mounted on flour barrels which had been rolled out to make operating tables." Given the crisis at hand, Shackelford and other youths may have watched surgeons perform gruesome operations.[20]

17-year-old Angeline Jackson, a domestic servant, lived at Captain David Smith's farm in 1862. On the morning of the battle, Jackson had just finished preparing a meal "when the rebells began to bring in the wounded" and Federal batteries "got to shelling pretty hard." With bleeding patients filling their yard and shells crashing nearby, the family decided it was no longer safe to remain at home. Jackson recalled, "I believe we left the house about 11 or 12 o'clock on the day of the battle; I remember I had the dinner all ready, except sitting at the table." Angeline and the Smiths "left the house and went west to Killionsburg on the Canal."

---

19 *New York Times*, September 23, 1862.

20 The claims of Capt. Smith, Mayer, Beeler, et al. mention Confederate hospitals on the properties. See also John H. Nelson, *As Grain Falls Before the Reaper: The Federal Hospital Sites and Identified Federal Casualties at Antietam* (Hagerstown, MD, 2004), 25-27; "Aged Woman Tells of Giving Food to Antietam Soldiers," *Morning Herald*, July 10, 1937; William "Bud" Shackelford interview, ANBL; Bushrod Washington James, *Echoes of Battle* (Philadelphia, 1895), 96. James wrote, "The two warehouses on the canal at Grove's Landing, one and one-half miles from Sharpsburg, were Confederate hospitals."

John L. Mayer owned a farm near Captain Smith. In September 1862, Mayer lived in Pennsylvania and rented his Sharpsburg land to Jacob Rodeniser. When casualties mounted during the battle, Confederate ambulances arrived on the Mayer-Rodeniser farm. Medical personnel filled the two-story "mansion house" with patients and unhinged doors to use as operating tables. The walls inside the home were soon "spattered with blood."

Something traumatized Jacob Rodeniser, but we don't know why he fled the home and never returned, despite having signed a lease to cultivate Mayer's farm until the spring of 1863. When a Union quartermaster agent later investigated Mayer's war claim, he learned that Rodeniser "left the community, and no one seems to know anything about him." Moreover, by abandoning the 101-acre tract, Rodeniser "neglected the crops" he toiled to plant and raise, losing a substantial amount of his annual income.[21]

*   *   *

To the ears of civilian and military witnesses alike, the Battle of Antietam screamed the sounds of sheer terror. The ominous report of artillery carried roughly twelve miles to Hagerstown, Maryland, near the Pennsylvania line, and even to Baltimore, some sixty miles distant. Across the Potomac River in Virginia, a witness remembered the "incessant explosions of artillery" and "shrieking whistles of the shells."[22]

South of Sharpsburg, on the farm of Reverend John A. Adams, evacuees "listened to the stunning thunder of the opposing batteries and to the rattle of musketry, the shots often coming so fast as to sound like the never-ending hum of thousands of angry bees."[23] Closer to the action, witnesses likened it to "a savage

---

21 Claims of David Smith (Nos. 1244, 1262, and 10237). Jackson and the Smiths may have trekked directly west to the cave along farm lanes, rather than the longer route via the Sharpsburg-Shepherdstown Pike and road to Grove's Landing; Claim of John L. Mayer (*RG* 123, Entry 22, Box 917, No. 8586). Jacob Rodeniser fled the farm "pending the battle." Claims testimonies and Washington County land records support that Mayer's land was north of Shepherdstown Pike and west of Captain Smith, adjoining the farms of Elias S. Grove and the C & O Canal.

22 Ernst, *TATC*, 146; Keith Snyder, Antietam National Battlefield ranger, televised interview, C-SPAN, September 16, 2012, 14:40–15:00, https://www.c-span.org/video/?307917-103/keith-snyder-battle-antietam; Mitchell, "A Woman's Recollections of Antietam," 690.

23 "Sharpsburg Citizen Tells Own Story," *The Daily Mail* [Hagerstown, MD], September 10, 1962, 12.

continual thunder," "a shower of hailstones on an enormous tin roof," and "a thousand storms in the region of Hades."[24] Colonel Stephen D. Lee warned a comrade after the battle, "Pray that you may never see another Sharpsburg. Sharpsburg was Artillery Hell."[25]

The feral growl of battle drew "hundreds of Marylanders" to the surrounding hills. One citizen recalled, "[M]any persons went to the top of Elk Ridge where the Union Signal Station was, and [had] a good view of the entire battle lines," above which rose "great columns of smoke and dust." Residents also gathered on Raleigh Domer's farm on Red Hill. Here, Sharpsburg resident Joe Marrow "observed the action of a Union battery of artillery" on John Ecker's farm. He also saw Federal artillery on Jacob F. Miller's farm firing at Confederate batteries. West of Philip Pry's house, Albert Deane Richardson, a *New York Tribune* correspondent, noted, "Five thousand spectators viewed the struggle from a hill comparatively out of range." Richardson mentioned that shells landed near the crowd of civilians, but "not more than three persons were struck there during the day."[26]

*   *   *

Townsfolk sheltering in Sharpsburg village heard the terrifying sound of missiles fired *at* them—and exploding far too close for comfort. "You can have no idea of the horrible noise the shells make," wrote an army surgeon at Sharpsburg, "when one passes over your head with its scream as if 50 Locomotive Whistles

---

24 Charles F. Johnson, *The Long Roll: Being a Journal of the Civil War, as Set Down During the Years 1861–1863* (East Aurora, NY, 1911), 191; Lew Wallace, et al. *The Story of American Heroism: Thrilling Narratives of Personal Adventures During the Great Civil War as Told by the Medal Winners and Roll of Honor Men* (Springfield, Ohio, 1897), 285; Gary W. Gallagher, "The Net Result of the Campaign Was in Our Favor: Confederate Reaction to the Maryland Campaign," *The Antietam Campaign*, 21.

25 Edward Porter Alexander, *Military Memoirs of a Confederate: A Critical Narrative* (New York, 1907), 247. Colonel Stephen D. Lee commanded a Confederate artillery battalion during the battle.

26 Reilly, *BOA*; *Valley Spirit* [Chambersburg, PA], September 24, 1862; Joe Marrow interview, January 24, 1934, "Civilian Reports," folder, ANBL. Marrow referred to the location as "Dommer's farm." Raleigh Domer's 60-acre property, adjoining Joseph Thomas on the south, sat atop Red Hill on modern-day Churchey Road, affording views of the Jacob F. Miller and John Ecker farms. However, Marrow may have also described Jacob Domer's farm, located south of Jacob F. Miller; Richardson, *The Secret Service*, 283-284. Richardson mentioned that "McClellan and his staff occupied another ridge half a mile in the rear." The large crowd may have gathered on or near the Alfred N. Cost farm.

were blowing at once." Another witness noted how the missiles "howled like demons" over Sharpsburg Heights before crashing into the town. Villager Jacob McGraw recalled that the artillery "made such a racket you'd think the earth was opening up." Samuel Michael hunkered in his parents' village cellar during the battle. He later wrote, "Such thundering and roaring you never heard since you been born. You would have thought the day of judgment had finally come if you would have been here."[27]

During the battle on the 17th, Federal artillery fired toward the town from sunrise to sunset. As on September 16, Union missiles overshot Confederate targets and struck the east walls of village dwellings, churches, and businesses. Some ripped through houses, continuing at deadly speeds and striking neighboring homes. Other projectiles lost momentum, coming to rest inside homes after plunging through roofs or penetrating walls. Numerous accounts support the conclusion that Federal shells struck virtually every structure in town.[28]

The September 17 shelling of Sharpsburg village began in the small hours of the morning. Jacob McGraw remembered, "[T]he artillery opened up before day … I went out to feed my horse, and on the way back a shell come mighty near 'getting' me. It bursted over my head and stunned me right smart."

At sunrise, "the booming of cannon" sent "shells and solid shot . . . whizzing into town shattering the houses and creating a sudden and frightful panic among the inhabitants." Teresa Kretzer recalled, "[A] cannon ball tore up the pavement out in front of our house. Oh my soul! [W]e thought we were gone. There was no more sleep, but most of us were awake anyhow." The Kretzers and their displaced guests slept overnight in the stone home's upper floor, but when Federal batteries erupted at first light, "we all flew to the cellar," recalled Teresa. "Very little was stored in there at that time of year. We carried down some seats, and we made board benches around, and quite a number of us got up on the potato bunks and the apple scaffolds." According to Teresa, food was in short supply, but stress

27 Bell Irvin Wiley, *The Life of Billy Yank* (Baton Rouge, 1952), 78; Alexander Hunter, "A High Private's Sketch of Sharpsburg," *Southern Historical Society Papers*, vol. XI, January to December 1883 (Richmond, VA, 1883), 15; Johnson, *BA*, 114; Samuel Michael to David Michael, November 27, 1862, WMR.

28 Alexander, "Destruction, Disease, and Death," 159; Cross, "The Strong Stone House;" Brian Baracz, Antietam National Battlefield ranger, phone communications with the author, May 31, 2018.

WOMEN AND CHILDREN OF SHARPSBURG TAKING REFUGE IN THE CELLAR OF THE KRETZER MANSION IN THAT TOWN, DURING THE BATTLE OF ANTIETAM—BURSTING OF A SHELL IN THE WINDOW OF THE CELLAR.
SKETCHED BY OUR SPECIAL ARTIST, MR. F. H. SCHELL.

Women and children of Sharpsburg taking refuge in the cellar of the Kretzer mansion in that town, during the Battle of Antietam—bursting of a shell in the window of the cellar. Sketch by Frank H. Schell. *Frank Leslie's Illustrated Newspaper.* October 25, 1862.

suppressed appetites. "We didn't have any breakfast—you bet we didn't—and no dinner was got that day, or supper . . . we had to live on fear."[29]

Dozens of residents squeezed into the Kretzers' basement. John Kretzer recalled that he sheltered "in the cellar of my house during the battle with 75 of our citizens." The underground space, Teresa Kretzer reflected, "was divided by massive walls in several rooms, in one of which was a splendid spring of running water." Incessant shell blasts, however, terrified the cellar's inhabitants. One shell "exploded at the corner of the house, causing a panic among" the huddled masses. "A number of babies were there, and several dogs," recalled Teresa, "and every time the firing began extra hard the babies would cry and the dogs would bark. Often the reports were so loud they shook the walls. Occasionally a woman was quite unnerved and hysterical, and some of those old aged men would break out in prayer."

29 Johnson, *BA*, 114, 120.

One of the babies was Susan Ward's infant daughter, born one week earlier. Susan feared the Kretzers' basement "was too damp for her in her delicate health or condition, so she and the babe were taken up into the kitchen." Soon though, "a shell came into the building, nearly blinding her with dust and smoke." The young mother quickly returned to the chilly cellar, and "said she would rather take her chances on taking cold and dying than to be killed with a shell or cannon ball."[30]

As artillery fire raked the town, Christina Watson fled to the cellar of Jacob H. Grove's house. "We carried boards down there," she recalled, "and spread carpets on 'em and took chairs down to set on. There was seven or eight of us, white and black, and we was all so scared we didn't know what we was doin' half the time." The jarring explosions "kept us in the cellar all day," remembered Christina. "The cannon sounded jest like thunder . . . sometimes we'd run up and look out of a window to see what was happening, but we didn't do that often—not the way them guns was firin'."

George Noyes, a member of General Abner Doubleday's staff, empathized with the trapped villagers. "I can imagine few situations more trying to the nerves than to be thus pent up in gloom while that tempest howled and shrieked through the air, or came hurtling in the rooms overhead." In one house, Noyes learned, a mother rushed her children to the basement "as soon as the first shell burst over the village; how they listened, expecting every moment to hear some of the shrieking fiends burst through their own walls."[31]

Explosions in the village drove Confederates into cellars. Teresa Kretzer remembered, "Six Rebel soldiers opened the basement door and said, 'We're comin' in, but we're not a-goin' to hurt you.'" Another soldier ran into Judge David Smith's cellar, joining Mrs. Smith and her children. Several Confederates ducked into a basement, surprising townsman Jacob McGraw. One of the soldiers, injured by an earlier shell explosion, asked McGraw to remove a log fragment embedded in

---

30 Claim of Joshua Newcomer (*RG* 123, Entry 22, Box 70, No. 272). John Kretzer testified in Newcomer's case; Cross, "The Strong Stone House;" Johnson, *BA*, 120; Reilly, *BOA*. Reilly gleaned the Susan Ward account from Anna Mary Kretzer McGraw, sister of Teresa Kretzer; Smith, "No Civilian Died." Smith wrote that the baby of "Mrs. Henry Ward" was three days old. Dr. Augustin A. Biggs, *The Obstetrical Records of Dr. Augustin Biggs, of Sharpsburg, Washington County, Maryland, 1836–1888*, medical ledger, WMR. Biggs recorded the birth of Ward's daughter on September 10, 1862.

31 Johnson, *BA*, 110; George Freeman Noyes, *The Bivouac and the Battlefield, Or Campaign Sketches in Virginia and Maryland* (New York, 1863), 237.

his arm. McGraw recounted, "I didn't dare refuse. I pulled him off his feet before I got it out."[32]

* * *

Union missiles killed several Confederates in Sharpsburg village during the battle. Dr. A. A. Biggs counted "sixteen rebels killed in town during the shelling." Among them, Biggs recalled, was "one man [who] had his leg shot off on my pavement, and another instantly killed just above my house." Biggs's twelve-year-old son, Charles, "saw a cannon ball come bounding up Main Street by the public square and hit a Confederate soldier, disabling him, and he made a feeble outcry from pain." Teresa Kretzer recounted, "A shell exploded right out here at our front gate and killed or wounded seven men." Across the street from Teresa, a shell fragment killed a Rebel near John Hamilton Smith's house.[33]

Federal ordnance crashed into all parts of the town. South of the public square, projectiles struck the homes of John Hill, Samuel McGraw, and James Marker, damaging Marker's tannery business. Another shell pierced Jacob Avey's farmhouse "and smashed a bedstead to pieces." On Sharpsburg's northernmost street, shells lodged in the eastern wall of William Gloss's brick house on Lot 80.[34]

Artillery rounds struck houses on East Main Street, including a stone dwelling owned by Henry Piper (Lot 154). Nearby, a "12-pound solid shot passed through both gable ends and through four rafters" in Adam Michael's house (Lot 55), then pierced the neighboring home of John Hamilton Smith, "tearing down the ceiling in an upper room." Shells even reached the western part of town, striking the house

---

32 Johnson, *BA*, 121; Reilly, *BOA*; Johnson, *BA*, 115.

33 A. A. Biggs to Elijah Kalb, September 29, 1862, WMR; Reilly, *BOA*; Johnson, *BA*, 122; Smith, "No Civilian Died," *Morning Herald*, January 25, 1951.

34 Cross, "The Strong Stone House;" Claim of James Marker (No. 1292). Marker's petition cites $50 for "Damages to two Houses & Tan yard property by shell." Marker's "Tan Yard Property" was located on Lots 8 and 9 in the village. See land records IN 11 / 200-1 and 75 / 611-612; Claim of Jacob Avey, Sr. (RG 92, Entry 843, Box 772, Book 304, Claim 243). Avey claimed $75 for "1 house damaged." Trowbridge in *The South*, 52, visited a farmhouse in 1865 that may have been Avey's; Cross, "The Strong Stone House." Cross described the house of "Mr. Elmer G. Boyer on Chapline street." The same year that Cross wrote his article, the National Park Service published "Building Survey of Sharpsburg, MD" (typescript, 1934, ANBL). The report noted that, in September 1862, Lot 80 "was known as the property of J. Gloss and was then a log construction. Today the place is a 2 story brick dwelling and is owned and occupied by Mr. Elmer Boyer;" Don Aines, "Many Sharpsburg Homes Have Civil War History," *Herald Mail* [Hagerstown, MD], September 13, 2013. The owner of Lot 80 showed Aines "five places where the brick work was damaged" during the battle.

on Lot 178E. Samuel Michael described the dwelling as "right smart riddled from the Yankee Shells."[35]

Dr. A. A. Biggs sheltered inside his stone house on Lot 47E. He wrote, "The shells were flying and exploding every moment around us. One shell passed through the parlor window and exploded, tearing up and destroying things at a great rate. In a few moments, I entered the room and found nothing was on fire." Biggs's daughter, Stella, remembered the explosion "practically destroyed everything" that was in the parlor. Outside, shells struck the family's stable and hog pen. When Dr. Biggs peeked outside to survey the damage, he recalled, "One shell exploded just over my head and some of the fragments struck the rim of my hat."[36]

Near Biggs's house, shells damaged all four buildings on Sharpsburg's public square. On the northeast corner, "a 12-pound solid shot came and went through" the cellar door" of Lot 49E, lodging inside the home. On the square's southwest corner, shells reportedly pierced Jacob H. Grove's brick house eleven times and "almost destroyed" the dwelling.[37]

Below Sharpsburg Heights, Union shells damaged Noah Putman's house on the north side of Main Street. On the south side, missiles battered the Lutheran Church and its adjoining graveyard, where "a number of the tombstones were shattered and broken to pieces."[38]

---

35 "WA-II-703 Piper House [Lot 154]," architectural survey file, MHT. The report cited Samuel Webster Piper, *Piper Family History*. The stone dwelling's masonry "was damaged by shelling;" Aines, "Many Sharpsburg Homes;" Smith, "No Civilian Died;" Samuel Michael to David Michael, November 27, 1862, WMR. In 1862, Adam Michael, Samuel's father, owned two lots in the village: Lot 55 (his primary residence) and Lot 178E. For information on Lot 178E, see land records IN 13 / 384-385 and IN 17 / 479.

36 A. A. Biggs to Elijah Kalb, September 29, 1862, WMR; 1934 interview with Stella Biggs Lyne, "Civilian Reports," folder, ANBL; Claim of A. A. Biggs (*RG* 92, Entry 843, Box 771, Claim 178). Biggs claimed "Destruction of house and furniture from explosion of shell." He also listed damages to his window and parlor ($30), carpeting ($15), a mirror ($10), stable ($4), and other damages ($5, possibly for his hog pen).

37 Reilly, *BOA*; Claim of Jacob H. Grove (*RG* 123, Entry 22, Box No. 228, No. 1267). Grove claimed $50 for "Damage to house by shell in Sharpsburg." Smith in "No Civilian Died" described damage to Jacob H. Grove's house and Lot 1 on the public square's southeast corner. Fred W. Cross in "The Strong Stone House" referred to shells damaging the house "on the northwest corner of the square," which is Lot 48E.

38 Claim of Nancy Miller (*RG* 92, Entry 843, Box 772, Book 304, Claim 233). Ms. Miller claimed $37 for "Damages to House that Putnam lives in." In 1862, Ann "Nancy" Miller owned Lot 63S (her primary residence) and Lot 94, which she rented to Noah Putman (also spelled Putnam). See land records IN 6 / 636 and IN 18 / 419; Fred W. Cross, scrapbook, ANBL; Smith, "No Civilian Died." Smith noted, "The tombstone of Mrs. Mary Knode, wife of

Sharpsburg, Md. Lutheran church. Federal artillery inflicted substantial damage to this house of worship on September 16 and 17. The church later served as a hospital for Antietam's wounded. Photograph by Alexander Gardner. *Library of Congress*

Some townsfolk ventured outside during the shelling. Alexander Hunter of the 17th Virginia walked to the rear of a "vine-covered cottage," where he found an old couple sitting on the back porch, "as calm and composed as if war and carnage had been a thousand miles away." The pair seemed unaffected by the cannon fire shaking "the very foundation of the house beneath their feet." Hunter "urged them to leave the place while there was still time." The old man replied, "[T]hey had no

the late Urias Knode of Sharpsburg, had a shell pass through one side of it, making a half round hole, and burying itself about two feet in the grave." Knode's grave and headstone were later relocated to Mountain View Cemetery; Reilly, *BOA*. Reilly wrote that the Lutheran Church's square cupola "was used by General Lee's army as their signal station." Federal batteries may have targeted the church, sending errant shots into the church's graveyard and the town below.

place to go, that this had been their home all their lives, they knew no other, and they would rather die here than leave it . . . they intended to stay."[39]

At the intersection of Main and Church streets, Lieutenant Henry Kyd Douglas, serving on Stonewall Jackson's staff, recognized a familiar face standing on the porch of Lot 7. It was Savilla Miller, daughter of Squire Jacob Miller, quite "unconscious to the danger she was in." Douglas knew the young woman, for he, himself, was a resident of the Sharpsburg area. The Confederate lieutenant urged Savilla to go indoors, but she ignored the advice, offering Douglas a glass of water. "As she approached me," he recalled, "a shell with a shriek in its flight came over the hill, passed just over us down the street and exploded not far off. My horse, 'Ashby,' sank so low in his fright that my foot near touched the curb." Savilla kept her composure, Douglas recalled. "She poured out the cooling drink and handed it to me without a word of fear or comment. Repeating my warning, I lifted my hat and went on my way to Dunker Church."

Other shells exploded near the Miller house, driving Savilla inside. One detonation tore "a portion of the wall" off the dwelling, while another blasted shrapnel on Squire Miller's back porch, cutting "the strap that held the cage" of Miller's pet bird—an African parrot named Polly.

Savilla reemerged in her father's doorway and watched "three Confederates . . . walking up the main street toward the old Lutheran church." A shell burst in front of them, "horribly mangling and killing the one in the center and stunning the other two." The surviving Rebels buried their comrade in Squire Miller's orchard.[40]

Artillery fire pounded Sharpsburg village throughout the day. One observer saw shells "dropping on the housetops, making a fearful noise as they tore up the plank, split the rafters, and sent the shingles flying in the air." Another witness remembered missiles exploding "over the town or in the streets, breaking windows, knocking down chimneys, perforating houses and roofs." A Confederate private wrote that the explosive echoes in town "reverberated among the houses and up the narrow street in a most terrifying manner."

---

39 Alexander Hunter, *Johnny Reb and Billy Yank* (New York, 1905), 286-287.

40 Douglas, *I Rode With Stonewall*, 170-171. Before the war, Douglas lived with his parents on their Ferry Hill farm, located southwest of Sharpsburg village near the Potomac River; Smith, "No Civilian Died;" Reilly, *BOA*. Reilly wrote that the parrot, owned by "Squire Miller," survived the battle and "lived to be nearly 100 years old." Some sources have associated the pet parrot's shrapnel account with David R. Miller and his father, Col. John Miller. Historical letters, however, clearly show that the bird belonged to Squire Jacob Miller. References to "Polly," the pet parrot, appear sporadically in the Jacob Miller family letters, WMR, from Mar. 1852–Nov. 1898.

Despite the danger of missiles and shrapnel raining from the sky, some townspeople fled the safety of cellars and raced toward the river. Samuel Cramer and his wife vacated their house on the western end of town, rushing south to Miller's Sawmill. The couple "had hardly left the house when a shell went into the building and exploded, tearing things to pieces."[41]

During the battle, "[A] young girl of apparently sixteen years appeared on the street bareheaded, her long hair streaming wildly." A Confederate recalled that the girl "tore frantically along, screaming piercingly, as a shell exploded over her head. Her presence at such a time gave rise to much conjecture which was never explained."

A North Carolina soldier, Jacob Nathaniel Raymer, watched panicked villagers flee town on September 17. "It was sad to see so many people deserting their homes," Raymer wrote. "The women and children, still in town, were running, crying and screaming so loud that their combined voices could be heard above the roaring battle and bursting of shells around us."[42]

*   *   *

Stragglers presented a significant challenge to both McClellan and Lee at Sharpsburg. Leading up to the battle, food in the Union army "had been so scarce that the men had continued in a state of ravenous hunger," recalled a Northern soldier. "The living—if the opportunity offers—empty the haversacks of the dead and the neighboring fields are scoured in search of corn, potatoes or anything that can be cooked for food." A similar problem presented in the Confederate army, many of whose soldiers hadn't eaten a substantial meal since entering Maryland. Subsequently, hundreds of Southern soldiers strayed from the ranks.[43]

---

41 Hunter, *Johnny Reb and Billy Yank*, 286; Douglas, *I Rode With Stonewall*, 170-171; Shotwell, *The Papers*, 1:349; Reilly, *BOA*. Reilly identified "Mrs. Cramer" as the mother of Martin Cramer. 1860 Federal census records place Samuel and Hester Cramer, the parents of Martin Cramer, at the western end of Sharpsburg. Martin Cramer testified that he lived in 1862 with Morgan and Andrew Rentch Miller, sons of Squire Jacob Miller, near Miller's Sawmill. The Cramers may have fled to Miller's Sawmill for this reason. See the claim of Morgan and Andrew Rentch Miller (RG 123, Entry 22, Box 541, No. 4295).

42 Hunter, *Johnny Reb and Billy Yank*, 286-287; Jacob Nathaniel Raymer, *Confederate Correspondent: The Civil War Reports of Jacob Nathaniel Raymer*, ed. E.B. Munson (Jefferson, NC, 2009), 41.

43 Matthew John Graham, *The Ninth Regiment, New York Volunteers (Hawkins' Zouaves): Being a History of the Regiment and Veteran Association from 1860 to 1900* (New York, 1900), 341-342.

Such disobedience incensed Robert E. Lee. Less than one week earlier, he wrote to Confederate president Jefferson Davis, "Our great embarrassment is the reduction of our ranks by straggling, which it seems impossible to prevent with our present regimental officers." Lee issued General Orders No. 102 on September 4, which warned officers that "any excesses committed will exasperate the people, lead to disastrous results, and enlist the populace on the side of the Federal forces in hostility to our own." By instructing quartermaster and commissary officers to purchase supplies from private citizens, Lee hoped to remove "all excuse for depredations." It was a good plan on paper. In the field, however, the ANV's food shortages and consequent straggling at Sharpsburg were so prominent, historian D. Scott Hartwig opined, that "not until the Appomattox Campaign would subsistence play such a pivotal role in the Army of Northern Virginia's operations."[44]

Scores of Confederates entered Sharpsburg's homes to satiate their appetites and slake their thirst. One Rebel scoffed at townsfolk who, before fleeing, locked their homes and nailed shut outbuildings to prevent troops from taking their food. "It was useless," remembered the soldier, "I verily believe every door in town was broken open, and, everything that could be eaten was consumed."

A newspaper reported that, in Sharpsburg, Rebels "carried off everything in the stores—robbed the women of . . . their meat, preserves, fruits, vegetables, and everything they could use." Confederates entered the dwelling of Judge David Smith and ate "every particle of food they had," leaving water from the well as "the only thing left to supply the wants" of the family. Dr. A. A. Biggs vented about the Rebels' plundering, writing, "All the fruit and vegetables of every description were devoured by them. Nearly every house was robbed of everything eatable."[45]

Behind the West Woods, Confederate cavalryman George Beale watched frightened women abandon "a brick house with chimneys at its farther end, and a flight of ten or twelve steps leading up to the front door." Soldiers wasted no time plundering the vacant home. "Many of our troops," Beale recalled, "could be seen ascending those steps or coming down them, in the latter case having their hands filled with meat, cans of fruit, honey, jars of pickle—whatever was eatable found in

---

44 *OR*, vol. 19, 2:606; Ibid., 592; Alexander, *Military Memoirs*, 244; Harsh, *Taken at the Flood*, 73; Hartwig, *To Antietam Creek*, 603-604.

45 Raymer, *Confederate Correspondent*, 41; *HFTL*, October 2, 1862, 2C; Biggs to Kalb, September 29, 1862, WMR.

the building. I am sure the supplies of the family were in a few minutes all seized by our men, and the home left as bare as Mother Hubbard's fabled cupboard."[46]

In addition to food, soldiers purloined civilians' horses during the battle. These animals were expensive to replace, endeared as family pets, and indispensable for business and travel. So when Henry F. Neikirk's horse vanished from his pasture on the morning September 17, he asked troops from the 12th Pennsylvania Cavalry if they had seen his equine. The men informed Neikirk that "his horse was in their Regt." They impressed the farmer's mount into military service, and offered no payment for the appropriation.

A Federal cavalryman arrived at Adam Hutzell's farmhouse the day of the battle "with a broken down horse." The trooper explained to Hutzell that he needed to exchange his mount for a fresh horse, and seized the farmer's prized roan stallion. In return, the man gave Hutzell the lame horse and a receipt to ensure later repayment.

The morning of the battle, Henry B. Rohrback's draft horse, a family pet named Dick, was "running at large" in a pasture near Lieutenant Samuel N. Benjamin's Union battery. After a Confederate shell killed one of Benjamin's artillery horses, the gun crew seized Dick. "He was turned into Benjamin's battery," recalled Rohrback. "The battery had a horse shot on the hill across from my house, and they got this horse and put him in its place—as fine a horse as I had . . . I saw him standing near their teams with government harness on him ready to hitch." Henry's son-in-law, Henry C. Mumma, also saw the soldiers seize Dick. "I saw him with the harness on. He went into the battery," Mumma testified. "I was going to stop and get a voucher for him, but it was a little too hot about that time. I called the women's attention to him. I said there is Dick in the battle."[47]

---

46 George Beale, *A Lieutenant of Cavalry in Lee's Army* (Boston, 1918), 48-49. Beale's account suggests that the farmhouse stood west of Lee's left flank. According to the Maryland Historic Trust's architectural survey reports, most of the extant homes near the West Woods were frame or log construction. These include the dwellings of Mary Locher (Alfred Poffenberger, tenant), WA-II-298; Heirs of Joseph Grove (Jacob Houser, tenant), WA-II-398; Andrew Rentch (Moses Cox, tenant), WA-II-407; and Jacob Nicodemus, WA-II-297 and Johnson, *BA*, 93-94. The exception—and perhaps the same house described by Beale—is the 1862 home of the heirs of Anthony Rowe, WA-II-408. James A. Rowe, along with his adult siblings and mother, owned and occupied a brick farmhouse on the Mercersville Road (now Mondell Road) opposite Moses Cox's farm and the western side of Nicodemus Heights. The 1860 Federal census for Sharpsburg misspelled the Rowes as "Bowers" and listed them in Dwelling #1521.

47 Claims of Henry F. Neikirk (H-4108 and H-4109); Claim of Adam Hutzell (*RG* 123, Box 540, Entry 22, No. 4292); Claim of Henry B. Rohrback (*RG* 123, Entry 22, Box 231, No. 1323). Congressional case depositions, quartermaster claims, land records, agricultural schedules, and

*   *   *

While rogue soldiers on both sides stole food and seized horses, the second stage of battle unfolded. Earlier in the morning, Maj. Gen. Edwin Sumner, commanding the U.S. II Corps, led the first of his three divisions into the West Woods and commenced an ill-fated attack. Sumner's other two divisions, trailing behind, veered south, toward the center of the Confederate line. This action initiated Antietam's second phase of battle, which began around 10:00 a.m.

Brigadier General William Henry French, commanding Sumner's second division, led the Union attack on Lee's center. French's men passed "within a few rods of the blazing barn and house of Mr. Mumma, feeling the scorching heat" before reaching the Roulette farm.

Two days earlier, William Roulette had escorted his family to safety, but he returned on the 16th to check on his property, and he spent the night at home. By morning, the battle began and Confederates deployed near the farmhouse, forcing Roulette "into the cellar for safety." When French's division traversed Roulette's property, they "cleared out the Johnnies," capturing Rebel pickets and driving the remainder off the farm, allowing Roulette an opportunity to escape. A U.S. army surgeon marching past the farmhouse, Dr. Thomas E. Bright of the 8th Ohio, recalled seeing Roulette emerge from the cellar, "and with hat in hand I think [he] did some of the tallest one man hollowing and tip-toe shouting I ever witnessed." Another soldier remembered that the farmer "quickly ran out of the cellar, shouting excitedly: 'Give it to 'em!' 'Drive 'em!' . . . 'Take anything on my place, only drive 'em! drive 'em!'"[48]

---

census listings reviewed in this study spell the surname as Rohrback. Although the Washington County land records index lists "Rhorback" in several records from 1865 to 1871, the deeds themselves cite Rohrback as the spelling. Another variation, Rohrbach, appears in Antietam battlefield maps and Ezra A. Carman's manuscript. An 1859 map of the Sharpsburg area also spells the name as Rohrbach. See Thomas Taggart and S. S. Downin, *A map of Washington Co., Maryland. Exhibiting the farms, election districts, towns, villages, roads, etc., etc.*, 1859, Map, *LC*, https://www.loc.gov/item/2002624033/.

48 "Letter from Dr. Ebright," *Holmes County Farmer* [Millersburg, OH], October 9, 1862. Regimental records also identify the army surgeon as Thomas F. Bright; Henry S. Stevens, *Souvenir of Excursion to Battlefields by the Society of the Fourteenth Connecticut Regiment and Reunion at Antietam, September 1891* (Washington, 1893), 51-52; *HFTL*, September 24, 1862, 2B; Stevens, *Souvenir of Excursion*, 51. Reilly in *The Battlefield of Antietam* reported that Captain Samuel Wright of the 29th Massachusetts "saw Mr. Roulette come out of the cellar and for a short while stand and look at them."

The Confederate line of battle stood south of Roulette's house, where Brig. Gen. D. H. Hill positioned his men in a sunken farm lane. This eroded road gave Hill's outnumbered Confederates—2,200 men, later reinforced with 3,400 additional troops from Major General Richard H. Anderson's division—a natural barrier against Union frontal assaults by 10,000 men in the combined divisions of French and Major General Israel B. Richardson.[49]

Similar to Antietam's morning phase, thousands of men fought at close range but in a space even more concentrated. Private J. Polk Racine, a U.S. soldier in French's division, described the horrors. "Oh, but the bullets did fly!," Racine wrote. "Men were falling all around us. Our bugler was standing near me, when a cannon-ball struck him in the head and cut it from his shoulders. I think I got some of the blood and brains in my face." Correspondent Albert Deane Richardson watched the action from a nearby bluff. He counted "more than sixty" cannon blasts to the minute and compared the musketry to "the patter of raindrops in an April shower."[50]

Numerous homes lay in the vicinity of this combat. Missiles and bullets pierced William Roulette's dwelling, "and one huge shell tore through the west side." Another shell "knocked to pieces" Roulette's safe containing cash and valuables. East of the house, the barn was "broken and torn by missiles."[51]

Near the sunken lane, Squire Jacob Miller's stone fence bordering Hagerstown Pike was "pretty well knocked to pieces, twenty od[d] balls and shells struck it, several took it nearly to the ground."[52] Henry Piper's farm, adjoining Squire Miller's

---

49 Carman, *The Maryland Campaign*, 2:297-298; "Tour Stop 8—The Sunken Road," web page, Antietam National Battlefield, https://www.nps.gov/anti/learn/photosmultimedia/tour-stop-8.htm. The Antietam National Battlefield is hereafter cited as ANB; Schildt, *Drums Along the Antietam*, 36-37; *The Daily Mail*, February 19, 1937, 16, alleged, "The old Bloody Lane road … was then called the Hog Trough road." This moniker, however, may not have existed in 1862. Mary Ellen Piper (E. P. to Sally Farran, October 4, 1862, *Dan Masters' Civil War Chronicles*) wrote shortly after the battle, "The lane that separates our farm from Mr. [William] Roulett's had been washed into a tolerably deep gulley, and this was used as a rifle pit."

50 J. Polk Racine, *Recollections of a Veteran of Four Years in Dixie* (Elkton, MD, 1894), 32; Richardson, *The Secret Service*, 284.

51 Stevens, *Souvenir of Excursion*, 64-66; Scanned claim of William Roulette, Frank Woodring, "Window to Yesterday," *Maryland Cracker Barrel* (Boonsboro, MD), vol. 21, August–September 1992, 16-17. Roulette claimed $30 for "Damages to house and barn" and $6 for "1 safe knocked to pieces by shell."

52 Jacob Miller to Amelia and Christian Houser, December 7, 1862, WMR. Miller owned several Sharpsburg tracts in 1862. One adjoined Henry Piper on the south and the Hagerstown

tract, fared worse. So many shells struck Piper's dwelling that there was "only one room in the house that a cannon ball had not penetrated."[53]

A Union soldier near the sunken lane noticed civilians' farm animals nearby, oblivious to the danger. "I saw a mare and colt, two or three cattle, and some sheep, pasturing," remembered the Federal. "They were between two fires—that is, getting our bullets and the enemy's. I saw the old mare stagger and fall, then all but the little colt fell at the first fire." Fifteen minutes later, the colt emerged from the smoky chaos and "ran down our line, apparently unhurt." But, caught in the death zone, the animal didn't last long. "The next day," the soldier recalled, "we found the little thing half a mile down the line. It was full of bullets."

An assistant surgeon, whose regiment fought at the sunken lane, remembered how "a fine, large, shaggy, black dog" approached a Union battery during the battle. When an unexploded Confederate shell crashed into the nearby soil, the dog dug at the projectile. While its "paws and nose were pressing into the earth," the shell exploded, "sending a cloud of earth and dog into the air." The surgeon recounted that "the nose and lower jaw of the dog were blown away by the explosion, but he lived and ran about for some time."[54]

Amid this chaos, a civilian drove a two-horse buggy onto the center of the battlefield. East of the sunken lane, Captain William M. Graham and his men of Battery K, 1st U.S. Artillery, watched a man drive "his carriage to my battery while under severe artillery fire." According to Graham, not only did the local ride willingly onto the battlefield, he "carried off my wounded who were suffering very much for the want of surgical attendance, and distributed ham and biscuits among the men of the battery." The resident returned a second time, and "one of his horses was wounded while performing this service." Graham did not identify the Samaritan, describing him simply as a gentleman "who resides near the battlefield."[55]

Pike on the east. This parcel includes what today is known as Battleview Market and Mountain View Cemetery. See land record IN 18 / 57.

53 E. P. to Sally Farran, October 4, 1862, *Dan Masters' Civil War Chronicles*; Claim of Henry Piper (No. 445). Piper claimed $25 for "Damage to Home & Barn."

54 Racine, *Recollections of a Veteran*, 32; William Child, *History of the Fifth Regiment, New Hampshire Volunteers* (Bristol, NH, 1893), 127.

55 James V. Murfin, *The Gleam of Bayonets: The Battle of Antietam and the Maryland Campaign of 1862* (Baton Rouge, 1965), 266. Murfin cited Graham's official report, dated October 4, 1862; Reilly, *BOA*. Reilly wrote of the Samaritan, "[N]o one today knows who he was or where he came . . . in 1910 the War Department made an effort, through Gen. Ezra Carman . . . to locate him; the

Federals eventually flanked the Confederates and poured enfilading fire into the sunken road. The Rebels' trench became a death trap. When the smoke cleared, piles of bodies and pools of blood filled the lane. Subsequent confusion sparked a Confederate retreat to the Piper farm. Union troops pursued, but Southern counterattacks, supported by artillery, forced the Federals back to the lane. In this way, Antietam's second phase of battle concluded. Of nearly 17,000 men engaged in the three-hour struggle, 5,500 were dead, wounded, or missing. Neither side gained ground or advantage.[56]

*   *   *

Antietam's third and final phase occurred south of Sharpsburg. Fighting began in the mid-morning at Antietam Creek, where General Ambrose Burnside's IX Corps attempted to seize the Lower Bridge from a small and stubborn Georgian defense. During this action, Confederate shells crashed onto farms east of the creek. South of the Lower Bridge, projectiles struck the farm of Noah Rohrback. One missile damaged the smokehouse while "two shells went through his barn."

Henry and Jacob Rohrback cultivated a farm northeast of the Lower Bridge. The family initially sought safety in the cellar, bringing mattresses with them for a modicum of comfort. Nevertheless, when shells exploded on the farm, General Burnside personally urged the occupants to evacuate. Earlier in the day, Union forces had impressed the Rohrbacks' draft horse into Lt. Samuel Benjamin's battery, leaving one lame horse to transport the family to safety. "Take him," Burnside reportedly implored, "and risk getting beyond the lines, it is safer to go than to stay."

Henry and Jacob Rohrback remained at the house, but purportedly escorted women of the family into a one-horse buggy. Henry's son-in-law steered the gimpy horse through the Rohrbacks' orchard, as shells exploded nearby. One witness inside the wagon recalled, in her later years, "I heard a terrible whistling and an explosion which sent the earth and stones in every direction. It was not very far

---

county papers were used to find out who he was, but with no success;" Bruce Catton, "Gallant Men in Deeds of Glory," *Life*, January 6, 1961, 68. Referring to the civilian, Catton wrote, "Nobody ever discovered his name." In 1962—not long after Catton's article attracted attention to the subject—a Keedysville resident alleged that the Samaritan was his grandfather, Martin Eakle, a miller from Eakles Mills. See "Confederate Extends Aid To Wounded Union Soldier," *Morning Herald* [Hagerstown, MD], August 30, 1962, 20-21.

56 "Tour Stop 8—The Sunken Road," ANB.

from us and we were all terrified." Fortunately, the "old lame horse" pulled the evacuees to a neighbor's house, safely distant from artillery fire.[57]

Hilary Watson sheltered on the Otto farm, west of the Lower Bridge. The slave remained on the property to guard the Ottos' horses, but when the shelling intensified, he at last evacuated. As Watson stepped outside, a shell "went between our house and the next, and busted. I could see the blue blaze flyin', and I jumped as high as your head," he remembered. Projectiles screeched above as Watson rounded up the horses. "I didn't like those shells a-flyin', and I got on one of the horses and led some of the others and went off across the Potomac to the place of a man who was a friend of my boss. There I stayed all day listenin' to the cannon."[58]

At 1:00 p.m., Burnside's IX Corps launched another frontal assault against 500 Georgians defending the Lower Bridge. The Union attack, supported by a flanking movement across John H. Snavely's farm, overwhelmed the Georgians. Burnside's men finally seized the bridge, but it was awfully late. To the benefit of Robert E. Lee, IX Corps consumed much time in taking the Rebel-held bridge and needed two additional hours to funnel across Antietam Creek.

Shortly after 3:00 p.m., Burnside ordered his forces to "attack Sharpsburg and the heights on the left." The mile-wide line advanced toward the town amid the fire from forty Rebel cannon. Elements of IX Corps crossed Catherine Tenant's 22-acre tract and approached Col. John Miller's stone mill complex. In September 1862, Col. Miller rented his mill to Solomon Lumm. On the day of the battle, Lumm, his wife, and two young daughters remained inside their stone home.[59]

---

57 Claim of Noah Rohrback (*RG* 92, Book H, Box 126, Claim H-3874); Hildebrand, "Recollections of Martha Ada Thomas, June 1934," *Antietam Remembered*, WMR. Martha Ada, Henry B. Rohrback's granddaughter, was three years old in Sep. 1862. Her detailed account, written years later, may stem from oral history rather than firsthand memory.

58 Johnson, *BA*, 107.

59 Carman, *The Maryland Campaign*, 2:440-441; "Tour Stop 10—The Final Attack," web page, ANB, https://www.nps.gov/anti/learn/photosmultimedia/tour-stop-10.htm. For details on the morning action at the Lower Bridge, see Carman, *The Maryland Campaign*, 2:409-430; Claim of Joseph Sherrick (*RG* 92, Book F, Box 89, Claim F-1433); Claim of Leonard Emmert (*RG* 123, Entry 22, Box 538, No. 4257). Emmert tenanted the 260-acre Sherrick farm in 1862, and testified that his cow and mare died during the battle; In Sep. 1862, Catherine Tenant owned a 22-acre tract on the battlefield situated between Joseph Sherrick's farm and Col. John Miller's stone mill. Catherine and her husband, Michael Tenant, resided on Lot 37W in Sharpsburg village. See land records IN 15 / 515, IN 19 / 674, 104 / 56, and 112 / 595; Claim of Solomon Lumm (No. 340). In war claims, land deeds, and other records, Lumm identified himself as Solomon S. Lumm.

After a sharp fight in the mill orchard, Confederates fell back and occupied the Lumm house. Colonel F. W. McMaster and soldiers from his 17th South Carolina Infantry converted the home "into a fort, and fought for some time." Lieutenant W. S. Moore of the 17th South Carolina recalled running inside "a rock house." Here, Col. McMaster ordered Moore and others "to raise the windows and shoot through; he also told some of the men to go up stairs and knock off some of the roof of the house, and ordered some men to go up and fire from the roof." The Lumms found themselves caught in the middle of the fighting. As Federals shot at the home, the South Carolinians let loose "a sharp and severe fire from the stone mill and house." Shells from both armies raked the Miller-Lumm property, striking the house, spring house, and barn. Projectiles set fire to frame outbuildings, including the stable, carriage house, corn house, and outhouse.

U.S. soldiers pushed across the stone mill complex, and Col. McMaster saw that "the enemy had almost entirely surrounded my little band." McMaster fled, joining other ANV forces in retreating toward the village. Soldiers from the 45th Pennsylvania stormed into Lumm's house and captured nearly a dozen South Carolinians, including Captain Hansford Twiggs.[60]

The IX Corps's push toward Lee's right flank, combined with Union artillery fire, forced Confederates on Sharpsburg Heights to withdraw into the village. Colonel Stephen D. Lee's battery and Brigadier General Richard B. Garnett's brigade, "outnumbered and outflanked," retreated amidst a barrage of shells. Garnett recalled, "[T]he main street of the town was commanded by the Federal artillery. My troops, therefore, passed . . . to the north of the town along the cross-streets." Captain Thomas H. Carter's battery followed Garnett's men into the north part of the village, halting on North Mechanic Street near Judge David Smith's house.

Near the southeast edge of Sharpsburg, the advance of Colonel Harrison S. Fairchild's brigade forced other Confederate batteries to fall back into the town. Captains James S. Brown and James Reilly withdrew their guns from the farm of Jacob Avey, Sr., and "went through Sharpsburg" from the Harpers Ferry Road

---

60 Carman, *The Maryland Campaign*, 2:441-442; Official report of Colonel F. W. McMaster, October 20, 1862, *OR*, vol. 19, 1:946; *Proceedings of a general court martial, in the trial of Col. F. W. McMaster, 17th regiment, S.C.V.* (Columbia, SC, 1863), 46; Claim of John Miller (No. 2227). Miller sought $200 for "Damages to the Mill the dwelling House Spring House and Barn." He also claimed $400 for "Burning by the shele on the day of the Battle of Antieatum a large frame stable carriage House Corn House [and] Out House;" Carman, *The Maryland Campaign*, 2:443.

(South Mechanic Street) to West Main Street. Captain Charles W. Squires's battery retreated north into the village, taking Church Street to East Main Street.[61]

*   *   *

The rising din of battle lured Teresa Kretzer from her cellar. She remembered climbing to the attic with another girl, where they "threw open the shutter and looked out toward the battleground. We were curious to know what was going on." The lasses observed "the blue uniforms and shining bayonets of our men." Being a Unionist, Teresa "thought it was the prettiest sight I ever saw in my life . . . I felt so glad to think that we were going to get them into town shortly."[62]

Teresa may have witnessed Fairchild's brigade advance onto Jacob Avey, Sr.'s farm, which overlooked part of the town. Fairchild's men pushed toward the Harpers Ferry Road into a tempest of artillery fire. A New York colonel reported, "A shell fell in my lines, killing eight men at one explosion, and a round shot took off private Conway's head." A member of the same regiment observed, "The whole landscape for an instant turned slightly red." Another IX Corps soldier compared the sounds to "all the demons of Hades howling an accompaniment . . . mingled with the groans, shrieks, curses, hurrahs and shouts of men, and the wailing cry of wounded animals."[63]

Fairchild's men charged the Confederate commands of brigadier generals Thomas Drayton and James L. Kemper. After a "short struggle" of hand-to-hand

---

61 Carman, *The Maryland Campaign*, 2:446, 451-452; "Map of the Battlefield of Antietam, Sept. 17th—4:20PM," United States War Department. Atlas of the battlefield of Antietam, prepared under the direction of the Antietam Battlefield Board, lieut. col. Geo. W. Davis, U.S.A., president, gen. E.A. Carman, U.S.V., gen. H Heth, C.S.A. Surveyed by lieut. col. E.B. Cope, engineer, H.W. Mattern, assistant engineer, of the Gettysburg National Park. Drawn by Charles H. Ourand. Position of troops by gen. E. A. Carman. Published by authority of the Secretary of War, under the direction of the Chief of Engineers, U.S. Army, 1908. [Washington, Govt. print. off, 1908] Map, *LC*, https://www.loc.gov/item/2008621532/ (hereafter cited as the Carman-Cope maps); Official report of Brigadier General Richard B. Garnett, November 7, 1862, OR, vol. 19, 1:897.

62 Johnson, *BA*, 122.

63 Edwin Forbes, *The battle of Antietam—Charge of Burnside 9th Corps on the right flank of the Confederate Army*, Sketch, *LC*, https://www.loc.gov/item/2004661896/. Forbes's sketch of combat on Jacob Avey, Sr.'s farm depicts the upper stories of several Sharpsburg village homes in the background; Carman, *The Maryland Campaign*, 2:449-454; Graham, *The Ninth Regiment*, 294, 318; Sears, *Landscape Turned Red*, 282; Jesse Leavenworth, "Civil War Stress," *The Hartford* [CT] *Courant*, June 1, 2009, https://www.courant.com/news/connecticut/hc-xpm-2009-06-01-civilwar-ptsd-0601-art-story.html.

combat at Avey's stone wall, the Federals drove Drayton's and Kemper's forces into Sharpsburg village. A historical map of the battle shows that Drayton's brigade retreated past the Avey farmhouse, and then continued up Granite Street (East High Street). Kemper's men ran northwest into town via Harpers Ferry Road (South Mechanic Street).[64]

Martin L. Fry, a Sharpsburg resident, observed fighting in the "out lots," which adjoined the southeast edge of town. Fry testified that a lane dividing the agricultural lots "was run over by the rebel army and fought over." Asked if combat destroyed crops in the out lots, Fry swore under oath, "Oh my God; yes . . . the fighting that I saw being done over it was sufficient to destroy anything."

As Drayton's and Kemper's Confederates retreated, parts of Thomas Welsh's Union brigade advanced into the orchard of Jacob Avey, Sr., joining Fairchild. Here, the combined forces "prepared to . . . advance into town." When Union skirmishers rushed down Avey's hill "to the first street" in the town's limits, some Federals, caught in the excitement of pursuit, chased the Confederates into the village. One of the charging Yankees "was killed in the street running from Avey's house." ANV troops captured other U.S. soldiers in town.[65]

Villagers heard the fighting swell as IX Corps pushed toward town. Some townsfolk, Teresa Kretzer recalled, "would come up and venture out under the porch, but they were afraid to stay out; and the danger wasn't just fancied either." Christina Watson stepped outside Jacob H. Grove's house at the public square and saw "an old colored man was comin' down the pavement with an iron pot on his

---

64 Carman, *The Maryland Campaign*, 2:453; "Map of the Battlefield of Antietam, Sept. 17th—4:20PM," Carman-Cope maps; A random sample of Washington County land records from 1856–1865 found nine deeds that refer to Sharpsburg village's southernmost road as Granite Street.

65 Claim of John Grice (*RG* 123, Entry 22, Box 692, Case No. 5872). Martin L. Fry testified in Grice's case. Land records show that Grice in 1862 owned several "out lots"—agricultural parcels measuring five to ten acres each, which adjoined the town on the south. Grice's out lots, numbered 1, 4, 10, 11, and 88, lay near the town's southern edge and Harpers Ferry Road; Carman, *The Maryland Campaign*, 2:443, 450-456. Based on the context of Carman's passage, the U.S. soldier may have died on Granite Street (East High Street) or South Church Street; "WA-II-723 Sharpsburg Historic District," architectural survey file, MHT, sec. 8, p. 3, https://mht.maryland.gov/secure/medusa/PDF/Washington/WA-II-723.pdf. Sharpsburg's out lots were "intended to be used by town dwellers for their kitchen gardens and the necessary livestock such as horse[s], cow[s] and hogs." Real estate laws forbid landowners from building houses on the out lots, but permitted a barn or stable; John Frye, Western Maryland Room, phone call to author, September 9, 2016. Mr. Frye, an esteemed Washington County historian, mentioned that Sharpsburg was the only town in the county that laid out agricultural out lots. Residential neighborhoods now stand on the former out lot grounds.

head. He said the Yankees had got the Rebels on the run, and there'd be fightin' right in the town streets."[66]

Jacob McGraw, hoping to catch a glimpse of the fighting, left the Kretzers' cellar and ran to his brother's home at the intersection of Mechanic and Antietam streets. "Two other men was with me," McGraw recalled, "and we was the only citizens in sight around the town. We hadn't been there but a very short time when half a dozen Confederates come down a cross street with eleven prisoners. One of the prisoners had his jaw shot off. I shall never forget how he looked."

As McGraw's group hurried through the village, a missile "went into a hogpen near us and killed two hogs." Another shell struck a soldier in the street "and turned him over and over like a wagon wheel." Then, as McGraw peeked around the corner of his brother's house, a projectile hit the building above his head, and the impact "sent down upon him a shower of bits of brick and mortar." Having seen enough, the young man "beat a hasty retreat" to the shelter of a cellar.[67]

Sharpsburg village was on the brink of becoming part of the battlefield. Ezra A. Carman, a veteran of the battle and renowned Antietam historian, wrote, "All was now confusion in the town; [Confederate] artillery was dashing to the rear through the rough and narrow streets." Carman noted that men from various Southern brigades "were retreating from Cemetery hill, filled the streets, broken in organization; Jones, Kemper, Drayton, Garnett and other officers endeavoring to rally them."[68]

* * *

The Union army's relentless artillery bombardment, which continued during the IX Corps's attack on Lee's right flank, set fire to several homes, barns, and outbuildings in the village. A Confederate soldier commented that the town was "enveloped in the flames of burning buildings, while flocks of terrified pigeons, driven hither and thither by the screaming and bursting of shells, flew round and round in the clouds of smoke." A townswoman recounted "how her husband was

66 Johnson, *BA*, 110.

67 Ibid., 115; Cross, "The Strong Stone House;" Fred W. Cross, scrapbook, ANBL. McGraw's account is a synthesis of the Clifton Johnson (*BA*) and Fred W. Cross interviews. McGraw told Cross that the incident near his brother's home occurred when "the attack of the 9th Corps was at its height, and Rodman's division was rapidly driving the brigade of D. R. Jones' Confederate division back toward the southerly side of the village."

68 Carman, *The Maryland Campaign,* 2:456. Cemetery Hill is a postwar moniker for Sharpsburg Heights.

forced to rush up and put out the fire caught from a shell which exploded in the second story." On Sharpsburg Heights, Susan Kennedy's house "was on fier up in the garret from the bursting of a shell but was put out by the soldiers." Shells crashed through the roof and upper windows of Dr. A. A. Biggs's home on West Main Street. "My house caught fire three times," the doctor wrote, "but I succeeded in putting it out."[69]

Ordnance set fire to the house of siblings Elizabeth and Harriet Good. They had fled before the battle, but four girls sheltering in Squire Jacob Miller's home noticed that the Goods' dwelling was in flames. The teenagers rounded up buckets and basins, and ran to the burning house. The Goods' lot adjoined the Big Spring, the town's primary water source. Despite the danger of shells falling into town, the four girls "carried water from the little spring . . . and put out the fire." The house again ignited, but the teens "repaired to the scene and this time they were successful in thoroughly extinguishing the flames."[70]

Jacob H. Grove's house survived nearly one dozen shell strikes, but his Pennsylvania-style barn did not. The large structure, situated on his village lot, contained grains, tools, chickens, and a two-horse carriage. During the battle, a missile ignited the barn. Grove's son, Robert, joined by neighbor John Benner and a Confederate soldier, tried extinguishing the blaze, but to no avail. When the flames threatened to spread to Grove's home, "the men jest had to get up on top of the house and spread wet blankets all over the roof," explained Christina Watson. "We couldn't save the barn," she lamented. "That burnt down to the ground, and the chickens and everything in it was burnt up. Oh! [I]t was an awful time."[71]

69 Carman, *The Maryland Campaign*, 2:451-452; Edward A. Moore, *The Story of a Cannoneer Under Stonewall Jackson* (New York, 1907), 154-155; Noyes, *The Bivouac and the Battlefield*, 237; Jacob Miller to Amelia and Christian Houser, December 7, 1862, WMR; Biggs to Kalb, September 29, 1862, WMR.

70 Smith, "No Civilian Died." The four teenagers, aged 13 and 14 years in Sep. 1862, were Jeanette Blackford, Maggie Hart, Jennie Mumma, and Clara Brining. The 1860 census lists Elizabeth and Harriet Good with two brothers, Jacob and William, in Dwelling #1646. Land records IN 8 / 96-98 and 85 / 266, along with Will liber H / folio 307, document the Good sisters' complex ownership of Lot 12. Some accounts have mistakenly identified the 1862 owner of Lot 12 as Aaron Good, a brother of Harriet and Elizabeth.

71 Johnson, *BA*, 109. Christina Watson implied that the barn caught fire on the 15th or 16th, but the accounts of John P. Smith and Jacob H. Grove support that it burned on the 17th. *The Daily Intelligencer* [Wheeling, WV], September 22, 1862, and *HFTL*, October 1, 1862, reported the destruction of Grove's barn. The *Intelligencer* described it as a "large barn situated in the centre of the town;" Biggs to Kalb, September 29, 1862, WMR. Biggs wrote, "J. H. Grove's house was set on fire and came very near setting the whole town on fire." Biggs may have

Union shells set fire to village buildings owned by three different widows. Near the public square, Catherine Rohrback's barn caught fire on Lot 2.[72] Ordnance also ignited Sarah Himes's home on Lot 181, located at the western end of town. An errant shell struck Margaret Shackelford's dwelling on Antietam Street, Lot 31, setting the widow's house on fire.[73]

Compared to the Union batteries, Confederate artillery inflicted minor damage to properties. Joseph Thomas owned a farm near the Middle Bridge, east of Antietam Creek. He reported that "the rebels threw shells into the field & destroyed some corn."

John Ecker's farm adjoined Thomas on the west and overlooked Antietam Creek. Infantry from the U.S. V Corps and guns of the Federal Reserve Artillery deployed on Ecker's ridge during the battle and drew fire from Confederate batteries. The Ecker family hid in their cellar while U.S. batteries fired near the brick farmhouse. John A. Miller, a grandson of John Ecker, was among those sheltering in the basement. He remembered, "A Union artillery battery, located not

---

mistaken Grove's house for the burning barn; Claim of Jacob H. Grove (No. 1267). Grove sought $1,500 for "One large swiser barn . . . burnt on the 17th day of Sept." Grove's two farms situated west of Sharpsburg were out of range from Union artillery, further supporting that the barn burned on his village lot.

72 Claim of Catherine Rohrback (*RG* 92, Entry 843, Box 772, Book 304, Claim 234). Rohrback claimed the $500 loss of "1 Barn Burned down by shells." The *Herald of Freedom and Torch Light*, October 1, 1862, incorrectly reported that the barn of "Daniel Rohrback [was] . . . destroyed by fire." Daniel Rohrback, Catherine's son-in-law, appears in her Sharpsburg household in the 1860 Federal census. Daniel owned no real estate in 1862, and his individual claim (*RG* 92, Entry 843, Box 772, Book 304, Claim 231) did not include a barn. Catherine Rohrback, the widow of William Rohrback, owned additional acreage on the battlefield in 1862, south of Sharpsburg, and her barn possibly stood in this location (see land records GG / 171, 74 / 31, and 1011 / 572). However, the context of the *Herald of Freedom and Torch Light's* article implies that the damage related to Sharpsburg village; *Antietam National Battlefield Historic Resource Study: Sharpsburg and the Battle of Antietam* (Washington, DC, 2008). This architectural study examined properties in Sharpsburg that stood in 1862. It noted that Catherine Rohrback's Lot 2E contained a "two-story, cut-stone, unbanked barn at the back of the lot."

73 Claim of Sarah Himes (*RG* 92, Entry 843, Box 772, Book 304, Claim 229). Himes claimed $350 for "House burnt by Shell; Claim of Margaret Shackelford (*RG* 92, Entry 843, Box 772, Book 304). Shackelford sought $200 for "House burnt by Shot and Shell;" *Herald of Freedom and Torch Light*, October 1, 1862. The newspaper reported the destruction of homes owned by "Widow Himes" and "Widow Shackelford." John P. Smith in "No Civilian Died" mentioned the fire damage to Shackelford's and Himes's houses; Hartwig, *To Antietam Creek*, 636. Supporting that Federal shells struck buildings at the western end of town, Robert E. Lee reportedly instructed General Lafayette McLaws on Sep. 17 to halt his command a safe distance from Lee's headquarters in the Town Woods. "Do not let them come quite this far," warned Lee, "as the shells from the enemy fall about here."

more than 100 yards away, was blazing away at the Rebels, and Confederates were trying to knock out the enemy battery. But our house was not hit, although a lot of cannon balls fell in many parts of the farm and not so far away from the house." Samuel Avey, John Ecker's son-in-law, recalled that "a line of battle formed by Fitz John Porters Corps extended over the farm, and several batteries were also on the farm." Additionally, Avey deposed, "There was considerable fighting done there on the evening previous and on the day of the battle." [74]

The combined fire of Confederate and Union batteries battered the house and mill complex of Joshua and Mary Ann Newcomer, located west of the Middle Bridge. The couple and their children fled to the farm of Philip Pry, which afforded a prime view of the battlefield.[75]

The Newcomers certainly worried about damages to their property, but they had more significant concerns. Their son, John Clinton Newcomer, was a Confederate in Robert E. Lee's army. He served in Cayce's Company, Purcell Artillery, A. P. Hill's division. John Newcomer wasn't the only Sharpsburg lad who enlisted in the unit. Joseph McGraw, who grew up in Sharpsburg village, served as a lieutenant in the same command.

Why did this matter? As IX Corps forces drove Lee's right flank into the village, with Union victory seeming imminent, A. P. Hill's Confederate division, along with Cayce's Company, Purcell Artillery, splashed across Blackford's Ford, arriving from Harpers Ferry.[76]

---

74 Claim of Joseph Thomas (*RG* 92, Book F, Box 76, Claim F-611); "Miller Recalls Antietam Battle," *Morning Herald* [Hagerstown, MD], September 17, 1948, 19; Claim of John Ecker (*RG* 92, Entry 812, Box 91, Claim F-1523). Samuel Avey testified "that during the war he lived in a tenant house on the farm of Claimant [Ecker], and was frequently employed by him as a farm hand."

75 Claim of Joshua Newcomer (*RG* 123, No. 272). Newcomer's son, Isaac Newcomer, testified that, during the battle, he "was at General McClellan's headquarters—Mr. Pry's house separated him from the farm—and at this point he could see and overlook the battle."

76 *CWSS*, M382, Roll 41. Private John Clinton Newcomer served in Cayce's Company, Virginia Light Artillery (Purcell Artillery); The Federal census in 1850 and 1860 lists Newcomer in his parents' Sharpsburg household—Dwelling #527 in 1850 and Dwelling #1742 in 1860; Washington County burial records cite Newcomer's interment with his parents, Joshua and Mary Ann Newcomer, at St. Paul's Reformed Church Cemetery near Clear Spring; Johnson and Anderson, *Artillery Hell*, 94, 106. A detachment of the Purcell Artillery remained at Harpers Ferry and it's unclear if Newcomer marched to Sharpsburg on the 17th; Carman, *The Maryland Campaign*, 2:465. Joseph McGraw's postwar correspondence with Carman gives weight to McGraw's presence in Sharpsburg on the 17th. For further reading on McGraw, see Fred W. Cross, "Joseph McGraw at Antietam," *Morning Herald*, two installments, February 1, 1934, and

Robert E. Lee, meanwhile, saw that his right flank was in peril. In response, he "ordered every gun that had wheels and horses to the south of the town," and then rode into Sharpsburg village and "gave his personal assistance in stopping stragglers and rallying the broken commands." Confederate officers, including Garnett, Jones, Kemper, and Drayton, joined Lee in rallying the troops and then rushed their regrouped forces to the Harpers Ferry Road.

Brigadier General Robert Toombs, arriving on Lee's crumbling right with a portion of his brigade, "found the enemy in possession of the ground" he was ordered to occupy, "including the eastern suburbs of the town of Sharpsburg." Rallied Confederate forces soon joined Toombs's command along the Harpers Ferry Road, while several Rebel batteries deployed near Sharpsburg's out lots.

As Lee's right reanimated, the 89th New York of Fairchild's brigade "pushed forward up the hill to the edge of town and not much over 300 yards from the town square." Before the regiment advanced into the village, the rallying Rebels threatened the New Yorkers' flank.[77]

A. P. Hill's division further strengthened Lee's right. The Confederates streamed up Miller's Sawmill Road, passing the farm of Henry V. S. Blackford. The farmer's son, William F. Blackford, "met the Confederate column as it came up the road . . . and an officer jokingly asked him if he didn't want to go up and see the battle." The curious lad followed Hill's forces for a spell, and then "beat a hasty retreat to Miller's [Saw]Mill." With the battle intensifying near the Harpers Ferry Road, Henry V. S. Blackford evacuated his family to Blackford's Ford.[78]

Around 4:00 p.m., the head of A. P. Hill's column crossed the Harpers Ferry Road and attacked the left flank of IX Corps. Two regiments defending the extreme Union left were partially blinded by the "very thick and high" corn in

February 15, 1934. See also Fred W. Cross, "A Forgotten Hero—Why Is No Mention Ever Made of Brave Major Magraw?" *Evening Times* [Cumberland, MD], April 30, 1906.

77 Carman, *The Maryland Campaign*, 2:456. For further details on Lee's movements during the battle's later stages, see Rossino, *Their Maryland*, 235-246; Official report of Brig. Gen. Richard B. Garnett, *OR*, vol. 19, 1:897; Official report of Brigadier General Robert Toombs, February 13, 1864, *OR*, vol. 19, 1:891-892. Two regiments from Toombs's Georgia brigade, earlier in the day, defended the Lower Bridge against Burnside's assaults; "Map of the Battlefield of Antietam, Sept. 17th—5:30PM," Carman-Cope maps; Carman, *The Maryland Campaign*, 2:454.

78 Fred W. Cross. "Recollections of Another Sharpsburg Boy," *The Daily Mail* [Hagerstown, MD], March 12, 1934, 4; Claims of Henry V. S. Blackford (*RG* 92, G-1630, G-1648, and G-1654). Testimony states that Henry V. S. Blackford evacuated to "protect his family and his horses." The Blackfords fled to the farm of Henry's brother, William M. Blackford, located at Blackford's Ford.

Joseph Sherrick's 38-acre field. The Rebels' "destructive volleys" fired into Sherrick's cornfield threw the Federals into confusion. The left flank crumbled, leaving advanced Union regiments near Sharpsburg village unsupported. The Confederate rally along the Harpers Ferry Road, combined with Hill's attack, effectively ended the IX Corps's assault. Union Brigadier General Jacob D. Cox recalled, "The mass of the enemy on the left still continued to increase; new batteries were constantly being opened upon us, and it was manifest the corps would, without re-enforcements, be unable to reach the village of Sharpsburg." Burnside had no choice but to call off the attack and withdraw his troops to Antietam Creek.[79]

* * *

As the sun set on September 17, one witness remembered that "the murmur of the night wind . . . was mingled with the groans of countless sufferers of both armies." Correspondent Charles Coffin observed, "Near the town, hay-stacks, barns, and houses are in flames . . . all the country is flaming, smoking, and burning, as if the last great day, the judgement day of the Lord, had come."

Confederate general James Longstreet rode through the battered village at day's end. "In going through the town," he recalled, "I passed a house that had been set afire and was still burning. The family was in great distress, and I stopped to do what I could for them."

A short while later, at Confederate headquarters, Longstreet and other officers gave their reports to General Lee. Most suggested the army return to Virginia, but Lee refused to relinquish the Confederacy's initiative. "If McClellan wants to fight in the morning," he purportedly said, "I will give him battle again."

---

79 Carman, *The Maryland Campaign*, 2:466-467. One of the regiments defending the Federal left, the 16th Connecticut, had never seen action before Antietam; Official report of Lieutenant Colonel Joseph B. Curtis, September 22, 1862, *OR*, vol. 19, 1:456-457; Claims of Joseph Sherrick (F-1433) and Leonard Emmert (F-1577 and No. 4257). As landowner and tenant, Sherrick and Emmert agreed to divide their corn yield evenly. Many writers have referred to the Sherrick-Emmert parcel as the "40-acre Cornfield"—an estimate that may stem from Ezra Carman's description (Carman, *The Maryland Campaign*, 2:462). However, Sherrick and Emmert estimated their field as 38 acres. Testimony alleged that combat destroyed some of the crop, and afterward, AOP forces seized the remainder of corn as horse forage "until the whole field was stripped." Thus, Sherrick and Emmert lost their total yield, and each claimed the loss of 19 acres of corn. Emmert testified, "[T]here were 38 acres planted in corn that year and that he [Sherrick] claimed 19 acres of that corn as his share." John Otto, appearing as a witness in Emmert's case, estimated the Sherrick-Emmert cornfield as "about 37 acres;" Official report of Brigadier General Ambrose P. Hill, February 25, 1863, *OR*, vol. 19, 1:981; Official report of Brigadier General Jacob D. Cox, September 20, 1862, *OR*, vol. 19, 1:426.

With the prospect of continued bloodshed in the morning, one officer present at headquarters described the somber moment. "A large number of general officers and staff officers were assembled about Gen. Lee. The occasional crack of a rifle, the groans of wounded men being carried by on stretchers, the crackling of the timbers of a burning house near by, which cast a lurid glare upon the group, made it a scene soon not to be forgotten."[80]

Throughout the area, flaming structures illuminated the darkening sky. A Federal lieutenant saw enemy troops moving across Sharpsburg Heights, silhouetted "by the light of blazing houses." Another witness observed, "The sky is bright with lurid flames of burning buildings." Elizabeth Miller Blackford, sheltering at her brother's farm near Miller's Sawmill, recalled, "[T]hat night I thought the whole town was on fire . . . I did not expect to see anything but embers when I returned the next day." Near the village, a Confederate noted, "[T]he scene of carnage was illuminated by the glare of half a dozen burning buildings, presenting a picture too horrible to attempt description."[81]

Structure fires dyed the night sky red. "There was a red haze on the sunset," recounted a villager. "[T]he brick of the church was red, and as far as I could see were suffering, crying or dead men . . . red, red, red. It was a red stew." An artillerist wrote, "Some of the enemy's shells set some buildings on fire in Sharpsburg and the flames threw a red glare on the sky that reflected a pale ghostly light over the battle plain strewn with the upturned faces of the dead."

Major Heros von Borcke observed, "[T]hroughout the evening the sky was reddened by the glare of the conflagration." He described the village as "a sad spectacle of death and destruction, as seen by the light of the yet glowing embers of its habitations, the greater number of which had been swept away by the flames." Von Borcke noted that the "unburied corpses of men and horses lay on every side

---

80 Coffin, *Following the Flag*, 204; Carman, *The Maryland Campaign*, 2:500; Longstreet, "The Invasion of Maryland," 314; Carman, *The Maryland Campaign*, 2:504-505; Owen, *In Camp and Battle*, 157, 142. Owen's map depicts a "Burning House" opposite the Shepherdstown Pike near Lee's headquarters at the western limits of town. Owen may have described the dwelling of Sarah Himes on Lot 181W, which stood in this vicinity.

81 Thomas H. Evans, "The Enemy Sullenly Held on to the City," *Civil War Times Illustrated*, April 1968, 32-40; Coffin, *Following the Flag*, 204; Elizabeth Miller to Amelia Houser, February 8, 1863, WMR; Raymer, *Confederate Correspondent*, 41.

Alonzo Fry (1859–1951), photographed in 1862, lived in Sharpsburg village at the time of the battle. We're left to wonder how the terror of Antietam impacted the mental health of Sharpsburg-area children. *Courtesy of Louise Benas*

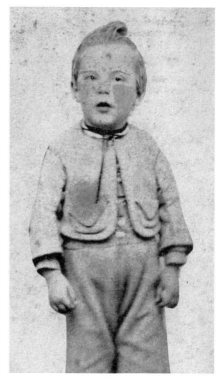

in the streets, while helpless women and children, who had lost their homesteads, were moving about amid the smouldering ruins seeking shelter for the night."[82]

After watching Confederates march past the public square, Christina Watson "went into the house and laid down, but I couldn't sleep none because I didn't know when they'd break in on me." Distant picket fire, which "kept up till ten o'clock," strained the nerves of villagers in the Kretzer cellar. To some, it seemed as though the fighting would never end. "Our neighbors who had been in the cellar didn't attempt to go home," recalled Teresa Kretzer. "Some of the older ones we accommodated in beds, others lay on the floors, but the best part of the people sat up all night and watched, for we didn't know what was going to come on us."

As night fell on Sharpsburg, a woman and her children emerged from their village shelter to aid the wounded. One of her children remembered "my mother laboring with three big baskets and I holding her pettiskirts . . . and all of us, my brother and sisters, too afraid to cry."[83]

The Battle of Antietam was over. While McClellan possessed the numerical advantage in all three phases, Lee successfully held his ground against the piecemeal attacks. In this sense, the battle was a draw with a horrific body count. In twelve hours of combat, military forces fired an estimated 50,000 rounds of artillery

---

82 Margaret Beltemacchi to Rep. Goodloe Byron, June 3, 1971, ANBL. Beltemacchi described "a little lady in her late eighties" known as "Grandma Siepel," who lived near the edge of town in 1862; George M. Neese, *Three Years in the Confederate Horse Artillery* (New York, 1911), 125-126; Von Borcke, *Memoirs,* 1:160, 162.

83 Johnson, *BA,* 111, 122; Margaret Beltemacchi to Goodloe Byron, June 3, 1971, ANBL.

and nearly four million bullets. By sunset, 23,000 men were dead, wounded, captured, or missing, making September 17, 1862, the deadliest day in American military history. For the civilians of Sharpsburg, however, the struggle had just begun.[84]

---

84 Carman, *The Maryland Campaign,* 2:601, 611-612. The estimates of bullets and artillery rounds fired during the battle are based on presentations by ANB park rangers during battlefield tours from 2006–2011. See also Keith Snyder, ANB park ranger, C-SPAN television interview, 5:05–5:15 and 7:00–7:35, https://www.c-span.org/video/?307917-103/keith-snyder-battle-antietam.

Chapter 3

War in All Its Hideousness:
The Battle's Aftermath

When the sun rose on September 18, civilians expected the battle to renew. It did not.

Several issues factored into McClellan's decision not to attack Lee on the 18th, including battered AOP commands, "greatly exhausted" reinforcements, and militia regiments "expected from Pennsylvania [but] never arrived." Another reason was low ammunition for the Federal Reserve Artillery, which expended most of its rounds from September 16–17. Lacking his long-range firepower, McClellan opted to remain idle on the 18th—a stroke of luck for Sharpsburg's residents in sparing their properties additional artillery damage.[1]

The armies licked their wounds and held their ground, but the day was not silent. Skirmish fire in the central and southern parts of the battlefield sparked early and rattled throughout the 18th. The musketry and cannonading pinned villagers in

---

1 Carman, *The Maryland Campaign*, 2:501-504; Rafuse, *McClellan's War*, 327-329; Harsh, *Taken at the Flood*, 437-440. Harsh explained several developments that factored into McClellan's decision not to attack Lee on Sep. 18; The U.S. war department shipped the AOP 2,500 rounds of Parrot ammunition, but this ordnance did not reach Sharpsburg until late on the 18th. For further reading, see Kevin Pawlak, "Railroads—Tracks to the Antietam: The Railroad Supplies the Army of the Potomac, September 18, 1862," online article, Emerging Civil War, October 27, 2018, https://emergingcivilwar.com/2018/10/27/railroads-tracks-to-the-antietam-the-railroad-supplies-the-army-of-the-potomac-september-18-1862/.

their cellars and prevented many evacuees from returning home. Gunfire in town further compounded the inhabitants' fears.[2]

Shots awakened Major Heros von Borcke, who spent the night of the 17th in a village stable. To von Borcke's surprise, he wrote, the firing "came from some of our men, who were amusing themselves with shooting the pigs and chickens, which, rendered homeless by the fire[s], were wandering about in a distracted condition." Von Borcke confronted the troops, who roasted meat "at several points among the ruins of the houses." The men wryly explained that the targeted animals were "poor little things" with "nowhere to go, and we ought to take care of them." Von Borcke knew the men were hungry, but he also complained about their "wanton disregard of the rights of property." The account, however, was not an isolated incident.[3]

According to eyewitnesses, Confederate soldiers—as they did from the 15th through the 17th—seized private property for personal gratification. "Stragglers were running around and robbing the houses of people who'd gone away," recalled Jacob McGraw, "and they got in my house and just took everything." Robert W. Grove, who sheltered in town from September 15–18, witnessed Confederates "foraging on the east side and west end of the village."

Sarah Cronise left batches of apple butter in her kitchen when she evacuated on the 16th. On the 18th, she left the Kretzers' cellar to check on her property. She found "three Confederate soldiers in the kitchen busily eating the unfinished apple butter right from the kettle on the stove. The finished crocks had all disappeared."

James Snyder left Reverend Adams's farm on September 18 to inspect his parents' house in the village. He discovered that "the doors and windows were all wide open and soldiers in gray were lounging all about the place." Inside the home, he found "everything in confusion" and observed that "the bureau drawers which had been so carefully locked, had been pried open with bayonets." James's father, Andrew Snyder, also returned home on the 18th. When Andrew approached his house, a Confederate tossed him a daguerreotype and said, "Here, old man, you can have this. It is no good to us." Studying the image, Andrew "was astounded to find

2 Graham, *The Ninth Regiment*, 330; Edward O. Lord, *History of the Ninth Regiment, New Hampshire Volunteers* (Concord, New Hampshire, 1895), 111; Official report of Major General David R. Jones, December 8, 1862, *OR*, vol. 19, 1:887; Official report of Lieutenant Colonel James M. Perrin, September 30, 1862, *OR*, vol. 19, 1:994; Harsh, *Sounding the Shallows*, 212; Reilly, *BOA*.

3 Von Borcke, *Memoirs*, 1:236-237.

on examination that it was a picture of his own wife which had been stolen from his house."[4]

*   *   *

As the hours ticked away on September 18, Gen. Lee altered the plans of his campaign. Rather than continue facing McClellan at Sharpsburg, Lee planned to march his ANV under cover of darkness to Blackford's Ford and cross the Potomac River to Virginia.

During the night of the 18th, the ANV's withdrawal from Sharpsburg was not stealthy; residents and Union soldiers heard wagons rumbling toward the river throughout the evening. Nevertheless, when the reports reached General McClellan, the Union commander chose to wait until sunrise to pursue, for it was unclear if Lee was leaving Maryland or shifting his line west.

By dawn on September 19, most of Lee's army had crossed into Virginia. The ANV's rearguard fired three parting cannon blasts, and then all became quiet.

Federal pickets crept across foggy fields and discovered the Rebels had vanished. Upon receiving this news, McClellan ordered cavalry to reconnoiter Blackford's Ford and then sent infantry and artillery west toward the river. Sharpsburg and its environs were now in the hands of the Army of the Potomac.[5]

To citizens in the region, the silence was deafening. "Everything was quiet," recalled Teresa Kretzer. "It was an unearthly quiet after all the uproar of the battle." Alex Davis described the stillness as a "queer thing," adding that the battle's thunderous racket had traumatized pets, livestock, and wildlife. "You couldn't hear

---

4 Johnson, *BA*, 116; Claims of David Smith (Nos. 1244, 1262, and 10237); Mumma, *Antietam: The Aftermath*, 43. Evidence supports that Sarah Cronise and her husband, William Cronise, owned and occupied Lot 2W in 1862, located five dwellings west of the John Kretzer home. See deed IN 19 / 647. See also Lake, Griffing & Stevenson *An Illustrated Atlas of Washington County, Maryland*, sheet 32 (Philadelphia, 1877), accessed at Johns Hopkins Sheridan Libraries, Baltimore, MD, 32-33, https://jscholarship.library.jhu.edu/handle/1774.2/32766. This illustration is hereafter referred to as the 1877 Sharpsburg village map. Dwelling #1636 in the 1860 Federal census for Sharpsburg shows the Cronises two entries from Catherine Rohrback, who owned Lot 2E in 1862 (see land records Y / 941-2 and 74 / 7); Cross, "A Sharpsburg Boy at Antietam." Andrew Snyder, Sr. in 1862 owned and occupied Lot 170 on West Main Street. See deeds IN 11 / 552-3 and 81 / 250. The 1860 Federal census for Sharpsburg lists the Snyders in Dwelling #1580 next to George Swain.

5 Harsh, *Taken at the Flood*, 444-448, 452; Carman, *The Maryland Campaign*, 2:508; Galwey, *The Valiant Hours*, 46; Kevin Pawlak, historian, Facebook message to author, July 9, 2019; McGrath, *Shepherdstown*, 53-54.

a dog bark nowhere," Davis recalled. "[Y]ou couldn't hear no birds whistle or no crows caw."

Word of the Confederate departure spread to evacuees sheltering at riverside caves and farms. Angeline Jackson was harboring on Adam Myers's farm, adjoining the Potomac, when the news arrived. "I remember this distinctly," Jackson testified, "for a Union officer rode into Mr. Myers' field and told us the Union forces were in possession, and we all went out and cheered him."

When Jackson and Captain David Smith's family returned to their farmhouse, they found it crowded with Confederate wounded, affording no space for the family. From there, Jackson recalled, the residents "gathered up our bundles and started for the village; we met the Union forces marching out on the Shepardstown road in great force . . . we came to the village and took room in Rev. Jacob Highburgers house."[6]

Hundreds of refugees began their journey home, but the going wasn't easy. Federal columns—tens of thousands of soldiers—clogged roads in all directions. Pickets prevented some residents from returning, requiring passes to cross through Union lines.[7]

Evacuees trekked home from Killiansburg Cave on September 19, and some civilians passed corpses along the route. When Maggie Grice Hoffmaster and her parents journeyed home from the cave, she recalled, "the dead lay so thick" that her family's horse "would be very careful not to step" on the bodies. The gruesome sights reportedly caused Maggie's father to faint off his horse.[8]

Henry Piper and his family approached their farm on the battlefield proper, but a long column of Federal troops blocked their path. Jeremiah Summers, a teenage

6 Johnson, *BA*, 123, 103; Claims of David Smith (Nos. 1244, 1262, and 10237). Adam Myers's farm adjoined the Potomac River, west of Capt. Smith's farm. Reverend Jacob Highbarger owned and occupied Lot 130E on West Main Street. See land records NN / 34, NN / 458-459, and 75 / 296. The 1860 Federal census for Sharpsburg lists Highbarger in Dwelling #1575.

7 Harsh, *Taken at the Flood*, 453-456; Murfin, *Gleam of Bayonets*, 306; Ernst, *TATC*, 156-157.

8 Reilly, *BOA*; Margaret "Maggie" Grice Hoffmaster was the daughter of John and Mary Grice, who lived on Lot 146 in Sharpsburg village. While not documented, Maggie may have described Confederate corpses staged near a field hospital, such as Grove's Landing; James, *Echoes of Battle*, 96. Dr. James served at Antietam as a volunteer surgeon with the U.S. Christian Commission. He wrote that the Grove's Landing warehouses were Confederate hospitals; William "Bud" Shackelford interview, ANBL. Shackelford stated that "the ware house" at Grove's Landing "was turned into a hospital on Wednesday;" "Aged Woman Tells of Giving Food to Antietam Soldiers." Susan Lopp Santman recalled seeing "many Confederate soldiers lying about on the ground near the Grove warehouse . . . some were dead, others were dying while still others, only slightly wounded, were weak from lack of food."

slave in 1862, recalled, "The Hagerstown Pike was so full of the Union forces moving toward Sharpsburg," that it delayed the residents from "passing across the road to the house."

The Pipers and their slaves eventually crossed the pike to find their fields "strewn with haversacks, canteens, guns, and other articles in every direction." Mary Ellen Piper wrote, "Trees and fences were knocked down and deep holes plowed in the earth by balls, shot, and shell. As we came home, my heart almost died within me. However, I did not think of turning back." Arriving home, Mary Ellen "could scarcely recognize the place," and found their yard "covered with bloody clothing, straw, feathers, and everything that was disgusting."[9]

Evidence supports that combat on September 17 damaged nearly every property on the battlefield. Unlike structures in the village and the West Woods area, which suffered damages from U.S. artillery, most battlefield farms received the wrath of infantry *and* artillery fire from *both* armies. Bullets peppered houses while shells struck buildings and splintered trees. Additionally, combat crushed crops, destroyed fencing, and killed livestock.

On the north end of the field, Joseph and Mary Ann Poffenberger found that shells had pierced their dwelling house, tenant house, barn, and ice house. David R. Miller and his family returned to find their granary and blacksmith shop wrecked, and their dwelling damaged. Combat had obliterated the Miller family's cornfield and covered their farm with corpses and dead horses.[10]

Federal artillery inflicted extensive damages to the Reel family's three farms. Brothers David, Samuel, and Henry Reel reported the destruction of two barns and one shop, along with shell damages to a third barn and two dwelling houses. Adding to the Reels' losses, the fires destroyed valuable contents inside the structures, including grains, tools, and equipment.[11]

---

9 Claim of Henry Piper (No. 445); E. P. to Sally Farran, October 4, 1862, *Dan Masters' Civil War Chronicles.*

10 Claims filed by John Otto did not cite damages to his buildings. Hilary Watson, though, in Clifton Johnson's *BA*, 107, observed shells "flyin' over the [Otto] house;" Claims of Joseph Poffenberger (No. 1300) and John Miller (No. 2227). Poffenberger reported $14 in damages to his ice house and barn, $5 to his dwelling house, and $15 to the tenant house. Colonel John Miller, referring to the farm tenanted by David R. Miller, claimed $25 in "Damage to Farm Dwelling House by the shells" and $40 for "Damage to Two one story Blacksmith shop & granary."

11 Claims of David Reel (D-6619), Samuel Reel (G-1923), and Henry Reel (Book 304, Claim 328). Fire destroyed the barns of David and Samuel Reel. Henry Reel reported $325 in damages to his house, barn, and fencing but did not specify what portion of this amount related to his

Antietam, Md. Real's barn. Federal artillery inadvertently destroyed several structures during the battle, including a barn owned by Samuel and Cerusha Reel. Photograph by Alexander Gardner. *Library of Congress*

Families on other parts of the battlefield discovered combat-related injuries to their properties. Noah Rohrback reported $45 in shell damages to his barn and smokehouse, while Henry Piper and William Roulette charged the U.S. a combined $55 for injury to their dwelling houses and barns. Joseph Sherrick reported only $8 for "Shelling house." Still, his 38-acre cornfield—which he owned jointly with tenant farmer Leonard Emmert—"was doubtless destroyed during the progress of

buildings. Samuel Reel lived opposite the ANB visitor's center. David Reel's farm adjoined the town of Sharpsburg at 5322 Sharpsburg Pike. A description of David Reel's home appears in "WA-II-1141 Pat Holland Property (D. Reel House)," architectural survey file, MHT. Land records chain this property's ownership, in part, from Patricia Holland in 1999 (1500 / 18-23), to Thomas H. Reel, son of David Reel, in 1882 (82 / 626-627), to David Reel's inheritance of the land in 1844 (Will liber D / folios 547-552).

the battle." In addition, there were "quite a number of men . . . killed in this field probably one or two dozen."[12]

The fighting caused severe injury to mill complexes on the battlefield. Colonel John Miller rented a ten-acre gristmill to Solomon Lumm in 1862. Miller reported $200 in shell damages to the mill, dwelling house, spring house, and barn. He claimed an additional $400 for the "Burning by the shele on the day of the Battle of Antieatum a large frame stable carriage House Corn House Out House & fencing."

Shot and shell also battered Joshua Newcomer's mill complex. He reported $15 for "Damages done to dwelling house by Shells and Rifle and Musket balls" and $40 for "Furniture in dwelling house destroyed or damaged by shells." Newcomer also claimed $25 in "Damage done to Mill House, barn and [cooper] shop by balls and shells." His son, Isaac Newcomer, surmised that "shells fired by the rebel army" inflicted most of the damages.

Joshua Newcomer also discovered that U.S. troops, to facilitate passage over Antietam Creek near the Middle Bridge, destroyed his mill dam and mill race. According to Isaac Newcomer, the soldiers "dug them away . . . and drew the water off between the two armies." Such damages incapacitated Newcomer's gristmill and were laborious to repair. Consequently, he sought $350 in reparations for his mill's dam and race.[13]

---

12 Claim of Noah Rohrback (H-3874). Rohrback charged the damages to the U.S., but Confederate artillery may have injured his buildings. A historic map depicts IX Corps artillery and infantry near Noah Rohrback's farmhouse. See "Map 9, September 17, 1862, 10:30 A.M," Antietam Battlefield Board, *Atlas of the battlefield of Antietam*, (Washington, 1904), Map, https://www.loc.gov/item/map05000006/; Claims of Henry Piper (No. 445 and Book 304, Claim 250). In Piper's latter claim, he sought $25 for "Damage done to House & Crib," caused by "Shell and Shot from the batteries at the battle of Sharpsburg;" E. P. to Sally Farran, October 4, 1862, *Dan Masters' Civil War Chronicles*. Mary Ellen Piper mentioned there was "only one room in the house that a cannon ball had not penetrated;" Woodring, "Window to Yesterday;" Claims of Joseph Sherrick (F-1433) and Leonard Emmert (F-1577 and No. 4257). John Otto, testifying in Emmert's claim, commented on the number of bodies in the Sherrick-Emmert cornfield. As described in Chapter One, Sherrick and Emmert estimated the size of their 1862 cornfield as 38 acres.

13 Claims of Joshua Newcomer (F-854, H-3618, and No. 272); Official report of Colonel Edward E. Cross, September 18, 1862, *OR*, vol. 19, 1:287. Cross ordered two companies from the 5th New Hampshire to destroy the Newcomers' mill-dam, "which backed up the waters of the creek." The men, however, were "unable to perform this duty for want of tools." Carman, *The Maryland Campaign*, 2:24; William A. Frassanito, *Antietam: The Photographic Legacy of America's Bloodiest Day* (Toronto, 1979), 87-88. Frassanito commented on a photograph taken near Newcomer's mill on Sep. 22, 1862. He noted that the New Hampshire soldiers failed to destroy Newcomer's dam for lack of proper tools, "but, judging from this photograph, the task was eventually completed by others, perhaps an engineer battalion then assigned to the Army of the

In terms of destruction, the Mummas suffered the worst. Fire destroyed the family's house and possessions, including their clothing, furniture, and beds. Additionally, the Mummas lost dozens of items, including an eight-day clock, sleigh blankets, a buffalo robe, parlor stoves, and three-ply carpeting. The blaze also consumed the barn, destroying grains, plows, wagons, and a McCormick reaper. Samuel Mumma, Sr. estimated his structural damages at $3,400 and petitioned the U.S. government for a total charge of $9,255.28. The losses translate to more than a quarter-million dollars in contemporary U.S. money.

Displaced by the loss of their home, the Mummas found shelter at the farmhouse of Joseph and Sarah Sherrick. But when Federal forces appropriated the Mummas' remaining property after the battle—grains, livestock, and fencing—Samuel Mumma, Sr. made no effort to request vouchers for his losses. His son, Samuel Mumma, Jr., explained, "He was living below Sharpsburg after the battle . . . he was an old man and very much discouraged by the loss of his house and barn." Mumma, Sr. later penned an affidavit, describing the "great distress and trouble one his age and condition in life would necessarily have an account of the great destruction of his property the fruit of a long life of labor toil and trouble."[14]

On the morning of September 19, civilians emerged from the cramped village cellars. Teresa Kretzer remembered, "The people who had taken refuge with us saw that the danger was over, and they scattered away to their homes." One can imagine the residents' thoughts while shuffling through the battered town as smoke drifted from the crackling embers of former dwellings. When Teresa and her father stepped outside, "We could see only a few citizens moving about," she recalled. But soon, a Federal officer emerged and asked "if any one was hurt in the town and said they had tried to avoid shelling it, and he was awful sorry they couldn't help dropping an occasional shell among the houses."

The Kretzers perhaps appreciated the officer's empathy, but "an occasional shell" does not accurately describe the U.S. artillery's damage to the town. Newspaper correspondents reported, "Nearly every house in Sharpsburg was struck by our shells" and only five dwellings "escaped uninjured." A Massachusetts

---

Potomac." According to Williamson's *PPT*, Newcomer's mill race damages convert to about $10,000 in modern U.S. real prices.

14 Claims of Samuel Mumma, Sr. (*RG* 92, D-1927 and D-1928). Mumma listed more than 160 items destroyed by the Sept. 17 fire; Otho Nesbitt, Diary, September 19, 1862, ANBL. Nesbitt wrote, "I saw Samuel Mumma's fine brick house and barn that was burnt;" Williamson, *PPT*. The monetary conversion is based on the relative value of the U.S. dollar in 1862, using the Consumer Price Index.

soldier, passing through town on the 19th, "noticed that nearly every house bore the marks of bullets and cannon balls; some of the houses are entirely destroyed." A member of the 118th Pennsylvania observed, "Few were the houses that had not been pierced by solid shot or shell." Dr. A. A. Biggs added, "Few houses escaped unhurt. As many as six shells passed through some houses and destroyed everything in their course." When New York civilian George Templeton Strong arrived in town after the battle, he noted, "Sharpsburg, a commonplace little village, was scarified with shot. In one little brick house I counted more than a dozen shot holes, clearly made probably by rifle projectiles. Here there was seen the more extensive ravage made by an exploding shell."[15]

Missiles scarred the town's houses of worship, ventilating the German Reformed Church and Lutheran Church. Town residences, though, fared the worst. Jacob Avey, Sr., Dr. A. A. Biggs, Jacob H. Grove, Susan Kennedy, James Marker, and Nancy Miller reported a combined $326 in shell damages to their homes and outbuildings. Two villagers, Catherine Rohrback and Jacob H. Grove, sought payment for their destroyed structures. Rohrback charged $500 for "1 Barn Burned down by shells" and Grove sought $1,500 for "One large swiser barn, corn house and other buildings burnt on the 17th day of Sept."[16]

15 Johnson, *BA*, 123; *Daily Intelligencer*, September 22, 1862; Royal W. Figg, *Where Men Only Dare to Go! Or, The Story of a Boy Company (C.S.A.)* (Richmond, 1885), 47. The estimate of five dwellings escaping injury also ran in the *Nashville* [TN] *Daily Union*, October 3, 1862, and the *Athens* [OH] *Messenger*, December 4, 1862; Timothy J. Regan, *The Lost Civil War Diaries: The Diaries of Corporal Timothy J. Regan*, eds. David C. Newton and Thomas Pluskat (Victoria, Canada, 2003), 90; Smith, *History of the Corn Exchange Regiment*, 52; Biggs to Kalb, September 29, 1862, WMR; George Templeton Strong, Diary, September 24, 1862, vol. 3, Sep. 11–Oct. 3, 1862, 428-429, New York Historical Society Museum & Library, Digital Collections, New York, NY, http://digitalcollections.nyhistory.org/islandora/object/nyhs%3A54776 (hereafter, NYHSM). Although dated Sep. 24, Strong's diary entry encompasses his visit to Sharpsburg, Maryland, from Sep. 20–24.

16 Smith, "No Civilian Died." Smith noted that an artillery round "passed through the walls of Christ Reformed Church and being spent dropped down in the church." This building in 1862 was known as the German Reformed Church; Claim of Jacob Avey, Sr. (Book 304, Claim 243). Avey charged $75 for one house damaged. Jacob is not to be confused with his son, Jacob Avey, Jr., who owned and occupied Lot 144 in Sharpsburg and filed his own claim for Antietam losses. See the claim of Jacob Avey, Jr. (*RG* 92, Entry 843, Box 772, Book 304, Claim 245); Claim of A. A. Biggs (Box 771, Claim 178). Biggs sought $64 for shell damages to his window, parlor, carpeting, mirror, stable, and other items on his town lot; Claim of Jacob H. Grove (No. 1267). Grove listed $50 for "Damage to house by shell in Sharpsburg;" Claim of Susan Kennedy (*RG* 92, Book F, Box 81, Claim F-865). Kennedy declared $50 for "Damages to dwelling House and out buildings by shot & shell;" Claim of James Marker (No. 1292). Among Marker's damages were $50 for "Damages to two Houses & Tan yard property by shell;" Claim of Nancy Miller (Book 304, Claim 233). Mrs. Miller sought $37 for "Damages to House that

Other townsfolk suffered catastrophic damages to their residences. A correspondent with the *Philadelphia Inquirer* observed that "houses once the home and pride of the peaceful farmer [were] now a mass of blackened ruins . . . all seem to convey to the mind a shuddering idea of the terrors and horrors of the late struggle." Elizabeth Miller Blackford wrote, "[T]he shels were all from the yankies that made all this distruction and distress . . . it was distressing enough to those pore people when they returned from the cave to see their homes in ashes."

Margaret Shackelford, a 46-year-old widow, found her house on Lot 31 destroyed by fire. Shackelford reported the loss of one "House burnt by Shot and Shell," along with her family's clothing, tables, sofas, desks, cupboards, a stove, rocking chair, four beds, 25 yards of carpeting, and other household items.[17]

Sarah Himes, another villager, also lost her house to fire. Appraisers estimated her losses at $1,067.27. Of this amount, Himes charged $350 for "House burnt by Shell." The fire destroyed food, furniture, dishware, and the family's clothing.[18]

Like the Mummas, the battle made the families of Margaret Shackelford and Sarah Himes homeless. It's unknown where the Shackelfords sheltered afterward, but the Himes family found temporary residence on the east half of Lot 178, owned by the Michael family in 1862.[19]

Putnam lives in;" Claims of Catherine Rohrback (Book 304, Claim 234) and Jacob H. Grove (No. 1267).

17 *Philadelphia Inquirer*, September 25, 1862; Elizabeth Miller Blackford to Amelia Houser, February 8, 1863, WMR; Claim of Margaret Shackelford (Box 772, Book 304). Land records IN 13 / 619 and 93 / 2 show that Margaret Shackelford in 1862 owned Lot 31 in Sharpsburg village. She owned no other real estate. Her husband, Coleman Shackelford, died in 1860. Appraisers in Shackelford's claim estimated the value of her destroyed house at $200—an exact match to her declared real estate in the 1860 Federal census; William "Bud" Shackelford interview, ANBL. William was Margaret Shackelford's oldest son. His interview notes, "Mr. Shackelford was living in Sharpsburg during the time of the battle . . . the house in which he was living during the battle was burned."

18 Claim of Sarah Himes (Book 304, Claim 229). Himes's claim cites that the fire was caused by "Damages done by the army of the Potomac on the 16th and 17th days of Sept 1862." The appraised value of her destroyed home, $350, exceeds Himes's $300 in real estate in the 1860 Federal census. John Himes, Sarah's husband, purchased Lot 181W via land records II / 682 and IN 6 / 416. He died in 1858. The 1860 census lists Sarah Himes in Dwelling #1711 with four children. The census shows Himes's dwelling near Joanna Kidwiler, who owned Lot 167W in 1862 (see land records IN 12 / 320 and 80 / 259). The 1877 Sharpsburg village map depicts Himes on Lot 181W, adjoining Joanna Kidwiler. The 1877 map also shows Margaret Shackelford on Lot 31. Thus, the two widows eventually rebuilt their houses and resumed the occupancy of their town lots.

19 Samuel Michael to David Michael, November 27, 1862, WMR. Samuel Michael wrote to his brother, David, "Your house that you lived in is also a hospital by the Yankees . . . Sallie Hines

Most of the village's buildings survived the battle but suffered damages, nonetheless. John and Eliza Benner discovered that a projectile crashed through their dwelling, "tearing its way through a featherbed, thence through the head board of the bed and into the floor, where its fury was spent."[20]

On Antietam Street, Aaron Fry noticed a shell had blasted "through the building, passed through a door and into a chest of bed clothes," boring a hole through the sheets. Judge David Smith, inspecting his home on Mechanic Street, found that "a cannon ball passed through his front door out of the rear door into his pantry and demolished his dishes and crockery ware."[21]

*   *   *

In New York City, a few weeks after the battle, photographer Matthew Brady exhibited grisly images of Antietam's dead, shocking visitors at his Manhattan gallery. The *New York Times* opined, "Mr. Brady has done something to bring home to us the terrible reality and earnestness of war. If he has not brought bodies and laid them in our door-yards and along the streets, he has done something very like it." What the *Times* overlooked was how such terrible sights affected the people of

---

now occupies it until spring." Adam Michael– the father of Samuel and David—resided in 1862 on Lot 55 in Sharpsburg village. Deeds IN 13 / 384-385 and IN 17 / 479 show that Adam Michael owned a second town lot in 1862, 178E. This property was across West Main Street from Sarah Himes's Lot 181W. No person named "Sallie Hines" appears in the 1860 or 1870 Federal census for Sharpsburg. However, Sallie was a common nickname for Sarah. Genealogical records reveal that Sharpsburg residents Sarah Webb, Sarah Reel, Sarah Hoffman, and Sarah Brashears all went by the nickname, Sallie. For further reading on the Sarah-Sallie connection, see David K. Israel, "The Origins of 10 Nicknames," December 16, 2015, online article, Mental Floss, https://www.mentalfloss.com/article/24761/origins-10-nicknames.

20 Smith, "No Civilian Died." John and Eliza Benner owned several lots in 1862. Deeds and census records suggest that the couple resided near the public square, on one of the four parcels of Lot 34. See land records IN 12 / 455 and IN 15 / 36. The 1877 Sharpsburg village map depicts John Benner as owning the two northern parcels of Lot 34. The Benner's granddaughter, Tena Blanche Spong, offered at public sale in the *Morning Herald*, September 24, 1931, 13, a "high post bed with shell hole in head-board (from Battle of Antietam)." The Boonsborough Museum of History displays a similar, Antietam-damaged headboard.

21 Reilly, *BOA*. Reilly wrote, "The day of the battle a solid shot was fired that went into the house on Antietam Street, then owned by Mr. Aaron Fry." In 1862, Aaron Fry owned Lot 25W. See land records TT / 797, 96 / 527-528, and WMCKK 1 / 122; *HFTL*, October 2, 1862, 2C. Reilly in *The Battlefield of Antietam* also reported Judge Smith's account, noting that the projectile "broke a jar of honey [and] struck the side of the closet," destroying dishes and crockery in the process.

Sharpsburg, who literally found bodies on their doorsteps—and inside their homes. The heirs of Col. Jacob Rohrback "found at their door one dead Confederate soldier and several others lying nearby in the street." Arriving home on East Main Street, the Grice family stumbled upon "three soldiers lying dead in the house and two in the yard."[22]

When Mary Ellen Piper returned to her parents' farmhouse, she "went up the steps and opened the dining room door and was thunderstruck. Great Heaven!," she wrote. "What a sight met my gaze. The room was full of dead men! Pools of blood were standing on the floor. I only looked one glance and passed on." Among the corpses in Piper's house were "three dead rebels, one of whom had crawled under the piano to die."[23]

Many civilians shared the same gory experiences. A young woman discovered two dead "rebs" in her village house, a sight she and her children "never wished to see again." A townsman stepped inside his home to find "two rebels . . . killed in the act of breaking open his safe." Near the Lower Bridge, Martha Rohrback returned home but could not access her front door, because "all around the porch and yard the dead soldiers lay so thick."[24]

---

22 *New York Times*, October 20, 1862; Reilly, *BOA*. Per Reilly, "Mrs. Mumma was Miss Gussie Rohrback and resided in the stone house now owned by Mr. John Early adjoining the new Dunkard Church in Sharpsburg." Land records cite that Augusta "Gussie" Rohrback and her family, known as the heirs of Colonel Jacob Rohrback, lived on Lot 52E in 1862. See the 1860 Federal census for Sharpsburg, Dwelling #1627, and 1870, Dwelling #173. See also "Lot 52, Brethren Church and 125 E. Main St. Randell-Reed house Deed Abstracts," Deed Chains and House Histories, Sharpsburg Historical Society, https://sites.google.com/site/davidhackley/ sharpsburghistory; The Grices in 1862 owned and occupied Lot 146 on East Main Street. See land records IN 3 / 134 and 103 / 79.

23 E. P. to Sally Farran, October 4, 1862, *Dan Masters' Civil War Chronicles*. Some families may have physically removed corpses and blood from their homes, but the Pipers did not. Rather, Mary Ellen wrote, "The officers had the dead removed from the house and I put the colored men to removing the carpets, charging them to clean the floor before they left;" Oliver Christian Bosbyshell, *Pennsylvania at Antietam: Report of the Antietam Battlefield Memorial Commission of Pennsylvania and Ceremonies at the Dedication of the Monuments Erected by the Commonwealth of Pennsylvania to Mark the Position of Thirteen of the Pennsylvania Commands Engaged in the Battle* (Harrisburg, Pennsylvania, 1906), 164.

24 *Timaru* [New Zealand] *Herald*, National Library of New Zealand, vol. 4, issue 93, February 23, 1866, 5, https://paperspast.natlib.govt.nz/newspapers/THD18660223.2.24. The article did not identify the woman; Biggs to Kalb, September 29, 1862, WMR. Biggs identified the townsman as James Hill, but no Sharpsburg resident by that name appears in the 1860 or 1870 census. Biggs may have referred to John Hill or Josiah Hill, both of whom headed households in Sharpsburg village during the Civil War; Hildebrand, "Recollections of Martha Ada Thomas," WMR.

Below Sharpsburg Heights, Anna Smith returned to her home on Lot 88E on East Main Street, finding a disemboweled corpse at the well, "his blood covering everything." A missile apparently struck the soldier, and then tore through her kitchen wall, where two Confederates had been foraging for food. To Anna's horror, she found that the shell killed both men inside her home. One of the soldiers was "torn to pieces" while clutching a bunch of onions.[25]

Mid-morning on September 19, V Corps marched up Boonsboro Pike en route to the Potomac River. As the Federals descended into Sharpsburg village, they crossed paths with civilians emerging from cellars or returning from evacuation sites.

Witnesses described the bustling activity. "It was a lively scene that morning," wrote one soldier. "The signal flags on top of the church-tower were wig-wagging like mad . . . orderlies and aids, bespattered from head to foot, were galloping here and there." The town's streets "were filled with wreckage. Here and there a wagon, a wheel, a dead mule, or a defunct caisson keeled up as though in its death agonies." A New York correspondent, having "dashed on a hurried trot through Sharpsburgh" on the 19th, reported, "Dead horses lay in the fields along the road. Hospital flags waved from chimney tops, where the Rebel wounded were left."[26]

Destruction abounded. Dr. Abner Hard of the 8th Illinois Cavalry observed, "[N]early every house and building gave evidence of the terrible battle, and several

25 Anna Smith's account is a synthesis of several sources. Reilly described the incident in *The Battlefield of Antietam*, noting that "Mrs. Emory Smith . . . lived in the frame house on the southwest corner of the alley on Main Street, opposite the old Lutheran graveyard." This description matches Lot 88E, co-owned in 1862 by Dr. A. A. Biggs of Sharpsburg and Mary Hill Bash of Pennsylvania. Anna Gloss Smith and her husband, Joseph Emory Smith, apparently rented Lot 88E in 1862. Land records IN 12 / 559-62 and IN 19 / 696 show that the Smiths purchased the property in 1867. Wilmer Mumma in *Antietam: The Aftermath*, 27-28, transcribed a 1926 letter penned by William I. Groninger of the 126th Pennsylvania. Groninger recalled entering town from the battlefield on Sep. 19, 1862, and stopping at a house "on the right side of the street." Here, Groninger observed "a dead man lying" near the draw well. Inside the home, he found "2 dead Confederates. A cannon ball had passed through the corner of the house, killed all three;" Oliver T. Reilly, "Fifty Years Ago at Sharpsburg," *Shepherdstown* [WV] *Register*, November 21, 1912, "Newspaper Articles," vertical file, WMR. William Coffin Reiff of the 9th Pennsylvania recalled that he marched into Sharpsburg village on Sep. 19 and noticed a dead Confederate near a well. Reiff entered the house and observed another lifeless Rebel clutching a "straw wisp of onions." Soon after grabbing the onions, Reiff surmised, the man was "was struck by a solid shot or shell and no doubt fell dead still clutching them."

26 Regan, *The Lost Civil War Diaries*, 90; McGrath *Shepherdstown*, 54-55, 60, cited a September 24, 1862 letter written by an unidentified member of the 4th Michigan, archived in the Michigan file, ANBL; John Lord Parker, *Henry Wilson's Regiment: History of the Twenty-Second Massachusetts Infantry* (Boston, 1887), 196; *New York Times*, September 25, 1862.

had been set on fire by the bursting of shells and were now mouldering ruins. Even the 'Liberty Pole' in the center of the town had been struck and shattered." A Pennsylvania soldier wrote of the village, "It is by no means a pretty place, nearly all the houses are considerably damaged by cannon fire and shells having passed through them."

Lieutenant Thomas H. Evans of the 12th U.S. Infantry noticed that many houses "were badly damaged by shot. A flagstaff had been cut in two, and one of the telegraph posts had a clean hole through it from one of our Parrott 10-pounders." A New York surgeon observed homes "battered into shapeless masses; the streets filled with disabled wagons; horses galloping about without riders; knapsacks, guns, and equipments cast away in the hasty flight . . . all helped to make up a scene of destruction such as has been rarely witnessed."[27]

Many townsfolk embraced the Federal troops. One soldier remembered, "The people welcomed the arrival of the Union army with every evidence of gladness, and hailed them as their deliverers. 'Bless God!' said one old lady, 'you've driven them away. I've been down in my cellar three whole days!'"

Joseph Collingwood recalled he "never saw people so overjoyed as they when we marched through. The women and children were crying, laughing, and shaking hands with the soldiers. It made the tears come into my eyes to see them." While passing through town on the 19th, a member of the 11th U.S. remembered, "[O]ur band blazed away in triumph & we felt happy and exultant. Women smiled and even cried with joy at the flag again, for they had been driven from home & were just coming back by the cart loads."[28]

V Corps infantry "marched in fours, three regiments abreast, filling the whole street solidly." Regimental flags waved, and "the bright sun reflected on the glistening bayonets." A Union soldier recalled, "The inhabitants hailed our appearance with the most enthusiastic demonstrations of joy. Pictures of

27 Abner Hard, *History of the Eighth Cavalry Regiment* (Aurora, Illinois, 1868), 187; Hartwig, *To Antietam Creek*, 764. Hartwig cited a September 1862 letter by Origen G. Bingham of the 137th Pennsylvania, Civil War Misc. Collection, USAHEC; Evans, "The Enemy Sullenly Held on to the City;" George Thomas Stevens, *Three Years in the Sixth Corps* (New York, 1870), 155. For details of the AOP's occupation of Sharpsburg village on Sep. 19, see McGrath, *Shepherdstown*, 53-60.

28 Warren Lee Goss, *Recollections of a Private. A Story of the Army of the Potomac* (New York, 1890), 117; McGrath, *Shepherdstown*, 55-56. McGrath's source is Joseph Collingwood to wife, September 21, 1862, Collingwood Family Papers, Huntington Library. McGrath also referenced John Ames to Mother, September 21, 1862, USAMHI; Joseph Keith Newell, *Ours. Annals of 10th Regiment, Massachusetts Volunteers in the Rebellion* (Springfield, Massachusetts, 1875), 144.

McClellan were trimmed with evergreens and national colors, and hung out on the battle-scarred houses; flags and handkerchiefs were waved from the shattered windows by women and children, as the army passed by."

U.S. troops marching through the town on the 19th learned that enemy soldiers looted many of the homes. Captain Joseph Collingwood of the 18th Massachusetts wrote, "The inhabitants were coming back, having been hid in caves on the Potomac . . . the Rebels had robbed them of everything." Timothy J. Regan recalled that nearly all the village houses "have been broken into in the absence of the owners, and robbed of everything moveable."

Union soldiers passed a villager "standing in the door of a house cursing the 'd—rebels' for a parcel of robbers, with the energy of a madman." Some troops "stopped long enough to hear him tell his listeners that [the Rebels] had torn the carpets off his floor, and taken the quilts and blankets off his beds." The enraged citizen wished that the Federals would "over take" the Confederates and "blow them to h—." While advancing through town on the 19th, a Michigan soldier noted, "Things look rough. Rebels have stripped houses of everything. Union sentiment is strong . . . children swear vengeance."[29]

One villager explained, "Them that stayed at home did not lose anything; but if the soldiers found a house deserted, that they robbed." John P. Smith added, "Many who left their houses, on their return after the battle found them ransacked and plundered of every thing of value by rebel stragglers."

Squire Jacob Miller noted that Susan Kennedy, who vacated her home on the 15th, returned to find it "plundered, her fine clothes struid all over the house and some carried off." Likewise, Elizabeth Miller Blackford found her smokehouse and cellar looted. Fortunately, she wrote, Confederates "did not get in the house, as they did many others and take their clothing, bedding, and every thing eatable."

Inside one dwelling, a witness observed "a scene of waste and confusion enough to sicken the coldest heart." Southern stragglers not only robbed the vacant home but vandalized it. "Magnificent mirrors had been wantonly broken in pieces," and paintings "by the first masters exhibited great rents, evidently made by

29 McGrath, *Shepherdstown*, 55; Regan, *The Lost Civil War Diaries*, 90; Daniel George Macnamara, *The History of the Ninth Regiment, Massachusetts Volunteer Infantry, Second Brigade, First Division, Fifth Army Corps, Army of the Potomac, June, 1861–June, 1864* (Boston, 1899), 221-222; John Milton Bancroft, Diary, September 19, 1862, 98, Auburn University, Civil War Diaries Collection, Auburn, AL, http://content.lib.auburn.edu/cdm/compoundobject/collection/civil/id/26093/rec/3.

sabre strokes and thrusts of bayonets." On the floor of the home, the witness found "several articles of female attire, thrown about in disorder."

The Confederate plundering infuriated Dr. A. A. Biggs. "They came upon like a gang of hungry wolves or hyenas," he wrote. "Nothing could be hid from their grasp. Some few that remained at home succeeded in saving what they had, but all who were forced to leave town lost everything." Continuing, Biggs ranted, "When [the Confederates] had possession of a house, it was stripped clean, even the children's clothes, knives, forks, dishes, and bed clothes—in fact nothing escaped, for what they could not use, they willfully destroyed. Two thirds of the families in the place had nothing but the clothes on their backs." According to Biggs, Rebels stole "money, jewelry, and all articles of any value" in some homes. "I never thought that human nature in a civilized land could lose, to such a degree, all sympathy for their fellow beings," seethed the doctor. "They entered several poor people's houses and robbed them of everything they had in this world. Stealing and plunder seemed to be their profession and design. They appear to have lost all feelings of humanity and self-respect."[30]

Due to delays and distances traveled on the 19th, some evacuees didn't return home until late morning. During this time, Union troops reportedly plundered vacant houses, taking items left behind by the Confederates. To be sure, rogue soldiers existed in the Army of the Potomac. At the onset of the 1862 Maryland Campaign, some of McClellan's men vandalized a house. A witness noted, "The furniture was smashed to kindling wood, the windows dashed to pieces by the butt-end of the muskets, [and] the plastering from the walls knocked off." The Federals reportedly left the place "so defaced and defiled that it discounted a hog-pen in filth."

Two months after Antietam, a Federal officer described United States troops ransacking the town of Fredericksburg, Virginia. "Boys came into our place loaded with silver pitchers, silver spoons, silver lamps and casters, etc.," the officer reported. "Splendid alabaster vases and pieces of statuary were thrown at 6 & 700 dollar mirrors. Closets of the very finest china were broken into and their contents smashed onto the floor and stamped to pieces. Finest cut glass ware goblets were hurled at nice plate glass windows." The major watched troops drag pianos into the

---

30 Trowbridge, *The South*, 51; John P. Smith, "Recollections of John P. Smith: The Battle of Antietam, the History of Antietam, and the Hospitals of Antietam," typescript, ANBL; Jacob Miller to Amelia and Christian Houser, October 1862, WMR; Elizabeth Miller Blackford to Amelia Houser, February 8, 1863, WMR; Shotwell, *The Papers*, 1:348; Biggs to Kalb, September 29, 1862, WMR.

street, and then "get on top of them and dance and kick the keyboard and internal machinery all to pieces." The U.S. soldiers, he wrote, "seemed to delight in destroying everything."[31]

Sandwiched between these two destructive accounts was Sharpsburg, where thousands of Federal troops straggled from their commands. After the Battle of Antietam, Brigadier General George G. Meade described these disobedient men as "the cowards, skulkers, men who leave the ground with the wounded and do not return for days, the stragglers on the march, and all such characters." Meade admitted such persons "are to be found in every army, but never in so great a ratio as in this volunteer force as ours."

The number of Sharpsburg homes pillaged by Federals is impossible to estimate, given that Southern stragglers plundered some of the identical dwellings. Several townsfolk, however, filed war claims alleging that U.S. soldiers took personal property. Joanna Kidwiler accused AOP troops of stealing her jewelry, Bible, hymn book, and photographs. David Pennel sought payment for three stolen musical instruments. Susan Kennedy claimed to have lost Sunday school books, daguerreotypes, and gold rings. One resident "was sorry she did not remain in the cellar of the house" during the battle to protect her belongings. When she returned, her food and possessions "had been swept away by the all-devouring armies."

Other citizens suffered similar losses. For example, Elijah Avey alleged that U.S. troops stole books and photographs, along with his entire silversmith inventory. The items included a silver-mounted guitar, seven silver watches, and one gold watch. Avey estimated his losses at $464.50, or $12,000 in contemporary money.

A family on East Main Street saw their store "looted by both armies." Then, compounding their misery, soldiers reportedly stole the family's pet dog and "tied him to the top of a cannon." The owner "ran out and tried to grab him but they pushed her away."[32]

---

31 Theodore Gerrish and John S. Hutchinson, *The Blue and the Gray: A Graphic History of the Army of the Potomac and That of Northern Virginia, Including the Brilliant Engagements of These Forces from 1861 to 1865* (Portland, Maine, 1883), 144-145. The major was Francis E. Pierce of the 108th New York; John Hennessy, "Civilians Endure the Battle of Fredericksburg," American Battlefield Trust, https://www.battlefields.org/learn/articles/voices-storm-0.

32 George Meade, *The Life and Letters of George Gordon Meade*, 2 vols (New York, 1913), 1:318; Claim of Joanna Kidwiler (*RG* 92, Entry 843, Box 772, Book 304, Claim 252); Claim of David Pennel (*RG* 92, Entry 843, Box 772, Book 304, Claim 248); Claim of Susan Kennedy (F-865).

United States forces also plundered homes on the battlefield. On September 19, Federal troops entered Joseph Sherrick's vacant dwelling and gorged on the family's food. "What a feast!" recalled Robert Goldthwaite Carter. "No crowd of schoolboys . . . ever acted so absurdly as did these rough, bronzed soldiers and recruit allies." Carter and his comrades "would seize a pot of jam, grape jelly, huckleberry stew, or pineapple preserve, and . . . shovel out great heaps of the delectable stuff, which rapidly disappeared into their capacious mouths." Joseph Sherrick corroborated Carter's account. He reported the loss of 30 jars of fruit, 25 glasses of preserves, 50 pounds of sugar, and 200 pounds of bacon.

Upon arriving home, Joseph and Mary Ann Poffenberger found their dwelling emptied of clothing, bedding, cookware, and food. Military forces undoubtedly seized some of the items for medical purposes. Still, soldiers took the couple's sleigh bells, shaving razors, books, and a hunting rifle, along with a silver watch, family Bible, and a "gold bracelet with diamond." One witness described the Poffenbergers' farm as "a perfect wreck after the battle, crops destroyed, house riddled, and everything taken out." Joseph Poffenberger testified, "The items of household goods &c were taken by the Federal army, the rebels were never on the place in large bodies."[33]

U.S. troops took other items from the community. Corporal Nathan F. Dykeman of the 107th New York Infantry stole the Dunker Church's Bible, keeping the book as a souvenir. Soldiers looted Daniel Miller's house, taking seventeen promissory notes and dealing Miller a blow in collecting monies owed to

---

The Act of July 4, 1864, did not consider claims for Confederate-related losses. Southern soldiers may have taken some of the items listed in Sharpsburg's claims, but petitioners or their attorneys charged the losses to the U.S. in an attempt to recoup the losses. Regardless, the 1864 act barred claims related to theft and depredations and did not recognize valuables and sentimental possessions as quartermaster supplies. Thus, even if U.S. forces took the personal property listed in the claims, the claimants received no payment; Trowbridge, *The South*, 51; Claim of Elijah Avey (*RG* 92, Entry 843, Box 772, Book 304, Claim 242); Williamson, *PPT*; Lloyd K. Hoffman, "The Hoffman Family: Two Hundred Years in America," unpublished manuscript, Ruth Scarborough Library, Archives and Special Collections, Shepherd University, Shepherdstown, WV, 40-42. The account did not specify whether Federals or Confederates took the dog.

33 Robert Goldthwaite Carter, "Four Brothers in Blue," *The Maine Bugle* (Rockland, ME, 1897), October 1897, 116-117; Claims of Joseph Sherrick (F-1433) and Joseph Poffenberger (No. 1300); "WA-II-279 Joseph R. Poffenberger Farm," architectural survey file, MHT, sec. 8, p. 3, https://mht.maryland.gov/secure/medusa/PDF/Washington/WA-II-279.pdf.

him. Miller ran a newspaper ad announcing the theft and also stopped payment on the notes, but it's unknown if he ever secured repayment of the loans.[34]

Troops from both armies despoiled Henry Piper's home. His daughter, Mary Ellen Piper reported, "The house had been pillaged from garret to cellar . . . in fact everything of any value whatever was gone . . . even down to our toothbrushes." Mary Ellen emphasized to her letter's recipient, "Do not understand me to say that all the damage was done by the Rebels; at least half was done by Federal forces."[35]

The unauthorized seizure of private property made lasting impressions on the Sharpsburg community. A correspondent for the *New York Times* opined, "The indiscriminate plundering by [U.S.] soldiers has resulted in creating and increasing local support for the Confederates, even among many of the area's lukewarm Unionists." Francis M. Miller, who lived near Miller's Sawmill, complained, "[W]hile the Confederate army occupied the farm they respected absolutely the property, but when the Union soldiers camped there it was another story. The Yankees ate all the vegetables from the garden, robbed the orchard of everything edible . . . and took from the place everything they wanted."

When a journalist asked a villager which army did most of the damage, she replied, "[T]hat I can't say stranger. The Rebels took; but the Yankees took right smart." Civilians felt a range of emotions upon finding their homes pillaged, but this particular woman was heartbroken. 'When we came back,' she recalled, "all I could do was just to set right down and cry."[36]

*   *   *

After marching through the town of Sharpsburg, advance elements of V Corps rushed toward Blackford's Ford. Around 12:30 p.m., Federal sharpshooters swarmed across William M. Blackford's farm. The troops deployed in the drained canal bed and opened fire on Confederate pickets across the Potomac River.

---

34 Allan Schmidt and Terry Barkley, *September Mourn: The Dunker Church of Antietam Battlefield* (El Dorado Hills, CA, 2018), 53-55. Dykeman's family returned the Bible to the Sharpsburg congregation in 1903; *HFTL*, October 22, 1862, 3F. Daniel Miller's advertisement specified, "During the battle of Antietam, on the 17th ult., my house was entered, and Seventeen Promissory Notes . . . together with other papers, were stolen."

35 E. P. to Sally Farran, October 4, 1862, *Dan Masters' Civil War Chronicles.*

36 Ernst, *TATC*, 193-194. Ernst cited a 1963 Ph.D. dissertation by Richard Ray Duncan titled *The Social and Economic Impact of the Civil War in Maryland*, 244; *Shepherdstown Register*, January 14, 1915; Trowbridge, *The South*, 51.

U.S. forces also descended upon Rev. Robert Douglas's Ferry Hill plantation, where they dug rifle pits in front of the house and "decorated the lawn" with "several rifled cannon, with their angry muzzles pointing across the Potomac." Artillery from both armies joined the fight, fraying nerves of local inhabitants.

William M. Blackford and his family lived next to Blackford's Ford. From September 15–18, Southern guards placed the Blackfords under house arrest to prevent them from reporting Confederate activity at the ford. Finally liberated on the 19th, the Blackfords found themselves in danger when U.S. troops, staged near their farm, drew fire from Rebels across the river.

At this time, William's brother, Henry V. S. Blackford, sheltered his family on William's riverside farm. When musketry and artillery fire erupted, the combined Blackford families found the "Artillery skirmish & sharpshooters fighting" too dangerous, and "every body about the place was obliged to seek shelter." Henry V. S. Blackford's son, William F. Blackford, recalled, "So many stray bullets were coming over" the river, that it forced the families to flee "across the fields to the Stephen P. Grove place." According to sworn testimony, the civilians fled on foot, and "the horses were altogether forgotten." The hasty evacuation indeed challenged Henry V. S. Blackford, who had a lifelong crippling disability.[37]

The ANV's swift withdrawal to Virginia on September 18 left behind thousands of wounded and straggling Confederates. As U.S. forces swept through the Sharpsburg area on September 19, they captured scores of Southerners. Frank Donaldson of the 118th Pennsylvania "found the houses crowded with wounded Confederates." Likewise, a Massachusetts soldier recalled, "[A]ll the houses, barns, and numerous tents along the road were filled with secesh wounded."

Two Confederates convalesced in the Maryland Hotel, situated on Sharpsburg's public square. When the "Advance Guard of Gen. McClellan's Army" entered Sharpsburg on the 19th, innkeeper Elias U. Knode snitched on the Southerners. Knode informed U.S. officers that "he had deluded 2 rebel soldiers to

---

37 McGrath, *Shepherdstown*, 69; Douglas, *I Rode With Stonewall*, 181; J. B. Moore, "Sharpsburg: Graphic Description of the Battle and Its Results," *Southern Historical Society Papers*, vol. 27, 213-214. Moore, a Confederate artillerist, described firing toward William M. Blackford's farm on Sep. 19; Claims of William M. Blackford (No. 1324) and Henry V. S. Blackford (G-1630, G-1648, and G-1654). As mentioned in Chapter One, Urias Knode testified that Blackford "was a cripple from childhood & very little about" during the war; Cross, "Recollections of Another Sharpsburg Boy."

remain there & rest, and if managed right, they could capture them, which they did."[38]

The AOP's occupation of Sharpsburg prompted pro-Union members of the community to rat out their Southern sympathizing neighbors. In his "advance through Sharpsburg" on September 19, First Lieutenant John Milton Bancroft of the 4th Michigan noted in his diary, "[A]s we go through women point out houses of those who have given the rebels shelter and where rebel flags are concealed." Federal forces paid visits to suspected Secessionists on account of the accusations, and these were by no means social calls.[39]

Reverend Robert Douglas, whose Confederate son served on Stonewall Jackson's staff, watched armed Union squads storm inside his Ferry Hill mansion. Soldiers searched Douglas's home, "invading the chambers of his wife and daughters—looking through the contents of their bureaus and wardrobes, and turning their beds upon the floor with their bayonets." Afterward, the troops insulted the women of the home and forbade Rev. Douglas from leaving. According to Henry K. Douglas, his father "became a prisoner in his own house; and if he walked out upon his land, he was either halted at his outer gate, or followed by a suspicious sentinel."[40]

Jacob Houser had a similar experience. Reportedly, "[A]ll his horses had been seized by the rebels before the Federal army got possession of the farm." After Sharpsburg fell into Union hands, "a near-by farmer" told U.S. authorities that Houser was a Confederate sympathizer. Federals responded to the allegation by entering and vandalizing the farmer's home. The damage was so extensive that the Housers' dwelling "had to be remodeled before they could return."[41]

John Grice, a Sharpsburg Democrat, escaped such misfortune. In 1862, Grice lived "right across the street" from William H. Standback, a free, African American

---

38 McGrath, *Shepherdstown*, 56, 60; Claim of Elias U. Knode (*RG* 92, Entry 812, Claim L-2074). Referring to Lot 49W on the northwest corner of Sharpsburg's public square, Benjamin F. Rohrback testified, "[D]uring the years 1860, 61 & 62, he [Knode] owned the only hotel in Sharpsburg." Likewise, Jacob Baker deposed that he lived in Sharpsburg during the war "directly opposite the 'Maryland Hotel' kept by Elias U. Knode." Leah Keedy owned Lot 49W in 1862 and possibly rented it to Knode.

39 McGrath, *Shepherdstown*, 60-62; Bancroft Diary, September 19, 1862, Auburn University.

40 John A. Marshall, *American Bastile: A History of the Illegal Arrests and Imprisonment of American Citizens During the Late Civil War* (Philadelphia, 1869), 156-164.

41 Reilly, *BOA*; Claim of Jacob Houser (F-814). Neighbor William F. Hebb testified that Confederates took all of Houser's horses. Additionally, Houser's claim listed $164 in "Damage to household & kitchen furniture."

laborer. "I remember when the Yankees were here," Standback recalled. "They were going to do something to him [Grice] . . . and I told them he was a nice man and they let him alone."[42]

Solomon Lumm wasn't as fortunate. On September 19, Union officers received a tip that Lumm sympathized with the South. Federals, commanded by "Colonel Scroggens," marched to Lumm's property and pillaged his house and gristmill. Lumm and his wife, Jennie, watched soldiers load the family's possessions into army wagons. The items included one dozen chairs, a fallen leaf table, and all clothing and shoes belonging to Jennie and her children. The soldiers didn't stop there. They took a rifle, a parasol, a tin stove, and the family's stash of gold and silver. Next, the troops set their sights on Lumm's gristmill, taking the scales, mill brushes, and a bolting cloth and then slashing the mill's elevator straps.

Lumm's neighbors—Hilary Watson, Michael Tenant, and Samuel Mumma, Jr.—later testified to have witnessed the plundering. Solomon Lumm testified that U.S. troops loaded his personal property into "seven or eight wagons." He estimated "there were fifteen or twenty engaged in the removal of goods and four or five hundred [soldiers] about the place." Compounding Lumm's losses, Federals seized his "transfer books belonging to the Mill." These records—daybooks, mill books, and a ledger—"were valuable to me," Lumm attested. "I lost all of two hundred dollars by the taking of these books, as there were accounts I could not collect without them, and never did collect for the same reason." Asked if he attempted to stop the plundering, Lumm replied, "I did protest against it to the men who were taking it . . . the men said they had to have it, and were going to take it." When Lumm pleaded with Colonel Scroggens "not to let his men take it, he gave me no reply . . . he did or said nothing to restrain his men in taking or destruction."[43]

In addition to harassing suspected Secessionists, Federal soldiers arbitrarily arrested civilians after the AOP occupied Sharpsburg on September 19. For instance, they detained Samuel Michael, a staunch Democrat, for "helping the Rebels to capture a cannon." The charges, Michael insisted, were "false and forged against me." Regardless, he "was marched in the rain one whole day in water four feet deep and had to sleep in my wet clothes until they dried on me. And had to sleep on the floor in mud two or three inches deep."

42 Claim of John Grice (No. 5872).

43 Claim of Solomon Lumm (No. 340). The identity of "Colonel Scroggens" is unclear. Michael Tenant's wife, Catherine Tenant, owned a 22-acre tract adjoining Lumm's mill.

Military forces also arrested Hiram Showman, a Democrat farmer who resided near Smoketown. Before the battle, Showman was on bad terms with his neighbor, Adam Hutzell, described as "one of the strongest Union men in the county." Resident Henry W. Mongan testified that Showman and Hutzell "were bitter enemies and were always quarreling." Showman's neighbor, Michael Miller, added, "There was a bitter feud between the two previous to the war, in so much even that they would not have division fencing together." The feud came into play shortly after the battle at Sharpsburg. Showman complained, "This man Hentzel [Hutzell]" told Federal officers "that I was a terrible rebel." As a result of the accusation, Showman "was arrested by the military authorities soon after the battle of Antietam" on suspicion of being "a rebel citizen of dangerous proclivities." Testimony in Showman's claim alleges that U.S. troops brought Showman before Major General John F. Reynolds and Gen. George Meade. Showman pled his innocence to the commanders and asked if Adam Hutzell was behind the arrest. "They would not tell me," Showman recalled, "and saw it was better for me not to know. There was no specific charge against me, except that it was said I was a rebel and I suppose Hentzel said that." After interviewing the farmer, Reynolds and Meade "came to the conclusion that he was not calculated to do any particular amount of mischief." To avoid future trouble, the generals ordered Showman "to go home and to behave himself, or that he would be attended to properly."[44]

Then there was Solomon Lumm. After U.S. forces pillaged his house and mill on September 19, rumors swirled that Lumm was "an accessory to the acts of the Confederates in loop-holing his barn and of firing from his barn on the union soldiers." This action supposedly occurred during the battle's afternoon phase, when IX Corps attacked the Confederate right and advanced toward the stone mill complex. Martin E. Snavely, who lived with his parents on the Belinda Springs farm, recalled, "A few days after the battle I was going over the field with some soldiers. They pointed out this roof with the holes in it. They said rebel sharpshooters and the man living there were firing on our troops." It's unknown where the rumor originated, but it led to Lumm's arrest.

"He passed right by my house," testified villager Jacob Lakin. "[T]he Union soldiers had him; they were guarding him on both sides; they were going towards the Union headquarters." The men marched Lumm past John Benner, one of the town's Republican Unionists. 'I saw Mr. Lumm," Benner testified, "after he was

---

44 Samuel Michael to David Michael, November 27, 1862, WMR; Claim of Hiram Showman (RG 123, Entry 22, Box 268, No. 1522); Claim of Adam Hutzell (No. 4292).

arrested by an Irish regiment of Union soldiers. They came by my property with him, taking him to Rev. Adams' farm, where General Burnside had his headquarters." The soldiers, Benner learned, intended to hang Lumm.

The guards escorted Lumm to Gen. Burnside's headquarters. Here, Lumm was "detained over night because it was found that port holes had been made in the roof of his house, and from them Union soldiers were fired upon and killed during the battle, as a result of which arrest the soldiers talked of hanging him."

By the next morning, word spread of the rumored execution. Martin E. Snavely remembered that U.S. troops came "to our spring for water, and I heard them tell my mother they were going to hang him [Lumm] that afternoon." So Snavely and other members of the community flocked to Adams's farm, finding Lumm "sitting there under guard . . . he had his mill suit on."

Lumm pleaded his innocence. "I was at home the day before and the day of the battle of Antietam," he admitted. "[T]here were holes made in there (roof of house or mill) but I do not know who made them; I do not know if there was any firing through them; I did not know anything about it until I got back there."

Luckily for Lumm, one of Sharpsburg's staunchest Unionists, Levin Benton, arrived at Burnside's headquarters and vouched for the miller. Military officials released Lumm that morning. Sharpsburg resident A. R. Renner deposed, "[H]ad it not been for him [Benton] and some others," Solomon Lumm would have "been hung or shot."[45]

*   *   *

Those traversing the battlefield on September 19 found death, destruction, and detritus in all directions. A group of Pennsylvania correspondents observed trampled crop fields "strewn with torn hats, coats, pants, shoes, canteens, haversacks, cartridge boxes, muskets, good and broken, broken gun carriages, etc." One of the reporters noted, "[F]or the first time, [we] realized the destructiveness

---

45 Claim of Solomon Lumm (No. 340). Lumm deposed that Union soldiers arrested him at "three or four o'clock" in the afternoon of Sep. 18. This date is incorrect, as Confederates held Sharpsburg on the 18th. Testimony in the claim of James Marker (No. 1292) supports that Gen. Burnside based his headquarters on Rev. John A. Adams's farm. Ezra Marker testified that, after the battle, "Burnside's headquarters were on the farm adjoining north of ours, John A. Adams's." Burnside later moved his headquarters to Raleigh Showman's farm; McMaster, *Proceedings of a General Court Martial*, 46. Colonel McMaster testified that, during the battle, he occupied Lumm's stone house and ordered some of his men "to go up stairs and knock off some of the roof of the house, and ordered some men to go up and fire from the roof." McMaster did not mention that Lumm or any other civilian shot at U.S. troops, but his testimony may explain the "port holes" in the dwelling.

Antietam, Md. Bodies in front of the Dunker church. *Photograph by Alexander Gardner. Library of Congress*

of war . . . all we had previously imagined sank into insignificance when the reality met our view. Such a sight cannot be described. It must be seen to be comprehended." Another witness recalled, "No matter in what direction we turned, it was the same shocking picture, awakening awe rather than pity, benumbing the senses rather than touching the heart, glazing the eye with horror rather than filling it with tears." Reflecting on such sights at Antietam, Lt. William H. Powell wrote, "[T]his was war in all its hideousness!"[46]

46 *Altoona* [PA] *Tribune*, October 2, 1862; *HFTL*, September 24, 1862, 2B; Samuel Fiske, *Mr. Dunn Browne's Experiences in the Army: The Civil War Letters of Samuel W. Fiske*, ed. Stephen W. Sears (New York, 1998), 11; *Altoona Tribune*, October 2, 1862; Noyes, *The Bivouac and the Battle-Field*, 216-217; William H. Powell, *The Fifth Army Corps (Army of the Potomac): A Record of Operations During the Civil War in the United States of America, 1861–1865* (New York, 1896), 303. Powell, a lieutenant in Sep. 1862, served at Antietam as an acting assistant adjutant general in Brig. Gen. George Sykes's division.

A Hagerstown reporter wrote, "The beautiful district of country over which the great battle of Wednesday raged presents a melancholy picture of devastation. A number of houses and barns were destroyed, fences scattered as if a tornado had swept them away . . . wreck, ruin and desolation meet the eye at every turn." Continuing, the reporter admitted, "We have hitherto read of and contemplated the ravages of war at a distance, but alas! [A] large portion of our fertile county has fallen a victim to them, and we now see and feel them in all their intensity."[47]

Ghastly sights greeted civilians who visited the battlefield. John Fisher, a resident of Sharpsburg village, discovered a "snout of a soldier's cap with the brains on." Sharpsburg youths, inspecting the ruins of David Reel's barn, sifted through the ashes and discovered "portions of bones of human beings"—Confederates burned alive when Reel's barn caught fire during the battle. Otho Nesbitt wrote in his diary on September 19, "I could sit on my horse and count 50 dead men. On the side 100 yards further I could do nearly the same." Nesbitt "saw probably 500 dead and from what others said, I didn't see more than half of the battle field for some said it extended far below Sharpsburg." The farmer "left about 12 o'clock for home, having satisfied myself in regard to the falling humanity."

Describing David R. Miller's cornfield, Dr. A. A. Biggs wrote, "Almost every step for several hundred yards around, dead rebels could be seen. The sight was awful." Biggs added, "The bodies of the men were laying around mangled in every conceivable manner. Legs off and heads and parts of heads off, and mortal wounds of every description."[48]

After finding her farm "dotted with dead," Mary Ellen Piper walked to the sunken road adjoining the property. "The lane that separates our farm from Mr. Roulett's had been washed into a tolerably deep gulley," she recalled, "and this was used as a rifle pit. The dead were lying so thick in this lane that it looked like the living mass." Everywhere she looked, Mary Ellen found death and destruction. "You could have walked five miles and not been off the battlefield," she wrote. "No tongue can tell or pen describe the horrors."[49]

Soldiers also commented on the horrid sights. A Pennsylvanian observed that "many of the bodies, struck by heavier missiles, were horribly torn and mangled.

---

47 *HFTL*, September 24, 1862, 2B.

48 Reilly, *BOA*; Ibid. Reilly's source for the burned barn account was Frisby Smith, son of Judge David Smith; Nesbitt Diary, September 19, 1862, ANBL; Biggs to Kalb, September 29, 1862, WMR.

49 E. P. to Sally Farran, October 4, 1862, *Dan Masters' Civil War Chronicles*.

There was a leg, with its ragged, bloody edges, severed near the thigh, evidently by a solid shot." Another soldier found a Confederate lieutenant "whose head had been taken completely off by a shell."

Lieutenant John C. Whiteside of the 105th New York Infantry described the grisly battlefield in a letter home. "Some had their heds bloon of[f]," he wrote. "[O]thers sculls broken and their brains dashed out, others fases shot of, others half the face gon, others bloon to pieces." Continuing, Whiteside admitted, "Oh! the sight of this battle field makes my blood chill when I think of it. If were in a thousand battles a gain, I never want to go over the battle ground until the dead is buried."[50]

The gruesome and stressful scenes overwhelmed some of the residents. Mary Ellen Piper recalled, after finding corpses in her battlefield home on September 19, that she "went to Sharpsburg. I did not return until Monday." Near Keedysville, Joshua and Ann Mary Wyand deemed "the sight of blood, the groans of the wounded and dying men" unbearable, which "caused [the] family to leave."[51]

After the battle, Henry A. Bamford and his wife, Maria, returned home. To their dismay, the couple reportedly found "nineteen Union soldiers . . . dead in their house." Perhaps wanting to distance themselves from further horrors, the Bamfords left Sharpsburg and relocated—permanently—to Pennsylvania. After fleeing with her children on the 16th, Harriet Houser later watched Federal troops ransack her home. As a result of the stress, Harriet "was taken suddenly ill from fright and could not be moved for weeks after the battle."[52]

---

50 Smith, *History of the Corn Exchange Regiment*, 46-47; *New York Times*, October 5, 1862; John C. Whiteside letter, October 4, 1862, University of Michigan, Bentley Historical Library, Ann Arbor, MI.

51 E. P. to Sally Farran, October 4, 1862, *Dan Masters' Civil War Chronicles*; Nelson, *As Grain Falls Before the Reaper*, 54. The Wyands boarded with family for three weeks until hospital personnel vacated their home. Nelson cited the claim of Simon Wyand (*RG* 92, Entry 561, Book G, Claim 1637). See also *RG* 92, Entry 843, Box 771, Claim 174. Simon Wyand owned the farm and rented it to his son, Joshua Wyand.

52 Reilly, *BOA*; Warner, Beers & Co. *History of Cumberland County, Pennsylvania. History of Cumberland and Adams Counties, Pennsylvania* (Chicago, 1886), 465-466. The account cited that medical forces converted the Bamford's house into a hospital, perhaps explaining why corpses were inside the building. The 1870 and 1880 Federal censuses for West Fairview, East Pennsboro Township, Cumberland County, PA, lists the family of H. A. and Maria Bamford in dwellings #126 and #285. Henry A. Bamford should not be confused with his father, an Irish immigrant of the same name, who appears in Sharpsburg's 1860 Federal census, Dwelling #1628. The location of Henry A. and Maria Bamford's Sharpsburg residence is not known. The 1860 census lists the couple in Dwelling #1351 near Miller's Sawmill on the Potomac River.

*   *   *

When combat ceased on September 17, most of the men killed in action lay between the lines. A few sporadic burials occurred on the 17th and 18th. Still, the vast majority of corpses lay exposed to warm temperatures and rain until the Union army gained possession of Sharpsburg on September 19. By this time, the bodies had rapidly decayed. A Connecticut lieutenant described "countless blackened corpses" scattered across the battlefield, while local farmer Otho Nesbitt noted that the lifeless figures were "all swelled and black and purple in their faces." Alex Davis recounted that "the flesh of the dead men had discolored so they looked like they was black people."[53]

The "bloat phase" of decay created gases that swelled some corpses twice their size and forced acidic foam from lifeless mouths. Sergeant Charles D. M. Broomhall of the 124th Pennsylvania was among the unfortunates assigned to burial duty. Studying a row of slain Confederates near David R. Miller's farm, Broomhall counted "ninety three of them, with their heads to the fence, on whom I could have walked without touching the ground, and they were not all the dead that were there." Civilians traversing the battlefield on September 19–20 would have observed the same haunting spectacle. In the eerie silence, Broomhall heard gaseous fluids bubbling in the mouths of the bloated corpses. He wrote, "Fermentation of the stomach had set in, and blubbers at the mouth were breaking all around you, making a slight noise in the breaking, giving a queer weird feeling to many a person, as one moved about among the dead."[54]

Postmortem vapors and secretions from bloated bodies attracted blowflies, which slathered corpses with maggots. In David R. Miller's cornfield, Otho Nesbitt "saw a man with a hole in his belly about as big as a hat and about a quart of dark-looking maggots working away." Dr. Daniel Holt of the 121st New York wrote, "I have seen, stretched along, in one straight line, ready for interment, at

---

53 Fiske, *Mr. Dunn Browne's Experiences in the Army*, 11; Nesbitt Diary, September 19, 1862, ANBL; Johnson, *BA*, 102.

54 Embriette R. Hyde, Daniel P. Haarmann, Aaron M. Lynne, Sibyl R. Bucheli, Joseph F. Petrosino, "The Living Dead: Bacterial Community Structure of a Cadaver at the Onset and End of the Bloat Stage of Decomposition," PloS One, October 30, 2013, https://www.ncbi.nlm.nih.gov/pmc/articles/PMC3813760; "The Stages of Human Decomposition," Aftermath, web page, https://www.aftermath.com/content/human-decomposition; Thomas G. Clemens, "Antietam Remembered," HistoryNet, August 25, 2010, https://www.historynet.com/antietam-remembered.htm. Clemens cited a letter from Charles D. M. Broomhall to Ezra Carman, dated June 29, 1891.

least a thousand blackened, bloated corpses with blood and gas protruding from every orifice, and maggots holding high carnival over their heads."

Bacteria and microorganisms in the decomposing bodies created the putrefaction phase of death. Here, internal decay transmitted foul-smelling fluids and gases. Historian William Frassanito wrote, "Decaying flesh and internal organs exude a disgustingly sour, pungent smell. Interspersed with the foul odors produced by decomposition was the distinctive odor of human excrement." Whenever a human dies, Frassanito explained, "the contents of the bowels (which were frequently diarrhetic) are usually evacuated as a result of internal gaseous pressure and the action of the death upon the muscles of the digestive system."

When multiplied by roughly 4,000 killed-in-action corpses, the malodor of Antietam's dead polluted the air for miles. A *New York Times* reporter noted, "As we approached Sharpsburgh, it was unnecessary to ask when we were coming near the great battle-field, for it could be distinctly smelt two miles off." Similarly, a group of Pennsylvania correspondents needed no visual proof they were nearing the battlefield. "Here our olfactory organs informed us," one of the journalists observed, "very perceptibly, that we were in the region" of decaying flesh, and "on every rise of ground thereafter we were greeted with the same stench."[55]

Up close, the putrid odor nauseated passersby. "Oh what a smell," one Union soldier recalled, "some of the men vomit as they went along." Lieutenant Origen Bingham led a burial crew from the 137th Pennsylvania. He requested permission from the provost marshal "to buy some liquor for our boys to keep them from getting sick when at this disagreeable labor."[56]

Sharpsburg villager John P. Smith recalled, "The stench arising from the battlefield was intolerable." According to civilian Jacob McGraw, "Lots of dead men got pretty strong before they was buried, the weather was so hot; and the stench was terrible—terrible!"[57]

---

55 Nesbitt Diary, September 19, 1862, ANBL; Daniel Holt, *A Surgeon's Civil War: The Letters and Diary of Daniel M. Holt, M.D.*, eds. James M. Greiner, Janet L. Coryell & James R. Smither (Kent, Ohio, 1994), 28; Frassanito, *Antietam*, 256; *New York Times*, October 4, 1862; *Altoona Tribune*, October 2, 1862.

56 Wiley, *The Life of Billy Yank*, 83; Drew Gilpin Faust, *This Republic of Suffering: Death and the American Civil War* (New York, 2008), 68-69; Alann Schmidt, "Battlefield Burials After Antietam: A Most Disagreeable Duty," blog, *Antietam Journal*, October 22, 2013, http://antietamjournal.blogspot.com/2013/10/v-behaviorurldefaultvmlo.html.

57 Ted Alexander, *The Battle of Antietam: The Bloodiest Day* (Charleston, SC, 2011), 102. Alexander cited "Recollections of John P. Smith," Smith file, ANBL; Johnson, *BA*, 117.

The burial of Antietam's dead began in earnest on September 19 with the interment of Federal corpses. Owing to the overpowering smell, burial crews rushed the inhumations, dragging bodies into mass graves. One of the soldiers tasked with this duty explained, "Time and circumstances forbade a more humane course than this." Another witness recalled, "Trenches were dug in which from fifty to eighty bodies were deposited. In some instances decomposition was so far advanced that holes were dug beside the remains, and then with pieces of boards were carefully rolled into the earthy receptacle."

Near Alfred Poffenberger's farm in the West Woods, Private Roland E. Bowen watched a burial crew pile his dead comrades in a mass grave. Upset by the crude interment, Bowen complained, "[T]his is not the way we bury folks at home." Near the sunken lane—now known as Bloody Lane—Josiah Favill of the 57th New York helped inhume hundreds of corpses in shallow trenches. "How many shattered hopes we buried there none of us may ever guess," wrote Favill. "War is certainly a dreadful thing, and a battlefield an ugly blot on civilization."[58]

Federals finished burying their dead on September 20. Next, they interred the enemy's corpses, assisted by Rebel prisoners. Dr. A. A. Biggs wrote after the battle, "Our neighborhood is one vast graveyard. The rebels are buried in ditches dug sufficient to hold as high as eighty piled in such a manner as to be barely covered sufficiently over the top layer of men."

Massachusetts civilian Oliver Wendell Holmes, Sr., while searching for his wounded son on September 21, observed "a long ridge of fresh gravel" marked with a single board reading, "The Rebel General Anderson and 80 Rebels are buried in this hole." Other graves, Holmes noted, "were marked with the number of dead under them." A Pennsylvania soldier recalled, "Just over there in Mumma's field in one ditch you placed 185 Confederate corpses, the one on top of the other, and indecorously covered them from sight with clay. In other ditches lesser numbers were similarly buried."

---

58 Bosbyshell, *Pennsylvania at Antietam*, 164; George H. Washburn, *A Complete Military History and Record of the 108th Regiment N.Y. Vols., from 1862 to 1894* (Rochester, NY, 1894), 26-27; Roland Bowen, *From Ball's Bluff to Gettysburg . . . and Beyond: The Civil War Letters of Private Roland E. Bowen, 15th Massachusetts Infantry 1861–1864*, ed. Gregory A. Coco (Gettysburg, PA, 1994), 128; Timothy Orr, "This is Not the Way We Bury Folks at Home: Killed in the West Woods, Part 3," blog, *Tales From the Army of the Potomac*, June 10, 2015, http:// talesfromaop. blogspot.com/2015/06/this-is-not-way-we-bury-folks-at-home.html?m=1; Josiah M. Favill, *The Diary of a Young Officer: Serving with the Armies of the United States During the War of the Rebellion* (Chicago, 1909), 189-190.

The AOP issued Union soldiers picks, spades, and shovels to facilitate burials. Apparently, though, given the vast number of dead at Antietam, some regiments lacked implements. Inventive soldiers bent bayonets into "body hooks," which they used to drag corpses into trenches. A member of the 27th New York recalled, "We had but few tools for digging, [and] it took most of the day to complete our wholesale interments."[59]

To hasten the burials, some soldiers confiscated tools from Sharpsburg farmers. Joshua Newcomer filed a claim for "Stone picks, mattock, shovels used by the Union troops to bury the dead." Newcomer's son, William, testified that his father's implements were "used in burying the dead, and that was the last he saw of them."

David R. Miller claimed that his "cart and gears were taken by the soldiers and were used for hauling some of the dead and wounded soldiers." A dozen other claimants alleged that Federals appropriated shovels, mattocks, spades, and digging irons after the battle. These residents, though, did not specify if soldiers took the tools for burial purposes. Likewise, the Union army confiscated plows from Daniel Poffenberger and Captain David Smith. Troops interred soldiers on both claimants' farms, but it's unclear if they used the plows to break ground for said burials.[60]

---

59 Louis C. Duncan, *The Medical Department of the United States Army in the Civil War* (Washington, DC, 1913), Chapter V, 32. Also supporting that Confederate prisoners buried their dead at Sharpsburg, the *New York Times*, September 29, 1862, reported that "rebels killed in that battle" were "buried by their own companions;" Biggs to Kalb, September 29, 1862, WMR; Oliver Wendell Holmes, Sr., *Pages From an Old Volume of Life. A Collection of Essays 1857–1881* (Boston, MA, 1863), volume VIII, 40-41. The sign Holmes described was inaccurate, for no Sharpsburg graves contained Confederate generals. See "Six Generals Killed at Antietam," web page, ANB, https://www.nps.gov/anti/learn/historyculture/ 6generals. htm; Bosbyshell, *Pennsylvania at Antietam*, 164.

60 "Curved Bayonet used to drag bodies for burial," online image, ANB, https:// www.nps. gov/museum/tmc/Antietam/Lesson3/Lesson3_attachments.pdf. The photo's caption cites that the bayonet was "found on the field after the battle" and "matched the description of bayonets bent and then used to drag bodies into mass graves;" William B. Westervelt, *Lights and Shadows of Army Life: As Seen by a Private Soldier* (Marlboro, NY, 1886), 24; Claims of Joshua Newcomer (No. 272), David R. Miller (*RG* 123, Entry 22, Book 228, No. 1266), Daniel Poffenberger (Box 771, Claim 333), and David Smith (Nos. 1244, 1262, and 10237); Maryland. Board of Trustees of the Antietam National Cemetery, Maryland (Oden Bowie), *A descriptive list of the burial places of the remains of Confederate soldiers: who fell in the battles of Antietam, South Mountain, Monocacy, and other points in Washington and Frederick counties, in the state of Maryland* (Hagerstown, MD, 1868), 13, 16, 22, 42, Western Maryland Historical Library, Hagerstown, MD (hereafter cited as WHILBR). The Confederate burial report is hereafter cited as the Bowie List. This

Antietam, Md. Miller house. David R. and Margaret (Pottenger) Miller had five children at the time of the battle, ages 4–13. Estimates vary as to whether this photograph was taken in 1862 or 1870. Nevertheless, some of the Miller children pictured in this image undoubtedly witnessed the horrors of Antietam's aftermath. *Library of Congress*

The omnipresent interments presented several problems to landowners. First, most graves were shallow, and it didn't take long for a cloudburst, windstorm, or foraging hog to knock away dirt and expose body parts. Oliver Wendell Holmes, Sr. noticed a grave onto which the burial party "had thrown some earth over him; but his last bed-clothes were too short, and his legs stuck out stark and stiff from beneath the gravel coverlet." Alex Davis remembered, "The trenches was so shallow that after the loose dirt which was thrown back had settled down heads and toes sometimes stuck out." When the 4th Maine Battery, Light Artillery, crossed the battlefield on September 19, one of the heavy guns accidentally rolled over a burial trench. The impact crushed the shallowly interred corpses. A Maine artilleryman remembered seeing "arms and legs fly up the same as sticks will when you drive over them and break them."[61]

Burial locations also challenged the civilians. Soldiers interred some corpses near dwellings and oft-used areas, such as gardens, barnyards, and farm lanes. Families, especially children, had to adjust to seeing graves and human remains outside their windows. Case in point, soldiers buried dead Confederates in the "truck patch in front of Capt. D. Smith's house," and "near the gate at Captain D. Smith's Carriage house." On Alfred Poffenberger's farm, witnesses observed exposed graves and skeletons next to the dwelling house and "just out side the garden fence." Similar sights presented on the farms of David Reel, Henry Piper, and David R. Miller.

In Sharpsburg village, troops buried three Confederates "in Daniel Poffenberger's town lot where he lives." They laid three other bodies to rest in

study, spearheaded by Maryland governor Oden Bowie, documented Confederate burial locations on various properties in Washington and Frederick Counties.

61 Holmes, *Pages From an Old Volume of Life*, 41; Johnson, *BA*, 101; Maine Artillery, *History of the Fourth Maine Battery Light Artillery in the Civil War, 1861–1865* (Augusta, ME, 1905), 130.

Squire Miller's orchard on his residential lot. On Susan Kennedy's village lot, an interment crew buried ten South Carolinians in the "little orchard, opposite her house." For Susan Kennedy, her children, and other civilians, we can only imagine their thoughts. Were they uncomfortable having graves so close to their homes? Were they concerned about the corpses' proximity to well water? Did they attempt to identify the remains and contact surviving loved ones?[62]

Burial crews overlooked some of the dead, leaving residents to dispose of the remains. Michael Tenant, whose wife owned a tract near Col. John Miller's stone mill, found a Union soldier "dead at his gate, shot by a Confederate sharpshooter in the mill." Tenant buried the soldier, "after much difficulty, in the hard limestone soil." Near Susan Kennedy's home, Dr. A. A. Biggs "scraped up the remains of a Confederate soldier who had been literally torn to pieces and buried him in a hole about two feet deep."

Alex Davis recalled, "[A]ll over the fields the bodies was picked up, but those right around the buildings was left. I suppose the soldiers thought that the people who owned the buildings would bury the bodies to get rid of 'em." Consequently, Davis had to inter 26 corpses. "I buried three bodies right behind our smokehouse," he remembered, "then four layin' at the back barn doors, and one near the well." Davis also "buried fifteen in a corner of a field that we'd ploughed and got ready to seed. Those fifteen were government soldiers, and they were very near all Massachusetts men." Davis found one corpse, described as "an awful big man," too heavy to drag into a grave. "I took cotton," he explained, "and tied up my mouth and nose and dug a grave right where he was a-layin' . . . then I shoved a board under him and got him to rollin', and he went into the grave. I'd rather not have buried him so near the well, but the water wa'n't very good anyhow."[63]

62 The Bowie List, 13, 23, 25, 35-37. "Capt. D. Smith" was David Smith. The list included "Mrs. Lucker" [Mary Grove Locher], who owned Alfred Poffenberger's farm in 1862. The property contained more than 100 Confederate corpses in various trenches and graves. See the Bowie List, 21-29, 32-33, 39; "Map of the Battlefield of Antietam," Lionel Pincus and Princess Firyal Map Division, New York Public Library Digital Collections, http://digitalcollections.nypl.org/items/185f8270-0834-0136-3daa-6d29ad33124f. Hereafter, this repository is described as *NYPL*, and the map is cited as the S. G. Elliott burial map. Elliott's map depicts 84 Confederates buried near the Locher-Poffenberger cabin, along with 54 Federal dead; Bowen, *From Ball's Bluff to Gettysburg*, 128; Orr, "This is Not the Way We Bury Folks at Home;" Bowie List, 42, 38, 45-46.

63 Carter, "Four Brothers in Blue," 332; Reilly, *BOA*. Biggs reportedly discovered the body parts "50 yards beyond the northwest corner of the National Cemetery and about 25 yards from the Keedysville pike." Oral history holds that the remains were "never taken up;"

Graves and burial trenches took up a considerable amount of acreage, including soil reserved for growing cash crops and subsistence. In 1864, cartographer S. G. Elliott depicted Antietam's burial locations, marking more than 5,800 bodies on the battlefield and its immediate vicinity. Although some of the remains lay in timber tracts, Elliott depicted most of the burials in farm fields and pasture land.

Some landowners filed claims for the appropriated acreage, given that the army converted portions of their farms into graveyards. Samuel Mumma, Sr. sought compensation for "land damaged" on account of the burials. William Roulette filed a $150 claim for "Burial ground for seven hundred soldiers." Colonel John Miller, meanwhile, petitioned the government for $1,000 on account of "Ground furnished to bury not less than 2000 soldiers, on Wright wing of Battlefield." These farmers, like many others, possibly lost potential income for their 1863 crops. The shallow burial trenches, after all, made plowing and seeding difficult, if not impossible.[64]

As burial duty continued, the decaying bodies attracted buzzards that floated over the battlefield. Correspondent Frank H. Schell sketched several dozen of the scavengers hovering over the corpse-filled Bloody Lane. Another observer noticed "large numbers of those harpies of the air; buzzards, awaiting an opportunity to descend to earth to partake of the cadaverous feast."

The "feast" included scores of animals killed during the battle. "Quite a number of cows, hogs, and other domestic animals were killed," reported a Pennsylvania journalist. Otho Nesbitt rode across the battlefield on September 19 and observed "a white bull or steer lying on his back all swelled up and 2 sheep nearby all swelled up ready to burst." Passing the charred remains of the Mumma farm, Nesbitt noticed "a small stable close by with a dead horse in that had busted the door half way open as he fell."[65]

Johnson, *BA*, 101-102. Alex Davis shared similar details in an interview with Fred W. Cross. See Cross, "Alexander W. Davis, of Sharpsburg."

64 S. G. Elliott burial map, NYPL; Claims of Samuel Mumma, Sr. (D-1927 and D-1928), William Roulette (Box 772, Claim 230), and John Miller (Case No. 2227). Colonel Miller's claim for lost acreage related to the farm tenanted by his son, David. R. Miller.

65 F. H. Schell, *Maryland and Pennsylvania Farmers Visiting the Battle-Field of Antietam While the National Troops Were Burying the Dead and Carrying Off the Wounded*, 1862, sketch, *LC*, https://www.loc.gov/item/2017650942/. Schell's sketch ran in *Frank Leslie's Illustrated Newspaper* on October 18, 1862; Bosbyshell, *Pennsylvania at Antietam*, 164; *Altoona Tribune*, October 2, 1862; Nesbitt Diary, September 19, 1862, ANBL.

Decaying army equines also polluted the landscape. George Templeton Strong, a member of the U.S. Sanitary Commission, arrived in Sharpsburg on September 21. He observed, "[S]cores of dead horses—swollen, with their limbs protruding at strange angles, the ground at their noses blackened with hemorrhage, lay all around." Captain David Been of the 14th Indiana remembered seeing "hundreds of dead horses strew in the fields in every direction." Likewise, 2nd Lieutenant Samuel Fiske of the 14th Connecticut described "hundreds of horses … all mangled and putrefying, scattered everywhere!"[66]

The number of Antietam's equine casualties is unknown. However, Dr. A. A. Biggs reported, "We had about 400 dead horses on the field." Fifty-one battery commanders reported the combined loss of nearly 300 artillery horses, killed or wounded. Additional evidence supports that other horses died during the battle while transporting officers, cavalry, and staff members. Also, artillery fire destroyed several equines on the streets of Sharpsburg village.[67]

The collective stench of dead humans and animals overwhelmed those living and bivouacking near the battlefield. Private George H. Washburn of the 108th New York remembered, "The bodies with hundreds of horses, cattle, and sheep that were in the fields . . . created an offensive odor, particularly evenings when a low dense fog prevailed, that was almost unendurable, and the boys remarked, 'It could be cut in chunks.'" In attempt to "ameliorate in a measure this rank stench,"

---

66 Strong Diary, September 24, 1862, NYHSM; Alexander, *The Battle of Antietam*, 102; Fiske, *Mr. Dunn Browne's Experiences in the Army*, 49.

67 Biggs to Kalb, September 29, 1862, WMR. Biggs's estimate may have been low. Researchers estimated that musketry and artillery killed 3,000–6,000 horses and mules at the Battle of Gettysburg. See Meg Groeling, T*he Aftermath of Battle: The Burial of the Civil War Dead* (El Dorado Hills, CA, 2015), 35. See also Blake A. Magner, *Traveller & Company: The Horses of Gettysburg* (Gettysburg, PA, 1995), 47. The S. G. Elliott burial map, NYPL, depicts 269 dead horses on the Antietam battlefield. However, soldiers and civilians may have burned, buried, or dragged away equine carcasses before Elliott surveyed the area circa 1863–4; Several battery commanders reported horse casualties in their official reports. Captain William M. Graham, 1st U.S. Artillery, Battery K, noted, "17 horses killed, and 6 horses wounded severely, some of which will probably die of the effects of their wounds" (*OR*, vol. 19, 1:344). Captain James Thompson, Pennsylvania Light Artillery, Independent Battery C, mentioned that "eighteen of my horses fell dead" during the battle (*OR*, vol. 51, 1:139). Lieutenant James Stewart, 4th U.S. Artillery, Battery B, cited the loss of "26 horses killed and 7 wounded" (*OR*, vol. 19, 1:229). Among the Confederate officers reporting equine casualties, Captain John P. W. Read, Pulaski (GA) Artillery, explained, in part, that he left a carriage and limber on the battlefield because "I had not the horses, having lost 20 killed and wounded in action" (*OR*, vol. 19, 1:867). Twenty more horses died in the Donaldson (LA) Artillery, based on the report of Captain Victor Maurin (*OR*, vol. 19, 1:848). Captain Stephen D. Lee, 2nd Battalion, Longstreet's Corps Artillery, wrote that "60 horses were disabled" during the battle (*OR*, vol. 19, 1:846).

Washburn added, "the carcasses of the animals were hauled together in lots, and rails piled upon them and fired."

Troops throughout the battlefield region burned the horses. Understandably, the carcasses were too large for burial and reeked worse by the day. Lieutenant Colonel J. W. Kimball, commanding the 15th Massachusetts Volunteers, recalled that his men "encamped upon the battle field" for three days after the battle. During this span, his regiment was "engaged most of the time in burying the dead," but "the dead horses were burned on the field where they lay and the fence rails in the vicinity were used for the purpose." Kimball's men may have taken some fencing from the nearby Nicodemus farmstead, for Alex Davis recalled, "Fully one third of the fences on our farm was gone. Some of the rails had been used to burn the dead horses."[68]

Soldiers didn't burn all the animals, leaving the unfinished task to residents. Samuel Mumma, Jr. and his father "dragged 55 dead horses from their farm to the East Woods, where they burned them." Jacob McGraw remembered "helping [to] drag the dead horses out of town." Using a four-horse team, McGraw's crew "hitch[ed] a log-chain around a dead horse's neck" and then pulled the carcass "over the hills." The townsfolk planned to burn the horseflesh with rails, but discovered that soldiers had confiscated most of the fencing in the vicinity. "We burnt what [horses] we could on the edge of town," McGraw remembered, "I s'pose we burnt ten or twelve, and we drug nearly as many more out on the farms so as to get the stench away from the town."[69]

Throughout late September, large pyres of horseflesh burned throughout the Sharpsburg area. A visitor traversing the battlefield observed dead equines "collected into a great pile which reached as high as the ruins of a barn." Great smoke clouds of miasmic stench permeated the region. Some witnesses recalled that "the odor of cooked meat even reached Hagerstown."

The widespread torching of carrion caused rumors to spread that Yankee burial squads set fire to Confederate corpses. Private George H. Washburn of the 108th New York Infantry recalled, "From such action arose a false report, that the Federals burned the bodies of their fallen foe." But was it a false report?

---

68 Washburn, *A Complete Military History and Record of the 108th*, 26-27; Claims of Samuel I. Piper (RG 123, Entry 22, Box 234, Case No. 1310) and the heirs of Henry Wade (RG 123, Entry 22, Box 741, Case No. 6585). Kimball testified in both cases involving Piper and the Wades; Johnson, *BA*, 100.

69 Reilly, *BOA*; Johnson, *BA*, 117.

While soldiers buried corpses in Sharpsburg, XII Corps troops on Maryland Heights interred Confederates killed during Stonewall Jackson's Harpers Ferry operation. The rocky hilltop, unfortunately, offered little soil for burial. "The only thing we could do," wrote Miles Clayton Huyette of the 125th Pennsylvania, "was to gather brush and logs and burn the bodies of the dead." J. Strait, a New York soldier, observed that burial squads on Maryland Heights "had just got the rebles burnt we saw the bones of them. The reasons they burn them," Strait reasoned, "is because they do not have time to bury them, but our men are all buried in one hole on top of the mountain."

At Sharpsburg, interment crews may have also burned some of the Confederate remains. On September 20, John C. Sunderlin of the 5th Vermont wrote in a letter home, "O the heaps and heaps of dead and dying . . . the air stank for five miles around caused by the dead bodies." Sunderlin recalled, "[W]e passed through the different fields, for the battle extended five or six miles," during which he observed burial crews "burning the bodies of men and horses that could not be moved, and the air stank so in some places that one could hardly breathe."[70]

Despite the combined efforts of troops and civilians, it took several days to finish burying the men killed in action. Soldiers completed most of the work by Sunday, September 21, but some corpses remained on the field. When Mary Ellen Piper arrived home on Monday, September 22, she recalled, "The dead had not all been buried when I returned."[71]

A few weeks after the battle, a *New York Times* reporter opined, "The living that throng Broadway care little perhaps for the Dead at Antietam . . . there is a confused mass of names, but they are all strangers; we forget the horrible significance that dwells amid the jumble of type." But the journalist emphasized

70 "Widow of Civil War Veteran Here For Commemoration," *Morning Herald* [Hagerstown, MD], August 13, 1937; Washburn, *A Complete Military History and Record of the 108th*, 26-27; B. W. Schulz and Rachel de Vienne, *A Separate Identity: Organizational Identity Among Readers of Zion's Watch Tower, 1870–1887*, 2 vols. (Morrisville, NC, 2014), 1:260. The authors cited a letter written by John C. Sunderlin, September 21, 1862. A partial transcription of the letter is archived at Raynor's Historical Auctions, Lot #235, "Antietam Dead Piled Up," http://www.hcaauctions.com/LotDetail.aspx?inventoryid=20312; Huyette, *The Maryland Campaign*, 57; Susan W. Frye and Dennis E. Frye, *Maryland Heights: Archeological & Historical Resources Study* (Washington, DC, 1989), 65-66. The authors cited J. Strait to his sister, October 19, 1862, personal collection of Dennis E. Frye.

71 Frassanito, *Antietam*, 256; E. P. to Sally Farran, October 4, 1862, *Dan Masters' Civil War Chronicles*. Mary Ellen Piper returned home on September 19, having sheltered during the battle on the farm of her uncle, Samuel I. Piper. Upon finding bodies inside her home, she boarded in Sharpsburg village until September 22.

that Antietam's dead represented more than a sterile list of names. Rather, "Homes have been made desolate, and the light of life in thousands of hearts has been quenched forever. All of this desolation imagination must paint—broken hearts cannot be photographed."

The battle's body count was heartbreaking indeed, as the local community witnessed firsthand. The dead, however, composed only a portion of Antietam's 23,000 casualties. In addition, thousands of wounded men urgently needed medical attention, and the Sharpsburg environs quickly became one vast hospital.[72]

---

72 *New York Times*, October 20, 1862; Frassanito, *Antietam*, 15-16.

$Chapter 4$

Putrid Mess:
Antietam's Hospitals

 **After Lee's** army withdrew to Virginia, the number of wounded soldiers in the Sharpsburg environs exceeded 9,500 Federals and 2,000 Confederates.

Adding to the casualties were U.S. troops wounded by artillery and skirmish fire on September 15–16 and fighting near Shepherdstown from September 19–20. In addition, hundreds of McClellan's non-wounded men fell sick to various diseases after the battle. The Army of the Potomac's medical department not only faced a monumental challenge in treating more than 11,000 patients, but it also lacked supplies, which exacerbated the emergency and burdened surgeons, soldiers, and civilians alike.[1]

---

1 "Casualties of Battle," web page, ANB, https://www.nps.gov/anti/learn/historyculture/casualties.htm. The Antietam National Battlefield estimates that 9,550 Union soldiers and 7,750 Confederates (17,300 total) suffered wounds during the battle. The Battle of Shepherdstown on September 20 sent more than 160 Federals to Sharpsburg's field hospitals. See Smith, *History of the Corn Exchange Regiment*, 95-96, and McGrath, *Shepherdstown*. 173, 217; Pawlak, *Shepherdstown in the Civil War*, 75, 87, 94-95, 106-107. Of the 7,750 Confederates wounded at Antietam, most of these men, to avoid capture, walked or rode in ambulances to Shepherdstown on September 18. Pawlak estimated that the total number of Confederates treated at Shepherdstown's hospitals, including casualties from South Mountain and the Battle of Shepherdstown, may have numbered as high as 5,000–6,000; Harsh, *Sounding the Shallows*, 202, 216-217. Harsh argued that it is "almost certain . . . that several thousand of the 6,000 prisoners captured by the Federals in the Maryland campaign must have come from the abandoned wounded at Sharpsburg;" Official report of Dr. Jonathan Letterman, March 1,

Before embarking on the 1862 Maryland Campaign, Dr. Jonathan Letterman, medical director of the AOP, found his department "in a most deplorable condition." When McClellan's army entered Maryland, Letterman reported that "no time could be allowed for medical officers again to equip themselves with the medicines, instruments, dressings, and stores necessary for the campaign in that State." As a result, Dr. Letterman directed the medical purveyor in Baltimore to ship railroad cars of medical stores to Frederick. Here, Letterman planned to pre-stage the supplies safely behind the lines in anticipation of an impending battle.

It was an excellent plan on paper. On September 8, however, Confederate engineers destroyed the Baltimore and Ohio Railroad bridge over the Monocacy River in a strategic move to injure the Union army's supply network. The severed railroad prevented the Baltimore supplies from reaching Frederick and log-jammed incoming train traffic, stranding some of the medical purveyor's boxcars between Baltimore and Frederick.

Adding to Dr. Letterman's woes, his department lacked an independent means of transportation, and thus the Baltimore supplies fell under jurisdiction of the quartermaster department. When Federal engineers finally repaired the railroad bridge on September 21, the quartermaster department switched the medical boxcars off the tracks to prioritize the shipment of ammunition and quartermaster stores to Sharpsburg.

Charles J. Stille, a member of the U.S. Sanitary Commission, complained that the medical supplies "did not reach the battle-field for many days." On September 21—four days after the battle—Stille observed that the urgently needed items still had not arrived at Sharpsburg. On this day, he added that the hospital supplies on hand at Antietam's hospitals "were not one tenth of what was absolutely needed."[2]

1863, *OR*, vol. 19, 1:111. Letterman estimated that his department treated 2,500 wounded Rebels after the Battle of Antietam, a figure that included casualties from South Mountain; Anna Holstein, *Three Years in Field Hospitals of the Army of the Potomac* (Philadelphia, 1867), 15. Holstein arrived in Sharpsburg shortly after the battle and observed that wounded Rebels "had been left by the thousands, and now had to be provided for;" *HFTL*, November 5, 1862. Seven weeks after the battle, countless Confederate patients at Sharpsburg had died of wounds or were transferred north for exchange as prisoners of war. Despite these departures, the *Freedom and Torch Light* reported that 1,400 Confederates remained in Sharpsburg's hospitals in early November.

2 Official report of Dr. Jonathan Letterman, *OR*, vol. 19, 1:106-107; Duncan, *The Medical Department*, Chapter V, 9, 34; "F-7-140 Frederick Junction (Monocacy Junction, Araby)," architectural survey file, MHT, sec. 8, p. 3. The report cited Jacob Engelbrecht's diary, Frederick County Historical Society, CD-ROM, 952, 998. Engelbrecht, a resident of Frederick, Maryland, observed cars passing over the repaired railroad bridge on Sunday, Sep. 21, 1862; Ira

Other factors contributed to the deficiency of hospital items. Dr. Letterman reportedly did not dispatch medical officers to Monocacy Junction to expedite the shipment of the supplies. Also, according to a member of the U.S. Sanitary Commission, none of the AOP surgeons "considered himself charged with the function of hurrying anything forward." Purchasing hospital stores from nearby towns was not an option because the government did not allocate the surgeons funds to obtain supplies.

Thus, desperately needed bandages, tents, hospital food, and other necessities sat idly along railroad tracks, dozens of miles from Sharpsburg. This snafu left Antietam's surgeons without critical supplies for thousands of patients. It would be days before these provisions reached Antietam's field hospitals.

Jonathan Letterman vented in his after-action report, "The failure of the railroad company to forward the supplies caused serious annoyance . . . great deal of confusion and delay was the consequence, which seriously embarrassed the medical department."[3]

Dr. Cornelius R. Agnew, a physician with the U.S. Sanitary Commission, witnessed the supply shortage firsthand. On September 20, Agnew and other volunteers arrived in Keedysville. Everywhere, he reported, "we were asked for chloroform and opiates, instruments and bedpans." Additionally, "[E]verything in the way of medical supplies was deficient . . . tourniquets were wanting in many instances; stimulants very deficient; concentrated food also scanty."

When Dr. Agnew compiled his report at Frederick two days later, he observed, "Many of the supplies are still here . . . awaiting transportation." Due to the delay, he concluded, "I solemnly affirm that great loss of life has occurred, and will occur, among the wounded, as the direct result of an inability on the part of the medical authorities to furnish, by rapid and independent means of transportation, the medical and surgical appliances needed within the two days subsequent to battles."[4]

K. Rutkow, *Bleeding Blue and Gray: Civil War Surgery and the Evolution of American Medicine* (New York, 2005), 199; Scott McGaugh, *Surgeon in Blue: Jonathan Letterman, the Civil War Doctor Who Pioneered Battlefield Care* (New York, 2013), 101-102; Charles J. Stille, *History of the United States Sanitary Commission: Being the General Report of its Work During the War of the Rebellion* (New York, 1868), 262-268.

3 Duncan, *The Medical Department*, Chapter V, 12, 20, 36; Official report of Dr. Jonathan Letterman, *OR*, vol. 19, 1:107.

4 George W. Hosmer, *Report of the Delegates from the General Aid Society for the Army at Buffalo, New York* (Buffalo, NY, 1862), 13-14. Hosmer cited Dr. C. R. Agnew to the U.S. Sanitary Commission, September 22, 1862; Duncan, *The Medical Department*, Chapter V, 20.

The *New York Times* also recognized the scant supplies at Sharpsburg, reporting the urgent need for medicines, clothing, bedding, candles, pails, and other items. Two days after the battle, Dr. Theodore Dimon of the 2nd Maryland Infantry "did not know where I should get a hundred things I needed for my wounded men." Dimon and his staff had no lanterns "to enable us at night to keep the wounds wet, turn over the wounded to ease their positions, or give them a drink." Also, his field hospital lacked vessels for wetting bandages and serving food and water. "We had one basin," wrote Dimon, "for dressing the wounds of one hundred and forty-seven men, and that had a hole in the bottom stuffed with rags."

Dr. James Oliver, while treating patients on Bishop John Russell's farm near Keedysville, penned his frustrations regarding the deficient supplies. "I wish to put on record the inefficiencies of the Medical Department at Washington at this time," complained Oliver. "Here was a hospital with about three hundred terribly wounded men. Requisition was made for mattresses and bedsteads but none were ever sent . . . we also made requisition for stoves to warm the tents, but none were ever sent."

When Clara Barton arrived at Sharpsburg with a wagonload of hospital items, Dr. James Dunn christened her "the true heroine of the age, the angel of the battlefield"—a moniker reflecting the urgent need for supplies. But Barton herself admitted that one wagon of bandages, lanterns, food, and wine would not remedy the emergency at hand. "After a time my stores for feeding the men began to give out," wrote Barton. "[O]f food I had naturally not enough for thousands, and by afternoon the line of wounded stretched out for five miles."[5]

*   *   *

The Army of the Potomac's medical department faced additional challenges during and immediately after the battle. Government-issued hospital tents lay stranded with other medical stores. Also, there was no rail transportation at Sharpsburg to evacuate the wounded to larger cities, which afforded ample shelter.

5 *New York Times*, October 1, 1862; Franklin Brigham Fay, *War Papers of Franklin Brigham Fay: With Reminiscences of Service in the Camps and Hospitals of the Army of the Potomac, 1861–1865* (Boston, 1911), 48; James Oliver, *Ancestry, Early Life and War Record of James Oliver, M.D.* (Athol, MA, 1916), 57; "Antietam: Clara Barton and the International Red Cross Association," online article, ANB; "Clara Barton at Antietam," online article, ANB, https://www.nps.gov/anti/learn/historyculture/clarabarton.htm.

With options limited, the AOP medical department forcibly converted all properties in the battlefield's vicinity into impromptu field hospitals. Military medical historian Louis Duncan aptly summarized the emergency by writing, "Every building between the Antietam and the Potomac was filled with wounded men."[6]

In a whirlwind of frantic activity, long lines of ambulances rumbled onto farmsteads, and hospital staff prepared properties for the reception of the wounded. As medical workers cleared out Henry F. Neikirk's barn, his "machinery and wagons were put out, and whilst moving said machinery some damages were done to a seeder and reaper." Captain David Smith's family had "some 400 bushels of wheat threshed in the barn." When Federals took possession of Smith's property on September 19, "a good deal of wheat was wasted" because "to make room for the wounded the wheat was thrown out."

Jacob H. Grove's 1862 wheat crop "was thrashed and in the barn" at the time of the battle. When medical forces pressed the farm into service, Grove's laborers helped move the grain out of the barn "to make room for the wounded." It didn't take long, though, for soldiers to feed the valuable crop to their horses. When Grove later hauled his wheat to a gristmill, he found that "it measured between 400 and 500 bushels short."

Due to the staggering number of wounded, the AOP's ambulance corps lacked enough vehicles to transport the soldiers. As a result, Union forces confiscated wagons from civilians. From David R. Miller's barn, soldiers took a horse cart to transport injured men, which they never returned. Samuel I. Piper alleged that Federals, needing "to take a sick man to the hospital," appropriated his horse, wagon, and harness. The property, Piper added, "was never returned to me." Union soldiers took Jacob H. Grove's two-horse wagon "from the barn-yard . . . for the transportation of the wounded soldiers." According to Grove, "I never saw anything of them afterwards."[7]

Medical personnel, to ventilate patients inside some of the buildings, shattered or removed fixed windows. For example, while converting Squire Jacob Miller's sawmill complex into a hospital, troops removed the windows but failed to replace them. A parishioner of Sharpsburg's Lutheran Church recalled that the building's windows "were pretty much broke and smashed out" by hospital personnel.

---

6 Duncan, *The Medical Department*, Chapter V, 7, 21.

7 Claims of Henry F. Neikirk (H-4108 and H-4109), David Smith (Claim F-846), David R. Miller (No. 1266), Samuel I. Piper (No. 1310), and Jacob H. Grove (No. 1267).

Likewise, the vestry of St. Paul's Protestant Episcopal Church sought compensation for "25 windows with glass and sash destroyed" by hospital staff.

Civilians sustained other property damages. At Smoketown, Dr. Letterman's men converted a tenant house on Catherine Showman's farm into a hospital. During the process, "the inside partitions of the house were knocked down" to clear space for the sufferers.[8]

While hastily clearing out houses for the wounded, medical staff tossed furniture outdoors and carried away beds and bedding for hospital use. Surgeons unhinged doors and mounted them on barrels to create makeshift operating platforms. At the homes of Stephen P. Grove, William Roulette, and George Miller, doctors performed grisly surgeries on the families' kitchen tables. Inside the Dunker Church, surgeons used the Elder's table "for the amputation of arms and legs."[9]

A reporter from the *New York Tribune* described the widespread crisis by writing, "Every private dwelling is filled with the wounded. Carpets are torn up, costly furniture removed, comfortable mattresses spread upon the floor awaiting the arrival of the ambulances." Samuel Beeler testified, "[T]he troops . . . committed depredations of all kinds, taking house hold furniture, etc." According to John Otto, soldiers seized "everything in and around his farm" for hospital use. The appropriations included "beds, furniture . . . and anything that would contribute to the comfort of the wounded, being either consumed entirely or rendered unfit for further use."

---

8 Snyder, *Trembling in the Balance*, 45. Snyder cited a letter from Jacob Miller to the C & O Canal's President and Directors, May 1, 1863, Ltre. Recd., C & O Co.; Claims of the Sharpsburg Lutheran Church (RG 123, Entry 22, Box 522, No. 4058) and St. Paul's Protestant Episcopal Church (RG 123, Entry 22, Box 1557, No. 13674); Nelson, *As Grain Falls Before the Reaper*, 67. Medical inspector W. R. Mosely toured Sharpsburg's Episcopal Methodist Church. He reported, "There is not a window in the building and no means of ventilation except by removing the whole or part of the canvas which occupies the place of glass and sash in the window frame;" Claim of Catherine Showman (RG 92, Entry 812, Book F, Box 85, Claim F-1176).

9 William "Bud" Shackelford interview, ANBL. Per Shackelford, "The doors were torn off and mounted on flour barrels . . . to make operating tables;" Schildt, *Drums Along the Antietam*, 163; "One Vast Hospital," educational brochure, ANB, https://www.nps.gov/museum/tmc/Antietam/Lesson2/Lesson2_attachments.pdf. The brochure cites Dr. Theodore Dimon's letter. He wrote, "Our amputating table consisted of a small door mounted on two barrels;" Hildebrand, "Mount Airy Has Its Moments of History," 83-85; John Banks, "Antietam: A Rare Piece of History from Roulette Farm?" blog, *John Banks' Civil War Blog*, October 24, 2013, http://john-banks.blogspot.com/2013/10/antietam-rare-piece-of-history-from.html; *Morning Herald*, August 31, 1962, 14. Soldiers allegedly carried George Miller's table "into the yard . . . for amputating the arms and legs of the soldiers."

When Lewis Blackford returned home on September 19, he "found his father's farm full with union soldiers, saw them brake several articles of furniture." On Stephen P. Grove's farmstead, patients reportedly used "all the beds and bedding on the place . . . rendering them useless." Other residents claimed to have lost their furniture and beds, including Nancy Miller, Michael Miller, and David R. Miller.[10]

Likewise, Henry Piper lost his "Homehold Kitchen furniture." Leonard Emmert testified that his furniture "was much damaged" by hospital use, and Bishop John Russell reported the loss of "5 beds used and taken away" by medical forces. On John C. Middlekauff's farm, the "beds and bed clothing were taken out and used for hospital uses," along with "the furniture of the house."[11]

Jonathan Letterman's department pressed dozens of properties into service for hospital use. Willing or not, most families in the Sharpsburg area found themselves boarding the wounded. Dr. Louis Duncan counted 71 field hospitals in the Antietam battlefield area, while other homes and farmsteads served as medical branches and dressing stations. In his ten-year study of Antietam field hospitals, John Nelson located 120 Federal infirmaries, with nearly 100 in the Sharpsburg-Keedysville vicinity.[12]

Medical personnel established large Union infirmaries on the farms of Bishop John Russell, near Keedysville, and Catherine Showman, at Smoketown. Other civilians hosted large hospitals on their farms, including Susan Hoffman, Samuel Poffenberger, Daniel and Michael Miller, Henry F. Neikirk, Sarah Snyder, Otho B. Smith, and George Line. At the last two locations, Otho B. Smith estimated that

---

10 *New York Tribune*, September 18, 1862; Claim of Samuel Beeler (*RG* 92, Entry 843, Box 772, Book 304, Claim 401); Claim of John Otto (*RG* 92, Book G, Box 98, Claim G-1857); Claims of Henry V. S. Blackford (G-1630, G-1648, and G-1654); Claims of Stephen P. Grove (*RG* 123, Entry 22, Box 804, Case No. 7354), Nancy Miller (Book 304, Claim 23), Michael Miller (*RG* 92, Book F, Box 89, F-1437 and F-1438), and David R. Miller (No. 1266).

11 Claims of Henry Piper (No. 445) and Leonard Emmert (F-1577); *Geeting, Ephraim and J. Russell, 1862-1863*, Record of accounts against the U.S. Government for supplies furnished to Locust Spring Hospital during and after the Battle of Antietam, Upper Midwest Literary Archives, Elmer L. Andersen Library, University of Minnesota, Minneapolis, MN (hereafter cited as Geeting and Russell accounts, UMLA). Ephraim Geeting was Bishop John Russell's son-in-law; Claim of John C. Middlekauff (*RG* 123, Entry 22, No. 321).

12 Duncan, *The Medical Department*, Chapter V, 21, 34; Nelson, *As Grain Falls Before the Reaper*, 5-6.

"1600 wounded were accommodated" on his farm. George Line remarked, "1700 wounded were dressed on his place so he was told by Dr. King."[13]

The day after the battle, a *New York Tribune* correspondent near the battlefield observed, "[T]he wounded are coming in by the thousands." Riding throughout the area, the same reporter "counted 1,250 wounded" on one farm. Next, he passed "three more hospitals, each having from six hundred to seven hundred in them, and long trains of ambulances standing in the road waiting to discharge their bloody loads." At each location, Federal surgeons were "covered with blood" while busily "amputating limbs, extracting balls, and bandaging wounds of every nature and in every part of the body."

A Pennsylvania journalist reported from Samuel Poffenberger's farm, "The scene beggars all description." He found that "every room in the house, the porticos in front and rear, the barn floor and mows, all the stables underneath the barn, the wagon-shed, and around the straw and grain stacks, were crowded with the wounded." Many patients, the journalist wrote, were "beyond the reach of medical skill and were now struggling in the last agonies of death."

At another location, a soldier recalled, "Every object in the landscape was tainted with the ravages of war." Everywhere, it seemed, there were "bloody and mutilated forms, some laughing and joking, some praying, some groaning, and some, alas, struggling with Death, with the death-rattle in their throats." A local newspaper reported, "From Hagerstown to the Southern limits of the county, wounded and dying soldiers are to be found in every neighborhood and nearly every house. The whole region between Boonsboro and Sharpsburg is one vast hospital."[14]

Most of the Confederate wounded convalesced at hospitals west of town. Other maimed Rebels sheltered in St. Paul's Protestant Episcopal Church in Sharpsburg village and on farms near the East Woods. Among the latter locations, George Line estimated that doctors cared for 115 Confederates on his farm, the prisoners having been "brought in by the federals."

---

13 Claims of Otho B. Smith (*RG* 92, Book F, Box 89, Claim F-1432) and George Line (F-1186 & F-1187). Surgeons referred to Bishop John Russell's farm as the Locust Spring or Crystal Spring Hospital. Catherine Showman's farm comprised part of Smoketown Hospital.

14 Figg, *Where Men Only Dare to Go*, 47-48. Figg did not cite the *Tribune's* date. The account appears in Edward A. Pollard, *Southern History of the War: The Second Year of the War* (New York, 1864), 137; *Altoona Tribune*, October 2, 1862; *The Valley Register* [Middletown, MD], September 26, 1862, 2A.

When George Templeton Strong inspected Otho B. Smith's farm near the Upper Bridge, he found "horrible congregations of wounded men there . . . in their bloody stiffened clothes." Union and Confederate patients lay in "barns & cowhouses . . . [and] the open air." Summarizing his visit, Strong wrote, "It was fearful to see Gustave Dore's pictures embodied in shivering agonizing suppurating flesh & blood."[15]

Medical personnel also commandeered homes in the town of Sharpsburg. Henry Piper recalled that "some of the private houses in the village" served as hospitals. The vestry of St. Paul's Church declared in its claim, "After the Antietam battle every building in Sharpsburg and vicinity that could be made available for such purpose was appropriated to hospital uses." Nurse Anna Holstein, referring to Sharpsburg village, observed that "half the houses in the place were crowded with our wounded troops." Samuel Michael found the dwelling on Lot 178 jammed beyond belief. He wrote to his brother, "Your house that you lived in is also a hospital by the Yankees. They had as high as ninety in there."[16]

The U.S. army also converted houses of worship into hospitals. For instance, at St. Paul's Protestant Episcopal Church, a villager recalled, "[In] order to better adapt the building to such purposes of a hospital and to afford more room, the pews were removed." Similarly, when the Dunker Church filled beyond capacity, medical staff carried the pews "out in the yard and placed [them] under the great oak trees."[17]

In the town of Keedysville, men from the AOP filled homes and other structures with wounded. These buildings included the Mount Vernon German

---

15 Mumma, *Antietam: The Aftermath*, 17. Julia Forrest Hebb volunteered at the "Confederate hospital . . . in the old Episcopal Church;" Holstein, *Three Years in Field Hospitals*, 15. Holstein wrote, "The Episcopal church in the town had also been taken for their [Confederate] use;" John Nelson, research materials from *As Grain Falls Before the Reaper: The Federal Hospital Sites and Identified Federal Casualties at Antietam*, vertical file, ANBL. Nelson's file includes Dr. Elisha Harris's "Field Records of Hospitals," archived in *RG* 94, Entry 544, *NA*. This document identified Union and Confederate infirmaries in the Sharpsburg environs. The claims of Capt. David Smith, John L. Mayer, and Stephen P. Grove show that Rebel hospitals operated on these farms. Also, the Bowie List for Confederate burials cites interments on properties west of Sharpsburg, including farms owned in 1862 by Elias S. Grove and Samuel Beeler; Claims of George Line (F-1186 & F-1187); Strong Diary, September 22, 1862, NYHSM.

16 Claim of Henry Piper (*RG* 123, No. 445); Claim of St. Paul's Protestant Episcopal Church (*RG* 123, No. 13674); Holstein, *Three Years in Field Hospitals*, 15; Samuel Michael to David Michael, November 27, 1862, WMR.

17 Claim of St. Paul's Protestant Episcopal Church (No. 13674); Schmidt and Barkley, *September Mourn*, 44-45.

Reformed Church, Jeptha Taylor's mill, Frederick Wyand's store, and the Keedysville schoolhouse. Like Sharpsburg, nearly all of Keedysville's farms served as hospitals. Medical forces also descended on Samuel Pry's mill complex, carrying patients into the gristmill, carriage house, barn, and cooper shop.[18]

At Smoketown, attendants brought sufferers into Catherine Showman's two-story tenant house and then appropriated her "negro house . . . for washing purposes." Federals transported injured men into Henry F. Neikirk's two dwelling houses, wagon shed, stables, and corn house. Afterward, they seized Neikirk's summer kitchen for cooking rations.

Near the Antietam Iron Works, Dr. Patrick Henry Flood's staff unloaded patients into John Snyder's barn. Dr. Flood's steward then expropriated Snyder's tenant house "for over two months, in which he cooked &c. for the hospital & the Doctor." On Susan Hoffman's farm, officers converted every building into a medical shelter. Patients filled Hoffman's brick house, bank barn, wagon shed, spring house, blacksmith shop, work shop, summer kitchen, bake house, and "two log buildings used as servant's quarters."[19]

After evacuating from September 15–19, many families arrived home to find their dwellings filled with Antietam's casualties. For instance, David R. Miller and his family allegedly returned from Pennsylvania two days after the battle "and where they left a home of comfort and ease, found it full of wounded and dying soldiers." As if the unexpected company wasn't startling enough, some civilians received troubling news. Due to the limited space inside the homes, surgeons asked the residents to find lodging elsewhere.

Many of the evicted families sought refuge with family or neighbors. For some, the displacement lasted only a few days. A woman in Sharpsburg village complained that the army "drove her out of her house, with her five children, and she never saw the inside of it again for a week." Other families endured longer evictions. Samuel and Catherine Poffenberger, for example, were "unable to take

---

18 Schildt, *Drums Along the Antietam*, 62; Reilly, *BOA*.

19 Claims of Catherine Showman (F-1176), Henry F. Neikirk (H-4109), and John Snyder (*RG* 92, Entry 561, Book F, Box 81, Claim F-859). Dr. Patrick Henry Flood served as regimental surgeon of the 107th New York and tended to General Mansfield's mortal wound during the battle; Claim of Susan Hoffman (No. 1318). Hoffman's case includes the testimonies of Andrew W. Reeder and Franklin T. Hine, who lived on Hoffman's farm at the time of the battle, working as farmhands.

up [their] abode" for nineteen days. Hospital forces also uprooted Otho B. Smith and his family, who boarded with nearby family for three weeks.[20]

Tenant farmers also lacked access to their dwellings. On Joseph Sherrick's farm, the army ousted Leonard Emmert and his wife and daughter for nearly a month. When the medical department sequestered Jacob H. Grove's two farms located west of the village, overseers E. W. Dorsey and Moses French "had to vacate" their tenant houses for eleven weeks "on account of said appropriation for hospital purposes."[21]

John Otto, along with his family and slaves, endured a seven-week displacement. During this span, the Ottos' "house, barn, beds, furniture & c. at the Burnside Bridge were used for hospital purposes to the exclusion of the family." Dr. James King and his staff cast out George Line and his household, who found temporary shelter with Line's father-in-law, Jacob Poffenberger. Captain David Smith's domestic servant, Angeline Jackson, testified that the Smiths weren't able to return "permanently back to our house on the farm" until mid-November on account of the medical occupation of their home. Jackson and the Smiths, during the interim, boarded with Reverend Jacob Highbarger on Lot 130E in the village.[22]

On Catherine Showman's farm, "the doctor in charge claimed full possession" of the two tenant houses. Consequently, Showman "had no chance to occupy" the buildings "all the time up to May 1/63." Susan Hoffman found the hospital occupation of her farm "a great personal inconvenience" as "she was practically kept out of the use of these buildings for several months." During this time,

20 Stephen H. Bogardus to *The Poughkeepsie Daily Eagle*, June 5, 1863, *Dear Eagle*, 72-73. Bogardus, a member of the Purnell Maryland Legion, fought in David R. Miller's cornfield at Antietam. In 1863, Bogardus visited Sharpsburg and toured the Miller cornfield. Afterward, he spoke with "the lady of the house." She told him that "eight thousand soldiers . . . were buried on the farm. Her house was used for a hospital, the family being away in Pennsylvania, and everything it contained being ruined." Bogardus noted that "the family returned on Friday after the battle," and found their dwelling "full of wounded and dying soldiers." Bogardus did not mention the Millers by name, but the context of his account suggests that he spoke with Miller's wife, Margaret Pottenger Miller. Her daughters in 1863 would have ranged in age from 5–14, likely making them too young to have been "the lady of the house;" *Timaru Herald*, February 23, 1866; Claim of Samuel Poffenberger (F-1434).

21 Claims of Otho B. Smith (F-1432), Leonard Emmert (F-1577), and Jacob H. Grove (No. 1267). Grove testified that his two tenant houses "were used for hospital purposes from September 17 to December 3, 1862."

22 Claims of John Otto (G-1857), George Line (F-1186 and F-1187), and David Smith (Nos. 1244, 1262, and 10237). Witness testimony cites that, in 1862, Capt. Smith and his wife, Ann, lived in Sharpsburg village. Their three sons, farm laborers, and domestic servant Angeline Jackson occupied the Smiths' farm west of town.

Hoffman and her family "were obliged to leave the farm and live during that time with the family of a neighbor."[23]

In most instances, surgeons allowed residents to remain in their homes, but there was a catch. According to Jacob McGraw, army doctors "would huddle the family all into one little room . . . while the rest of the house was used to shelter wounded soldiers." Surgeons, stewards, and army cooks also boarded with civilians, crowding dwellings furthermore. William Roulette testified that Union medical officers used "the whole business" on his farm, occupying his "House, Barn and outbuildings for Hospital purposes."[24]

When injured men from IX Corps filled Henry B. Rohrback's house, Martha Ada Mumma Thomas recalled that her family was "all crowded into a bedroom in the rear." She remembered that "the kitchen was in use by the army cooks . . . and [we] did not know what was taking place." John P. Smith described his parents' house in Sharpsburg village, writing, "Two rooms in the house . . . were used by the Federal Army, one as a hospital, the other by the ladies of the Relief Association." Hosting twenty patients and six volunteers, the Smiths occupied what little space remained in the dwelling.[25]

Smaller families may have adapted to the temporary arrangement, but many households included five to ten children, extended family members, slaves, and domestic help. Confining such groups into small spaces created cramped conditions. This inconvenience paled in comparison to what the wounded men endured, but it was uncomfortable, nonetheless.

At the home of Stephen P. and Maria Grove, "The family were allowed three [of ten] rooms, and everything on the place was used as a hospital." The Groves' household included three children and five slaves. Further crowding their allocated space, Stephen P. Grove testified that "several of my neighbors also took shelter in my house." These guests may have been villagers displaced by artillery destruction or hospital eviction. It's unknown how long the dislocated neighbors stayed with the Groves, but surgeons and their patients reportedly boarded inside the dwelling house for 92 days.[26]

---

23 Claims of Catherine Showman (*RG* 92, F-1176) and Susan Hoffman (*RG* 123, No. 1318).

24 Johnson, *BA*, 116-117; Claims of William Roulette (No. 4299 and F-618).

25 Hildebrand, "Recollections of Martha Ada Thomas;" Smith, "Reminiscences of Sharpsburg."

26 Claim of Stephen P. Grove (*RG* 123, No. 7354).

These living arrangements were temporary, but tensions sometimes arose. One example involved Jeptha Taylor. The young miller lived in Keedysville with his wife, Mary, and a one-year-old daughter. When an army surgeon named Dr. Chamberlain commandeered Taylor's mill complex, Jeptha and Mary "kindly gave permission." However, when Taylor asked to keep two rooms for his family, Dr. Chamberlain refused. Worse, the doctor "forcibly took possession" of the couple's private space and "used insulting and abusive language to his [Taylor's] wife."

As the Taylors adapted to their stressful living arrangement, they learned that Chamberlain was a drunk. Not only did the surgeon intoxicate himself while performing surgeries, but he allowed his staff to drink freely, as well. On one occasion, Chamberlain "exposed his person [penis]" to Mary Taylor, and then urinated "on a foot bridge over the mill race" by the Taylors' front door.[27]

After filling battlefield-area buildings, hospital workers carried hundreds of wounded men onto lawns, farm fields, and orchards. The medical department needed to bed these outdoor patients but lacked cots and bedsteads in the battle's immediate aftermath. To remedy the situation, the AOP medical department targeted Sharpsburg's straw supply.

Straw, the threshed stalks of wheat and other cereal grains, served multiple purposes to Washington County residents. They scattered it to bed animals and stuffed it into mattresses and ticks. They also weaved straw into rugs and thatched it on roofs.

Antietam Valley farmers in 1862 harvested two types of straw: wheat and rye. The 1860 agricultural schedule for Sharpsburg reported nearly 67,000 bushels of wheat, compared to 4,800 bushels of rye. Given that almost every farmer in the area raised the grains, straw gleaned from threshing served families' financial and practical purposes. During and after the battle, though, hospital forces descended upon farmsteads and seized mass quantities of straw. They layered the dried plant on floors of houses, barns, and churches and spread it on farm fields for patients placed outdoors.[28]

---

27 Nelson, *As Grain Falls Before the Reaper*, 51-52. Nelson cited two letters from A. J. Atkinson to Dr. Jonathan Letterman dated October 20 and October 28, 1862, Medical Officers Files, *RG* 94, *NA*. The identity of Dr. Chamberlain is not known. Atkinson worked under Chamberlain and declared the surgeon "drunk and unfit to administer medicine."

28 1860 Federal census, non-population schedule 4, productions of agriculture, Sharpsburg District. Hereafter cited as the 1860 agricultural schedule; The 1862 market value is based on dozens of Sharpsburg-area claims involving losses of wheat and rye. Land record IN 11 / 458 cites an 1856 bill of sale that included straw carpet, and September 1862 photographs show

David Spong alleged that U.S. forces seized a portion of his wheat straw "for the use of the hospitals in the vicinity." Stephen P. Grove sought repayment for "3 Tons of Straw for wounded . . . taken by Dr. Rauch." Also, John J. Keedy, who briefly hosted McClellan's headquarters, lost "two tons straw, rye straw . . . used for as bedding for wounded soldiers."[29]

Correspondent Charles Coffin, surveying Susan Hoffman's farm, observed, "it was an appalling sight . . . the wounded were lying in rows waiting their turn at the surgeon's tables. The hospital stewards had a corps of men distributing straw over the field for their comfort." When Letterman's department finally ceased hospital operations on the farm, Hoffman claimed to have lost twenty tons of straw.[30]

On other farms, AOP hospital attendants confiscated unthreshed grains. Farmers coveted these cereals because the stalks still contained kernels intended for market sale and family flour. Still, unthreshed wheat and rye offered more density than threshed straw and thus served as a makeshift solution for bedding and sheltering the wounded.

Medical forces seized unthreshed wheat on William Roulette's farm to construct "temporary straw sheds" to shelter "hundreds of wounded and dying men." Otho B. Smith tenanted the farm of his father, Dr. Otho J. Smith. According to a postwar investigation, hospital staff seized Otho B. Smith's unthreshed wheat to bed the patients. Not only did blood soak the bedding, but surgeons poured water on wounds, causing the runoff to spill onto the valuable grain. Moreover, the investigation of Smith's claim found that "the blood of the wounded and the water used to cool their wounds caused the wheat in the straw . . . to spoil."

Rather than make the ailing soldiers sleep on wet bedding, Smith's "straw was changed every day and the dirty straw was burned." Additionally, hospital attendants confiscated "a large amount of wheat in the straw . . . to make temporary

---

straw-thatched roofs in the Sharpsburg-Keedysville area. See Alexander Gardner, photographer. *Keedysville, Md., vicinity. Smith's barn, used as a hospital after the battle of Antietam.* Keedysville Maryland United States, 1862. September. Photograph, *LC*, https://www.loc.gov/item/2018666244/. See also James F. Gibson, photographer. *Antietam, Maryland. Bridge across the Antietam. Northeast view.* United States, 1862. Sept. Photograph, *LC*, https://www.loc.gov/item/2018671863/; Johnson, *BA*, 94. Alex Davis remarked that the roof of Jacob Nicodemus's barn in 1862 "was thatched with rye straw."

29 Claims of David Spong (*RG* 92, Entry 797, Book 54, Box 15, Claim 54-1462), Stephen P. Grove (No. 7354), John J. Keedy (54-1488), Catherine Showman (F-1185), John Otto (G-1857), and Samuel I. Piper (D-2392). The six claimants reported a combined loss of 98 tons of straw. U.S. forces used the straw as bedding in camps and field hospitals.

30 Claim of Susan Hoffman (No. 1318).

sheds for the wounded and sick that could not be accommodated in the buildings." Medical forces used the wheat to make "roof shanties" and "shelter roofs" for the patients.

Otho B. Smith watched his grain supply shrink daily. He ultimately lost sixteen tons of wheat straw—a sizeable portion that detracted from his earnings as a tenant farmer.[31]

On the farm of George Line, U.S. forces took "five tons of straw . . . to lay the wounded on." The quantity, though, was not sufficient to bed the hundreds of patients on Line's farm. As a result, Dr. James King ordered attendants to seize unthreshed wheat from the barn as "bedding for the wounded." As opposed to straw, the expensive grain was "cool and pliable to the body [and] made a most beneficial bed." Ultimately, George Line lost 350 bushels because "wheat used in that way was completely ruined, it being soaked with blood and water."[32]

*   *   *

To be sure, the AOP's medical supply shortage from September 16–23, 1862, impacted the Sharpsburg community on many levels.

"For the first few days" after the battle, Dr. Jonathan Letterman reported, "the supplies of some articles became scanty, and in some instances very much so." Making matters worse, Letterman added, large amounts of hospital stores "had been lost and in various ways wasted, and not unfrequently all the supplies for a regiment had been thrown away for want of transportation, and, of course were not on hand when wanted." The deficiency burdened surgeons responsible for thousands of unfortunates. "The fear of the supplies becoming exhausted," Letterman wrote, "for the difficulty in procuring them was well known, caused uneasiness on the part of some medical officers."

---

31 Bosbyshell, *Pennsylvania at Antietam*, 165; Claim of Otho B. Smith (*RG* 92, F-1432). Smith salvaged some of his unthreshed wheat straw because blood did not tarnish it. However, his sixteen tons of threshed straw, used as bedding, was allegedly ruined; Alexander Gardner, photographer, Keedysville, *Maryland vicinity. Straw huts erected on Smith's farm used as a hospital after the battle of Antietam*, United States, 1862. Sept. Photograph, LC, https://www.loc.gov/item/2018671857/.

32 Claims of George Line (*RG* 92, F-1186 and F-1187); Based on the vast amount of straw claimed by battlefield-area residents, 100 tons is a conservative estimate. Susan Hoffman and Otho B. Smith lost a combined 36 tons of straw for hospital purposes, and there were more than one hundred other farmers in the vicinity. In addition, this 100-ton estimate does not include straw seized by soldiers for bedding in camps.

Army surgeons rapidly expended their on-hand items and sorely lacked bandages, dressing, and tourniquets. The doctors could not afford to wait for the quartermaster department to deliver supplies from Monocacy Junction because hundreds of men needed immediate care. So what was the stop-gap solution? Sharpsburg.

Unofficially, the medical department turned the battlefield's community into an emergency supply depot. Hospital forces entered dozens of homes, seizing clothing, bedding, and other household items. They shredded the civilians' cloth into bandages and dressing, scraped it into lint, used it as tourniquets, or gave it to patients lacking clean garments.[33]

Alex Davis recalled, "The soldiers had taken every stitch of mine and the old man's clothing, and they'd torn up the old woman's clothing and used it for bandages." Joseph Poffenberger, Samuel D. Piper, and William Roulette alleged that armed forces took all the clothing in their homes. The three farmers estimated their losses at about $100 each, which converts in modern U.S. currency to roughly $2,800. Similarly, Catherine Avey Highbarger claimed the loss of "clothing and beading" valued at $102.25. This amount implies that troops took all she owned.[34]

Dozens of civilians listed clothing in their claims. The items included calico dresses, cassimere pants, capes, veils, and a roundabout jacket. Other residents listed childrens' clothing in their claims, along with fur coats and ladies' undergarments. Mary Ellen Piper complained, "Our clothing was taken, and what they could not take was torn up." She described some of the missing items as "stockings, shawls, dresses, bonnets."[35]

---

33 Official report of Dr. Jonathan Letterman, *OR*, vol. 19, 1:109, 113; Fay, War Papers, 47; Steiner, *Report of Lewis H. Steiner, M.D.*, 34. The U.S. Sanitary Commission and other relief agencies partially remedied Dr. Letterman's supply shortage. The agencies delivered food, clothing, bandages, bedding, and medicines to Antietam's hospitals. These provisions, though, according to Dr. Elisha Harris, did not arrive in sufficient quantity until "eight days from the occupancy of the field of Antietam by our force."

34 Johnson, *BA*, 100; Claims of Joseph Poffenberger (No. 1300), Samuel D. Piper (Claims D-2392 & D-2393), and William Roulette (No. 4299); Williamson, *PPT*; Claim of Catherine Highbarger (*RG* 92, Entry 843, Box 772, Book 304, Claim 254). Genealogical and census records support that the claimant was Catherine Avey Highbarger, daughter of Jacob Avey, Sr. and widow of Joseph Highbarger, who died in 1854. She may be the same person as Kate Avey, listed in her parents' dwelling in the 1860 census. Supporting this argument, Catherine Highbarger's claim cites that her 1862 residence was a "House & farm being on part of the battle field."

35 Claim of George Roderick (*RG* 92, Entry 843, Box 772, Book 304, Claim 232); Claim of Joanna Kidwiler (*RG* 92, Entry 843, Box 772, Book 304, Claim 252); Claims of Samuel

Nurse Anna Holstein recalled that a great need for patients after the battle was "beds, pillows, clothing, covering." Similar to civilian clothing, medical staff addressed the shortage by taking bedding from citizens.

When troops began carrying away Henry Piper's linens, he "prevailed on these soldiers to leave some of the bedding in the home for the use of my family." Soldiers later returned some of the items. Ultimately, though, the family lost coverlids, quilts, woolen blankets, and feather pillows. These items, Henry Piper explained, were all "taken for the use and comfort of wounded in the hospitals near by."[36]

Similarly, Dr. Letterman's men confiscated chaff ticks from the home of Samuel Poffenberger and took sheets from William Unger, which they "used for bandage[s]." When Alex Davis returned home, he discovered that "we had no beds or and no bed-clothing. There wa'nt a pillow in the house, and no sheets, no blankets, no quilts or coverlids. There was only bedticks—just them left." Daniel and Levi Middlekauff swore under oath that their parents' "blankets were taken away entirely" by hospital personnel. The losses included "9 bed quilts"—sentimental coverlets that had been in the Middlekauff family for years—which were "torn and used to bandage the sick and wounded."[37]

Soldiers also seized textiles for hospital needs. Odd as this may appear, medical officers at the Battle of Fredericksburg "appropriated supplies of all kinds in the town." One surgeon recalled finding "a large quantity of ribbons," which he used to treat the wounds of his patients.[38]

After the Battle of Antietam, Confederate troops allegedly took from Henry Piper "every stich of muslin, linen and calico . . . for binding up their wounds." In addition, U.S. forces took muslin from the homes of Joanna Kidwiler and George Roderick. They also carried away calico and flannel from Joseph Poffenberger's dwelling. For families like the Poffenbergers, who lost considerable amounts of

---

Poffenberger (F-1434) and Susan Kennedy (F-865); Anna Cueto, curator of the Washington County Historical Society, email message to author, June 20, 2017. Ms. Cueto helped to identify several items listed in Sharpsburg's war claims. Cassimere was a popular nineteenth-century wool fabric; E. P. to Sally Farran. October 4, 1862, *Dan Masters' Civil War Chronicles.*

36 Holstein, *Three Years in Field Hospitals,* 16; Claim of Henry Piper (*RG* 92, Book 304, Claim 244).

37 Claims of Samuel Poffenberger (F-1434) and William Unger (*RG* 92, Entry 843, Box 771, Claim 181); Johnson, *BA,* 100; Claim of John C. Middlekauff (*RG* 123, No. 329).

38 Duncan, *The Medical Department,* Chapter VI, 20.

clothing, the appropriation of fabrics may have deprived them of the means to make new garments.[39]

Field hospitals were so short of supplies that surgeons used any materials available. Medical staff seized window curtains from the homes of Barney Houser, Ephraim Geeting, and Samuel D. Piper. From the windows of Samuel Poffenberger's house, troops tore down oil cloth window blinds and twenty-two paper blinds.[40]

Claimants lost table covers, bed valances, cloth napkins, and towels. Soldiers also took carpeting from the residents. Among them, Elijah Avey claimed the loss of wool carpet and rag carpet. Bishop John Russell noted that 45 yards of his carpeting was "used and taken away" by personnel at the Locust Spring hospital. On their Mount Airy farm, Stephen P. Grove and his wife, Maria, willingly "cut up their Brussels carpet for the sick and wounded."[41]

Most of the civilian claims relating to Antietam do not specify whether or not troops took items for U.S. hospital purposes. Evidence proves that soldiers from both armies carried off household items for personal gratification and, without a doubt, Confederate medical personnel confiscated supplies from Sharpsburg's homes to treat the Southern wounded. Nonetheless, the sweeping appropriations deprived countless families of clothing, bedding, and textiles.

Adding to the civilians' hardships, hospital personnel inflicted various damages to buildings. For example, surgeries spilled blood onto the floors of homes and churches. George Line, Samuel Poffenberger, and John L. Mayer reported blood-related damages to their houses. Also, Steven P. Grove testified that his walls were "defaced by blood stains." At the Dunker Church, a soldier

39 Bosbyshell, *Pennsylvania at Antietam*, 164; Claims of Joanna Kidwiler (Book 304, Claim 252) and George Roderick (Book 304, Claim 232); Claim of Joseph Poffenberger (No. 1300).

40 Barney Houser, inventory of losses, Robert Eschbach collection, courtesy Robert Eschbach, hereafter cited as *Houser's Account*. For further reading on Barney Houser's losses, see John Banks, "What Army Borrowed From Private Barney Houser at Antietam," blog, *John Banks' Civil War Blog*, May 21, 2013, http://john-banks.blogspot.com/2013/05/what-army-borrowed-from-private-barney.html; Geeting and Russell accounts, UMLA. Ephraim Geeting was Bishop John Russell's son-in-law; Claim of Samuel D. Piper (Piper, *Piper Family History*). Piper listed the loss of curtains in a "Copy of Bill sent to the U.S. Government;" Claim of Samuel Poffenberger (F-1434).

41 Claim of Elijah Avey (Book 304, Claim 242); Geeting and Russell accounts, UMLA, Claim of Stephen P. Grove (No. 7354).

recalled that blood "laid thick and hard all over the floor and pews and furniture for weeks."[42]

In addition to blood, pus stained the floors of buildings. Many wounds became swollen with painful abscesses, requiring surgeons to drain the infected matter. One army doctor, tending to a patient in a Sharpsburg church, "opened the leg above the knee . . . and evacuated more than a pint of pus." At another field hospital earlier in 1862, the incised wound of a septic arthritis patient gushed "about two quarts of pus." Several miles north of Sharpsburg, a Williamsport resident found the floor of one church "in bad shape and horribly stained" because "the pus from the wounded soldiers went on the floor." Caretakers "threw chloride of lime" on the floor, hoping to remove the discoloration, but the combination of pus and lime "made stains which never came out."[43]

At some locations, hospital personnel befouled or damaged home interiors. Samuel Michael ranted, "The hospital was continued in our parlor for several weeks. I do not know how many has died in it . . . it looks like a hog pen." In addition, the floors of William Roulette's house were "covered with the blood and dirt and litter of a field hospital."[44]

Before the battle, Frederick Wyand's new store was "regarded as the best house in Keedysville." Afterward, hospital personnel "left it filthy, and damaged it." Similar issues occurred in Susan Hoffman's home. Hospital use allegedly caused "hard damage" to the dwelling. Hoffman's son recalled that the house "was not fit for occupation for a period of six months because it had to be re-papered, repainted and renovated generally."

Medical workers spared John Otto's house from such damages. The residents, notwithstanding, came home to a shocking surprise. Hilary Watson recounted that

---

42 Claims of George Line (F-1186 and F-1187), Samuel Poffenberger (F-1434), John L. Mayer (No. 8586), and Stephen P. Grove (*RG* 123, No. 7354); Schmidt and Barkley, *September Mourn*, 44-45.

43 Nelson, *As Grain Falls Before the Reaper*, 58-64; Bonnie Brice Dowart, "Disease in the Civil War," online article, Essential Civil War Curriculum, https://www.essentialcivilwar curriculum.com/disease-in-the-civil-war.html; Nelson, *As Grain Falls Before the Reaper*, 71-72. Nelson noted that the stain might have happened during the Gettysburg Campaign, although minor skirmishing occurred in Williamsport during the Antietam Campaign.

44 Samuel Michael to David Michael, November 27, 1862, WMR; Stevens, *Souvenir of Excursion to Battlefields*, 64-65.

their home "had been used as a hospital, and whatever had been left in it was gone."[45]

*   *   *

The community had good reason to be upset with the Northern and Southern armies. Military and medical forces had damaged buildings, confiscated possessions, and drove families from their domains. Nevertheless, evidence shows that most of the Sharpsburg-area civilians pitched into the crisis to help the wounded soldiers.

Their volunteering took many forms. Some residents cooked and nursed, while others scraped lint or hauled supplies. Henry Piper stated that he and his family "did all we could for the wounded in the hospitals . . . people in the neighborhood & in the village took turns about in this work. I was in the hospitals on this business often." Piper's youngest daughter, Susan, helped "carry food to the Union soldiers in company with other ladies of the [German Reformed] congregation." In Keedysville, a Pennsylvania soldier recalled, "Here the boys were most liberally supplied with hot cakes and bread by Mr. John Cost, a good Union citizen of that place, and from where Captain Byrnes got liquor enough to give the men a ration."

On the south end of the battlefield, Jacob F. Miller's family cooked for Dr. Theodore Dimon and his patients of the 2nd Maryland Infantry. Next door, Martha Rohrback "worked with her assistants all night . . . they baked bread in the big brick oven all day and gave it out to the soldiers, both blue and gray."[46]

North of the battlefield, Barbara Pry and her mother "baked bread day after day to feed the sufferers." Elias Eakle testified that he "kept a man six weeks at my house, he had his leg broke and [I] attended to him in my room." Another family fed sixty convalescents, buying flour at their own expense to make bread. One

---

45 Claims of Frederick Wyand (*RG* 123, Entry 22, Box 1625, Case No. 14112) and Susan Hoffman (No. 1318).

46 Claim of Henry Piper (No. 445); Claim of the Sharpsburg German Reformed Church (*RG* 123, Entry 22, Box 1208, Case No. 11014); Evan Morrison Woodward, *Our Campaigns: or, The marches, bivouacs, battles, incidents of camp life and history of our regiment during its three years term of service* (Philadelphia, 1865), 201; Schildt, *Drums Along the Antietam*, 165; Hildebrand, "Recollections of Martha Ada Thomas."

Elizabeth (Keedy) and Henry Piper were among the local civilians who volunteered at field hospitals after the battle. *Sharpsburg Historical Society*

person in the household recalled that her father "had a fine flock of sheep at that time and killed them all to feed the sick."[47]

On Henry F. Neikirk's farm, Martha Schlosser gave up her tenant house to accommodate the sufferers. At night, she "went to one of the neighbors & during day time she was at her house cooking for the attendant and nursing the wounded." Martha's sympathies for the ailing men hit home. Her only son, Henry Schlosser, moved to Illinois before the war. Shortly before the Antietam battle, he enlisted in the 92nd Illinois Infantry. Surely missing her boy, one can picture Martha's thoughts while nursing the wounded lads inside her home. One may also imagine her heartbreak upon learning that Confederates captured Henry and sent him to his eventual death at the Andersonville military prison in Georgia.[48]

47 Reilly, *BOA*; Claim of Elias Eakle (*RG* 92, Entry 812, Box 91, Claim F-1523); Williams, HWC, vol. 1, 2:361. Williams interviewed an unidentified woman. In 1862, she was a child living with her family "not far from the northern limit of Antietam battlefield."

48 Claim of Martha Schlosser (*RG* 92, Entry 843, Box 771, Claim 170). Schlosser filed her losses in the claim of her brother, Henry F. Neikirk (H-4108 and H-4109). The 1850 Federal census for Subdivision 2, Washington County (encompassing Sharpsburg), lists Henry Schlosser next to Henry F. Neikirk in Dwelling #801. The Federal 1860 census for Foreston, Illinois, places Henry in his half-brother's household, Dwelling #3364. Martha Schlosser's claim cites that her son served in the 115th Illinois and "fell victim to the horrors of Belle Isle."

Sharpsburg villagers did their part in volunteering, as well. Jane Show Bolinger "went out upon the battlefield and administered to the wants of the injured and dying." When later asked if he aided the Union army, John Grice replied, "Certainly; I think I done as much in the hospital as any man." Jacob Avey, Sr. helped by "feeding the Federal soldiers and hauling them around in his hack." John Kretzer's family boarded Colonel John Franklin Farnsworth of the 8th Illinois Cavalry. Farnsworth convalesced with the Kretzers for several weeks while suffering from debilitating varicose veins.[49]

The dire circumstances forced some civilians to cast aside political differences. In Jacob H. Grove's house, Dr. A. A. Biggs, a fervent Unionist, teamed up with Grove, a staunch Democrat who hosted Robert E. Lee days earlier. Biggs worked at Grove's home as surgeon-in-charge. Grove and his family, meanwhile, nursed wounded men of the U.S. army. A Union lieutenant recalled that Grove cared for the Federals "during the whole time they remained in his house, as so much as a gentleman possibly could do." Among the patients was "a N.Y. Zouave . . . who was shot through the knee." Jacob H. Grove and his family supposedly nursed the New Yorker for three months.[50]

Other Sharpsburg residents suspended their political sentiments to aid the soldiers. Dr. Otho J. Smith, a pro-South Democrat, treated U.S. patients at his farm near the Upper Bridge. One witness recounted that Dr. Smith devoted time to "saving of the lives of the wounded federals." In one instance, "a young soldier of some Ohio Regt. was shot in the bowels, and . . . [was] given up by the federal surgeons." Dr. Smith, however, "took charge of the case & after untold labor &c, saved the man."

Military records show that Corporal Henry Schlosser enlisted in the 92nd Illinois in August 1862, was captured at Dug Gap in the Chickamauga Campaign, and died at Andersonville on June 28, 1864. Schlosser is buried at Andersonville National Cemetery in grave number #2585. See the roster of the 92nd Illinois, Co. E., 343, archived at Civil War Index, https://civilwarindex.com/armyil/rosters/92nd_il_infantry_roster.pdf. See also "Henry Schlosser," *CWSS*, https://www.nps.gov/civilwar/search-soldiers-detail.htm?soldierId= B84C87CD-DC7A-DF11-BF36-B8AC6F5D926A.

49 "Wedded 65 Years," *Pittsburgh Press*, December 4, 1927, 101. The article spotlights Jane Show and John C. Bolinger, who lived in Sharpsburg in 1862. The couple married in 1863. Jane was the daughter of Samuel and Elizabeth Show, who owned town lots 40 and 41 in 1862. See land records IN 16 / 313 and IN 17 / 496; Claims of John Grice (No. 5872), Jacob Avey, Sr. (No. 9908) and John Kretzer (*RG* 92, Entry 797, Box 54, Claim 54-1471); Hard, *History of the Eighth*, 196. For details on Farnsworth's illness, see Jack D. Welsh, *Medical Histories of Union Generals* (Kent, Ohio, 1996), 113-114.

50 Claim of Jacob H. Grove (*RG* 123, No. 1267).

North of Sharpsburg, Joseph Stonebraker—whose family sympathized with the South—boarded seventeen sick men from the 145th Pennsylvania and 8th New York. Another Southern-leaning Democrat, Daniel Poffenberger, nursed a U.S. lieutenant for "three or four weeks." Poffenberger also "filled some several hundred ticks for the Union Hospital." He stuffed the cloth sacks with his own straw and received no payment for his services.[51]

The inhabitants ministered to Rebel patients, as well. Susan Lopp Santman, the wife of a Union private, saw "many Confederate soldiers lying about on the ground near the Grove warehouse." She recounted that "some were dead, others were dying while still others, only slightly wounded, were weak from lack of food." Despite her U.S. sympathies, Susan helped the Southern sufferers. She and other volunteers left Grove's Landing, ignoring protests from "a man from Sharpsburg with Union convictions [who] told us we should not help the 'Rebels.'" Reaching town, Susan discovered that "the shells exploding in the village had killed a large number of chickens. Some of these were brought to us and I remember that we made chicken broth." The ladies gathered what flour they could find and "made quite a large quantity of bread in a bake oven." When Susan delivered the food to Grove's Landing, the famished Confederates "ate it with big gulps."[52]

To expedite the shipment of supplies to field hospitals, medical officers leaned on the community for help. As a result, several civilians volunteered their time, wagons, and horses to travel afar and pick up hospital provisions.

Jacob Nicodemus of Springvale transported "supplies from Hagerstown to Cold Spring hospital near Keedysville." The aged farmer performed the service for twenty days without pay. Samuel Poffenberger hauled "hospital stores for Smoketown Hospital" with his four-horse team. Poffenberger's near-neighbor, Adam Showman, made "nine trips hauling from Hagerstown to Smoketown Hospital." Showman "started every day at 4 o'clock in the morning and got back at 9 o'clock p.m." He drove his "six horses and his wagon" twenty-four miles

---

51 Claim of Otho J. Smith (*RG* 92, Book K, Box 157A, Claim K-1565); Claim of Joseph Stonebraker (*RG* 92, Entry 843, Box 771, Claim 173). Joseph Stonebraker of the Bakersville area is not to be confused with Joseph R. Stonebraker, author of *A Rebel of '61*. The 1860 Federal census lists the former in Tilghmanton, Dwelling #1108. The latter lived with his parents in Funkstown, Dwelling #833; Claim of Daniel Poffenberger (No. 1505).

52 "Aged Woman Tells of Giving Food to Antietam Soldiers," *Morning Herald*, July 10, 1937, 10C.

round-trip. Additionally, Showman paid the Hagerstown Pike tolls out of his pocket while furnishing "his own board and forage."[53]

Stephen P. Grove made thirty-two trips to Hagerstown to procure supplies for the hospital on his farm. In addition, Grove testified that he and his wife "labored and toiled" for the wounded. He added, "We gave them food, beds as far as we could, tore up our fine carpets for their sake and kept back nothing which could add to their comfort." Grove remarked that he "cheerfully furnished them with a barn nearly full of hay, wheat, oats, also fuel—and in fact everything raised on my farm cattle included."[54]

Not all citizens aided the wounded. Sergeant Jonathan Stowe of the 15th Massachusetts, suffering from infection after losing his leg, lay ailing among other unfortunates in Susan Hoffman's barn. Stowe complained, "Hard to get nurses . . . people come in from all parts of the country. Stare at us but do not find time to do anything." It's unknown if Stowe referred to local inhabitants or civilians from outlying towns. Nonetheless, some visitors to Antietam's field infirmaries kept their distance from the suffering men.

At least one family protested against the military medical takeover. After Federal hospital authorities impressed Adam Michael's home, the Southern-leaning Democrats resisted. "On Monday they forced a hospital in our house," Samuel Michael wrote to his brother. "Kate and Mother fought them hard." The Michaels eventually relented, and U.S. forces filled the home with patients.[55]

Ultimately, evidence implies that most inhabitants living near the Antietam battlefield ministered to the sufferers of both armies. The civilians' deeds did not go unnoticed. General Joseph Hooker recognized Samuel Pry for "his attentions

53 Duncan, *The Medical Department*, Chapter V, 34. Duncan noted that the civilians' hauling helped the ambulance corps devote its attention to the wounded; Claims of Jacob Nicodemus of Springvale (G-1854, G-1855, and F-613). "Cold Spring" was another name for the Locust Spring hospital on Russell's farm. Jacob was the son of Valentine Nicodemus. He is not to be confused with another Jacob Nicodemus, son of Conrad Nicodemus, who lived near the Antietam battlefield in 1862. Land records and war claims differentiate the two cousins as "Jacob of V" and "Jacob of C." For this study, the two men are cited as Jacob of Springvale and Jacob of Sharpsburg; Claims of Samuel Poffenberger (F-1434) and Catherine Showman (F-1176). Adam Showman was the son of Catherine Showman.

54 Claim of Stephen P. Grove (*RG* 123, No. 7354). Testimony in the claim cites that Dr. John Henry Rauch supervised the field hospital on Grove's Mount Airy farm.

55 Nelson, *As Grain Falls Before the Reaper*, 12-13; Samuel Michael to David Michael, November 27, 1862, WMR.

Citizen volunteers assisting the wounded in the field of Battle. Sketch by Alfred R. Waud.
Library of Congress

and liberal kindness to the wounded and sick of our army." Dr. Jonathan Letterman reported that the "kindness exhibited by the people" facilitated the medical department's care of Antietam's patients. A soldier in the 13th Massachusetts praised "the generosity shown by the people." He recalled that citizens not only brought "food and supplies from their homes" for the wounded, "but for the men who had escaped that misfortune."[56]

Three days after the battle, Dr. C. R. Agnew, a member of the U.S. Sanitary Commission, reported that the wounded were "receiving the kind service of the farmers' families." Dr. Louis C. Duncan also commended Sharpsburg's civilians. "Judged by the commendatory notices," Duncan wrote, "the people here were more generous to the sick and wounded of this army than those in [Gettysburg] Pennsylvania the next year."

56 Claim of Samuel Pry (81-1489). Pry's case file contains a letter from General Joseph Hooker to Montgomery C. Meigs, dated July 2, 1866. The letter pertains to Pry's property losses at Antietam; Official report of Jonathan Letterman, *OR*, vol. 19, 1:112; Davis, *Three Years in the Army*, 150.

Newspaper correspondents also praised the citizenry. After the battle, one journalist observed that "nearly the whole population" ministered to the wounded. A Hagerstown reporter commented that Confederate patients received "kind treatment . . . from our own surgeons, as well as from benevolent citizens." Similarly, a New York Tribune correspondent reported, "The inhabitants in all these villages are laboring day and night to relieve the dying and the suffering. A more Christian people, in the practical significance of that word, I never saw."[57]

* * *

Civilians witnessed horrible sights at Antietam's hospitals. Mary Ellen Piper "stopped a few minutes to look at the wounded" and found it "sickening in the extreme." At Grove's Landing, Susan Lopp Santman watched surgeons perform "emergency operations out in the open and in the warehouse." In her later years, Susan reflected that she "would like to forget some of the more terrible things connected with the battle which she saw."

When Angela Kirkham Davis and other volunteers arrived on George Line's farm after the battle, "a ghastly gruesome sight met our gaze," Davis wrote. "About two thousand pallid, death-like looking men, mangled, bleeding and torn, were lying all around on the ground." Surgeons amputated limbs in the open. Nearby, "a pile of severed hands, arms and legs [was] lying on the ground." Davis described it as a "horrible and sickening scene to behold such as I wish to never see again." Struggling to stomach the images, she recalled, "I staggered from the carriage but exercising all of my will power, kept from fainting."[58]

Limb amputations were a common sight at Antietam's hospitals. During the battle, Minie balls, made of soft lead, shattered bones and shredded soft tissue. Historian John Nelson wrote of Minie ball wounds, "The destruction was often so complete that surgeons had no chance of reconstructing a limb. Out would come the dirty saw, and there would go the appendage." Other lead projectiles, such as

---

57 Hosmer, *Report of the Delegates*, 10-11; Duncan, *The Medical Department*, Chapter V, 21; "Louis Caspar Duncan, M.D.," U.S. Army Medical Department, Office of Medical History. Accessed at https://history.amedd.army.mil/booksdocs/rev/MedMen/LouisCDuncan.html; *The Valley Register*, September 26, 1862, 2A; *HFTL*, November 5, 1862, 2C; *New York Tribune*, September 18, 1862.

58 E. P. to Sally Farran. October 4, 1862, *Dan Masters' Civil War Chronicles*; "Aged Woman Tells of Giving Food to Antietam Soldiers;" Angela Kirkham Davis, "War Reminiscences," letter, WMR, 40. Davis and the other volunteers lived in Funkstown, located between Hagerstown and Boonsboro.

musket balls and case shot, caused similar damage. Consequently, doctors removed limbs from dozens of soldiers.[59]

In a few cases at Antietam, surgeons performed amputations without sedating the patient with chloroform vapors—making it an unimaginably painful procedure. A New York journalist on September 18 described a Confederate officer of the 27th Alabama enduring "the amputation of his leg without the use of chloroform." The correspondent observed, "Every muscle of his face was contracted, his jaws looked as if in a death spasm, but no sound of pain issued from him." Despite the patient's silence, he wore "an expression of physical agony."

Maria Hall, a volunteer nurse, entered a residence near the Sharpsburg battlefield and found "a surgeon operating at that hour without the merciful aid of chloroform. The supply was exhausted." Hall stepped outside to grab a bite of food, for she "had eaten nothing since breakfast." She found the meal, however, difficult to stomach on account of the amputation in progress. While Hall and others were "listening to the groans from the house," she recalled, "our hearts sickened, and the food and tears mingled."

Some army doctors chose to postpone surgeries until shipments of medicine arrived. On September 24, a member of the U.S. Sanitary Commission reported, "The want of chloroform was the most serious deficiency in the regular medical supplies and, as the result, amputations which should have been primary will now be secondary or impossible."[60]

Using what chloroform was available, army surgeons and Sharpsburg's physicians performed hundreds of operations. Dr. A. A. Biggs served as "the Surgeon in charge" at Jacob H. Grove's house, where "several amputations took

---

59 Terry Reimer, "Wounds, Ammunition, and Amputation," online article, National Museum of Civil War Medicine, November 9, 2007, http://www.civilwarmed.org/surgeons-call/amputation1/; Robert G. Slawson, "The Story of the Pile of Limbs," online article, National Museum of Civil War Medicine, December 6, 2018, http://www.civilwarmed.org/surgeons-call/limbs/; John H. Nelson, "Battle of Antietam: Union Surgeons and Civilian Volunteers Help the Wounded," HistoryNet, https://www.historynet.com/battle-of-antietam-union-surgeons-and-civilian-volunteers-help-the-wounded.htm.

60 Figg, *Where Men Only Dare To Go*, 48. Scharf in *HWM*, 1:252, also described the Alabaman's amputation, citing the *New York Tribune*, September 18, 1862; United States Sanitary Commission, "Appeal to the Public, With Letters Concerning Army Operations in the Relief Work of the Commission in Maryland (September 24, 1862)," *Documents of the U.S. Sanitary Commission* (New York, 1866), vol. 1, doc. 48, 12; John Banks, "Our Hearts Ached With Pity: A Journey with an Antietam Nurse," blog, *John Banks' Civil War Blog*, May 30, 2017, http://john-banks.blogspot.com/2017/05/our-hearts-ached-with-pity-journey-with.html. Banks's source was *The Republican*, (Springfield, MA), January 10, 1887.

place in the house." Christina Watson, one of Grove's slaves, recalled, "[T]he doctors was cuttin' off people's legs and arms and throwin' 'em out the do' jest like throwin' out old sticks."[61]

Antietam's medical teams, operating on a seemingly endless line of patients, tossed aside freshly severed limbs because no time allowed for hygienic disposal. Subsequently, body parts piled outside the field hospitals, rotting in the sun and attracting swarms of flies. "Just outside of the hospital tent," recalled a Union private, "was a pile of legs and arms about three feet in height." At a Confederate hospital near Sharpsburg village, a cannoneer remembered that "the heap of amputated legs and arms increased in size until it became several feet in height." On William Roulette's farm, "piles of amputated legs and arms were in evidence, inviting even from stolid hearts, commiseration, pity, tears."[62]

One family found a Confederate's arm "under the table in their parlor when they returned after the battle." Martha Rohrback, meanwhile, came home to find "a pile of arms and legs" on her porch. A soldier inside Mrs. Rohrback's home, Private Philo Stevens Pearce of the 11th Connecticut, assisted surgeons with amputations. Pearce recalled holding chloroform on the patient's faces, but the vapors soon made him dizzy. "I staggered outside," he recounted," "and when I came to my senses, I was laying on arms and legs."[63]

The severed limbs decomposed for days after the battle, fouling the air with stench. Daniel Holt, a surgeon with the 121st New York, complained in a letter home, "I have seen arms, legs, feet and hands lying in piles rotting in the blazing heat of a southern sky unburied and uncared for, and still the knife went steadily in its work adding to the putrid mess."

---

61 Claim of Jacob H. Grove (*RG* 123, No. 1267). Grove's son, Robert W. Grove, testified about Dr. Biggs and the amputations in the house; Johnson, *BA*, 111.

62 Mark Nickerson, "Recollections of the Civil War by a High Private in the Front Ranks," unpublished manuscript, U.S. Army Military History Institute, Brake Collection, Carlisle, PA (hereafter, USMHI); Moore, *The Story of a Cannoneer*, 159; Bosbyshell, *Pennsylvania at Antietam*, 164.

63 Ezra E. Stickley, "The Battle of Sharpsburg," 67; Hildebrand, "Recollections of Martha Ada Thomas;" Philo Stevens Pearce, "Civil War Memories of Mr. Philo Stevens Pearce," typescript, Harris-Elmore Public Library, Grace Luebke Local History Room, Elmore, OH, 14. This repository is hereafter cited as HEPL. For additional details on Private Stevens's experiences at Antietam, see John Banks, "Teenager's Antietam: Close Calls, Slumber on Amputated Limbs," blog, *John Banks' Civil War Blog*, September 15, 2018, http://john-banks.blogspot.com/2018/09/teens-antietam-close-calls-slumber-on.html.

Near the West Woods, resident Martin E. Snavely remembered seeing limbs "piled up several feet high at the Dunkard Church window where the amputating table sat." Church members reportedly "took wheel barrow loads of arms and legs" and buried them in the nearby woods. To expedite the removal, Union officers ordered troops "to burn or bury" the decaying limbs. Such disposal may have brought minor relief to the community, but the gruesome horrors in Antietam's hospitals continued.[64]

*   *   *

On September 22, 1862, army surgeon William Child wrote, "The days after the battle are a thousand times worse than the day of the battle . . . the dead appear sickening but they suffer no pain." On the contrary, he opined, "the poor wounded mutilated soldiers that yet have life and sensation make a most horrid picture." Anna Holstein concluded the same. The Pennsylvanian nurse worked in Sharpsburg's hospitals and needed few words to summarize her experience. "The name of Antietam," Holstein wrote, " is ever associated in my mind with scenes of horror."

As Dr. Child and Holstein alluded, Sharpsburg-area hospitals presented shockingly graphic scenes. Several accounts showcase what residents may have witnessed while aiding the wounded or hosting field infirmaries.[65]

While lying in a Keedysville home, Captain Norwood Hallowell recalled that surgeons "scooped out the maggots from my side and arm which had been generated by the wound." At another location, an Irish Brigade chaplain came across "one poor man with a bullet in his forehead, and his brains protruding from the hole made by the ball." The dying soldier "was speechless and deaf, and had lost his senses entirely."[66]

Dr. Theodore Dimon treated a patient "who was in an uncontrollably restless state . . . I had to strip him and wash him, for he was covered with faeces." The man died within the hour. West of Sharpsburg, a Georgian reported, "I write at a

---

64 Holt, *A Surgeon's Civil War*, 28; Reilly, *BOA*; Schmidt and Barkley, *September Mourn*, 44-45, 52.

65 William Child, *Letters From a Civil War Surgeon: The Letters of Dr. William Child of the Fifth New Hampshire Volunteers*. Transcribed by Timothy C. Sawyer, Betty Sawyer, Merrill C. Sawyer (Solon, Maine, 2001), 34; Holstein, *Three Years in Field Hospitals*, 11.

66 Norwood P. Hallowell, *Reminiscences Written for My Children by Request of Their Mother* (West Medford, MA, 1897), 18; William Corby, *Memoirs of Chaplain Life: Three Years with the Irish Brigade in the Army of the Potomac*, ed. Lawrence Frederick Kohl (New York, 1992), 113.

hospital in the midst of the wounded and dying. Amputated arms and legs, feet, fingers and hands cut off, puddles of human gore, and ghastly gaping wounds." Continuing, the Georgia journalist wrote, "There is a smell of death in the air, and the laboring surgeons are literally covered from head to foot with the blood of the sufferers."[67]

A reporter from Pennsylvania saw "men wounded in every conceivable manner, with shot and shell, in the head, body, arms and legs." A Confederate patient was missing "both eyes and . . . part of his nose." The reporter observed another man who "had been shot through the head just below the temples," but was seen "walking about the barn, talking with his companions and seemingly giving it little attention." Yet another soldier "had been struck with a piece of shell which carried away one side of his face and part of his skull." The patient was still alive, "but evidently could not last long."[68]

In Sharpsburg's German Reformed Church, Dr. E. M. McDowell recorded several unfortunate cases. From one soldier's wound oozed "a black serious unhealthy discharge." On another patient, lice crawled upon "ulcers on the scrotum which is swelled and purplish." Inspecting an amputee's limb, McDowell found the stump "covered with maggots, some of which had burrowed 2 or 3 inches up under the skin." The poor man, described as "filthy dirty," also had "shocking bedsores full of maggots."

Curiosity drove a Union rookie, Private Mark Nickerson, to peek inside a hospital tent near the Sharpsburg battlefield. One soldier's leg "had been taken off above the knee, and a surgeon and his assistant were taking up the arteries." Another man, Nickerson recounted, had his "eye gouged out by a piece of shell, while two doctors were consulting as to whether the eye would have to be taken out entirely or put back into place." Yet another patient suffered from a "bullet hole in his forehead." He was barely alive, the private wrote, "and it was a mistake to have brought him here." After seeing enough of the "horrors of war," Nickerson concluded, "I never had any desire . . . to look into a hospital tent after a battle."[69]

---

67 Nelson, *As Grain Falls Before the Reaper*, 34. Nelson cited James I. Robertson, "A Federal Surgeon in Sharpsburg," *Civil War History* (Kent, OH, 1960), vol. VI, No. II, 134-151; "Letter From Maryland," *Mobile* [AL] *Daily Advertiser and Register*, October 2, 1862.

68 *Altoona Tribune*, October 2, 1862.

69 Nelson, *As Grain Falls Before the Reaper*, 58-64; Nickerson, "Recollections of the Civil War," USAMHI.

When the Confederate army departed Sharpsburg on September 18, Private Randolph Shotwell passed a sergeant sitting in an ambulance. Upon closer inspection, Shotwell was horrified to discover that "the poor fellow's whole lower jaw had been knocked off, carrying tongue and teeth with it, leaving the moustache, clotted with blood; arching over a frightful chasm of tangled muscles and arteries."

A Philadelphia reporter visited the "Concentrating Hospital" in Sharpsburg village. Inside, Private William Kidd of the 16th Mississippi Infantry convalesced. The correspondent learned that grape shot destroyed Kidd's cheek, brow, nose, and right eye. His upper jaw "fell down over the lower jaw and chin, leaving his palate and throat exposed." Despite the shocking wound, the maimed Mississippian was "so far recovered as to walk the streets of Sharpsburg."[70]

With ghastly sights came horrid smells. Hospitals reeked of infected wounds, body odor, vomit, feces, chloroform, rotting limbs, and death. Several locations lacked bedpans. One soldier complained, "Very meager are accommodations—no chamber pots & nobody to find or rig one up. How ludicrous for 2 score amputated men to help themselves with diarrhea." On September 20, a hospital volunteer found that many "poor fellows, with broken and lacerated and broken thighs, had to be carried out of barns into the open fields to answer the call of nature."

Some of the wounds emitted a nauseating stench. A soldier in Susan Hoffman's barn observed, "The horrid smell from the mortifying limbs is nearly as bad as the whole we have to contend." After the battle, Jacob McGraw visited Henry B. Rohrback's farm and found General Isaac Rodman laying inside the house "in a dying condition." Rodman's wounds, McGraw recalled, "became so offensive" that the Rohrbacks "were obliged to set the dining table on the porch, as it was impossible to partake of food inside the house."[71]

By sharing homes with patients or volunteering in hospitals, families saw the suffering up close. The sounds were often distressing and heartbreaking.

A New York nurse, accompanied by the women and children of "a good farmer's house," ventured to the Dunker Church to help the injured soldiers.

---

70 Shotwell, *The Papers*, 1:358; *HFTL*, November 5, 1862, 2C. The "Concentrating Hospital" was St. Paul's Episcopal Church in Sharpsburg village, which housed wounded Confederates after the battle.

71 Gerrish and Hutchinson, *The Blue and the Gray*, 146; Nelson, *As Grain Falls Before the Reaper*, 12-13; Duncan, *The Medical Department*, Chapter V, 28; Frassanito, *Antietam: The Photographic Legacy*, 257; Fred W. Cross, "Gallant Officers at Antietam," *Morning Herald* [Hagerstown, MD], February 13, 1934, 8.

However, the nurse recalled, "[T]he shrieks and moans of the poor fellows who had been wounded were too much for us, so we were ordered to retreat." Mary Ellen Piper reflected, after visiting a hospital, "My heart bled to see human beings in such a state of suffering... you could hear nearly all of them calling their dear old mothers' names, or their wife, sister, or some other absent loved one."[72]

After Charles F. Johnson of IX Corps sought treatment on a Sharpsburg farm, he noted, "[T]he sights were terrible, but the sounds were more so... the groans of the poor fellows around me are heart sickening to the extreme." Another soldier, E. Livingston Allen, watched a hospitalized man in his throes of death, calling "Mother! Mother! MOTHER!" Allen described the affecting scene, writing, "Brave hearts trembled—strong men wept—indescribable emotions swept over mind and heart." Anna Holstein comforted a dying New Yorker in a Sharpsburg village hospital. When death approached, the boy's thoughts drifted to his family back home. "This will kill my mother," he exclaimed. "[O]h, break it gently to her."[73]

*   *   *

Hundreds of soldiers died in Antietam's hospitals. A conservative estimate suggests that 1,000–2,000 men succumbed to wounds or sickness in Sharpsburg-area homes, churches, and field infirmaries. Other sources propose higher mortality rates for the 17,300 wounded.[74]

---

72 Anna P. Erving, *Reminiscences of the Life a Nurse in Field, Hospital and Camp during the Civil War* (Newburgh, NY, 1904), 48; E. P. to Sally Farran. October 4, 1862, *Dan Masters' Civil War Chronicles.*

73 Ernst, *TATC*, 155. Ernst cited a letter written by Theodore J. Vanneman on September 18, 1862, ANBL; Johnson, *The Long Roll*, 196-197; E. Livingston Allen, *Descriptive Lecture: Both Sides of Army Life, the Grave and the Gay* (Poughkeepsie, NY), 1885, 2; Holstein, *Three Years in Field Hospitals*, 18.

74 "Confederate Soldiers Killed at Antietam," WHILBR, http://www.whilbr.org/ confederateSoldiers/index.aspx. WHILBR estimated that 20 percent of Antietam's 17,300 Union and Confederate wounded, or 3,460 men, may have died of wounds; F. R. Freemon, *Gangrene and Glory: Medical Care During the American Civil War* (Chicago, 2001), 215. Freemon wrote that, before Sep. 1862, wounded soldiers suffered a mortality rate of 25 percent. The number dropped to 13 percent thereafter; The Antietam National Battlefield estimated that 3,650 U.S. and C.S. soldiers died in action on Sep. 17. The 1864 S. G. Elliott Antietam battlefield burial map, NYPL, depicts the interment of 5,844 soldiers. While we cannot take Elliott's estimate at face value, one can surmise that his map's higher number of burials reflects soldiers who died of wounds or sickness after the battle; "The Army of the Potomac: Reports from the Various Camp Hospitals," *New York Times*, October 12, 1862. *The Times* referred to

As hospital deaths continued in the weeks following the battle, army personnel created small graveyards on the farms of Catherine Showman and Bishop John Russell. At the Methodist Episcopal Church in Sharpsburg, medical staff buried 29 Confederates in the adjoining Lot 135.

U.S. forces confiscated lumber from the community to make coffins for soldiers who died in hospitals. Henry F. Neikirk testified that he "had a pile of boards close to the barn, perhaps some 500 feet . . . it was used for coffins to bury the federal dead." On William M. Blackford's farm, Union troops loaded 1,400 feet of Blackford's plank into an army wagon. They explained to the farmer that they needed the lumber "for the use of the hospital for making caskets or coffins."

Medical staff inside Sharpsburg's Methodist Episcopal Church reportedly tore out the benches "to make coffins to bury the dead soldiers." In the town's Lutheran Church, a congregation member testified, "The benches were torn out and the seats and backs were used for making coffins for the soldiers, many of whom died in the church." The parishioner added that the ends of benches "were used for head boards to mark the head of the soldiers' graves in the Lutheran grave yard adjoining the church."[75]

It's impossible to gauge how the battle and its aftermath impacted the psychological health of the Sharpsburg community—especially children and teenagers. William Miller, seven years old in 1862, remembered seeing "amputating tables" on his front porch. The blood, he recalled, was "so thick against the walls for weeks after." Did young Miller witness the amputations? Did he watch soldiers suffer and die? Likewise, Frank H. Schell's September 1862 sketch shows a civilian child studying corpses in Bloody Lane. If the scene unfolded as depicted, what lasting impressions did it make on this young mind?

One of the patients in Philip Pry's home was Gen. Israel Richardson, who suffered from a mortal wound. A witness, referring to Richardson, "could hear his groans the whole time I was in the house." After the general died inside the

---

surgeon reports furnished by Jonathan Letterman. It reported the deaths of more than five hundred Union soldiers at various Sharpsburg-Keedysville hospitals.

75 Bowie List, 40-41; Reverend John A. Adams owned Lot 135 in 1862. See land records IN 8 / 248-249 and 87 / 583. The 1877 Sharpsburg village map depicts Lot 135 as vacant. Claims of Henry F. Neikirk (H-4108 and H-4109) and William M. Blackford (No. 1324); Scharf, HWM, 2:1210; Claim of the Lutheran Church of Sharpsburg (No. 4058).

MARYLAND AND PENNSYLVANIA FARMERS VISITING THE BATTLE-FIELD OF ANTIETAM WHILE THE NATIONAL TROOPS WERE BURTING THE DEAD AND CARRYING OFF THE WOUNDED, FRIDAY, SEPT. 19. FROM A SKETCH BY OUR SPECIAL ARTIST, MR. F. H. SCHELL.

Maryland and Pennsylvania farmers visiting the battle-field of Antietam while the National troops were burying the dead and carrying off the wounded. Sketch by Frank H. Schell.
Library of Congress

dwelling, oral history cites that the Prys' six young children "were afraid to go in the room afterward" and the space was "kept closed for years."[76]

William F. Blackford, 15 in 1862, lived near the battlefield on Miller's Sawmill Road. While visiting a hospital on Stephen P. Grove's farm, Blackford "found a North Carolina boy lying wounded on the ground just at the left of the kitchen door." After the Confederate complained of feeling cold, Blackford "helped him

76 Reilly, *BOA*. William Miller, a son of Michael Miller, lived in 1862 on the Daniel Miller farm near the East Woods; Schell, *Maryland and Pennsylvania Farmers Visiting the Battle-Field of Antietam While the National Troops Were Burying the Dead and Carrying Off the Wounded, LC*; Charles S. Wainwright, *A Diary of Battle: The Personal Journals of Colonel Charles S. Wainwright, 1861–1865*. ed. Allan Nevins (New York, 1962), 104. Wainwright described Richardson's suffering in a diary entry dated September 19, 1862; Walker and Kirkman, *Antietam Farmsteads*, 135-136; Fred W. Cross, scrapbook. Pry descendants showed Cross "the big east chamber where Gen. Richardson lay wounded and [died]."

into the kitchen and got him a seat near the fireplace." The two lads conversed, and the young soldier told Blackford about "his mother in far off North Carolina and said he wished he might see her again." But, unfortunately, whatever bonds may have formed between the Sharpsburg youth and North Carolinian were short-lived. "The next morning," Blackford recalled, "he was dead."[77]

Seventeen-year-old John P. Smith watched a Confederate die on Henry Reel's farm during the battle. Afterward, he witnessed the death of Union soldiers in his Sharpsburg village home, where medical forces established a hospital. Smith reflected on "an affecting sight" in which a dying private was "begging God's forgiveness of his sins that he might be saved."

On the verge of death, another soldier in Smith's house clutched photographs of his wife and children and asked those present to bury him with the pictures. Smith recalled that the images were "all he had of his distant home." We can only imagine how these sorrowful accounts affected John P. Smith. He later reflected, "[S]even brave boys died in the hospital in our house."[78]

Youths in the Sharpsburg-Keedysville area witnessed artillery explosions, shrieking patients, horrible wounds, dead bodies, and other upsetting scenes. Unfortunately, it is not known how Antietam affected the mental health of these young eyewitnesses. Ted Alexander, a former chief historian at Antietam National Battlefield, observed, "There probably is not enough evidence to develop a modern psychological study of how the [Antietam] battle impacted anyone, let alone children." Accordingly, Alexander wrote, "We may never know if manifestations such as alcoholism, domestic violence, crime, or an increase in the 'lunatic' population were caused by the battle."[79]

*   *   *

The medical department's takeover of the Sharpsburg environs saved the lives of countless soldiers. Residents, for the most part, understood the emergency at hand. They complied with the army's stressful demands, furnished supplies to

---

77 Cross, "Recollections of Another Sharpsburg Boy."

78 Smith, *Reminiscences of Sharpsburg*; Holstein, *Three Years in Field Hospitals*, 20-23. Smith identified the soldiers, both privates in the 32nd Massachusetts, as James Carey and J. T. Bourne. Smith noted that hospital staff buried Bourne with his family photographs in Sharpsburg's Lutheran graveyard.

79 Alexander, "Destruction, Disease, and Death," 173.

hospitals, and ministered to the wounded. Still, families hoped and prayed that the Union army would soon leave the region and stop appropriating property from the community.

However, as days passed, it became clear that George McClellan's Army of the Potomac wasn't going anywhere. Faced with a shortage of commissary and quartermaster supplies, tens of thousands of Federal troops began setting up camp for an indefinite stay at Sharpsburg.

Chapter 5

Destitute State:
The Army of the Potomac's Supply Crisis

After V Corps rushed to Blackford's Ford on September 19, some locals may have wondered if McClellan's army might leave the area by chasing the Confederates into Virginia. However, according to some historians, Robert E. Lee was not ready to surrender the initiative.

After withdrawing from Maryland, Maj. Gen. J. E. B. Stuart, under Lee's orders, led an expedition to Light's Ford, located 25 miles north of Blackford's Ford. Late on the 19th, Stuart's forces re-crossed the Potomac River, occupied the Maryland town of Williamsport, and established a foothold for the ANV's potential reentry into the Old Line State.

When George McClellan received word of the enemy's presence at Williamsport, he rushed cavalry and infantry to Light's Ford. The Federals arrived near Williamsport on September 20, beating the ANV's main body to the river ford and blocking Lee's path for reentering Maryland. McClellan may have been pleased with the results, but other events on September 20 did not bode well for the AOP commander.[1]

---

1 Harsh, *Taken at the Flood*, 445-446, 448-452, 462, 466-467, 475; Dennis E. Frye *Antietam Shadows: Mystery, Myth & Machination* (Sharpsburg, MD, 2018), 181-182. The Union forces at Williamsport included Major General Darius Couch's division (of IV Corps), supported by VI Corps.

Near Sharpsburg, a portion of V Corps splashed across Blackford's Ford to glean intelligence on what McClellan believed was a disorganized and disheartened foe. The reconnaissance mission on September 20, later developing into the Battle of Shepherdstown, saw A. P. Hill's Confederates maul the probing Federals. The Southern forces drove Union soldiers over cliffs and shot others midstream as they retreated across the Potomac to Maryland.

The events on September 20 factored into McClellan's post-battle strategy. He had already met his objective of the Maryland Campaign, which was "to preserve the National Capital and Baltimore, to protect Pennsylvania from invasion, and to drive the enemy out of Maryland." If he pondered rushing his army into Virginia to attack Lee, the clash at Shepherdstown showed McClellan that the enemy was by no means demoralized.

Ruling out an immediate advance, McClellan decided, "[T]he first thing to be done was to insure Maryland from a return of the enemy." J. E. B. Stuart's brief occupation of Williamsport suggested that Lee might attempt to reenter Maryland at a different ford. To prevent this possibility, McClellan stretched his army along the Potomac River to defend major crossing points from Williamsport to Harpers Ferry.[2]

At Williamsport, Brigadier General John R. Kenly's Maryland brigade arrived from Hagerstown to guard Light's Ford. This movement allowed VI Corps and Major General Darius Couch's division (of IV Corps) to establish camps between Williamsport and Bakersville.[3]

I Corps, meanwhile, encamped south of VI Corps, from Mercersville to Grove's Landing.

V Corps sprawled across riverside farmsteads west and south of Sharpsburg village, from Captain David Smith's farm to the Blackford's Ford vicinity.[4]

---

2 Official report of Major General Fitz John Porter, October 1, 1862, *OR*, vol. 19, 1:339-340; Official report of Brig. Gen. Ambrose P. Hill, *OR*, vol. 19, 1:982; Rafuse, *McClellan's War*, 331; McGrath, *Shepherdstown*, 91-94; Official reports of Major General George B. McClellan, September and October 1862, August 1863, *OR*, vol. 19, 1:82.

3 *OR*, vol. 19, 2:356-357. Kenly's brigade marched from Hagerstown to Williamsport on Sep. 21; Robert S. Westbrook, *History of the 49th Pennsylvania Volunteers* (Altoona, PA, 1897), 126-127. Westbrook wrote on Sep. 23, "[W]e left camp at 2 P. M. and marched back toward Sharpsburg, and halted at sunset about one-half mile from the river." On Sep. 24, Westbrook cited the regiment's camp as "Near Bakersville;" Edward H. Fuller, *Battles of the Seventy-Seventh New York State Foot Volunteers* (New York, 1901), 9.

4 Claim of Samuel I. Piper (No. 1310). Evidence shows that Brigadier General James B. Ricketts's division encamped on Piper's farm for six weeks following the battle. Ricketts

Last, IX Corps made its temporary home south of V Corps, stretching its camps from the farms of John H. Snavely and Rev. John A. Adams to the mouth of Antietam Creek.[5]

To guard waterway crossings south of IX Corps, McClellan sent XII Corps to Maryland Heights and ordered II Corps to Harpers Ferry. A brigade of Federal cavalry, meanwhile, bivouacked near Sharpsburg Heights and the town's out lots.[6]

---

established his headquarters in Samuel I. Piper's house; Claim of William I. and John U. Cox (M-901). The Cox brothers alleged that the men of "Genl Ricketts and Meade" appropriated their property. Urias Knode testified, "[A]ll this was after the battle of Antietam, the soldiers staying for some 4 or 6 weeks;" Franklin B. Hough, *History of Duryée's Brigade, During the Campaign in Virginia Under Gen. Pope, and in Maryland Under Gen. McClellan, in the Summer and Autumn of 1862* (Albany, NY, 1864), 122-124; Nancy Husky, "Coffman Farm: From Deer Path to Tourism—How a Transportation Network Shaped a Homestead," thesis, University of Leicester, 2004. Husky cited that the 97th New York of Duryee's brigade, Ricketts's division, encamped on David Coffman's farm at Mercersville from Sep. 23 through Oct. 26; Claim of William F. Hebb (*RG* 92, Book F, Box 89, Claim F-1417). The investigating quartermaster agent reported, "After the rebels had crossed the Potomac, Gen. Reynolds division encamped on claimant's farm and while there encamped the Federal forces did a great deal of damage to claimant;" Claims of Samuel D. Piper (Claims D-2392 and D-2393 and Case. No. 440). General Abner Doubleday testified that his command encamped on Samuel D. Piper's farm after the battle. Doubleday boarded in Piper's house; Claim of Jeremiah P. Grove (G-1632). Grove's claim noted that a portion of Gen. Reynolds's command encamped upon the farm, "the said Genl Reynolds having his head quarters thereon." Grove and his siblings resided on the Mount Pleasant estate near Grove's Landing; Claim of Samuel Reel (No. 3209). Testimony cites that I Corps forces encamped "for six weeks after the battle" on Reel's farm and adjoining properties.

5 IX Corps moved its headquarters to Rev. John A. Adams's farm on Sep. 19. From Sep. 19 to about Sep. 26, encampments of IX Corps spanned from John H. Snavely's farm to the mouth of Antietam Creek. On or about Sep. 26, IX Corps moved its camps south near Antietam Iron Works and farmsteads owned by the Showman and Wade families; Official report of Brigadier General Orlando B. Willcox, September 21, 1862, *OR*, vol. 19, 1:432-433; Byron M. Cutcheon, *The Story of the Twentieth Michigan Infantry, July 15th, 1862, to May 30th, 1865* (Lansing, MI, 1904), 30-32; Edward O. Lord, *History of the Ninth Regiment*, 133-134, 146; Graham, *The Ninth Regiment*, 333-334, 340; Bernard F. Blakeslee, *History of the Sixteenth Connecticut Volunteers* (Hartford, CT, 1875), 21; Sworn testimonies by Sharpsburg residents John Benner, Martin A. Snavely, and Ezra Marker in the cases of Solomon Lumm (No. 340) and James Marker (No. 1292) identify Rev. John A. Adams's farm as the post-battle headquarters of General Burnside. Adams lived south of John H. Snavely's farm on the Harpers Ferry Road.

6 The *New York Times*, October 4, 1862. *The Times*, referring to Sharpsburg village, reported, "On the heights immediately overlooking the town is a brigade of cavalry, under the gallant Col. Farnsworth;" Claims of Henry Piper (No. 445), Catherine Tenant (*RG* 92, Entry 797, Book 54, Box 15, Claim 54-1464), and Joshua Newcomer (No. 272). Evidence in these claims supports that Col. John F. Farnsworth's cavalry brigade encamped near Sharpsburg village for an extended period after the battle. Men from the 8th Pennsylvania Cavalry reportedly bivouacked on the properties of Joshua Newcomer and Catherine Tenant, and the 8th Illinois Cavalry encamped near Sharpsburg's out lots. Joshua Newcomer's daughter testified that "Major Keenan" boarded at her parents' house after the Confederates left Maryland on Sep. 18. She

From a strategic standpoint, McClellan's defensive web along the Potomac forced Robert E. Lee to suspend his plans for reentering Maryland. Consequently, the commander withdrew his Confederate army farther south into Virginia. Satisfied with his defense of the river, McClellan planned to prepare his army "for a definite offensive movement, and to determine upon the line of operations for a further advance."

Such preparations would not happen anytime soon. Inhabitants hoping to see the Union army leave the area watched with concern as thousands of soldiers marched to new positions surrounding Sharpsburg, lit campfires, and awaited further orders.[7]

*   *   *

As Federal columns marched to new positions, army wagons rumbled through the area, and ambulances continued traveling to and from field hospitals. The heavy traffic congested local thoroughfares and blazed new roads across farm fields which "extended everywhere among the camps." A Massachusetts soldier recalled that Sharpsburg's roads were soon "covered with fine dust, which rose in clouds when it was stirred by the movements of the trains, or by the horses of mounted officers or men." The dust became so thick, the New Englander wrote, that "we lived all day long in an atmosphere of dirt, which when moved by fresh winds, drove and drifted about to our exceeding discomfort."

Local civilians also noticed the traffic and dust. Squire Jacob Miller wrote, "[T]he number of waggons I might say [number in the] thousands and perhaps near on to a hundred thousand." In addition, Miller observed that hundreds of horses pulled the wagons, "traveling back and forward day and night which raised a dust almost to suffocation at times."

The movements not only crowded local roadways but also jammed streets in the town. "The little village of Sharpsburg," reported a Hagerstown newspaper, "is literally overwhelmed by the army. Soldiers swarm everywhere, and divisions move in so many directions that the eye becomes confused in the attempt to study out or

---

may have alluded to Colonel Peter Keenan, who commanded the 8th Pennsylvania Cavalry. Seven claimants accused the 8th Illinois Cavalry of taking large amounts of grains and fencing from Sharpsburg's out lots and farms south of the town. Additionally, evidence in the claims of Henry Piper, Catherine Tenant, and Samuel Swain shows that Col. Benjamin Davis's small cavalry brigade, the 3rd Pennsylvania and 8th New York, also bivouacked at Sharpsburg after the battle and took supplies from civilians.

7 *OR*, vol. 19, 1:82.

detect the purpose of what is going on." Describing traffic clogging Main Street, Teresa Kretzer recalled, "So constant was the coming and going of troops and army conveyances . . . that we didn't get to speak to our neighbors across the street for weeks."[8]

Military and medical forces sprawled over Sharpsburg-area farmsteads. South of Sharpsburg, resident Eli Wade saw IX Corps encampments on various farms. "For six weeks after the battle of Antietam," Wade testified, "Gen. McClellan's Army in great numbers was all through that section camping on or near the rest of the farmers."

Near the tiny hamlet of Bakersville, north of the battlefield, John E. Knode recalled that VI Corps troops "were camped all over the farm pretty much for some weeks." A Federal staff officer remarked about Bakersville, "[Our] staff and attendants double its population."[9]

The same scenarios presented west and south of Sharpsburg village. The farms of Capt. David Smith, John L. Mayer, Squire Jacob Miller, John H. Snavely, and Rev. John A. Adams hosted Confederate encampments or hospitals days earlier. From September 19 and beyond, U.S. infantry, cavalry, and artillery smothered these same properties.

Mary S. Grove, referring to John L. Mayer's property, recalled seeing soldiers from Brigadier General Andrew A. Humphreys's division (V Corps) "encamped all over the farm." Squire Jacob Miller wrote to his family in Iowa, "The Federal troops are encamped from Harpers Ferry to Hancock, some places thicker than others." Miller explained, "Around town they are very thick, the outlots are full. [T]he Groves & farms are all full our wilson farm is full Ottos and Shericks farms are full one regiment had encamped in our fiel[d] adjoening town."

Residents like Miller fretted over the army's continued encampment at Sharpsburg. Rogue soldiers and medical personnel had already taken property from dozens of homes. Could residents salvage what remained of their food, crops,

---

8 Francis J. Parker, *The Story of the Thirty-Second Regiment Massachusetts, Infantry* (Boston, 1880), 108-111; Jacob Miller to Amelia and Christian Houser, October 1862, WMR; *HFTL*, October 2, 1862, 3A; Johnson, *BA*, 124.

9 Claim of Raleigh Domer (*RG* 92, Entry 797, Book 92, Box 211, Claim 92-551); Claims of the heirs of Henry Wade (*RG* 92, Entry 812, Book G, Box 106, Claim G-2394 and G-2398); Claim of John E. Knode (*RG* 123, Entry 22, Box 917, Case No. 8587); Noyes, *The Bivouac and the Battlefield*, 261-262.

and fencing while surrounded by Union camps? Would the army pay civilians for the appropriations? More importantly, how long did McClellan intend to stay?[10]

*   *   *

It is not within the scope of this study to judge Gen. McClellan's idleness after the battle. It's necessary, though, to examine some of the challenges the AOP faced from September 19–October 26, which factored into its prolonged encampment along the river. Consequently, the presence of so large an army—encamped for so long a time—inflicted devastating property losses on Sharpsburg and its neighboring communities.

First, McClellan reported that his army was "exhausted by a series of severe battles, destitute to a great extent of supplies, and very deficient in artillery and cavalry horses." Second, rumors of the enemy's strength may have given McClellan concern about immediately crossing into Virginia. He reported to Major General Henry W. Halleck from September 21–25 that the enemy was "receiving re-enforcements," "expected to give us another battle," had "large forces between Shepherdstown and Martinsburg," and was "anxious for us to cross the river."[11]

In defense of McClellan, evidence shows that many men in the AOP were, in fact, "destitute to a great extent of supplies." Quartermaster officers and corps commanders attempted to procure items from Washington after the battle but encountered transportation delays and other issues.

The Confederates' destruction of the Monocacy Junction bridge, as evidenced, delayed AOP medical stores from reaching Sharpsburg. Additionally, this damage disrupted shipments of quartermaster supplies to McClellan's army. Inflicting further injury to Federal supply lines, Confederates destroyed the pontoon bridge and Baltimore and Ohio [B & O] Railroad bridge at Harpers Ferry and then wrecked sections of the C & O Canal. Until engineers repaired the bridges and

---

10 Claim of John L. Mayer (No. 8586); Jacob Miller to Amelia and Christian Houser, October 1862, WMR. Squire Miller's "Wilson Farm," tenanted in 1862 by his son, Francis M. Miller, lay near Miller's Sawmill. See "Wilson-Miller Farm," https://mht.maryland.gov/secure/medusa/PDF/Washington/WA-II-332.pdf.

11 *OR*, vol. 19, 1:82; *OR*, vol. 19, 2:339, 346, 353, 358. Halleck served as general-in-chief of all Union forces.

canal, the AOP would have to draw supplies from depots at Frederick and Hagerstown.[12]

On September 21, Lieutenant Colonel Rufus Ingalls, chief quartermaster of the AOP, wrote to the quartermaster general in Washington, "We are more than twenty miles from the Frederick and 15 from the Hagerstown depots." He added, "The country here on both sides of the Potomac is exhausted of all supplies. It would be found impracticable to supply so large an army beyond the river with wagons." Making matters worse for Ingalls, he quickly learned, supplying the AOP from regional depots was no easy feat.[13]

In the weeks following the battle, quartermaster officers in Washington shipped supplies to the depots in Hagerstown and Frederick. Yet, George McClellan insisted that no such shipments arrived. "Several instances occurred," complained McClellan, "where these [wagon] trains went back and forth from the camps to the depots as often as four or five different times without receiving their supplies." McClellan grumbled that despite the numerous requests, "I was repeatedly told that they had filled the requisitions at Washington and that the supplies had been forwarded. But they did not come to us, and of course were inaccessible to the army."[14]

Following the battle, correspondence between Rufus Ingalls and quartermaster officers in Washington reveals several instances in which shipments of clothing and other supplies were delayed or misrouted for various reasons.

Based on the distances between regional depots and AOP encampments, the quartermaster department dedicated the Hagerstown storehouse to troops in the Sharpsburg region, while the Frederick depot supplied II Corps and XII Corps at Harpers Ferry. Trains, however, sometimes routed supplies to the wrong depots. Other times, lengthy delays resulted, frustrating Lt. Col. Rufus Ingalls. He ranted in various messages to his department during this time, describing the holdups as "outrageous," "painful," and "disgustingly slow."[15]

Ingalls later reflected that the labor of "arranging and perfecting this system of transportation . . . for the distribution of these vast supplies to the different portions of the army, was excessively onerous night and day." In addition to

12 OR, vol. 19, 2:333, 342-343.

13 OR, vol. 19, 2:339-340.

14 OR, vol. 19, 1:74-75.

15 OR, vol. 19, 2:388, 408, 409.

problems shipping horses to McClellan's army, Ingalls recalled that "there was great delay in receiving our clothing. The orders were promptly given by me and approved by General Meigs, but the [rail]roads were slow to transport." Ingalls admitted, "[T]here has, doubtless, been some suffering in particular commands," but "such commands make no effort to help themselves in the proper way, but content themselves with suffering and grumbling."[16]

The 4th Rhode Island Infantry was one such grumbling command. Before marching to Sharpsburg, the regiment's historian recalled, the soldiers' baggage, tents, and commissary supplies "were transported in the wagons following so far in the rear that they reached us only at infrequent and uncertain intervals."

The 107th New York shared the Rhode Islanders' sentiments. "Just as we went into the Antietam fight," Captain Newton T. Colby recounted, "the men were ordered to take off and pile up their overcoats—tents and blankets and of course—after the battle they were missing." Worse, upon leaving their camp near Washington, Colby's regiment was "ordered to leave their baggage—consisting of carpet bags and trunks and knapsacks behind." When the regimental baggage finally arrived at Sharpsburg, Colby recalled, "such a looking lot of plunder I never saw—scaracly [scarcely] a man in the regiment but had lost something . . . knapsacks had been torn open and plundered of anything valuable."

Before joining McClellan's army at Sharpsburg, the 16th Maine faced a similar quandary. The men obeyed orders to leave their knapsacks, overcoats, and tents near Washington, but "in our greenness," the regiment's historian recalled, "we expected they would follow us in a few days." After reaching Sharpsburg on September 19, the poorly equipped Mainers found themselves exposed to the elements. "The condition of the regiment was most deplorable," the 16th Maine's historian recounted. Lacking their supplies, the men stripped crop fields to assemble shelters "made from cornstalks and boughs."[17]

Similar problems affected other regiments after the battle. According to McClellan's generals, the quartermaster department in Washington failed to forward supplies to entire divisions, leaving thousands of men without shoes,

---

16 *OR*, vol. 19, 1:95; *OR*, vol. 19, 2:492.

17 Henry J. Spooner, *The Maryland Campaign with the Fourth Rhode Island, Personal Narratives of Events in the War of the Rebellion: Being Papers Read Before the Rhode Island Soldiers and Sailors Historical Society* (Providence, RI, 1903), 13; Newton T. Colby, *The Civil War Papers of Lt. Colonel Newton T. Colby, New York Infantry* (Jefferson, NC, 2003), 181. Colby ranked as Captain during the 1862 Maryland Campaign, per the roster of the 107th New York; Abner R. Small, *The Sixteenth Maine Regiment in the War of the Rebellion, 1861–1865* (Portland, ME, 1886), 33, 36-37.

clothing, blankets, and tents. "By some fatality, or by general crowding," wrote Brig. Gen. Alpheus Williams, "we are lacking much. There seems to be an unaccountable delay in forwarding supplies." Williams added, "I have sent requisition upon requisition; officers to Washington; made reports and complaints, and yet we are not half supplied."

Major General John F. Reynolds took command of I Corps after Gen. Joseph Hooker suffered a wound during the battle. Reynolds reported that his quartermaster found "no shoes, tents, blankets, or knapsacks at Hagerstown . . . this leaves many of the men yet without a shoe." Major General William Buel Franklin, commanding VI Corps, grew so impatient with the Hagerstown depot shortages that he requested supplies from Chambersburg, Pennsylvania.

Brigadier General George Meade wrote to his wife, "We have been detained here by the failure of the Government to push forward reinforcements and supplies." Meade complained that he sent telegrams to Washington weeks earlier requesting supplies, but none had yet arrived. "What the cause of this unpardonable delay is I can not say," the general complained, "but certain it is, that some one is to blame, and that it is hard the army should be censured for inaction, when the most necessary supplies for their movement are withheld, or at least not promptly forwarded when called for."[18]

*   *   *

Indeed, the AOP's supply shortages wreaked havoc on the Sharpsburg community. But the army's size also factored into the crisis. Union troops came and went from Sharpsburg from September 17–October 26, but the military population near the small village remained colossal.

Chaos and casualties inflicted by Antietam's combat on September 17 created low field returns on September 18. Nonetheless, the numbers increased as convalescents and stragglers returned to their ranks. I Corps, for example, listed

---

18 Williams, *From the Cannon's Mouth*, 140; Rafuse, *McClellan's War*, 353; *OR*, vol. 19, 1:75; Meade, *The Life and Letters*, 1:320-321. Rufus Ingalls opined that "these delays are not all chargeable to our department." See Rufus Ingalls to Montgomery C. Meigs, Oct. 26, 1862, *OR*, vol. 19, 2:491-493. James V. Murfin in *Gleam of Bayonets*, 317, cited Ingalls's Oct. 26 report, arguing, "There is abundant evidence that the Federal army was well supplied" after the Battle of Antietam, and "not a single requisition from the Army of the Potomac can be cited as purposely delayed."

6,364 men and officers present for duty on September 18. Four days later, the figure swelled to 15,239.[19]

Antietam Valley residents experienced minor relief from the military crowding on September 19, when McClellan sent XII Corps to Maryland Heights. Two days later, II Corps marched to Harpers Ferry. The departure of these two corps removed about 22,000 men and officers from the Sharpsburg vicinity.

Additionally, the divisions of Couch (IV Corps) and Major General George Morrel (V Corps) joined the AOP late on September 17. These forces missed the battle but added more than 12,000 men to camps near Sharpsburg and Bakersville. Also, a division commanded by Brig. Gen. Andrew Humphreys (V Corps) reached Sharpsburg on September 18, and, as mentioned earlier, Brig. Gen. John R. Kenly's Maryland brigade arrived in Williamsport on September 21.[20]

Shortly after the battle, thousands of reinforcements arrived in Sharpsburg to further swell the AOP's ranks. On September 19, the 16th Maine Infantry, having been detached on railroad duty, joined I Corps, Brigadier General George Hartsuff's brigade. The newly formed 36th Massachusetts and 20th Michigan marched to IX Corps headquarters on September 21 and 24, respectively. Around the same time, recruits joined the 9th New York Infantry, nearly doubling "the then effective strength of the command."[21]

The previous winter, the 12th Indiana Infantry camped at Sharpsburg. At that time, residents expressed concerns over hosting so large a military force. One regiment, after all, nearly equaled the district's small population. After Antietam, more than 140 U.S. regiments encamped near the town, along with cavalry, dozens of batteries, and thousands of wounded patients. Sharpsburg, formerly a quiet hamlet of 1,200 inhabitants, rapidly transformed into a bustling military city.[22]

---

19 *OR*, vol. 19, 2:349.

20 *OR*, vol. 19, 2:336. The Sep. 20 returns for II Corps and XII Corps show an aggregate of 21,987 men present for duty; Hartwig, *To Antietam Creek*, Appendix B. Referring to returns on Sep. 2, 1862, Hartwig listed the strength of Couch and Morrel's divisions as 6,400 and 6,100, respectively. The AOP's returns on Sep. 20 (*OR*, vol. 19, 2:336) show Couch's present-for-duty strength as 7,219; *OR*, vol. 19, 1:368-370.

21 Official report of Brig. Gen. Orlando B. Willcox, *OR*, vol. 19, 1:432; Small, *The Sixteenth Maine Regiment*, 35-36; Henry S. Burrage, *History of the Thirty-Sixth Regiment Massachusetts Volunteers 1862–1865* (Boston, 1884), 14-15; Graham, *The Ninth Regiment*, 334; Cutcheon, *The Story of the Twentieth Michigan Infantry*, 30-32.

22 The estimate for the number of AOP regiments at and near Sharpsburg includes I and V Corps (encamped near the village), IX Corps (near Antietam Iron Works), and VI Corps (near Bakersville). As noted, several new regiments joined the aforementioned army corps at

To provide for so large a force, quartermaster general Montgomery C. Meigs proclaimed that supplying McClellan's army "must be continuous, like that of a great city whose population it equals in number." Historian Ethan S. Rafuse noted that the population of Washington, DC in 1860 "was only 61,122." By comparison, returns show that AOP forces near Sharpsburg and Bakersville on September 30 had ballooned to 70,470 present for duty.[23]

The AOP's strength continued to grow when 20 new regiments arrived in early October. Of these, 13 commands totaling 12,066 men reported to Sharpsburg and Bakersville. At this time, one study argued, there were more people concentrated "within a five-mile radius of Sharpsburg than in Pittsburgh, Detroit, Milwaukee, Rochester, or Cleveland." The bigger problem, the study noted, was that these larger cities were "established urban centers" capable of supplying large quantities of sustenance and supplies. However, the rural community of Sharpsburg and its neighboring hamlets "lacked the commercial ties and transportation networks" to feed and supply the tens of thousands of military guests.[24]

Medical personnel, meanwhile, continued to control battlefield-area farms and churches as field hospitals. Letterman's department gradually transferred most of Antietam's patients to cities such as Frederick, Baltimore, and Washington. Still, thousands of wounded remained in the Sharpsburg-Keedysville environs, along with hundreds of medical workers and ambulance corps personnel. The staff at Smoketown Hospital, for example, included eleven surgeons and "121 attendants, 10 ward masters, seven washers, 31 cooks, bakers and water carriers, four butchers, one ward master-in-chief, one commissary sergeant, and two stewards." All of these hospital workers, like their patients, required a constant supply of food.[25]

Sharpsburg after Sep. 17. According to the AOP's order of battle in September 1862, I, V, VI, and IX Corps contained, in total, more than 140 infantry regiments.

23 *OR*, vol. 19, 1:22; Rafuse, *McClellan's War*, 357; *OR*, vol. 19, 2:374. The September 30 aggregate of 70,470 men consists of I and V Corps at Sharpsburg (31,370 men), IX Corps and McClellan's headquarters staff three miles south of Sharpsburg (16,532 men), and VI Corps three miles north of Sharpsburg (22,568 men).

24 *OR*, vol. 19, 2:368-369, 373-374. Twelve regiments joined I, V, and VI Corps at Sharpsburg, and the 37th Massachusetts joined Couch's division (IV Corps) at Bakersville; Judkin Browning and Timothy Silver, *An Environmental History of the Civil War* (Chapel Hill, NC, 2020), 78-79.

25 Official report of Dr. Jonathan Letterman, *OR*, vol. 19, 1:110-111. It's unclear how many medical personnel and regional volunteers worked in Antietam's field hospitals. In Oct. 1862, Dr. Letterman's staff in Frederick, Maryland numbered nearly one thousand; John H. Nelson, "Antietam Hospital," WHILBR. Nelson cited a Nov. 1862 letter from W. R. Mosely, assistant

It took nearly six weeks for the quartermaster department to remedy the AOP's supply problems. Finally, on October 26, Rufus Ingalls reported to Washington, "It has been my pride to know the fact that no army was ever more perfectly supplied than this has been, as a general rule." To be sure, Lt. Col. Ingalls, railroad officials, and quartermaster officers in Washington worked tirelessly to supply the massive AOP after the battle. Regardless, evidence does not support that these efforts "perfectly supplied" McClellan's army before October 26.

William H. Powell, who served in V Corps at Sharpsburg during the supply shortage, criticized Ingalls's department. Powell wrote, "Day after day passed without receiving supplies. General McClellan wrote, urged, and got into a snarl with the quartermaster's department, the officers of which insisted that the stores had been shipped." The items technically had been shipped, Powell explained, but only a short distance, as "upon investigation, train loads of supplies for the army were found on the tracks at Washington, where some of the cars had been for weeks." Powell noted that "this delay continued until the 26th of October." Coincidentally, October 26 was the same date Rufus Ingalls declared the AOP as being "perfectly supplied."[26]

Subsequent investigation found that shipments "intended for General McClellan's army in the field . . . had been by some means or other diverted for the use of the troops in the [Washington] fortifications, and thus had failed to reach him." Given the countless requisitions sent to Washington by McClellan's division and corps commanders, some critics questioned how vast quantities of supplies could have been misrouted to the wrong commands or stranded on the railroad tracks of Washington. Historian George Ticknor Curtis declared that "the forts around Washington must have been gorged with supplies, while General McClellan's army in the field was left destitute. Was this a blunder of 'red tape,' or was it intentional?"[27]

Arguments aside, evidence supports that elements of the AOP experienced a supply crisis after the Battle of Antietam. Moreover, these shortages were not limited to the medical and quartermaster departments. Subsistence, too, was lacking.

---

medical inspector, to J. J. Milhau. For further reading, see http://www.whilbr.org/itemdetail.aspx?idEntry=2345&dtPointer=0.

26 *OR*, vol. 19, 2:492-493; Powell, *The Fifth Army Corps*, 310-311.

27 George Ticknor Curtis, *McClellan's Last Service to the Republic* (New York, 1885), 61-73.

Since the onset of the Maryland Campaign in early September, many soldiers suffered without regular rations, given that commissary wagons remained miles behind the mobile army. Unfortunately, hunger among the ranks continued throughout September and October 1862. Lieutenant Matthew Graham of the 9th New York Infantry recalled that local roads from September 15–17 were "fully occupied by the moving troops, or reserved to be used for the rapid transfer of regiments and batteries to critical points as they may be needed." Being a lower priority, the commissary trains were "compelled to hover on the fringe of the army," causing "considerable suffering from hunger."

Graham explained that the commissary shortage "still continues for some days after the battle has been fought. Then every energy is exerted in caring for the wounded and in bringing up ammunition to fill the empty ammunition chests and cartridge boxes . . . it is a very difficult matter to get anything to eat at such times."[28]

Commissary wagons, though, were not a long-term solution to feeding so large a force. McClellan considered bringing supplies up the C & O Canal, but Confederate saboteurs disabled the waterway earlier in September. This destruction prevented canal shipments from reaching the Sharpsburg area until mid-October.[29]

Colonel Henry F. Clarke, the AOP's chief commissary of subsistence, thus depended on railroad shipments from Washington to feed McClellan's army. Yet, like the AOP's medical and quartermaster departments, Clarke encountered shipping delays after the Confederates destroyed the Monocacy River bridge on September 8.

To better serve McClellan's forces in the Sharpsburg-Bakersville region, Clarke's personnel established a commissary depot in Hagerstown on September 21. Notwithstanding, the AOP's subsistence department ran into similar transportation issues that plagued the medical and quartermaster departments. Rail shipments to Hagerstown were slow and circuitous, and miscommunications caused delays.[30]

28 Graham, *The Ninth Regiment*, 341-342.

29 *New York Tribune*, September 15, 1862; Timothy R. Snyder and Jim Surkamp, "Destroy the C & O Canal—Fall, 1862," blog, *Civil War Scholars*, April 4, 2014, http://civilwarscholars.com/2014/04/destroy-the-co-canal-fall-1862-by-t-r-snyder-and-jim-surkamp/; *OR*, vol. 19, 2:339, 342-343; Snyder, *Trembling in the Balance*, 140-142.

30 *OR*, vol. 19, 2:450, 467-468; *OR*, vol. 11, 1:172-173.

Distance compounded the problem, as twelve miles separated the hungry troops at Sharpsburg from the Hagerstown commissary depot. Rufus Ingalls recognized that such distance affected the supply network. "It can thus be easily seen," Ingalls explained, "how far from our depots an army can be supplied by wagons. When the supplies in trains become exhausted, an army must be at or near another source of supply, as a matter of course."

Dr. Jonathan Letterman concurred with Ingalls, for his medical department encountered challenges in feeding the wounded. "The difficulty of supplying the hospitals with food," Letterman reported after the battle, "was a much greater one than that of providing articles belonging to the medical department, and was a matter of very great concern." Letterman blamed much of subsistence shortage on "the distance of the depot of supplies."[31]

Despite these challenges, little evidence exists in the *Official Records* to support that the AOP suffered from a food shortage after the battle at Sharpsburg. By contrast, Major Alexander E. Shiras, acting commissary general of subsistence in Washington, informed the secretary of war, Edwin M. Stanton, that no such problem existed at all. "I have the honor to state," Shiras reported on October 25, "there has been no failure nor neglect of the Subsistence Department to furnish subsistence for the army under command of General McClellan, and that all requisitions for its subsistence on this department have been promptly met."

Accounts from members of McClellan's army, nevertheless, tell a different tale than Shiras's report. Alfred Pleasonton, commander of McClellan's cavalry, complained to Washington on September 20 that his men had "nothing to eat for two days." The cavalry's constant movement from the Maryland Campaign separated men from their commissary supplies. A Massachusetts cavalryman recalled, "Rations for the men and horses were issued only once from September 4 until September 19." During this time, the horseman explained, "Both men and horses had to be fed by a country nominally loyal to the Union."

On September 22, McClellan wrote to Henry Halleck, "[T]he entire army has been greatly exhausted by unavoidable overwork, hunger, and want of sleep and rest. When the enemy recrossed the Potomac the means of transportation at my

---

31 Official report of Lt. Col. Rufus Ingalls, February 17, 1863, *OR*, vol. 19, 1:94-98. Another commissary depot at Monocacy Junction supplied the forces at Harpers Ferry and Maryland Heights; Official report of Dr. Jonathan Letterman, *OR*, vol. 19, pt. 1:109-110. Letterman's department also encountered wagon shortages to haul supplies.

disposal was inadequate to furnish a single day's supply of subsistence in advance."[32]

Some regiments waited until late September for rations to arrive. After the 9th New York established its camp near Antietam Iron Works on September 26, the regiment's historian recalled that "rations began to be issued here in the quantities somewhat approaching the regular army allowance." The New Yorkers, he added, "had the first opportunity to fully satisfy their hunger . . . since the 9th or 10th of September."

Unfortunately, many rations shipped to Sharpsburg were inedible. One resident recalled that patients convalescing in her barn "got their rations but would not eat them and we had to provide more palatable food." Private Charles Johnson of Hawkins' Zouaves complained in late September, "[I]t is absolutely impossible for me to stomach the miserable rations we get here."

Another soldier at Sharpsburg opened a box of hardtack in early October. He found the food "to be alive with worms, many of which had been luxuriating there since the Peninsular campaign." The fare was no better for members of the 4th Maine Battery, Light Artillery. "The pork we have received had been poor and the hard bread wormy," recalled one of the artillerymen. "I have sat down to supper with a cup of coffee and put my hard bread into it and seen the worms half an inch long crawl out."[33]

The distant commissary wagons, inedible rations, and commissary department's transportation challenges forced many troops into fits of hunger. "How those men suffered!" recalled Abner Small of the 16th Maine. "Hunger, daily felt, was nothing compared with it." A soldier from the 126th Pennsylvania wrote from Sharpsburg on September 21, "We are having pretty rough times . . . most of the time commissary wagons fail to keep up with us, so we have none too much to eat."[34]

As hunger in the AOP persisted, foraging parties—authorized and unauthorized—took food from nearby homes and fields to satiate their appetites.

32 OR, vol. 19, 1:23-24; OR, vol. 19, 2:334, 342, 347; Benjamin W. Crowninshield, *A History of the First Regiment of Massachusetts Cavalry Volunteers* (Boston, 1891), 76.

33 Graham, *The Ninth Regiment*, 340; Williams, HWC, vol. 1, 2:359-362; Hussey, *History of the Ninth Regiment*, 206-207; Johnson, *The Long Roll*, 199-200; Maine Artillery, *History of the Fourth Maine Battery Light Artillery*, 131.

34 Small, *The Sixteenth Maine Regiment*, 37-38; *Valley Spirit*, September 24, 1862.

For example, several accounts show that soldiers sneaked into Sharpsburg's fields, stole corn or wheat, and then grated it into meal.

A few residents witnessed the appropriations. West of the West Woods, farmer Urias Knode watched General Ricketts's troops take William Cox's corn "for the 'men's' purposes' by grading it . . . after the battle of Antietam." On his farm near Bakersville, Thomas Barnum saw members of VI Corps confiscate his threshed wheat from the "shed at my stable." Barnum remembered that the men "ground it up in coffee grinders and baked cakes of it."[35]

Some soldiers offered payment to local folks for the appropriated food. Sergeant Austin Stearns recalled that "Turkeys, Geese, Chickens were taken whenever found . . . in fact everything that was eatable was procured, sometimes by paying cash and at other times by promises to pay when change could not be made."

However, based on Sharpsburg's war claims, the vast majority of AOP forces took food from private citizens without permission or payment, and rarely issued receipts to document the appropriations. A historical account written by survivors of the 9th New Hampshire Infantry cites, "After the severe engagement at Antietam there was, throughout the army, necessarily some relaxation of the stern discipline usually observed." As officers struggled to "bring order out of the chaos that reigned everywhere," many soldiers straggled in search of food. After all, the New Hampshire account noted, "the somewhat scanty rations made the surrounding country a tempting field for foraging."[36]

In truth, there was an alarming number of Federal stragglers after the battle. On September 20, the AOP reported 53,530 men and officers absent from I, V, VI, IX Corps, and McClellan's headquarters. By September 30, some men had returned to their units, but more than 52,000 remained absent. These figures only relate to

---

35 Carter, *Four Brothers in Blue*, 122; Small, *The Sixteenth Maine Regiment*, 49-50. Small's placement of quotation marks around the word "bought" may imply sarcasm; Austin C. Stearns, *Three Years With Company K*, ed. Arthur A. Kent (Cranbury, N.J., 1976), 133-34; Claims of William I. and John U. Cox (M-901) and Thomas Barnum (RG 123, Entry 22, Box 83, Case No. 333).

36 Stearns, *Three Years With Company K*, 137-138. Stearns didn't specify if the foraging related to Sharpsburg or a later campaign. A discussion of the AOP's non-payments and receipts for Antietam-related appropriations appears in Chapter Eleven; Lord, *History of the Ninth Regiment*, 147. Lord did not belong to the regiment. The book's introduction explains that health problems prevented three regimental historians from completing the written history, and Lord took over thereafter. He based the work on evidence compiled by the previous historians and communicated with a committee of 9th New Hampshire veterans.

commands near Sharpsburg and Bakersville, not including Couch's division or cavalry, which reported thousands more men absent on September 20 and 30.[37]

Soon after the battle, Brig. Gen. George Meade wrote from Sharpsburg, "The development here made of straggling and abandoning their commands on part of the officers and men is so startling . . . how this serious and terrible evil can be cured is a difficult question to solve." Meade found the epidemic beyond the army's control, blaming much of it on "the inefficiency of the officers commanding them—I mean regimental and company officers." He added, "Nothing, in my judgment, short of taking life will have any effect."[38]

In examining the AOP's returns on September 20 and 30, the number of men reported absent near Sharpsburg is quite alarming. Where, exactly, did these 50,000 men go? How many of them remained in the area? More importantly, from where did they draw rations?

On September 29, Seth Williams, an adjutant assistant general on McClellan's staff, informed Maj. Gen. Edwin Sumner of II Corps that the Harpers Ferry region needed "to be thoroughly scoured by parties of cavalry, for the purpose of arresting all marauders and stragglers that may be found on the highway, in the fields, in the woods, or in or about the dwellings of the inhabitants." It was feared, Williams explained, "that many of our men have absented themselves from their regiments, and are actually living upon the people of the country. All marauders and stragglers that your parties may find, the commanding general wishes you to have promptly brought to trial."

Such marauders pillaged the Sharpsburg area, as well. Mary Lee, a nurse based near Keedysville, "commenced preparing food for the wounded," but was "greatly annoyed by a gang of villainous camp followers, who hung around her fires and stole everything from them if she was engaged for a moment." After she complained to hospital authorities, Major General John Sedgwick, one of the patients at the infirmary, "immediately responded to her request, by authorizing her to call upon the first soldier she could find for the purpose, and she had no further annoyance."

Three days after the battle, Maj. Gen. Henry Halleck notified Brigadier General George Stoneman that complaints arrived in Washington alleging "that

37 OR, vol. 19, 2:336, 374. The Sep. 30 report shows an aggregate absence of 52,031 men in I, V, VI, and IX Corps, along with McClellan's headquarters staff. This figure does not include men reported as sick, arrested, or assigned to special duty.

38 OR, vol. 19, 2:348; Meade, *Life and Letters*, 1:317-318.

the troops of your division are pillaging and plundering the country. Stringent measures must be resorted to enforce order." Stoneman, commanding a division of III Corps at Poolesville, Maryland, refuted the allegations. He replied, "The whole country is covered with stragglers from General McClellan's army, and they are the depredators."[39]

*   *   *

Before September 15, 1862, Sharpsburg's farmsteads, out lots, and village lots overflowed with food. Thousands of cattle, swine, sheep, and poultry roamed pastures and barnyards. Cured meats hung in smokehouses. Jarred foods filled cellars. Orchards brimmed with apples and acres of potatoes awaited harvest.

To hungry soldiers, the Antietam Valley was a smorgasbord free for the taking. Confederates had already plundered food from many properties. Now, United States forces seized what remained. Stragglers, foraging parties, commissary officers, army butchers, and hospital cooks took food from nearly every family in the area. The Sharpsburg region stood no chance of weathering the storm, prompting a local newspaper to report, "The two armies of from nearly eighty to a hundred thousand each have . . . devoured everything within reach."

Before examining the omnipresent appropriations, it's important to remember that the AOP commissary department did not establish a depot at Hagerstown until September 21—four days after the battle. We also must revisit Rufus Ingalls's message to Quartermaster General Meigs written the same day, September 21. Ingalls reported from Sharpsburg, "The country here on both sides of the Potomac is exhausted of all supplies." Given that the "country here" included Sharpsburg and its neighboring communities, how did the area become "exhausted of all supplies" just four days after the battle?

More than two hundred claimants from the Sharpsburg, Keedysville, and Bakersville region, supported by sworn testimonies of several hundred witnesses, alleged that McClellan's army ravaged properties from September 15–October 26 to offset supply shortages in the medical, quartermaster, and commissary departments.[40]

39 *OR*, vol. 19, 2:335, 370; Linus P. Brockett and Mary C. Vaughn, *Woman's Work in the Civil War: A Record of Heroism, Patriotism and Patience* (Boston, 1867), 484.

40 *The Valley Register*, September 26, 1862. 2A; *OR*, vol. 19, 2:339-340. Regarding Sharpsburg / Antietam claims filed at the NA in Washington, DC, the author located 176 July Fourth claims

Describing her parents' losses, Mary Ellen Piper wrote, "[I]f you would have gone from cellar to garret, not a mouthful could have been found to eat. Our cattle had been killed; the sheep, hogs, chickens, and everything were gone. We had 300 chickens, besides turkeys, geese, etc., but now we have not one." John C. Middlekauff experienced similar losses. He alleged that I Corps took all "the eatables in the home . . . such as flour, corn meal, milk, butter, preserves and such things, as were laid away."[41]

Samuel Michael described the losses on his father's Sharpsburg farm, writing that U.S. troops "killed nearly all of our hogs and sheep and 1 steer and 1 cow. Stole all our beef and took all of the apples . . . our loss is upwards of 2 thousand dollars. They have refused to pay us anything yet." Soldiers from IX Corps seized all the potatoes, apples, and livestock from Washington C. Snively's farm. A quartermaster officer, Captain Theron E. Hall, reported, "This case seems to be an extreme one. I have investigated it and . . . have no hesitation in recommending the payment of the bill."[42]

Another resident remembered, "The locusts which settled down in clouds upon the land of Egypt could not have made things disappear before them as these soldiers did . . . the meat house was broken open and every pound of bacon was taken except a few hams which had been concealed in the garret."

Alex Davis experienced the same misfortune. After returning to the Nicodemus farmhouse after the battle, Davis recalled, "there wa'n't enough food in the house to feed a pair of quail." Dozens of items had disappeared, including 50 pounds of butter, 75 pounds of lard, 20 gallons of wine, and a half-barrel of whisky.

(RG 92) and 70 congressional cases (RG 123). The author also separated Antietam losses from the Gettysburg Campaign in 1863, which also affected many Sharpsburg-area residents.

41 E. P. to Sally Farran, October 4, 1862, *Dan Masters' Civil War Chronicles*; Claim of John C. Middlekauff (No. 329).

42 Samuel Michael to David Michael, November 27, 1862, WMR; Claims of Washington C. Snively (RG 92, Book H, Box 121, Claim H-3458 and Claim L-3128). Snively alleged that IX Corps forces took the property on or about Sep. 20, but did not specify where the appropriations occurred. The 1860 Federal census lists Snively in his father's household in Eakles Mills. Jacob Snively, Washington's father, owned several properties in Sep. 1862, including a parcel near the Middle Bridge, adjoining the lands of Philip Pry and Alfred N. Cost. See land records IN 14 / 602-3, WMCKK 4 / 245, and 85 / 249. Jacob died in Oct. 1862. In his last will (Will liber E / folios 638-640), he devised to Washington his 160-acre Home farm and a tract adjoining the heirs of Peter Showman.

"We had just baked eight or ten loaves of bread the day before, and pies," Davis recalled. "Those things was all gone."[43]

Sharpsburg's war claims are rife with commissary losses. Perhaps the most expensive food taken by soldiers at Antietam was livestock, starting with beef.

At the onset of the 1862 campaign, the AOP commissary department herded hundreds of military cattle into Maryland to feed McClellan's soldiers. Notwithstanding, traffic during the battle's aftermath delayed most of the stock from reaching regimental camps. To address the shortage until the herds arrived, army butchers and hospital cooks slaughtered dozens of milch cows, heifers, steers, bulls, bullocks, and calves belonging to private citizens.

Mary Ellen Piper recalled, "I saw the Union soldiers butchering some of the cattle, when we came back, in the barn field . . . I remember four of the calves were slaughtered in the orchard back of the blacksmith shop." Henry B. Rohrback deposed under oath, "Ten head of fat cattle and three cows . . . were shot down on the night of the battle." United States troops, Rohrback explained, "swarmed over our farm and shot down the cattle . . . they shot the cows down at the granary close to the house."

On the burned property of Samuel Mumma, Sr., U.S. forces drove the farmer's steer and calf to a field hospital on Henry F. Neikirk's farm. There, army personnel slaughtered the bovines. Henry F. Neikirk later told authorities, "[S]ome cattle were killed in my field and [Mumma, Sr.] recognized the hides as being the hides of his cattle. Hancock's corps was encamped on my farm and some of the medical directors told me . . . that cattle were needed and they were taken for supplies."

Robert W. Grove watched AOP forces seize and slaughter "2 or 3 beeves" owned by Captain David Smith, one of which "was a large white steer which I remember well, which was kept in the barn." When this incident occurred, Robert testified, Sharpsburg villager James Marker purchased the hides "from some one having charge of the slaughter."

James Marker worked as a tanner in 1862 and saw the opportunity to acquire leather for his trade. Robert W. Grove was with "Mr. Marker when he bought the hides." Along with purchasing the skins of Capt. Smith's cattle, Grove recalled, Marker also bought the hides "from some of my father's cattle and from the cattle of the neighbors around," which Union forces had killed. In other words, Grove alleged, AOP butchers confiscated and slaughtered privately owned livestock, paid nothing to the farmers, and then sold the animals' skins for profit.

---

43 Williams, *HWC*, vol. 1, 2:359-362; Johnson, *BA*, 97-98.

A sample of 36 Sharpsburg claimants alleges that AOP forces destroyed 214 cattle from September 15–October 26. Combat killed a few of these ruminants during the battle. However, claims testimonies allege that soldiers seized most of the 214 cattle for commissary purposes.[44]

The AOP's destruction of bovines impacted livestock owners on different levels. First, beef cattle and milch cows provided subsistence to farm families and reaped additional income on the market. Second, the beasts were expensive to replace. Calves, heifers, young cattle, and small steers ranged from $5–$20 per head, depending on the weight. Milch cows and large steers, though, cost from $25 to $50—or about $700 to $1,400 per head in 2022 money.[45]

Swine, which included hogs, sows, pigs, and shoats (young, weaned hogs), were a primary food staple for Sharpsburg families. Farmers also fattened hogs throughout the fall and winter to sell their animals at the market.

According to war claims filed by 55 claimants, the AOP seized and slaughtered 954 swine during their stay in the battlefield area, taking the animals from farmsteads and village lots. The 954 figure equates to forty-five percent of the total 2,117 swine reported in the 1860 agricultural schedule for Sharpsburg District.[46]

At Lock 39 on the C & O Canal, Henry Marion Johnson recalled that U.S. soldiers "started to tear down the fence around the hog pen to get at the hogs." Henry's mother told one of her sons to summon an officer. She then "grabbed up an axe and ran out after the men." Johnson's mother supposedly "bluffed them away from the hogs until the officer came. He sent the men back to camp and told her if any more came to molest her, she would be within her rights to kill them because they had orders not to destroy or steal anything." No further incidents occurred at the Johnson residence. Other civilians were less fortunate.

---

44 Claims of Henry Piper (No. 445), Henry B. Rohrback (No. 1323), and Samuel Mumma, Sr. (No. 334). Hancock's brigade (VI Corps, Second Division) encamped at Sharpsburg from Sep. 17–22 before moving to Bakersville. See *OR*, vol. 19, 1:379; Claims of David Smith (Nos. 1244, 1262, and 10237). Robert W. Grove identified the tanner as "James Macker," who owned a "tan yard in the village." The sampled war claims are located in record groups 92 and 123 at the *NA* in Washington, DC. Of note, Sharpsburg farmers in the 1860 agricultural schedule reported the combined ownership of 1,419 ruminants, including milch cows and other cattle. Comparatively, then, the sampled amount of 214 animals destroyed by the AOP amounts to fifteen percent of Sharpsburg's bovines.

45 Williamson, *PPT*.

46 1860 agricultural schedule, Sharpsburg District. The claims are located in record groups 92 and 123 at the *NA*.

Several farmers lost between 30 and 50 swine each. Joshua Newcomer claimed that Federals took 67 of his animals after the battle, comprised of 42 hogs and 25 shoats. Daniel B. Grim, Newcomer's neighbor, testified that he saw AOP forces skin Newcomer's porkers. "There were so many soldiers," Grim added, "and they took whatever they could get." Another neighbor, Henry Piper, swore to have witnessed U.S. troops shoot Newcomer's swine. Asked what the soldiers did with the animals, Piper replied, "They ate them."[47]

Samuel I. Piper watched hungry Federals destroy ten of his hogs. "They were taken out of the field," he explained. "They killed them as they wanted them and ate them. On one occasion I heard some shooting and I saw five of them had a hog down and when I got back they were gone, hog and skins. The soldiers killed them at different times."

Jessie D. Price, a farmhand, watched commissary staff from Abner Doubleday's division confiscate and kill Samuel D. Piper's "fat hogs and stock hogs." These men, Price remarked, slaughtered 22 hogs "at different times . . . sometimes two and sometimes more at a time as they were wanted, quite a number of these would be netted at 200 pounds and upwards. I saw them slaughter these hogs."[48]

Sheep were another vital resource to farmers, raised for mutton, milk, tallow, and wool. Families used the latter for personal use and market sale, evidenced by Sharpsburg's production of 4,963 pounds of wool in 1860.

After the battle, 29 farmers claimed the loss of 413 lambs, rams, and ewes, which represents forty-four percent of the 940 sheep reported in Sharpsburg's 1860 agricultural schedule. Among the hardest hit were William M. Blackford, from whom U.S. forces took 33 sheep, Catherine Showman (27 sheep), and Capt. David Smith (23 sheep).[49]

On the farm of Jacob F. Miller, Henry M. Miller, Jacob's son, remembered seeing men from IX Corps chasing "after them [sheep] in the field shooting them."

---

47 Henry Marion Johnson interview, ANBL; Claims of Joshua Newcomer (*RG* 92, F-854 and *RG* 123, No. 272).

48 Claims of Samuel I. Piper (No. 1310) and Samuel D. Piper (No. 440). Price testified that, in 1862, he lived in a tenant house on Samuel Reel's farm, which overlooked Samuel D. Piper's property.

49 1860 agricultural schedule, Sharpsburg District; L. G. Connor, "A Brief History of the Sheep Industry in the United States," *Agricultural History Society Papers* (Washington, DC, 1921), vol. 1, 128-132; Claims of William M. Blackford (No. 1324), Catherine Showman (F-1185), and David Smith (Nos. 1244, 1262, and 10237).

Item 1.   I should say that from the fact that she was prac-

tically kept out of the use of these buildings for sev-

eral months, the sum of from six to seven hundred dollars

would be a fair rent;

Item 2.   and that the repairs could not have cost less than three

hundred dollars. (P. 9 Record.)

I was on her farm and had helped thresh her grain.

I saw them killing her stock on the day of the battle

and a day or two after. The soldiers killed the cattle,

SHEEP, and HOGS, and used them on the place. I was on

STOCK.   the place almost daily and was a witness to the whole

matter.   The farm was in the rear of the Federal lines

of battle. (P. 10 Record.)

They killed two HEIFERS, one STEER, ten SHEEP and

eighteen HOGS. I worked on the farm and knew how much

stock they had and in this way am able to state how

much stock was taken. These animals were all used on

the premises.

The HOGS were two years old and the SHEEP were full

grown. I would say they were worth five dollars each.

At the time these things were taken the soldiers in the

hospitals were in need of fresh meat and in fact of all

kinds of supplies and they were obliged to take supplies

wherever they could find them. (P. 10 Record.)

(8)

Partial testimony of farmhand John H. Myers in the congressional case of Susan Hoffman. After the war, Myers was one of many residents to testify in claims cases involving the U.S. Army's appropriation of civilian livestock. *NARA*

Later, when a claims attorney asked Jacob F. Miller what soldiers did with his sheep, the farmer replied, "They killed them and eat them . . . every time we came home, some of them would be missing."

Miller's neighbor, Henry B. Rohrback, reported the loss of 31 sheep. Rohrback stated that Northern forces drove the animals "to the hospital on Mr. [Joseph] Thomas's place," and then added, "They were the finest sheep in the neighborhood." William H. Thomas corroborated the allegation. He testified to have witnessed Federals slaughter Rohrback's sheep "at our place in the family grave yard where they had a hospital."

William Roulette also lost sheep after the battle. He deposed that "Colonel Irving, of a Pennsylvania regiment, told me that they used the sheep because they didn't have rations . . . he said they needed them. He said to me, I will see, or help see, that you are paid for them." Irving's men killed and consumed a dozen of Roulette's sheep, but the promised payment never came. Jacob Myers, a tenant farmer living on Roulette's farm in 1862, recounted, "The sheep were all gone; wasn't any left . . . they were very fine ones, about as fine as I ever saw."[50]

AOP troops also seized civilians' poultry and slaughtered the birds by the thousands. "We had four geese and 'bout sixty chickens," Alex Davis recounted. "[T]he soldiers got 'em all except one hen." Troops on the Nicodemus farm "had done their chicken-killin' in the room where we had our winter kitchen," Davis explained. "They'd taken the dough scraper and put it on a chicken's neck and hit it a whack with the rollin'-pin, and that rollin'-pin was all bruised up. They were dirty butchers, and the floor was ankle deep easy with heads and feet, entrails and feathers."

Davis's account was one of many. Solomon Lumm recounted that U.S. soldiers took his chickens and ducks under cover of darkness. He added, "some they killed and others were tied in bunches, and taken away." Samuel I. Piper swore that Federals "took 35 turkeys and 200 chickens. The soldiers ate them . . . the turkeys and chickens were taken by private soldiers just as they wanted them."

---

50 Claims of Jacob F. Miller (No. 4294), Henry B. Rohrback (No. 1323), and William Roulette (No. 4299). Roulette may have confused "Irving" for Col. William H. Irwin (VI Corps, Second Division), whose brigade remained at Sharpsburg from Sep. 17–22, 1862. Jacob Myers testified that he worked for Roulette in Sep. 1862 and the context of his statement suggests that he lived on the Roulette farm. Upon returning to Roulette's farmstead the night of the battle, Myers stated, "Mr. Roulette sent me down to put up the fence around the corn . . . I went down and everything was black. They were burning the fence rails and everything. I got as far as the house where I lived and got back to the barn where they had carried a great many wounded."

William Roulette's claim states that U.S. troops appropriated 350 chickens, 25 ducks, and eight turkeys. Joshua Newcomer claimed the loss of twelve turkeys and "200 chickens of large size." Likewise, George Line swore that his 250 chickens were "used in the hospital."[51]

Dozens of citizens claimed similar losses. In fact, 37 claimants alleged that U.S. soldiers destroyed 2,906 chickens after the battle. This figure may have included roosters, which Private Philo S. Pearce of the 11th Connecticut recalled confiscating from civilians earlier in the Maryland Campaign.

If this figure is accurate, it may explain why some residents recalled seeing few domestic fowl in the battle's aftermath. Alex Davis remembered, "The farmers didn't have no chickens to crow." Also, Dr. A. A. Biggs wrote, less than two weeks after the battle, "At present, it is a strange sight to see fowl of any description."[52]

*   *   *

Based on the losses reported, McClellan's army allegedly shot down so many farm animals after the battle that Sharpsburg's citizens may have wondered if skirmishing had returned to the area. For example, William M. Blackford claimed the loss of 66 head of livestock, which were taken by "the Pennsylvania Corn Exchange Regiment, Martin's Battery, and others." Blackford testified that the AOP's "supply trains did not get up for a couple of days, and during that time they used this stock as rations for the soldiers . . . all these animals were butchered on my premises and fed to the troops."

Describing Raleigh Showman's losses, John Snyder remembered seeing "a great portion of the hogs and sheep shot down & taken by the troops." Among Captain David Smith's losses were seven cattle, 23 sheep, and 15 hogs. Solomon Renner testified that Union forces "stripped [Smith's] farm of everything that was

---

51 Johnson, *BA*, 98; Claims of Solomon Lumm (No. 340), Samuel I. Piper (No. 1310), William Roulette (No. 4299), Joshua Newcomer (F-854), and George Line (F-1187).

52 1860 agricultural schedule, Sharpsburg District; Pearce, "Civil War Memories," HEPL, 9; Johnson, *BA*, 103; Biggs to Kalb, September 29, 1862, WMR. The author accessed the sampled claims in *RG* 92 and *RG* 123 at the *NA*. Among the total losses were 157 turkeys, 52 ducks, and 31 geese. Adding to the poultry losses, structure fires during the battle killed a number of birds. For example, Samuel Mumma, Sr. declared the loss of 200 chickens and Sarah Himes claimed 50 hens and five geese. After Jacob H. Grove's barn caught fire, Christina Watson recalled in Clifton Johnson's *Battleground Adventures*, 109, "the chickens and everything in it was burnt up."

In 1862, Jane Sinclair was a 45-year-old slave owned by Stephen P. and Maria Grove. She resided with the Groves in their Mount Airy dwelling southwest of Sharpsburg village.
Sharpsburgh Museum of History

on it." After the troops left, Renner recalled that Captain Smith "hadn't a horse on the farm nor a hog."[53]

Jane Sinclair, a slave on Stephen P. Grove's farm, watched U.S. military personnel shoot all of Grove's hogs, sheep, and cattle. "He had fifteen or sixteen hogs," Sinclair deposed, "and a lot of pigs, which they killed on the farm, and eat up there. The meat was used in great part in the hospital on the place, as there were several hundred wounded there." Sinclair saw Federals "get all the cattle also. They were butchered by the troops on the place, and the meat was used in the hospital. This was done just after the battle of Antietam."[54]

Susan Hoffman attested that military and medical forces killed 31 head of livestock on her farm. Her son, Euromus F. Hoffman, recalled seeing U.S. troops shoot down a fat, red steer "and use the meat in the hospital." Euromus also deposed that Federals consumed the Hoffman's six-week-old calf and then killed "eighteen hogs a day or two afterwards. They shot them down and used them on the place." Additionally, medical personnel "killed ten sheep at the same time and used them in the same manner."

As hard as it was to watch soldiers kill his mother's livestock without permission or payment, Euromus Hoffman seemed to grasp why the slaughtering occurred. "The army had just had a battle," he testified, "and a great many wounded were on the farm and they not only wanted any kind of fresh meat they could get for them, but many of the troops were without immediate supplies."[55]

53 Claims of Willliam M. Blackford (No. 1324), Raleigh Showman (F-1183), and David Smith (Nos. 1244, 1262, and 10237).

54 Claim of Stephen P. Grove (No. 7354).

55 Claim of Susan Hoffman (No. 1318).

Thomas Barnum remembered, "Immediately after the Antietam Battle, the 1st New Jersey Brigade under the command of Col. Talbart, Major Henry, Quartermaster Wheeler, Commissary B. F. Painter, encamped in my yard and fields and stables. These men came to me and told me that they wanted food for their men and horses, that they were starving and said if I did not sell it to them that they would take it."

With options lacking, the African American farmer handed over his livestock, consisting of nine cattle, 16 sheep, and 18 hogs. In exchange, the officers promised to give Barnum, at a later time, a voucher documenting the transaction. Denied payment, one can only speculate what thoughts raced through Barnum's mind as military personnel killed the animals inside his shed, which they "used as a regular slaughter house." In all, VI Corps forces appropriated the farmer's "hogs, chickens, Turkeys, ducks, whole patch potatoes," along with garden vegetables, sheep, and cattle. This food, Barnum testified, was "all he had at the time for himself and family to live on."[56]

Joseph Poffenberger's farmhand, Isaac Malott, watched men from I Corps gun down Poffenberger's livestock, comprised of seven head of cattle, 15 sheep, and 20 swine. These animals "were all taken by the troops in a body," Malott recalled. "There were plenty of officers present. They said their wagon supplies had not come up, that they were out of rations, and they must have food for themselves." The farmhand testified that military personnel "slaughtered them on the premises, and issued them to the troops." U.S. officers paid Poffenberger nothing, and the farmer helplessly watched troops kill his stock. "I was with Mr. Poffenberger at the time they were taken," Malott recalled. "He was so distressed that he could not eat."[57]

Farmers did not raise all of their livestock for meat and market sale. Milch cows (dairy cows), for example, provided families with milk and butter. Other animals were revered possessions or endeared pets. Reverend John A. Adams, for instance, owned a "fine large Alderny Bull Ayshire Cross," which he described as "very

---

56 Claim of Thomas Barnum (No. 333). "Col. Talbart" was likely Colonel Alfred T. A. Torbert, who commanded the New Jersey brigade in Slocum's division, VI Corps.

57 Claim of Joseph Poffenberger (*RG* 123, No. 1300). Arthur Kenney operated the Hagerstown Pike toll-gate across from Poffenberger's farm in 1862. Kenny testified that an officer asked him "to tell Mr. Poffenberger that he was obliged to kill his cattle for the use of the United States troops Hookers corps that he could come to Harpers ferry and get his money for them." Poffenberger's claim (No. 1300) suggests that he did not receive payment for his livestock in 1862, because he pursued compensation for said losses into the early 1890s.

valuable." After the battle, troops killed and consumed the prized bull. When Federals appropriated a herd of cattle from James Marker's farm near the Antietam Iron Works, Susan Marker recalled, "I saw them driving them away, and I remember how I begged them to leave one that was a pet." Susan didn't specify whether she saved her pet cow, but the Marker family lost 24 head of cattle to the Union army.[58]

Some civilians discovered that soldiers took only a portion of the meat after killing the animals. On Henry B. Rohrback's farm, U.S. forces "shot down everything they came across," including 26 swine. The Rohrbacks later found their butchered livestock and "saw several of the hogs where they only used the hind quarters."

On the same subject, Alex Davis recalled that explosions spooked Jacob Nicodemus's hogs off the farm during the battle. Davis later found that troops killed the swine but "took the hams off and let the rest of the carcass lay. More was wasted than was saved." Based on Rohrback's and Davis's accounts, the soldiers' negligence caused a considerable amount of meat to rot, thus wasting ribs, loins, shoulders, and bacon.[59]

Normally, Sharpsburg's farmers used all parts of their livestock, processing lard from swine and tallow from beef and mutton. They reserved heads and organs for consumption and ground other parts into sausage. Farmers hung most of their meat in smokehouses to be smoked or air-dried. Captain David Smith's smokehouse, Robert W. Grove remembered, "hung full of bacon and hams, [and] cured meat" before the battle. The smokehouse "was made of brick and it was 14 or 15 square," Angeline Jackson recalled, and "had a cellar under it where we kept our winter apples; there were joice or beams placed at the eves or square above, upon which the bacon was hung." Continuing, Jackson stated, "We usually killed 12 or 15 hogs and I believe this was the bacon from that number, except the odds and ends that had been consumed."

Similar to livestock, McClellan's men took vast quantities of cured meat from the Sharpsburg neighborhood. Before Captain Smith's family evacuated their farm on September 17, Angeline Jackson "took down 11 hams and threw them below into the cellar among the apple barrels, so that they might not be so easily

---

58 Claim of John A. Adams (*RG* 92, Book G, Box 99, Claim G-1933). Adams's bull may have been a cross of two Scottish breeds, Ayrshire and Alderney; Claim of James Marker (*RG* 123, No. 1292).

59 Claim of Henry B. Rohrback (*RG* 123, No. 1323). Rohrback's son-in-law, Henry C. Mumma, described the wasted meat; Johnson, *BA*, 100.

discovered." She recounted that "the bacon, sides of meat and shoulders still hung so full it did not show that any had been taken, one would hardly have noticed." The captain's son, David M. Smith, remained at home and "succeeded in preventing the rading of the smoke-house" by Confederates. Afterward, when the family returned, Angeline Jackson recalled that the meat "was all taken by Union forces after they came in."[60]

Other farmers alleged that U.S. troops took similar quantities of preserved meat, which included bacon, hams, shoulders, cured veal, and dried beef. Samuel D. Piper, Henry Piper, Stephen P. Grove, William Roulette, and Joseph Poffenberger reported a combined loss of 2,390 pounds of preserved meats. In Joseph Poffenberger's claims case, farmhand Isaac Malott asserted, "I saw his bacon taken. They took all he had on the place. The troops used it there the day after the battle." The Nicodemus family also lost cured meats, including "every piece of bacon from the smoke-house."[61]

*   *   *

Sharpsburg's gardens in 1862 varied in size. Some townsfolk cultivated gardens on their residential lots. Wealthier villagers owned out lots and small tracts adjoining the town, in which they raised larger quantities of vegetables, possibly for additional income. Before the battle, one of Squire Jacob Miller's daughters wrote, "My garden is very backwards . . . I set 113 cabbages, 96 beet[s] and 50 some tomato out yesterday and the rain will be good for them."[62]

60 Wilmer Mumma, *Out of the Past: A Collection of Creative Writings of a Human Interest Nature, Spotlighting the Historic Sharpsburg, Maryland Area*, 2 vols. (Sharpsburg, MD, 1993), WMR, 1:35; *HFTL*, February 20, 1856, 2C, and February 13, 1861, 2C. The articles cite that the Michael family's hogs weighed 498, 545, 568, and 710 pounds; Stephen P. Grove, *Ledger of Stephen P. Grove of Mt. Airy, Sharpsburg, Washington County, Maryland*, business ledger, WMR; Claims of David Smith (Nos. 1244, 1262, and 10237).

61 Claims of Samuel D. Piper (No. 440), Henry Piper (No. 445), Stephen P. Grove (No. 7354), William Roulette (No. 4299), and Joseph Poffenberger (No. 1300); Johnson, *BA*, 98.

62 Reverend John A. Adams owned a vacant lot in Sharpsburg and may have dedicated it for growing vegetables and other crops. Land records IN 8 / 248-249, IN 17 / 135, and 87 / 583 describe Lot 135, adjoining St. Paul's Episcopal Church, as "Reverend John A. Adams's farm." The 1877 Sharpsburg village map does not depict a dwelling on Lot 135, and the property remained in Adams's family until 1885; Undated "Letter from Millie" to Amelia Houser, WMR. "Millie" may have been Savilla Miller, Squire Miller's daughter, who lived with her father in 1862. "Millie" reported the burials of two residents, Alfred Showman's child (Charlie Showman, who died on May 9, 1862) and Hezekiah Myers' wife (Mary E. Myers, who died on

Farm families, meanwhile, raised vegetables, herbs, and other plants on small beds near their dwellings. They also cultivated larger plots called "garden trucks" or "truck patches" to grow crops for market sale.

In the fall of 1862, soldiers and medical personnel plundered gardens, out lots, and truck patches. Villager Joanna Kidwiler blamed troops for "distroying [her] garden." From Samuel Poffenberger's garden, they took grapes, beets, white beans, and onions. Solomon Lumm accused U.S. forces of confiscating "four squares of cabbages in the garden about thirty heads to the square." Members of McClellan's army reportedly took from John L. Spong 250 heads of cabbage and from William Roulette "1 wagon load of pumpkins."[63]

William M. Blackford and Jacob Avey, Sr. claimed that Union military personnel wiped out their truck patches. At the same time, William Unger, John Russell, and Ephraim Geeting reported the loss of garden trucks. Leonard Emmert, meanwhile, testified that Federals did "great damage" to his garden while confiscating vegetables "for Hospital purposes."[64]

Nearly all of Sharpsburg's farmers grew potatoes in 1862. Most patches were one acre or more, producing large yields for additional income and winter subsistence. Sharpsburg's residents grew two types of potatoes: Irish and sweet. The former variety predominated, as farmers grew 4,892 bushels of Irish potatoes in 1860. By contrast, seven people in 1860 reported ninety combined bushels of sweet potatoes. In 1862, though, many farmers lost their potato crops because soldiers stripped the patches clean.

Jeremiah Summers stated that Henry Piper's spuds "were all dug and used by the Union forces. I saw them digging many times. I also helped plow the field after the Union forces had moved away and we only found about two bushels remaining in the whole field . . . it was a very fine field of Irish potatoes." Daniel Grim swore

---

May 20, 1862), suggesting that she wrote the letter in late May 1862. The letter doesn't specify where the garden was located. The Millers resided in town on Lot 7 in 1862, but Squire Miller owned several properties in 1862, including two farms south of the village, three smaller tracts, and Lot 182 in the village. See land records 86 / 556, 84 / 586, 84 / 671, 82 / 29, 79 / 661, and 79 / 167.

63 Claims of Joanna Kidwiler (304-252), Samuel Poffenberger (F-1434), Solomon Lumm (No. 340), John L. Spong (*RG* 92, Book D, Box 46, Claim D-946), and William Roulette (No. 4299). Lumm's plot may have been a "four square garden," consisting of raised beds and separated by walkways.

64 Claims of William M. Blackford (No. 1324), Jacob Avey, Sr. (Book 304, Claim 243), and William Unger (Box 771, Claim 181 and Claim K-516); Geeting and Russell accounts, UMLA; Claims of Leonard Emmert (Claim F-1577 and Case No. 4257).

to have seen U.S. troops unearth Joshua Newcomer's crop from a patch of three or four acres. "It was a good crop of potatoes that year," Grim pointed out, "and they were big ones. It was an extra new kind of potato."[65]

Mary Grice recalled seeing Federals on Benjamin F. Rohrback's out lot after the battle. "There was a little over four acres in potatoes" in Rohrback's field, she recalled. "I saw five Union soldiers digging these at one time, and I told them they ought not take them, but they said they were very fine potatoes." Grice added, "I saw a large crowd at another time when one came to me and asked if I had any bread, that they had taken about all the potatoes."

William M. Blackford claimed the loss of "fifty bushels of potatoes . . . which were dug up and eaten by the soldiers . . . they were all the potatoes I had. They took them all." On Jacob H. Grove's farm adjoining the Shepherdstown Pike, Grove's overseer, Elias F. Bussard, testified, "I saw the Union soldiers digging them [potatoes] with their bayonets."[66]

Jacob F. Miller was one of the few persons to raise yams at the time of the battle. He testified that men from IX Corps "took a patch of sweet potatoes." Asked if he saw "any officer in charge of a squad of soldiers taking this property," Miller replied, "I frequently saw General Burnside; he camped on my sweet potato patch after the battle of Antietam, and I was acquainted with him."

The widespread appropriation of potatoes deprived families of an essential staple for winter meals. Squire Jacob Miller wrote to his daughter in Iowa that the Federals "have taken all our potatoes not only ours but every bodys within their range. So I suppose we will have to send out to you for potatoes and corn this winter." Being one of the wealthier persons in the community, Miller had the funds to ship food to Sharpsburg. Many other residents could not afford such a luxury.[67]

Civilians also grew apples and other orchard fruits. Sixty-six percent of Sharpsburg's farmers reported bushels of such produce in 1860, and at least one Sharpsburg town lot contained an orchard in 1862. Farmers reserved a portion of

---

65 1860 agricultural schedule, Sharpsburg District; Claims of Henry Piper (No. 445) and Joshua Newcomer (No. 272).

66 Claims of Benjamin F. Rohrback (*RG* 123, Entry 22, Box 537, Case No. 4234), William M. Blackford (No. 1324), and Jacob H. Grove (No. 1267).

67 Claim of Jacob F. Miller (No. 4294). Henry B. Rohrback, Miller's adjoining neighbor, testified, "[T]roops lay all over Mr. Miller's and my property and the batteries were all placed on the hill and the line of battle was on the hill between his and my farm." Rohrback added, "Burnside had his headquarters up there at the claimant's [Miller's] place;" Jacob Miller to Amelia and Christian Houser, October 1862, WMR.

each year's harvest for personal consumption, storing apples in cellars to last throughout winter and early spring.[68]

Nonetheless, during and after the battle, AOP forces swept through Sharpsburg's orchards, picking large quantities of fruit for subsistence. Thirty-six claimants petitioned the U.S. government for a total loss of 6,005 bushels of apples, or about 167 bushels per farmer. Claimants charged the government 50, 60, or 75 cents per bushel, depending on the size of the fruit.[69]

Witness testimonies cite that Federals stripped orchards clean on some farms, leaving nothing for the families. James Marker deposed under oath that his "orchard was full of apples," but soldiers "took them all." Jacob F. Miller stated that Colonel Hugh Ewing's command from IX Corps "just cleaned the orchard . . . the trees were just bending and breaking down." Miller estimated the loss at two hundred fifty bushels, which he described as "a low estimate . . . as near as we could get to it." Later describing the loss, Miller testified, "Colonel Ewing had his headquarters there in the orchard, and he came and told me, if we couldn't keep the soldiers out of here to shoot them. I said, Don't shoot them . . . let the apples go."

---

68 1860 agricultural schedule, Sharpsburg District; Smith, "No Civilian Died." Smith wrote that soldiers buried a Confederate in "the orchard of Squire Jacob Miller." The Bowie List for Confederate burials, page 38, lists three burials "in Squire Miller's orchard in town." Susan Kennedy's town lot adjoining the Lutheran Church also contained an orchard. See "Map 3: September 17, 1862, 6:45 to 7 A.M.," Map, Antietam Battlefield Board, *Atlas of the battlefield of Antietam* (Washington, 190), https://www.loc.gov/item/map05000006/. In the claims of Captain David Smith (Nos. 1244, 1262, and 10237), Angeline Jackson testified, "[W]e kept our winter apples" in a cellar in Smith's smokehouse. Likewise, in a prewar letter (Adam Michael to David Michael, August 20, 1857, WMR), Adam Michael wrote, "We had apples of last year to eat up to the first day of June." Another resident (Joseph R. Stonebraker, *A Rebel of '61*, 32) remembered having bins in his cellar "that were so full of fruit, that the apples commenced to decay faster than they could be used, and . . . the family ate rotten apples the whole winter through."

69 The aggregate sample of 6,005 bushels is derived from claims filed in *RG* 92 and *RG* 123 at the *NA*. This figure exceeds the amount of orchard fruit reported by Sharpsburg's farmers in 1860. However, Maryland's orchard yields varied year-to-year, depending on weather, diseases, insect infestation, and the destruction of trees by insect borers. For example, based on the 1871 report of the U.S. Department of Agriculture, Maryland's orchardists reported 90–150 bushels of apples per acre. By comparison, Henry B. Rohrback testified (Book 304, Claim 235) that his orchard in Sep. 1862 contained 40 bushels of apples per acre. Thus, the lower yields of fruit in Sharpsburg's 1860 agricultural schedule may reflect a poor harvest. See also Mohammad Hamid Alta'i, "Geographical Analysis of Washington County, Maryland, and Its Fruit Industry," thesis, University of Maryland, 1953, 154, https://drum.lib.umd.edu/handle/1903/17807?show=full. In comparing yields from 1900 to 1950, Alta'i found "fluctuations in productions from year to year," the apple trees having a "pronounced tendency to produce heavily in alternate years."

Miller's neighbor, Henry B. Rohrback, testified that Union soldiers "swept the whole orchard. We had as fine an orchard loaded with fruit as I ever saw. In two days there was not one of them." Rohrback claimed that troops took four hundred bushels of apples in "four wagon loads." The orchard was ten acres, explaining the high yield of fruit.[70]

The same story unfolded throughout the Antietam Valley. South of Sharpsburg, Hezekiah Myers witnessed Union troops take "200 bushels of apples out of my orchard right immediately after the battle when they were laying there." In some cases, officers assigned guards to protect the orchards. Samuel Pry "had a guard for awhile," but it did little to prevent soldiers from picking the fruit. Thus, Pry concluded, "[I]t was no use to try to keep apples."

Samuel Michael wrote that U.S. troops "took all of the apples—hardly left the trees stand." Jacob Avey, Sr. sought payment for "150 apple trees of fruit." When Samuel I. Piper testified in his claims case, he deposed, "My apples were on the trees. The orchard was full and they cleared it. They used them for food . . . there were 72 trees in the orchard and they were pretty full that fall."[71]

Along with apples, some residents grew peaches, quinces, berries, and other fruit. Families preserved a portion of their harvests by drying or pickling the fruit or cooking it into jam and butter. Civilians alleged that soldiers confiscated large amounts of such foods in September and October 1862.

Samuel and Catherine Poffenberger sought reparations for more than 100 quarts of fruit, including blackberry jam, plum butter, dried currants, and dried cherries. Joseph Poffenberger lost thirty gallons of fruit butter made from peaches, plums, and apples. Likewise, Samuel D. Piper claimed the loss of "preserves & jellies" and "apple butter for hospital." Dozens of claimants listed comparable losses.[72]

Shells damaged a few commercial beehives during the battle. Afterward, troops seized at least 25 other hives from various farms to obtain honey as

---

70 Claims of James Marker (No. 1292), Jacob F. Miller (No. 4294), and Henry B. Rohrback (No. 1323).

71 Claims of Hezekiah Myers (No. 1301) and Samuel Pry (Box 771, Claim 182); Samuel Michael to David Michael, November 27, 1862, WMR; Claims of Jacob Avey, Sr. (Book 304, Claim 243) and Samuel I. Piper (No. 1310).

72 Claims of Samuel Poffenberger (F-1434), Joseph Poffenberger (No. 1300), and Samuel D. Piper (Piper, *Piper Family History*). At least nine claimants grew peaches in 1862, including Noah Rohrback and John J. Keedy. Susan Kennedy had an orchard on her Sharpsburg Heights tract, in which she grew apples, pears, peaches, and quinces. Joshua Newcomer grew "apples, peaches and all kinds of fruit" in his twenty-acre orchard.

subsistence in camps and hospitals. Joseph Thomas and Jacob F. Miller claimed the loss of "2 Hives Bees with Honey" and "3 Hives bees." Thomas Fisher, William Hebb, and Henry Piper also accused soldiers of taking their hives. Similarly, Joshua Newcomer lost "6 patent bee hives filled with bees & honey."

The loss of hives, of course, reduced the number of bees to pollinate crops and orchards on the farmers' properties. The appropriations also may have deprived beekeepers of potential income, as the 1860 agricultural schedule shows that sixteen Sharpsburg farmers produced 985 pounds of honey.[73]

Sharpsburg farmers produced an aggregate of 36,875 pounds of butter in 1860, averaging 350 pounds per farmer. They sold much of it to the community and local peddlers known as "butter men." U.S. soldiers reportedly confiscated butter from Susan Kennedy, George Roderick, and John C. Middlekauff. Likewise, John J. Keedy and Samuel D. Piper claimed that troops took a combined 180 pounds of butter. In his parents' claims case, G. Findlay Smith testified, "I know that mother had . . . a 100 lb. Firkin of butter ready for the butter man, and in the cave, and that these were taken by the Union forces."[74]

Civilians often rendered tallow (fat from cattle and sheep) for making candles and soap. They also reserved lard (fat from swine) for cooking, extra income, and other purposes. While encamped at Sharpsburg, McClellan's army reportedly appropriated the animal fats from various properties. Among them, soldiers seized 300 pounds of lard from Henry Piper's and William Roulette's farms, and "two 100 lbs tin cans" of lard from Capt. David Smith's cave.[75]

---

73 Claims of Joseph Thomas (F-611), Jacob F. Miller (No. 4294), Thomas Fisher (*RG* 92, Book H, Claims H-4113 and H-4114), William Hebb (F-1417), Henry Piper (No. 445), and Joshua Newcomer (F-854). Additionally, Sarah Himes (Book 304, Claim 229) reportedly lost 12 beehives, but these may have perished during her house fire on Sep. 17; Alan E. Fusonie, Leila Moran eds., *Heritage of Agriculture in Maryland, 1776–1976* (Beltsville, MD, 1976), 36-38. Newcomer's patent hives may have resembled L. L. Langstroth's moveable frame hive, invented in 1851; Kelby Ouchley, *Flora and Fauna of the Civil War: An Environmental Reference Guide* (Baton Rouge, LA, 2010), 157-160; 1860 agricultural schedule, Sharpsburg District. While 16 beekeepers reported yields of honey in 1860, only one farmer reported beeswax as an agricultural product.

74 1860 agricultural schedule, Sharpsburg District; Claims of Susan Kennedy (F-865), George Roderick (Book 304, Claim 232), John C. Middlekauff (F-1587), John J. Keedy (No. 2157), and Samuel D. Piper (Piper, *Piper Family History*); Claims of David Smith (Nos. 1244, 1262, and 10237). Similar to the Nicodemus family in the West Woods, Capt. David Smith's family stored some of their perishable foods inside a cave on their farm.

75 Claims of Henry Piper (No. 445), William Roulette (Woodring, "Window to Yesterday," 16-17), and David Smith (Nos. 1244, 1262, and 10237).

Combined, Henry Piper, Leonard Emmert, Thomas Fisher, Joseph Thomas, and John Russell lost 171 pounds of tallow. Other farmers listed tallow among their losses, as well. The medical department may have appropriated the rendered fat for making candles. However, lamps and lanterns were safer alternatives for illuminating barns filled with beds of straw, on account that "one drop of hot flaming tallow" might "transform the place into a crematorium."[76]

Soldiers carried off all types of food from the Sharpsburg vicinity. For example, claimants listed large quantities of salt, sugar, molasses, coffee, and flour among their losses. Barrels of pickles and herring went missing, as did dozens of eggs. Essentially, military and medical forces, being desperately short of subsistence, took whatever they could find. Clara Barton remembered searching through a home near the Antietam battlefield. "[W]e went into the house to reconnoiter for food," Barton recalled. "[D]own in the cellar we found three barrels of Indian meal and a bag of salt; there were three or four great kettles in and about the house, and we made gruel, gruel, gruel."[77]

*　　*　　*

Sharpsburg's inhabitants in 1862 obtained drinking water from wells and springs. When thousands of soldiers and army animals occupied their farms, citizens grew concerned about their water supply. In the neighboring communities of Middletown and Shepherdstown during the 1862 Maryland Campaign, nervous residents locked or removed pump handles to prevent soldiers from bleeding wells

76 Claims of Henry Piper (No. 445), Leonard Emmert (Claim F-1577 and Case No. 4257), Thomas Fisher (H-4113 and H-4114), and Joseph Thomas (F-611); Geeting and Russell accounts, UMLA; Reilly, *BOA*. After the battle, Maggie Grice Hoffmaster recalled that the only food remaining in her parents' cupboards was "beef tallow, like we used to make candles with;" Morris Fradin, "The Story of Clara Barton," United States Senate, *Hearing Before the Subcommittee on Parks and Recreation of the Committee on Interior and Insular Affairs. S.3700. A Bill to Provide for the Establishment of the Clara Barton House National Historic Site* (Washington, DC, 1974), 49; Schildt, *Drums Along the Antietam*, 151. Schildt wrote that Barton brought a shipment of lanterns to Sharpsburg because "she had learned a lesson on the last battlefield. Candlelight is undependable and can easily start a fire in a pile of straw."

77 The commissary items appear in various claims archived in *RG* 92 and *RG* 123, *NA*. Military personnel purportedly confiscated an aggregate of 645 pounds of sugar from William Roulette (Woodring, "Window to Yesterday," 16-17), Henry Piper (No. 445), and Joseph Poffenberger (No. 1300); Susan Kennedy (F-865), William Roulette (Woodring, "Window to Yesterday," 16-17), and Samuel Poffenberger (F-1434) claimed to have lost dozens of eggs; "Antietam: Clara Barton and the International Red Cross Association," ANB; "Clara Barton at Antietam," ANB.

dry. Groundwater recharged over time, but the military's continual crowding of wells limited the civilians' access to water.[78]

Many town lots in Sharpsburg contained wells, but the village's Big Spring, located on Lot 13, supplied water to most townsfolk. A few days after the battle, villager Martin L. Fry testified that he saw U.S. soldiers lead "a great number" of army horses to "the big spring in the village of Sharpsburgh." Another resident noted there was "almost a continuous line of men [troops], horses and mules going to the spring for water" after the battle. Such congestion may have temporarily prevented inhabitants from retrieving water for their families and horses.

Claims evidence shows that soldiers also flocked to springs on the farms of John H. Snavely and Henry F. Neikirk. Likewise, a Pennsylvanian on William Roulette's farm observed, "The walled spring below the house was dipped almost dry by men in quest of its precious water for the laving of wounds and quenching of thirst."[79]

The AOP's continual drawing of well water caused some residents to worry. One woman living near the battlefield recalled that her well "was so constantly pumped that it was necessary to place a guard there so that enough water could accumulate for the use of the family." Worse, the soldiers' overuse threatened to break pumps and handles. A New York soldier, George H. Washburn, recalled, "In the barnyard of the 108th hospital was a large pump, we manned the huge handle thereof vigorously two hours or more for water for the suffering."

---

78 A. D. Kenamond, *Prominent Men of Shepherdstown During Its First 200 Years* (Charles Town, WV, 1963), 90; Pawlak, *Shepherdstown*, 100; Smith, *History of the Corn Exchange Regiment*, 37. When residents of Middletown removed the handles from their wells, members of the 118th Pennsylvania Infantry retaliated by dumping "stones, earth and rubbish" into the wells. The soldiers assumed the Marylanders dismantled the wells for political reasons but later learned the residents were loyal citizens who feared for their water supply.

79 Claim of Samuel Swain (*RG* 92, Book N, Box 242, Claim N-2188); Reilly, *BOA*. Big Spring was also known as Great Spring; Vernell and Tim Doyle, *Sharpsburg* (Charleston, SC, 2009), 9, 12, 52; "History of Sharpsburg," Sharpsburg, Maryland website, http://sharpsburgmd.com /history/. Sharpsburg's founder, Joseph Chapline, selected the village's site "because of the 'great spring' of water located there;" Claim of Solomon Lumm (No. 340). Martin E. Snavely, incorrectly identified as Martin A. Snavely, lived on the Belinda Springs farm in 1862 and testified in Lumm's case; Blakeslee, *History of the Sixteenth Connecticut Volunteers*, 21. Col. Edward Harland's brigade encamped on Snavely's farm until Sep. 26, and then relocated to the Antietam Iron Works vicinity; Claims of Henry F. Neikirk (H-4108 and H-4109). Father William Corby of the Irish Brigade, incorrectly identified as "Corly," testified that wounded soldiers "used up about all the products of the [Neikirk] farm besides enjoyed the water of his excellent spring;" Bosbyshell, *Pennsylvania at Antietam*, 165.

Jacob H. Grove pursued payment of $20 for the troops' damage to his pump and well. Also, Jacob Houser and Capt. David Smith sought compensation for damages to their pumps. According to Samuel I. Piper's sworn deposition, General Ricketts's command "used up and expended" his pump "in the public service in raising water for the use of the Army." Piper testified that Rickett's men "used my pump continually while they lived there and when they left I had to get a new pump. It cost me ten dollars to get it fixed."[80]

In addition to crowding springs and wells, soldiers confiscated milk to quench their thirst. Several claimants listed crocks of milk among their Antietam losses, and Squire Jacob Miller complained about Federals "milch[ing] our cows" without permission. Another resident remembered that her "cows had to be guarded to keep the soldiers from milking them" because "there was a soldier all the time tugging at each one."[81]

Military and medical forces took other beverages from inhabitants, such as wine. Most of it was made from grapes, although some farmers kept cherry and blackberry wine in their homes. In addition, soldiers carried off "half a barrel of whiskey" from Jacob Nicodemus of Sharpsburg and fifty gallons of rye whisky from Joseph Poffenberger.[82]

Sharpsburg's farmers pressed a portion of their yearly apple harvest into cider, barreling the beverage as non-alcoholic juice or fermenting it into hard cider and applejack brandy. Citizens also aged cider into vinegar, which they used as a preservative for pickling meat, fish, cucumbers, cabbage, and other foods.

During and after the battle, AOP troops expropriated barrels of cider and vinegar from various homes. For instance, after U.S. soldiers slaughtered Joshua

---

80 Williams, HWC, vol. 1, 2:361; Washburn, *A Complete Military History and Record of the 108th Regiment*, 25; Claims of Jacob H. Grove (No. 1267), Jacob Houser (F-814), David Smith (Nos. 1244, 1262, and 10237), and Samuel I. Piper (No. 1310). Lieutenant Colonel G. S. Jennings of the 26th New York refuted Piper's allegation. He stated that one of his men fixed the pump and reported that it was "in good order when we left there."

81 Claimants who lost milk included Susan Kennedy (F-865), William Unger (Box 771, Claim 181 and Claim K-516), Samuel Poffenberger (F-1434), Bishop John Russell, and Ephraim Geeting (Geeting and Russell accounts, UMLA); Jacob Miller to Amelia and Christian Houser, December 7, 1862, WMR; Williams, HWC, vol. 1, 2:359.

82 Johnson, *BA*, 97-98; Claim of Joseph Poffenberger (No. 1300). Other claimants reporting the loss of wine included Henry Piper (No. 445), Henry B. Rohrback (No. 1323), Samuel D. Piper (Piper, *Piper Family History*), Bishop John Russell (Geeting and Russell accounts, UMLA), Thomas Fisher (H-4113 and H-4114), Henry Piper (No. 445), and William Roulette (No. 4299).

Newcomer's swine, the troops stole three barrels of Newcomer's "cider vinegar" to pickle the pork for later use in camps and hospitals.

Before the AOP took possession of Capt. David Smith's farm, Angeline Jackson remembered seeing "3 of 4 barrels of vinegar in the smoke-house" and "several barrels of cider laying out side in the sun to make vinegar." Each barrel contained forty gallons. After U.S. troops occupied the farm, the barrels vanished. Jackson confessed, "I don't know what became of said vinegar or cider . . . but know it was there." Another Sharpsburg farmer, Leonard Emmert, swore under oath that AOP personnel carried off his subsistence, including vinegar. Emmert explained that the troops "used a good deal of [his] vinegar in the Hospital. I saw them take it . . . we wanted some and they would not let us have any."[83]

* * *

Sharpsburg-area citizens lost enormous amounts of food during the Battle of Antietam and its aftermath. Although Confederates plundered homes from September 15–18, war claims evidence alleges that troops of the AOP appropriated the vast majority of food during their weeks-long encampment after the battle. Thus, combined, the Union and Confederate armies ate families out of house and home.

The subsistence nourished hungry soldiers and likely saved lives in Antietam's field hospitals. Most aptly summarized by a member of the 2nd Massachusetts, Sharpsburg "gave a refreshing respite from the hardships which had been the regimental lot since the early summer." Part of the reason why the New Englanders enjoyed their stay, the historian explained, was because "fruitful Maryland made up the shortcomings of the commissariat."[84]

Civilians complained to army surgeons, officers, and corps commanders about their heavy losses. Eventually, word reached George McClellan that his troops were committing widespread depredations. To address the "stragglers and

---

83 Claim of Joshua Newcomer (No. 272). Newcomer's neighbor, Daniel Grim, testified regarding the pickled pork; Claims of David Smith (Nos. 1244, 1262, and 10237) and Leonard Emmert (Claim F-1577 and Case No. 4257). U.S. forces may have needed vinegar for medicinal, cleaning, or commissary purposes. For further details, see Tom Klas, "Vinegar Use in the Civil War: A Compilation on the Federal Army Issue," The Authentic Campaigner, https://www.authentic-campaigner.com/forum/showthread.php?8326-Vinegar-Use-in-the-Civil-War-A-Compilation-on-Federal-Army-Issue-by-Tom-Klas.

84 George A. Thayer, *History of the Second Massachusetts Regiment of Infantry: Chancellorsville* (Boston, 1882), 4.

pillagers" wreaking havoc on Sharpsburg during the two weeks following the battle, McClellan issued General Order No. 159 on October 1. Here, he addressed his "corps and otherwise insubordinate commanders to the subject, and to impress upon them the absolute necessity of holding the different commanders responsible for this direct and flagrant violation of orders."

McClellan began his order with a simple reminder, "We are now occupying a country inhabited by a loyal population, who look to us for the preservation of order and discipline." Nevertheless, he wrote, "instead of suffering our men to go about in small parties, lawlessly depredating upon their property." In an attempt to stop the plundering, McClellan planned to send armed patrols daily "to arrest all officers and soldiers who are absent from the limits of their camps without written permission from corps, division, or brigade commanders."

Continuing, McClellan demanded that his corps commanders, upon receipt of the order, "furnish evidence . . . that it has been published to every company under their command." Finally, McClellan concluded his mandate with the resolve "to put a stop to the pernicious and criminal practices of straggling and marauding, and he will hold corps commanders responsible for the faithful execution of this order."[85]

According to a 9th New Hampshire historian, McClellan's mandate "brought the men back into line and restored the old-time regime." Unfortunately, for residents of the Sharpsburg region, the October 1 order came too late. Soldiers had already decimated the food supply. Based on the staggering amount of commissary supplies listed in the civilians' quartermaster claims and congressional cases, McClellan's army expropriated Sharpsburg's subsistence until nearly everything was gone.

Normally, the Antietam battlefield region's residents would have entered the cold months of winter with smokehouses stocked full of meat, barnyards packed with livestock, cupboards filled with jarred foods, and cellars stuffed with potatoes and apples. The winter of 1862–63 offered no such luxuries. By relinquishing their property to aid the AOP's supply crisis, inhabitants lost subsistence and potential income while receiving in exchange the mere verbal assurance of later payment by Uncle Sam. The sacrifice of serving McClellan's army cast many Antietam Valley families into troubled circumstances.

Dr. William Child wrote to his wife from Smoketown Hospital on September 30, "You have no idea of the damage done just by the passage of an army through

---

85 Lord, *History of the Ninth Regiment*, 147; OR, vol. 19, 2:376.

their own land even when all is done possible to save property. The man with whom I stop has not an apple, peach, sweet or Irish potato left. He would have had a great quality of each had no army passed this way." Expressing concern two weeks after the battle, Dr. A. A. Biggs wrote, "We have nearly the whole of McClellan's army quartered here, at Harper's Ferry, and Williamsport . . . we are all in a destitute state, and if the government don't relieve us, this neighborhood is ruined."

The people of Sharpsburg did indeed face ruin. However, Dr. Biggs did not realize when he penned the letter that George McClellan and his idle army had not finished appropriating property from the community. In fact, they were just getting started.[86]

---

86 Lord, *History of the Ninth Regiment*, 147; Child, *Letters From a Civil War Surgeon*, 39; Biggs to Kalb, September 29, 1862, WMR.

Chapter 6

The Ravages of This War:
Sharpsburg's "New Normal"

Horses were central to the lives of local citizens. The animals transported riders and pulled wagons, hacks, sleighs, and buggies. They lugged coal from Grove's Landing, hauled crops to Sharpsburg's market, and pulled coffins to graveyards.

Farmers in the Antietam Valley "use no oxen," Dr. William Child observed. Instead, they owned "horses for draft" which "weigh from 1200 to 1400 each and are stout fat animals." As Dr. Child noted, draft horses were the "engines" of local farming. Without the massive beasts, farmers lacked the means to plough fields, power threshing machines, and haul grains to gristmills.[1]

Sharpsburg's farmers in 1860 reported ownership of 614 horses, averaging six equines per farm. Most villagers also possessed horses, but the 1860 report did not include those figures. Thus, residents in the community may have owned more than 700 horses.[2]

Horses were also the backbone of the military. The animals carried generals and cavalry troops, pulled cannon and caissons, and hauled ambulances and supply wagons. The fighting at Antietam destroyed many equines and separated others

---

1 Child, *Letters From a Civil War Surgeon*, 60.

2 Johnson, *BA*, 94-95; 1860 agricultural schedule, Sharpsburg District; 1860 Federal census, Sharpsburg. The C & O Canal Company employed Sharpsburg residents as boatmen, canal laborers, lock keepers, and boat cooks. Many crews consisted of the captain's wife and children.

from their commands. However, the biggest killer of McClellan's horses occurred after the battle in the form of malnutrition and disease.

Poor diet debilitated hundreds of horses in the AOP. A Union cavalryman recalled that, for most of September 1862, "the horses were fed almost exclusively upon corn stalks and blades." *A New York Times* correspondent, roaming through Sharpsburg's cavalry camps after the battle, reported, "I could not help being struck with the miserable condition of our horses; many of these poor generous brutes being more fit for a slaughter house than for a charge upon the enemy." The journalist observed the "wretched, cadaverous animals munching their coarse fare of dry corn straw." He noted, "[F]or a whole fortnight, and during such tremendous labor, the poor brutes have not had more than three feeds of grain!"

McClellan's equine shortage worsened after sending 1,000 of his healthy mounts on a desperate chase into Pennsylvania. In early October, Confederate general J. E. B. Stuart circumvented the AOP's defense of the Potomac River, leading 1,800 horsemen into Maryland, north of Williamsport. From there, the Rebel troopers dashed north and raided Chambersburg, Pennsylvania. Stuart had already ridden around McClellan's army in June 1862.

When McClellan learned that the enemy had invaded Pennsylvania, he ordered "all the cavalry that could be collected to pursue Stuart." The Yankees, though, failed to catch the Confederate raiders, who slipped across the Potomac near Poolesville and escaped into Virginia.

Stuart's raid made national headlines and embarrassed McClellan. Moreover, "the severe labor" of pursuing Stuart, along with scouting and reconnaissances, "worked down the horses," McClellan reported, "and rendered many of them unserviceable."

In response to his equine shortage, the AOP commander made numerous requests to the war department for new horses. "I have in camp 267 horses," he informed the war department in late October. "[O]f these, 128 are positively and absolutely unable to leave the camp, from the following causes, viz, sore-tongue, grease, and consequent lameness, and sore backs . . . the horses, which are still sound, are absolutely broken down from fatigue and want of flesh."

The report soon reached President Abraham Lincoln. He replied to McClellan, "I have just read your despatch about sore tongued and fatigued horses. Will you pardon me for asking what the horses of your army have done since the battle of Antietam that fatigue anything?"[3]

---

3 *Philadelphia Inquirer*, October 27, 1862; *New York Times*, October 4, 1862; Harsh, *Taken at the Flood*, 478; Sears, *Landscape Turned Red*, 327-328; *OR*, vol. 19, 2:417, 484-485. McClellan

*   *   *

With respect to Lincoln, he perhaps did not realize the severity of diseases plaguing the AOP's horses, primarily the illnesses described by McClellan as "sore-tongue" and "grease."

One of the deadliest epidemics to sicken army animals after the battle was greasy heel, also known as pastern dermatitis. Captain Benjamin W. Crowninshield of the 1st Massachusetts Cavalry declared the greasy heel epidemic as "disastrous." He blamed Maryland's rough roads for inflicting "irritation to the horses' feet," which became wounded by "marching without horseshoes." Ultimately, Crowninshield reflected, "Nearly half of the horses of the Army of the Potomac were rendered unserviceable" by greasy heel after the Antietam battle, "and vast numbers died."[4]

Other equines fell victim to "sore tongue." This contagious virus, also known as vesicular stomatitis, reportedly sickened countless horses during an 1862 outbreak. The condition progressed rapidly. Often, a seemingly healthy horse would suddenly develop an ulcerated mouth and swollen throat and then drop dead the next day.

Hoof and mouth diseases sickened thousands of Federal army horses during Antietam's aftermath. By late September, the 1st Massachusetts Cavalry "was practically unhorsed. The camp became a hospital for sick horses," Benjamin Crowninshield recalled. "It was sad to see so fine a regiment, so well drilled and fitted for active service, in this short period rendered almost useless." In one squadron of seventy men, "only nineteen had horses fit to march."[5]

---

estimated that his available cavalry, when he ordered them to pursue Stuart, "only amounted to less than 1,000 men."

4 Alexander, *The Battle of Antietam*, 108; "Greasy Heel," online article, EquiMed, July 22, 2014, http://equimed.com/diseases-and-conditions/reference/greasy-heel; Crowninshield, *A History of the First Regiment*, 76-77. Greasy heel is also known as soft hoof, mud fever, and dew poisoning. In some instances, infection manifests in cracked hooves and spreads up the animals' pasterns. Other times, microbes infect the horses' lower legs after prolonged contact with mud or wet pasture. The blisters eventually burst, covering the heels with an oozing discharge that resembles grease. From there, the infection worsens, crusting into painful lesions that ultimately lame the horses. Further research may shed light on the possible correlation between shoeless horses and greasy heel after the battle at Sharpsburg. Many AOP horses did, in fact, lack horseshoes at that time. See Wainwright, *A Diary of Battle*. 107, 114-115.

5 "Vesicular Stomatitis Virus," online article, Swine Health Information Center, College of Veterinary Medicine, Iowa State University, November 2015. 6, https://www.swinehealth.org/wp-content/uploads/2016/03/Vesicular-stomatitis-virus-VSV.pdf. Clinical history cites

McClellan's chief quartermaster, Lt. Col. Rufus Ingalls, also recognized the epidemic. "A most violent and destructive disease made its appearance at this time," Ingalls reported, "which put nearly 4,000 animals out of service. Horses reported perfectly well one day would be dead or lame the next . . . they were attacked in the hoof and tongue." In the war claim of Sharpsburg villager Samuel Swain, Major Charles Treichel of the 3rd Pennsylvania Cavalry testified that, after the Battle of Antietam, "the hoof disease was very bad, and they were probably short of horses and may have taken some [from civilians], and they shot about 250."[6]

Treichel's testimony is telling because he admitted that AOP cavalry, to address their shortage of horses, "may have taken some" from the Sharpsburg community. Civilians had previously lost horses to marauding soldiers during the battle. Also, Confederates seized at least twenty equines before leaving Maryland on September 18. During the AOP's encampment at Sharpsburg from September 15–October 26, quartermaster claims and congressional cases allege that U.S. forces appropriated dozens of horses from private citizens.[7]

Union artillery took some of the animals. For example, villager John L. Spong petitioned the government for "1 Artillery horse taken by Gen. F. J. Porter's command" on September 22, 1862. After Federals took Capt. David Smith's horse from his village stable, members of the U.S. artillery seized four other horses from Smith's farm. The family retrieved one of the mares, but could not locate the other animals.[8]

McClellan's cavalry also confiscated horses from Sharpsburg residents. Samuel D. Piper remembered that his bay horse "was taken out of my stable on the 19th

---

that "a large suspected epidemic" of VSV, known as "sore tongue," plagued U.S. horses in the year 1862; "Sore Tongue in Horses," *American Turf Register and Sporting Magazine* (Baltimore, MD, December 1830), vol. 2, no. 4, 169; Crowninshield, *A History of the First Regiment*, 84.

6 *OR*, vol. 19, 1:95; Claim of Samuel Swain (*RG* 92, N-2188). Swain's claim includes testimony from "C. Treichel, late Major, 3d Pa. Cav."

7 The number of civilian-owned horses taken by Confederates at Sharpsburg in Sep. 1862 is not known. Claimants George Line, Jacob H. Grove, and Capt. David Smith deposed that they lost five horses each to the ANV. Jacob Houser and Benjamin F. Rohrback alleged that Southern troops stole an unspecified number of horses. William M. Blackford testified that Confederate soldiers stole one of his horses on Sep. 18.

8 Claim of John L. Spong (*RG* 92, D-946). Spong's evidence proved his case, and the U.S. quartermaster general awarded him $150.00 via Treasury settlement No. 4824; Claims of David Smith (Nos. 1244, 1262, and 10237). Smith's son, David M. Smith, testified that Confederates took five of his father's nine horses during the ANV's occupation of Sharpsburg. U.S. forces seized Smith's remaining four equines "after the battle of Antietam."

September 1862 by a squad of U.S. cavalry." Jessie Price saw Piper's horse taken, which he described as "a number one horse." Similarly, Joshua Newcomer swore that he "had ten or eleven horses in a pasture field, [and] two or three were taken by the [U.S.] soldiers." Newcomer recovered all of the animals except his "extra sorrel horse," described as "six years old in fine condition, the best horse he owned." Newcomer testified that it "was taken from the field for cavalry use."

Near Blackford's Ford, William M. Blackford lost a "fast racking and trotting mare," which he declared as "one of the finest animals in the county." The farmer accused the 1st New York Cavalry of taking his animal. When an investigator later questioned the allegation, Blackford emphasized, "I know it was the First New York Regiment that took the mare because they were dismounted and came with the Berdan Sharp-Shooters."[9]

Blackford's brother, Henry V. S. Blackford, sought payment for two horses "alleged to have been taken Sept. 19, '62 by the 3d Pa. Cavly. Col. W. H. Averill." Initially finding five mounts missing, Blackford and his sons "instituted a search for the animals & succeeded in finding three of them" in possession of the 3rd Pennsylvania Cavalry. The horsemen returned three animals to Blackford after the farmer proved ownership. Unfortunately, the Blackfords, "after the most thorough search," failed to locate their other horses.[10]

Samuel Swain, a canal boatman by trade, also suffered the loss of horses. Swain attested that "two or three days after the battle of Antietam, his three horses were impressed into U.S. service out of the pasture." He explained that Confederates did not take his animals "because the horses were still in pasture after the rebels had left; that two were sorrels, and one a bay mare."

Testifying in Swain's case, resident Martin L. Fry swore that the equines "were appropriated to the use of the 3d Penna Cav'y; that he saw said horses on frequent

9 Claims of Samuel D. Piper (No. 440), Joshua Newcomer (No. 272), and William M. Blackford (No. 1324). Daniel S. Mumma testified in Blackford's case, "I saw the cavalry soldier on her. She was in the [U.S.] service as a cavalry horse . . . this soldier to all appearances was not a straggler. He was in camp with his company . . . I passed and repassed this camp every day;" Smith, *History of the 118th Pennsylvania Volunteers*, 91-94. Smith wrote that the 1st New York Cavalry guarded the Potomac River and Blackford's Ford after the battle. The New Yorkers granted a parley to Lt. Henry Kyd Douglas of the ANV, allowing the Confederate to cross the river to meet with his Sharpsburg mother.

10 Claim of Henry V. S. Blackford (RG 92, G-1648). Lieutenant Colonel Samuel M. Owen commanded the 3rd Pennsylvania Cavalry at the time of the battle, on account that Colonel William Averell was absent with malaria. See "Samuel Wilson Owen," Antietam on the Web, http://antietam.aotw.org/officers.php?officer_id=333. Blackford's mention of Averell correlates with the colonel's return to command in late September 1862.

occasions in use by said regiment." Moreover, Fry remembered that "many federal cavalrymen were dismounted in the battle of South Mountain Antietam, and had received no fresh supplies except such as they took from farms and citizens in the neighborhoods." Swain, meanwhile, never saw his horses again and lost his remaining mounts during a Confederate raid the following summer.[11]

The AOP took other horses from local inhabitants. Joseph Poffenberger testified that David R. Miller's horses were "all taken by the Union soldiers." On Moses Cox's farm near Nicodemus Heights, farm laborer William Show saw Cox's horse "taken by a man who had an order from Genl. Meade." Also, two mares and a black mule belonging to Jacob C. Grove "were impressed into & for the good of the U.S. service by Capt. Russell, several days after the battle of Antietam, to supply the place of horses alleged to have been lost at that time." Grove asserted that he "saw soldiers of Capt. Russell's command take his bay horse on the same day the federals reached his warehouse and he was unable to get a receipt on account of the confusion existing. All his horses were about the warehouse."[12]

A U.S. army messenger supposedly seized a roan horse from Adam Hutzell's stable during the battle and gave the farmer a receipt in exchange. Hutzell later complained to a Union officer, who requested the voucher so "he could attempt to secure payment for the horse." Hutzell handed over the document—his only proof of the appropriation. To Hutzell's chagrin, the receipt, like his prized roan horse, "was never seen again."[13]

Horses required extensive tack for carrying riders, comprised of saddles, pads, bridles, and harnesses. When soldiers appropriated the animals, they rode off with the gearing as well. The 1862 market price for a good, average horse in Sharpsburg was around $125. After adding tack, though—much of it made of leather—a fully

---

11 Claim of Samuel Swain (*RG* 92, N-2188). Testimony cites that U.S. troops seized Swain's horses "on the farm of H. V. S. Blackford about 1 mile S.W. of Sharpsburg." Henry V. S. Blackford owned two properties in 1862: his farmstead southeast of town (see land records IN 14 / 655 and WMCKK 2 / 439), and a tract two miles west of town, adjoining the Chesapeake and Ohio Canal (IN 11 / 239). Neither property is "1 mile S.W." of Sharpsburg, so it's not clear where the horses pastured at the time of the impressments.

12 Claim of David R. Miller (F-1499); Claim of Moses Cox (*RG* 92, Entry 812, Book G, Box 95, Claim G-1657). William Show "lived & worked on claimants place in Sept. & Oct. 1862;" Claim of Jacob C. Grove (G-1649). Grove identified the officer as "Capt. Russell commanding an Independent Company of Infantry in the Army of the Potomac." This officer may have been Captain Charles Sawyer Russell, 11th U.S., First Battalion, Co. A, V Corps.

13 Claim of Adam Hutzell (*RG* 123, No. 4292).

Sharpsburg villager Jacob McGraw, photographed by Fred Wilder Cross in 1920.
Boonsborough Museum of History

equipped mount was worth $135–140, or about half the cost of a frame dwelling house in Sharpsburg village.

The AOP's appropriation of horses presented many hardships to civilians. Farmhands and day laborers, for example, needed transportation to work odd jobs on multiple farms. Yet, these low-paid workers may have lacked the funds to replace stolen equines. Farmers also encountered challenges, for they relied on horses for many essential tasks, including hauling crops to the market. According to Jacob Houser's war claim, he "could not have hauled [his] wheat any place to sell it, because all his horses had been seized."

Canal workers faced similar dilemmas. Jacob McGraw recalled that, after the battle, U.S. troops "took five mules of mine out of a field where I kept 'em. Them were mules that did my towing on the canal." Kathleen Ernst wrote that the military's appropriation of mules "destroyed McGraw's livelihood as a boatman on the C & O Canal."[14]

Battlefield-area inhabitants spent substantial time searching for their stolen animals, traveling from camp to camp, from Williamsport to Harpers Ferry. Michael Miller petitioned the U.S. government for two horses confiscated after the

---

14 Claims of Jacob Houser (F-814) and the heirs of Joseph Grove (No. 9057). War claims filed by Josiah Hill, Adam Hutzell, William M. Blackford, and Henry Piper reveal that superior horses sold from $140–250 each in 1862; Johnson, *BA*, 116; Ernst, *TATC*, 196. More than thirty claimants reported the loss of horse tack. In addition, petitioners accused U.S. troops of confiscating wagons for use in hauling army supplies. Sharpsburg's claims are also rife with wagon gearing (halters, collars, breast plates, straps, and lead harnesses), which farmers fastened to horses for pulling wagons and ploughs. Other items reportedly seized by U.S. troops included yokes, driving lines, spare wheels, doubletrees, wagon jacks, fifth chains, whips, and check lines.

battle. One he never found. For the other, he claimed $15 for one horse "taken and recovered at cost." This amount, quite a sum in 1862, suggests that Miller may have invested considerable time and travel to locate his animal.

Those who located their horses needed to prove ownership before Union authorities released the equines. When Alex Davis found his horses at a VI Corps camp near Williamsport, he and a friend complained to the captain in charge. The officer told the Sharpsburg men "to come with me to the corral where we keep our horses, and if you see yourn there, take 'em." Davis retrieved his mounts but recalled, "[T]he soldiers stood around and looked at us pretty hard while we rode off with them."

James Marker didn't have to look far for his animals. He discovered four of his missing horses at "Burnside's headquarters . . . on the farm adjoining north of ours, John A. Adams's." The troops "gave two of them back," Marker's son recalled, but "the other two they kept."

Adam Michael's family experienced a similar misfortune, having lost six horses to Union soldiers after the battle. Michael's son, Samuel, scoured the area and finally located "four of these horses in possession of McClellan's troops at Bakersville 6 miles distant." However, when Michael tried to retrieve the animals, VI Corps officers denied the request, explaining, "[T]he army was greatly in need of horses." Worse for Adam Michael and his family, officers refused to pay for the animals' $600 aggregate value, a loss equaling about $16,000 in modern money.[15]

War claims reviewed for this study show that the Federal and Confederate armies appropriated at least eighty horses from the Sharpsburg community. This figure was undoubtedly higher if we consider overlooked claims and unreported thefts. For instance, Squire Jacob Miller and David Reel listed no horses in their claims. Still, Squire Miller wrote in October 1862, "They have taken a great many horses from farmers. nine head from us. all David Reels." Additionally, Miller wrote, [T]he rebels got many of the horses."

An early historian of the battle, Oliver T. Reilly, estimated "there were only three horses left in the town" when the AOP finally left the area. Corroborating

---

15 Claim of Michael Miller (F-1438); Johnson, *BA*, 96-97; Claims of James Marker (No. 1292) and Adam Michael (*RG* 92, Entry 820, Box Number 199, Claim Number 199-161). In addition to refusing to pay Michael for the horses, officers furnished no receipt to document the appropriation; Williamson, *PPT*.

Reilly's statement, Dr. A. A. Biggs wrote in late September 1862, "Nearly all the horses are taken away."[16]

The widespread loss of horses, mules, and tack inflicted financial strain on the community while impacting farming, canal operations, and transportation. It also affected civilians emotionally, for some of the animals were pets that had been in families for years.

Martha Ada Mumma Thomas recalled that all of her grandparents' horses "were taken but 'Jack' and he being such a pet we saved him by putting him in the cellar." Another resident, Samuel Michael, informed his brother that Federals seized "six head of horses—even old Confidence and Jane. The others was young blooded horses that I raised since you are absent."

Henry Piper described his roan mare, Diamond, as a "perfectly sound . . . [and] superior animal and worth $200." Shortly after the Pipers returned to their farm on September 19, the family watched a squad of troopers take Diamond from her stable. "I saw the horse taken myself," Henry Piper testified, "and know they were Union Cavalry." Oral tradition holds that Mrs. Piper begged one of the soldiers "to let the horse go, as he was a pet." The Yankee ignored her pleas, then "politely tipped his hat and with the horse bid her adieu."[17]

*   *   *

To local folks, the army's sweeping expropriation of personal property seemed never-ending. Based on the staggering amount of food and livestock seized by military and medical personnel, it perhaps comes as no surprise that civilians also declared significant losses of cooking, eating, and drinking wares. From September 15–19, army traffic prevented the forwarding of regimental wagons containing cooking utensils, and the medical department's commissary wares lay stranded with other supplies at Monocacy Junction. Consequently, the AOP temporarily depended on the local community for such supplies.

16 Jacob Miller to Amelia and Christian Houser, October 1862, WMR. In the 1860 agricultural schedule for Sharpsburg, David Reel reported the ownership of five horses; Biggs to Kalb, September 29, 1862, WMR; Reilly, BOA; Philadelphia Inquirer, October 27, 1862. Of note, a correspondent reported that some of the AOP's horses became "mysteriously transferred into the hands of sundry citizens." U.S. forces later recovered many of the animals.

17 Hildebrand, "Recollections of Martha Ada Thomas," WMR; Samuel Michael to David Michael, November 27, 1862; Reilly, BOA; Claims of Henry Piper (Claim 304-244 and Case No. 445). Piper deposed, "I saw her [Diamond] afterwards at the camps of the Union Cavalry." His attempts to retrieve the horse were unsuccessful.

John C. Middlekauff testified that the AOP took possession of his dwelling and barn for hospital purposes from September 16–October 10, 1862. During this time, all of his "cooking utensils were used" by the army but not returned. Troops carried off similar items from other homes. Joseph Poffenberger lost china dishes and all his "kitchen ware for cooking." Soldiers took from George Roderick 36 pieces of silverware, 15 baking pans, and a dozen plates. In addition to losing a set of dishes, Leonard Emmert sought payment for "Queensware & stoneware," while Barney Houser claimed the loss of kettles, waffle irons, and a dutch oven.[18]

Claimants accused soldiers of seizing all types of kitchenware, including bread pans, pie plates, copper boilers, meat crocks, and tumblers. Henry Piper's losses included "Glasses, Goblets & Decanters," along with earthenware and his entire "lot of Kitchen ware."

From Samuel and Catherine Poffenberger's home, AOP personnel carried off ladles, dippers, iron pots, Queensware, and valuable silverware. Samuel Poffenberger clarified that soldiers took these items "for their use as hospital supplies. I know that the supplies were used in the hospitals, or some of them, because Dr. Shadduck told me they used everything in the house as hospital supplies." Similarly, Susan Kennedy, in addition to losing her Britannia silverware, filed a claim for 19 silver spoons of various sizes valued at $35—almost $1,000 in 2022 money.[19]

The civilians' inventories of Antietam-related losses allege that U.S. forces carried away many household possessions, including personal items for grooming and hygiene. Residents also lost dozens of brooms after the battle, along with soap—and lots of it. Samuel D. Piper requested reimbursement for one barrel of soap and Henry Piper accused troops of taking 25 pounds of soap. Also, William

---

18 Claims of John C. Middlekauff (No. 329), Joseph Poffenberger (No. 1300), George Roderick (Book 304, Claim 232), Leonard Emmert (F-1577), and Barney Houser (*Houser's Account*). English potter Josiah Wedgwood debuted Queensware in the mid-1700s. By the 1860s, Queensware was a catch-all term for cream-colored china.

19 Claims of William Roulette (Woodring, "Window to Yesterday," 16-17), Henry Piper (No. 445), Samuel Poffenberger (F-1434), Susan Kennedy (Claim F-865); Anna Cueto, curator, Washington County Historical Society, email message to author, June 20, 2017. Britannia, a silver alloy, was more affordable than wares made from coin silver or Sterling silver. The high prices in Poffenberger's and Kennedy's claims suggest that their silverware consisted of pure, coin silver; Williamson, *PPT*; Sally M. Miller, A. J. H. Latham, Dennis O. Flynn, *Studies in the Economic History of the Pacific Rim* (New York, 2003), 227. The authors, referring to the U.S. Commerce Department, wrote, "The price of silver in New York in 1862 averaged $1.35 per fine ounce."

Roulette, Samuel Poffenberger, and Leonard Emmert lost a combined 130 pounds of hard soap.[20]

In early October 1862, *New York Times* reported that Antietam's hospitals urgently needed candles and lanterns. Accounts from medical personnel showcase this demand. Immediately after the battle, Dr. Theodore Dimon lacked lanterns for night work in his field hospital, and he mentioned candles being scarce. At another hospital, Clara Barton remembered that army surgeon James Dunn worked a night shift with a mere "bit of tallow candle." Dr. Dunn told Barton that the "two inches of candle is all I have or can get."[21]

These same items appear in civilians' claims petitions, reflecting expropriations by military forces. Daniel Mose, Joanna Kidwiler, Frederick Wyand, and William Roulette lost more than one dozen pounds of candles. Samuel D. Piper and Joseph Poffenberger declared the combined loss of 70 pounds of lamp lard. Other claimants alleged that troops took kerosene, candlesticks, and glass lamps.[22]

Other items lacking in the hospitals, the *New York Times* cited, included "wash basins . . . pails, bed-pans, and urinals." To supply these needs, soldiers and hospital staff seized a variety of vessels from the community. Solomon Lumm, William Roulette, and Daniel Mose claimed that the AOP took a combined twelve wash tubs and wash basins. Susan Kennedy sought repayment for a washing machine taken and not returned. From Ephraim Geeting, soldiers seized "1 Large tub" and "Wash bord & pitchers." Other residents lost cooking and stable buckets.[23]

20 Claims of Henry Piper (No. 445), Samuel Poffenberger (F-1434), and Joseph Poffenberger (No. 1300). The three claimants lost various personal items, including mirrors, brushes, razors, and a "shaving apparatus;" Residents who lost brooms included Samuel Poffenberger (F-1434), Bishop John Russell, and Ephraim Geeting (Geeting and Russell accounts, UMLA). Frederick Wyand and Catherine Rohrback also listed brooms in their petitions; Claims of Samuel D. Piper (Piper, *Piper Family History*), Henry Piper (No. 445), Solomon Lumm (N-546), William Roulette (No. 4299), Samuel Poffenberger (F-1434), and Leonard Emmert (Claim F-1577 and Case No. 4257). Some families made their own soap in large batches, which may explain the hundreds of pounds claimed.

21 Fay, *War Papers*, 48; Barton, *The Life of Clara Barton*, 200; "Antietam: Clara Barton and the International Red Cross Association."

22 *New York Times*, October 1, 1862; Claims of Daniel Mose (*RG* 92, Entry 843, Box 772, Book 304, Claim 263), Joanna Kidwiler (304-252), Frederick Wyand (No. 14112), and William Roulette (No. 4299); Claims of Samuel D. Piper (Piper, *Piper Family History*) and Joseph Poffenberger (No. 1300).

23 *New York Times*, October 1, 1862; Claims of Solomon Lumm (N-546), William Roulette (Woodring, Frank. "Window to Yesterday"), Daniel Mose, (Book 304, Claim 263), Susan Kennedy (F-865), and Joseph Thomas (F-611); Geeting and Russell accounts, UMLA.

Lieutenant Colonel David Hunter Strother of McClellan's staff wrote on September 20, "An old woman came up this morning examining all our tents for a tin bucket she had lost. She says a soldier borrowed it for General McClellan. Some waggish thief has doubtless visited her." It may seem odd that a civilian would go to such extremes to locate a trivial object. Nonetheless, when considering that soldiers plundered homes of pots, pitchers, basins, and other vessels, a bucket may have been the woman's only means of carrying water to her house.[24]

Compounding discomfort for civilians, McClellan's forces carried off cookstoves and heating stoves. George F. Noyes of Abner Doubleday's staff recalled, "Two of our lieutenants had confiscated somewhere a sheet-iron stove with a long piece of pipe, which, when thrust horizontally out of their tent-flaps, looked like a gun protruding from an embrasure."

Other members of the army took similar articles. Medical staff at Sharpsburg's German Reformed Church borrowed Barney Houser's cookstove but failed to return it. Jacob C. Grove claimed the loss of two stoves. Morgan Miller, meanwhile, testified that his two cookstoves were "taken to camp and used by Q Master."[25]

Jacob H. Grove swore under oath that his "dining table and stove were taken from my farm-house." Grove later found the items in an officer's shanty. Seeking reimbursement for his bake oven, Col. John Miller alleged that U.S. troops "used it till destroyed." Likewise, Solomon Lumm testified that United States forces wrecked two of his cooking appliances, "one a ten-plate stove and one a cook stove." Both ovens, Lumm deposed, "were so broken that I had to sell them for old iron. I paid nine dollars for the ten plate stove and fifteen dollars for the cook stove. I got one half cent per pound for the old iron."[26]

*   *   *

24 Claim of Joseph Poffenberger (No. 1300); Geeting and Russell accounts, UMLA; Claims of Joanna Kidwiler (304-252) and Samuel Poffenberger (F-1434); David Hunter Strother, *A Virginia Yankee in the Civil War: The Diaries of David Hunter Strother*, ed. Cecil D. Eby Jr. (Chapel Hill, NC, 1961), 114.

25 Noyes, *The Bivouac and the Battlefield*, 262; Nelson, *As Grain Falls Before the Reaper*, 38. Nelson noted that after the battle, Dr. James Oliver of the 21st Massachusetts "made requisition for stoves to warm the tents, but none were ever sent;" Claims of Barney Houser (*Houser's Account*), Jacob C. Grove (G-1649), and Morgan and Andrew Rentch Miller (No. 4295).

26 Claims of Jacob H. Grove (No. 1267), John Miller (No. 2227), and Solomon Lumm (No. 340). Some Washington County bills of sale from 1850–60 refer to ten-plate stoves as "tin plate stoves."

Dwelling houses in the battle's aftermath remained crowded beyond belief. In addition to patients and surgeons packing homes, AOP officers squeezed inside dwellings for quarters, meetings, and meals. Isaac Newcomer, a son of Joshua Newcomer, recalled that after the battle, "[T]here were a number of officers boarding at his father's house . . . among them were Majors, captains, lieutenants, and there may have been colonels."

Isaac's sister, Josephine Newcomer Miller, attested that Federals occupied her parents' farm "for 3 or 4 weeks . . . there was a great number of them encamped on the farm." During this span, she remembered seeing many Northern officers in her home. "One was Major Keenan," Josephine recalled. "These officers were back and forth from the house. They took their meals three times a day at my father's house."[27]

Near Bakersville, Captain Alfred Torbert established his headquarters near Thomas Barnum's farm. According to Barnum, Torbert's headquarters were "only a little distance from my house . . . it was about two stone throws [away]." Consequently, Torbert and his staff occasionally quartered in Barnum's house, sharing the space with the farmer's wife and children. Barnum recalled, "[W]hen the day was bad they would use my best room for their headquarters; they would set their tables in my house and eat there."[28]

U.S. generals encamped on various farms after the battle. George McClellan established AOP headquarters on the Home farm of Kesia Showman, located on modern-day Mills Road. South of this property, in the vicinity of Antietam Iron Works, Gen. Ambrose Burnside relocated IX Corps headquarters to the farm of Kesia Showman's son, Raleigh Showman.

During I Corps's six-week encampment, Samuel I. Piper frequently conversed with Brig. Gen. James Ricketts, "who had his headquarters at my house." Near Sharpsburg village, Piper's nephew boarded Gen. Abner Doubleday, who "resided at Mr. [Samuel D.] Piper's house for a month or more." Stephen P. Grove also accommodated Federal brass. He wrote, "I willingly gave up my large and commodious house to Genl [Fitz John] Porter for his headqua[r]ters, and my wife

---

27 Claim of Joshua Newcomer (*RG* 123, No. 272). "Major Keenan" was probably Peter Keenan, who commanded the 8th Pennsylvania Cavalry. Regimental records indicate that Keenan may have ranked as captain while occupying the Newcomers' house. Newcomer's near neighbor, Catherine Tenant (*RG* 92, 54-1464), alleged that the 8th Pennsylvania Cavalry took grains and fencing from her property after the battle.

28 Claims of Thomas Barnum (*RG* 92, 131-1078 and *RG* 123, No. 333).

and little children took a back room." The Groves also boarded surgical staff and displaced neighbors, further crowding the quarters.[29]

Throughout the region, the Union army commandeered homes and outbuildings for various purposes. In the vicinity of Bakersville, farmer Elias Eakle testified that "the government had my barn there as a storage for their guns." Squire Jacob Miller complained that "Provost Gards [were] occupying our basement story and washouse to cook and wash in."[30]

After the AOP occupied the Samuel Grove heirs' farm, soldiers seized a tenant house on the property "for holding Court Martial." A postwar investigation found that the Groves' building was "occupied by the federal troops . . . for two or three days. Said house was used for purpose to hold Court Martial."[31]

A number of blacksmith shops stood on farms and village town lots. As per the 1860 Federal census, twelve Sharpsburg residents made their living as blacksmiths and thus depended on the workshops. After the battle, though, military forces utilized the outbuildings for various needs and seized supplies from the shops.

Examples include William Roulette, who sought repayment for "75 Pounds Iron taken from Blacksmith shop." Second, Henry F. Neikirk testified that his

---

29 The 1862 ownership of the Showmans' Home farm is complex. David Showman, the husband of Kesia Showman, owned a vast amount of acreage upon his death in 1858. Afterward, as Otho Showman explained, "My mother was entitled to her dower of one third but in lieu thereof we paid her a certain sum of money each year during her life time in pursuance of a verbal agreement entered into between us." In 1859, land record IN 13 / 740 transferred David Showman's "dower of his widow, Kezia Showman, to his five children." However, Kesia continued to own interest in her husband's estate. The 1860 Federal census for Sharpsburg lists her with $7,350 in landholdings. Also, Kesia Showman filed a claim (*RG* 92, Entry 843, Book 50, Box 772, L-304, Claim 268) for 605 panels of fencing destroyed by "the Army of the Potomac in the months of September & October 1862." Only landowners could file claims for fencing, which suggests that Kesia owned or co-owned her Home farm when McClellan established his AOP headquarters on the property after the battle; "198—Burnside's Headquarters, circa 1840. South of Sharpsburg, MD," online article, Washington Historical Trust, http://washingtoncountyhistoricaltrust.org/198-burnside-headquarters-circa-1840-south-of-sharpsburg-md/; Claim of Samuel I. Piper (No. 1310); Claims of Samuel D. Piper (Claims D-2392 & D-2393 and Case No. 440). George F. Noyes, an officer on Doubleday's staff, wrote that the division's camp on Oct. 12 moved closer to Sharpsburg, where "the general hired rooms in a house, and the staff encamped in a field close by." See Noyes, *The Bivouac and the Battlefield*, 256; Claim of Stephen P. Grove (No. 7354).

30 Claim of Elias Eakle (No. 1291); Jacob Miller to Amelia and Christian Houser, October, 1862, WMR; Claim of Stephen P. Grove (No. 7354).

31 Claims of Jeremiah P. Grove (*RG* 92, Book G, Box 94, Claim G-1632) and Jacob C. Grove (G-1649). Further research may reveal details of the court-martial. It possibly involved I Corps, given that Gen. John F. Reynolds reportedly based his headquarters on the Samuel Grove heirs' farm after the battle.

"blacksmith shop & tools were used" for twenty days. During this time, Neikirk saw "Dr. Walker, Chaplain of the 81 Pa Vols shoe some horses there." Third, Raleigh Showman and his brothers filed a claim for the IX Corps's "Use of blacksmith shop for 3 weeks" and appropriation of thirty bushels of coal from said building. Last, on Lot 38 in Sharpsburg village, V Corps soldiers impressed Peter Beeler's blacksmith shop, using it "for mechanical purposes [and] repairs."[32]

Mill operators encountered similar interruptions. Samuel Pry and Joshua Newcomer typically profited in the months of September and October by grinding threshed grains. After hospital forces converted their gristmills into field hospitals, business ground to a halt.

Inflicting further setbacks to millers and their clients, soldiers confiscated some of the mills' inventories. For example, at Solomon Lumm's mill, U.S. troops seized barrels of flour, grain bags, mill brushes, scales, and bolting cloths. Civilian John Otto delivered his rye harvest to a nearby gristmill before the battle, intending to pick up the ground meal later. Instead, to Otto's dismay, soldiers confiscated his rye as "forage for the army horses."[33]

Storeowners also lost heavily. Confederates reportedly plundered two Keedysville stores owned by John Cost and Frederick Wyand. After the Union army occupied the town, medical forces impressed Wyand's store as a field hospital. According to Wyand, construction of his brick building "had just had just been completed when the Surgeon of McClellan's Army took possession of it." One soldier estimated the "Wyand store building . . . had 243 wounded in it for awhile," which certainly delayed the launch of the new business. Wyand suffered more misfortunes when U.S. medical staff appropriated items in the store left behind by Confederates, such as candles, kerosene, and tools.[34]

32 Claims of William Roulette (No. 4299), Henry F. Neikirk (H-4109), Raleigh Showman (F-1183), Peter Beeler (*RG* 92, Entry 812, Box G, Claim G-1771). Neikirk possibly misidentified the chaplain or regiment. The 81st Pennsylvania's roster lists Stacy Wilson as chaplain from 1861–1864.

33 Claims of Samuel Pry (95-1691 and 81-1489); Nelson, *As Grain Falls Before the Reaper*, 29; Claims of John Otto (G-1857), John Miller (No. 2227), and Solomon Lumm (No. 340). Col. John Miller rented the mill to Lumm in 1862, and both listed mill-related damages in their separate claims. Other mills suffered losses after the battle. For example, the AOP seized Squire Jacob Miller's sawmill for hospital purposes. Thereafter, pickets used the building as a rendezvous, prolonging the interruption of Miller's business. See Snyder, *Trembling in the Balance*, 45.

34 Claims of Frederick Wyand (*RG* 92, G-1624 and *RG* 123, No. 14112); James, *Echoes of Battle*, 95. Testimony in Wyand's claim suggests that his store's construction was "practically

In Sharpsburg village, an AOP quartermaster based his headquarters in Jacob H. Grove's store. Testimony does not clarify whether Grove continued running the shop during the occupation, but U.S. troops interrupted business at another village store. Soon after the battle, Squire Jacob Miller wrote that soldiers forced Hilliard F. Hebb "to moove all his goods out of the store and they occupy the room as a store for themselves."[35]

Brothers William M. Cronise and Benjamin F. Cronise operated two dry goods stores in Sharpsburg village in 1862. Two months before the battle, Benjamin Cronise opened an additional shop in the Confederate town of Shepherdstown, Virginia. The risky venture backfired. Cronise was "arrested by a squad of Ashby's Cavalry" and his entire "stock of goods . . . valued at about $2,000 were all seized and removed by order of the rebel authorities."

Benjamin's brother, William Cronise, suffered losses during the Antietam Campaign. Dr. A. A. Biggs wrote, "Wm. Cronises' store was broken open and all his goods taken." Biggs did not allude to whether Federals, Confederates, or both looted William's store, but woes for the Cronise brothers continued. Three days after the battle, the U.S. Sanitary Commission commandeered one of the Cronise-owned stores in the village for use as a supply depot.

Dr. C. R. Agnew, a member of the commission, reported, "I took on Saturday a store at Sharpsburgh, hiring it of a Union citizen of the name of Cronise." The following day, Agnew and others unpacked the commission's supply boxes "and filled the shelves and bins" inside Cronise's shop. Agnew did not specify which Cronise brother owned the store, nor did he mention whether he paid Cronise for the occupancy. Regardless, the commission's supplies took up most of the space.

---

completed" when U.S. forces commandeered the building. Washington County land record IN 16 / 236 cites that Wyand purchased the lot in May 1862.

35 Claim of Jacob Avey, Sr. (No. 9908). Robert W. Grove, a son of Jacob H. Grove, testified in Avey's case that "Q.M. Lieut. Coburn had his head quarters in our store" after the Battle of Antietam. Grove may have referred to Lieutenant Colonel Albert V. Colburn, an assistant adjutant general on McClellan's staff. In Jacob H. Grove's claim (No. 1267), John F. Delauney testified that Grove "resided in Sharpsburg" in 1862 and "at one time kept store." Another son of Jacob H. Grove, James H. Grove, lived in Hagerstown during the war. From 1861–69, James owned part of Lot 1 on Sharpsburg's public square, opposite Jacob H. Grove's home (see land records IN 15 / 502 and WMCKK 1 / 263). Thus, the Groves may have operated their store on Lot 1; Jacob Miller to Amelia and Christian Houser, October 1862, WMR. Squire Miller described the storeowner as "H. T. Hebb," but no such person lived in Sharpsburg during the war. Hilliard F. Hebb, though, appears in 1860–70 census listings as a merchant in Sharpsburg village. Land records suggest that Hebb resided on Lot 49E on the public square in 1862.

Supporting this argument, the *New York Times* reported that the U.S. Sanitary Commission's depot in Sharpsburg village included "28,763 pieces of dry goods," along with "shirts, towels, bed ticks, and pillows, 30 barrels of linen bandages and lint, [and] 3138 pounds of farina." To create room for so many items, Cronise likely removed some or all of his goods from the building—assuming that soldiers had not already plundered the store of its inventory.[36]

Disruption of the Chesapeake and Ohio Canal caused various hardships to Sharpsburg's populace. Because Confederates sabotaged the waterway earlier in the 1862 Maryland Campaign, the bed near Sharpsburg remained dry from early September through mid-October 1862. This damage brought canal operations to a standstill.

Much of the canal's freight involved coal mined in Cumberland, Maryland, located about eighty miles northwest of Sharpsburg. Subsequently, Sharpsburg's boatmen earned their living by freighting the mineral fuel from Cumberland coal companies to ports in Georgetown, Alexandria, and Washington, DC. Canal boats were expensive, valued on average at $1,500 (about $42,000 in 2022 U.S. money). Boatmen mortgaged the vessels, paying their grantors a share of wages earned from each round-trip shipment. Standard terms required boat captains to pay higher installments until completing a prearranged number of trips, after which the payments decreased. The sabotaged canal, however, cost boatmen potential wages and prolonged their higher installments.[37]

The suspension of canal operations affected many workers, including lockkeepers, laborers, and cooks. Among the latter was Mary Moore, a single

---

36 *HFTL*, June 4 and June 11, 1862. Confederates detained Cronise for one week in Martinsburg, VA, and then released him; Biggs to Kalb, September 29, 1862, WMR; Land records for brothers William and Benjamin Cronise, along with the last will and testament of their father (George Cronise, will liber E / folio 475) cite the brothers' ownership of village lots 2W and 48W in Sep. 1862. Census and tax records list William and Benjamin Cronise as merchants in 1850 and 1860. Both listed their occupation in 1870 as "retired dry goods merchant." Federal census records from 1860–1880 list the brothers in separate households, possibly the locations of their stores, given the proximity to the town's public square. Benjamin F. Cronise (Dwelling #1564 in 1860 and Dwelling #109 in 1870) is associated with Lot 48W. William M. Cronise (Dwelling #1636 in 1860 and Dwelling #147 in 1870) possibly lived and operated his store at Lot 2W; United States Sanitary Commission. *Documents of the U.S. Sanitary Commission*, vol. 1., doc. 48, 11-12; *New York Times*, October 1, 1862.

37 Harland D. Unrau, *Historic Resource Study: Chesapeake & Ohio Canal. United States Department of the Interior, National Park Service* (Hagerstown, MD, 2007), 736-740. For examples of Sharpsburg's canal boat mortgages, see Washington County land records IN 15 / 551, IN 16 / 474 and LBN 1 / 318; Williamson, *PPT*; *New York Tribune*, September 15, 1862; Snyder and Surkamp, "Destroy the C & O Canal."

mother of three children, employed in 1860 as "Cook on Boat." With canal business halted, Moore may have struggled to make ends meet, especially if soldiers had plundered her home of food.

Had Rebels not damaged the canal, Timothy Coin would have busied himself tending Lock 40, located northeast of Samuel I. Piper's farm. Instead, the Irish lockkeeper watched military forces take over his home. Coin, his wife, and two children shared their small lockhouse with Union hospital staff "for a month or more, and there were at times as many as 16 sick & wounded soldiers in the house."[38]

Under normal circumstances, Samuel Swain, a canal boatman living in Sharpsburg village, would have freighted coal to the capital cities. Instead, Swain pastured his remaining horses near the Potomac River "in the month of September 1862 owing to the interruption to his business on the canal."

The drained waterway impacted ancillary businesses associated with the canal industry, such as laborers who hauled coal from Grove's Landing and workers employed in riverside stores. For example, Daniel S. Mumma in 1862 "was engaged at Grove's warehouse in selling flour," and Nathan Highbarger "worked as a carpenter in the shop belonging to the C & O Canal." Both men may have lost income due to the weeks-long cessation of canal business.

Also, the dry canal prevented farmers from exporting threshed grains to the District of Columbia region. Soon after Confederates drained the canal, *The Evening Star* in Washington reported, "This suspension of navigation with the up country of course cuts off arrivals of flour and grain from the fine grain-growing country in Maryland . . . lying near the Potomac."

Even after engineers repaired the waterway in mid-October 1862, heavy rains delayed business from fully resuming. Thereafter, boat crews shared the canal with small military steamers rushing supplies to McClellan's army and navigated between contending pickets guarding both sides of the Potomac River. Of course,

---

38 The 1860 Federal census for Sharpsburg lists Mary Moore and her children in Dwelling #1320; Claim of Timothy Coin (*RG* 92, Box 578, Claim 212-719); The 1860 Federal census lists the Coins in Dwelling # 1534; "Life as a Lock Keeper on the C & O Canal," online article, C & O Canal Trust, February 29, 2016, https://www.canaltrust.org/2016/02/life-as-a-lock-keeper-on-the-co-canal/. The average lockhouse measured 30 feet by 18 feet and contained two stories. Lock 40 is west of Nicodemus Heights at C & O Canal mile marker 79.41. Reilly (*BOA*) referred to it as the "Timothy Coin Lock." Timothy Coin died in 1866, and Henry Johnson tended Lock 40 thereafter, explaining why some Antietam battlefield maps refer to Lock 40 as "Johnson's Lock."

Abner and Magdalena (Emmert) Highbarger lived in the town of Sharpsburg at the time of the battle. Abner, a carpenter by trade, was likely among the local workers affected by the AOP's occupation of the area. *Courtesy of David Zeller and Mary Stephanos*

many canal boatmen remained out of work due to the military's appropriation of their mules and horses.[39]

The stifling military and medical presence affected Sharpsburg's daily life, as well. It suspended school services and denied church congregations the use of their houses of worship. It also disrupted the livelihoods of countless workers, including coopers, carpenters, seamstresses, and shoemakers.

Also, the armies' movements through Western Maryland during the 1862 campaign interrupted mail service and newspaper production. For instance, in the town of Frederick, *The Examiner* ceased printing from September 10–24 on account that "the Rebel occupation of Frederick and sacking of the *Examiner* office prevented publication." In Hagerstown, the editors of the pro-Union *Herald of Freedom and Torch Light* stopped the press and fled town when the Confederate army approached. Similarly, the proprietor of Middletown's *Valley Register* "skeddadled" to Pennsylvania for fear of the "pack of drunken Rebels." When the editor resumed printing on September 19, he reported, "We are yet without a regular mail."[40]

---

39 Claims of Samuel Swain (N-2188) and William M. Blackford (No. 1324). Daniel S. Mumma testified in Blackford's case; Claim of Benjamin Graves (*RG* 92, Book F, Box 78, Claim F-713). Nathan Highbarger testified in Graves's case; Unrau, *Historic Resource Study: Chesapeake & Ohio Canal*, 736; Lee and Barbara Barron, *The History of Sharpsburg, Maryland* (Sharpsburg, MD, 1972), 68. Sharpsburg had no railroad during the war, and thus merchants often moved goods on the C & O Canal. Stephen P. Grove's ledger is rife with sales transactions involving coal, hatchets, ladders, sarsaparilla, whisky, salt, and barrels of mackerel. He likely imported his goods to Grove's Landing, located near his home. During the war, hostilities interrupted canal commerce, and Grove's sales dropped. He recorded few transactions from September–December 1862. See Grove, *Ledger of Stephen P. Grove of Mt. Airy*. For further reading on goods sold in the mid-1800s, see *Ledger of B. F. Rohrback, Merchant of Sharpsburg, Washington County, 1856–1885*, WMR.

40 Sharpsburg's 1860 census reported about sixty different occupations. Farming, by far, employed most of the workers; *The Examiner* [Frederick, MD], September 10 (24), 1862; *HFTL*, September 10 (24), 1862; *The Valley Register*, September 19, 1862.

The military's arbitrary arrests of civilians also continued. Henry Marion Johnson, who lived with his parents at Lock 39 on the C & O Canal, recalled that Federal authorities arrested his father, Henry Johnson, Sr., on suspicion "that he was sending messages to the Rebels across the river." Johnson, Sr. "was first held in the orchard of the Douglas place [Ferry Hill]." Thereafter, soldiers imprisoned him in Frederick, some twenty miles distant. After a few weeks, Henry recalled, his father "was allowed to walk home."[41]

At Ferry Hill, Union forces kept hawkish watch on Rev. Robert Douglas. U.S. officers knew that Douglas's son, Lt. Henry Kyd Douglas, served on General Stonewall Jackson's staff in the ANV. Hence, after the AOP occupied Sharpsburg on September 19, Federal officers put the Confederate-sympathizing minister under house arrest. They also ordered the Douglas family to close their Virginia-facing shutters out of concern they might signal intelligence to Rebel friends across the Potomac.

According to Henry Kyd Douglas, on "one stormy night," wind blew open one of the shutters. Mrs. Douglas passed by the window holding a candle and caught the eye of a Federal sentinel. The next morning, U.S. officers arrested Rev. Douglas "for giving signals to the enemy." Provost guards marched Douglas to Berlin, near Harpers Ferry, where the minister refused to take the oath of allegiance "as the price of his release." Thereafter, he was "sent to Fort McHenry without further parley."

Meanwhile, Douglas's wife and daughter worried over the reverend's whereabouts while finding themselves "absolutely unprotected." Other Secessionist families may have felt the same. When Robert Douglas's arrest made national headlines, the *New York Times* reported that "numerous traitors" remained in Sharpsburg "and are only awaiting a favorable opportunity to impart valuable information to the rebels."[42]

*   *   *

---

41 Henry Marion Johnson interview, ANBL. Johnson stated that the arrest occurred "during the time of the battle."

42 Smith, *History of the 118th Pennsylvania Volunteers*, 91-93. The New York pickets agreed to the parley because "all their officers were in Sharpsburg at a dinner;" Stonebraker, *A Rebel of '61*, 43-45; Douglas, *I Rode With Stonewall*, 181-182; *New York Times*, November 4, 1862; Max L. Grivno, *Historic Resource Study: Ferry Hill Plantation*, United States Department of the Interior, National Park Service, Chesapeake & Ohio National Historic Park (Hagerstown, MD, 2007), 60-61. Authorities released Rev. Douglas from Fort McHenry in Dec. 1862.

As news of the battle spread throughout the Northern and Southern states, civilians from outlying towns flocked to Western Maryland. Hagerstown, having the nearest railroad depot to Sharpsburg, became congested with incoming travelers en route to the battlefield.

Emotions ranged among the out-of-towners, from anguished families to excited tourists. All was turmoil. A New York Times correspondent observed on September 26, "I found Hagerstown completely overwhelmed with visitors, some from mere curiosity, others in pursuit of the graves of their relatives and friends." The journalist found it "quite impossible to obtain a shelter anywhere." Hiring transportation to the battlefield was equally as challenging. "[B]ands of people were running about in bewilderment," the *Times* reported, "imploring of every owner of a trap—no matter if only a donkey cart—to take them to Sharpsburgh at the rate of $2 apiece or anything else they chose to name."

A group of Pennsylvanians found "a perfect jam of people in Hagerstown ere we arrived, and each succeeding train added to the number." The visitors struggled to find rides to the battlefield. "[E]very horse and vehicle in the town and neighborhood," one traveler complained," had been pressed into the service of Uncle Sam, or hired at the most exorbitant prices." The Pennsylvanians eventually secured transportation and joined the flood tide of people rushing to Sharpsburg.[43]

The region soon became "a crowded scene of chaos," overrun by "gawkers, souvenir hunters, sutlers, regional volunteers, newspaper correspondents and relatives of soldiers." Combined with 75,000 troops and thousands of wounded, the throngs of visitors "congested area roads, disrupted daily business and further depleted the local food supply."

Two weeks after the battle, the *Herald of Freedom and Torch Light* described the masses. "Strangers from every part of the loyal states continue to visit the battle field in large numbers," during which "every vehicle and horse seemed to be pressed into the service, and one continued stream of humanity flowed down the Sharpsburg turnpike."

A New York journalist reported, "We had proceeded hardly two miles from the [Hagerstown] village before we were met by long rows of supply wagons, ambulances filled with wounded, and groups of Maryland soldiers who having obtained leave of absence were wending their way homeward." As the New Yorker pressed toward Sharpsburg, he discovered that "the number of vehicles and

---

43 *New York Times*, October 4, 1862; *Altoona Tribune*, October 2, 1862.

soldiers increased, almost blocking up the way and indicating the near presence of the battle-field."

Military trains on the narrow turnpike moved "at a snail's pace," causing impatient travelers to "lose their temper" and "curse the road because it was not built with direct reference to the very emergency of travel which has arisen." A Hagerstown resident among the masses recalled, "The road was so full of men and wagons that we could hardly travel."[44]

Some of the visitors arrived on the battlefield to gawk at the carnage and search for souvenirs. "The battle-field of Wednesday is daily trampled by a small army of curiosity seekers," a local newspaper reported. "They come from the West, North and East, and win their way here by all sorts of contrivances. The conveyances from Frederick and Hagerstown come out loaded down, and many more even walk."

Captain George F. Noyes, an I Corps artillery officer, remembered seeing "the van of that immense army of visitors, which for several weeks came pouring in to visit Antietam." Lieutenant Josiah Marshall Favill of the 57th New York noted, "The country people flocked to the battlefield like vultures." Several sightseers, Favill remembered, "stood around, dazed and awe-stricken by the terrible evidence of the great fight." At the same time, hundreds more "were scattered over the field, eagerly searching for souvenirs in the shape of cannon balls, guns, bayonets, swords, canteens, etc."[45]

Some out-of-towners arrived with more noble intentions, bringing food and supplies to Dr. Letterman's medical department. The volunteers hailed from different states and included nurses, physicians, relief agency delegates, and politicians. E. W. Funk, Mayor of Hagerstown, recalled that on Friday, September 19, "I was on the battlefield, and also on the farm of said [Joseph] Poffenberger." Augustus Bradford, Governor of Maryland, "accompanied by some fifteen or

44 Susan W. Trail, "Remembering Antietam: Commemoration and Preservation of a Civil War Battlefield," Ph.D. Dissertation, University of Maryland, 2005, 62-63; *New York Times*, October 5, 1862; Ernst, *TATC*, 167. Ernst cited the diary of John Koogle, Sep. 18, 1862, WMR; *HFTL*, October 1, 1862, 2C and October 22, 1862, 2B; Alexander, *The Battle of Antietam*, 152. Alexander noted that heavy traffic brought profits to the Hagerstown and Sharpsburg Turnpike Company, which levied tolls on their new, macadamized thoroughfare connecting the two towns. However, the tolls came with a tradeoff as the constant tread of horses and wagons damaged the road.

45 *HFTL*, October 2, 1862, 3A; Noyes, *The Bivouac and the Battlefield*, 220; Favill, *Diary of a Young Officer*, 190.

twenty Surgeons," arrived in Sharpsburg on September 21 "with a large quantity of medical stores and other provisions for the wounded soldiers."

One account claimed that Governor Andrew Curtin of Pennsylvania volunteered at Sharpsburg after the battle. While there, Curtin helped a maimed patient of the 28th Ohio into an ambulance, whose blood stained the governor's "hands and clothing." Curtin later learned, purportedly, that the soldier was a female in disguise named Catherine E. Davidson, who had followed her fiancé into the battle.[46]

From September 19 through mid-October, volunteers, tourists, and reinforcements passing through Sharpsburg gaped at the war-torn village. Many townsfolk lacked the money to repair artillery damages, given the more significant need to replace food, clothing, and other property taken by military forces. Outsourcing the renovations to contractors was also expensive, as soldiers appropriated large quantities of building supplies for use in camps and hospitals, spiking the prices for materials and labor. When describing the high cost of repairs after the battle, Jacob McGraw stated, "[Y]ou could not get a mechanic hardly at all here then and when you did you had to pay about three dollars a day."

The town of Sharpsburg, meanwhile, was an eyesore. On October 6, a private in the 96th Pennsylvania noted, "[A]t sharps burg the houses are rittled with balls and shells nearly all the gimleys [chimneys] . . . of the brick houses are all racket and the streets are laying full shells and Balls I never seen such a sight."[47]

Few village homes had space for boarding out-of-town guests because many residents already shared their dwellings with wounded soldiers and medical staff. Nevertheless, some villagers still managed to board the travelers, cramping quarters in the process. Anna Holstein, a nurse from Pennsylvania, along with five other volunteers and crates of supplies, jammed into one room inside Barney Houser's house on West Main Street. Holstein described the accommodations as an "uncomfortable little place . . . crowded with boxes and swarming with hospital flies."

46 Claim of Joseph Poffenberger (RG 123, No. 1300); HFTL, September 24, 1862; Linus P. Brockett, *Lights and Shadows of the Great Rebellion: Or, The Camp, the Battle Field and Hospital, Including Thrilling Adventures, Daring Deeds, Heroic Exploits, and Wonderful Escape of Spies and Scouts, Together With the Songs, Ballads, Anecdotes, and Humorous Incidents of the War* (Philadelphia, 1866), 358-360. According to Brockett, Davidson lost her arm to amputation after the battle. Her unidentified fiancé was reportedly killed at Antietam.

47 Claim of the Sharpsburg Lutheran Church (No. 4058); Alexander, "Destruction, Disease, and Death." 143. Alexander's source is an Oct. 7, 1862 letter by Private Daniel Faust, ANBL.

Due to the area's food shortage, Sharpsburg's hosts had little to offer their boarders. A Pennsylvania correspondent wrote, "[I]nstead of 'beef a'la mode,' we get mule fricassee, and instead of old Java, or Mocha coffee, we get unadulterated breakfast beverage from new crop acorns . . . commend us to Sharpsburg luxuries 'till the last syllable of recorded time.'"

Other guests described the artillery damages. A chaplain from the 97th New York "staid at Sharpsburg over night" and observed that "every house . . . is pierced with cannon balls & shells." A *Philadelphia Inquirer* correspondent found that artillery during the battle threw "nine hissing meteors . . . entirely through" his guestroom," puncturing "two loop-holes in the east wall, which ventilates it in the latest and most popular Sharpsburg style."

A New York journalist struggled to find a vacancy in town but finally secured lodging in "an unassuming private little house in one of the side streets." He found "there was not a single pane of glass" in his room, as ordnance had shattered the windows. One shell, he deduced, "had entered one window, torn away the architecture and a square yard of the wall, and burst apparently in the center of the room." The explosion "knocked to atoms" the bedroom, piercing walls with a dozen holes and blasting shrapnel through the floor and ceiling. "Another shot," he noted, "had gone right through the bedstead and feather-bed which was offered me . . . passing clean through the wall behind." Such damage was not an isolated case, though. The New Yorker concluded, "[T]his house is only a specimen of many others in the place."

Indeed, artillery damage left many houses poorly insulated as cold autumn temperatures approached. Primitive as boarders found the lodging, at least their stays were brief. For Sharpsburg residents, the crude accommodations were their indefinite reality. Describing her home after the battle, Mary Ellen Piper wrote, "I tell you we are living in style now; no carpet on the floor in some of the rooms and only one room in the house that a cannon ball had not penetrated."[48]

---

48 Holstein, *Three Years in Field Hospitals*, 12; John Ferguson to "Kate," October 16, 1862. John V. Ferguson letters, transcribed by Leith Regan, New York State Military Museum, Division of Military and Naval Affairs, Saratoga Springs, NY, http://dmna.ny.gov/historic/reghist/civil/infantry/97thInf/97thInfFergusonLetters.pdf; *Philadelphia Inquirer*, October 27, 1862, 1. Testimony from Elias U. Knode's war claim (L-2074) cites that there was only one hotel operating in Sharpsburg village in Sep. 1862—the Maryland Hotel, located on Lot 49W. After the battle, the town's overcrowding prompted other villagers to capitalize on the situation by renting rooms to travelers; *New York Times*, October 4, 1862; *Philadelphia Inquirer*, October 27, 1862; E. P. to Sally Farran, October 4, 1862, *Dan Masters' Civil War Chronicles*.

*   *   *

Among those rushing to the battlefield area were kinfolk hoping to locate and care for wounded soldiers. Some visitors hailed from Confederate states and crossed the Potomac River at Blackford's Ford under flags of truce. The arriving relatives from the North and South added to the masses congesting the Antietam Valley.

A few days after the battle, George Templeton Strong of the U.S. Sanitary Commission squeezed up a crowded street in Sharpsburg village, passing "ambulance, army wagons, beef cattle, staff officers, recruits, kicking mules, &c &c &c." Amid the turmoil, Strong spotted a familiar face, Arabella Barlow. She also belonged to the sanitary commission and had arrived in Sharpsburg to nurse her wounded husband. Despite the troops, wagons, and animals choking the road, Strong noted that Mrs. Barlow appeared "serene & self-possessed as if walking down Broadway." Unfortunately, not all visitors shared the same demeanor.[49]

Joyous as some reunions may have been at Antietam's hospitals, many relatives were appalled by the crude conditions and demanded the discharge of their kin for recovery at home. Others, having learned in advance that their husbands, sons, or brothers died during the battle, made the solemn journey to seek the remains. Compounding their anguish, countless persons could not locate the bodies, as thousands of soldiers lay in unmarked graves.

For those who located their fallen loved ones, the scenes were understandably upsetting. One resident remembered a New Hampshire man arriving on her farm to claim the body of his son. "His grief," she recalled, "was very affecting." Villager John P. Smith escorted an Ohio woman to Smoketown Hospital to locate her wounded husband. When they arrived at the infirmary, an army surgeon broke the news that her husband "had died two days before her arrival and was buried." The doctor led John P. Smith and the stunned woman to the hospital's impromptu cemetery. "At the sight of the grave," Smith remembered, "she threw herself prostate upon it and wept in bitter agony."[50]

49 Pawlak, *Shepherdstown*, 115; *New York Times*, October 8, 1862; Strong Diary, September 22, 1862, NYHSM. The context of Strong's passage places him in Sharpsburg village. Arabella Barlow traveled to Sharpsburg to nurse her husband, Colonel Francis C. Barlow, who suffered a wound during the battle. Colonel Barlow jointly commanded the 61st and 64th New York at Antietam.

50 Official report of Dr. Jonathan Letterman, *OR*, vol. 19, 1:112; Williams, HWC, vol. 1, 2:362; *Antietam Valley Record*, October 31, 1895; Holstein, *Three Years in Field Hospitals*, 13.

Out-of-town mourners often lacked independent transportation to locate graves, exhume corpses, and transport remains to distant depots for shipment home. Consequently, some visitors paid local civilians for the grim services. Martin E. Snavely of Sharpsburg "hauled a six-horse load of coffins containing dead soldiers to Hagerstown . . . to be shipped home by friends who had come to look after them." A New Hampshire soldier hired Sharpsburg villager Samuel Show to locate and exhume the corpse of Corporal Charles M. Noyes of the 9th New Hampshire.[51]

Oral tradition cites that Sharpsburg villager Aaron Fry "assisted in locating many dead ones for friends." On one occasion, Fry helped a "Northern man" find his brother's grave near Burnside Bridge. Accepting ten dollars for the job, Fry dug up the remains and helped the man arrange shipment to the deceased's hometown, "like hundreds of others did [for] their friends."[52]

Private Robert Hubbard of the 14th Connecticut was among the hundreds of soldiers buried on William Roulette's farm. Hubbard's family paid Roulette to disinter the remains, buy a coffin, haul the body to Hagerstown, and arrange freighting on the Cumberland Valley Railroad. "Dear Friends," Roulette wrote to the Hubbards, "I have received your draft of $70.00 and have forwarded the remains of your brother by express." To reduce the family's expenses, Roulette bypassed the local undertaker's inflated rate and bought a coffin "from the cabinet maker at first cost which saved $15.00." Roulette mailed the change to the Hubbards, along with a brief note. "The battle caused considerable destruction of property here," wrote Roulette. "My nearest neighbor lost his house and barn to fire. I lost valuable horses, some sheep and hogs. Please write as soon as you receive this and inform me whether all is right."

Another resident, Aaron Good, invested time compiling the names and locations of Antietam's dead. He then used this information to profit. "In the village of Sharpsburg resides a man named Aaron Good," a newspaper reported, "who has a list of the names of all the Union soldiers buried there, and by his help the graves can easily be found, but he demands a large fee for his services."

Despite the entrepreneurial slant, Good's efforts brought closure to some families, including George and Margaret Wilson. The New York couple paid Good to exhume and ship home their son, Sergeant George Wilson, Jr., of the 82nd New York Infantry. "We received the remains of our son George," wrote the Wilsons to

---

51 Reilly, *BOA*; Lord, *History of the Ninth Regiment*, 123-124.

52 Reilly, *BOA*.

Good. "On their arrival we felt satisfied that you had transacted your part of the contract faithfully and honorably, and . . . paid that respect to the remains of one whom we had loved so dearly."[53]

The exhumations of Antietam's dead continued for weeks, recalled Capt. George F. Noyes. Traffic on the Hagerstown Turnpike, meanwhile, resembled "almost one continual funeral procession, bearing away to the north, the bruised bodies of the North's bravest sons." Dr. Alfred Castleman, a surgeon in the 5th Wisconsin, VI Corps, rode to Sharpsburg on September 28 in search of medicine. "The smell was horrible," wrote Castleman. "The road was lined with carriages and wagons conveying coffins and boxes for the removal of dead bodies, and the whole battle-field was crowded with people from distant States exhuming and removing the bodies of friends. 'Twas a sad, sad sight."

On October 1, the *Herald of Freedom and Torch Light* reported, "Friends and relatives of fallen soldiers are removing their bodies to their homes, and daily and hourly hearses may be seen slowly wending their way from the battle field with the remains of some fallen hero." One month later, the same newspaper observed, "The remains of the dead . . . continue to be removed by their friends. Last week we saw two ladies riding from that vast graveyard in a one-horse vehicle, both being seated upon the coffin which contained the remains of a relative."

While appearing to onlookers as an endless cortege, the removal of Antietam's dead was far from complete. In fact, when a cartographer visited the battlefield several months later, he estimated that more than 5,800 soldiers remained buried in Sharpsburg's soil.[54]

By late September, the patient population in Sharpsburg-Keedysville hospitals had thinned considerably. Many AOP convalescents rejoined their commands, while others with minor injuries relocated to regional hospitals. Confederate prisoners who recovered from their wounds traveled to Baltimore and Fortress Monroe for exchange.

In early October, *Hagerstown's Herald of Freedom and Torch Light* reported, "The [Union] wounded in the late battle at the Antietam creek are being rapidly removed

---

53 Clem, "Farmer Cheers Federals at Antietam." Clem cited William Roulette's letter to the Hubbard family, dated December 31, 1862; *HTL*, May 6, 1863, and June 14, 1865; George & Margaret Wilson to Aaron Good, June 4, 1863, "George Wilson, Jr.," web page, Antietam on the Web, http://antietam.aotw.org/officers.php?officer_id=8190.

54 Noyes, *The Bivouac and the Battlefield*, 220; Alfred L. Castleman, *The Army of the Potomac: Behind the Scenes* (Milwaukee, WI, 1863), 236-237; *HFTL*, October 1, 1862, 2D, and November 5, 1862, 2B; S. G. Elliott burial map, NYPL.

from the temporary hospitals in the vicinity of the battle field to Frederick and Washington in one direction, and to Hagerstown, Chambersburg, Harrisburg and Philadelphia in another." Although ambulances were "constantly moving over the various roads leading to and from the neighborhood of the recent engagement," there were "still a number of wounded left in temporary hospitals at Sharpsburg, Keedysville, Boonsboro', and intermediate points between these places." By mid-October, one correspondent estimated, "There are about 2,500 Union and rebel patients in the hospitals in and about Sharpsburgh."

Due to the reduced patient load in the battleground vicinity, the medical department consolidated the remaining wounded at the larger field hospitals, such as Smoketown, Locust Spring, and Mount Airy. Smaller field infirmaries subsequently ceased operations, allowing many families to regain full possession of their homes.[55]

Despite the downsized patient population and astounding amount of property taken from private citizens, supply problems persisted in Sharpsburg-area hospitals. Fortunately for Dr. Jonathan Letterman's medical department, help arrived.

Approximately three days after the battle, regional volunteers and relief agency delegates began arriving in the Antietam Valley with subsistence and provisions. The U.S. Sanitary Commission was among the first on the scene, "supplying the wounded with indispensable comforts before the Government could act." Most of the commission's supplies arrived "within ten days of the battle." Artillery officer George F. Noyes praised the sanitary commission. He wrote, "[N]o one could visit these hospitals without becoming a firm believer in the importance and value of this institution . . . within three days its forty agents had distributed food and clothing among eight thousand wounded men."

The U.S. Sanitary Commission did not act alone. Scores of nurses, including Clara Barton and Anna Holstein, traveled to Sharpsburg with supplies, as did the U.S. Christian Commission, which sent over seventy delegates to the battlefield. Nurse Maria Hall was among those who established a "ladies aid" station at Smoketown Hospital. She recalled, "[T]he Pennsylvania farmers, and some good friends from Montgomery County, Md., visited the camp and always brought substantial gifts of food for the wounded." In addition, Hall remembered giving

---

55 Duncan, *The Medical Department*, 35, 41-42; *HFTL*, October 1, 1862, 2D; *New York Times*, October 16, 1862.

"bread and butter parties," where volunteers served "from 600 to 700 sandwiches" to the patients.

The donated supplies brought temporary relief to wounded sufferers, but these provisions were "insufficient to relieve the distress." For example, several days after the battle, Anna Holstein learned that soldiers at Antietam "were actually dying for food, home comforts, and home care." She and other Pennsylvania volunteers arrived in Sharpsburg on October 6 to find that "a sad want of suitable food and medical stores was still felt." As days passed, Holstein recalled, "the short supply of medicine, food, and clothing continued."[56]

The need for subsistence and supplies, combined with overcrowding of the battlefield region, caused local prices to skyrocket. In early October, Mary Ellen Piper wrote, "Everything is remarkably high priced." Likewise, Anna Holstein noted that food "was almost impossible to buy at any price." The great demand prompted merchants in outlying towns to spike their rates. In Frederick, Dr. Lewis Steiner with the U.S. Sanitary Commission complained about shopkeepers' steep prices for brown sugar, coffee, and other dry goods. "The outrageous attempt to take advantage of the troubled condition of the community," Steiner vented, "had excited considerable indignation."

Hagerstown, too, was affected. The *Herald of Freedom and Torch Light* reported, "In consequence of the immense accession of soldiery and other strangers to our population, the prices of everything which enters into the consumption of a family have greatly advanced." The newspaper added, "Country produce of every description, as well as Groceries and Dry Goods, are sold at prices which have never before prevailed here, and which render living a very expensive affair." Exacerbating the problem, the *Freedom and Torch Light* opined, "A considerable proportion of our people seemed to have turned hucksters, buying and selling to the army at heavy profits, which has the effect of very greatly increasing prices."[57]

---

56 *New York Times*, October 1, 1862; Noyes, *The Bivouac and the Battlefield*, 244-245; William Howell Reed, *The Heroic Story of the United States Sanitary Commission, 1861–1865* (Boston, 1910), 18; United States Christian Commission, *United States Christian Commission for the Army and Navy: First Annual Report* (Philadelphia, 1863), vol. 1, 24; Edward P. Smith, *Incidents of the United States Christian Commission* (Philadelphia, 1869), 41; Banks, John. "Our Hearts Ached With Pity;" Holstein, *Three Years in Field Hospitals*, 11, 17.

57 E. P. to Sally Farran, October 4, 1862, *Dan Masters' Civil War Chronicles*; Holstein, *Three Years in Field Hospitals*, 12-13; Steiner, *Report of Lewis H. Steiner, M.D.*, 17. Steiner commented on the high prices after Confederates marched through Frederick in early September 1862; Ernst, *TATC*, 197; *HFTL*, October 15, 1862.

To be sure, hucksters descended upon the Sharpsburg region. When word of the battle spread to outlying towns, opportunists loaded commissary supplies into wagons, traveled to field hospitals and army camps, and sold food at inflated prices.

A horseman from the 3rd Pennsylvania Cavalry penned in his diary, "Citizens can be seen pouring into camp from every quarter this morning, with provisions for sale, such as pies, bread, cakes, of most every description; in short, everything good in the eatable line." While encamped near Blackford's Ford, Private Robert Goldthwaite Carter of the 22nd Massachusetts recalled that the hucksters "mostly came from Pennsylvania, and asked exorbitant prices for everything. One dollar a pound for butter, six small cakes for fifty cents, etc., was a fair sample of the outrageous advantage and monopoly which these non-combatant sharks seized upon."[58]

Sharpsburg-area residents who salvaged food from the raiding armies also took advantage of the high demand. Greed surely motivated some civilians to price-gouge the soldiers, while others may have charged steep prices to offset their property losses. Private Charles Johnson of Hawkins' Zouves recalled, "I was without a cent of money which would have enabled me to buy something from the neighboring farms to tempt my miserable appetite."

While encamped near Sharpsburg, Benjamin Crowninshield of the 1st Massachusetts Cavalry occasionally procured "bread and other provisions from the houses," but found that the homeowners often charged "exorbitant prices." In Keedysville, Ann Sophia Knadler sold pies and rolls to the 9th New York State Militia. Her prices charged are lost to time, but if she gouged the New Yorkers, they might have had the last laugh. According to local lore, "[Q]uite a number of them were Bowery men and they had a lot of counterfeit money that they passed on."

In early October, the *New York Times* reported, "The citizens of Sharpsburgh are rapidly replenishing their purses from sales made to the soldiers. Anything in the shape of edibles finds a ready market, and commands a good price." The *Times* noted that ladies of the village sold bread to regional peddlers for twenty-five cents a loaf. Yet, when the townswomen learned that peddlers were reselling the bread to U.S. soldiers at double the price, they cut off sales to the hucksters. According to

---

58 Regimental History Committee, *History of the Third Pennsylvania Cavalry, Sixtieth Regiment Pennsylvania Volunteers, in the American Civil War, 1861-1865* (Philadelphia, 1905), 138; Carter, *Four Brothers in Blue*, 122-123.

the *Times*, the Sharpsburg women declared "that Union men should not be imposed upon and robbed, [and] it is was in their power to prevent."[59]

*   *   *

Abraham Lincoln was among those who traveled to Sharpsburg after the battle. The U.S. president, accompanied by a small entourage of political friends, journeyed to Harpers Ferry on October 1 and then rode to the Antietam battlefield on October 2. Upon arrival late in the day, George McClellan and his staff escorted Lincoln to a "high knoll" on or near Philip Pry's farm, where the group briefly viewed the battleground. From there, the commander-in-chief asked to see "where Hooker went in," referring to the northern end of the battlefield. Accounts conflict as to what transpired next.

Colonel Charles S. Wainwright alleged that Lincoln's party became separated en route to the battlefield, and thus the anticipated tour never took place. However, Brigadier General Jacob D. Cox claimed that he was among the officers who led Lincoln "over the route which Sumner had followed in the battle." The presidential party, Cox wrote, crossed Antietam Creek near Keedysville. From there, they followed "the hollows and byways to the East Wood, and passed through this and the cornfields which had been the scenes of Hooker's and Mansfield's fierce fighting." The president, meanwhile, seemed "observant and keenly interested in the field of battle, but made no display of sentiment."

Journalists followed the group. The Washington *Evening Star* reported that during the afternoon of October 2, "General McClellan conducted the President over the Antietam battle-field, accompanied by a brilliant array of officers, including McClellan's staff." After escorting President Lincoln past the northern part of the battleground, General Cox recalled, "We visited the Dunker Church."

---

59 Johnson, *The Long Roll*, 199; Oliver T. Reilly, "Sharpsburg Letter," *Shepherdstown* [WV] *Register*, March 15, 1934, 8, "Newspaper Articles," vertical file, WMR. Reilly did not mention Mahlon Knadler's wife by name. Land and genealogical records, though, identify her as Ann Sophia Carr Knadler. See also Williams, HWC, vol. 2, 1:928; *New York Times*, October 4, 1862. There were undoubtedly civilians in the Sharpsburg community who shunned the wounded, hoarded food and supplies, or sold subsistence at high rates to the troops. Still, the author found very few accounts supporting such behavior. By contrast, author Gregory A. Coco, while researching the Gettysburg Campaign, located "over 75 negative comments toward Pennsylvanians, usually directed by the soldiers or medical personnel against the German inhabitants of the county." See Gregory A. Coco, *A Strange and Blighted Land: Gettysburg: The Aftermath of a Battle* (El Dorado Hills, CA, 2017), 248-254.

Oral tradition holds that, during Lincoln's stop at the church, "he addressed a number of civilians."[60]

During his visit to Sharpsburg, Lincoln likely witnessed the same desolation described by other observers in October. "[T]here was plenty yet to prove the awful scene which had so recently been enacted," the *New York Times* reported on October 4. "[F]ences torn down, and left in pell-mell confusion; canteens, haversacks, riddled caps, blood-stained shirts, and fragments of shell and cannon balls laying in every direction." A Philadelphia journalist reported, "Evidences of that great fight are yet everywhere visible," including "dead horses, and alas! long rows of graves and ditches."

Weeks after the battle, AOP surgeon Dr. William Child noted that trampled crop fields, fenceless farms, burned houses, the stench of death, and "the general ruin in every direction proclaimed the awful nature of war." Similarly, an *Altoona Tribune* correspondent observed in early October that the numerous graves and burial trenches "gave to every field the appearance of a vast cemetery," and thus showcased the raw "destructiveness of war."

As daylight faded on October 2, President Lincoln's party concluded their battlefield tour and rode to AOP headquarters on the Showman family's Home

60 Charles S. Wainright, *A Diary of Battle*, 109-111. Wainwright noted that Lincoln "suddenly changed his mind" about seeing the battleground and returned to AOP headquarters. However, Wainwright's editor on page 111 wrote that Wainwright, a conservative Democrat, gave "a prejudiced account of the President's visit;" Jacob D. Cox, *Military Reminiscences of the Civil War*, 2 vols. (New York, 1900), 1:364-365; *The Evening Star* [Washington, DC], October 3, 1862. *The Evening Star* reported that Lincoln left Harper's Ferry at noon on Oct. 2 and toured the Sharpsburg battlefield on the same day "during the afternoon;" Meade, *The Life and Letters*, 1:317. Meade wrote, "I had the distinguished honor of accompanying him [Lincoln] to the battle-field, where General McClellan pointed out to him the various phases of the day;" George B. McClellan, *McClellan's Own Story* (New York, 1887), 655. McClellan wrote to his wife, "The Presdt was very kind personally . . . I showed him the battle fields & am sure he departed with a more vivid idea of the great difficulty of the task we had accomplished;" Ward Hill Lamon, *Recollections of Abraham Lincoln*, ed. Dorothy Lamon Teillard (Washington, DC, 1911), 147-148. Lamon wrote that Lincoln's party arrived in Sharpsburg late on Oct. 2, "reaching there only in time to see very little before night;" E. Russell Hicks, "The Church and the Battlefield," *Church of the Brethren Gospel Messenger* (Elgin, IL), vol. 101, no. 6, February 9, 1952, 12-15; Schildt, *Drums Along the Antietam*, 253; *Morning Herald*, January 28, 1946. James Peterman, a Sharpsburg villager, claimed to have seen Lincoln "near the famous Dunkard Church;" Philip B. Kunhardt, Jr., Philip B. Kunhardt III, and Peter W. Kunhardt, *Lincoln: An Illustrated Biography* (New York, 1992), 321. The Kunhardts wrote that, at some point during the battleground tour, the president "shucked off his boots" before "wading in a brook on the Antietam battlefield." The Kunhardts cited no source for this account.

farm, located south of the village. Here, the Washington guests slept for the next two nights.[61]

During the president's visit to Sharpsburg, U.S. soldiers sabotaged a peddler's wagon, causing it to capsize. As troops confiscated bread loaves, "General Burnside's carriage, in which he was escorting the President . . . suddenly appeared." Burnside was reportedly escorting Lincoln to an IX Corps camp when the dignitaries drove upon the scene of plunder. The troops' misbehavior reportedly outraged the general. Not only did the looting embarrass him in front of the president, but it occurred in the wake of McClellan's General Order No. 159, which addressed depredations among the ranks. Consequently, Burnside berated the men, "using decidedly pointed and vigorous language in doing it." While this occurred, a witness recalled, "The President neither said or did anything to indicate that he was especially interested in the affair, he simply looked on."[62]

On the morning of October 3, IX Corps artillery "thundered forth a salute" for President Lincoln during his review on the Showman family's Home and Antietam farms. One witness recalled seeing Lincoln ride past the soldiers on a "dark chestnut horse" while "the bands played their loudest and sweetest strains, and from thousands of throats rose cheer on cheer."

The artillery salute, we can only presume, drew the attention of Kesia Showman and her adult sons, Otho and Raleigh. The Showmans' slaves and neighbors may have also gathered on nearby knolls to watch the spectacle. But, while the grandeur may have captivated some residents, neighboring families who suffered from military depredations, like the Wades, Markers, and Snyders, perhaps

---

61 *New York Times*, October 4, 1862; *Philadelphia Inquirer*, October 27, 1862; Child, *History of the Fifth Regiment*, 130; *Altoona Tribune*, October 2, 1862; *The Evening Star*, October 3, 1862. The *Evening Star* reported that, after Lincoln toured the battlefield on Oct. 2, he "returned to Gen. McClellan's headquarters, where he will pass the night in camp;" Cox, *Military Reminiscences of the Civil War*, 1:364-365. After visiting the Dunker Church on Oct. 2, Cox wrote that he and Lincoln's party "returned to camp by Bloody Lane and the central stone bridge." Various sources cite that McClellan established his headquarters on the Showman family's Home farm, located on present-day Mills Road. Widow Kesia Showman and her sons, Raleigh, Otho, and Alfred, owned several farms in 1862. Testimonies in the claim of Raleigh Showman (F-1183) alleged that the family's "'Home Farm' [was] where Genl. McClellan had his Head Quarters," and where Federal troops established a signal station. For further details on the property, see Save Historic Antietam Foundation, "SHAF acquires historic signal station site," November 10, 2000, http://shaf.org/historic-signal-station-site/. See also "WA-II-108 Showman Farm," architectural survey file, MHT, https://mht.maryland.gov/secure/Medusa/PDF/Washington/WA-II-108.pdf.

62 Graham, *The Ninth Regiment*, 341-346; *OR*, vol. 19, 2:376.

longed for better days when livestock, long slaughtered by this time, occupied the pastures instead of a martial review.

After Lincoln looked over IX Corps, McClellan escorted the president and his retinue north, riding through Sharpsburg village. Soldiers may have tipped local folks of the anticipated route, given that civilians supposedly lined the roads to steal a glimpse of the president.

Similar to previous rallies in Sharpsburg, in which enthusiastic villagers cheered the 9th New York State Militia in 1861 and greeted V Corps after the Battle of Antietam, patriotic townsfolk embraced the United States president. Among the eager masses was a *New York Times* reporter, who wrote that Abraham Lincoln "entered the village of Sharpsburgh at 11 1/2 A.M., to the great delight of the citizens, many of whom had never before seen either the President or Gen. McClellan." Noting the town's small population, the *Times* observed, "[W]hat few inhabitants it contains did their utmost, by cheering, waving flags and handkerchiefs, to express their unbounded gratification at being honored by such distinguished visitors."[63]

After Lincoln's party "moved slowly through the village," they continued up the Sharpsburg-Shepherdstown Pike to the Mount Airy farm of Stephen P. and Maria Grove. There, the president met with Major General Fitz John Porter and reviewed V Corps troops encamped in the vicinity. Similar to the earlier IX Corps review, "The customary salute of twenty-one guns was fired" to honor the president. Earlier in the war, an artillery salute might have thrilled the local populace. But two weeks after weathering the violent bombardment of shot and shell, the sudden cannon blasts on October 3 possibly jarred the nerves of nearby villagers.

During Lincoln's stop at Mount Airy, the president "talked with Mr. and Mrs. Grove in the hall" of their home. One source alleges that, during the conversation, the president placed his hand on the head of the Groves' daughter, Louisa, and "expressed his regrets . . . for the destruction and inconvenience the battle had brought to them."

---

63 Census records and claims testimony place Kesia Showman's other son, Alfred Showman, near Jones's Crossroads during the war. The 1860 slave schedule for Sharpsburg lists Raleigh Showman as owning twelve slaves; Lord, *History of the Ninth Regiment*, 148-149; Burrage, *History of the Thirty-Sixth Regiment*, 16. The regimental historian of the 36th Massachusetts cited, "The President arrived on the ground shortly after nine o'clock" on Oct. 3 "and passed us in review about ten;" *New York Times*, October 3, 1862. It's not known what route Lincoln took from the Showmans' farms to Sharpsburg village.

Antietam, Md. President Lincoln and Gen. George B. McClellan in the general's tent. Alexander Gardner took this October 1862 photograph on or near the Showman family's Home farm, located southeast of the battlefield on modern-day Mills Road. *Library of Congress*

Before leaving the Grove farm, Lincoln posed for photographs with Federal officers, including George McClellan, Dr. Jonathan Letterman, and Captain George Armstrong Custer. A correspondent traveling with the presidential party observed Lincoln address Confederate wounded, telling them they were "enemies through uncontrollable circumstances and he bore them no malice," offering to "take them by the hand with sympathy and good feeling."[64]

Concluding the Mount Airy visit, the president "next proceeded to review Gen. Reynolds, formerly Hooker's corps." These forces formed on various farms located west of the West Woods. According to an early historian of the town, Lincoln reviewed a portion of I Corps on the Moses Cox farm, which adjoined Nicodemus Heights on the west. While not confirmed by evidence, I Corps artillery probably thundered a salute to the president. This sound was all too familiar to nearby farm families who fled their homes days earlier amid terrifying cannonading.

After Lincoln reviewed I Corps, the presidential party continued north to Bakersville. Here, another artillery salute greeted the chief executive upon his arrival to review Maj. Gen. Franklin's VI Corps. Lincoln's visit to Bakersville completed his army corps reviews for the day. But as daylight faded on October 3, the president's work was far from finished. He returned to McClellan's headquarters with important business remaining.[65]

Lincoln's ulterior motive in visiting Sharpsburg was to urge McClellan to move. During the visit, the president met with the AOP commander to gauge the army's condition and inquire when it could embark on a new campaign. Later, McClellan wrote to his wife that the president was trying "to push me into a premature advance into Virginia." He sensed that Lincoln "was fully satisfied with

---

64 *New York Times*, October 3, 1862 and October 10, 1862. A Grove descendent alleged that Lincoln's interaction with wounded Confederates took place at Mount Airy. Evidence confirms that Confederates convalesced at Mount Airy for several weeks after the battle. However, the *New York Times* did not specify a location. Rather, it cited that the incident occurred "after leaving Gen. Richardson . . . in a house in which there was a large number of Confederate wounded;" Interview with Mrs. A. D. Grove, January 12, 1934, "Civilian Reports," folder, ANBL; Schildt, *Drums Along the Antietam*, 248; John W. Schildt, *Antietam Hospitals* (Chewsville, MD, 1996), 35-36.

65 *New York Times*, October 3, 1862; *The Evening Star*, October 4, 1862. *The Evening Star* reported that Lincoln began reviewing the AOP corps "with Gen. Burnside, near the mouth of the Antietam" and concluded "with that of Franklin, at Bakersville;" Reilly, *BOA*. Reilly wrote that Lincoln reviewed I Corps "on the Moses Cox farm, near the Norfolk and Western Railroad now, on the hills northwest of the Roulette crossing." According to war claims, Moses Cox (G-1657) rented his farm from Andrew Rentch (No. 4235) in Sep. 1862. The Rentch-Cox farm adjoined Nicodemus Heights on the east and modern-day Mondell Road on the west. "Northwest of Roulette's Crossing" likely refers to the postwar bisection of Mondell Road and the Norfolk and Western Railroad. In 1862, this land was part of Jacob Houser's farm, which adjoined the Rentch-Cox farm on the east. Houser's farm later devised to the Roulette family, perhaps explaining the name "Roulette's Crossing." See land records LBN 2 / 619 and 77 / 662. See also Williams, HWC, vol. 2, 1:951-952.

my whole course . . . that the only fault he could possibly find was that I was perhaps too prone to be sure that everything was ready before acting." Lincoln, meanwhile, told his personal secretary, John Hay, "After the battle of Antietam I went up to the field to try to get him [McClellan] to move . . . but when I came back he began to argue why he ought not to move." Ultimately, Lincoln desired action, but McClellan was not yet ready to advance.[66]

Abraham Lincoln departed Sharpsburg on October 4, making a short stop near the Middle Bridge and Antietam Creek. Local lore holds that the president, suffering from thirst, asked a resident for a glass of milk. The woman informed her distinguished guest that no milk was available "because the soldiers had taken all of the cows." Notwithstanding, Lincoln procured a drink from another civilian. William "Frisby" Keplinger allegedly fetched water for the president from a spring located "about 150–200 yards East of the Middle Bridge."[67]

Continuing, Lincoln and his party rode to the house of Philip and Elizabeth Pry. Here, the president met with Maj. Gen. Israel Richardson, who lay mortally wounded inside the home. During Lincoln's stop at the house, Elizabeth Pry served "a fine breakfast" to the guests. According to the Prys' granddaughter, Lincoln expressed his gratitude by mailing Elizabeth a note of thanks bearing his signature.[68]

66 Sears, *Landscape Turned Red*, 324; McClellan, *McClellan's Own Story*, 627; William Roscoe Thayer, *The Life and Letters of John Hay*, 2 vols. (Boston, 1908), 1:132-133. Lincoln and McClellan may have met several times between Oct. 1–4. Alexander Gardner captured an image of one said meeting inside McClellan's tent. See Alexander Gardner, *President Lincoln and Gen. George B. McClellan in the general's tent; another view.* Antietam Maryland United States, 1862. October 3. Photograph, https://www.loc.gov/item/2018666253.

67 "WA-II-1145 Keedysville Historic District," National Register of Historic Places Registration Form, MHT, sec. 8, p. 15. The source for the milk account was Mary Arita Van Rensselaer, *History of Keedysville*. The civilians mentioned in the account, cross-referenced with genealogical records, likely refer to Van Rensselaer's great-grandparents, Jacob and Sarah Staub. See https://mht.maryland.gov/secure/medusa/PDF/Washington/WA-II-1145.pdf. Supporting this argument, Robert Goldthwaite Carter (*Four Brothers in Blue*, 325) recalled halting during the battle between "the Pry house" and "that of [John] Eckers, 350 yards directly in our rear, occupied at this time by Straub, or Staub." The 1860 Federal census for Sharpsburg lists Jacob and Sarah Staub (spelled "Stopp") in Dwelling #1410 near Joseph Parks, who managed Philip Pry's Lower farm in 1862; Interview with J. A. Miller, January 9, 1934, "Civilian Reports," folder, ANBL. William "Frisby" Keplinger, son of David Keplinger, appears in the 1860 Federal census for Sharpsburg, Dwelling # 1449. The census lists the Keplingers near Daniel B. Grim, who testified that he lived near the Middle Bridge in Sep. 1862.

68 Lamon, *Recollections of Abraham Lincoln*, 148; Schildt, *Drums Along the Antietam*, 175; Janet Heim, "Unsung Heroines Offered Care, Compassion after Battle of Antietam," *Herald Mail*

Upon leaving the Pry house on October 4, Maj. Gen. McClellan escorted President Lincoln and his entourage up the Boonsboro Pike to tour the South Mountain battlefield. McClellan then returned to AOP headquarters while the presidential party rode to the Frederick railroad depot to board a train for Washington.

Meanwhile, people living in the Sharpsburg area may have wondered if the president noticed their dire circumstances. Lincoln, after all, had ridden through the shell-torn village and visited several farms stripped of fencing, grains, and livestock. Certainly, folks hoped that the U.S. president and his government might offer relief to ameliorate their sufferings—financial hardship being one concern, lack of subsistence being another.

*   *   *

Hunger plagued the battlefield region during the Army of the Potomac's six-week encampment. On September 24, the *New York Times* observed, "The residents of this section of Maryland have suffered terribly since its occupation by the two armies. In many cases families which, a few days ago, were in comfortable circumstances are now wanting the necessaries of life." The *Herald of Freedom and Torch Light* reported two weeks after the battle, "The consumption of food of every description by the two armies has been so enormous, that the inhabitants, even the wealthiest of them, have scarcely been able to procure subsistence enough to keep soul and body together." To aid the sufferers, the newspaper implored its readers "who have, in the Providence of God, thus far escaped the ravages of this war, to extend some relief to the poorer classes of them."

In Sharpsburg village, Maggie Grice Hoffmaster remembered, "[A]ll that we had to eat was bread, and to put on this all we had was beef tallow." Fortunately, a neighbor, Levin Benton, brought the Grices "a basket full of provisions." Another civilian wondered "how we ever managed to keep enough food in the house for the family to live upon. There was a constant demand upon us."

Describing David R. Miller's losses, Henry F. Neikirk deposed that Miller's farm "was completely stripped by the troops, leaving but little for himself & family to subsist upon." Federals also plundered the home of Joseph Poffenberger, carrying off all things edible. "[W]hen I returned to my house," Poffenberger later

---

[Hagerstown, MD], September 12, 2012. Per the Prys' granddaughter, Hazel Pry Moreno, Elizabeth Pry lost Lincoln's note during the family's postwar move to Tennessee.

testified, "it was completely empty. I had nothing left. I lived on army crackers that I found on the battle field for five days."

William Houser remembered that U.S. soldiers "destroyed lots of their household goods and what was left was hauled away by their neighbors and kept." As a result of the depredations, Houser recalled, "The only thing the parents had left was five hungry children."[69]

Some people leaned on their neighbors, church congregations, or extended families for help. Others bartered with what goods they had left. Martha Ada Mumma Thomas remembered, "We had potatoes and some had milk so we exchanged." Trading with neighbors was merely a stopgap, however. Martha recalled, "[T]he time came when there was no coffee, sugar, milk, or eggs, but we existed somehow."

Some civilians traveled afar for food or dipped into savings to pay inflated rates for eatables. Hiram Showman's claim cited, "[T]he corn bought by him at some 8 or ten miles from his home during the winter following the battle of Antietam must certainly have been more expensive than he raised in 1862, for corn was rather scarce in this county that winter."

Mary Grice, describing inflated prices after the battle, testified, "I paid one dollar and a half a bushel for potatoes in Frederick County, there were no potatoes here at that time." Grice added, "[W]e lost all of our corn and we had to buy corn and paid Eli Wade one dollar a bushel, in Sharpsburg for what we used. At that time fodder was sold for ten dollars a ton I heard."[70]

To satiate their appetites, Keedysville-Sharpsburg residents may have scoured their farms for potatoes and apples overlooked by the troops. They may have also joined soldiers in foraging for walnuts, which grew in abundance in the Antietam Valley.

Although Maryland's fishing season ran from March through early June, plenty of fish populated the Potomac River and Antietam Creek during the fall, such as shad and Potomac herring. A few residents maintained "fish pots"—V-shaped

69 Lamon, *Recollections of Abraham Lincoln*, 148; *New York Times*, September 24, 1862; *HFTL*, October 1, 1862; Reilly, *BOA*; Williams, HWC, vol. 1, 2:359-362; Claims of David R. Miller (F-1499) and Joseph Poffenberger (No. 1300); Reilly, *BOA*.

70 Jacob Miller to Amelia and Christian Houser, October 1862, WMR; Hilldebrand, "Recollections of Martha Ada Thomas;" Claims of Hiram Showman (No. 1522) and Benjamin F. Rohrback (No. 4234). Mary and John Grice testified in Rohrback's case. Before the battle, Sharpsburg's typical market price for standing corn was sixty cents per bushel. Thus, Eli Wade, who lived south of the village, sold some of his corn at a sixty percent markup after the battle.

weirs made of stacked stones that funneled trout, bass, sunfish, and American eels into an apex, where civilians speared or netted the fish. Water levels in the Potomac typically ran low during the late summer and early fall, causing the "rocks in the weirs to extend above the water line." This made it easier to trap fish, but may have also caught the eye of hungry troops, thousands of whom encamped along the same waterway.[71]

Sharpsburg civilians hunted for food, but the battle's thunderous racket spooked away much of the wildlife. "The rabbits had run off," Alex Davis recounted, "but there was a few around . . . not many." Several weeks after the battle, resident William "Bill" Marker hunted on William Roulette's farm. Marker, a 25-year-old farmer, tracked a rabbit "into a stonepile." While trying to flush it out, Marker's revolver "fell out of his pocket [and] discharged and the ball went through his heart." Another civilian, Joe Marrow, was also hunting that day. He stumbled upon the bloody scene, finding Marker "lying about six feet from the pistle." Marrow summoned Dr. A. A. Biggs, but it was too late—William Marker was dead.

Squire Jacob Miller reported the tragedy in a letter to his relatives, noting that the deceased "leaves a widow and two children," adding, "Bill was a good citizen." Mary Marker had already lost an infant son earlier in 1862. After burying her husband, she faced an uncertain future as a pregnant widow raising two toddlers.

Meanwhile, Sharpsburg's scarcity of subsistence continued. The *Herald of Freedom and Torch Light* summarized the direful circumstances:

[T]he region of the country between Sharpsburg and Boonsboro has been eaten out of food of every description. The two armies . . . have swept over it and devoured everything within reach . . . The amount of personal property—horses, cattle, hogs, sheep, corn, hay,

---

71 John Ferguson to "Kate," October 16, 1862, New York State Military Museum; Child, *Letters From a Civil War Surgeon*, 59-60; Ouchley, *Flora and Fauna of the Civil War*, 142-143; *HFTL*, May 26, 1858 and June 9, 1858; Don Peterson, *Native American Fish Traps in the Potomac River, Brunswick, Maryland* (Brunswick, MD, 2018), 5, 11-12, 17, https://www.brunswickmdhistory. com/images/3/3d/Book-Fish_traps-bhc-consolidated.pdf. Native Americans may have originally built the stone traps maintained by Sharpsburg civilians during the Civil War. Fish pots went by various names, including eel pots, fish dams, and fish traps; Piper, *Piper Family History*. Brothers Henry and Samuel I. Piper, along with two other farmers, "[H]ad a fish-pot located in Antietam creek at horseshoe bend on a farm of Jacob A. Myers" and another "fish pot was located on [the] Samuel I. Piper farm about 300 ft. below [the] canal lock." Holmes, "My Hunt After the Captain," 63; Reilly, *BOA*. Captain Albert H. Van Deusen of the 97th New York told Reilly that, while he encamped on David Coffman's farm after the battle, troops "would almost daily go to the canal for bathing and to wash some clothes." The C & O Canal, which adjoined the Potomac River, remained drained for several weeks after the battle due to Confederate-related damages.

and other provender—which was taken from the farmers, was enormous, the whole lower portion of our county has been stripped of every description of subsistence, and what our people in that section of the county will do to obtain food for man and beasts during the approaching winter, God alone knows.

Sharpsburg's residents were not alone in suffering from hunger after the battle. Beasts—any civilian-owned horses and livestock remaining in the area—required daily forage to survive. These animals, however, shared the same farms with the "engine" of McClellan's army—horses, mules, and army beef cattle, which suffered from woefully insufficient quantities of forage sent from Washington.

As if things couldn't get any worse for local farmers, Federal forces turned loose thousands of army animals into Sharpsburg's cornfields, hay mows, and wheat stacks, threatening to destroy what remained of the 1862 harvest.[72]

72 Johnson, BA, 103; Jacob Miller to Amelia and Christian Houser, December 7, 1862, WMR; The Maryland Free Press [Hagerstown, MD], December 12, 1862. The 1860 Federal census for Sharpsburg lists William Marker and his wife, Mary, in Dwelling #1617 with a five-month-old son, Charles. Burial records cite that the Markers' infant son, James, died earlier in 1862. In 1864, Mary Marker lost a daughter named Williana of unknown causes. Mary remarried in 1870 to Joseph C. Christian and moved to Mount Carroll, Illinois; HFTL, September 24, 1862.

Chapter 7

Heart-Rending Disaster:
The Devastation of Farmsteads

When the armies gathered at Sharpsburg in 1862, U.S. army surgeon Thomas T. Ellis noticed, "[N]early every part of the valley is under cultivation." The agricultural landscape "varied into squares of the light green of nearly ripened corn, the deeper green of clover, and the dull brown of newly ploughed fields."[1]

As Ellis described, Antietam Valley farmers diversified their crops, subdividing properties into multiple fields to grow various foods for humans and animals. For example, James Marker, Samuel Mumma, Sr., and Joshua Newcomer segmented their farms, respectively, into six, nine, and eleven fenced fields, which contained crops, pastures, and orchards.

Most residents practiced the same farming techniques, including Sharpsburg villagers who owned out lots. These five and ten-acre parcels were more affordable than farmsteads but contained similarly divided fields for growing different grains. Dozens of townsfolk, like Magdalene Jones, John Kretzer, and John Grice, depended on crop income from their out lots.

Proceeds from farming were also crucial to tenant farmers. Along with their wives and children, these hard-working folk resided upon and cultivated their landlords' farms. The sharecroppers lived rent-free in crude tenant houses, usually

---

1 Thomas T. Ellis, *Leaves from the Diary of an Army Surgeon; Or, Incidents of Field, Camp, and Hospital Life* (New York, 1863), 262.

owing half the grains grown to the landowners while keeping the hay crops for themselves.

Some tenants couldn't afford to hire help for cultivating the large farms, so they bartered with local farmhands, giving part of their share in exchange for assistance in seeding, cutting, and stacking grains. Sharpsburg's tenants who "farmed on the shares" included David R. Miller, Otho B. Smith, Michael Miller, Samuel Poffenberger, Thomas Barnum, Moses Cox, and William Unger.[2]

In mid-September 1862, fall harvest was in full swing, in varying phases. Aside from seeding in the spring and cutting in the summer, no other time of year challenged Sharpsburg's farmers and their laborers like September. Their tasks involved threshing wheat, oats, and rye. They also ploughed wheat fields in preparation for seeding, stored first-growth hay crops in mows, picked orchard fruit, and prepared to harvest the annual corn crop. In September 1862, however, the Northern and Southern armies interrupted everything.

"At the time of the battle," Alex Davis explained, "we'd thrashed our rye and oats, but our wheat was standing in stacks beside the farmyard. Our corn was on the stalk in the field, and there was sixteen acres of it." Dr. William Child wrote, "It may not be uninteresting to know that this battle of Antietam was fought upon the best agricultural region of the states, producing abundantly of wheat, corn, oats, rye," and other products. Child described local citizens as "refined, wealthy, well educated, hospitable, sensible and kind." Their farms, he added, "indicate thrift, their barns plenty, and their dwellings taste and love of ease and comfort . . . and most excellent and durable fences surround their lands and gardens."

Eight days after the battle, Dr. Child starkly contrasted his description of the Antietam Valley. "The whole country on and about the field is as thickly settled

---

2 In addition to subdividing their properties, farmers rotated crops each year to enrich the soil with nutrients and reduce weed and insect infestation; Claim of John Kretzer (*RG* 92, 54-1471). Kretzer stated that he "is a blacksmith by trade and lives on income from his farm." Land records show Kretzer's 1862 ownership of eleven out lots and a 13-acre tract adjoining Sharpsburg village; Tenant-landlord agreements varied. Most contracts required tenants to stock farms with their own animals and pay landlords half the grains raised. David R. Miller, though, only owed two-fifths to his father. The agreements usually devised the full hay crop to tenants, while some landlords like Susan Kennedy kept fifty percent of all crops, including hay. Most of the nonlandowners farmed under tenant agreements. Others, like Jacob Houser, Alfred Poffenberger, and Jacob H. Cost, rented their farmsteads, paying $325–$400 per year to landlords while keeping all the crops raised.

with wealthy, industrious farmers," he wrote. "See the produce of their last year's labor is destroyed."[3]

*   *   *

When the Army of the Potomac entered Maryland in early September 1862, it included more than 30,000 horses and mules. These equines, Gen. McClellan explained, didn't only transport officers, cavalry, artillery, and commissary stores. They also hauled "quartermaster's supplies, baggage, camp equipage, ambulances, reserve ammunition, forage for officers' horses, &c." Additionally, McClellan's commissary department herded hundreds of beef cattle into the Old Line State. These ruminants, like the equines, all needed food.

To address the challenge of feeding so many animals, McClellan issued a circular on September 9, instructing quartermasters "to take measures at once to provide what forage may be necessary for their respective corps from the country in the vicinity of their camps . . . and to draw as little from the Depots as possible."

In short, the circular mandated that the AOP's animals would live off the crops of farmers during the campaign. To ensure fairness to the civilians, McClellan ordered his brigade quartermasters to "make the purchases of forage, pay for the same in money, or in lieu thereof, will issue to the owners certificates." Additionally, McClellan emphasized, all vouchers given to civilians when cash payments were not possible must include the "date and place of purchase," the farmer's name, type of forage, and other details.

Moreover, the circular stipulated that any receipts issued "will be paid on presentation in Washington at the Office of Gen McClellan's Chief Quartermaster." Fixed prices applied to forage seized "in stack and hauled by our team." The AOP would reward higher payments to farmers who delivered forage to camps. Last, McClellan's circular concluded, "Farmers will be encouraged to bring in supplies and Quarter Masters and their Wagon Masters and Agents must visit them to examine the Country and make necessary arrangements." Such was the plan on paper as the Army of the Potomac entered Maryland.[4]

---

3 Johnson, *BA*, 94; Child, *History of the Fifth Regiment*, 130; Child, *Letters From a Civil War Surgeon*, 37, 60.

4 *OR*, vol. 19, 1:80; Claim of Jeremiah P. Grove (*RG* 92, G-1632). Grove's case file contained a copy of McClellan's circular dated Sep. 9, 1862. This document should not be confused with McClellan's other circular issued on Sep. 9, which addressed straggling. See *OR*, vol. 19, 2:225.

By October 1, the AOP reported 32,885 equines assigned to headquarters, cavalry, horse artillery, Couch's division, and six different army corps. Of this total, there were 22,493 horses and 10,392 mules. McClellan assigned most of these equines to army corps in the Sharpsburg environs, and the remainder belonged to II Corps and XII Corps in the Harpers Ferry area. By occupying an agricultural region, there was only one logical place to stage all these beasts: on local farmsteads.

To present an idea of how McClellan's animals overwhelmed the battlefield region, IX Corps and AOP headquarters, south of Sharpsburg, reportedly had 4,579 combined horses and mules. In the Bakersville-Williamsport area, VI Corps and Couch's division possessed 2,938 animals. I Corps and V Corps, near Sharpsburg and the battlefield, reported 8,378 equines.

In addition, McClellan's cavalry had 8,300 horses, many of which belonged to regiments encamped near Sharpsburg village. There were also army beef cattle in Sharpsburg, which possibly numbered in the thousands. These bovines, known as "beef on the hoof" and "self-propelled rations," provided fresh meat to the troops. During the Peninsula Campaign a few months earlier, McClellan reported, "a large herd of 2,500 beef cattle was, by the chief commissary, Col. Clark[e], transferred to the James River without loss." It's not farfetched to estimate that McClellan brought a similar number of cattle into Maryland during the 1862 campaign. Allegations in Sharpsburg's war claims, after all, reported multiple herds, some numbering as high as five hundred head.

Calculating the totals of AOP horses, mules, and cattle, more than 18,000 army animals may have been in the Sharpsburg-Bakersville vicinity on October 1. By comparison, Sharpsburg's farmers in 1860 reported less than 3,500 equines and bovines. McClellan's hungry animals, significantly greater in number than Sharpsburg's 1860 total, smothered farms north, south, and west of town.[5]

Based on the United States Army's forage regulations in 1861, military horses required 26 pounds of daily food, consisting of "fourteen pounds of hay and twelve pounds of oats, corn or barley." The army recommended 23 pounds of daily forage for mules, being "fourteen pounds of hay and nine pounds of oats, corn, or barley."

---

5 OR, vol. 19, 1:94-98. Lt. Col. Rufus Ingalls reported that "many of the cavalry and artillery horses present" in the 32,885 figure "were unfit for a march." Said animals, nonetheless, required forage to survive; Rodney C. Lackey, *Notes on Civil War Logistics: Facts & Stories*, United States Army Transportation Corps, https://transportation.army.mil/History/PDF/Peninsula%20Campaign/Rodney%20Lackey%20Article_1.pdf; McClellan, *McClellan's Own Story*, 423; 1860 agricultural schedule, Sharpsburg District.

Applying these regulations to the AOP, let's use I Corps and V Corps as examples. Both encamped at Sharpsburg after the battle. On October 1, the two corps had an aggregate total of 8,378 animals—2,946 mules and 5,432 horses. Based on the recommended allowances, rations for these equines equate to 141,232 pounds of daily forage for horses and 67,758 for mules. This computes to 208,990 pounds or 105 tons of daily forage for only two army corps. The estimate does not include AOP cavalry horses, beef cattle, and animals belonging to II, VI, IX, and XII Corps.[6]

Such demand for forage was not unfounded in the Federal army. During the Peninsula Campaign earlier in 1862, McClellan's chief quartermaster, Brigadier General Stewart Van Vliet, reported that "every horse consumes 26 pounds of forage" and for the entire campaign, "over 500 tons were required daily by the army."

In April 1863, a quartermaster in the Army of the Cumberland recalled that his on-hand supplies of 24,000 bales of hay and 200,000 sacks of grain were inadequate to feed the military animals. "The amount necessary to supply such an army," he recalled, "is almost beyond belief, and must be seen to be realized." Subsequently, "For three months the army was entirely supplied with forage from the country in which it was quartered."

Major General Henry Slocum confiscated forage from private citizens during the 1865 Savannah Campaign and estimated "the amount of grain taken from the country at 5,000,000 pounds; fodder, 6,000,000 pounds; besides the forage consumed by the immense herds of cattle that were driven with the different columns."[7]

The same challenges applied to McClellan's army after the Battle of Antietam. The war department shipped forage to Western Maryland, but the insufficient quantities failed to meet the AOP's demands. In October 1862, Brig. Gen. George

---

6 *OR*, vol. 19, 1:97-98. The equine estimate for I Corps and V Corps is based on returns from October 1, 1862. By November 1, both corps had acquired an additional 500 animals; *United States War Department, Revised United States Army Regulations of 1861, With an Appendix Containing the Changes and Laws Affecting Army Regulations and Articles of War to June 25, 1863* (Washington, DC, 1863), 166, Paragraph 1121; *OR*, vol. 29, 2:422. In 1863, the U.S. Army reduced the allowance to 24 daily pounds of grain for horses and 23 pounds for mules. When long forage wasn't available, the army recommended short forage at 18 daily pounds for horses and 15 pounds for mules.

7 *OR*, vol. 11, 1:159; John Fitch, *Annals of the Army of the Cumberland* (Philadelphia, 1864), 267-268; Charles Elihu Slocum, *The Life and Services of Major-General Henry Warner Slocum* (Toledo, OH, 1913), 252; *New York Times*, October 4, 1862.

Meade complained, "Our artillery horses and train animals have been literally starving, and have been suffering for the want of forage." Major General John F. Reynolds expressed concern over the "the difficulty . . . [in] getting forage for the artillery horses." Similarly, Rufus Ingalls notified a Baltimore quartermaster in October, "There has been great deficiency of forage, particularly hay, for four days past." Ingalls wrote in another dispatch, referring to the depot quartermaster in Hagerstown, "Captain [George W.] Weeks reports that his forage does not arrive promptly."

Two weeks after the battle, a Northern correspondent observed underfed cavalry horses at Sharpsburg. He opined, "[I]t really did seem cruel that in this region of overflowing plenty, and with all the money our people are squandering upon the army, the horses . . . should have no better nourishment to live upon." One reason, the reporter noted, "is the atrocious prices which the farmers here are charging for their corn. For a small stack—just as it is cut down, and about fifty bushels—they charge $110."

Compared to the AOP's well-documented deficiency of food, clothing, and medical supplies, correspondence in the *Official Records* reveals no urgent want of forage from September 15 through early October. But yet the army's concern for animal feed spikes after that, as do local prices for forage. There may be a simple explanation for this anomaly: by early October 1862, McClellan's horses, mules, and beef cattle had devoured the majority of Sharpsburg's grains. Thus, once again, willing or not, farmers near the Antietam battlefield supplied the needs of the AOP.[8]

*   *   *

Indian corn was an essential crop to Antietam Valley residents, for it served several purposes. Farmers sold it at market, ground it into meal, and fed it to livestock and poultry, storing the dried ears in cribs to last until the next harvest.

Unlike the popular variety of sweet corn, Sharpsburg's farmers grew field corn, also known as dent corn or cow corn. Field corn was dry and hard at maturity, making it ideal for livestock feed and long-term storage. While it wasn't a staple food, Sharpsburg residents consumed some of the ears in the early summer when the immature kernels still contained moisture. Many folks called this subsistence

---

8 *OR*, vol. 19, 2:320-321, 460, 480, 492; *New York Times*, October 4, 1862.

"roasting ears." The Michael family described eating green field corn, noting, "We eat roasting ears about the 15th of July."[9]

Corn yields varied by year, depending on weather and other factors. Excellent seasons, according to local newspapers, produced sixty to ninety bushels per acre.[10]

Adam Hutzell recalled that he "often raised 50 bushels per acre," and George Line recounted, "Sometimes we raise fifty and sixty bushels." The 1862 corn crop was average due to a moderately dry summer and minor damage by hailstorms. Consequently, war claim testimonies reveal that the 1862 yields averaged 25–40 bushels per acre.[11]

Nearly every farmer living near the Antietam battlefield grew Indian corn, and at the time of the battle, the crop was close to reaching maturity. Nevertheless, for most farmers in the region, there would be no corn harvest in 1862.

Military forces at Sharpsburg destroyed cornfields by trampling the crop during the battle, picking ears for human consumption, and feeding the plants to

---

9 Sharpsburg's corn was non-hybrid, producing stalks of varying height. Farmers spaced their plants in check-row designs, providing ample room to drive single-horse cultivators through the rows to weed their fields; Adam Michael to David Michael, August 20, 1857, Michael Family Letters Collection, WMR; Samuel Michael to David Michael, August 7, 1865, WMR. The soldiers' consumption of immature corn during the 1862 Maryland Campaign is well documented. William Owen, a Confederate in the Washington Artillery, nicknamed it "The Green-Corn Campaign." (Owen, *In Camp and Battle*, 130); Civil War Digest, "Civil War Cornfields—Like Antietam—Vol. II, Episode 19," YouTube video, September 14, 2016, https://www.youtube.com/watch?v=3LoBGQ-docQ; Kevin Pawlak, "What Did Antietam's Cornfield Look Like in September 1862?" blog, *Antietam Brigades*, March 1, 2020, http://antietambrigades.blogspot.com/2020/03/what-did-antietams-cornfield-look-like.html.

10 High corn yields appear in the Hagerstown newspapers, *Herald of Freedom and Torch Light*, November 6, 1860, and *Herald of Freedom*, October 29, 1851 and November 26, 1851; Adam Michael to David Michael, August 20, 1857, WMR; Samuel Michael to David Michael, August 7, 1865, WMR. Hail in 1862 damaged some crops in Washington County, per the *HFTL*, June 18, June 25, and July 23. The same newspaper cited drought on Aug. 20 and Sep. 3. By comparison, modern Maryland yields often average 180 to 250 bushels per acre. See Rachael Jackson, "Corn and Soybean Harvest Could Be Second-Largest in State History," *Capital News Service*, November 12, 2004, https://cnsmaryland.org/2004/11/12/corn-and-soybean-harvest-could-be-second-largest-in-state-history/. See also Hannah Himes, "Aw, Shucks: Maryland Farmer Wins National Corn Yield Contest," *U.S. News*, December 28, 2019, https://www.usnews.com/news/best-states/maryland/articles/2019-12-28/aw-shucks-maryland-farmer-wins-national-corn-yield-contest.

11 Claims of Adam Hutzell (F-1538) and Joseph Poffenberger (No. 1300). George Line testified in Poffenberger's case. Several claims cases contain testimony describing Sharpsburg's corn yields in 1862. See the claims of John U. and William I. Cox (M-901), Joshua Newcomer (F-854), Jacob Avey, Sr. (No. 9908), Samuel Mumma, Sr. (No. 334), Jeremiah P. Grove (G-1632), and John Roulette (*RG* 92, Entry 812, Box 169, Claim L-830).

army animals. Farmers living on and near the battlefield experienced compounded losses. For instance, combat and Confederate movements crushed cornfields belonging to David Reel, Alfred Poffenberger, and Jacob Nicodemus. After the AOP occupied the same farms later, soldiers fed the remaining standing corn to their horses and mules.[12]

Likewise, Joshua Newcomer alleged that U.S. forces "fed their horses all of my corn and pasture that had not been previously ruined . . . during the skirmishing and progress of the battle." Describing Newcomer's corn losses, neighbor Daniel B. Grim attested that AOP animals "gobbled it all up" because "the mules were as hungry as the soldiers."[13]

William Unger incurred similar damages. The tenant farmer stated that "the Divisions of Genls. French and Richardson, and he thinks the Irish Brigade, marched over this farm through every field" during the battle and his corn "was very much injured." On September 19, Unger recalled, the remainder of his crop "was cut off by the soldiers, carried out of the field and fed to their horses."[14]

In 1862, tenant farmer Leonard Emmert planned to split the proceeds of his corn crop with landlord Joseph Sherrick. Instead, based on their claims for damages, the Emmert-Sherrick cornfield "was fought over and the growing crop more or less injured." When Emmert returned home two days after the battle, he found AOP forces loading his remaining corn into army wagons. These Federals, Emmert testified, "were hauling and carrying it away for several days until the

---

12 Claim of David Reel (No. 6619). Reel's son, Thomas H. Reel, deposed that the ANV posted a battery "right back of the corn field; there was a great deal of running over the fields by a portion of Jackson's command." Later, U.S. cavalry seized the corn "and then had their stock to run in on the fodder;" Claim of Alfred Poffenberger (M-917). After Confederates destroyed part of Poffenberger's corn, the remainder "was taken from the field by the [U.S.] troops and fed to their horses in lieu of their usual supply of forage from the regular source." Poffenberger named Major George Breck of the 1st New York Artillery, Battery L, as one of the officers who authorized the appropriation of his corn; Claim of Jacob Nicodemus of Sharpsburg (RG 92, Book 95, Box 238, Claim 95-1683); Johnson, BA, 100. AOP forces reportedly took 350 bushels of Nicodemus's corn after ANV batteries trampled "a good deal" of the field. But, Alex Davis remarked, "[W]e got enough at the ends of the field to see us out the year."

13 Claim of Joshua Newcomer (No. 272). Newcomer identified Battery B, Rhode Island Light Artillery, as one of the commands that confiscated his 900 bushels of corn for animal feed.

14 Claim of William Unger (RG 92, K-516). In 1862, Unger tenanted Susan Kennedy's farm, which adjoined Henry F. Neikirk on the west. Susan Kennedy lived in a townhouse on the eastern end of Sharpsburg village.

whole field was stripped." Ultimately, he "did not get any of this corn except for a wagon load with husks on, which he fed to the pigs."[15]

David R. Miller, whose tenant farm stood in the epicenter of Antietam's combat, reported the loss of only five bushels of corn—a minuscule amount compared to his neighbors. How could this be? Primary sources describe heavy fighting in Miller's cornfield during the battle, which likely obliterated most of the crop. War claims, though, barred citizens from filing combat-related damages. Thus, in all likelihood, Miller could not pursue reparations for his wrecked corn, except for five bushels seized by Federal soldiers as forage.[16]

Throughout the area, claimants lost considerable amounts of corn to encamped Federals. To give an example, the quartermaster department's investigation of Jacob Houser's claim found that his "entire crop was cut by [U.S.] troops . . . and fed to the horses in the adjoining fields." Next door, Cerusha Reel suffered similar losses. "I saw them in the corn field hauling the corn away when I came home," Reel testified. "I saw 18 or 20 wagons in there when I came home I counted them." Asked to explain her knowledge of the yield—595 bushels from seventeen acres—she answered, "[I]t was good corn, I am used to seeing corn growing and estimating."[17]

Federals took from Jacob A. Myers "at least 100 bushels of corn which they fed to their horses" because "their supply train not having arrived." Near Bakerville, Eliza Davis reported that "Genl Slocum's command" confiscated "her entire crop of growing corn" because "the troops being without forage for some days after the

---

15 Claims of Leonard Emmert (F-1577) and Joseph Sherrick (F-1433).

16 Claim of David R. Miller (F-1499). Neither Miller's board of survey appraisal, quartermaster claim, nor congressional case mentioned his cornfield, nor did the congressional lawsuit filed by his father, Col. John Miller. The five bushels listed in David R. Miller's claim may have been the surviving remnants of his ravaged cornfield, which troops fed to AOP animals as forage on or after Sep. 19. Sources supporting this argument include the official report of Maj. Gen. Joseph Hooker, *OR*, vol. 19, 1:218, and Schell, "Sketching Under Fire at Antietam," 425. On Sep. 17, Schell observed in Miller's field only "a few stalks defiantly standing" amid "a maze of broken, tangled fragments." Interestingly, Oliver Wendell Holmes, Sr., who toured the battlefield on Sep. 21, 1862, allegedly "wandered about" in Miller's cornfield, noticing, "[T]here was every mark of hard fighting having taken place here, [but] the Indian corn was not generally trodden down." Holmes, who may have mistakenly described a different cornfield, found that Miller's "corn stalks were left standing very generally, as if they had been trees." See Holmes, *Pages From an Old Volume of Life*, 41, 169.

17 Claim of Jacob Houser (F-814); Reilly, *BOA*. Houser's son, William, told Reilly that U.S. forces "put a drove of fat cattle in the cornfield;" Claim of Samuel Reel (No. 3209).

battle were compelled to subsist their horses off the farmers in the neighborhood."[18]

Not far from Eliza Davis, tenant farmer John C. Middlekauff and farmhand Isaiah Shaw harvested their 1862 corn crop when AOP wagons rolled onto the farm. Troops began cutting corn from the same field and loading it into the wagons. "[W]e had to quit husking it," Middlekauff recalled, because "they were hauling it away as fast as we could husk it."[19]

Complaining of the widespread damages, Squire Jacob Miller wrote to his family that U.S. forces "have taken every corn field within their reach fodder and all." Miller himself was among the victims, having lost corn on his three farms.

Miller also made an important point by mentioning "fodder and all." Ears of corn comprised only part of the plant's value. The leftover stalks, leaves, and husks—known as fodder—served as nutritious feed for livestock, especially cattle. During harvest, farmers cut, gathered, and bundled the stalks (commonly called "stocks" by locals). Once the stacked shocks dried, farmers removed the ears and scattered the remaining silage in barnyards. On average, one acre of corn produced one ton of fodder, which sold in 1862 for $5 per "load," a word that Sharpsburg folks used to describe one ton.[20]

Most of the farmers who reported the destruction of corn also lost fodder. Several claimants stated that AOP animals wiped out their cornfields, "fodder and all."[21]

18 Claims of Jacob A. Myers (*RG* 92, Box 242, Book N, Claim F-2190) and Eliza Davis (*RG* 92, Book F, Box 92, F-1536).

19 Claim of John J. Middlekauff (*RG* 123, Entry 22, Box 228, Case No. 1261). John C. Middlekauff is not to be confused with Joseph Poffenberger's adjoining neighbor of the same name. The former tenanted his father's farm, John J. Middlekauff, near Fairplay, located three miles north of Poffenberger. Isaiah Shaw testified in the case.

20 Jacob Miller to Amelia and Christian Houser, October 1862, WMR; Claim of Jacob Miller (*RG* 123, Entry 22, Box 541, Case No. 4296); Perry C. Wheelock, *Farming Along the Chesapeake and Ohio Canal, 1828–1971*, U.S. Department of Interior, National Park Service, Chesapeake & Ohio Canal National Historical Park (Hagerstown, MD, 2007), 25; "Farming in Maryland," *The Cultivator: A Monthly Journal for the Farm and Garden* (Albany, NY, April 1862), vol. 10, 115; "Corn Harvesting Machinery," *The American Thresherman* 10, no. 4 (Madison, WI, 1910), 3. The magazine described corn fodder as "beyond a doubt . . . as nutritious as good hay."

21 Claims of John A. Wade (*RG* 123, Entry 22, Box 741, Case No. 6586) and Raleigh Showman (F-1183). In John A. Wade's case, testimony alleged that AOP "team horses and cavalry" consumed two cornfields, fodder included. In Raleigh Showman's claim, Noah Rohrback testified that "Col. Hayes of the U.S. Artillery turned his horses into the field and cleaned it up—fodder and all." Rohrback may have referred to Lieutenant Colonel William Hays, who commanded the Artillery Reserve in V Corps; Claim of William M. Blackford (No. 1324). V

John Roulette, who tenanted a farm owned by Martin Eakle near Antietam Iron Works, testified that General Burnside's chief quartermaster commandeered the Roulette-Eakle cornfield for forage purposes. Soon thereafter, troops "removed the fences permitting their horses to run in the fields and consume it . . . not leaving a single bushel on the ground."

Near Antietam Iron Works, the 6th New York Cavalry bivouacked on John Snyder's farm. His daughter, Eveline Snyder Friese, recalled, "My father had a field of thirteen acres of corn, which had been cut just before the army came. It was all taken by the army, fodder and all and fed to the army horses. I saw this with my own eyes." Providing further details, Eveline remarked, "The officers and soldiers were all around and they made no secret of their actions. My father did not get any corn or fodder either one from this field. It was all the corn he had."

The army appropriated standing corn and fodder throughout the battlefield region. Stephen P. Grove alleged that Union troops "took the crop . . . and fed it to their horses." When the equines finally left his farm, Grove recalled, there was "nothing left but the butts." Near Sharpsburg's out lots, John H. Snavely remembered that "Saturday morning after the battle [September 20] his corn field was all right." Soon after, though, Alfred Pleasonton's cavalry, along with Federal teamsters, "took all of the corn not leaving a single blade nor ear."[22]

McClellan's forces also seized leftover livestock feed from the previous harvest, known as "old corn." Similar to standing corn and fodder, soldiers fed old corn ears to AOP animals. Near the Lower Bridge, Henry B. Rohrback accused the Union army of taking "300 bushels old corn" from his crib. On the neighboring farm of his brothers, Noah and Elias B. Rohrback, 125 bushels of old corn "was taken from the crib in U.S. wagons and in bags, the men who took said corn belonged to the 12th Ills. Cavy. and to some Md. Cavalry." Across Antietam Creek, John Otto testified, "[O]ne hundred bushels of old corn . . . was stored in my barn on the farm at Burnside Bridge, and was taken for the use of and was consumed by the army animals." Many other claimants reported losses of their old corn.[23]

Corps forces allegedly fed Blackford's corn to the "horses of the cavalry and artillery," destroying all 25 acres, "fodder and all."

22 Claims of John Roulette (L-830), John Snyder (Claim F-589 and Case No. 6617), Stephen P. Grove (No. 7354), and John H. Snavely (*RG* 92, Entry 820, Claim F-1441).

23 Claims of Henry B. Rohrback (Book 304, Claim 235), Noah Rohrback (H-3874), and John Otto (G-1857). Other petitioners who requested reimbursement for old corn included Susan Kennedy (F-865), Martha Schlosser (Box 771, Claim 170), Henry Griffith (*RG* 92, Entry 812, Box 576, Claim 212-707), James Marker (No. 1292), Morgan and Andrew Rentch Miller (No.

The army's sweeping appropriations in September and October 1862 drove up the local prices of corn and fodder. Hiram Showman recalled, "[C]orn was rather scarce in the country that winter." Similarly, after AOP equines consumed Benjamin F. Rohrback's crop, he testified, "I never got an acre of corn of said field; I was obliged to haul my corn from Frederick County." When the U.S. quartermaster department later questioned the high fodder prices charged in Samuel Mumma, Sr.'s claim, his son explained, "[W]e got as much as $10 a load for it hauled to Sharpsburg the following year. That year fodder was very scarce after the armies were here and commanded a high price."

Corroborating the scarcity of corn and fodder, eighty claimants living near Sharpsburg reported an aggregate loss of 43,902 bushels of standing corn, all reportedly taken by the AOP after the Battle of Antietam. Individually, each claimant lost about 549 bushels. By comparison, each Sharpsburg farmer in 1860 reported an average yield of 668 bushels. Based on corn's 1862 market price of sixty cents per bushel, the confiscation of 43,902 bushels dealt the claimants a combined loss of $26,341.

Civilians sought reimbursement for their confiscated fodder, as well. According to 58 claimants, AOP personnel seized 807 acres of fodder or fourteen acres per person. Applying the 1862 price of five dollars per ton, each petitioner lost about $70 in corn fodder.

The total amount of appropriated old corn is unknown. Overall, war claims suggest that the average farmer lost more than $400 in standing corn, fodder, and old corn after the battle. For comparative purposes, $400 converts to more than $11,000 in modern currency. Unfortunately for Sharpsburg's farmers, their corn crops were insufficient to satiate the appetites of McClellan's horses, mules, and cattle. As a result, other crops—like hay—met similar fates.[24]

*　　*　　*

4295), and Jacob H. Grove (No. 1267). Typically, farmers fed old corn to poultry and swine, and sometimes cattle. In addition, claimants reported the loss of dried corn reserved for human consumption. Among them were Samuel Mumma, Sr. (D-1927 and D-1928), Samuel Poffenberger (F-1434), and Henry Piper (No. 445). Families likely reserved dried corn for grinding into meal.

24 Claims of Hiram Showman (No. 1522), Benjamin F. Rohrback (No. 4234), and Samuel Mumma, Sr. (No. 334); 1860 agricultural schedule, Sharpsburg District; Claim of Joseph Poffenberger (No. 1300). George Line testified in Poffenberger's case; Williamson, *PPT*.

Sharpsburg-area residents raised two types of hay in 1862: timothy and clover. Timothy hay, a fast-growing grass, served as feed for horses, sheep, and cattle. In addition, farmers often mixed timothy with clover hay—a protein-rich legume—for young stock and lactating or pregnant animals.

Assisted by slaves, family, and hired help, farmers tackled their first hay growth in June, cutting and then stacking it into massive, multi-ton ricks. By mid-September, the cured stacks towered in the fields. Residents began transferring some of the timothy and clover into haymows inside barns and hauling other portions to market. Every wagonload of Sharpsburg's hay "was good for at least one ton," reported Victor Vifquain of the U.S. quartermaster department. "There is no doubt of this. I have myself seen these people haul the hay . . . and the loads are really astonishing." Hay at this stage was most valuable. Samuel Poffenberger explained, "[T]he clover hay was gathered and stacked about the last of June . . . when the hay is first cut in the spring it is not worth as much as it is in the fall when it is cured and dried."

The army's confiscation of hay inflicted twofold damages to local families. First, troops fed first-growth timothy and clover as forage. Second, they pastured military animals on second crops of hay grown for the following year's seed. Farm families usually reserved several tons of hay for feeding horses and livestock throughout the winter and spring. As an example of the large quantities grown, the 1860 agricultural schedule for Sharpsburg shows that 94 farmers produced 1,614 tons of hay, an average of 17.17 tons per person. After the Antietam battle, 86 Sharpsburg-area claimants alleged that the AOP appropriated a combined total of 1,432.25 tons. In other words, each claimant lost 16.65 tons of hay, which closely matches the average amount grown in 1860.[25]

These losses, however, did not include hay seized by Confederates from September 15–18, the quantity of which is not known. Several claimants admitted that Rebels took some of their hay. Still, these amounts paled compared to AOP

---

25 In the claims of David Smith (Nos. 1244, 1262, and 10237), Angeline Jackson testified, "[T]he hay crop was cut with scythes that year [1862]. We did not have machines for cutting hay then; we had quite a number of hands mowing and getting the hay." Claim of David R. Miller (No. 1266). Samuel Poffenberger testified in Miller's case; Claim of Otho B. Smith (F-1432). Agent Vifquain conducted on-site investigations of dozens of Sharpsburg-area farms, including Smith's. Vifquain reported in Smith's claim, "Every load [of hay] was good for at least one ton . . . I have no doubt but what every load would weigh 1 ½ tons as taken from the field; but of course it shrinks in volume and in weight as it cures in the barn, but the shrinkage never amounts to more than 1/6 in weight, and 1/5 in volume;" 1860 agricultural schedule, Sharpsburg District.

appropriations, given the Federals' 41-day-long stay at Sharpsburg after the battle. U.S. forces seized copious amounts of hay during this time, and the army animals ate it in droves.[26]

Benjamin F. Rohrback testified, "[O]n the second day after the battle of Antietam the village of Sharpsburg was filled with Union soldiers who supplied themselves with forage from all the stables in the village." Referring to the Maryland Hotel on the public square, Rohrback remembered seeing "some cavalry soldiers carry in the arms and feed to their horses in the street some hay from [Elias U.] Knode's stable." Knode himself explained the appropriation, recalling that "the Advance Guard of Gen. McClellan's Army" took two tons of timothy hay from his lot on September 19. He remembered that "a number of Gen. McClellan's soldiers came to his house, saying they must have hay." On John L. Highbarger's town lot, F. H. Parker, identified as "2d Lieut. of Ordnance," seized hay from Highbarger's stable "for the use of Government team engaged in hauling ammunition for the Army of the Potomac."[27]

Countless commands took hay from battlefield-area residents. Near Bakersville, men from Captain William Hexamer's New Jersey Light Artillery, Battery A, appropriated six tons of timothy and clover from Thomas Barnum. Nearby, the 145th Pennsylvania Infantry and 8th New York Cavalry occupied part of Joseph Stonebraker's farm. These troops, Stonebraker alleged, took "20 to 25 cwt of hay . . . without my consent."[28]

---

26 Claimants who mentioned Confederate appropriations of hay included Samuel I. Piper (D-2392), Hezekiah Myers (No. 1301), Alfred Poffenberger (M-917), and Stephen P. Grove (No. 7354). Myers stated that the Rebels took "probably a quarter of a ton" of his hay. Grove's claim cites that Captain Colin McRae Selph, an ANV quartermaster, appropriated 10,000 pounds of Grove's hay "just before the battle of Antietam . . . from a rick in the orchard." In 1861, Selph supervised the production of the Confederacy's first battle flags. See *Southern Historical Society Papers*, vol. 37 (Richmond, VA, 1909), 255-256. See also Kent Masterson Brown, *Confederacy's First Battle Flag: The Story of the Southern Cross* (Gretna, LA, 2015).

27 Claims of Elias U. Knode (L-2074) and John L. Highbarger (*RG* 92, Book 54, Box 15, Claim 54-1476 filed as 54-1487).

28 Claims of Thomas Barnum (Claim 131-1078 and Case No. 333); Claim of Joseph Stonebraker (*RG* 92, Box 771, Claim 173). CWT is a hundredweight or one hundred pounds. "20 to 25 cwt" measures one to one and one-half tons. Stonebraker sought $15 for the hay taken, and the price of hay in 1862 was $15 per ton; Samuel P. Bates, *History of the Pennsylvania Volunteers, 1861–65; Prepared in Compliance with Acts of the Legislature*, 5 vols. (Harrisburg, PA, 1870), 4:518-519. The 145th Pennsylvania arrived in Sharpsburg during the battle. It was "immediately moved into position, filling a gap which then existed between the Union right and the Potomac, holding the tow-path and the road which runs along under the high bluff skirting the river . . . this position was held, and picket duty performed in face of the enemy, until the

On the property of Cerusha and Samuel Reel, farmhand Jessie Price remembered that the Reels "had a stack of hay to best of my knowledge 7 or 8 tons down from the barn a piece." After the battle, Price testified, "I seen the wagons drive in." He watched government soldiers confiscate the Reel's hay and "take it away every bit of it . . . I stood and saw them load the hay and drive it down the lane." Cerusha Reel also witnessed the appropriations. "I know we had the timothy hay—I helped to put it there myself," she recalled. "Each stack was two rails long. I helped to haul it out and stack it myself."[29]

Having been cut before the battle, part of David R. Miller's hay crop grew in the "Dunker Church field." This tract might have been the triangular field near the Dunker meeting house, where more men fell during the battle than Miller's "Bloody Cornfield." On or about September 20, Colonel Joshua T. Owen of the Philadelphia Brigade authorized the appropriation of Miller's entire crop, leaving "no hay in the barn or in the rick." Farmhand John H. Gatrell saw U.S. forces haul Miller's hay "in the direction of Sharpsburg, they were hauling several days; it was taken away with government wagons." Another farmhand, William Waterman, tried to stop the troops. "I saw this taken," Waterman testified, and "told them not to take it, as it was all Mr. Miller had to feed his stock on." The young farmhand's efforts were in vain, he recalled, "because when I told these men not to take it, they cursed me and then I did not go any further."[30]

---

morning of the 19th." This was the Mercersville-Bakersville vicinity, where Stonebraker's farm was located. Also supporting Stonebraker's allegations, the 8th New York Cavalry rode from Greencastle, Pennsylvania, to Sharpsburg during the battle, arriving in the afternoon, and took a position "on the right flank of the army." See Henry Norton, *Deeds of Daring, or History of the Eighth N.Y. Volunteer Cavalry* (Norwich, NY, 1889), 35-36.

29 Claim of Samuel Reel (3209). Regarding Cerusha Reel's estimate that "each stack was two rails long," more than one dozen witnesses testified in Antietam-related claims regarding the loss of worm and post and rail fencing. Their testimonies reveal that fence rails in 1862 averaged nine to eleven feet in length.

30 Thomas G. Clemens, "Antietam Rebirth," online article, Historynet.com, September 2017, https://www.historynet.com/antietam-rebirth.htm. Clemens wrote that the "44-acre triangular property . . . originally part of the David R. Miller Farm . . . was the scene of intense fighting early in the battle and experienced more casualties than the Cornfield itself;" Claim of David R. Miller (No. 1266). The triangular field adjoined the "Bloody Cornfield" on the south and the Dunker Church tract on the northeast. ANB estimates the triangular field's size as 44-acres. Along with two witnesses in the claim, Miller estimated the "church field" as 40–50 acres. Records show that Col. Joshua T. Owen took command of the Philadelphia Brigade after the battle. William Waterman lived on David R. Miller's farm in Sep. 1862 and testified that he "resided at claimant's house."

vinced that the claim was just.

Proof of administration on the estate of David R. Miller, deceased, issued to Buchanan Schley and William P. Miller, were filed in this Court December 18, 1899.

EVIDENCE UNDER RULES.

Deposition filed for claimant September 27, 1888:

DAVID R. MILLER: 69 years; retired farmer; resident of Sharpsburg, Maryland; I am the claimant; prior to and during the war of the rebellion I resided on my farm on the Hagerstown Pike, two mile north of Sharpsburg; that farm contained 265 acres; part of the hay was put in the barn and part of it ricked out, one mow of the barn was filled with that hay and two sheds; it was grown in the church field, 40 acres in that field, in the year of the battle of 1862; Gen. Hooker's corps, I talked with the general at the time and Gen. Joshua T. Owen took it; he gave me his affidavit; 60 tons were taken and fed to their horses; I saw them feed it; hay was worth $10 a ton; this hay was worth that; there were 60 tons or more of that hay with clover seed in it; it was fed; it would have produced 90 or more bushels of seed; the same soldiers took that, Gen. Hooker's troops and the Irish brigade; the officers came with them when they took it; this clover seed was worth from $12 to $15 per bushel(?); officers were present when the clover hay was taken; the blacksmith tools were taken by soldiers, but I cannot tell you by whom; they were worth $75 to $100; the cart and gears were taken

-2-

A page from *David R. Miller vs. the United States.* NARA

AOP wagon masters and teamsters confiscated hay from dozens of farms, feeding some of the roughage to ambulance horses. For example, C. A. Cunier, wagon master of an ambulance train, took eight hundred pounds of hay from William Roulette on September 22, and "teamsters of the Ambulances" seized one ton of clover hay from Jacob Snyder's barn. Abraham Hammond planned to haul his hay "3 miles to put it on the market." Nonetheless, a witness explained, "the ambulance corps took hay [from Hammond] every day for some 4 weeks," confiscating all twelve tons.[31]

Throughout the area, civilians incurred heavy hay losses to AOP medical and military personnel. One woman recollected that "every pound of hay from the barn was taken by the soldiers," and Hilary Watson remembered that "every bit of our hay and stuff had been taken to feed the army horses." Jacob H. Grove alleged that United States troops seized all forty tons of his hay and "fed it to their mules." John H. Snavely, meanwhile, lost 33 tons of clover and "prime Timothy" to Federal cavalry. Snavely described this hay as "all he had."[32]

Officers commandeered Joseph Poffenberger's barn after the battle, the structure serving "as a place of rendezvous for the quartermasters to get their forage." Poffenberger watched army wagons haul away 20 tons of hay "to the different places in the camp," confiscating "the entire crop." On another farm, elements of Gen. Israel Richardson's command pitched into William Unger's hay, described as "a large rick . . . containing 12 or 15 loads or tons." These troops, Unger alleged, "fed it to the cav. and arty horses which lay there as thick as bees."[33]

The resulting shortage of clover and timothy inflated the price of hay remaining in the area, which generally sold for $12–$15 per ton. Cerusha Reel remembered that, after Antietam, "Hay was then selling from $20 to $25 per ton." Civilians still possessing horses and livestock struggled to afford these prices,

---

31 Claims of William Roulette (F-618), Jacob Snyder (F-1537), and Abraham Hammond (*RG* 92, Book F, Box 89, Claim F-1430).

32 Williams, HWC, vol. 1, 2:359; Johnson, *BA*, 108. Watson referred to John Otto's hay. After a quartermaster agent investigated Otto's claim (*RG* 92, G-1857), he concluded, "there is no doubt that the claimant supplied large quantities of forage and fuel to the U.S. troops;" Claims of Jacob H. Grove (No. 1267) and John H. Snavely (F-1441). First Lieutenant Richard Byrne of the 5th U.S. Cavalry receipted Snavely for a portion of the hay, without any payment, to document the transaction. The receipt identified the officer as "R. Byrne 1st Lieut. Commr Co 'C' 5th Cav. . . . acting as Provost Guard to this Division."

33 Claims of Joseph Poffenberger (No. 1300) and William Unger (K-516). Unger, a tenant farmer, attested in his claim, "[T]his hay was his own; [he] had already hauled three tons to Mrs. [Susan] Kennedy her share."

forcing them to travel afar for better bargains. "One trouble, after the battle," Alex Davis explained, "was to get feed for our stock. I had to ride a whole day to buy some hay, and there'd been a lot made, too, but it had been taken for the army horses." Likewise, after U.S. troops took twenty tons of timothy from Hiram Showman's mow, the farmer testified, "I was obliged to buy my hay" because "the army took every bit of it."

A quartermaster who investigated Hiram Showman's claim had previously interviewed scores of claimants regarding their Antietam-related property losses. The agent reported to his superiors in Washington, "It is undoubtably true that the hay of this claimant was all taken by our men." Moreso, he reasoned, "[I]t is nevertheless such a notorious fact that all the hay in this country was accaperated for the use of the army, that I can not very well overlook it."

As a result of the widespread expropriations, claimants accused the AOP of confiscating nearly 1,500 tons of first-growth timothy and clover hay. High as these losses seem, they only represented part of the 1862 hay crop destroyed by military forces. At the time of the battle, Sharpsburg's secondary crop, raised strictly for seed, was still growing in the field.[34]

In September 1862, pastures brimmed with second growths of clover, which contained the seeds for the following year's crop. Yet, when military forces drove their horses, mules, and cattle into Sharpsburg's meadows, the animals consumed both the clover and the seed, putting the community's 1863 crop at risk.

On some properties, soldiers and animals combined to destroy pastures. Brothers Noah and Elias B. Rohrback observed that "[Colonel Rutherford B.] Hayes Regt. and some other troops camped on . . . and destroyed" their "17 acres clover land." In addition, the Rohrbacks' other clover field of fourteen acres "was pastured down" by more than 200 horses from the 23rd Ohio. Also, U.S. soldiers crushed Joseph Sherrick's clover pasture by "encamping thereon." Otho B. Smith, meanwhile, testified that "the ambulance corps camped on a 16 acre field of clover seed ready to cut and destroyed it."[35]

---

34 Claim of Samuel Reel (No. 3209); Johnson, *BA*, 117; Claim of Hiram Showman (No. 1522). Online translations define acaparar (Spanish) as hoarding and acaparat (Romanian) as seizing. The hay totals cited are based on war claims archived in record groups 92 and 123 at the NA in Washington, DC. The agent's reference to "country" related to the Sharpsburg region rather than the U.S.

35 Claims of Noah Rohrback (H-3874), Joseph Sherrick (F-1433), and Otho B. Smith (F-1432). Clover, being a legume, also served as an essential fertilizer for Sharpsburg's farmers, as it released nitrogen into the soil. Farmers also used manure to fertilize their fields.

Animals of the AOP damaged the majority of pastures. When troops fed their horses all thirty acres of David R. Miller's clover, it constituted "the entire produce of the field for that season." Near Mercersville, a witness saw AOP personnel drive "a couple of hundred gray mules . . . and a quantity of horses" into John E. Knode's pasture. Samuel Mumma, Jr., describing his parents' losses, recalled, "[T]here was 25 or 30 acres of pasture on the place which was pastured by the government horses." Some of the meadow, Mumma explained, "was the second year crop" and had not yet been cut. Unfortunately, army horses "were turned in on the fields and kept there until it was gone."[36]

The AOP's cattle also destroyed Sharpsburg's clover pastures. For instance, Moses Cox lost fifty-nine acres of clover hay to "200 head of [cattle] stock." Also, on the nearby farm of his brothers, John and William Cox, army butchers established a "slaughter pen" in a ten-acre clover field, "which was fed upon by the army cattle."

McClellan's bovines grazed on the farm of Samuel I. Piper. "There was a large herd of beef cattle fed on the place for 4 or 5 weeks," Piper alleged, and the ruminants "consumed the growing grass on the whole place." Another farmer, Morgan Miller, claimed damages for "64 acres pasture used for 500 cattle." John Otto suffered similar losses. He recalled seeing "a large amount of stock on my property, as high as five hundred head of cattle at one time together with horses and mules."[37]

Thousands of McClellan's animals grazed on Sharpsburg-area pastures. Robert W. Grove, describing his father's damages, recalled that army personnel "turned their horses and cattle . . . into a fifty acre field of clover, the second crop, and used it all." Describing the encampments of AOP headquarters and IX Corps on his family's farms, Otho Showman testified, "184 acres of clover was pastured by beef

---

36 Claim of David R. Miller (No. 1266). The 1860 agricultural schedule for Sharpsburg included a separate category for clover seed, listing it among other crops such as corn and wheat. David R. Miller estimated his 30-acre field to be "well filled & would have yielded at least 3 bushels to the acre;" Claims of John E. Knode (No. 8587) and Samuel Mumma, Sr. (No. 334).

37 Claims of Moses Cox (G-1657), John U. and William I. Cox (M-901), Samuel I. Piper (D-2392), Morgan and Andrew Rentch Miller (No. 4295), and John Otto (G-1857). In 1862, John Otto owned a 67-acre farm near Burnside Bridge, a 51-acre farm adjoining Miller's Sawmill Road, and a 132-acre tract adjoining the Showman family's Home farm, southwest of Sharpsburg. The large herd of cattle described by Otto likely belonged to AOP headquarters, which based itself on and near the Showmans' lands after the battle. See land records IN 8 / 362, 76 / 689, IN 10 / 235, 91 / 266-7, MM / 417, and WMCKK 2 / 405.

cattle belonging to the army." In addition, Showman stated, "the animals belonging to the cavalry were also turned in upon it, and that it was entirely consumed."

On John J. Keedy's farm, where McClellan based his headquarters before and during the battle, "a sixteen acre field of clover was pastured by the beef cattle of the army during their stay here." Keedy's son deposed, "The field was pastured off clean, so that nothing was saved." Similar damages occurred when Federal teamsters parked 25 wagons near Joseph Poffenberger's clover field. "All the horses of said wagons were turned into it," farmhand Isaac Malott recounted. The animals grazed in the twenty-acre meadow for twelve days. During this time, Malott recalled, "I saw them pasture his farm off as bare as a floor."[38]

*   *   *

Western Maryland civilians also grew rye and oats. Families reserved some of their rye grain for making bread and whiskey, while oats served as supplemental horse feed. When the armies arrived at Sharpsburg, farmers were threshing their oat and rye crops, storing the grains in barns and granaries. Unthreshed oats, meanwhile, lay bound in sheaves and stacked in fields.

Like appropriating corn and hay from the community, McClellan's army seized oats and rye to feed army animals. Hiram Showman, whose farm adjoined the Keedysville-Bakersville Road, recalled seeing U.S. army wagons, "a very long train of them . . . in the road on my farm." The wagon masters, Showman testified, fed his unthreshed oats to their horses. Jacob Snyder farmed along the same road and recalled that his 25 bushels of oats "were in Sharfs [sheaves] & in the barn & were taken out of the barn when it was used for a hospital." Afterward, Snyder added, "the oats was fed to the horses."[39]

<hr />

38 Claims of Jacob H. Grove (No. 1267), Raleigh Showman (F-1180 and F-1183), John J. Keedy (54-1488), and Joseph Poffenberger (No. 1300).

39 Claims of Hiram Showman (No. 1522) and Jacob Snyder (F-1537). Sharpsburg's annual yields of oats and rye were much smaller than corn, hay, and wheat. As described in Chapter Four, the AOP's medical department seized rye straw for use as hospital bedding. Supporting Sharpsburg's consumption of rye whiskey, Joseph Poffenberger's claim (No. 1300) cited the loss of "50 gallons rye whisky." For further reading, see Jack Sullivan, "Outerbridge Horsey IV: A Blueblood and His Booze," blog, *Those Pre-Pro Whiskey Men!*, April 29, 2011, http://pre-prowhiskeymen.blogspot.com/2011/04/outerbridge-horsey-iv-blueblood-and-hi s.html. During the Civil War, Outerbridge Horsey IV operated a rye whiskey distillery in Burkittsville, located ten miles from Sharpsburg.

Samuel Poffenberger remembered that he threshed his oats "on the Monday previous to Antietam," carrying 25 bushels "from the meadow to the bin." When he returned home on September 19, "said oats were gone." Poffenberger's neighbor, Simon Morrison, testified, "I helped him thresh the oats. We had threshed them a day or two before the army came. I saw them [soldiers] take the oats and saw part of them fed."

Isaac Malott was present on Joseph Poffenberger's farm when Federals seized the grains. "[T]he oats and rye were fed about the barn the day of and the day after the battle," the farmhand deposed. "I saw them take his oats from the barn along with the wheat and rye." Jacob Eakle, who lived north of Joseph Poffenberger, visited the farm shortly after the battle and watched AOP personnel cut a hole in the barn to access the grains inside. "I saw boards cut away from the barn," Eakle recalled, "as if they were to take feed out." Once soldiers broke into the structure, Joseph Poffenberger observed that army animals "near the barn were fed from it right there."[40]

On Jacob H. Grove's farm, U.S. troops "took all the rye and oats," feeding their horses "at least 100 bushels of rye in the boxes and chop-chests." Similarly, medical staff carried off 63 bushels of Bishop John Russell's rye, which was "used to feed ambulance horses." Michael Miller claimed that U.S. soldiers took 10 bushels of rye grain and 23 bushels of rye chop from his stable. Also, William M. Blackford recalled that his 140 bushels of rye "was in the granary measured, and was taken by the cavalry and fed to their horses."[41]

Jacob Houser swore that AOP forces fed forty bushels of his rye to their horses. Houser was "positive of the quantity because he measured it as it was threshed in the machine." Supporting his allegation, William F. Hebb "was visiting the residence of Mr. Houser when the troops of the 1st Corps Army of the Potomac came with some 3 or 4 wagons to haul away wheat & c." Hebb noticed the appropriations "in particular at the time because he thought it was an unusual proceeding to feed wheat & rye to horses."[42]

---

40 Claims of Samuel Poffenberger (No. 4298) and Joseph Poffenberger (No. 1300).

41 Claim of Jacob H. Grove (No. 1267); Geeting and Russell accounts, UMLA; Claims of Michael Miller (F-1438) and William M. Blackford (No. 1324).

42 Claim of Jacob Houser (F-814). In describing his threshed rye, Houser stated, "He was obliged to pay what is called toll, that is 6 bushels for every 100 bushels threshed by the machine, which belonged to another party."

Reflecting the AOP's dire need for forage, McClellan's men confiscated bran particles from mills and stables. Civilians reserved these wheat by-products as horse feed, which they described as offal, middlings, millfeed, shorts, and shipstuff. Solomon Lumm sought repayment for four bushels of shorts and two bushels of middlings, which were "taken in the night" by Federal soldiers and "fed to their horses by these troops." Henry Piper reported the appropriation of "3 bu[shels] offals." Before Samuel Poffenberger evacuated his farm on September 16, "he had in his stable about 25 bushels of middlings & 15 bushels of ship stuff," described as "ground feed" and "horse feed." When Poffenberger returned home on September 19, though, the medical department occupied his farm and all the horse feed had vanished.[43]

*　　*　　*

Washington County farmers planted their annual wheat crop in the fall of each year. The grain remained dormant during winter, sprouted in the spring, and matured in early summer. Harvest took place in June or July, when farmers and their hands cradled the wheat, bound it in bundles, and stacked it in "ricks" to dry. One resident recalled, "It was a pleasant sight to see twenty or more cradlers in line mowing down the golden grain, all keeping time to the leader's stroke, and the gleaners in their wake, binding the swath into sheaves." From there, farmers and their laborers stacked wheat conically to shed rainfall and protect the unthreshed grains from molding or sprouting.

In a typical year, the wheat stacks dried by September. After threshing the cured grain—separating seeds from straw and chaff—farmers measured the kernels in bushels. From there, they sold most of the proceeds to mills and markets while saving some of the grain for family flour (or "bread purposes," as one resident described). Being Sharpsburg's primary cash crop, wheat provided substantial income to farm families, especially during good years. 1862 reportedly

---

43 Claims of Solomon Lumm (N-546), Henry Piper (No. 445), and Samuel Poffenberger (F-1434). For further reading on offal and middlings, see *The American Miller and Processor* (Chicago, September 1, 1913), vol. 41, 722-723. See also Joy L. Harwood, Mack N. Leath, Walter George Heid, *The U.S. Milling and Baking Industries*, United States Department of Agriculture, Economic Research Service (Washington, DC, 1989), 24; Sharpsburg war claims show that soldiers took several dozen grain bags from civilians after filling them with confiscated feed. Among the claimants who lost grain sacks were Raleigh Domer (92-551), Henry V. S. Blackford (G-1630, G-1648, G-1654), Josephus Clopper (RG 92, Book G, Claim G-1916), Thomas Fisher (H-4113 and H-4114), Samuel D. Piper (D-2393), Michael Miller (F-1438), and Solomon Lumm (N-546).

produced a strong yield, described by resident Moses Cox as "an extra good one . . . above the average." Unfortunately for citizens of the Antietam Valley, their supply of corn, hay, oats, and rye did not provide enough forage for the large population of military animals. Consequently, McClellan's army confiscated the 1862 wheat crop from farmsteads throughout the battlefield region.[44]

West of Sharpsburg village, Samuel Beeler raised "a very fine crop of wheat from 30 or 35 acres . . . all of which was stacked near and inside the Barn." Troops seized Beeler's "whole crop," he alleged, and fed it "to the horses of McClellan's army." William M. Blackford suffered a similar misfortune. In September 1862, he had a rick of 800 bushels "on the back part of my farm" and 200 bushels in his barn and granary. AOP forces confiscated the wheat for cavalry and artillery horses, Blackford deposed. "They took it all."[45]

Farmers throughout the area filed similar claims. Medical forces fed 100 bushels of John Russell's golden grain to "hospital horses." From Noah Rohrback's wheat stacks, Northern troops pulled bundled sheaves of wheat through "the hole in the rick" and fed it "as roughness for the horses." On his "Lime Kiln" tract near the Antietam Iron Works, John A. Wade alleged that 700 bushels of wheat were "fed to the horses belonging to the United States Cavalry." Likewise, Philip Pry deposed that his "wheat in the rick was consumed by the Cavalry of the 12th and 13th Pa Cavy and the Ambulance Corps," who "encamped and remained near the rick until it was all eaten up [because] Forage was very scarce."[46]

Angeline Jackson remembered that Captain David Smith's sons were "threshing at the time the Federals came in. He [Smith] had the best crop that year he had ever had." Jackson recounted, "[T]he wheat crop had all been gathered from the fields and was in the barn and in two large stacks or ricks near the barn."

44 Stonebraker, *A Rebel of '61*, 31; Claim of John A. Wade (G-2400). Four farmhands signed an affidavit swearing that they "worked on the [John A. Wade] farm for years and plowed the ground and put out the crop of wheat in the Fall of 1861 & the corn crop in the spring of 1862;" Sharpsburg farmers in the 1860 agricultural schedule reported an aggregate of almost 66,000 bushels of wheat; Claims of Stephen P. Grove (No. 7354) and Jacob Houser (F-814). Moses Cox appeared as a witness in Houser's claim. While not documented in claims testimonies, Sharpsburg's farmers may have crowned their stacks with capsheaves to create rain runoff and protect the wheat from moisture.

45 Claims of Samuel Beeler (201-56) and William M. Blackford (No. 1324).

46 Geeting and Russell accounts, UMLA; Claims of Noah Rohrback (H-3874), John A. Wade (No. 6586), and Philip Pry (G-1759); Alexander in "Destruction, Disease, and Death," 156, noted that the 12th and 13th Pennsylvania Cavalry served as McClellan's escort at Antietam.

Brothers Philip and Samuel Pry, shown here in their later years, lost large amounts of property to the AOP during and after the battle. According to their separate war claims, the Pry brothers' heaviest losses were wheat, corn, hay, and straw. *Courtesy of Betsy Webb*

Confederates hadn't taken any of the crop, she deduced, because, "I went out there to get some my clothing after the rebels left, and the ricks of wheat were standing there yet, unthreshed." After U.S. troops seized the wheat in Capt. Smith's barn, they tore into the stacks in the field, pulling off the outer layers that protected the grains from moisture. With Smith's wheat exposed, rainfall spoiled what remained of the crop, on account of "the stacks having upset and the rain making it sprout."[47]

On September 19, Moses Cox watched men from Gen. Abner Doubleday's command "loading 8 to 10 army wagons with wheat from Jacob Houser's barn." The soldiers continued until "the entire crop was taken . . . [for] the horses of Doubleday's command." Houser learned that the army seized his grain to "supply an urgent want occasioned by the failure of the regular supply trains to reach them, during and immediately after the battle of Antietam." Similarly, Joseph Poffenberger lost his entire wheat crop to elements of I Corps. "I saw the soldiers take it away," Poffenberger recalled. "I went to a general of the army and asked him to save my wheat; he told me they needed it for the horses."

Another farmer, Samuel Mumma, Sr., lost 80 bushels of wheat inside his barn when it caught fire during the battle. His remaining crop survived the flames, being stacked in the field. Regrettably, it didn't last long. "All this forage," Mumma testified, "was taken immediately after the battle of Antietam" on account that the army's "supply trains were irregular and often interrupted and delayed, and . . . the necessities of the army were great and pressing." Mumma's son, Samuel, Jr., deposed that U.S. soldiers took the unthreshed wheat "out of the ricks and hauled it to General Sumner's camp." Afterward, he recalled, "I went to General Sumner and he referred me to his Quarter Master and he said they would have to have it and

47 Claims of David Smith (Nos. 1244, 1262, and 10237).

would pay for it." Such reparation might have helped the homeless family rebuild their burned buildings. The promised payment, however, never came.[48]

Not all of Sharpsburg's wheat became food for AOP animals. Witnesses observed troops carry off bushels of the valuable grain for use in camp. For example, when Henry W. Mongan of the 3rd Maryland Infantry bivouacked on Hiram Showman's farm during the battle's aftermath, he "saw the men take all they wanted, such as wheat in the bundles." Mongan recalled, "We made beds out of the wheat." In Keedysville, C. M. Keedy deposed that there was "a large stack of wheat" on his father's farm, "the crop of thirteen acres." When McClellan established his headquarters on the property, Keedy recounted that soldiers "got on the stack and pitched the sheaves down, and fed it to the horses[49]

In addition to appropriating threshed wheat from the community, the AOP's encamped troops carried off straw for use as bedding in camps. Many civilians had already lost straw to the medical department and now watched infantry, cavalry, and artillery forces take what remained. Samuel I. Piper recalled, "I had threshed a crop of wheat in the field right where they were encamped . . . the straw was ricked up and they used it while they lay there." Soldiers used some of Piper's straw "for bedding in the tents."

According to William M. Blackford, V Corps forces took 20 tons of straw "from his barn-yard" because "the weather got cold and disagreeable, and they used the straw in their tents." Federals took ten tons of wheat straw from Samuel D. Piper "from the rick in the barn-yard" and used it "for bedding and coarse forage." John Grice caught U.S. troops confiscating 60 tons of straw from his out lot, "I saw them taking it from the rick," Grice testified, but "they drove me away from there." Scores more claimants reported straw losses during McClellan's six-week encampment. From Squire Jacob Miller's three farms, the commands of Meade and Sykes reportedly took 52 tons. Jacob Houser, meanwhile, claimed the loss of 50 tons of straw to the commands of Ricketts and Doubleday. Near Houser's farm, James A. Rowe and Moses Cox reported a loss of 82 tons.[50]

---

48 Claims of Jacob Houser (F-814), Joseph Poffenberger (No. 1300), and Samuel Mumma, Sr. (D-1927, D-1928 and 113-1024). Poffenberger estimated his loss at 500 bushels, as the wheat had previously "been measured for the [threshing] machine."

49 Claims of John J. Keedy (No. 2157) and Hiram Showman (No. 1522).

50 Claims of Samuel I. Piper (D-2392), William M. Blackford (No. 1324), Samuel D. Piper (No. 440), John Grice (No. 5872), Jacob Houser (F-814), Jacob Miller (No. 4296), James A. Rowe (*RG* 92, Entry 797, Book 113, Claim 113-76), and Moses Cox (G-1657).

To present a sample of the AOP's destruction of threshed wheat, 57 Sharpsburg-area claimants filed an aggregate loss of 12,909 bushels or 226 bushels of grain per claimant. By comparison, 103 farmers living near the battlefield in 1860 reported 65,683 bushels, averaging 638 bushels of wheat per claimant. Priced at around $1.25 per bushel in 1862, each farmer lost roughly $283 in potential wheat income. This amount converts to almost $8,000 with inflation. The sampled losses do not include wheat appropriated by Dr. Letterman's medical department or the Confederate army. As financially damaging as wheat appropriations were to the community, they only represented the 1862 crop. During Antietam's aftermath, the numerous Federal encampments put the 1863 wheat crop in peril.[51]

*   *   *

"Very few of our farmers have as yet sown their wheat," reported the Middletown Valley Register on October 10, 1862, because the AOP's occupation "prevented many farmers from working while the farms of others were thrown open and their fields trampled down." Squire Jacob Miller corroborated the Register's concern. "[V]erry fiew farmers can sow any wheat where ever the soldiers are encampt," he complained. "[W]e want to sow eighteen acres. Francis cant sow any. Morgan and Rench will sow some, and many farmers cant sow an acre." Dr. A. A. Biggs summarized the emergency more succinctly: "All is lost, and in all probability, the farmers will not be able to put out any grain this fall."[52]

Sharpsburg's farmers usually planted their annual wheat crop in October. After the battle, though, they faced several challenges in sowing seeds for their 1863 wheat. First, the clock was ticking, and it was necessary to seed the soil a week or two before the first killing frost. Sowing too early exposed wheat shoots to destruction by Hessian fly larvae, and thus timing was crucial. Second, farmers could not plant wheat until soldiers ceased camping on their ploughed fields. Third, the military encampments compacted tilled soil to the extent that some fields required reploughing before seeding could commence. Such work would take days, though, and little time remained before the planting window closed.[53]

51 1860 agricultural schedule, Sharpsburg District; Williamson, *PPT*.

52 *The Valley Register*, October 10, 1862, 2A; Jacob Miller to Amelia and Christian Houser, October 1862, WMR; Biggs to Kalb, September 29, 1862, WMR.

53 Thomas J. Basden, A. O. Abaye, and Richard W. Taylor, "Chapter 5: Crop Production," abstract, University of Maryland Extension, 105, https://extension.umd.edu/sites/extension.

Consequently, dozens of farmers failed to plant wheat in October 1862, which resulted in no crop—and no wheat income—in 1863. Samuel I. Piper was among those affected. He pursued repayment from the United States government for being "unable to put in his crop of winter wheat by reason of the occupation of his farm by the U.S. Army." Similarly, Peter Beeler was unable to plant on his "17 acres seed ground," and John L. Mayer sought reparations for "Loss of next years crop of wheat from inability to seed by reason of military occupation."[54]

Near Bakersville, Eliza Davis claimed $42.50 for "Damage by occupation of land prepared for seed." Correspondingly, Otho Showman sought $675 for acreage "despoiled from seeding" due to the AOP basing its headquarters on Showman's property. Another claimant, David R. Miller, "could not get a [wheat] crop on account of the troops" damaging his ploughed field. North of Sharpsburg, Federals encamped on two farms owned by Andrew Rentch, preventing his tenants from planting the 1863 wheat crops. As a result, Rentch claimed the $575 loss of "25 acres plowed not seeded" and "75 acres ground prepared by Tenant."[55]

---

umd.edu/files/_docs/programs/anmp/MANMChapter5.pdf; Bob Kratochvil, "10 Steps to Profitable Wheat Production," blog, *Maryland Agronomy News*, University of Maryland, August 2, 2017, http://blog.umd.edu/agronomynews/2017/08/02/10-steps-to-profitable-wheat-production/. The flies' larvae feed on young wheat stems. This problem appears in Hagerstown newspapers from 1846–1857 and dates to the 1700s, when Thomas Jefferson sought a solution for destroying the pests. See "Hessian Fly," Thomas Jefferson Encyclopedia, The Jefferson Monticello, https://www.monticello.org/site/research-and-collections/hessian-fly; Jeff Semler, phone communications with author, September 16, 2021. Semler is an extension agent with Agriculture & Food Systems, University of Maryland Extension, in Washington County. He stated that Washington County farmers typically do not plant wheat before Oct. 1 due to the Hessian fly threat; U.S. Department of Agriculture, *Soil Survey of Washington County, Maryland* (Washington, DC, 1919), 9. The 1919 survey cited Oct. 20 as the average date of Keedysville's first killing frost. Of note, General McClellan's forces did not begin departing the Sharpsburg-Keedysville area until Oct. 26, 1862.

54 Claims of Samuel I. Piper (D-2392), Peter Beeler (G-1771), and John L. Mayer (No. 8586). The annual wheat harvest affected the local economy. For example, heavy rain reportedly stunted the 1859 yield. As a result, Adam Michael informed his son (Adam Michael to David Michael, December 26, 1859, WMR), "Everything is dull, especially money matters, and more so than they have been for a long time." Furthermore, Squire Jacob Miller (Jacob Miller to Amelia and Christian Houser, August 10, 1859, WMR) complained to his family in 1859 that "[W]heat failed which wound up money matters verry close which threw everybody out of market in buying land." Thus, farmers who failed to plant wheat for 1863 certainly suffered setbacks in attempting to recover from Antietam-related property losses.

55 Claim of Eliza Davis (Citizens' appraisement, Joseph Davis collection, Kingsport, TN). Davis donated a copy of his papers to the WMR; Claims of Raleigh Showman (F-1183), David R. Miller (F-1499), and Andrew Rentch (No. 4235).

In early October, shipments of tents began trickling into McClellan's camps and field hospitals. When Brigadier General Abram Duryée's brigade received their shelters at Mercersville on October 11, the regiment withdrew from riverside woodlots to "a ridge in the open fields, about half a mile from their former site, and over-looking the battle field."

Near Sharpsburg village, medical personnel erected "three large hospital tents" on the farm of Elias S. Grove. Nearby, troops pitched ninety-two tents on Stephen P. Grove's farm. In this vicinity, "stretching for some fifteen miles along the course of the river," recalled Col. Francis J. Parker of the 32nd Massachusetts, "the various corps were encamped in due form." From a vantage point, Parker observed an "array of white tents, and could see the bounds of each regiment, brigade, or division." During the night, "the lines of lighted tents would show from a distance, like an army of glow-worms."

Three miles south of the village, a member of the 9th New Hampshire remembered viewing IX Corps camps from atop a high bluff. "[A]s far as the eye could reach," he observed, farm fields were "dotted over with white tents, and fairly alive with men, either busy about their daily tasks or marching and countermarching in regular columns." In abundance nearby were "the baggage and supply trains, the wagons arranged in line with military precision, and surrounded by a circle of noisy, hungry mules. At intervals could be seen the parks of artillery, and in the neighboring wood were the numerous camps of the cavalry." After nightfall, "under the soft, white light of the moon the scene took on a touch of romance, which was not wholly lost when the camp-fires burned brightly, and each tent displayed its bit of candle."[56]

Romantic as these scenes appeared to soldiers, local farmers saw the ubiquitous camps as destructive to clover fields and impediments to sowing wheat. Worse, the military concentrations trampled freshly-tilled land, packing soil so firmly that many farmers needed to replough their fields before planting wheat. Also damaging the land was the AOP's supply train of 3,219 wagons. Most of these heavily weighted transports belonged to commands near Sharpsburg. Combined

---

56 Hough, *History of Duryée's Brigade*, 122-124; Claims of Elias S. Grove (*RG* 123, Entry 22, Box 804, Case No. 7356) and Stephen P. Grove (No. 7354). Stephen P. Grove sought rent for "Lawn covered with tents for 92 days;" Parker, *The Story of the Thirty-Second Regiment*, 108-111; Lord, *History of the Ninth Regiment*, 149-151. Also supporting that tents arrived in early October, Dr. Jonah F. Dyer, based near Smoketown, wrote on Oct. 1, "[T]he tents are now being put up. The wounded will be much better off in tents than in houses or barns." See Jonah F. Dyer, *The Journal of a Civil War Surgeon*, ed. Michael B. Chesson (Lincoln, NE, 2003), 42.

with cavalry, foot soldiers, batteries, and ambulances traveling to and from camps, the wagon traffic blazed roads across farms and carved ruts into crop fields.

Describing the Samuel Grove heirs' property, Jacob McGraw recalled that Federals "used the entire farm that could be wagoned over for roads when they had to haul anything to their camps." Similarly, Samuel Reel's land incurred "damage from [military] traveling," and John J. Keedy sought reparations for "25 acres ploughed ground trampled." North of the battlefield, Levi Middlekauff remembered that "the Federal Army passed in columns over" his father's farm, "and that they made several roads through it."[57]

William Roulette accused the U.S. army of making "roads through fields and tramping ploughed fields so that they must be ploughed over." Near Keedysville, Ephraim Geeting claimed a $200 loss on account of "55 acres of ground prepared for seeding unable to sow in consequence of the ground run over by the army." Samuel Mumma, Sr., who had already lost significant acreage to burials, suffered additional damages to his farm that included "land damaged by traveling," "roads through farm," and "49 acres of ground encumbered so that it can not be seeded."[58]

Ploughing in the mid-nineteenth century was an arduous task, and, not surprisingly, some farmers filed labor claims for the time required to re-till compacted fields. Among the claimants were Samuel Poffenberger, who sought $24.00 for "reploughing 12 acres of ground," and Henry B. Rohrback, who charged the U.S. $20.00 for "reploughing 20 acres of fallow grass." Numerous civilians witnessed the trampled fields. On one farm, a resident remembered, "In an incredibly short time a splendid field of luxuriant verdue had been beaten down as hard as a turnpike road and every blade of grass had disappeared. It was years before the most careful cultivation could restore the land to anything like its former productive condition." Through great efforts her family loosened the soil, but "the land broke up in great clods and lumps which had to be pulverized with axes and mallets. And it was not only the fields in which the encampment was that were injured," she recalled. "[R]oads were made across all the fields in every direction."

---

57 *OR*, vol. 19, 1:95. Rufus Ingalls reported, "In the beginning of October [1862] . . . there was with the army immediately present under General McC about 3,219 baggage and supply wagons;" Claims of the heirs of Samuel Grove (No. 9313), John J. Keedy (No. 2157), Samuel Reel (G-1923), and John C. Middlekauff (F-1587).

58 Claim of William Roulette (Woodring, "Window to Yesterday"). Geeting and Russell accounts, UMLA.

Newspaper correspondents also noted the land damages. In early October, the *New York Times* reported that some Sharpsburg farms contained "battered corn, fairly trampled into the earth" and "deep ruts formed by the heavy wheels of artillery." On October 2, the *Altoona Tribune* noted that crop fields near the battlefield "were tread into the dust and the whole face of the country resembled a wide wagon road."[59]

Such was the destruction of Sharpsburg's crops and farm fields after the Battle of Antietam. Testimonies in war claims are rife with allegations that McClellan's army stripped entire grain crops from farms. Thomas Barnum reported that men from VI Corps "took and consumed nearly the whole of the year's products of the farm, wheat, hay, straw, corn and fodder." Samuel E. Sherwin deposed that "the troops took everything" from the farm of John E. Knode. Likewise, one of William Wade's witnesses, William C. Bussard, testified, "I suppose they used whatever they needed in the way of forage. Mr. Wade raised large crops of corn, hay, wheat, rye, etc. I know when the Federal troops left the farm there was little or nothing upon it."

To better comprehend the collective loss of Sharpsburg's grains, let's combine the losses cited in previous samples for corn, fodder, hay, rye, oats, and wheat. In a sample of 150 claims reviewed at the National Archives in Washington, civilians of the Sharpsburg environs claimed that the AOP took 4,226 tons of grains from September 15–October 26. Evidence suggests that troops fed the majority of this forage to military animals.

Earlier in this chapter, we applied the United States Army's daily forage requirements to the equines in I Corps and V Corps. Those horses and mules needed 105 tons of forage per day. By dividing the total amount of sampled appropriations—4,226 tons—by 105 tons of daily forage, said grains would have fed the army animals for 40.24 days. Interestingly, I Corps and V Corps encamped near Sharpsburg for 41 days, from September 19–October 26, 1862.

Granted, this formula only applies to two army corps. The daily need for forage was much higher when we consider animals assigned to other elements of the AOP, such as cavalry, headquarters, VI Corps, XI Corps, the ambulance corps, commissary department, and Reserve Artillery—along with the two army corps based near Harper's Ferry.

---

59 Claims of Samuel Poffenberger (F-1434) and Henry B. Rohrback (Book 304, Claim 235); Williams, HWC, vol. 1, 2:359-360; *New York Times*, October 4, 1862; *Altoona Tribune*, October 2, 1862.

Monetarily, based on 1862 market rates, the 4,226 tons of crops totaled $69,876. With inflation, this amount converts, in 2022 U.S. relative value, to almost $2 million. While incomplete, this figure presents a rough estimate of what McClellan's army may have taken from the community insofar as grains and feed crops are concerned. The Hagerstown *Herald of Freedom and Torch Light* reported something along the same line in early October 1862, estimating that "a million of dollars will not more than cover the total loss inflicted upon our county" by the two armies. And because "the necessary and unnecessary destruction of property has been enormous," the newspaper predicted, "the county will not recover from the effects of this heart-rending disaster for years to come—probably not in our day and generation."

Combining the crop appropriations with other military-related losses like livestock, horses, orchard fruit, clothing, and structures destroyed by fire, one gets a partial sense of the overall financial hardship inflicted on civilians. But Sharpsburg's property losses were far from over. As temperatures dropped throughout October, the Army of the Potomac's need for fuel increased, and the region's fencing and timber were about to go up in smoke.[60]

---

60 Claims of Thomas Barnum (No. 333), John E. Knode (No. 8587), and William Wade (No. 9314); Williamson, *PPT*; Farmers calculated their losses in a variety of ways, such as measuring ricks, acreage, haymows, and wagonloads. It's impossible to gauge how close these estimates were to the exact quantity of 4,226 tons. Conversions are based on the U.S. short ton, 2,000 pounds equaling one ton. The claimed losses, in tons, consisted of corn (1,537), fodder (807), hay (1,432) oats (42), rye (21), and wheat (387); United States Department of Agriculture, Economic Research Service, "Weights, Measures, and Conversion Factors for Agricultural Commodities and Their Products," (Washington DC, June 1992). Pounds-per-bushel conversions included corn ears (70), wheat (60), rye (56), and oats (32). Sharpsburg claimants calculated fodder and hay losses in tons. See https://www.ers.usda.gov/webdocs/publications/41880/33132_ah697_002.pdf?v=0.; *HFTL*, October 1, 1862.

Chapter 8

Like Frost Before a Burning Sun:
The Destruction of Landscape

Antietam is well known for its trees, given that part of the battle raged in the East and West Woods. But timber covered dozens of farms in 1862. It also lined the Potomac River and sprawled across Elk Ridge and Red Hill. Various hardwoods colored Sharpsburg's landscape in 1862, including white oak, black oak, chestnut, hickory, walnut, and locust. Some visitors to the area marveled at the timber. "The forest trees here," Dr. William Child wrote in September 1862, "are all large and hardwood. There is but little if any pine. You might drive a wagon among the trees anywhere."

Washington County residents cared for their woodlots by weeding the undergrowth and felling as few trees as possible. Like Lavinia Grove, Colonel John Blackford, and Henry Wade, landowners long-deceased took pride in their decades-old hardwoods, and willed the towering trees to offspring for constructing future barns and fences. When civilians chopped their timber, they cut the stumps low to the ground to obtain as many cords as possible. If residents came across unusually high stumps, they immediately knew that outsiders—soldiers, especially—had cut their trees.[1]

---

1 Child, *Letters From a Civil War Surgeon*, 59-60; Last will and testament of Lavinia Grove (Will Book E / 314-315); Claims of William M. Blackford (No. 1324) and the heirs of Henry Wade (No. 6585); "Forestry in Germany," *Consular Reports: Commerce, Manufactures, Etc.* (Washington, DC, January–April, 1903), Vol. LXXI, 81. The Antietam Valley residents' careful management of timber tracts resembled forestry in Germany, from where many Sharpsburg families

Samuel Mumma, Sr. and his wife, Elizabeth (Miller) Mumma, photographed before the war. After finding their farmhouse and barn in ruins, the Mummas watched Federal soldiers carry off their remaining property, including cordwood, livestock, grains, and fencing. *ANB*

Typically, landowners felled a few trees each spring to obtain winter firewood. They then cut and stacked the wood to cure over the summer. Stephen P. Grove needed "four or five cords to last him a year," while C. M. Keedy recounted, "About a dozen cords were cut each Spring for use the following winter." Samuel Mumma, Sr. cut fifteen cords of wood early in 1862, "which he intended for the use of his own family that coming winter." It was generally his father's habit, Mumma's son recalled, "to have fine wood cut and corded" in the spring "so that the wood would be dry or partly so by winter."

In September 1862, the community's cordwood was almost ready to use in fireplaces and cookstoves. Nonetheless, most of this firewood vanished after soldiers arrived in the Antietam Valley.[2]

"Wherever an army camps, it uses and cuts wood." Such was the U.S. quartermaster department's explanation for confiscating fences, firewood, and timber from civilians after the Battle of Antietam. During the AOP's encampment near Sharpsburg, soldiers indeed used wood, destroying copious amounts as

---

descended. German farmers kept their timber tracts "free from weeds, undergrowth, washouts, and dead and decayed wood." By cutting timber "as close as possible to the ground," they saved "millions of feet of lumber per year." Thus, the consular report cited, "high stumps are a rarity."

2 Claim of the heirs of Samuel Grove (No. 9313). Robert W. Grove testified regarding Stephen P. Grove's firewood, referring to him as "Uncle Stephen;" Claims of John J. Keedy (54-1488) and Samuel Mumma, Sr. (113-1024). Antietam Valley property owners often felled a few extra trees each spring, selling corded wood for extra income to the community. Firewood in 1862 sold for $3.50 per seasoned cord. Modern estimates describe one cord of wood as 128 cubic feet, cut and stacked in a pile measuring eight feet long, four feet wide, and four feet tall. In a sample of 33 Sharpsburg claimants, the majority used oak as firewood, while Catherine Showman, Henry Shamel, Rev. John A. Adams, and a few others reserved hickory logs for the winter of 1862–63.

temperatures dropped throughout October. Seasoned cordwood, because it was cut and ready to burn, was the first to go.[3]

John Otto recalled that his thirteen cords of wood "was cut and seasoned and was piled in my yard for winter use." After the battle, though, Otto's firewood "was burned for fuel in the Hospital and by soldiers around my house." Another claimant, John Snyder, had reserved some of his seasoned oak for "delivery at market," but Federals took Snyder's entire supply. Likewise, Adam Hutzell's 30–35 cords were "racked for sale and for private use," but "the wood was taken by General Ricketts Corps and hauled to their camps 2 1/2 miles below his farm."[4]

Soldiers seized firewood from several dozen battlefield-area residents. For example, Catherine Showman lost ten cords of wood reserved "for winter use." Samuel Mumma, Sr. had fifteen cords of "good solid and sound oak wood . . . but instead of using it himself it was furnished and used by the army." Widow Martha Schlosser, who lived alone, kept one cord "laying by the house." Federals confiscated her stack and used it "for cooking purposes." Joseph Poffenberger's winter stash of oak and hickory was "cut and ricked in a little patch of timber." Did I Corps forces leave any firewood for Poffenberger and his wife? Not so, deposed their farmhand. "It was all taken. Not a stick being left."[5]

As crucial as cordwood was to civilians, John S. Grove offered it to the army in an attempt to save his father's fencing. "We had been clearing a piece of [wooded] ground," John recalled, from which "the wood was all hauled out and ranked up. When they were taking the fences, I told them to take these," referring to the family's winter logs. Union troops agreed to the deal and hauled the Groves' firewood to their camp. However, it wasn't long before the soldiers returned and seized the worm rails on Elias S. Grove's farm—along with other fencing in the Sharpsburg environs.[6]

* * *

In September 1862, omnipresent fence lines covered Sharpsburg's landscape. Miles of fencing lined turnpikes and farm lanes, and miles more enclosed farmsteads, village lots, and out lots. Farmers divided their multiple fields with

3 Claim of the heirs of Henry Wade (G-2394).

4 Claims of John Otto (G-1857), John Snyder (No. 6617), and Adam Hutzell (F-1538).

5 Claims of Catherine Showman (F-1185), Samuel Mumma, Sr. (113-1024 and D-1927/1928), and Martha Schlosser (H-4109).

6 Claims of Joseph Poffenberger (No. 1300) and Elias S. Grove (No. 7356).

interior fencing known as cross fence or middle fence. To bound perimeters and separate properties, landowners and their adjoining neighbors jointly built division fence, also described as party or law fence. Farms, in other words, typically contained thousands of rails. Given the amount of exterior and interior partitions, it wasn't uncommon for large farmsteads to have several miles of fencing, which varied in type.

The most common fence on Sharpsburg's farms in 1862 was worm fence, also known as Virginia, snake rail, and split rail fence. Due to the problematic abundance of limestone in Washington County's soil, landowners preferred worm fencing because it required no digging. Relying on local timber, farmers sawed oak or chestnut logs into lengths of ten to twelve feet, then split them into rails measuring four or five inches thick. They stacked rails into interlocked panels and secured the sections with wooden stakes called riders. To stabilize the fence, farmers angled each panel in a zigzag design, allowing gravity to hold together the rails.[7]

Farmers knew what materials comprised the fences and knew the length of each panel. Moses Poffenberger remembered that Capt. David Smith's worm fence required "two pannels or 18 rails to the rod and 4 stakes." Likewise, Eli Wade explained the dimensions of his worm fence. "I made the calculation of nine rails and two stakes, or eleven rails to the panel," he recalled, which measured "five steps to the rod and twenty two rails to the rod . . . it would take eighteen rails and four stakes to the rod to construct a good fence as that was."[8]

Post and rail fences, sturdier than worm fencing, often bounded property lines, farm lanes, and turnpikes. Nonetheless, building post and rail was arduous and required laborers to dig post holes in the rocky soil. Locals preferred soil-resistant locust wood for the posts, boring each piece with holes before driving them vertically into the ground. Cutting the wood, tapering and inserting rails, securing posts, and leveling panels took great lengths of time. Sharpsburg's war claims show

---

7 Adjoining landowners split the maintenance and repair of division fences; "Hand Split & Snake Rail Fence," online article, Ed Arey & Sons, Inc., http://edareyandsons.com/products/hand-split-snake-rail-fence/; Vernon M. Briggs, Jr., "Rail Fences," *Railroad Brotherhoods*, Cornell University, ILR School, 1976, 3, http://digitalcommons.ilr.cornell.edu/articles/142/.

8 Claims of David Smith (Nos. 1244, 1262, and 10237) and the heirs of Henry Wade (No. 6585). Catherine Showman, Henry B. Rohrback, and Samuel Beeler used oak wood for worm fences in 1862. By contrast, John J. Keedy, Jacob Nicodemus of Springvale, and the heirs of Samuel Grove made their rails with chestnut. Others, like John Ecker, Susan Kennedy, Joshua Newcomer, and Henry Piper, mixed chestnut and oak for their worm fences. A rod is a unit of measurement containing 16.5 feet.

that this type of fence in 1862 often contained five, six, or seven oak rails to the panel. Alex Davis recalled that Sharpsburg's post and rail "was 10 feet to the panel … rails in that day were 11 feet long—now they make them 12."[9]

Other types of fences stood on Antietam Valley properties in 1862. First, a cheaper alternative to post and rail fencing was post and board, for which farmers used 14–16 foot planks instead of rails. William M. Blackford, John C. Middlekauff, and Capt. David Smith fenced part of their farms with post and board, and several out lot owners preferred this type of partition. Also, historical photographs from September 1862 show post and board fencing along sections of Antietam Creek.[10]

Second, cap fence, known as capped or yoke fence, divided several fields on the farms of Otho B. Smith, Samuel Beeler, Lafayette Miller, and Stephen P. Grove. This type of partition resembled worm fencing. Farmers reinforced the panels, though, by bracing each angle with two stakes. From there, they placed fitted, wooden caps over the stakes to lock them together. Residents also built paling fence, also known as plank or picket, around gardens, small fields, and village lots. Last, random sections of uncut stone fences stood on several properties on and near the battlefield. While the types of Sharpsburg's fences varied, all suffered damages to McClellan's army in the fall of 1862.[11]

9 Claims of the heirs of Samuel Grove (*RG* 92, G-1633 and *RG* 123, No. 9313). Alex Davis testified in the case. Various sources describe Sharpsburg's post and rail fencing in 1862. See the claims of the heirs of Samuel Grove (No. 9313), John J. Keedy (54-1488), Washington C. Snively (H-3458), and Samuel I. Piper (D-2392). Photographic examples appear in Alexander Gardner, *Antietam, Maryland. Bodies of dead, Louisiana Regiment.* Photograph, 1862, *LC*, https://www.loc.gov/item/2018671466/. See also Gardner, *Antietam, Maryland. Sherrick's house, near Burnside bridge.* Photograph, 1862, *LC*, https: //www.loc.gov/item/2018671858/. Also see Gardner, *Sharpsburg, Md. Lutheran church.* Photograph, 1862, *LC*, https://www.loc..gov/item/2018666247/.

10 Several claims cite the 1862 value of post and board at eighty cents to one dollar per panel, compared to post and rail's price of $1.50 to $1.75 per panel; Claims of John Kretzer (54-1471), William M. Blackford (No. 1324), John C. Middlekauff (F-1587), and David Smith (Nos. 1244, 1262, and 10237); Unrau, *Historic Resource Study: Chesapeake & Ohio Canal*, 747; Gardner, Alexander. *Antietam, Maryland. View on Antietam creek.* Photograph, 1862, *LC*, https://www.loc.gov/item/2018671478/; Gardner, *Antietam, Maryland, Antietam Bridge, eastern view.* Photograph, 1862, *LC*, https://www. loc.gov/item/2018671864/.

11 Claims of Otho B. Smith (F-1432), Samuel Beeler (Book 304, Claim 401), John Miller (No. 2227), and Stephen P. Grove (No. 7354); S. Edwards Todd, *The Young Farmers' Manual* (New York, 1860), 76-80, https://catalog.hathitrust.org/Record/001504435; Briggs, "Rail Fences, 3; Calvin Goodrich, "Rural Fences of Michigan," *Michigan Alumnus Quarterly Review*, University of Michigan, Volume 49, December 19, 1942, 250-252; Stone fencing claimants included Catherine Rohrback (Book 304, Claim 234), Henry Piper (No. 445), William Roulette (Book 304, Claim 230), and Squire Jacob Miller (Jacob Miller to Amelia and Christian Houser,

*   *   *

Eight days before the battle, George McClellan issued General Orders No. 155. This decree warned AOP troops that upon entering Maryland, "All damages to fences or crops, all marauding and trespassing will be prevented as far as possible . . . the sentence of death will be executed if awarded by the court, with promptness and as publicly as possible." Based on the army's subsequent destruction of Sharpsburg's fences, McClellan, at the time he issued the order, may not have envisioned camping in Western Maryland for six weeks with no supply of firewood. Consequently, threats were lifted and Sharpsburg's fences became free game.[12]

Appropriations of fencing were commonplace during the war. Historian Joan E. Cashin wrote that soldiers frequently took rails "without getting an officer's permission or giving out documents to civilians." A running joke among troops was to "only take the top rail" of worm fences until nothing remained of the loosely stacked panels. While campaigning in Virginia in 1862, Private Anthony W. Ross of the 73rd Ohio recalled that each man in his brigade burned an average of five fence rails per day. If one does the math, a single brigade could destroy more than 50,000 rails in one week.

During the fighting on September 17, Northern and Southern soldiers dismantled worm panels for passage, stacked rails as breastworks, and burned the wood in campfires. Shot and shell also splintered some of the partitions. These damages, though, paled in comparison to the AOP's subsequent six-week encampment. More than 100 claimants alleged that McClellan's forces stripped farms of fencing for use in camps and hospitals. After burning the community's cordwood and worm rails, troops dismantled post and rail panels, pulled hundreds of locust posts from the ground, and carried off scores of fence gates. The widespread devastation stripped away miles of fencing, leaving farmers little to divide crop fields and protect future harvests. To locals, the barren landscape was

---

October 1862, WMR). Additionally, John Grice (*RG* 123, No. 5872) claimed damages to "twenty rods of stone fence" on his out lot. Replacing the stone barriers was laborious and expensive. A witness in Grice's case recalled that it "cost him, I reckon, three dollars a yard to put up."

12 *OR*, vol. 19, 2:226-227.

unrecognizable. Many compared it to a "common" or "commons," referring to the antiquated "open-field" system of farming that used no fences.[13]

Hospital personnel took some of the partitions. George Line saw troops haul "a great many" of his 5,000 worm rails "to the Smoketown hospital about one-half mile distant." Line's neighbor, Catherine Showman, filed a claim for "7713 Oak Rails used for fuel for the use of the 'Smoketown Hospital.'" Also, Otho B. Smith, having lost one-third of the fencing on his 180-acre tenant farm, testified that some of the confiscated rails "were used as fuel by the attendants to Dr. Grants hospital in 1862."[14]

Other elements of the AOP seized fencing for use in camps. When soldiers bivouacked on Adam Michael's 70-acre farm south of town, they also tore down interior fences and confiscated the perimeter fencing. Michael testified, "[T]hey burned all the fences on the place . . . fully 4000 rails were used for fuel" and "all the outside and cross fences were taken." Near Michael's tract was John H. Snavely's farm, where U.S. troops burned a "string of fencing at least one half a mile long." A quartermaster agent later examined Snavely's farm and concluded that "Federals encamped right by claimants fencing and while there . . . used some 9630 rails."

Magdalene Jones, a Sharpsburg villager, owned several out lots in 1862. She alleged that her acreage "was entirely stripped of fencing by U.S. troops and used as fuel" and consequently lost "40 panels of fence averaging eight rails per panel." After a quartermaster agent inspected Jones's property, he reported to Washington, "I made a measurement of the lines and find that this [forty panels] is a fair estimate." Jones's damages were one of many. On Catherine Tenant's tract between Lumm's mill and the Sherrick farm, "the fences around her property were nearly all burned." Susan Kennedy accused soldiers of confiscating various fencing,

13 Joan E. Cashin, *War Stuff: The Struggle for Human and Environmental Resources in the American Civil War* (Cambridge, UK, 2018), 100; Earl McElfresh, "Only Take the Top Rail," *Civil War Times*, April 2008, https://www.historynet.com/take-top-rail.htm; Open-field farming dates to the Middle Ages. Before Maryland established fence laws to protect crops from livestock, early settlers may have practiced this farming method, based on the frequent mention of "common" and "commons" in Sharpsburg's claims testimonies. For further reading on open-field farming, see Rowland E. Prothero, *English Farming: Past and Present*, (London, 1912), 224-252; Claimants who lost fence gates included William F. Hebb (Book 304, Claim 254 and F-1417), John L. Mayer (No. 8586), John Miller (No. 2227), and Jacob H. Grove (No. 1267).

14 Claims of George Line (F-1187), Catherine Showman (F-1185), and Otho B. Smith (F-1432).

including sawed palings, plank, worm, and post and rail. These troops, she claimed, destroyed all fences on both of her properties, along with 184 locust posts.[15]

Confederates burned rails during their stay in Sharpsburg, but the amount cannot be quantified. Benjamin F. Rohrback lost "nearly all the fencing" on his out lot acreage and admitted that Rebels "no doubt . . . burned a few [rails]." Still, he noted, "their chances for destruction were nothing as compared with that of the federals." During the battle, Rohrback deduced, "a few gaps were made by the rebels to facilitate their maneuvers," but "the rails burned . . . were used only by their stragglers, the regular rebel camp was about one mile from my land." After the ANV left Sharpsburg, Rohrback found that his "plank fence was not touched by the rebels at all, and was only destroyed one week after our [U.S.] army got there." In total, he concluded, "the federals . . . burned between two and three thousand rails."[16]

South of the out lots, the farm of Hezekiah Myers "was in possession of the rebel forces" from September 15–18, and afterward, was "occupied by the Union forces who remained there for several weeks." During these spans, he attested, "the fencing on the farm was burned by both armies." Myers estimated that Union cavalry destroyed 2,400 rails and 25 locust posts, using everything as fuel "except twenty panels of plank which were cut up for tent stakes by the 8th Illinois cavalry." He remembered seeing troops struggle to dismantle his post and rail fencing and recalled, "[T]hey had to split the posts to get out." Concluding his testimony, Myers complained, "I have never been paid a cent for this stuff."[17]

In the case of Samuel Grove's heirs, the family summoned eleven witnesses to describe the AOP-related damages to their 329-acre Mount Pleasant farm. Jacob C. Grove, one of the heirs, swore under oath that "[T]he fencing was all destroyed after the battle of Antietam: some 30,000 or 40,000 rails." A quartermaster agent found that the property contained a "great deal" of fencing "on account of roads cutting the farm in two different places." Alex Davis described the layout. "I knew the fence lines," he testified. "On the east side and south side there would have been about one and a half and 2 miles on the river road; along the river about 80 rods; along the Lafayette Miller farm about one-half mile." Davis reckoned that the "party fence between the Grove and [Captain] Smith farm was about a mile—half

15 Claims of Adam Michael (199-161), John H. Snavely (F-1441), Magdalene Jones (*RG* 92, Entry 797, Book 54, Claim 54-1470), Catherine Tenant (54-1464), and Susan Kennedy (F-865).

16 Claim of Benjamin F. Rohrback (*RG* 123, No. 4234).

17 Claim of Hezekiah Myers (*RG* 123, No. 1301).

This prewar photograph of Colonel John Miller and his wife, Mary (Knode) Miller, is sometimes confused for their son and daughter-in-law, David R. and Margaret Miller. Colonel John Miller owned four Sharpsburg farms in 1862, all of which suffered extensive damages during the Antietam campaign. *ANB*

of this Mr. Grove had to make." In addition, the property "had four cross fences on the east side of the river road, each 80 rods long; on the west side of the river road there were four cross fences each 80 rods." Davis concluded by remarking, "The farm was thoroughly fenced and a good one too before the Union troops first occupied it . . . there was no fencing left on the farm after the last Union forces left."

Although Confederates briefly occupied the farm, the Groves' witnesses swore to have seen only a few Rebel campfires and insisted that Union forces destroyed most of the rails. Mayberry Beeler declared, "The [Groves'] fencing between Sharpsburg and the Potomac was cleaned up entirely." Van S. Brashears remembered "there was very little fence left" on the place "when the Union troops left; it was pretty much all gone." Robert Leakins deposed that Northern troops took some of the Groves' rails to "make water closets" but burned most of the fences as firewood. "After the Union troops left," Leakins recalled, "it looked like a prairie—no fencing at all; the soldiers burnt it up; they tore it all down nearly." The witnesses agreed that the heirs of Samuel Grove lost between eight and nine miles of fences.[18]

18 Claims of the heirs of Samuel Grove (*RG* 92, G-1633 and *RG* 123, No. 9313). Martin L. Fry witnessed "rebel camps" between Sharpsburg village and the Potomac River prior to the battle, but he opined that the Confederates "had not destroyed any fencing or wood" on the Groves' farm. William Shoppert, who operated a blacksmith shop near the Groves' property in 1862, deposed, "[T]he rebels camped all over the place at the time of the Antietam battle," but they "had no fires that he saw . . . only behind his shop," where "they burned palings from Mr. Dan Poffenbergers fence." By mentioning water closets, Robert Leakins may have referred to sinks (field latrines). The "river road" most likely refers to the (Snyder's) landing road, which connected Sharpsburg village to Grove's Landing.

As shown, claimants did not make such allegations by themselves. Hundreds of witnesses swore to have observed the appropriations. In addition, U.S. quartermaster agents toured the affected properties and concluded that AOP forces inflicted severe damages to Sharpsburg's fencing. For example, Col. John Miller claimed to have lost 61,956 rails after the battle, consisting of "all the fencing on the Land" of his four farms and out lot acreage. When a quartermaster agent investigated Miller's properties, he found the estimate accurate. The U.S. government paid the colonel $1,929, valued at more than $54,000 in modern U.S. currency. Another landowner, Samuel Mumma, Sr., found that most of his fences survived the fire on September 17. Once the Union army occupied the farmstead, though, he estimated that the Federals destroyed "nearly all the fencing I had on my farm." Mumma recruited his neighbors, Henry F. Neikirk, William Roulette, and Henry Piper, to appraise the damages. Under sworn oath, the men found "the places being well marked where the panels came from" and estimated that U.S. forces burned nearly 1,300 panels of Mumma's fence.[19]

After a quartermaster agent investigated Hiram Showman's losses, he reported to his department that Federals took all the fencing "along the Keedysville Road." Explaining his findings, the agent wrote, "I have myself stepped and rode along that part which is reported as having been taken . . . 100 panels, as charged for, is a moderate charge." Another quartermaster agent, Madison Sallade, examined "the [fence] lines burned" on Samuel I. Piper's farm. Afterward, Sallade reported that he was "well satisfied that the number of panels set forth in the appraisement are not in excess of what were taken by the troops." In total, Piper lost 1,699 panels totaling 18,081 rails.

Countless witnesses took sworn oaths in Sharpsburg's war claims. Samuel Reel claimed the loss of 10,780 rails. One of his witnesses, Jessie Price, deposed, "I remember it as though it was yesterday . . . I seen the Union forces tear the fences down and burn them up, I was right there, they used the fences for cooking." Price added, "I saw them take them 50 or 60 times, saw them taking it all the time they were there, until they [the fences] were nearly all gone."[20]

---

19 Claim of John Miller (*RG* 123, No. 2227). Payment to Miller for the 61,956 rails "was approved . . . and closed by Treasury settlement No. 356;" Williamson, *PPT*. Miller's estimate is based U.S. real prices using the Consumer Price Index; Claims of Samuel Mumma, Sr. (113-1024 and D-1927/1928).

20 Claims of Hiram Showman (No. 1522), Samuel I. Piper (D-2392), and Samuel Reel (No. 3209). Reel stated that "Col. Rufus Ingalls Chief Quartermaster of the Army of the Potomac" authorized the appropriation of his fencing.

In another case, Capt. David Smith testified that V Corps soldiers, while encamped on his 140-acre farm, confiscated "all the fencing outside and inside, and used it as fuel." Witness Mayberry Beeler saw Federals take Smith's fences "at different times . . . and they continued the use of the same until I do not believe there was a rail or fence post left on the farm." According to Angeline Jackson's deposition, Smith's stripped fencing made it appear as though "the farm was laid out as a common." In Joshua Newcomer's claim, his daughter, Josephine, recalled, "I was out on the farm on one occasion and saw the [AOP] camp fires and other fires going and saw when the rails had been taken." Describing James Marker's losses, Susan C. Marker stated, "I was on the farm near Antietam Iron Works all the time . . . and I know the Union Army took all the fences. I saw them taking the fences, and burning them for fuel."[21]

Neighboring James Marker were three farms owned by the heirs of Henry Wade. Eli Wade deposed that "General Burnside's Corps encamped on these farms for several weeks after the battle of Antietam in 1862." With so many troops concentrated on the farmsteads, Wade testified that his family's "wheat, corn, hay, straw and fencing disappeared before them like frost before a burning sun." From the 290-acre Antietam farm, "[T]he Federal army took all the fencing off it except a few panels of post and rail fence around the buildings. It was taken in September and October, 1862 . . . they took fifty thousand rails." On the 266-acre Home farm, Wade asserted, "Gen. Burnside's Corps and others took thirty-two thousand rails."

These were hefty allegations. To support their case, the Wade heirs recruited witnesses to corroborate their losses. Farmhand William C. Bussard "lived with the Wade heirs part of the time during the war" and saw troops "hauling rails from their different farms." Bussard noted, "[T]hese farms were turned into commons on account of being stripped of rails." Samuel Drenner and James Friese lived on adjoining farms. Drenner told investigators, "I know that the Union army was there and rails on the Wade farms were used. The farm was laid bare." James Friese added, "I knew the farm and knew every fence row on it. I know that this fence that I measured was taken by the Federal army . . . there were twelve lines of fence taken, three deep the long way and six the short way." Two members of the Potomac

---

21 Claims of David Smith (*RG* 92, F-846 and *RG* 123, Nos. 1244, 1262, and 10237), Joshua Newcomer (No. 272), and James Marker (*RG* 123, No. 1292). Describing Newcomer's land, witnesses stated that in 1862, the "Sharpsburg and Boonsboro pike ran through the farm" and was bordered on both sides by post and rail fencing. In addition, Newcomer's farm was "divided into seven [fenced] fields." In James Marker's case, Susan C. Marker stated that the 153-acre farm "was divided into six fields on the East side of the [Harpers Ferry] road and two fields on the West side of the road," and "bounded on the north by the land of Rev. Adams."

Home Brigade, James Wilson and Martin L. Fry, also supported the Wades' case. The Sharpsburg soldiers declared in a joint affidavit, "When Genl. Burnside's army first took possession" of the properties, "the fencing and the farms were in good order. When the troops left, the land was almost in the state of a Commons."

To further prove their losses, the Wade heirs asked quartermaster agent Madison Sallade to count his steps along the fence lines and estimate the panels burned. After agreeing to the tedious task and taking "unusual pains to make a thorough investigation," Sallade reported to the quartermaster general's office. "I visited the farms and counted and measured the panels of fencing burned," he wrote. "[A]ll of the rails were burned on the Antietam farm, with the exception of three or four hundred. The Home farm fared somewhat better, but lost heavily."

Proving that the AOP destroyed the fencing was one challenge of many. The Wades, like other families, had no 1862 crops to sell because the Federals reportedly took everything from their farms. Worse, without partitions to enclose their fields, they could grow no crops for 1863. As Eli Wade explained, their farms "had to be refenced before they could be cultivated" to prevent animals from destroying the crops. Unfortunately, these expenses were beyond what most families could afford. Obtaining financial assistance from the government was an option, but claims investigations took ages to complete. This dilemma prevented Henry Wade's heirs from farming for several years, and their fenceless properties were "not enclosed until 1866."[22]

*   *   *

Soldiers created additional problems by tearing down fences that enclosed pastures, barnyards, and cornfields. This destruction set loose surviving livestock, and the animals wandered into unfenced cornfields to graze. Army horses and cattle joined the farmers' livestock in feasting on what remained of the 1862 crops. For instance, on Adam Hutzell's farm, "owing to the destruction of the fences by the troops the cattle of the neighbors got into the corn . . . and destroyed portions."

---

22 Claim of the heirs of Henry Wade (No. 6585). The heirs were Nancy Wade, widow of Henry Wade, sons Eli, William, and John A., and daughters Elizabeth Jane, Mary Ellen, and Susan. Eli Wade estimated the 50,000 rails by walking along the fence lines with his appraisers and counting 11,363 steps. Next, Wade "made the calculation of nine rails and two stakes, or eleven rails to the panel, five steps to the rod and twenty two rails to the rod, making fifty thousand rails." In addition to their three farms near Antietam Iron Works, the Wade heirs owned a fourth tract in 1862 known as the Upper farm, which adjoined the property of Noah and Elias B. Rohrback.

Jacob Snyder suffered the same misfortune. After his "fencing had all been knocked down," U.S. troops drove forty head of army cattle into Snyder's cornfield to graze. Worse for the farmer, troops dismantled the fencing on neighboring farms. As a result, civilians' cattle roamed loose and "destroyed the remainder" of Snyder's unprotected corn.

In a similar case, Thomas Barnum observed AOP teamsters turn their horses into his cornfield. "I could not tell how many horses," Barnum recollected, but they "were frequently in the fields; the fences were away and they could go wherever they please." Likewise, Rev. Robert Douglas complained in late October that U.S. soldiers "have intirely divested my farm of its fences, even my private garden is thrown open to the ravages of stock."[23]

With no fence rails to contain livestock, some privately owned animals wandered into army camps and became meals for the troops. Henry M. Miller recalled, "It was impossible for me to see" where his parents' hogs fled "because the fence was cut down and they run in every direction." With 4,200 rails destroyed, the Millers also lost their sheep. "The fence was all taken," Jacob F. Miller complained, "and we couldn't keep them [sheep] anywhere; we stabled them up at last or we wouldn't have saved any of them."[24]

Replacing fences put great physical and financial demands on Sharpsburg-area inhabitants. Farmers who lost perimeter and interior partitions labored to cut down trees, haul and split logs, reset posts, and rebuild miles of fencing.

To recoup some of these costs, several farmers petitioned the U.S. government for the labor and expense of restoring their lands. Brothers Henry and Samuel I. Piper sought payment for "hauling & rebuilding fence," which included more than 1,300 worm and post and rail panels on Samuel's farm alone. William F. Hebb's charge involved "hauling and building" 130 panels of post fence and an unknown number of worm panels. Samuel Poffenberger claimed $15 for twenty days labor for replacing his fences, and Jacob H. Grove sought compensation for "rebuilding fences on said farms by hauling the rails, posts, boards and paying for labor." After Jacob Nicodemus lost "fully one third of the fences" on his farm, Alex Davis

<hr/>

23 Claims of Adam Hutzell (F-1538), Jacob Snyder (F-1537), and Thomas Barnum (No. 333); Robert Douglas to Fitz John Porter, October 24, 1862, *NA*.

24 Claim of Jacob F. Miller (No. 4294). Miller testified that AOP troops shot and consumed the loose animals.

remembered that "it was quite a job to make them rails, and quite a job to lay a fence up again."[25]

While AOP soldiers encamped on the farm of Jacob Avey, Sr., the 71-year-old farmer and his neighbors watched troops destroy the fencing. "I saw them burning rails from his fence," recounted Robert W. Grove. "[H]is farm contained about seventy-five or eighty acres; there was hardly a rail left on the place." After Union forces left the area, Avey purchased a tract of "Antietam Works" mountain land, possibly to obtain wood for new fencing. The physical demands of rebuilding, nevertheless, proved to be too much. "It killed my old father," a daughter lamented. "He overworked getting the fences up again, and it wore on him so he died within a year." Jacob Avey, Sr. passed away on October 12, 1863.[26]

Some families like Henry Wade's heirs faced financial difficulties in replacing their fences. Stephen P. Grove declared in his claim, "After the battle of Antietam, Gens Porter's and Sykes Command . . . laid on or near my farm for 42 days, burned up all my fencing so as to render it impossible to farm for three years" because "there was no enclosure or way of fixing it up, & c." Grove's brother, Elias S. Grove, lived across the Shepherdstown Pike in 1862. In consequence of losing an estimated 10,284 rails after the battle, Elias sought $1,300 from the government because "all the fencing [was] burned" and his crop fields "could not be farmed [for] four years," until he obtained the money to re-fence his land.[27]

The same military appropriations occurred throughout the community. Squire Jacob Miller informed his daughter in Iowa that Yankees "commit all kinds of depredations" and "burn our rails, board, and pale fence." Echoing Miller's sentiments, Dr. A. A. Biggs wrote to his uncle, "For five miles around, nearly all the fences are gone, and this seems as one vast plain." A local woman remembered, "The fencing was swept from the farm as if by a conflagration. It all went into the camp fires." Describing the soldiers' damages to his father's farm near Fairplay,

---

25 Claims of Henry Piper (No. 445), Samuel I. Piper (D-2392), William F. Hebb (Book 304, Claim 254 and F-1417), Samuel Poffenberger (F-1434), and Jacob H. Grove (No. 1267); Johnson, *BA*, 100.

26 Claim of Jacob Avey, Sr. (*RG* 123, No. 9908); Trowbridge, *The South*, 52. The woman did not identify her father by name. Avey bought the Antietam Works tract in Dec. 1862 via land record IN 16 / 508-509. Scharf in *HWM*, 2:1210, listed the Oct. 12, 1863 death of "Jacob Eavey," age 72, with burial in Sharpsburg's Methodist graveyard. Lucy Grayson Ditto in "Journal of Deaths in Sharpsburg" cited the same date. Avey's case no. 9908 cited, "The claimant in this case was an old man of about seventy years of age when the war broke out and died two years before its close."

27 Claims of Stephen P. Grove (No. 7354) and Elias S. Grove (No. 7356).

John C. Middlekauff testified, "They took all the fencing on the farm. They just cleaned up the fences from there to Sharpsburg." At Bakersville, Sergeant William Remmel of the 121st New York wrote in his diary, "The general appearance of things here at present is that of disorder . . . farms which one month ago were in a high state of culture, are now to be seen without a sign of cultivation—everywhere with rails and paths and fences almost entirely burned for wood." Unfortunately for the farmers, Remmel wrote, "[S]uch are the effects of war. Destruction follows in every form."

The community's ubiquitous fencing previously aided navigation by marking farm lanes, country roads, and turnpikes. When soldiers stripped farmsteads and thoroughfares of all posts, rails, and palings, they transformed the region into an unrecognizable plain. "The battle made quite a change in the look of the country," remembered Alex Davis. "The fences and other familiar landmarks was gone, and you couldn't hardly tell one man's farm from another, only by the buildings, and some of them was burnt." It was easy to become disoriented without fencing to divide properties and mark roadways, especially in poor light. "You might be out late in the day and the dark would ketch you," Davis recalled, "and things was so torn and tattered that you didn't know nothin'. It was a strange country to you. I got lost three or four times when I thought I could go straight home."[28]

In a sample of 75 claims shelved at the National Archives, civilians accused Federal troops after the Battle of Antietam of destroying 615,885 fence rails and locust posts, an average loss of 8,200 rails per claimant. This number primarily reflects worm and post fencing. Factoring in cap, board, and paling rails, the total amount of fences destroyed in the area possibly measured 200 miles or more.[29]

By comparison, Virginia civilians in November 1864 blamed General Philip Sheridan's command for 100 miles of "fencing destroyed." A quartermaster in the Army of the Cumberland, while encamped in Nashville in November 1862, estimated to have appropriated "at least 200 miles of fencing, mostly cedar rails . . .

---

28 Jacob Miller to Amelia and Christian Houser, December 7, 1862, WMR; Biggs to Kalb, September 29, 1862, WMR; Williams, HWC, vol. 1, 2:359-362; Claim of John J. Middlekauff (No. 1261); William Remmel, *Like Grass Before the Scythe—the Life and Death of Sgt. William Remmel, 121st New York Infantry*, ed. Robert Patrick Bender (Tuscaloosa, AL, 2007), 14; Johnson, *BA*, 100.

29 The sample is based on Sharpsburg / Antietam war claims archived in record groups 92 and 123 at the National Archives in Washington, DC. Among the heaviest sufferers were five claimants who owned fourteen farms near Sharpsburg: the heirs of Henry Wade, Raleigh Showman and his brothers, Andrew Rentch, Col. John Miller, and Jacob H. Grove. These claimants alleged that the AOP destroyed an aggregate of 240,477 fence rails.

Alexander W. "Alex" Davis, photographed by
Fred Wilder Cross in 1922.
Boonsborough Museum of History

board fences, and all other lumber found in the county," to make "bunks, cots and coffins."[30]

The exact amount of fencing destroyed by McClellan's soldiers after the Antietam battle is not known. But, if there was a bright side to the widespread destruction, at least Sharpsburg and its surrounding environs had an abundance of timberland, from which civilians could draw wood to refence their properties. Nevertheless, as days passed in October, residents listened with marked concern to the sound of army axes and crashing trees.

*   *   *

Artillery fire at Antietam disfigured many trees, but the Army of the Potomac inflicted far more damages to timber from September 19–October 26. Tens of thousands of encamped soldiers, after all, required a significant amount of fuel for cooking and warmth. So, after burning all available cordwood and fences, the troops set their sights on Sharpsburg's hardwoods, which grew on privately owned lands. Out came the axes, and down went the trees—hundreds of them.

Several dozen residents petitioned the government for damages to their timber tracts from September 19–October 26, 1862. Reverend Robert Douglas noticed V Corps troops chop down trees on his land. Hoping to stop the soldiers, after suffering the loss of his barn and fences, he penned a plea to Maj. Gen. Fitz John Porter. "[N]ow the Army is cutting down my timber," Douglas wrote in late October 1862, "so that I will have nothing left to rebuild my barn or reconstruct my fences . . . I hope you will be pleased to take some measures at once to stop the destruction of my timber, as it is useless for me to speak to any but yourself upon

---

30 William G. Thomas, III, "Nothing Ought to Astonish Us: Confederate Civilians in the 1864 Shenandoah Valley Campaign," ed. Gary W. Gallagher, in *The Shenandoah Valley Campaign of 1864* (Chapel Hill, NC, 2006), 241. Thomas cited the *Staunton Republican Vindicator*, November 18, 1864; Fitch, *Annals of the Army of the Cumberland*, 269.

the subject." It's not known if Gen. Porter intervened, but Federal authorities arrested Rev. Douglas four days later on suspicion of aiding the Confederate cause.[31]

U.S. troops felled hardwoods on Jacob H. Grove's 75-acre tract on Maryland Heights before the battle. Soon after, V Corps troops destroyed a "large quantity of green timber locust trees" on Grove's South farm, located west of Sharpsburg. Elias F. Bussard stated that he visited Grove's farm "right after the battle of Antietam" and "saw the United States soldiers cutting, hauling and using this timber for fuel." To estimate the damages, Grove hired a professional surveyor, Samuel S. Downin, who "carefully measured said piece of land . . . with proper instruments" and concluded, "the wood has been cut from 15 acres."[32]

Near Grove's South farm, V Corps troops toppled trees on the tract of Capt. David Smith. In the span of six weeks, Smith alleged, soldiers "cut and used ten acres of good timber consisting of hickory, oak & maple trees," all taken with Gen. Porter's "knowledge and by his consent." Moses Poffenberger recounted that the Union army "took nearly all the timber in this vicinity during the war. Troops were encamped in this vicinity most of the time and they got their fuel in this way." Captain Smith's 14-acre woods, Mayberry Beeler remembered, contained "fine timber, composed of white oak, black oak and walnut and probably some other kinds of trees. [It was] a valuable and choise timber tract." Beeler noticed a "Massachusetts Regiment encamped in said timber after the battle of Antietam and I saw them cutting and using said timber at different times." He described Smith's woodland as being "entirely destroyed by Union forces."[33]

Soldiers caused similar damages to Smith's neighbors, the heirs of Samuel Grove. Known also as the "Town Woods" and "Jerry Grove's Woods," the Grove heirs' timber stretched from the Potomac River to the town limits. Two African American residents, Robert Leakins and D. B. Simons, testified on behalf of the Groves. "I lived in this town during the war," stated Leakins. "I knew the Samuel Grove farm . . . this was good timber, a beautiful woods." "The Samuel Grove farm," added Simons, was "the farm I worked on . . . I don't think there was any better timber in this locality." Jacob McGraw described the Grove heirs' woods as

31 Robert Douglas to Fitz John Porter, October 24, 1862, *NA*; Accounts vary as to whether Union soldiers or local Unionists torched Douglas's barn in 1861. See *HFTL*, November 27, 1861, 2C, and Grivno, *Historic Resource Study: Ferry Hill Plantation*, 8, 60-61.

32 Claim of Jacob H. Grove (*RG* 123, No. 1267).

33 Claims of David Smith (*RG* 92, F-846 and *RG* 123, Nos. 1244, 1262, and 10237).

"the best tract of timber land I ever saw," comprised of "white oak, black oak, hickory and walnut." He compared it to forests on Red Hill, Elk Ridge, and South Mountain, on which three-fourths of an acre "made 29 or 30 cords of wood and between 6 and seven hundred rails." This mountain land, McGraw opined, "was nothing to compare with the timber on the Grove land."

One of the Groves' witnesses testified, "General Lee's headquarters were on the Samuel Grove farm during the battle of Antietam." Lee indeed based his headquarters on the Groves' property—specifically, in a cluster of oaks near the village—but witnesses did not believe the Confederates encamped in the area long enough to destroy any timber. "The land between Sharpsburg and the Potomac was covered with rebel camps previous to the battle of Antietam," Martin L. Fry remembered, but "the rebels had not destroyed any fencing or wood on the ground in Mr. Grove's woods." After Lee's army departed Sharpsburg, I Corps forces encamped on the Samuel Grove heirs' farm. True, the 12th Indiana, during the previous winter, felled dozens of trees on the property. However, Robert W. Grove testified, "There were a great many more [I Corps] men than the 12th Indiana . . . these men cut more timber than the Indiana men. I saw this myself." After the battle, Grove "saw the ground cut over" an expanse of "12 or 15 acres." McClellan's soldiers, he added, "burnt it for fuel and building small cabins."

Alex Davis agreed, stating, "I know every foot of the Samuel Grove farm . . . these men [after the battle] used about as much timber and rails for fuel as the others did." Robert Leakins knew that locals did not chop down the Groves' trees because of "the high stumps where they had been cut." Ultimately, the heirs of Samuel Grove accused the AOP of destroying eleven acres of standing timber. If we consider Alex Davis's estimate that "fairly good timber" contained "100 to 105 trees to the acre," the Groves may have lost more than 1,000 trees.[34]

The dense timber on the Grove heirs' farm stretched north onto adjoining tracts. David Reel, in addition to his farm near the battlefield, owned part of this forest at the time of the battle. He claimed that McClellan's forces hacked down 156 "beautiful prime trees . . . right after the battle of Antietam." The woods also

---

34 Claims of the heirs of Samuel Grove (*RG* 92, G-1633 and *RG* 123, No. 9313). Alex Davis deposed, "The large timber they burnt for fuel; the wood was green and they used rails to make it burn. There was fine big white oaks, black oaks, hickory and walnut . . . it ought to make nearly 100 cords to the acre . . . it was good and stood very thick on the ground." Lee's "Oak Grove" headquarters were located on the north side of the Sharpsburg-Shepherdstown Pike, one-quarter of a mile west of the town limits. Commands accused of felling the Groves' trees included the "2nd N.Y. [Cavalry] Regt & 12 Penn Cavalry." Both regiments supposedly destroyed timber through Dec. 1862.

sprawled onto the 140-acre farm of Colonel John Miller, tenanted by his son, Lafayette Miller. One citizen described Miller's timber as the "Big Woods" and a section of these hardwoods, Col. Miller testified, was felled "by the forces under command of Gen'ls. Reynolds and Meade." "I saw them cutting pretty often," testified Lafayette Miller. "[T]hey were chopping the wood and burning it whenever [I] went out into the woods . . . every couple of days." Lafayette recalled that the troops camped on his farm "about six weeks" after the battle, during which time, "they used the fence, and they were about two weeks on that, and the other four weeks they used the timber." William F. Hebb and Henry Piper assessed Colonel Miller's timber damages and jointly swore in a signed affidavit, "[W]e did appraise and count the trees cut by the stumps left." They presented their findings to Col. John Miller, who filed a claim for "Cutting down & Burned the Timber 475 Trees."[35]

Troops in the divisions of Couch and Slocum destroyed 80 acres of "green wood" on Andrew Rentch's farms in the Downsville-Bakersville area. Rentch also suffered losses on his Sharpsburg farm, tenanted by Moses Cox. Trees on this property, Rentch attested, were "damaged during the months of September & October 1862 . . . by the Military of the United States Gen. Ricket's Division."

West of the West Woods, I Corps forces presumably destroyed hundreds of trees. William F. Hebb deposed that, on his property alone, soldiers from Meade's and Reynolds's divisions chopped down more than 1,000 hardwoods that varied in size. One of Hebb's appraisers, Henry Piper, helped "count the [felled] 1200 trees and recalled they averaged 1.5 feet in diameter." A quartermaster agent later inspected Hebb's woodlot. After observing hundreds of stumps, the agent concluded, "[A] good deal of lumber was . . . cut by the Federals . . . the trees were oak, hickory, locust & c. I recommend that the claimant be allowed this [full] amount."[36]

Next door, Samuel I. Piper accused Ricketts's division of inflicting similar damages. Piper claimed the loss of 135 locust trees and 100 oaks and hickories "cut

---

35 Claims of David Reel (No. 6619) and John Miller (No. 2227). Trees were considered part of the real estate, explaining why Col. Miller, as landowner, claimed the timber damages. Lafayette Miller, as tenant, owned two-fifths of the crops grown. Alex Davis testified in the Samuel Grove heirs' case (No. 9313) that Confederates encamped from Sep. 15–18 "on Lafayette Miller's farm in the big woods; the big woods was nearly a mile from the Grove farm."

36 Claims of Andrew Rentch (No. 4235) and William F. Hebb (F-1417). Henry Piper testified that he counted 1,200 stumps on Hebb's farm, but Hebb later revised his losses to 1,116 trees. Hebb's claim specifies, "Alleged to have been taken during the period from Sept. 17 to Oct. 1862 by Genl. Reynolds and Meade, Army of the Potomac."

down and burned right on the ground where they were encamped." Testifying on Piper's behalf, farmhand John Francis swore to have seen "Union soldiers cutting the standing timber for fuel at various times." Neighbor William I. Cox deposed, "I saw where his timber had been cut. I saw the stumps. It looked exactly like an army had cut it. There was nobody there that could have done it except the army."

South of Sharpsburg village, brothers Otho and Alfred Showman sought repayment for the AOP's destruction of "good standing timber" on their Home farm. Near the crest of these heights, the Showmans attested, one and one-half acres of timber "was cut from mountain land by the Signal Corps." After Noah Rohrback appraised the losses, he testified that the "standing timber had been cut and slashed in every way . . . by the Signal Corps, in order that their signals might be seen at a distance." Suppose the Showmans were upset in losing an acre of valuable timber. In that case, it's hard to imagine their reaction upon learning that Federals decimated 50 acres of woodland on their River farm, located near Mercersville. Otho Showman claimed that this tract contained "good heavy black and white oak and hickory," which soldiers "used in the construction of winter huts and for fuel; that they culled from the entire tract of timber land, taking the best timber."[37]

*   *   *

The construction of winter huts was not limited to the Showmans' farm. After the battle, AOP soldiers built log quarters on other farms along the Potomac, from Mercersville to Antietam Iron Works. Compared to shelter tents, these crude huts provided better protection from the elements but required a significant amount of timber to build. Colonel Henry Lee Scott, in his *Military Dictionary* written in 1864, estimated, "[I]t would require 12 trees to build up one side," of a single log hut, "or

---

37 Claim of Samuel I. Piper (No. 1310). Piper swore in his affidavit, "[T]hinks that the troops were known as Genl Ricketts Division of Genl Hookers Corps of the Army of the Potomac;" Dennis E. Frye, email message to author, February 14, 2022. Frye confirmed that Alexander Gardner photographed the AOP signal station on the Showman family's Home farm in early Oct. 1862 during President Lincoln's visit. In his writings, Frye refers to the unnamed high ground as "Showman's Knoll." For further details on the AOP signal station atop Showman's Knoll, see Frye, *Antietam Shadows*, 190-192; Claim of Raleigh Showman (F-1183). Claim F-1183 also includes the property losses of Raleigh Showman's brothers, Otho and Alfred Showman, who served as administrators of the claim after Raleigh's death in April 1863. In addition to describing timber felled for constructing the AOP signal station, the claim cites that the Showmans' 403-acre River farm, located "near Dam. No. 4," was tenanted in 1862 by Martin Slifer. Federal soldiers burned much of the River farm's timber "during the winter after the battle of Antietam."

48 to make all four walls." The initial step for building such quarters, Private Philo Stevens Pearce of the 11th Connecticut remembered, was to cut logs "about the size of our bodies." Next, Pearce explained, "[W]e laid them up in a log house style, a little higher than our head," and erected a "ridge pole through the center high enough to get a good slant to put the roof in a good position." The men then secured their shelter tents over the pole to create a roof. Finally, Stevens completed construction by caulking gaps and building a "fireplace at one end with split logs and put mud up our chimney." He described the quarters, which held six men during the Fredericksburg Campaign, as "quite comfortable."[38]

While encamped at Sharpsburg after the battle, Colonel Francis J. Parker of the 32nd Massachusetts, V Corps, recollected, "As the weather grew cooler . . . we began to construct defences against the weather, and the acting adjutant even dreamed of a log hut." The adjutant was not alone in his thinking. Near Bakersville, Corporal William B. Westervelt of the 27th New York, VI Corps, noted, "Some of us built log huts in place of tents." At Blackford's Ford, despite "frequent rumors of the enemy's reappearance about the Shepardstown Heights," a Massachusetts soldier recalled that "the men were snugly housed in quarters of boards and logs."

After constructing cabins, some soldiers built furnishings for their quarters using locally confiscated lumber and various army materials. "[T]he manufacture of furniture became an extensive occupation," Col. Francis J. Parker recalled, "It was quite wonderful what results could be obtained in both of these industries by the use of barrels and hard-bread boxes. Of the barrels we made chimneys and chairs; and of the boxes, tables, washstands, cupboards, and the walls and clapboards of our dwellings."[39]

Having recovered from a wound received during the battle, Captain Robert Gould Shaw rejoined the 2nd Massachusetts at their encampment near Blackford's Ford. Shaw informed his mother, "We have a very pretty camp, near the river, and only have to step out of the woods to see the Rebel outpost on the other side." Shaw's comrade, Private Henry Newton Comey, wrote in a letter home, "I am building a nice house for winter quarters, good enough for a prince. I shall be ready to receive visitors when I get it done. I am going to have a nice fireplace, etc."

38 Henry Lee Scott, *Military Dictionary: Comprising Technical Definitions; Information on Raising and Keeping Troops; Actual Service, Including Makeshifts and Improved Matériel; and Law, Government, Regulation, and Administration Relating to Land Forces* (New York, 1864), 139; Pearce, "Civil War Memories," HEPL, 19. Pearce occupied the cabin from Nov. 9, 1862–Feb. 6, 1863.

39 Parker, *The Story of the Thirty-Second Regiment*, 107-110; Westervelt, *Lights and Shadows*, 25; Thayer, *History of the Second Massachusetts*, 4; Parker, *The Story of the Thirty-Second Regiment*, 107-110.

During his stay at Sharpsburg, Comey noted, "[W]e played ball, tossed quoits, and even watched a horse race."

Private Robert Goldthwaite Carter of the 22nd Massachusetts wrote in his diary on October 24, "Near Sharpsburg . . . the general appearance of things indicated a movement, but at headquarters they are building log huts and seem as contented and happy as possible." To keep warm, Carter observed, the men "are cutting down everything here in the shape of trees; we burn black walnut sticks to make coffee, as if it didn't cost anything." The soldiers took advantage of Sharpsburg's abundant timber and constructed dozens of log huts. A member of the 2nd Massachusetts Infantry remembered, "[T]he men made themselves as comfortable as they could, and 'built a city.'"[40]

The soldiers' destruction of Sharpsburg's trees prompted residents to file claims for their losses. Colonel John Miller's damages included "Timber cut down for Building Cabbins." Brothers William I. and John U. Cox alleged that "a good deal of young timber had been cut to build quarters" for soldiers "encamped on the place." A neighbor, Urias Knode, helped appraise the brothers' losses and found that government soldiers chopped down 91 trees on the Cox farm. Knode "went over the timber and counted the stumps," he recalled, noting "it was an easy matter to recognize stumps cut by the soldiers, for they were cut . . . higher."

Maria Grove accused V Corps troops of destroying fifteen acres of "large oak timber" on her Mount Airy farm, which they "used in building winter quarters." She remembered seeing "a good deal of it . . . hauled off the premises to build winter quarters for the troops encamped on the farm of Rev. R. Douglas, a short distance from my husband's farm." This timber, Maria recalled, "was in sight of the dwelling-house" and "about one mile from market." She added, "These troops cut all the timber on the plantation but about nine acres."

---

40 Robert Gould Shaw to Sarah Blake Shaw, November 3, 1862, in Robert Gould Shaw Letters to His Family, Houghton Library, Harvard University, Cambridge, MA. Shaw wrote the letter "Near Sharpsburg, Md." He later took command of the 54th Massachusetts Infantry, an African American regiment. In 1863, Shaw was killed in action during an assault on Fort Wagner in South Carolina; Lyman Richard Comey, *A Legacy of Valor: The Memoirs and Letters of Captain Henry Newton Comey, 2nd Massachusetts Infantry* (Knoxville, TN, 2004), 84-91. Comey rose to the rank of captain. Quoits is a ring-toss game, similar to horseshoes; Carter, *Four Brothers in Blue*, 146; Alonzo H. Quint, *The Record of the Second Massachusetts Infantry, 1861–1865* (Boston, 1867), 144-145, 149. Quint wrote that the 2nd Massachusetts constructed the huts while encamped at "Blackburn's [Blackford's] Ford . . . near Sharpsburg." The regiment, Quint noted, remained on guard duty at this location from Oct. 30–Dec. 12, 1862. Further details of said guard duty are described in Chapter 10.

Near Antietam Iron Works, scores of hardwoods grew on four farms owned by the heirs of Henry Wade. On one farmstead was a "Chestnut tract . . . of full growth" that "had not been touched for twenty five or thirty years." On the Wades' Home farm, Eli Wade recalled, stood a tract of "prime oak timber . . . of a splendid character." This woodlot was so dense, he deposed, "that it was almost impossible to drive a wagon through the woods." The majority of trees "were very tall and large and of such a character that his [late] father had intended selecting the material from them to build 4 barns." Raleigh Domer declared that he "was frequently employed on the farm of Hy. Wade" and was "perfectly familiar with the property." He described the woodland as "a better character than the average in that locality; the timber was of a very thick growth." Domer recollected that "Old Mr. Wade in his life time took great care of his timber tract, not allowing any trees to be cut on it." Another neighbor, James Brown, "heard Mr. Henry Wade in his life-time boast that he had the finest timber in his section of the country."

While camping south of Sharpsburg, U.S. soldiers reportedly cut between twenty to thirty acres of timber on the Wades' Home Farm "for building winter quarters and for fuel." Eli Wade deposed, "It was cut in the fall of 1862 . . . it was oak and hickory and would yield one hundred cords per acre." The Wade heirs estimated that soldiers destroyed 3,000 cords of timber valued at $3,000. Before leaving the area, a Union quartermaster offered the Wades "$1500 as compensation for the timber cut." The family, though, found "the sum totally inadequate" and "declined the offer."

Consequently, the Wades filed a $3,000 claim against the U.S. government and asked near neighbors to appraise their damages. Martin Eakle "estimate[d] the value of this timber . . . to have been one hundred dollars per acre for the timber alone." Eakle explained, "The value of cleared land in that vicinity at that time was about fifty dollars per acre." However, because soldiers "had left very high stumps standing, the labor and expense of removing these necessarily lessened the value of the land." To further assess the marred real estate, the Wades hired James Brown, a surveyor from Boonsboro. Brown found "that this timber land . . . was not worth more than half as much as cleared land on account of the expense of removing the stumps which were very high, as is usually the case when cutting is done by the army." Ultimately, the destruction cost the Wades valuable timber while decreasing their real estate's value because the acreage contained neither hardwood trees nor cleared cultivable land. "It would not pay to cut them," Wade testified in 1876, referring to the high stumps, "for which reason no attempt has ever been made to cultivate an acre of it up to this day."[41]

---

41 Claims of John Miller (No. 2227), William I. and John U. Cox (M-901), Stephen P. Grove (No. 7354), and the heirs of Henry Wade (G-2394 and No. 6585).

Finally, there is the case of William M. Blackford. The farmer described his property as containing 230 acres, "about one hundred and sixty of which were under cultivation, and the balance very heavily timbered. I inherited it from my father, who died in 1839." Of Blackford's 70 acres of timber, he testified that "over half of it was cut [by soldiers] . . . it was a very fine and heavy piece of timber which had been saved up for years by my father and myself, and was very valuable." Of this prized forest, "Not less than thirty-three acres were cut in the fall and winter of 1862 for fuel and winter quarters." Granted, Blackford lost 250 cords of standing timber to the 12th Indiana during the previous winter "without any arrangement being made for payment." However, after the Battle of Antietam, V Corps troops felled "33 acres heavy timber, 3,300 cords of wood." Urias Knode, an appraiser, testified, "We estimated it at thirty three acres actually cut by the army. It was cut by the troops, and a great deal of the best of it was used up to build winter quarters, and also part of it was used for fuel." Also, Blackford and his appraisers reported, Federals used some of the logs to make a "military bridge."

Blackford's timber damages continued after the AOP departed the region. "When the main army moved," Blackford recalled, "two Maine Batteries, the 13th New Jersey Regiment, and the 22nd Massachusetts Regiment remained until the latter part of January, 1863. These commands encamped immediately upon my place" to picket Blackford's Ford and other crossing points. During this time, a member of 4th Maine Battery, Light Artillery, remembered camping near "Blackford's Ford" and constructing "tents of all styles of architecture." Soon after, he recalled, the artillerymen were "enjoying the luxury of bunks raised about a foot or eighteen inches from the ground and with straw to sleep on."

The unpaid loss of 33 acres of mature timber not only impacted William M. Blackford financially. This land was his ancestral forest—cherished property he possibly intended to pass along to his children—and half of it was gone. Describing the woodland's prewar condition, Blackford lamented, "It was a piece of the finest timber in the county."[42]

*   *   *

---

42 Claim of William M. Blackford (*RG* 123, No. 1324); Maine Artillery, *History of the Fourth Maine Battery*, 35. The other battery Blackford described may have been the 6th Maine Battery, Light Artillery. Urias Knode, explaining the $4,950 appraisement of Blackford's timber, deposed, "[W]ood was worth in Sharpsburg $3 per cord [in 1862], and it cost 50c per cord to cut it, and $1 per cord to deliver it, so that wood was worth $1.50 per cord in the tree." Blackford's claim did not specify where the military bridge was located.

Federal soldiers confiscated all types of building materials from the community to construct cabins. Ezra Marker deposed that his father's 1,000 feet of lumber "was taken from the hay house to build winter quarters over on the Wade farm, the next farm south of us." Otho Showman testified that U.S. soldiers used 1,400 feet of his lumber "in the erection of tents, that it was new oak lumber." Referring to his farm near Miller's Sawmill, Morgan Miller recalled, "I had a good deal of lumber taken from my boat yard on the canal," which "was used for building quarters to some Massachusetts Rgt . . . I have seen the soldiers of that command take the lumber."[43]

In the case of Jacob H. Grove, Mayberry Beeler testified that Grove "had a brick kiln on his place," but Union soldiers "took all his bricks for use at their camps." Jacob H. Grove explained, "There were three and a half arches of brick when the troops came there . . . they were taken for making brick-ovens and all sorts of purposes . . . an arch of brick contains 10 to 12,000 bricks. I put 10,000 each in mine." Grove's farmhand swore that V Corps troops, "after the Sharpsburg battle . . . dug pitts . . . [and] hauled stone and brick for flues and chimneys & c."[44]

AOP forces also seized shingles and staves to build structures. William M. Blackford, for example, accused Northern troops of taking 3,000 barrel staves, described as "new staves . . . taken by the army to roof a commissary-house, or store, which had been erected by Gen. Porter's Corps." Blackford also lost 3,000 shingles, which were "taken and used in the same manner as the staves, that is, for building a store-house for commissary supplies for Gen. Porter's Corps." It's not clear why soldiers took 80 mulberry casks from Bishop John Russell, but they may have used the barrel wood for fuel, roofing materials, or other construction purposes.

Along with building a commissary storehouse from appropriated materials, Porter's men, according to Robert W. Grove, "built a hospital on Steven Grove's place from wood taken from Jacob C. Grove's place." Referring to the Samuel Grove heirs' farm, Alex Davis recalled, "There were a few trees left standing here

---

43 Claims of James Marker (No. 1292), Raleigh Showman (F-1183), and Morgan and Andrew Rentch Miller (No. 4295).

44 Claim of Jacob H. Grove (*RG* 123, No. 1267). By "brick-ovens," Grove possibly alluded to fireplaces, which troops built onto their log huts. For more details on the AOP's construction of winter quarters, see Kristopher D. White, "The Rebirth of the Army of the Potomac (part three): Camp Health and Winter Huts," blog, *Emerging Civil War*, June 23, 2016, https://emergingcivilwar.com/2016/06/23/the-rebirth-of-the-army-of-the-potomac-part-th ree-2/.

and there, such as gums and hickorys. [Soldiers] made winter quarters with it, their stables, etc." The same troops used Jacob H. Grove's timber to construct "shops, stables, sheds" on the property and hammered "posts for cavalry horses" into Grove's farm fields.[45]

Archeological evidence from the AOP's campsites in Stafford County, Virginia, during the winter of 1862–63 reveals that Union forces used various tools to build temporary log quarters. Among the excavated items were felling axes, pick-axes, hatchets, spades, shovels, and mattocks. In all likelihood, McClellan's army used similar tools to build cabins at Sharpsburg in the fall of 1862. Branches of the army had the equipment for these tasks, especially the engineers and pioneers. Nonetheless, foot soldiers may have lacked enough tools to chop down hundreds of trees, notch logs, cut out doorways, nail lumber, and build furniture. For instance, one account cited that a single company in the 13th Massachusetts, I Corps, was only supplied with "6 saws, 2 hatchets . . . 2 shovels, 2 axes, and 2 picks." Based on the previous estimate of 48 trees required for one six-man cabin, troops after the Sharpsburg battle may have taken tools from local inhabitants in order to build dozens of log quarters.[46]

Near I Corps encampments, James A. Rowe, Jacob Houser, and Samuel I. Piper claimed to have lost axes, shovels, and mattocks. Susan Kennedy sought payment for a spade, broad axe, and digging iron taken and not returned. Morgan Miller lost a screw wrench, hatchet, and "1 cross bar and screw used for building." When soldiers took over 4,000 feet of lathe, plank, and scantling from Bishop John Russell's farm, they also confiscated "1 keg nails."[47]

Also, nearly twenty farmers accused McClellan's men of seizing sets of carpenter and blacksmith tools, some of which "were taken away piecemeal & used by the army and never returned." Further research is required to link the confiscated tools and implements to the army's construction of log quarters.

45 Claims of Robert Douglas (*RG* 92, Entry 843, Box 772, Book 304, Claim 398) and William M. Blackford (No. 1324); Geeting and Russell accounts, UMLA; Claims of the heirs of Samuel Grove (No. 9313) and Jacob H. Grove (No. 1267).

46 Paul A. Boccadoro, "Examination of Original Tools Excavated From Federal Camps," online article, The Liberty Rifles, https://www.libertyrifles.org/research/uniforms-equipment/original-tools; Paul A. Boccadoro and John C. Holman, "U.S. Army Tool Contracts, 1863–1865," online article, The Liberty Rifles, https://www.libertyrifles.org/research/uniforms-equipment/tool-contracts.

47 Claims of James A. Rowe (No. 1303), Jacob Houser (F-814), Samuel I. Piper (D-2392), Susan Kennedy (F-865), and Morgan and Andrew Rentch Miller (No. 4295); Geeting and Russell accounts, UMLA.

Certainly, military forces may have needed them for other purposes, such as repairs or shoeing horses. Regardless, the appropriations affected citizens who needed axes, saws, hammers, and other tools to replace fences and rebuild structures.[48]

After confiscating what building materials and tools they could find, soldiers reportedly dismantled outbuildings and canal boats, carrying away lumber, logs, and weatherboarding for fuel and construction purposes. Josiah Hill swore that Federals boarded his canal vessel and "tore the stern and middle cabins out of the boat and carried the lumber to a field and built shelters with it," using some of the boards "for floors for the tents." Hill added, "[I]t cost me $84.00 to have the boat repaired." Jacob H. Grove, meanwhile, lost a canal boat when troops demolished the vessel and used the wood "for shanty purpose[s]."[49]

These were not isolated incidents. Soldiers needing lumber and fuel damaged several structures in the Sharpsburg community after the Antietam battle. Jacob H. Grove accused military personnel of tearing off his "weather boarding from barn." Similarly, Daniel Poffenberger reported the loss of "weather-boarding taken off barn floor." Michael Kidwiler, who worked for Poffenberger in 1862, testified regarding the weatherboarding, "I saw them tearing it up and burning it." On some farms, soldiers knocked down entire buildings to obtain lumber and firewood. "Several of my out houses," wrote Rev. Robert Douglas to General Fitz John Porter, "have been in part or in whole demolished by the pickets . . . for instance my pig sty is entirely torn down also my ice house & part of my blacksmith shop."[50]

Morgan Miller blamed Federal troops for "1 Warehouse torn down and materials used for W[inter] quarters." In addition, soldiers demolished Miller's blacksmith shop for the same purpose. After troops dismantled the buildings, Miller recounted, they used the lumber, floorboards, and windows to construct shanties on the adjoining farm of William M. Blackford.

Miller's father, Squire Jacob Miller, fared no better. After soldiers used a building at Miller's Sawmill for a field hospital and picket rendezvous, they carried

48 Claim of Henry Piper (RG 123, No. 445).

49 Claims of Josiah Hill (No. 8532) and Jacob H. Grove (No. 1267). In addition, Elijah Avey (Book 304, Claim 242) and Timothy Coin (212-719) accused U.S. troops of damaging a sleigh and skiff, respectively. However, it's not known how soldiers used the wood.

50 Claims of Jacob H. Grove (No. 1267) and Daniel Poffenberger (No. 1505); Robert Douglas to Fitz John Porter, October 24, 1862, NA.

away the structure's doors, flooring, windows, and weatherboarding to construct huts in their camp.[51]

Describing damages to James Marker's farm, Samuel Highbarger recalled, "I knew James Marker very well and did work for him. I built a hay shed on his farm at Antietam Iron Works." Highbarger described the shed as "20 by 40 and 12 feet to the square, and constructed on locust post[s] planted in the ground." This building, Highbarger deposed, "was made of one inch yellow pine weather borded and covered with lap oak shingles." Its roof consisted of "six inch plates and railing to we[a]therboard too—there was about twenty one hundred and eighty feet of weatherboarding, exclusive of rafters, laths and shingles, but including plates and railing." In the end, though, Highbarger's time and labor were all for naught. IX Corps soldiers emptied the structure of hay, tore down the shed, and burned the lumber, weatherboards, and shingles in campfires. William "Bud" Shackelford, who worked for the Markers in 1862, summed up the destruction by testifying, "[T]hey took the hay and the shed."

The heirs of Henry Wade charged the U.S. government $600 for "Two houses torn down and material used to make winter quarters, etc." Eli Wade, along with witness Raleigh Domer, deposed that Federals demolished the tenant dwellings. Domer testified that troops "tore down two houses and took the lumber to their camp." Eli Wade added, "There was two houses taken from this farm at the same time," made of frame and log. Wade swore under oath that both structures were "taken down and taken away" and "used for building winter quarters." The AOP soldiers responsible for the damages neither sought permission nor offered payment. When Madison Sallade of the U.S. quartermaster department investigated the Wade heirs' case, evidence convinced him that Federal soldiers destroyed the two houses.[52]

The heirs of Samuel Grove incurred minor injuries to their warehouse when Confederates occupied the property. The damages worsened, though, when Federals encamped on the farm. AOP troops tore logs and lumber from the Groves' barn, tenant house, and warehouse. They also destroyed a stable and a "water house and spring house," which were "taken for fuel."

Other buildings in the vicinity suffered a similar fate. West of Sharpsburg, Jacob H. Grove charged the U.S. government for "2 small houses burnt on farm for fuel." Nearby, soldiers tore down a two-story, log tenant house on John L.

---

51 Claim of Morgan and Andrew Rentch Miller (No. 4295); Snyder, *Trembling in the Balance*, 45.

52 Claims of James Marker (No. 1292) and the heirs of Henry Wade (No. 6585).

Mayer's property. When a quartermaster agent later interviewed Mayer's neighbors, he found that "a great portion of said log house was . . . torn down and consumed for fuel." Additionally, the agent learned that "several of the outbuildings" on Mayer's farm, "after having been vacated and abandoned as hospitals, were entirely demolished and burned up about said premises" by the men of Porter's V Corps.[53]

*　　*　　*

It is difficult to estimate the total number of trees destroyed by McClellan's army after the Battle of Antietam. Some claimants quantified their losses in cords, while others only listed the number of timber acres decimated. Also, citizens like the Samuel Grove heirs and William M. Blackford suffered losses to their woodland at various times from 1861–63. Still, war claims evidence provides a general sense of the overall damages. For example, William F. Hebb and Lafayette Miller sought payment for the combined destruction of 1,500 trees in September and October 1862. At least 20 other claimants reported Antietam-related losses of hardwood timber, and several others accused U.S. troops of chopping down their orchard trees. In the end, AOP soldiers encamped at Sharpsburg after the battle, along with XII Corps commands stationed near Blackford's Ford and Antietam Iron Works in November 1862, possibly destroyed more than 5,000 trees.[54]

As extreme as this seems, deforestation by the Federal Army was not uncommon during the Civil War. In September 1862, Major General William Tecumseh Sherman explained to civilians in Memphis, Tennessee, that armies "will naturally clear the ground of houses, fences, and trees. This is waste, but is the natural consequence of war . . . generally war is destruction and nothing else." Private Philo Stevens Pearce of the 11th Connecticut estimated that, during the Fredericksburg Campaign in 1862–63, "I believe our army must have cut down 200 acres of pine timber for fuel and buildings." Likewise, a quartermaster in the Army

---

53 Claims of the heirs of Samuel Grove (G-1633), Jacob H. Grove (No. 1267), and John L. Mayer (No. 8586).

54 Claims of William F. Hebb (F-1417) and John Miller (No. 2227). The Samuel Grove heirs, Henry Wade heirs, Jacob H. Grove, and William M. Blackford alleged that AOP forces destroyed a combined 106 acres of prime timber after the Antietam battle. As mentioned previously, Alex Davis testified in the Samuel Grove heirs' case that "fairly good timber" contained "100 to 105 trees to the acre." Among the claimants who accused AOP troops of chopping down orchard trees were John C. Middlekauff, who sought payment for "30 fruit trees destroyed" (F-1587), and Stephen P. Grove, who reported, "Orchard destroyed—100 good size trees" (No. 7354).

of the Cumberland recalled that "the needs of the Union army were great, and . . . of fuel the consumption is enormous." While based in Nashville in November 1862, he estimated that "eighteen thousand cords of wood have been consumed, and to this must be added the large forests that have been cut down and burned."[55]

The army's destruction of Sharpsburg's timber had lasting effects on the community, stripping the landscape of trees while negatively impacting land values, wood prices, and wildlife habitats. More than three decades after the battle, Maria Grove testified, "[S]uch timber is now worth about one hundred dollars per acre, as it is very scarce." In the immediate sense, though, many families lacked heating and cooking fuel for the looming winter of 1862–63. For wealthier families, hauling wood from nearby towns was an option, but troops stole so many horses from the community that some folks may have lacked animals to pull wagons. Residents could have used coal as a secondary heating source, but damages to the C & O Canal during the 1862 Maryland Campaign suspended coal shipments to Sharpsburg-area wharves. Once engineers repaired the canal, coal freighting halted again when the U.S. army built a river-spanning pontoon near Harpers Ferry. Consequently, the stoppage caused coal companies in Cumberland, Maryland, to temporarily cease production, forcing frustrated coal miners to leave the area and seek work in Pennsylvania. This chain of events left Sharpsburg residents without coal, which increased the demand for wood and further spiked local timber prices. John Grice recounted that fence wood after the battle increased to "six dollars here; I sold it at that price; our supply of coal was cut off for nearly two years; this advanced the price of wood."[56]

After soldiers vacated their log quarters, landowners salvaged wood from the huts to obtain winter fuel. Robert W. Grove recounted that his uncle, Jacob C. Grove, "used some of the [reclaimed] timber for fire wood, and sold a good deal of it right here in town." In addition, Robert testified, "[P]art of it was taken to our place" and more "was taken . . . to Uncle Stevens," referring to Stephen P. Grove. Jacob C. Grove could have salvaged wood to sell to the community, but Union forces torched some of the log huts upon departure. Van S. Brashears recollected, "I suppose that the soldiers built 25 or 30 shacks or houses on this place. They did not leave them all when they left; they set fire to some of them and burnt them."

55 Cashin, *War Stuff*, 99-100; William T. Sherman, *Memoirs*, 2 vols. (New York, 1891), 1:276-278; Stevens, "Civil War Memories," 19; Fitch, *Annals of the Army of the Cumberland*, 269.

56 Claim of Stephen P. Grove (No. 7354); Snyder, *Trembling in the Balance*, 142; Claim of Benjamin F. Rohrback (No. 4234). John Grice testified in Rohrback's case.

Brashears further explained, [S]ome were standing and some were knocked down and set fire to. They were all burnt . . . it was said at the time that these shacks contained vermin and were burned on that account."

William M. Blackford used logs and lumber from the soldiers' cabins to warm his home and rebuild fences. Unfortunately, this did not bode well with his adjoining neighbor, Morgan Miller. This lumber consisted of Morgan Miller's warehouse, which troops tore down and carried to their camp on Blackford's farm. "[W]hen the army left," Miller recalled, "I could not get my lumber back because the camp had been made on Wm. Blackford's land, and he would not let me remove them."[57]

*　*　*

As property losses continued to mount, civilians asked officers to end the depredations, pay for property taken, or provide written documentation of the appropriated items. Among the residents was Joseph Poffenberger, who "made complaint about the taking" to "one of the high officers." When the confiscations continued, Poffenberger "then went to General Meade, with whom he was personally acquainted." Meade instructed the farmer "to make out a bill of all the property taken and that the Government would compensate him for it." The general also told Poffenberger "to submit the list to him and that he would endorse it," but before Poffenberger calculated his losses, "the General had gone."

Samuel I. Piper deposed that, after losing large amounts of property, "I went to see general ricketts several times, who had his headquarters at my house and he said to keep a record and the Court of Claims would rectify everything." Near Mercersville, Josiah E. Davis spoke directly with VI Corps generals about his mother's losses. "I talked with Bartlett on the farm of Mr. Rench," Davis testified. "[I]t was the day that they moved in that I talked with Franklin; I talked with Slocum at different times, up to the time that he left about the first of November." Despite the frequent conversations, it's not known if the generals offered Davis any payment or vouchers. Adjoining Davis's farm was Thomas Barnum, who met with "Quartermaster Wheeler" and "Commissary B. F. Painter" about his losses of grain and livestock. The officers, Barnum recalled, ensured "they would give me

---

57 Claims of the heirs of Samuel Grove (No. 9313) and Morgan and Andrew Rentch Miller (No. 4295).

satisfactory papers . . . where I would receive compensation for the goods they had taken." Such papers, however, were never provided.[58]

After AOP soldiers stripped Mary Grice's out lots of grains and potatoes, she voiced concerns to nearby officers, who referred her to army headquarters. "I talked to Gen. McClellan," Grice testified, "and I asked about paying for my property and he said the government would pay for it" at a later time. The Mummas, meanwhile, failed to prevent Union troops from confiscating livestock, grains, fence rails, and what remained of the family's property. Samuel Mumma, Jr. recalled, "I talked with both general Meade and Sumner and they said they were out of supplies and that they must have what they could get from my father and that the Government would pay for it." Encouraged by the promise of eventual payment, the Mummas "did not object any more."

Being a strong Union man, Henry Piper remained patient with the appropriations until Federals fed most of his grains to army animals. "I talked with several officers & especially with quartermasters in relation to the taking & use of my property," Piper recalled. "They told me they were in great need of all kinds of forage and that they must have it." Piper later admitted, "I was unacquainted with the way and manner of doing business with the quartermaster and did not know the way to proceed to get pay for my property; neither did I know of any way of preventing the army taking & using the same according to their needs."

Thomas Fisher fretted over the valuable grains "taken from his farm, which lay near 'Burnside's Bridge' on the Antietam Battle field." Yet, he was "promised by Genl. Burnside, who visited his house at the time, that he should be paid fully." Content with assurance from high command, Fisher "therefore gave himself no further concern about it." Jacob F. Miller also complained to Gen. Burnside. After IX Corps soldiers stripped Miller's farm of fruit, potatoes, and livestock, Miller testified, "I talked with Mr. Burnside; I got acquainted with him and stated the whole thing, and all the satisfaction I got was he said: Very good, I would be paid [later] for all of it. He knew it was taken, every bit of it."[59]

Some officers assigned guards to watch over the citizens' property. After "squads of 20 to 30" carried away bundles of hay from Jacob A. Myers's barn, he lodged a complaint and "Genl. Wilcox sent a guard to protect his property."

---

58 Claims of Joseph Poffenberger (No. 1300), Samuel I. Piper (No. 1310), and Thomas Barnum (No. 333). Josiah Ellsworth Davis, a son of Eliza Davis, testified in Barnum's case.

59 Claim of Benjamin F. Rohrback (*RG* 123, No. 4234). Mary Grice appeared as a witness in Rohrback's claim; Claims of Samuel Mumma, Sr. (No. 334), Henry Piper (No. 445), Thomas Fisher (H-4113 and H-4114), and Jacob F. Miller (No. 4294).

William F. Hebb "was able to save much of his property" after obtaining a guard . . . furnished by Genl. Reynolds." On the neighboring farm of Samuel I. Piper, a Union soldier remembered that Piper's cordwood "was guarded by our troops and no one allowed to touch it but the people in the house."[60]

In the chaos following the battle, though, civilians found it challenging to obtain guards promptly. Consequently, troops hauled away much of the private property before sentinels were assigned. Tenant farmer William Unger, hoping to preserve what remained of his grains, "made a complaint to an officer, who put a guard over his wheat before it was all taken." On the farm of Henry V. S. Blackford, nearly everything on the property was "destroyed or greatly damaged by the troops." Fortunately, Blackford "procured a guard from Genl. Porter . . . to save the rest of the wheat, hay, rails & c." In a similar case, John C. Middlekauff "complained to Gen. George Meade" about the loss of his grains. To appease the worried farmer, Meade "gave him a guard to protect the barn, to keep the men from carrying the wheat out." Nonetheless, by the time the sentry arrived, "the property had been taken."[61]

Obtaining guards did not always guarantee the protection of property. After John J. Keedy noticed a Federal wagon train park along his twelve-acre cornfield, he grew "alarmed at the great number of teamsters penetrating said field" to gather corn for their horses. Keedy then "applied for a guard which was immediately furnished him and placed around the field . . . but nevertheless the teamsters would get in."

In early October, Dr. Abner Hard of the 8th Illinois Cavalry recalled that his regiment moved to a new camp in Sharpsburg, "situated in a field where there was no timber, and where all the fences were protected by the infantry guards." Concocting a plan "to procure a few boards with which to make bunks, tables &c.," one of Dr. Hard's comrades approached a sentinel guarding the fence, "taking with him a colored man, a hatchet and a bottle of whisky." After a brief conversation, "the bottle was drawn from the Doctor's pocket, and the sentinel was seen to imbide a deep draught, and then walk leisurely round to the opposite side of the

60 Claims of Jacob A. Myers (F-2190), William F. Hebb (F-1417), and Samuel I. Piper (No. 1310).

61 Claims of William Unger (K-516), Henry V. S. Blackford (Claims G-1630, G-1648, G-1654), and John C. Middlekauff (No. 329).

stack." With the fence being conveniently unguarded, "The colored boy at once set to work tearing off the boards, which were soon brought to our tent."[62]

Promises of later payment and appointments of guards did little to quell the collective temper of the ravaged community, especially those intensely loyal to the Union. As AOP forces continued commandeering property throughout late September, patience grew short, and civilians became more vocal in their complaints. William M. Blackford recalled, "[W]hen I found out they had taken everything I had I went and hunted up some of the quartermasters. They gave me no satisfaction, some saying I must identity myself, & c.; some would say that when they got ready to move they would give me proper vouchers." Unsatisfied with verbal promises, Blackford went to the headquarters of Fitz John Porter, where "Col. Webb, of his staff, laid my case, and Gen. Porter sent for me. He told me that he would select three officers from his Pennsylvania Regiments to appraise the value of what crops had been taken, and that he would endeavor to get officers who had been farmers."[63]

* * *

What William M. Blackford described was a board of survey, which Maj. Gen. Porter authorized on September 30 via Special Order No. 136. Porter appointed three Pennsylvania officers to the board, Captain Samuel Conner of the 62nd, Captain David A. McManigal of the 131st, and Chaplain Orson B. Clark of the 83rd. These men convened "for the purpose of appraising and ascertaining, if possible, the amount of damages accruing to certain property in this vicinity by troops in the service of the United States." The board notified "sundry persons within the limits of the 5th Army corps" to record their losses in writing, obtain certificates of loyalty to the U.S., and recruit witnesses to appraise items taken or damaged. Upon meeting all of these requirements, petitioners could submit requests for board of survey investigations.[64]

After reviewing claimants' petitions, interviewing witnesses, and touring properties, the military board conferred internally upon monetary awards and drafted their findings in triplicate. They issued one copy to the claimants. The other

---

62 Claim of John J. Keedy (No. 2157); Hard, *History of the Eighth Cavalry Regiment*, 197.

63 Claim of William M. Blackford (*RG* 123, No. 1324).

64 Claim of Israel Smith (*RG* 92, Entry 843, Box 772, Book 304, Claim 392). The claim's envelope incorrectly identified "Abram Smith" as the petitioner. Israel Smith lived near Capt. David Smith in 1862 and his case file includes a copy of Porter's Special Order No. 136.

papers they forwarded to the corps quartermaster and quartermaster general's office in Washington. Porter's board inspected farmsteads west and south of Sharpsburg. In the case of William M. Blackford, he testified that Porter's three officers "came to my premises, and remained three days, and made a thorough inquiry into my losses and appraised the same."[65]

Battlefield residents and persons living northwest of Sharpsburg village fell under the jurisdiction of I Corps. To appraise these properties, Maj. Gen. John F. Reynolds issued Special Order No. 22 and appointed three officers from Meade's division to "estimate the damages." It started as a minor assignment for Reynolds's board, but when other inhabitants learned of the opportunity to recoup losses, the number of survey requests spiked. "There being but three different properties named in the original order," reported a board officer, "yet by subsequent orders from head quarters the number has been increased to over twenty." One of the orders involved Moses Poffenberger. After growing concerned about his father's mounting losses, Poffenberger recounted, "I went to General Meade's headquarters, and he told me he was about to pay, when he said no, I will put your father's name on the Board of Survey and they will call on you."

Throughout the first week of October, military boards from I Corps and V Corps reviewed claim requests, convened on various farms, and obtained sworn statements of neighbors. For civilians seeking payments for their losses, these surveys presented several drawbacks. One, the officers needed substantial time to investigate each property, and there were dozens of requests. If the AOP departed Sharpsburg before completing the inspections, some civilians would lack authorized claims. Two, the monetary awards were only recommendations, for the boards were not authorized to dole out cash payments. Three, the board's findings were sometimes below the amounts requested by claimants. Last, many residents had surveys conducted in early October, but the AOP continued to appropriate grains, fencing, and timber thereafter. None of these latter losses appeared in the original appraisals, and officers denied requests for second surveys.[66]

---

65 Claims of William M. Blackford (No. 1324) and David Otto (*RG* 92, Entry 843, Box 772, Book 304, Claim 403). David Otto, the son of John Otto, resided near Sharpsburg's out lots in 1862. The document furnished to Otto by the military board was "signed in Triplicate," with "One copy furnished to Brig. Gen. Ingalls, One copy furnished to David Otto, One copy on file at these Head Quarters."

66 Claim of Henry Piper (No. 445). Piper's case file included a copy of Reynolds's Special Order No. 22, which identified the board's officers as "Major Snodgrass, 9th Regiment, P.R.C.; Major Briner, 3rd Regiment P.R.C.; Captain McPherson, 5th Regiment P.R.C." Additional

Throughout October, more civilians requested military appraisements, reflecting the broad scope of the army's damages. In response, Maj. Gen. Reynolds appointed an additional board via Special Orders No. 36, led by Major Alexander Biddle. On October 23, Maj. Biddle's board of survey dispatched a written notice to residents "that the Board would meet at the Stone Hotel in Sharpsburg on the following morning" to consider claims for "all the claimants in the neighborhood."

The following day, suppliants and witnesses crammed inside of Elias U. Knode's Maryland Hotel to present their cases. One of the first to appear was Anna Stonebraker, wife of Joseph Stonebraker. Her three witnesses, after "being sworn according to Articles of War No. 73," informed the board that the "articles set down in Mrs. Stonebraker's claim . . . were used by the troops of the U States and the valuation was just and true." After interviewing Stonebraker and her appraisers, the officers cleared the room to confer privately. They determined her claim was valid, scheduled an appointment to inspect Stonebraker's farm, and summoned the other claimants back inside the hotel. On went the slow process. Serving as a witness in Alfred N. Cost's case, John J. Keedy swore that Cost's "post and worm fence, fodder, corn and clover are not over the quantities he knows to have been on the property." Samuel Cost, having "walked back and forward over the fields" of his son's farm, told the board, "[N]ot an item is set down which is not correct" in the claim because Alfred N. Cost's farm "was full from end to end" with United States troops. Other residents presented cases throughout the long day, and the board scheduled appointments to tour their farms.

The following day, Maj. Biddle's board surveyed the properties. They "rode to the farm of A. N. Cost and examined the premises where the alleged damage was done." The officers "saw the lines where the fence had been destroyed, the remnant of the fields of corn and fodder, the field of Broom Corn, the clover field, the orchard and made a general examination of the premises." Alfred N. Cost and his witnesses priced the losses at $945, but the board of survey found the amount excessive and recommended an award of $771.

---

research may determine whether Generals Franklin and Burnside ordered boards of survey to appraise properties near Bakersville and Antietam Iron Works, where VI Corps and IX Corps encamped; Claims of Daniel Poffenberger (No. 1505) and Henry V. S. Blackford (G-1630, G-1648, and G-1654). Lewis M. Blackford, a son of the claimant, deposed that a board of survey appraised his father's losses on Oct. 1, 1862, but "the troops continued after that date to hold possession and took forage, fuel & c." To document the appropriations, Blackford "called upon Col. Norton Ch. Qr. Mr . . . for another Board to assess these losses; was told that it was impossible as they expected marching orders every day." Lieutenant Colonel C. B. Norton was the chief quartermaster of V Corps.

From there, the officers "rode over the farm of Samuel Pry" and conducted another survey. Pry estimated his damages at $1,992.25, but the board determined that a "payment of $1618.00 . . . would compensate Samuel Pry for injury sustained by him." The officers then investigated properties owned by brothers Jacob H. and Aaron Cost, where U.S. forces reportedly destroyed fences and corn. On the former farm, they recommended a $442 settlement to Jacob H. Cost, who sought $592.60. Upon reaching Aaron Cost's property, the board "rode over the farm . . . round his boundaries and examined his corn field—the apparent injury to which was not less than his estimate." That afternoon, the officers toured several other farmsteads, concluding on Anna Stonebraker's property, then "returned to camp at dark and adjourned." Such was a day's work for a military board at Sharpsburg.[67]

The price difference was a point of contention for farmers like the Cost brothers and Samuel Pry, who believed their submitted claims were accurate. Major James McKinney Snodgrass of the 9th Pennsylvania Reserves, who served as president of General Reynold's first board of survey, reported in late October, "It will be seen there is a great discrepancy between our valuation and the assessment made by the individuals themselves." Having witnessed the army's devastation to the community during his inspections, Snodgrass wrote, "[A]ll we can say, on our part is, we have endeavored to act conscientious between man and man and between the citizen and the government."

There were undoubtedly opportunists in the Sharpsburg community, as shown in previous accounts of residents selling bread at high prices. However, there were also persons, illiterate or otherwise, who placed their claims in the hands of legal advisors. As word of the board of survey appointments spread throughout the region, attorneys began running notices in local newspapers for "Collection of Claims Against the U.S. Government." Among the lawyers advertising their services to Washington County residents were George French, William M. Tice of Hagerstown, and John V. L. Findlay of Baltimore. No evidence supports that these attorneys convinced claimants to inflate their losses. Nevertheless, it may explain,

---

67 "Proceedings of a Board of Survey Convened in Conformity with Special Order No. 36," October 22, 1862 (*RG* 92, Entry 843, Box 771, NARA). Officers who made up the third board of survey were identified as "Lt. Col. Clark, 3rd Regt. P.R.V.C., Lt. Col. McCalmont, 142nd P.V., Major Biddle, 121st P.V;" *New York Times*, October 16, 1862; Claim of Aaron Cost (*RG* 92, Entry 843, Box 771, Claim 180). See also *RG* 92, Entry 797, Book 95, Box 230, Claim 95-1029.

in part, why a national newspaper accused the people of Sharpsburg of submitting fraudulent claims.[68]

"That the majority of the people in Sharpsburgh are loyal to the Union is not doubted," reported the *New York Times*, but "with few exceptions the parties presenting estimates of damages are desirous of obtaining more than the full value of the property taken or destroyed." Continuing, the *Times* vented, "When professed Union people attempt to rob the Government by making false statements, we have good reason to suppose that a small pecuniary inducement would transform them into avowed rebels." According to the article, "Numerous instances occur in which most outrageous frauds have been attempted upon the Government." Not only did civilians supposedly make "double charges" for their property, they "placed fabulous prices to goods and commodities which they never had in their possession."

To illustrate its point, the *Times* spotlighted widow Sarah Himes, whose home on West Main Street burned down during the battle. Himes submitted a certified appraisement of $1,059 in losses, which included the dwelling, clothing, food, furniture, kitchenware, and other items. "The house for which she [Himes] claims $400," the *Times* argued, "was a rude, dilapidated structure, built mostly of logs, and resembling a hut, and worth not over half the sum named." Additionally, "[T]he furniture and some other articles were greatly overestimated," the home's interior "was not of sufficient capacity to contain all the articles enumerated," and the house was "burned by the rebels."[69]

It is not known where the *New York Times* gleaned its information on Sarah Himes. True, a fire destroyed the widow's house during the battle, but no evidence supports that Confederates burned down the dwelling. Regarding the "greatly overestimated" amount of household items, Himes listed double the amount of carpeting claimed by Margaret Shackelford, who also lost her house to fire. Still, the chairs and furniture listed in Himes's claim were no different from quantities cited in bills of sale for Sharpsburg village residents from 1856–1862. Also, Margaret Shackelford listed the same number of beds, tables, and bureaus in her appraisal of losses.

Himes did inflate the price of her dwelling. In the 1860 Federal census, she declared $300 in real estate, but her claim for damages listed the house's value as

---

68 Claim of Henry Piper (No. 445); *HFTL*, October 8, 1862, 2E, October 15, 1862, 2D, and October 22, 3F.

69 *New York Times*, October 16, 1862.

$350 (rather the *Times'* assertion of $400). Thus, she exaggerated the home's price by 15 percent. We'll never know if Himes did this on her own accord or through the advice of her appraisers or attorney; nonetheless, it was an apparent discrepancy, and the *Times* was justified in reporting it. However, did the newspaper have other evidence to back its allegations of "numerous instances" of "outrageous frauds"? If so, any claimants attempting to defraud the military boards would have needed to convince their witnesses—who had claims of their own—along with Sharpsburg's justice of the peace, to conspire with their schemes.

A review of 39 board of survey reports relating to the Battle of Antietam found no evidence of fraudulent claims. In fact, the military boards recommended awards to all thirty-nine claimants. In 13 cases, the boards awarded the total prices charged. In 21 other cases, the claimants' original amounts submitted were not located, so it's unclear if the boards awarded full or partial settlements. In four cases involving the three Cost brothers and Samuel Pry, the board reduced the claimed amounts by an average of 18 percent. Like Sarah Himes's 15 percent difference, this inconsistency does not support the "double charges" reported by the *Times*. Of the 39 claims, Henry Reel was the only case involving a significant disparity, but the board still awarded the farmer $922 rather than rejecting his claim.

Decisions like this did not sit well with the *New York Times*, which blamed the military boards for being "too liberal with those claiming damages" and accused the officers of "being indolent and careless, or wishing to rid themselves of the business as soon as possible." Careless or not, the V Corps and I Corps boards completed their surveys in October.[70]

Due to the submission of so many claims and the AOP's eventual departure from Sharpsburg, the boards did not complete all the survey requests, leaving several cases unexamined. Without official documentation of their losses, civilians like Susan Hoffman, Philip Pry, and Joseph Sherrick faced uphill battles in securing claims payments from the United States government.

The military boards forwarded their completed reports to the AOP's chief quartermaster, Lt. Col. Rufus Ingalls. After reviewing the papers, Ingalls wrote to Lieutenant Colonel C. B. Norton, chief quartermaster of V Corps. "I am well

---

70 Claim of Sarah Himes (Book 304, Claim 229). The *Times* accused Himes of claiming the loss of 18 chairs, but her certified appraisement only lists 11. Bills of sale for Sharpsburg residents' furniture from 1856–62 include IN 9 / 612, IN 11 / 515, IN 12 / 246, IN 13 / 730, IN 15 / 478, and IN 15 / 501; Claims of Margaret Shackelford (Box 772, Book 304) and Henry Reel (Book 304, Claim 328). The board reduced Reel's claimed amount by seventy-one percent; *New York Times*, October 16, 1862.

aware," Ingalls admitted, "that the loyal people of this section of Maryland have suffered severely during this campaign and doubtless to any extent beyond any relief they will ever obtain." Ingalls expressed "regret that they cannot receive full compensation now for their losses, but no disbursing officer with this Army is authorized to pay any claims for damage." The requested payments, he concluded, "can only be settled by express authority of Congress" and "should be referred to the proper authorities at Washington."

We can only guess how Sharpsburg claimants responded upon learning that the government would not promptly pay their board of survey awards. Now at the mercy of Washington's claims system, those needing immediate financial settlements would have to wait, and wait, and wait. In the interim, Sharpsburg's formerly picturesque landscape resembled a fenceless wasteland, blemished with acres of tree stumps, stripped cornfields, and shallow graves. Families devoid of food and firewood huddled inside of cold homes. With temperatures dropping, stressed and malnourished civilians—who lost clothing, coats, and blankets to army appropriations—struggled to maintain their health. As if circumstances were not bleak enough, the unthinkable happened: a deadly disease outbreak swept across the region.[71]

---

71 "Proceedings of a Board of Survey." General Joseph Hooker forwarded a list of unexamined claims to quartermaster general Montgomery C. Meigs on Mar. 14, 1863; Claim of Samuel Beeler (RG 92, Book 304, Claim 401). Beeler's case file included correspondence between Norton and Ingalls from Oct. 23–26, 1862.

Chapter 9

Beautiful Corpse:
Antietam's Disease Outbreak

cological conditions in Sharpsburg after the battle were abysmal. Decaying flesh polluted the air, while excrement from military men and animals attracted disease-spreading insects and contaminated the groundwater. The resulting outbreak sickened hundreds of soldiers and civilians, taking the lives of many. Writing from the Susan Hoffman farm on October 1, Dr. Jonah Franklin Dyer expressed concern for his wounded patients, writing, "I hope that all will soon be removed, as the atmosphere of the whole neighborhood is tainted."[1]

Many written works have documented that disease killed more soldiers in the Civil War than combat. Contagious conditions like malaria, smallpox, and yellow fever sickened soldiers in army camps, hospitals, and prisons throughout the four-year conflict. Insofar as Antietam's outbreak is concerned, evidence shows that typhoid fever, diarrhea, and dysentery were primarily to blame for the epidemic that sickened hundreds of people after the battle.

In November 1862, assistant medical inspector Dr. W. R. Mosely toured Smoketown hospital, noting the cases. Mosely counted 479 patients, 247 of whom suffered from sickness rather than wounds. The main problems, he reported, were typhoid fever, diarrhea, and dysentery. After examining hospitals in Hagerstown, Mosely listed the same three conditions as the leading cause of illness, with

1 Dyer, *The Journal of a Civil War Surgeon*, 42.

Dr. John Aiken's Ward I of Smoketown Hospital, photographed after government-issued hospital tents arrived in the Sharpsburg area. *William Smith Ely Collection, Miner Library History of Medicine Section, University of Rochester Medical Center*

diphtheria present in some cases. Of 67 patients in the Williamsport area, the inspector noted that 64 ailed from typhoid fever or diarrhea.

Paralleling Dr. Mosely's observations, an environmental study of the Civil War determined that the primary causes of Antietam's outbreak were "typhoid and chronic diarrhea." Also, in his study of Antietam-area hospitals, John Nelson located several cases of typhoid fever and diarrheal disease. Another researcher found that "most of the men who died on Maryland Heights during the fall of 1862 died from typhoid fever." Let us examine these illnesses.[2]

According to the World Health Organization, diarrhea is caused by a "host of bacterial, viral and parasitic organisms, most of which are spread by faeces-contaminated water." The intestinal infection often occurs "when there is a shortage of adequate sanitation and hygiene and safe water for drinking, cooking and cleaning." Dysentery is similar to diarrhea but involves bloody excrement.

Both types of diarrheal disease cause frequent, watery stools that expel water, salt, blood, and electrolytes necessary for survival. Without antibiotics, which did not exist in 1862, prolonged symptoms can prove fatal. In cases of acute diarrhea, which lasts less than two weeks, one medical historian estimated that "3 of every 1,000 afflicted died," while the number increased to 17 of every 1,000 in cases of

---

2 Nelson, *As Grain Falls Before the Reaper*, 5, 15, 48, 71, 110-449. Nelson cited W. R. Mosely to J. J. Milhau, November 14, 1862 (*RG* 94, Entry 623, File D, Box 1, *NA*); Browning and Silver, *An Environmental History of the Civil War*, 78-79; Jim Sundman, "Disease: A Tale of Two Regiments (Part 2)," blog, *Emerging Civil War*, January 16, 2012, https://emergingcivilwar.com/2012/01/16/disease-a-tale-of-two-regiments-part-2/.

acute dysentery. In chronic cases, diarrhea and dysentery combined had an 11.6 percent case-fatality rate in the year 1862.[3]

The deadliest threat to soldiers and civilians after the battle at Sharpsburg was typhoid fever. Not to be confused with typhus (which is transmitted by fleas and lice), typhoid fever was caused by *Salmonella typhi*. Typhoid carriers shed the bacteria through feces and often transferred the fecal bacteria to their hands through inadequate handwashing after bowel movements. As a result, *Salmonella typhi* spread to others through person-to-person contact or by ingesting fecal-contaminated food or water. For instance, caregivers handling soiled linens, clothing, or bedpans of typhoid patients exposed themselves to infection, as did those who sponged the sweaty sufferers with typhoid-contaminated water. Also, some of those infected were asymptomatic. If these unwary carriers prepared food for others, they could spread the disease, akin to "Typhoid Mary" in the 1900s.[4]

Physicians during the Civil War could not definitively diagnose typhoid fever but were able to identify symptoms that distinguished it from similar maladies. For example, in its early stage, typhoid caused malaise and a steadily rising fever. Temperatures remained consistently high thereafter, which differed from intermittent fever caused by malaria. Additional traits included abdominal pain and diarrhea. Delirium, known as "typhoid toxemia," was another distinguishable sign, as were lung congestion and rose-colored spots on the chest.

Without vaccines and antibiotics, there was no cure for typhoid fever. As the disease progressed, diarrhea and delirium worsened. Symptoms in some patients included "vomiting of green or black matter" or "coughing up thick, foul-smelling phlegm." Late-stage typhoid often caused intestinal bleeding and perforated the small intestine, releasing fecal matter into the abdominal cavity. Upper respiratory infections progressed from bronchitis to a condition called "typhoid pneumonia." *Salmonella typhi* truly wreaked havoc on the body, evidenced by its high death rates

3 "Diarrhoeal Disease," web page, World Health Organization, May 2, 2017, https://www.who.int/en/news-room/fact-sheets/detail/diarrhoeal-disease; Alfred Jay Bollet, *Civil War Medicine: Challenges and Triumphs* (Tucson, AZ, 2002), 284, 330.

4 Wiley, *The Life of Billy Yank*, 134; F. Marineli, G. Tsoucalas, M. Karamanou, and G. Androutsos, "Mary Mallon (1869–1938) and the History of Typhoid Fever," Annals of Gastroenterology, 26(2), 2013, 132-134, https://pubmed.ncbi.nlm.nih.gov/24714738/. Mary Mallon, known also as "Typhoid Mary," was an asymptomatic cook who infected several dozen people with typhoid fever; Thomas Ruby, Laura McLaughlin, Smita Gopinath, and Denise Monack, "Salmonella's Long-Term Relationship with its Host," FEMS Microbiology Reviews, Volume 36, Issue 3, May 2012, 600-615, https://doi.org/10.1111/j.1574-6976.2012.00332.x; Charlotte A. Aikens, "Protection Against Typhoid," *The Trained Nurse and Hospital Review*, Vol. XLIX, (New York, July 1912), 99.

among whites in the Union army. One account found that case mortality rates among hospitalized white soldiers were 32.6 percent in 1862 and 44 percent in 1863. Similar death rates applied to African American troops and Confederate soldiers.

Typhoid fever infected Washington County residents before and after the war. Newspaper articles and obituaries, though, do not support that it sickened as many Western Marylanders as cholera, consumption, and scarlet fever. But if *S. typhi* was not a typical public health threat to Sharpsburg, why did it sicken so many people after the Battle of Antietam?[5]

* * *

Underneath the Antietam battlefield region is a bed of soluble limestone known as karst. Within this terrain, the Antietam National Battlefield cited, the "slightly acidic groundwater dissolves the soft stone, carving out spaces and cavities below the surface." These underground features, through which groundwater travels, include "sinkholes, rock outcrops, sinking streams, caverns, and many fissures."

Surface contaminants on this type of terrain are capable of creating a public health problem. Rainfall can wash surface pollutants into the karst cavities, "which are direct channels to the groundwater." From there, Washington County researchers found that these "contaminants and/or pathogens can travel long distances very quickly, intersecting a drilled well" and other sources of drinking

---

5 "Typhoid Fever and Paratyphoid Fever," Centers for Disease Control and Prevention, https://www.cdc.gov/typhoid-fever/sources.html; "Correspondence: Albany Military Hospital," *Medical and Surgical Reporter* (Philadelphia, August 10, 1861), vol. 6, no. 19, 432-434; "Hints and Observations on Military Hygiene, Relating to Diet, Dress, Exercise, Exposure, and the Best Means of Preventing and Curing Medical and Surgical Diseases in the Army," *Medical and Surgical Reporter*, vol. 6, no. 12, June 22, 1861, 263-268; R. K. Nair, S. R. Mehta, and S. Kumaravelu, "Typhoid Fever Presenting as Acute Psychosis," Armed Forces India, 2003, 59(3), 252-253, https://doi.org/10.1016/S0377-1237(03)80023-0; Rutkow, *Bleeding Blue and Gray*, 226-227; Michael Walsh, "Typhoid Fever," online article, Infection Landscapes, November 10, 2011, http://www.infectionlandscapes.org/2011/11/typhoid-fever.html; Jim Sundman, "Disease;" Bollet, *Civil War Medicine*, 330. Another study found that Union soldiers infected with typhoid fever during the Civil War suffered a 36.92 percent case mortality rate. See Joseph F. Siler and John S. Lambie, Jr., "Typhoid and the Paratyphoid Fevers," U.S. Army Medical Department, Office of Medical History, https://history.amedd.army.mil/booksdocs/wwi/communicablediseases/chapter1.html.; Historic Newspaper Indexing Project, Washington County Free Library, Hagerstown, MD. This database includes Washington County newspapers from 1845–65.

water. Making matters worse, the underground pathways "do not provide a treatment zone to remove pathogens present in surface water before the water reaches a well." Without adequate filtering, runoff can carry "harmful pathogens that could cause human illness" into the public supply of drinking water.[6]

As mentioned earlier, Sharpsburg had an abundance of springs and wells at the time of the battle. Big Spring in the village provided drinking water to many inhabitants, but the fountain was susceptible to contamination. During the summer of 1904, for instance, "[T]here was a typhoid epidemic which some persons attributed to the use of spring water. At that time there was a general cleaning out of the privy vaults and hog pens that line the run," which contaminated Big Spring and made numerous villagers ill. Another Sharpsburg outbreak occurred in 1966 involving infectious hepatitis, which sickened several dozen townsfolk. An investigation determined that "the risk of hepatitis among persons who obtained drinking water from a particular source, the Big Spring, was more than four times higher than that of persons who obtained drinking water from other sources." This was no anomaly, the investigators reported, because "the Big Spring has shown evidence of fecal contamination for many years."

It is not known when Sharpsburg's first waterborne outbreak occurred. However, in 1862, the colossal amount of deadly microorganisms created by the armies could have poisoned Big Spring and every other water source in the vicinity.[7]

The smell of death hung over Sharpsburg's scarred landscape long after hostilities ceased on September 17. "The stench," complained Dr. A. A. Biggs in

---

6 "Cave / Karst Systems," web page, ANB, April 10, 2015, https://www.nps.gov/ anti/ learn/nature/cave-karst-systems.htm; "Source Water Assessment Report: Washington County, Maryland," Washington County Health Department, Environmental Health Division, April 2006, 3-7; Koosha Kalhor, Reza Ghasemizadeh, Ljiljana Rajic, and Akram Alshawabkeh, "Assessment of Groundwater Quality and Remediation in Karst Aquifers: A Review," Groundwater for Sustainable Development, Volume 8, April 2019, 104-121, https:// doi.org/10.1016/j.gsd.2018.10.004; "Water-Related Diseases and Contaminants in Public Water Systems," Centers for Disease Control and Prevention. https://www.cdc.gov/ healthywater/drinking/public/water_diseases.html. Modern studies found that these microorganisms can cause hepatitis, giardiasis, cryptosporidiosis, Legionnaires' disease, and other ailments.

7 Horatio N. Parker, Bailey Willis, R. H. Bolster, W. W. Ashe, and M. C. Marsh, *The Potomac River Basin*, Department of the Interior, United States Geological Survey (Washington, DC, 1907), 234; Theodore R. Whatley, George W. Comstock, Howard J. Garber, Fernando S. Sanchez, Jr., "A Waterborne Outbreak of Infectious Hepatitis in a Small Maryland Town," American Journal of Epidemiology, Volume 87, Issue 1, January 1968, 138-147, https://doi.org/10.1093/oxfordjournals.aje.a120794.

late September, "is becoming so disagreeable, particularly after sundown, that we can hardly endure it." Alex Davis also suffered in the miserable atmosphere. The farmhand recounted that the horrible odor "hung on for a month, there was so many dead men and horses that was only half covered. The stench was sickening." The rancid smell even permeated inside homes. "We couldn't eat a good meal," Davis remembered, "and we had to shut the house up just as tight as we could of a[t] night to keep out that odor. We couldn't stand it, and the first thing in the morning when I rolled out of bed I'd have to take a drink of whiskey. If I didn't I'd throw up before I got my clothes all on."[8]

On September 25, Dr. William Child wrote from Smoketown Hospital, "It is awful about here now. The odor from the battlefield and hospitals is almost insupportable." Child later added, "[T]he odors were oppressive and deathly, and that dead men and horses were left unburied and unburned for days." When a *New York Times* correspondent approached Sharpsburg on September 26, he reported, "[I]t was unnecessary to ask when we were coming near the great battle-field, for it could be distinctly smelt two miles off." Upon arrival, the New Yorker observed the "charred remains of horses every where, and others again laying in all sorts of attitudes, just as they fell . . . poisoning the air for miles around."[9]

As noted, rotting horseflesh caused much of the miasma. Soldiers and citizens tried to reduce the stench by setting fire to the carrion, but the number of carcasses was purportedly too extreme to finish the job. "In all directions lay dead horses, some of which had been partly burned," observed a Pennsylvania correspondent on September 23, "but the task of thus destroying them was evidently too great for the force detailed for that purpose and they had been left to the elements and the buzzards." Consequently, Daniel Faust of the 96th Pennsylvania Infantry wrote on October 7, "[T]he battle ground is laying full of dead horses." On October 25, a *Philadelphia Inquirer* correspondent reported, "[A]lmost every field is arabesque with dead horses." Months later, in 1864, cartographer S. G. Elliott inspected the battlefield's graves. While doing so, he counted the remains of 270 horses scattered about the combat zone.[10]

---

8 Biggs to Kalb, September 29, 1862, WMR; Johnson, *BA*, 101.

9 Child, *Letters From a Civil War Surgeon*, 37; Child, *History of the Fifth Regiment*, 130; *New York Times*, October 4, 1862. President Abraham Lincoln, who toured the Antietam battlefield on October 2, 1862, may have experienced the same sickening stench.

10 *Altoona Tribune*, October 2, 1862; Alexander, "Destruction, Disease, and Death," 142; *Philadelphia Inquirer*, October 27, 1862; S. G. Elliott burial map, NYPL. Because Elliott specified

If scores of equines rotted on the battlefield in September and October 1862, the decay process released disease-causing microbes into the soil, regardless of whether the animals were buried or not. According to an agricultural study, "The potential for contamination exists when livestock mortalities are buried." Another study found that "carcass fluids can leach into and pollute groundwater, while "bacteria and viruses can be transmitted to surface water." Meanwhile, while carcasses polluted the battlefield in 1862, the AOP's living horses posed a similar threat.[11]

As mentioned previously, there were 18,000–20,000 horses and mules attached to McClellan's army near Sharpsburg on October 1, 1862. In addition, Robert E. Lee's Army of Northern Virginia brought 16,000 mules and horses into Maryland. Based on these estimates, the combined armies at Sharpsburg from September 15–18 possibly totaled 30,000 equines—and these animals produced an awful lot of waste.[12]

The Virginia Cooperative Extension estimated, "On any given day, the average 1,000-pound horse will produce approximately 50 pounds of manure." The Penn State Extension reported similar yields, citing that a 1,000-pound horse "produces about 31 pounds of feces and 2.4 gallons of urine daily, which totals around 51 pounds of total raw waste per day."

One could argue that the military equines at Sharpsburg, having unlimited access to civilian-owned grains and pastures, might have produced similar amounts of waste. Blake Magner, though, in his study of horses at Gettysburg, estimated that military horses and mules excreted "twelve to fifteen pounds of manure per day," an average of 13.5 pounds daily, along with two gallons of urine. Admittedly,

---

the locations of "Union Graves" and "Rebel Graves," his reference to "Dead Horses" may imply that the carcasses were unburied.

11 Saquib Mukhtar, "Routine and Emergency Burial of Animal Carcasses," online article, Texas A & M AgriLife Extension, https://agrilifeextension.tamu.edu/library/ranching/routine-and-emergency-burial-of-animal-carcasses/; Rachel Freedman and Ron Fleming, "Water Quality Impacts of Burying Livestock Mortalities," online article, Ridgetown College, University of Guelph, Ontario, August 2013, https://www.ridgetownc.com/research/documents/fleming_carcassburial.pdf.

12 Alexander, "Destruction, Disease, and Death," 157. The estimate of McClellan's equines after the battle does not include horses and mules assigned to II Corps and XII Corps at Harpers Ferry. From Sep. 15–18, per Joseph Harsh in *Taken at the Flood*, 369, a portion of Lee's artillery guarded fords at Williamsport, Falling Waters, and Blackford's Ford. Thus, not all of the ANV's horses were at Sharpsburg during the battle.

Magner's figures are less than the extensions' estimates, but let's take a conservative approach and apply them to Antietam.[13]

Based on 13.5 pounds of daily manure per animal, the estimated 30,000 Union and Confederate horses and mules in Sharpsburg from September 15–18 would have produced, over the course of four days, 1,620,000 pounds of manure and 240,000 gallons of urine. Incredibly, this was only a fraction of what followed.

From September 19 through October 7, approximately 18,000 horses, mules, and cattle in McClellan's army defecated and urinated in the Sharpsburg area. Although IX Corps and part of VI Corps left the area in early October, more than 8,000 equines attached to I Corps and V Corps remained until October 26.

Based on the figures above, military animals near the Antietam battlefield possibly produced more than 4,100 tons of manure and 1.25 million gallons of urine from September 15–October 26. These estimates do not include waste from the large herds of AOP beef cattle or the hundreds of horses brought to Sharpsburg after the battle by regional volunteers, journalists, soldiers' relatives, peddlers, and tourists.[14]

The staggering amount of animal waste not only fouled the air but created a serious health risk. Pathogens in manure, such as *E. coli* and *giardia*, can leach through karst terrain into shallow groundwater tables. "Agricultural run-off poses a severe threat to groundwater in many karst systems," one hydrologist reported. "Studies in Mammoth Cave National Park, which is surrounded by agricultural areas, have recorded high levels of manure, fecal coliforms . . . pesticides and herbicides in the cave system after rainfall events." Another groundwater study found, "Shallow aquifers in karst areas are probably the most vulnerable in the world to groundwater contamination." This pollution is caused, in part, by "contaminants from agricultural activities" and "bacteria from livestock waste."

In Washington County, where Sharpsburg is located, water quality specialists determined that "large scale feeding operations" were a potential source of

---

13 Crystal Smith, "Horse Manure Management," online article, Virginia Cooperative Extension, May 1, 2009, https://www.pubs.ext.vt.edu/406/406-208/406-208.html; "Horse Stable Manure Management," online essay, Penn State Extension, September 25, 2019, https://extension.psu.edu/horse-stable-manure-management; Magner, *Traveller & Company*, 47-48. By comparison, Magner estimated that the Union and Confederate armies brought more than 70,000 horses and mules to Gettysburg.

14 *OR*, vol. 19, 1:97-98. The estimated number of AOP equines is based on returns reported on October 1, 1862. On this date, McClellan's army had, in total, 32,885 horses and mules. Although hoof and mouth diseases killed untold numbers of military equines after the battle, the AOP's returns by November 1, 1862, show an increased total of 37,897 horses and mules.

contamination because karst features were vulnerable to "receiving contaminated run off and delivering the contamination directly into the aquifer." The presence of coliform bacteria and E. coli in groundwater, the specialists concluded, was "likely to be associated with the fecal pollution originating from the gastrointestinal tract of warm-blooded animals."

Thus, if army animals produced 4,100 tons of manure in six short weeks, this may have potentially sickened civilians and AOP forces with diarrheal disease and other illnesses. However, many other contaminants fouled the groundwater in September–October 1862.[15]

*   *   *

As discussed in Chapter Six, even after relatives retrieved the remains of their loved ones in the weeks following the battle, thousands of corpses remained. In 1864, cartographer S. G. Elliott depicted the burials of 5,844 Union and Confederate bodies near the battlefield. The scope of Elliott's map was limited, though, and did not include several locations featured in the Bowie List of Confederate burials. Thus, if we combine Elliott's estimate with the Bowie List's burials, there might have been more than 6,000 soldiers buried in Sharpsburg's karst topography at the time of the 1862 outbreak.[16]

Most of the remains lacked coffins, and bodily fluids discharged from corpses would have contacted the soil. Could this have factored into Sharpsburg's 1862 epidemic? Historian Ted Alexander wrote, "[O]nly diseases commonplace before a disaster are likely to be a threat after the event transpires." Supporting Alexander's argument, the World Health Organization cited, "The widespread belief that corpses pose a risk of communicable disease is wrong. Especially if death resulted

15 Christine Skelly, "One Horse or a Hundred: Manure and Water Don't Mix," online article, Michigan State University, October 23, 2015, https://www.canr.msu.edu/resources/one_horse_or_a_hundred_manure_and_water_dont_mix_wo1020; Jeff Jack, "Environmental Problems in Karst Lands," online article, Prentice-Hall, Inc., https://wps.prenhall.com/wps/media/objects/2894/2963555/update13.html; Kalhor, et al, "Assessment of Groundwater Quality;" Kristina Perry, "Contamination and Collapse: Human Settlement and Karst," abstract, San Francisco State University, May 21, 1999, http://online.sfsu.edu/jerry/geog810/1999/Perry.html; "Source Water Assessment Report," 2, 4, 7.

16 S. G. Elliott burial map, NYPL. The scope of Elliott's map did not include a number of Confederate burial sites described in the Bowie List, such as the Locust Spring and Smoketown hospitals, and farms of Susan Hoffman, Capt. David Smith, Elias S. Grove, and the heirs of Samuel Grove.

from trauma, bodies are quite unlikely to cause outbreaks of diseases such as typhoid fever, cholera, or plague." The International Committee of the Red Cross concurred, reporting, "The bodies of people who have died in a disaster do not cause epidemics." In a disaster—or a major battle—those who perish "are not likely to have epidemic-causing diseases such as cholera, typhoid, malaria or plague."[17]

There may be an exception to this reasoning. The International Committee of the Red Cross cited that corpses can potentially pass along illness to survivors, on account that "dead bodies often leak faeces, which may contaminate rivers or other water sources with diarrhoeal diseases." Given the high rate of infectious ailments throughout the war, some Union and Confederate soldiers killed at Antietam may have carried typhoid fever or chronic diarrhea / dysentery at the time of their deaths. If these corpses leaked feces before or after burial, rainfall could have potentially washed *S. typhi* bacteria into the karst groundwater. Farfetched as this may sound, it's not conjecture. One researcher in Paris, responding to an outbreak of typhoid fever among persons living near a graveyard, discovered "sweet-tasting water and an unpleasant smell exuding from wells situated close to cemeteries." Another study in Berlin found a connection between "the increased number of typhoid fever cases observed between 1963 and 1967 among people living around a cemetery." Groundwater tests in this vicinity "showed quantities of bacteria 60 times higher than those found in natural water." Similarly, other experts opined that typhoid-infected feces from Antietam's dead could have potentially contaminated the groundwater.[18]

17 Alexander, "Destruction, Disease, and Death," 157; "Water Sanitation Hygiene: Are There Disease Risks From Dead Bodies and What Should Be Done For Safe Disposal?" web page, World Health Organization, https://www.who.int/water_sanitation_health/ emergencies/ qa/emergencies_qa8/en/; "Why Dead Bodies Do Not Cause Epidemics," web page, International Committee of the Red Cross November 13, 2013, https:// www.icrc. org/en/doc/resources/documents/faq/health-bodies-140110.htm; U.S. Depart- ment of Transportation, *Mass Casualties, a Lessons Learned Approach: Accidents, Civil Unrest, Natural Disasters, Terrorism, National Highway Traffic Safety Administration* (Washington, DC, 1982), 189; "Management of Dead Bodies: Frequently Asked Questions," web page, World Health Organization, November 2, 2016, https://www.who.int/hac/techguidance/management-of-dead-bodies-qanda/en/.

18 "Why Dead Bodies Do Not Cause Epidemics," International Committee of the Red Cross; Józef Zychowski, Tomasz Bryndal, "Impact of Cemeteries on Groundwater Contamination by Bacteria and Viruses—a Review," *Journal of Water and Health*, vol. 13, issue 2, June 1, 2015, 285-301.doi: https://doi.org/10.2166/wh.2014.119.; Dr. Michael T. Osterholm, infectious disease expert, email message to author, June 8, 2020. Dr. Osterholm, at the time of this study, was director of the Center for Infectious Disease Research and Policy at the University of

Other pollutants festered at Sharpsburg's hospitals. According to Ted Alexander, "thousands of severed human appendages, sometimes buried and often not . . . posed as much of a health threat as dead bodies." Livestock carrion may have added to the problem. Army butchers were encouraged to bury animal carcasses "at a sufficient distance from camp" with "at least four feet of earth," but it's unclear if the slaughtermen at Sharpsburg complied.[19]

A more likely cause of the 1862 disease outbreak was human feces, as thousands of Union soldiers defecated on Sharpsburg's karst terrain for weeks after the battle. The U.S. Sanitary Department warned in its "Rules of Health," issued in 1862, that "inattention to nature's calls is a frequent source of disease" and "men should never be allowed to void their excrement elsewhere than in the regular established sinks." In camps, "no refuse, slops, or excrement should be allowed to be deposited" near the tents. At camps and hospitals, police parties were encouraged to inspect the sinks daily and throw lime or other disinfecting agents into the sewage to prevent it from "becoming offensive and unhealthy."[20]

This was sound advice, but was it heeded?

One source argued that Federal and Confederate troops throughout the war "defecated and urinated where and when it suited them, with little regard for the health hazards their excrement created." At Cold Harbor in 1864, medical director Thomas A. McParlin reported to Major General George Meade, "Very few regiments provided sinks for the men, and their excreta are deposited upon hill sides to be washed from thence into the streams, thus furnishing an additional

---

Minnesota. He wrote, "*S. typhi* can survive in the environment for some time." Hence, if Antietam's corpses had typhoid-infected fecal matter on them, in close range to karst groundwater tables, "the graves could theoretically be a source" of a typhoid outbreak; J. Scott Shipe, water infrastructure science consultant, email messages to author, June 2020. Shipe has extensive knowledge of karst topography in Washington County. In an Antietam-related case study, he determined that an "epidemiological investigation was never formally conducted after the battle, but the shallow source of groundwater would have been highly polluted" with concentrated matter from human corpses and dead horses. In addition, Sharpsburg's 54-degree groundwater was the ideal temperature for "keeping any bacteria thriving for months." Shipe wrote that the highly polluted groundwater "would have easily made the strongest person's immunity fail."

19 Alexander, "Destruction, Disease, and Death," 166; Nelson, *As Grain Falls Before the Reaper*, 67, 15; Isabella Fogg (Maine Sanitary Commission) to J. W. Hathaway, November 10, 1862, Miscellaneous Civil War Documents, Digital Maine Repository, Augusta, ME, https://digitalmaine.com/cw_misc_doc/10/.

20 Daniel Butterfield, *Camp and Outpost Duty for Infantry* (New York, 1862), 108.

source of contamination to the water." The runoff, McParlin observed, caused a rash of illnesses among his men, with "diarrhea being especially prevalent."[21]

Similarly, an army surgeon observed men neglecting to use their sinks, instead "going out into the bushes, and not infrequently some 30 or 40 feet from some of their tents and relieving themselves." Consequently, he reported, "[H]uman excrement has been promiscuously deposited in every direction, until the atmosphere . . . is so heavily loaded with effluvia that is sickening."[22]

Other problems occurred with the sinks. On Maryland Heights in the fall of 1862, shallowly dug latrines "overflowed with the heavy rains that fall, contaminating the campground," and reportedly sparking an epidemic of typhoid fever. Dr. Joseph Janvier Woodward of the U.S. surgeon general's office inspected various Federal camps throughout the war. Latrine management, on paper, stipulated that "when the trench is two-thirds full it should be covered to the surface with earth and a new one dug." In person, though, Woodward found "sinks full to overflowing are allowed to remain," making it "impossible to approach them without nausea." Consequently, he wrote, "[L]arge numbers of the men will not use the sinks under these circumstances, and every grove, every clump of bushes, every fence border in the vicinity is resorted to for the purpose." Sick men, Woodward, noted, also neglected to use the unkept sinks. Anyone walking near hospital wards found the air "poisoned by putrid exhalations from the liquid discharges of diarroea, dysentery, and fever cases."[23]

After the Battle of Antietam, similar conditions may have prevailed at Sharpsburg, as thousands of encamped soldiers, wounded men, and hospital personnel evacuated their bowels on the karst landscape for six weeks. Human feces, whether deposited in sinks or random locations, put nearby springs and wells at risk because the excreta potentially contained different pathogens. Along with *Salmonella typhi*, feces carried *Entamoeba histolytica*. During the war, this parasite caused amoebic dysentery, considered "the most lethal of diarrheal infections due to its infestation of not only the intestines, but the lungs, brain, and other important organs." One witness may have stumbled into evidence of such while traversing

21 Browning and Silver, *An Environmental History*, 78-79; Thomas A. McParlin to George Meade, June 5, 1864, *OR*, vol. 36, 1:247. Meade served as brigadier general at Antietam, and was later promoted to major general.

22 "How Parasites Changed the American Civil War," online article, National Museum of Civil War Medicine, June 1, 2018, https://www.civilwarmed.org/parasites/.

23 Sundman, "Disease;" Joseph Woodward, *Outlines of the Chief Camp Diseases of the United States Armies* (Philadelphia, 1863), 49-50.

the Sharpsburg battlefield in late September 1862, coming across "a ribbon of dysenteric stools."

Indeed, in September and October 1862, there was a mind-boggling amount of disease-spreading matter lying a few inches above the Antietam Valley's groundwater. One karst study concluded that surface runoff from rainfall could carry pathogens "into the aquifer and then to a spring in only a few hours." Proving the rapid contamination rate, Washington County researchers conducted a dye test that clocked the karst groundwater flow at fifty feet per hour. The study found that "contamination at the surface can reach a well in this region in a matter of hours or days."[24]

As infectious agents poisoned Sharpsburg's drinking water in 1862, human feces and horse manure remaining on the surface attracted an entirely different problem—the housefly.

According to medical historian Bonnie Brice Dowart, houseflies throughout the Civil War "play[ed] a crucial role in spreading diarrhea/dysentery." When flies fed on infected stools and then landed on food, they potentially contaminated the subsistence with pathogens like *Shigella* and *Salmonella*. One modern study extracted dozens of bacterial strains from houseflies, finding *Bacillus* and *Staphylococcus* the most prevalent.[25]

Another historian, Vincent J. Carillo, argued, "Two conditions are required to produce a typhoid epidemic: an abundance of fly-breeding material and the presence of typhoid-infected human feces to which the flies have access." Cirillo cited that "horse manure piles," of which there was plenty at Sharpsburg after the battle, "were the chief oviposition sites, and camp sinks (pit latrines) the richest source of typhoid germs." Further examining the housefly-typhoid relationship, Carillo found that the insect can "disseminate germs through defecation and regurgitation." In addition, the housefly's "habit of walking, feeding, and breeding on manure, human excrement, garbage, and carrion makes it an ideal disease vector." The pests' preferred meals are freshly excreted human stools, but "when

---

24 "How Parasites Changed the American Civil War;" Richard Carr, "Excreta-Related Infections and the Role of Sanitation in the Control of Transmission," online article, World Health Organization, 2001, https://www.who.int/water_sanitation_health/dwq/iwachap5.pdf; Strong Diary, September 22, 1862, NYHSM; "Source Water Assessment Report," 3, 6.

25 Dorwart, "Disease in the Civil War;" Mansour Nazari, Tahereh Mehrabi, Seyed Mostafa Hosseini, and Mohammed Yousef Alikhani, "Bacterial Contamination of Adult House Flies (Musca Domestica) and Sensitivity of These Bacteria to Various Antibiotics, Captured from Hamadan City, Iran," *Journal of Clinical and Diagnostic Research*, 2017, 11(4), DC04–DC07, https://doi.org/10.7860/JCDR/2017/23939.9720.

disturbed, these voracious scavengers, with feces-laden bodies, migrated to food preparation and eating areas." In the late 1800s, medical officer Alfred Woodhull described the houseflies' route from latrine sinks to army kitchens as a "literal highway of disease."[26]

Supporting Woodhull's observation, a Union hospital steward based in Vicksburg during the war recalled, "No care whatever was used in disposing of the bowel discharges from typhoid patients." Houseflies, he noted, "were everywhere in great numbers . . . the wonder is we were not all infected; for there was nothing to prevent them from coming direct from the bowel discharges to our food."[27]

The large concentration of people in camps and hospitals at Sharpsburg, along with Federal reinforcements and civilian visitors streaming into the area, also accelerated the epidemic. One historian pointed out that this crowded environment was ideal for diseases to expand, akin to a "gigantic petri dish."

With soldiers drinking contaminated water and houseflies carrying deadly microbes from feces to food, Antietam's epidemic erupted. Infection spread through hospitals, sickening patients recovering from combat wounds. Diseases raged through camps, infecting scores of McClellan's men. Colonel Louis C. Duncan, medico-military historian, estimated that sick troops accumulated in Sharpsburg's field hospitals "at a rate of four or five hundred a day." Anna Holstein recalled that "scores of fever-patients came pouring in" to battlefield-area hospitals, and "some new regiments went down by hundreds."[28]

Along with diarrhea and dysentery, *Salmonella typhi* infected Federal troops and medical workers throughout the region. In October, a Northern correspondent reported from Harpers Ferry, "There are a good many cases of Typhoid fever." Near Sharpsburg, as the "nights grew bitterly cold," a member of the 22nd Massachusetts remembered, "the sick grew numerous. Many were sick with typhoid fever, and our condition at all times in this camp are mentally, morally and

26 Vincent J. Cirillo, "'Winged Sponges': Houseflies as Carriers of Typhoid Fever in 19th- and Early 20th-Century Military Camps," *Perspectives in Biology and Medicine*, Vol. 49, no. 1, Johns Hopkins University Press, 2006, 52-63, doi:10.1353/pbm.2006.0005. Cirillo cited Alfred A. Woodhull, *Military Hygiene for Officers of the Line* (New York, 1909), 313.

27 Charles B. Johnson, *Muskets and Medicine* (Philadelphia, 1917), 159-160.

28 Freemon, *Gangrene and Glory*, 205; Duncan, *The Medical Department*, 33; Holstein, *Three Years in Field Hospitals*, 17.

physically bad." In a letter home, army surgeon Daniel Holt wrote, "Last night a man died of typhoid fever, and quite a number look as if they would soon follow."[29]

Private Henry B. Paulding of the 18th Massachusetts initially suffered from a combat wound but "was suddenly attacked by a fever, which in a few days proved fatal." He died on October 11 in Sharpsburg's Lutheran Church hospital. Another soldier from the 11th Connecticut died on October 14 "of wounds received in the forearm and Typhoid Fever contracted at Sharpsburg."[30]

Rachel P. Evans, a volunteer nurse from Pennsylvania, took ill in Sharpsburg with "unmistakable symptoms of camp fever" that proved nearly fatal. Another volunteer, Clara Barton, "collapsed from lack of sleep and a budding case of typhoid fever."[31]

In an attempt to contain the outbreak, hospital staff isolated some of the typhoid sufferers. One location, described as a "miserable little log-house near the Potomac River," contained 30 soldiers who "lay upon the floor, ill with fever." Another hospital near Blackford's Ford sheltered fever patients from the 13th New Jersey, several of whom died in the house. Medical workers also requisitioned homes in Sharpsburg village, crowding fever patients into one or two rooms while families continued occupying the same dwellings. This cramped living arrangement placed civilians in close range of dangerous bacteria.[32]

After the medical department commandeered the home of John Hamilton Smith, they allocated one room to Anna Holstein's relief association. The other room, John P. Smith recalled, was "devoted to fever-patients," in which a "narrow entry separated our room from the one where twenty men laid upon the floor." Around the same time, Anna Holstein remembered, Adam Michael's home next door "was filled in like manner" with infected patients. A few days later, Holstein

---

29 *New York Times*, October 28, 1862; Carter, *Four Brothers in Blue*, 123; Holt, *A Surgeon's Civil War*, 33.

30 *The Plymouth* [MA] *Rock*, November 27, 1862. Paulding's obituary appears in the Find a Grave database, https://www.findagrave.com/memorial/8236025/henry-b_-paulding; John Banks, "Antietam: Two Rural Graves, Two Tragedies," blog, *John Banks' Civil War Blog*, August 18, 2013, http://john-banks.blogspot.com/2013/08/antietam-two-rural-graves-two-tragedies.html. The soldier was Corporal William D. Warrimer. Banks posted a scanned image of the letter.

31 Holstein, *Three Years in Field Hospitals*, 21; "Clara Barton at Antietam," ANB.

32 Holstein, *Three Years in Field Hospitals*, 18-24; Samuel Toombs, *Reminiscences of the War: Comprising a Detailed Account of the Experiences of the Thirteenth Regiment New Jersey Volunteers* (Orange, NJ, 1878), 33. The deaths occurred from Nov. 8–Dec. 5, while the 13th picketed Blackford's Ford.

recalled that the fever patients in Adam Michael's home "were all moved into our house," referring to the Smiths. Not surprisingly, the families of John Hamilton Smith and Adam Michael soon became violently sick—along with other citizens in the battlefield region.[33]

Among those affected was John J. Middlekauff, who lived near Fairplay. "He was sick—I do not know how many months," resident Ezra Nally remembered. "He was sick in the fall of 1862. I saw him very often before he got sick—worked for him a great deal." Jeremiah Kuhn ran Sharpsburg's post office in 1862, but fell ill after the battle. "Mr. Koons was Postmaster," Moses Poffenberger recalled, and "I was assistant, but he was sick most of the time." Another resident remembered caring for U.S. troops suffering from "fevers and various ailments." The patients, she recounted, "made it sickly at our home," and "although the greatest care was taken and disinfectants were used liberally all about the house, my little sister was taken with typhoid fever and was very ill."[34]

Certainly, other residents contracted health problems. If hundreds of soldiers caught diseases after the battle, one could assume that the outbreak affected the local community on a similar scale. But where lies the evidence? Do any primary sources support that civilians, like the soldiers, went down by the hundreds?

As a matter of fact, yes—a Sharpsburg physician documented the cases day-by-day as the epidemic unfolded.

*   *   *

"My name is Augustin A. Biggs," stated Sharpsburg's doctor in August 1888. "[M]y occupation is M.D. I am 75 years of age" and during the Civil War, "I was a doctor of medicine by profession and practice and have been in this place since 1836."[35]

---

33 Claim of John H. Smith (*RG* 92, Book F, Box 86, Claim F-1205). John Hamilton Smith's claim cited $170.16 in hospital rent; Smith, *Reminiscences of Sharpsburg*. John P. Smith, a son of John Hamilton Smith, wrote, "I know that one of the doctors . . . had charge of the Lutheran Church Hospital, as it was called, and the hospital in our house;" Holstein, *Three Years in Field Hospitals*, 19-20.

34 Claims of John J. Middlekauff (No. 1261) and Hezekiah Myers (No. 1301). Poffenberger did not specify when Kuhn was sick, but Dr. A. A. Biggs's medical daybook cites several appointments with Kuhn in Dec. 1862; Williams, HWC, vol. 1, 2:359-362.

35 Claim of John Miller (*RG* 123, No. 2227). A. A. Biggs testified in Miller's case on Aug. 15, 1888.

A page from the medical daybook of Dr. Augustin A. Biggs.

John Clinton Frye, Western Maryland Room

In 1862, Dr. A. A. Biggs lived on West Main Street in Sharpsburg village with Elizabeth (Wagner) Biggs, his second wife, and four children. The 49-year-old physician was "a man of medium height, squarely built, and of great physical strength." He made daily house calls in 1862–1863, seeing patients on weekends and holidays, as well. His wide territory included Sharpsburg, Keedysville, and parts of Rohrersville, Tilghmanton, and Bakersville. While working this vigorous schedule, Biggs documented his appointments in medical daybooks. In these chronological entries, he logged the dates, the names of the household heads, and the dispensed medicines or types of procedure. In some entries, he listed the household member treated, identifying them as "wife," "child," or first name.

From March 1 through September 14, 1862, Biggs made 1,427 house calls in 198 workdays. This schedule computes to a daily average of 7.20 patients. He performed various procedures, ranging from diagnosing ailments and delivering babies to lancing abscesses and extracting teeth. From March 1–September 14, Dr. Biggs's busiest time was May, in which he averaged 10.61 daily house calls. His slowest month was July, for which he recorded, on average, 5.61 house calls per day. In the 14 days preceding the Battle of Antietam, he completed 8.8 appointments per day.[36]

Granted, the Sharpsburg community was not free of sickness before the battle. In May 1862, five children died. A few weeks later, diphtheria claimed the lives of two other Sharpsburg youths. However, Dr. Biggs's daybook entries, cross-referenced with local death records and newspaper articles, do not support the presence of a significant disease outbreak in the weeks preceding the battle.[37]

The Antietam Campaign interrupted Biggs's medical practice, and he recorded no entries from September 15–19. During this time, the doctor and his family sheltered inside their stone home in Sharpsburg village. From September 20–30,

36 Williams, HWC, vol. 2, 1:838; Dr. Augustin A. Biggs, Daybooks and Ledgers, Vol. 2, 2/23/1862–8/7/1863, WMR, hereafter cited as the Biggs daybook. These books are part of a large collection spanning Biggs's career, including medical appointments and finances. In Biggs's daybooks, he listed his patient appointments chronologically, by day. He often listed neighboring residents on the same pages, which suggests that Biggs made house calls, traveling from home-to-home, instead of conducting in-office appointments. Fifty-four entries from Aug. 1862–May 1863 noted cash payments, with no dosage or procedure listed. In addition, Biggs logged more than 200 vaccines in Mar. and Apr. 1862. Neither the billing transactions nor the vaccines are factored into the total number of house calls cited.

37 Lucy Grayson Ditto, "Journal of Deaths in Sharpsburg," Sharpsburg Historical Society. The Sharpsburg Historical Society is hereafter known as SHS, and the notebook is hereafter cited as the Ditto journal; Smith, *Reminiscences of Sharpsburg*, 76. Two daughters of Mortimer and Lucinda Shuford died of diphtheria during the summer of 1862.

Biggs only saw 53 patients in 11 days. This lower average of 4.8 daily appointments might correlate, in part, with military traffic congesting local roads during the battle's aftermath, hindering the doctor's ability to make his usual rounds.

Interestingly, his treatments changed in late September. In the six weeks preceding the battle, his most commonly administered medications were calomel, quinine, opium, potassium chlorate, and a calomel-opium combination written as *cal et opii*. He dispensed these drugs evenly, and each constituted 4–9 percent of all medicines administered from August 1–September 14. From September 20–30, though, his administration of quinine and potassium chloride dropped to zero. Meanwhile, opium, calomel, and *cal et opii* jumped to 25 percent of all medicines prescribed. This marked the beginning of an unusual trend.

In the first half of October, Biggs's average of daily appointments increased to 11.43. From October 16–31, this figure climbed to 15.94 house calls per day. Similar patterns continued in November. During the first half of the month, the physician logged 19.3 daily appointments. The peak occurred on November 15, when he completed 30 house calls in a single day.

Of his 407 logged entries for October and November, he administered opium and *cal et opii* 16.5 percent of the time. Also present in his logs but less frequent were quinine, calomel, turpentine, potassium chloride, and blue mass.[38]

December's house calls declined to 9.94 appointments per day but remained above the pre-battle average. Biggs's dosage of opium and *cal et opii* also dropped in December. After that, his leading medicine was quinine, followed by potassium chloride, turpentine, calomel, and blue mass. From January–May 1863, the daybook entries returned to pre-battle averages. No unusual trends appear in these five months, and Biggs documented 6.62 daily appointments.

To summarize Biggs's daybook entries, his daily appointments from March 1–September 14, 1862, and January 1–May 31, 1863, were 7.20 and 6.62, respectively, averaging 6.91. From October–December 1862, he logged 13.74 entries per day—about twice the usual amount.

It is also essential to consider the number of households needing medical attention. In the six weeks before the battle, from August 1–September 14, Biggs's daybook contains 133 accounts, each assigned to a different head of household. From October 21–December 2, the height of the outbreak, there were 160 accounts. In other words, the number of households needing medical aid increased

---

38 Biggs daybook, WMR. Biggs's low number of patient visits from September 20–30 may also reflect his need to address the substantial artillery damages to his Sharpsburg village home.

by 17 percent, and Biggs's daily appointments doubled. So from a public health standpoint, something was clearly wrong in the community. But what specifically sickened these people? Evidence suggests that the major diseases reported in Antietam's field hospitals—typhoid fever, diarrhea, and dysentery—also infected the local population. Dr. Biggs's dispensed medicines shed light on this connection.[39]

Opium, being an anodyne, provided pain relief. It was also a sedative, and physicians frequently prescribed it to slow bowel movements in cases of diarrhea. Calomel was a mercury-based cathartic. Nineteenth-century doctors, largely unaware of mercury's poisonous effects, used calomel to treat various ailments, including diarrhea, fevers, and pneumonia.

Blue mass and blue pill also contained mercury. Doctors often used these purgatives to treat constipation, as well as diarrhea and dysentery. Dr. Biggs also dispensed *cal et opii*—a mixture of calomel and opium. One historical source cited that physicians administered calomel and opium pills to treat peritonitis and bilious colic. Symptoms for both of these conditions include diarrhea, abdominal pain, and fever.

Quinine, an antipyretic, prevented malaria and helped control fevers. In 1855, a physician reported that quinine "has lately been highly recommended in typhoid fever." Likewise, Civil War historian Bell Irvin Wiley listed "blue pill and quinine" as a standard treatment for typhoid sufferers. Potassium chlorate served as a diuretic to increase urine production and an antipyretic to reduce fevers. A medical book from the Civil War period cited that potassium chlorate "has been especially recommended by some in various forms of cachexia," including "typhoid and eruptive fevers." Other sources associate potassium chlorate with the treatment of diphtheria.[40]

Oil of turpentine, a diuretic, antipyretic, and stimulant, was used for numerous health problems, including dysentery and typhoid fever. A Union hospital steward recalled after the war, "In that era most medical men regarded turpentine as little

---

39 Biggs daybook, WMR.

40 Terry Reimer, director of research, National Museum of Civil War Medicine, email messages to author, June 2020; Dr. Jonathan S. Jones, medical historian, email messages to author, June 2020; Bollet, *Civil War Medicine*, 235-242; W. W. Hall, *Health at Home, or Hall's Family Doctor* (Hartford, CT, 1879), 730-740; Henry Hartshorne, *Essentials of the Principles and Practice of Medicine: A Handbook for Students and Practitioners* (Philadelphia, 1881), 602-618; Wiley, *The Life of Billy Yank*, 137-139; Henry Beasley, *The Book of Prescriptions: Containing 2900 Prescriptions Collected from the Practice of the Most Eminent Physicians and Surgeons* (Philadelphia, 1855), 281, 287.

short of a sheet-anchor in the treatment of typhoid, and needless to say, it was a standard remedy in our regimental hospital."[41]

Dr. Biggs's daybook chronicles dozens of families who required extensive care during the outbreak. Villagers were particularly vulnerable, perhaps from drinking contaminated water from the Big Spring or wells located on town lots. Some of the afflicted townsfolk included the families of Judge David Smith, Jacob H. Grove, Rhinehart Line, and Levin Benton. Another household in the village, headed by widow Elizabeth Miller Blackford, was among the sickest.

The daughter of Squire Jacob Miller, Elizabeth Miller Blackford lived in Sharpsburg village with four daughters and two sons. We don't know how many people in her household became infected in late 1862, but two daughters—Helen, 24, and Jeannette, 15—were among Dr. Biggs's patients. Describing Elizabeth's family, Squire Miller wrote that "Hellen and Janet" suffered from a "severe attack of the tayfoy fevour."

Dr. Biggs made 26 calls to Widow Blackford's home between November 7–30. During the first week, he dispensed quinine, calomel, and muriatic acid. Doses of turpentine oil, quinine, anodyne, morphine, and opium appear in Blackford's entries for the remainder of the month. Everyone in the household survived, but her daughter Jeanette recovered slowly. In early February 1863, Elizabeth wrote to her sister in Iowa, "[Y]ou know I have had much to contend with much sickness . . . Jennette has gone up to stay awhile with cousin Harriet she was sick so long I thought a change would be an advantage to her."[42]

Other villagers experienced similar health crises. John P. Smith recalled, "The latter part of the year 1862 was exceedingly sickly, owing it is thought to the stench caused by Sept. 17, 1862." Smith knew this personally, for he, his parents, and siblings became seriously ill during the hospital occupation of their home. Their adjoining neighbor, Samuel Michael, wrote in November 1862, "John [H.] Smith

41 Johnson, *Muskets and Medicine*, 157-60; Michael A. Flannery, *Civil War Pharmacy: A History of Drugs, Drug Supply and Provision, and Therapeutics for the Union and Confederacy* (Carbondale, IL, 2017), 122. Per Flannery, doctors used oil of turpentine to treat "intestinal fluxes" like dysentery as well as fevers, "especially typhoid;" Hartshorne, *Essentials*, 617; Bollett, *Civil War Medicine*, 236. Bollett wrote, "Turpentine was used orally for chronic diarrhea and, sometimes, typhoid fever."

42 Biggs daybook, WMR. Biggs listed Blackford initially as "Mrs. F[ranklin] Blackford" and thereafter as "Mrs. Blackford." Franklin Blackford, a son of Col. John Blackford, died in a hunting accident in 1852; The 1860 Federal census for Sharpsburg lists Elizabeth Blackford and her six children in Dwelling #1571. The four daughters were unmarried in 1862 and likely lived with Elizabeth; Jacob Miller to Amelia and Christian Houser, December 7, 1862, WMR; Elizabeth Miller Blackford to Amelia Houser, February 8, 1863, WMR.

was sick with the same fever but is up and about the room. Mary and little John [P. Smith] is both poorly." In early December, Squire Jacob Miller wrote, "[N]early all or quite all of John Smith famly wore down [with fever] but are getting better."

Dr. Biggs ministered to the Smiths nineteen times between November 26 and December 10. His notation of the word "family" on November 29 suggests that the entire household—both parents and four children—may have been sick. Dosing them with quinine, opium, camphor, turpentine, and a hydrochloric acid solution, Biggs helped the Smiths overcome their life-threatening fevers.[43]

Farm families also fell ill. Dr. Biggs logged thirteen house calls to Henry Piper's farm from September 27–December 7. At least one appointment involved Henry's wife, Elizabeth. The doctor primarily medicated the Pipers with opium and calomel for ten weeks, suggesting that diarrhea or dysentery may have sickened the family. Next, Biggs dosed Joseph Poffenberger and his wife with the same medicines, giving them opium in five of six visits and calomel once. In mid-October, he prescribed opium to the household of Samuel Mumma Sr., citing an unidentified daughter as one of the patients.

The treatment plan differed for the family of Philip and Elizabeth Pry. Dr. Biggs made nine visits to the Pry house between October 14–23, administering quinine and turpentine, indicating that fever possibly sickened one or more of the Prys. David R. Miller's family presented a similar challenge. Biggs made 18 house calls to the Miller farm from November 5–December 2. After initially giving them opium, Biggs switched to different drugs as their afflictions progressed, including quinine and potassium chloride, which were associated with treating fevers. The Millers overcame whatever plagued them, but other families weren't as fortunate.[44]

---

43 John P. Smith, "Register of Persons Who Have Died in Sharpsburg, Washington County Maryland and Surrounding Neighborhood From the Year 1831," loose-leaf notebook, 1904, Washington County Historical Society. This notebook is hereafter known as the Smith register and the repository is cited as WCHS; Samuel Michael to David Michael, November 27, 1862, WMR; Jacob Miller to Amelia and Christian Houser, December 7, 1862, WMR; Biggs daybook, WMR. Neither Biggs nor Smith mentioned a specific illness, but Smith wrote that fever-sickened soldiers convalesced in his home. Also, Bigg's dispensed medicines are associated with treating typhoid fever. In *The Book of Prescriptions*, 21, Beasley wrote that tonics of hydrochloric acid, given "in small doses and properly diluted," were often given for "malignant typhus and scarlet fevers."

44 Biggs daybook, WMR; Claim of David R. Miller (F-1499). Miller neglected to include hay losses in his citizens' appraisement "because it was made up at Sharpsburg, Md. at a time when he was sick at home & therefore not present & the oversight was not discovered until some time afterward." The majority of Sharpsburg's citizens' appraisements took place between Oct. 1862–Jan. 1863, roughly the same span in which Biggs treated Miller's household.

Based on his daybook entries, Dr. Biggs traveled to the home of William and Margaret Roulette seven times from October 14–19. He dispensed opium during the first appointments, but it's not clear what medications followed. On October 21, the couple's youngest child, Carrie May Roulette, died at the age of one. Later, William wrote about his daughter's death, describing her as "a charming little girl 20-months-old . . . just beginning to talk."[45]

How many other civilians died during the 1862 epidemic? Dr. Biggs's daybook provides valuable insight regarding illnesses but lists no mortality statistics. Fortunately, other records exist that shed light on the deaths of Sharpsburg citizens after the battle.

One source is Washington County burial data. When examining the number of Sharpsburg-area burials from 1850–1870, records show an increase of interments in Mountain View Cemetery and the Mumma graveyard from October 1862–April 1863.[46]

Fairview Cemetery in Keedysville tells a similar story. Established in 1872, Fairview contains prewar and Civil War-period remains transferred from local graveyards. Of these, records show 110 deaths from the years 1850–61 and 1864–70. This 18-year sample averaged 6.11 annual interments. From September 1862–April 1863, there were 23 burials—an increase of 73 percent.[47]

---

45 E. P. to Sally Farran, October 4, 1862, *Dan Masters' Civil War Chronicles*; Claim of Henry Piper (No. 445); Biggs daybook; Wiley, *The Life of Billy Yank*, 138-139; William Roulette to Mary Hubbard, December 31, 1862, cited in Clem, "Farmer Cheers Federals at Antietam;" Ditto journal; *Maryland Free Press*, October 31, 1862. The newspaper announced, "Near Sharpsburg, on the 21st inst., Carrie May, youngest daughter of William and Margaret Ann Rulett, aged 1 year, 7 months and 27 days."

46 Samuel Webster Piper, *Washington County Cemeteries—Samuel Piper and the DAR*, Volume 1, 1936, WHILBR, https://digital.whilbr.org/digital/collection/p16715coll31. These burial records are hereafter cited as WCC; Maryland Tombstone Transcription Project, Washington County, online database, http://www.usgwtombstones.org/maryland/maryland.html. Burial records for smaller graveyards in Sharpsburg, on church lots and farms, revealed no spikes in 1862; Mountain View Cemetery, established in 1883 on a former tract of Squire Jacob Miller, contains many remains formerly interred in Sharpsburg's church graveyards. Mountain View records cite 4.38 yearly interments from 1853–61, and 3.0 annual burials from 1863–68. This combined average is 3.69 deaths per year. By comparison, records cite seven burials from October 1862–April 1863; Douglas M. Mumma, *The Mumma Graveyard, Antietam National Battlefield, Sharpsburg, Maryland*, typescript, Mumma.org, July 2014, https://www.mumma. org/archives/MummaCemetery.pdf. The Mumma graveyard, situated on the Antietam battlefield, shows an average of 1.6 interments per year from 1797–Oct. 1862, and Feb. 1863–1964. In 14 weeks, from Nov. 1862–Jan. 1863, there were six burials.

47 "WA-II-1112 Keedysville Survey District," architectural survey file, Maryland Historical Trust, sec. 8, p. 10; WCC, WHILBR; Maryland Tombstone Transcription Project.

Two death registers, written by John P. Smith and Lucy Grayson Ditto, also shed light on the number of civilian deaths from late 1862 through early 1863. By cross-referencing both registers, we find the following. From 1852-61 and 1865-75, Smith and Ditto logged 530 deaths in the Sharpsburg area. In this 21-year sample, there were approximately 25 mortalities each year. From October 1862–April 1863, there were 37 deaths in a six-month span.[48]

Thus, Dr. Biggs's daybook entries, burial records, and local death registers all show increases in sickness and death in the Sharpsburg community from October 1862–April 1863. To further support this argument, a closer look at the cases is necessary.

*   *   *

One of the first civilian deaths after the Battle of Antietam may have occurred on Lot 74W on the "back street" of Sharpsburg village, known today as West Chapline Street. Benjamin and Elizabeth Highbarger Bender, their last name also known as Painter, married the year prior. They were the parents of a one-year-old daughter, Perdida May. Dr. Biggs logged no visits to the Benders' home in the six weeks preceding the battle, suggesting that the family had no serious medical issues at the time. However, on September 23, six days after the battle, the Benders summoned Dr. Biggs to their home, and the physician returned the following day. On September 25, Perdida May Bender died.[49]

From October 13–15, Dr. Biggs logged seven house calls with the Benders' relatives, who lived nearby. Samuel Painter, Benjamin Bender's father, resided next door on Lot 73. Biggs gave Painter *cal et opii* and opium, perhaps to treat diarrhea or a related bowel problem. He dispensed opium and potassium chlorate to John Bender, Benjamin's uncle. He also treated the household of Elizabeth Bender's

---

48 Smith register, WCHS; Ditto journal, SHS. John P. Smith witnessed the battle and later recorded local deaths from 1831 until 1904. Ditto, a postwar resident of Sharpsburg, edited Smith's work and added deaths after 1904. These chronological records list the name of the deceased, date of death, and place of burial. For some the entries, Smith and Ditto noted ages of the deceased, maiden names, and names of parents and siblings.

49 Biggs daybook, WMR. Perdida May Bender's death appears in the Smith register, Ditto journal, and WCC. Benjamin Bender's parents, Samuel and Elizabeth Bender / Painter, owned Lots 73 and 74 in 1862. See land records IN 8 / 32, WMCKK 1 / 727, and IN 17 / 166 (Lot 74), and IN 4 / 417 and 102 / 83 (Lot 73). Benjamin and Elizabeth Bender lived in their respective parents' households in 1860 and owned no real estate in 1862. The 1870 census lists the couple next to Benjamin's parents (Lot 73) and the 1877 Sharpsburg village map depicts them on Lot 74W.

brother, Samuel Highbarger. Like the Benders, Samuel and Helen Highbarger do not appear in Biggs's daybook before the battle. On October 14, though, the physician made an emergency call to the couple's home on West Main Street. Their infant died two days later.[50]

The demise of these two Sharpsburg children was possibly a coincidence—or not. During the same span, ill fortune struck Roger and Elizabeth Willet, the Highbargers' near-neighbors. Biggs logged no entries for the Willets in August or September, but he documented two visits to their home on October 15 and 17. On October 19, their son died. John H. Willet was only 21.[51]

Other deaths in the village occurred around this time. Ann Teresa Jackson Gloss was 23 years old in 1862. She and her husband, David Gloss, had a seven-month-old boy, John Francis. Census records suggest that the couple lived with Ann's mother on Lot 121 in the southwest part of Sharpsburg village—a house that Dr. A. A. Biggs visited on November 2.

The Sharpsburg doctor first treated Ann Gloss with opium, then returned to administer quinine and camphor twice the following day. Sadly, her health continued to decline. Over the next five days, Biggs made ten house calls to the Gloss-Jackson household, dosing the young woman with more opium and quinine. On November 9, Ann passed away—but sickness in the household continued. Biggs returned on November 15, writing the word "child" in the daybook entry. He tended to the young patient again on the 18th, but could not save him. 7-month-old John Francis Gloss succumbed to illness the same day.[52]

---

50 Biggs daybook, WMR; Smith register, WCHS; Ditto journal, SHS; WCC, WHILBR. The deceased child may have been Cora, Franklin, or Margaret Highbarger. All three infants are buried with their parents, but the children's death dates are unknown. Land records IN 12 / 214 and 74 / 657 confirm the Highbargers' 1862 ownership of Lot 127W. Helen Highbarger later purchased Lot 39 via WMCKK 3 / 170.

51 The 1860 Federal census for Sharpsburg lists the Willets four dwellings from Samuel Highbarger, and near Abner Highbarger, Samuel Swain, and Col. John Miller, all of whom lived on West Main Street. John Willet's headstone inscription lists his Oct. 19 death. Ditto cited Willet's death as Nov. 10 and WCC cited Nov. 25.

52 Biggs daybook, WMR; WCC, WHILBR; Smith register, WCHS. The Jackson-Gloss household appears in the 1860 Federal census for Sharpsburg, Dwelling #1723. Land records UU / 318 and 99/500 show the Jackson family's ownership of Lot 121. Angeline Jackson, testifying in David Smith's claims (Nos. 1244, 1262, and 10237), recalled, "[M]y sister Mrs. Ann Terressa Jackson Gloss, died Nov. 9, 1862, and I distinctly remembered that we returned to the farm a few days after her funeral." Angeline added, "I have examined the family record in the Bible at my brothers house here in Sharpsburg in order to fix the exact date of the death of my sister, and I know it is correct."

In 1862, Adam Michael owned two village lots and three farm tracts in Sharpsburg. The retired farmer and his wife, Nancy Reel Michael, resided on Lot 55, next to John Hamilton Smith. Four of the Michaels' adult children, Elizabeth, Samuel, Kate, and Caleb, lived with their parents in 1862. Another son, David Michael, resided in Indiana. After the battle, medical forces converted Adam Michael's town lots into hospitals, establishing a fever ward in the primary residence. Nancy Michael and her daughters protested the takeover, to no avail. Hospital staff filled the home with diseased soldiers, and typhoid fever eventually infected the family.

The Michaels first appear in Dr. Biggs's medical logs on October 21. Over the course of seven weeks, the physician made 44 visits to the Michaels' home, often treating them twice, and sometimes thrice, in a single day. One of the first patients was Elizabeth Michael, the oldest daughter, to whom Biggs prescribed calomel on October 21 and quinine and other medicines thereafter. Samuel Michael recalled that his sister Elizabeth "had been sick and was doing very well on Sunday previous to her death," he wrote to his brother. "She walked out into the garden and looked at her flowers. I was certain that she was going to recover." Elizabeth Michael passed away on October 24. According to Samuel, she "died from the typhoid fever the Doctor say."

Salmonella typhi also infected Kate and Caleb Michael. In ten visits from November 12–18, Biggs treated the siblings with quinine, turpentine, and morphine. During this time, unfortunately, typhoid fever spread to Nancy Michael, their mother. Dr. Biggs visited the ailing Michaels ten times in a one-week span. Despite Nancy's poor health, she managed to look over her children and "made soup while the old man held her up for Caleb and Kate." Dr. Biggs aggressively treated the family twice daily from November 26–30, and six times the first week of December. Both siblings survived.

Nancy Michael's symptoms worsened, though. Battling typhoid, grieving the loss of her daughter, and caring for Kate and Caleb exhausted the poor woman. The presence of dying soldiers inside the home added to her stress. "[S]he heard it upstairs," Samuel Michael wrote, referring to hospital activity, "and it frightened her and she just gave way." Furthermore, *S. typhi* likely perforated Nancy's intestines. "Mother complained but a short time," Samuel explained to his brother. "[W]as taken with three very severe hemorrages of the bowels—took place about 12 o'clock at night, the first one."

With bedridden siblings and a feeble father, Samuel Michael undertook most of the nursing duties by himself. "The night that she had her hemorrages," he recalled, referring to his mother, "I had nobody to assist me in the room—Kate not able to be up. I called the old man and got him to assist me, but I never experienced such a night as that was." Samuel spared his brother the graphic details of what he witnessed that evening, writing, "I had to do what I never expected I would have to do." Nancy Michael made it through the terrible night, but "died the next day 10 minutes before two." Concluding the tragic news to his brother, Samuel wrote, "She was a beautiful corpse."[53]

Deaths in the community continued. "The house across the way from mine was a hospital," Jacob McGraw remembered, "and the family there got what the doctors called camp fever, and some of 'em died." Among other casualties in late-1862 were William Show's child, who died on November 18, and John Shay, Jr., who passed away on December 9. John S. Reel, son of Henry Reel, received multiple treatments from Dr. Biggs in December but died on the 15th. Biggs also tended to Captain David Smith and his sister, Elizabeth Smith, several times from December 12–17, dosing each with potassium chloride and quinine. The captain overcame his ailment, but Elizabeth Smith died on December 17.[54]

People also became sick in nearby Tilghmanton. Over eight days in mid-October, tenant farmer Robert C. Albert and his wife, Ann, lost two sons, ages one and two. In the same locality, several members of the Manor Church died within a short time. "We feel bereaved," an obituary lamented, "at the departure of so many of our dear members in so short a span, yet we sorrow not as those who have no hope." The obituary did not mention the causes of deaths, but we should not rule out infectious maladies. Richard Clem, a Washington County historian, toured a Bakersville cemetery containing graves of Tilghmanton-area residents. He observed, "In studying dates of death, the increase in local burials following Antietam became evident . . . civilians contracted typhoid, diphtheria and scarlet

53 Biggs daybook, WMR. Biggs listed Caleb and Kate under Adam Michael's account, supporting that both siblings lived in their father's household in 1862; Claim of Adam Michael (199-161). Samuel Michael testified, "During the late rebellion he lived with his father, Adam Michael, in Sharpsburg, Md.;" Samuel Michael to David Michael, November 27, 1862, WMR; Williams, HWC, vol. 2, 1:764-765; Jacob Miller to Amelia and Christian Houser, December 7, 1862, WMR. Nancy (Reel) Michael was the sister of farmers David, Samuel, and Henry Reel.

54 Johnson, BA, 117; Biggs daybook; Ditto journal; WCC; Smith register; In the claim of Moses Cox (G-1657), William Show testified "that he worked and resided on claimant's farm during and after the battle of Antietam." Reilly in BOA wrote that John Shay, Sr., in 1862 "lived at the edge of town as you go out the Harpers Ferry Road." This matches Lot 21, where the 1877 village map depicts Shay residing. Solomon Renner testified in David Smith's claims, "The Captain lived in town at the time" of the battle. Elizabeth Smith's 1862 residence is unknown.

fever while caring for wounded soldiers who carried these highly contagious diseases."[55]

South of Tilghmanton lived John C. Middlekauff and his family. A karst topographical study found that the Middlekauff farm is part of a Duffield rock outcrop complex, which allowed "pollution to enter the water easily at a rate of 2 inches per hour and reach the shallow groundwater table below the surface that supplied drinking water to the families." In 1862, the study argued, groundwater near the Middlekauff farm's springhead and wells may have been only "30–42 inches under surface in the wet months of the year." Purportedly, rainfall after the battle washed contaminants from nearby graves, camps, and hospitals "into the sinkholes near the springhead on the farm." Primary sources do not confirm whether this drinking water or another contagion sickened the Middlekauffs, but typhoid fever ravaged the family.

The 1860 Federal census for Sharpsburg lists John C. Middlekauff with his wife Elizabeth, two sons, and three daughters, Barbara, Kate, and Emma. In 1862, another daughter, Ann Mary Middlekauff Wyand, lived near Keedysville with her two-year-old daughter, Emma Kate, and husband, Joshua Wyand. After the battle, disease spread to both households. In a two-day span, November 25 and 26, Ann Mary and Emma Kate Wyand passed away. A newspaper grouped mother and daughter in the same obituary, reporting that Ann Mary died "of typhoid fever."

Salmonella typhi then spread to John C. Middlekauff's home. Kate Middlekauff died on December 5 at the age of 18. Less than two weeks later, 19-year-old Barbara Middlekauff perished. It's not known how the sickness infected others in the household, but John C. Middlekauff couldn't evade the deadly disease. After losing three daughters and one granddaughter, the 57-year-old farmer died on January 6, 1863. The *Maryland Free Press* reported that Middlekauff passed away "at his residence, 3 miles North of Sharpsburg, of typhoid fever." Not including the death of Emma Kate Wyand, the newspaper informed its readers that in six weeks, "four members of the family have been removed by the hand of death, first three

55 *Maryland Free Press*, October 31, 1862 and November 7, 1862. The 1860 Federal census, Tilghmanton district, lists the Alberts in Dwelling #1293 and the 1870 census lists them in the same area. The deceased sons were Lewis and George Albert; "Obituaries," *Gospel Visitor* (Columbiana, OH), Vol. XIII, January 1863, 63, https://archive.org/details/gospel3112kurt/page/n69/mode/2up; Richard Clem, "Misery Lasts Long After Antietam Battle," *Washington* [DC] *Times*, September 22, 2007, https://www.washingtontimes.com/news/2007/sep/22/misery-lasts-long-after-antietam-battle/.

adult daughters, and now the father—May the Lord comfort the bereaved family in their sore afflictions."[56]

*   *   *

Several women in the community gave birth during the epidemic, exposing newborns to dangerous diseases. Rhinehart Line's wife, Dr. Biggs observed, "had typhoid fever for several days before confinement." After delivering a boy, her "fever continued about three weeks after confinement." Nevertheless, Mrs. Line and her baby survived.

Mary Jane Rohrback Mumma, 25, lived near the Lower Bridge with her parents, Henry B. and Martha Rohrback. Mary Jane's husband, Henry C. Mumma, and their daughter, Martha Ada, also resided in the household. On November 4, Dr. Biggs helped Mary Jane deliver a daughter, but the baby only "lived a few hours and died." Mary Jane may have suffered from an illness at the time of delivery, for Biggs noted, "Mothers health not very good previous." The next night, Mary Jane "was found delirious" and the following morning presented symptoms of jaundice. Despite Biggs's treatments, the young woman remained "insensible," fell into a "profound coma," and died on the fourth day after delivery.

After the war, Mary Jane's husband testified in Henry B. Rohrback's claims case for Antietam-related damages. Asked if the Union army had a hospital on the Rohrback farm, Mumma replied, "Yes, sir. I think that is where my wife caught her death. They brought the wounded soldiers in there and she contracted a disease from them. She had the jaunders."[57]

---

56 *Maryland Free Press*, January 2, 1863, 2A, and January 16, 1863, 3B; Mumma, *The Mumma Graveyard*, WCC, WHILBR. The 1860 Federal census for Sharpsburg lists the Middlekauffs in Dwelling #1485 and the Wyands in Dwelling #1441; J. Scott Shipe, "Sharpsburg Maryland—Typhoid Waterborne Outbreak—1862–63. Historical Analysis," YouTube video, *Water Advocacy*, February 20, 2019, https://www.youtube.com/watch?v=XgqCIvo5lJ0; Shipe, email messages to author.

57 Biggs, *The Obstetrical Records of Dr. Augustin Biggs, 1836–1888*, entries 1315 and 1354; Biggs daybook; Hildebrand, "Recollections of Martha Ada Thomas;" Claim of Henry B. Rohrback (No. 1323); Biggs's obstetrical records list Mary Jane's death as Dec. 10, but WCC, Smith's register, and Biggs's daybook support that she died on Nov. 10. The deceased newborn, per WCC and Samuel Webster Piper's *Piper Family History*, was also named Mary Jane. Biggs did not specify the mother's cause of death, but delirium is a common symptom of typhoid fever. Jaundice, in rare cases, can accompany *S. typhi*. See "Typhoid Fever With Jaundice," World Health Organization, https://applications.emro.who.int/imemrf/Professional_Med_J_Q/Professional_Med_J_Q_2015_22_4_439_442.pdf.

Soon after Mary Jane's death, Dr. Biggs returned to Henry B. Rohrback's farm several times to treat an unidentified household member. The family's sickness abated but may have spread to Henry's brothers on the adjoining property.

Noah and Elias B. Rohrback jointly owned the farm south of Henry B. Rohrback. Elias was 41, unmarried with no children, and lived with Noah and his family. On November 4, the same day that Mary Jane Mumma gave birth to her sickly child, Elias B. Rohrback requested medical help. From November 4–20, Dr. Biggs visited Elias sixteen times. Drugs given during the first week included opium, camphor, anodyne, and "tannin" (tannic acid, an astringent). Afterward, he treated Rohrback with quinine, blue mass, and muriatic acid. None of these medications helped the farmer shake off the disease, and Elias B. Rohrback died on November 21.[58]

The outbreak affected other residents east of Antietam Creek. Joseph and Mary Thomas, the parents of three boys, lived between Henry B. Rohrback and John Ecker. The Thomas's house after the battle, their claim alleged, "was used as a hospital for several weeks." On October 1, Dr. Biggs began treating the Thomas household. His ongoing care of the family lasted nearly three months. On November 11, Franklin Thomas died at the age of 16. Surviving family members still needed medical aid, and Biggs continued making house calls to the Thomas farm until December 22.[59]

The Sharpsburg doctor also tended to Jacob Snively, a 77-year-old resident of Eakles Mills. In six treatments from October 10–17, Biggs dosed the retired farmer with opium, astringents, and tannic acid, but Snively died on October 17.[60]

From October 5–26, Dr. Biggs made 15 calls to the home of Alfred and Elizabeth Stine Keedy, who lived in the Keedysville area with five children. Biggs did not specify how many family members were sick, but Elizabeth Keedy died on October 26. Afterward, Biggs's continued visits to the Keedy's home suggest that other family members remained ill. Elizabeth Keedy's older brother, Harmon Stine, also took a turn for the worse. On October 21, Biggs medicated the

---

58 Biggs daybook; Smith register; Ditto journal. The 1860 Federal census for Sharpsburg lists Elias and Noah Rohrback in Dwelling #1452. Elias never married, and devised his estate to Noah in his last will and testament, dated Nov. 12, 1862 (Will liber E / folio 644). Flannery in *Civil War Pharmacy*, 119, described camphor as a stimulant and an anodyne, "used frequently in the treatment of typhoid."

59 Biggs daybook; Claim of Joseph Thomas (*RG* 92, F-611).

60 Biggs daybook. The 1860 Federal census for Sharpsburg lists Jacob Snively in the household of his son, Washington C. Snively, Dwelling #1505.

35-year-old farmer with opium, and gave Stine other medicines in six appointments over the next nine days. Harmon Stine died on October 30, four days after the death of his sister.[61]

Before the battle, some residents suffered from various illnesses, which weakened their immune systems and made them vulnerable to catching a secondary infection. Martha Anna "Georgia" Buchanan, a 20-year-old granddaughter of Col. John Miller, may have been one of these persons. Described as a "beautiful and accomplished lady," Georgia was among those who sheltered in Killiansburg Cave from September 15–18. While exposed to the elements, the lass presented signs of being unwell. One villager feared that "pore Georgia . . . would die there she was so much exasted." Young Georgia survived the cave but died on January 31, 1863. Her cause of death is unknown, but if she was sick before the battle, a subsequent infection like typhoid fever or dysentery could have proved fatal.[62]

84-year-old Daniel Miller was another member of the community who suffered from an underlying problem before September 17. A brother of Squire Jacob Miller, Daniel evacuated his Willow Spring farm near the East Woods on September 16. Afterward, the medical department took possession of Daniel's farm, forcing him to shelter with his son-in-law, Henry F. Neikirk. Squire Miller described Daniel's health in a letter to his daughter. "He was not well when he left home, the day before the big battle . . . when he got back he went to Henry Newkirks and continued there the balance of his time."

Whatever ailed Daniel Miller before the battle was not debilitating. Dr. Biggs dosed him on September 6 and 14 with buchu extract, a diuretic for treating bladder and urinary tract issues. After the battle, Biggs gave Daniel another dose of buchu on October 1 and an unknown medication the following day. Biggs did not log other appointments with Miller in October, perhaps a sign that the elderly man's health was improving.

---

61 Biggs daybook; Smith register; Ditto journal.

62 Elizabeth Miller Blackford to Amelia Houser, February 8, 1863, WMR; *Maryland Free Press*, February 13, 1863, 3A; Smith register; *Antietam Valley Record*, September 12, 1895. John P. Smith wrote in the *Valley Record*, "Among the number who sought refuge in this cave was Miss Georgianna Buchanan, daughter of Dr. James Buchanan." Smith's death register cites, "January 31—Georgiana Buchanan, dau of Dr. Buchanan." The 1860 Federal census for Sharpsburg lists Martha Buchanan in her mother's house, Dwelling #1695. The households of Roger Willet and Samuel Highbarger—where two persons died of possible disease in Oct.-Nov.1862—are listed on the same census page.

Squire Miller wrote that Daniel "came to town several times after he got back," but was soon "taken with a diarear [diarrhea] which was a very common complaint with the troops and Citizens. Both armies were afflicted with the disease." Miller recalled that Daniel "took sick on Monday or Tuesday and continued getting worse with sick vomiting spells." The days cited were probably Monday, November 10 and Tuesday, November 11, on which Dr. Biggs drugged Daniel Miller with opium and anodyne. "I sent once to see him on Thursday," Jacob Miller wrote, "and found him ill but he could still converse yet on almost any subject, but the next day I found him worse and so he continued failing."

Biggs treated Daniel daily from November 12–16, dispensing quinine and morphine, to no avail. "Your Unkle Daniel Miller is no more," Squire Miller informed his daughter. "He departed from us on Sunday 16th day of November last, between the hours of twelve and one o'clock, and was buried on Monday about the same hour of the day." In Daniel's final hours, Jacob recalled, he "appeared anxious this warfare should be settled but now it is nothing to him whether it is settled or not."[63]

As diarrhea, dysentery, and typhoid fever infected citizens and soldiers near Sharpsburg, other diseases swept across Western Maryland. On October 10, 1862, the Middletown *Valley Register* reported, "We bear a great deal of sickness in this vicinity at this time. The Diphtheria and Scarlet Fever prevails to a considerable extent in both town and country." On November 5, the *Herald of Freedom and Torch Light* estimated that 600 to 800 soldiers convalescing in Hagerstown "exhibit almost every form of disease and suffering."[64]

Scarlet fever infected persons in Boonsboro and other outlying towns, while diphtheria spread to the Antietam battlefield vicinity. Dr. T. H. Squire, based at the Locust Spring hospital on Bishop John Russell's farm, reported that "Private O. M. W." of the 16th Connecticut died of diphtheria on November 3. Isabella Fogg, a volunteer from Maine, visited soldiers at Smoketown hospital and found "that diphtheria has broken out among them, and in nearly every case proves fatal." One

---

63 Biggs daybook; Jacob Miller to Amelia and Christian Houser, December 7, 1862, WMR; Claims of Henry F. Neikirk (H-4108 and H-4109); *Maryland Free Press*, December 5, 1862; Williams, HWC, vol. 2, 1:752; F. R. Mason and Kathryn Garst, *The Michael Miller and Susanna Bechtol Family Record* (Bridgewater, VA, 1993), 77-79; Flannery, *Civil War Pharmacy*, 119. Flannery wrote that the fluid extract of buchu, a flowering plant, was "used in urinary tract and bladder infections."

64 *The Valley Register*, October 10, 1862; *Herald of Freedom and Torch Light*, November 5, 1862, 2C.

of the men, Fogg, reported, was "seized suddenly with diphtheria, caused by exposure, and lived but two or three hours."[65]

In the Keedysville-Boonsboro area, Daniel and Susan Thomas lost three children in three weeks. The first to pass was Hugh Thomas, age three, who died of diphtheria on November 7. His four-year-old brother, Daniel, died four days later, and sister Dora Bell, age one, passed away on November 23. Also near Keedysville, at the home of Christian Deaner, two young ladies died on the same day. Anna Catherine Storm and Mahala Young, ages 11 and 14, passed away on December 21.[66]

In the Sharpsburg-Rohrersville vicinity lived Daniel B. Grimm. The 44-year-old tailor raised six children with his second wife, Anna. Dr. Biggs began aggressively treating the family on November 1. Over the next three weeks, he logged 19 appointments, prescribing potassium chloride, quinine, muriatic acid, and a chloride soda solution. Susan Grimm, 19, died on November 10. Her five-year-old brother, Daniel, followed two weeks later. Their cause of death, based on the medicines Biggs dispensed, may have been diphtheria.[67]

Historian Kathleen Ernst wrote that epidemics after the battle "ravaged the county for months." Environmental researchers studying Antietam's aftermath sided with Ernst, finding that the Sharpsburg region suffered from illness "throughout the winter of 1862–63," until steady rainfall in the spring "helped

---

65 *Herald of Freedom and Torch Light*, November 5, 1862, 2F. The newspaper reported that 3-year-old Katie H. Smith of Boonsboro died "after a brief illness of scarlet fever;" Jacob Miller to Amelia and Christian Houser, December 7, 1862, WMR. Squire Miller, referring to his grandchildren in Boonsboro, wrote, "Jacob and Annmarys children nearly all or perhaps all had Scarlet fevour but are all getting well." Ann Mary Miller, Squire Miller's daughter, appears with her husband, Jacob H. Mumma, in the 1860 Federal census for Boonsboro, Dwelling #1225; *Catalogue of the Surgical Section of the United States Army Medical Museum* (Washington, DC, 1866), 275; Isabella Fogg to J. W. Hathaway, November 10, 1862. Further research may reveal additional cases of diphtheria at Sharpsburg in 1862–63.

66 *Maryland Free Press*, December 12, 1862, 3A. The newspaper published the deaths of the three Thomas children on the same date. The 1860 Federal census for Boonsboro lists Daniel and Susan Thomas and sons Daniel and Hugh in Dwelling #1439; *Maryland Free Press*, January 9, 1863. The 1860 Federal census for Boonsboro lists Christian Deaner's household in Dwelling #1406, and cites Ann C. Storm in her parents' household, Dwelling #1533. Mahala Young lived in Thomas Reeder's household in Pleasant Valley, Dwelling #1051.

67 Biggs daybook, WMR; Ditto journal. Potassium chloride and muriatic acid appear in Civil War-era formulas for diphtheria, but other diseases may have killed the Grimms. See Pascal Harrison Owen, *A Monograph on Diphtheria: Its History, Diagnosis and Treatment* (Montgomery, AL, 1861), 24-32. See also Reuben Ludlam, *A Course of Clinical Lectures on Diphtheria* (Chicago, 1863), 118-124.

flush out streams and replenish groundwater." According to local lore, "Some residents believed that the town did not recover until well after the war ended."[68]

Although daily appointments in A. A. Biggs's daybook returned to pre-battle averages in late 1862 and early 1863, his dispensed medicines and repeated visits to the same households propound that dangerous diseases remained in the area.[69]

For example, on December 19, Dr. Biggs began treating 20-year-old Cyrus Hoffman, the son of Susan Hoffman. Over the next two weeks, Biggs peppered the lad with different drugs, but his condition didn't improve. To get a second opinion, Biggs consulted with another local physician, Dr. Otho J. Smith, who owned a farm adjoining the Hoffmans. The subsequent treatment plan ranged from quinine and turpentine to veratri viride, morphine, and blistering. Nothing worked, and Cyrus Hoffman died on January 2, 1863.[70]

Barbara Ann Cost, the wife of Jacob H. Cost, met a similar fate. She gave birth to a child, Rolla, at the time of the battle but fell ill thereafter. Dr. Biggs began treating the Costs in November 1862, but his visits increased in December and January. At one point, he gave a "cough mixture" to someone in the home. Whatever sickness took hold of Barbara proved to be too strong. She died on February 18 at the age of 33. Biggs continued making calls to the Cost farm afterward, treating the family seven times from February 20–March 1. He

---

68 Ernst, *TATC*, 185. Ernst also described a smallpox outbreak in the Hagerstown area in late January 1863. On January 27, Otho Nesbitt of Clear Spring wrote, "The small pox is in town … Tis said there is one or 200 cases in Hagerstown. Persons are getting vaccinated everywhere." Another Clear Spring resident wrote in late January 1863, "The small pox that terrible disease is fearfully on the increase in town and even those that have been vaccinated have taken it. I dread it very much." Ernst cited Otho Nesbitt's diary, Jan. 27, 1863, and "Sister M." to Dr. Edward Kershner, Jan. 1863. Both sources are archived at the Clear Spring Historical Association, Clear Spring, MD. The same virus may have spread to the Sharpsburg environs, as Lucy Ditto noted in her journal that Mrs. James Groome died of smallpox on December 27; Browning and Silver, *An Environmental History*, 80.

69 Biggs daybook, WMR.

70 Claim of Susan Hoffman (*RG* 123, No. 1318); Biggs daybook; WCC. Biggs consulted with Dr. Smith on Dec. 26, 1862. Hoffman's formal name was Uriah Cyrus Hoffman, but the 1860 census and Dr. Biggs's daybook refer to him as Cyrus; Flannery in *Civil War Pharmacy*, 121 and 283, noted several conditions treated with veratri viride, including pneumonia, influenza, jaundice, and dysentery; Terry Reimer, email message to author, June 29, 2020. Blistering involved mechanical cupping or applying a chemical compound. This treatment "was done on the assumption that counter-irritation would relieve the primary irritation, or that it would draw blood to the affected area to promote healing." It was a very painful procedure and Biggs likely used it as a last resort.

dispensed opium, camphor, and an expectorant during this time and resorted to blistering on March 1. The following day, five-month-old Rolla Cost passed away.[71]

Elizabeth "Betsy" Good, 37, also died in early 1863. Unmarried with no children, Betsy co-owned and occupied Lot 12 in Sharpsburg village. Dr. Biggs treated her several times from January 29–February 8 with veratri viride, quinine, and valerian root. She died on February 8.[72]

Disease also spread to the household of Stephen P. and Maria Grove. Biggs paid thirteen visits to the Groves' Mount Airy farm throughout the first half of March, treating an unnamed child with quinine and blistering. Burial records show that the young patient did not pull through. Stephen Hays Grove, just shy of turning three, died on March 17, 1863.[73]

Raleigh Showman, one of the biggest landowners and slaveowners in Sharpsburg, required little medical care throughout late 1862 and early 1863. By March 29, though, the 49-year-old farmer had fallen gravely ill. During the next nine days, Dr. Biggs treated Showman with calomel, colchicum, phosphate ammonia, *cal et opii*, and turpentine—none of which proved effective. Raleigh Showman succumbed to illness on April 8, leaving a pregnant wife, Elizabeth Piper Showman.[74]

---

71 Claim of Jacob H. Cost (*RG* 92, Book 95, Box 230, 95-1028). Cost claimed rent for "House, barn outbuildings . . . for Hospital purposes;" Williams, HWC, vol. 2, 1:933-934. Williams wrote that "over 500 wounded soldiers were cared for" on the Jacob H. Cost farm; Biggs daybook. Under Jacob H. Cost's account, Biggs noted "wife" on Dec. 31; Piper, *Piper Family History; Maryland Free Press*, February 27, 1863; Ditto journal; WCC; "Fairview Cemetery Records," Town of Keedysville, Online database, https://keedysvillemd.com/portfolio/fairview-cemetery-records/. Based on Rolla Cost's Mar. 2, 1863 death date and lifespan of five months and 13 days, he may have been born on Sep. 17, 1862. Barbara Ann Cost was the daughter of Henry and Elizabeth Piper.

72 Biggs daybook. Valerian root is a sedative and antispasmodic. See Chapter Two for details of Elizabeth Good's co-ownership of Lot 12. Ditto's journal cites Good's death on Feb. 1, but Biggs's daybook shows that he treated her until the 8th, listing her as "Betsy Good." WCC and Elizabeth Good's last will and testament (E / 667-668) also support her Feb. 8 death.

73 Biggs daybook, WMR; Ditto journal, SHS; WCC, WHILBR.

74 Biggs daybook; Smith register; Piper, *Piper Family History*; Dennis E. Frye, *Antietam Revealed: The Battle of Antietam and the Maryland Campaign As You Have Never Seen It Before* (Collingswood, NJ, 2004), 146. Frye, a former chief historian at Harpers Ferry National Historical Park, owned Raleigh Showman's Civil War-era house at the time of this study. He wrote, "Diseases brought by the armies into the Antietam Valley proved more dangerous to the population than the battle . . . disease killed the wife of Henry Mumma, the wife and daughter of Samuel Michael and Raleigh Showman—to name only a few." Samuel Webster Piper in *Piper Family History* noted that, roughly one month after Showman's death, Elizabeth Piper Showman gave birth to Raleigh Showman, Jr., on May 13, 1863. Flannery in *Civil War Pharmacy*, 119-120, described

Sharpsburg villager Harriet (Ashkettle) Benton, the wife of Levin Benton, was among the patients listed in Dr. Biggs's daybook during the 1862-1863 disease outbreak. Harriett survived the war, became Sharpsburg's postmistress, and certified the loyalties of several residents who filed claims for Antietam-related losses. *Trish Worthington Cobb and Liane Murphy Glasrud*

The fate of Sharpsburg's African Americans during the 1862–1863 disease outbreak is unknown. Unfortunately, slaves and free persons of color do not appear in local death registers, burial records, or obituaries from 1861–1865. Also, of the dozens of "free black" households in Sharpsburg, only one person—Levi Lee—appeared in Biggs's daybook from September 1862–April 1863. Dr. Biggs treated slaves in eight different households during the 1862–63 outbreak, but he did not identify the patients by name. Based on the multiple appointments and drugs dispensed, some of these African Americans may have suffered from life-threatening illnesses—and some may have perished. For instance, Biggs logged 16 visits to the farms of James A. Rowe and Raleigh Showman to treat a "servant boy" and "servant girl," giving them quinine, opium, and calomel, and one blistering procedure. It is not known if the children survived.[75]

colchicum as a sedative and an anodyne, while ammonia, a stimulant, was often used to treat severe lung congestion. Hartshorne in *Essentials of the Principles and Practice of Medicine*, 431 and 433, associated ammonia's use with chronic bronchitis and typhoid pneumonia.

75 Biggs daybook, WMR. Biggs identified Levi Lee as "colored." Entries for the unnamed servants appear in accounts of the following slaveowners: Susan Hoffman, Col. John Miller, Urias Knode, Henry Piper, Samuel I. Piper, James A. Rowe, Raleigh Showman, and Mary Rohrback (identified as "Mrs. Jacob Rohrback"); Dr. Emilie Amt and Edith Wallace, email messages to author, June 2020. These two historians have extensive knowledge of African American history in Western Maryland. Both confirmed the lack of prewar and Civil War-era marked graves of Sharpsburg-area slaves and free blacks. According to WCC, the Tolson's Chapel and Red Hill "colored" cemeteries, located in Sharpsburg and Porterstown, contain only postwar interments. See also Michael Trimkey and Debi Hacker, "Preservation Assessment of Tolson's Chapel Cemetery," MHT, 2013, 13-14; Further research of Dr. Biggs's obstetrical records may shed light on the rate of infant mortality from Oct. 1862 through Apr. 1863.

We will never know how many civilians died during Antietam's disease outbreak. But the evidence clearly shows that numerous residents in the Sharpsburg area from October 1862–April 1863 contracted sicknesses and lost their lives. Squire Jacob Miller described the epidemic in a letter to his relatives. After detailing several accounts of disease-related illnesses and deaths, Miller wrote, ["M]any other citizens and hundreds of soldiers have been taken with the same, and many died, it is an army disease [and] thus ads an addition to the Horrers of war."[76]

*   *   *

Ted Alexander wrote that the Battle of Antietam "influenced the economy, ecology, health, and the collective psyche of the community." This argument also applies to the 1862–63 epidemic, which affected civilians on multiple levels. Along with battling sickness and losing loved ones, residents incurred debt by missing work and accumulating medical bills. The sudden loss of breadwinners cast young mothers like Ann Sophia Ecker into uncertain futures. Soon after losing her husband and daughter to disease, Ann sold her possessions at public sale in Keedysville, parting with the family's horses, livestock, wagons, farm equipment, and "household and kitchen furniture."[77]

Other residents suffered various hardships that added to their stress. For example, Rev. Robert Douglas wrote in November 1862, "I am frequently called to visit the sick or bury the dead." Federal authorities, though, held the minister under house arrest due to his pro-South sympathies, preventing him from providing comfort to those in need. Consequently, Douglas bemoaned, "I can neither go nor send to [S]harpsburg."[78]

After Elizabeth Michael died of typhoid fever in October, her parents tried to arrange a funeral. However, the U.S. provost guard, "stationed across the street" in the home of Squire Jacob Miller, "refused for a time to let the daughter's body be removed from the house." Adding to the family's woes, after Nancy Michael died in November, the family had no place to hold services because the medical

---

76 Jacob Miller to Amelia and Christian Houser, December 7, 1862, WMR.

77 Biggs daybook; *Herald of Freedom and Torch Light*, December 17, 1862, 2D. Ann's husband and daughter, Elhanan and Isadora Ecker, died on November 26 and December 7 after repeated treatments from Dr. Biggs.

78 Alexander, "Destruction, Disease, and Death," 151; Robert Douglas to Fitz John Porter, October 24, 1862, *NA*; Biggs daybook, WMR.

department had converted all local churches into hospitals. Samuel Michael informed his brother, "Mother was buried today by Mr. Adams and Shufford. We could not have no funeral for neither of them [reverends] had no place to preach."

Samuel Michael's letter showcases another way in which civilians suffered during the outbreak. For households with multiple bedridden persons, heavy demands fell on the caregivers. "I could get nobody to come to help in the house," Samuel recalled. "It keeps me busy milking and waiting on them day and night. Caleb and Kate are improving slowly, Kate more than Caleb. I believe they will both get well if I will be able to hold out in nursing them."[79]

Typhoid fever inflicted lasting damage to some individuals who survived the disease. In addition, we don't know what effects mercury medicines had on Sharpsburg's patient population. Lingering effects from typhoid fever, along with possible poisoning from calomel and blue mass, may have slowed recoveries in some persons or caused long-term impairments.

From November 11, 1862–May 23, 1863, Dr. Biggs dispensed opium and other drugs to Rev. John A. Adams and his wife. The sporadic daybook entries suggest that the couple's afflictions were not dire. Still, the combined stress from the battle, military appropriations, and sickness had lasting effects on the couple. "My health has been . . . feeble during the winter and spring," Adams wrote in May 1863. "Mrs. Adams, too, since the Battle of Antietam, has not recovered from the severe shock and remains exceedingly delicate and nervous."[80]

Biggs only tended to Joseph and Mary Ann Poffenberger five times in October and November 1862, so one might assume that their conditions were minor. However, less than two years later, Mary Ann Poffenberger died at the age of 46. Her cause of death is unknown, but a Maryland Historic Trust study of the Poffenberger farm opined, "[I]t is possible that Mary Ann's illness was the result of

---

79 Jacob Miller to Amelia and Christian Houser, December 7, 1862, WMR; Williams, HWC, vol. 2, 1:764-765. It is unclear why provost guards prevented the Michaels from removing Elizabeth's body from the home. The Michaels were Democrats and deemed by some townsfolk as disloyal. Thus, the guards may have acted out of spite; Samuel Michael to David Michael, November 27, 1862, WMR. Samuel referred to Rev. John A. Adams and Rev. Mortimer Shuford. Sarah Himes later helped Samuel care for his family. He wrote, "Sally done a great deal for me—baked for me and made soup for our sick. The Doctor told me that he thought she would take the same disease."

80 John A. Adams to Bishop William Rollinson Whittingham, May 26, 1863. Cited in Canon David Churchman Trimble, *History of St. Paul's Episcopal Church* (1998), 16. In addition to suffering from mercury poisoning, some Sharpsburg-area patients after the battle may have developed addictions to opium or morphine.

the rampant disease that took soldier and civilian alike following the Antietam battle."[81]

Another example relates to the Michael family. When Squire Jacob Miller wrote about the typhoid-related deaths of Nancy and Elizabeth Michael, he mentioned that "the other daughter [Kate] and Kalille [Caleb] wore both down and verry ill at the same time but are getting better." Nonetheless, neither of the siblings fully recovered. Kate Michael died less than two years after the battle, on August 12, 1864. Richard Clem, in his research of the Michael family, noted that "Kate never completely recovered from typhoid." Meanwhile, her younger brother, Caleb Michael, lived until 1907 but remained debilitated. Washington County biographer Thomas J. C. Williams wrote in the early 1900s, "Mr. Michael was seized with camp fever soon after the battle of Antietam, and has never fully recovered from it."[82]

One chilly morning in late October, amid a driving rainstorm that washed more pathogens into the groundwater, a distinct rumble caught the ears of local inhabitants. Families peering through rain-streaked windows observed snakelike columns of armed forces marching past their homes, along with wagons, artillery, and army animals. Civilians had seen plenty of military movements in the weeks following the battle, such as reinforcements arriving from Washington or divisions relocating camps. This time, though, all columns moved south. Whether or not local citizens grasped the magnitude of the moment is unknown, but one thing was clear: George McClellan's Army of the Potomac was leaving Sharpsburg. What residents soon learned, however, was that the war—and their Antietam-related hardships—were far from over.

---

81 Biggs daybook; Ditto journal; WCC; "Joseph R. Poffenberger Farm, WA-II-279," MHT, sec. 8, p. 3.

82 Richard Clem, "Civilians Fall Victim at Bloody Antietam," *Washington* [DC] *Times*, January 2, 2004, https://m.washingtontimes.com/news/2004/jan/02/20040102-091328-1739r/; Williams, HWC, vol. 2, 1:765; Another example of typhoid fever's damaging effects is the case of Dr. William Sheffield, who contracted *Salmonella typhi* while treating patients at Harpers Ferry after the Battle of Antietam. Sheffield never fully recovered, and the disease made him an invalid. See *Index to the Reports of Committees of the House of Representatives for the First Session of the Forty-Ninth Congress, 1885–1886* (Washington, DC, 1886), vol. 2, report no. 654.

Chapter 10

A Tossed and Broken Sort of Place: Continuation of Hardships

n October 31, 1862, an article in the *Maryland Free Press* caught the eyes of Washington County residents. "From what we can gather from the Northern newspapers and from our own observations here," the *Free Press* announced, "we are induced to believe that an onward movement of the Army is in progress. This will be gratifying intelligence to the whole country, but particularly to the Farmers of this county, who have already suffered greatly, [and] began to have dim visions of the Army in winter quarters in their midst."[1]

The movement was weeks in the making. After J. E. B. Stuart's Pennsylvania raid in early October 1862, McClellan sent two divisions of VI Corps north toward Hagerstown and Hancock. Next, he ordered IX Corps (which had moved to Pleasant Valley on October 7) south to Berlin, Maryland. Meanwhile, I Corps and V Corps remained near Sharpsburg, and elements of VI Corps continued encamping near Bakersville.[2]

---

1 *Maryland Free Press*, October 31, 1862, 2B.

2 *OR*, vol. 19, 2:447; Crowninshield, *A History of the First Regiment*, 81; Westbrook, *History of the 49th Pennsylvania Volunteers*, 126-129; Frederick David Bidwell, *History of the 49th New York Volunteers* (Albany, NY, 1916), 23; *OR*, vol. 19, 2:394; Official report of Brig. Gen. Orlando B. Willcox, September 21, 1862, *OR*, vol. 19, 1:432-433; Graham, *The Ninth Regiment*, 333-334, 340, 351; Members of the Regiment, *A History of the Eleventh Regiment, Ohio Volunteer Infantry* (Dayton, OH, 1866), 79-81. The source cites that the Kanawha Division detached from IX Corps on

In late October, McClellan launched a new offensive against the ANV, known as the 1862 Loudon Valley Campaign. First, he ordered I Corps and VI Corps to support IX Corps in Berlin. He then instructed V Corps to march to Harpers Ferry, joining II Corps and XII Corps.[3]

On October 26, Maj. Gen. John F. Reynolds's I Corps left the Antietam Valley. Troops marched "in a furious rain to [the town of] Sharpsburg," taking the Lower Bridge Road to Rohrersville. Abner Small of the 16th Maine Infantry recalled that his regiment "marched through the village of Sharpsburgh in a torrent of rain—on through mud ankle deep, through Rhorersville, over South Mountain, through Thornton's Gap, and came to a halt about 8 P.M."[4]

Colonel Francis Parker of the 32nd Massachusetts, V Corps, remembered, "We were really getting to be very comfortable in the latter days of October, 1862 … [when] orders began to intimate that we would not live always in that neighborhood." When V Corps left Sharpsburg on October 30, Parker recalled, "[T]he whole army drew out like a great serpent, and moved away down the Potomac to Harper's Ferry."

As I, V, and VI Corps marched south, McClellan ordered IX Corps into Virginia. He notified Washington on October 26, "Two divisions and one brigade

---

Oct. 8 and marched to Hagerstown, en route to West Virginia; Camille Baquet, *History of the First Brigade, New Jersey Volunteers From 1861–1865* (Trenton, NJ, 1910), 56-57. Baquet wrote that Torbert's brigade of VI Corps encamped at Bakersville from Sep. 23 until Oct. 31; Brig. Gen. John Newton's brigade also encamped near Bakersville throughout October. See Bates, *History of the Pennsylvania Volunteers*, 3:336. See also "32nd New York Infantry Regiment's Civil War Historical Sketch," New York State Military Museum and Veterans Research Center, https://museum.dmna.ny.gov/unit-history/infantry/32nd-infantry-regiment/historical-sketch.

3 *OR*, vol. 19, 2:394; Rafuse, *McClellan's War*, 349, 364-368.

4 Benjamin F. Cook, *History of the Twelfth Massachusetts Volunteers (Webster Regiment)* (Boston, 1882), 75; Timothy J. Reese, *Sealed with Their Lives: The Battle for Crampton's Gap* (Baltimore, MD, 1998), 227-228; Small, *The Sixteenth Maine Regiment*, 50. In referring to "Thornton's Gap," Small likely described Crampton's Gap; Claims of Washington C. Snively (H-3458 and L-3128) and Henry Griffith (212-707). Snively and Griffith lost considerable amounts of fence rails and other property when part of Reynolds's command encamped on their properties while departing Sharpsburg. Griffith, an African American farmer, stated that the damages occurred on "Sunday night Oct. 26th 1862" while the troops were marching from "Sharpsburg to Berlin." Snively added, "It was a cold and rainy night." Land record IN 12 / 472 cites Henry Griffith's 1862 ownership of a tract near Mount Briar.

of cavalry have crossed the Potomac at Berlin . . . other troops will be pushed across as rapidly as possible."[5]

After reaching Berlin, I Corps and VI Corps followed IX Corps into Virginia. Upstream, at Harpers Ferry, II Corps and V Corps crossed the Shenandoah River. On November 2, McClellan informed President Lincoln, "The last division of this army is now crossing the river."

For people in Sharpsburg, the sudden departure of McClellan's army seemed surreal, given that the small community lived among the martial mass of humanity for almost seven weeks. On October 26, Anna Holstein watched I Corps depart, and "by the evening of the same day their camping-grounds were nearly all vacated." On October 30, Holstein wrote, "[T]he last of the troops were moving," referring to V Corps, and soon "the town looked deserted."

Even though McClellan's men had appropriated so much property during their stay, Teresa Kretzer reflected, "[W]e became much attached to them. When they went away it left us decidedly lonely here." The army's withdrawal also magnified the loss of Sharpsburg's horses, livestock, and poultry, the sounds of which had wafted across farmsteads for generations. All of this was gone, replaced with an eerie stillness that unnerved some residents. "When night come," Alex Davis recalled, "I was so lonesome that I see I didn't know what lonesome was before. It was a curious silent world."[6]

After the AOP marched to Harpers Ferry and Berlin, some field hospitals in Sharpsburg and Keedysville continued to operate. "We stayed until the town was deserted," Anna Holstein recounted. "[T]he few [wounded] that were left being taken to 'Smoketown' and 'Locust Spring.' Our services no longer required, we went home the last of November."[7]

Inhabitants of Sharpsburg continued battling typhoid fever and other diseases amid December's freezing temperatures. "[L]ast night, wrote Squire Jacob Miller on December 7, "I think was the coldest night we have had for years and continued cold all this day." However, the bone-chilling weather was the least of Sharpsburg's problems.

Although the AOP had crossed into Virginia, XII Corps remained at Harpers Ferry to defend against enemy raids. Brigadier General George H. Gordon's

---

5 Westervelt, *Lights and Shadows*, 25; Stearns, *Three Years With Company K*, 136; Parker, *The Story of the Thirty-Second Regiment*, 110.

6 OR, vol. 19, 2:494, 531; Holstein, *Three Years in Field Hospitals*, 21-22; Johnson, *BA*, 124, 103.

7 Holstein, *Three Years in Field Hospitals*, 24.

brigade, detached from XII Corps, deployed along the upper Potomac River, from Dam No. 4 near Mercersville to Antietam Iron Works. Most of Gordon's regiments encamped at Sharpsburg, and over the next several weeks, burned fence rails and felled trees. The 2nd Massachusetts, 13th New Jersey, and 107th New York guarded Blackford's Ford, as did the 4th and 6th Maine Batteries, Light Artillery. The 3rd Wisconsin encamped at Antietam Iron Works, where troops "cut beautiful cedar trees from a neighboring forest . . . and made excellent quarters for officers and men."[8]

"We have still got two Regiments a long the canal," Squire Miller wrote in December 1862. These troops, Miller complained, commandeered his barn and wagon shed for their commissary supplies and "use our sleigh shed and chicken house for horse stables, they still occupy our blacksmith shop and the house oposit the horse stable." Inside Squire Miller's village home, Federals occupied "our basement story for a provost gard of forty od Soldiers, [and] our wash house to cook and wash in."[9]

In mid-December, residents were relieved to see Gordon's brigade join the AOP in Virginia. "Suddenly there came orders to move," wrote Chaplain Alonzo Quint of the 2nd Massachusetts. On December 12, Quint recalled, "[T]he regiment left its huts and cabins. They were good; but the owners, being about to leave town, had no further use for them." Captain Henry Newton Comey of the 2nd Massachusetts regretted parting with his log shelter, which he constructed with William M. Blackford's timber. "It is unknown to me," Comey grumbled, "why we must now leave these cabins and huts which we built for winter quarters, but this is the army way." Before the 3rd Wisconsin left their camp at Antietam Iron Works, one soldier recounted, "Ruefully the men burned the cedar cabins, built with so many days labor."

Despite the departure of these troops, some soldiers stayed to picket the river, where they "remained until the latter part of January, 1863." Other forces arrived

8 Jacob Miller to Amelia and Christian Houser, December 7, 1862, WMR; After McClellan ordered the majority of his army into Virginia, he placed Major General George W. Morrell in command of Union forces defending the Upper Potomac. McClellan then assigned Gordon's brigade to Morrell's command. See *OR*, vol 19, pt. 2, 512-514, 529; United States Army, 13th New Jersey Regiment, *Historical Sketch of Co. "D," 13th Regiment, N. J. Vols: Part of the 3d Brigade, 1st Division, 12th Army Corps, U. S. A. with the Muster Roll of the Company* (Newark, NJ, 1895), 19-20; Toombs, Reminiscences of the War, 32-34; Claim of William M. Blackford (No. 1324); Maine Artillery, *History of the Fourth Maine Battery*, 35; Edwin E. Bryant, *History of the Third Regiment of Wisconsin Veteran Volunteer Infantry 1861–1865* (Madison, WI, 1891), 137-138.

9 Jacob Miller to Amelia and Christian Houser, December 7, 1862, WMR.

On this and the following page. Original citizens' appraisement of Margaret Shackelford. The widow sought compensation for the destruction of her Sharpsburg village home and personal property consumed in the house fire. Three "good and loyal" residents—Samuel Show, James Marker, and Rhinehart Line—served as Shackelford's appraisers and signed the document before Sharpsburg's justice of the peace, Jacob Good. *Author's collection*

during the winter of 1862–63, including portions of Major General Robert H. Milroy's command and the 12th Pennsylvania Cavalry. Depredations to Sharpsburg's trees and fences continued throughout the winter, albeit on a much smaller scale than the fall of 1862.[10]

As described earlier, military boards of survey appraised civilian losses in early October 1862. Property losses incurred after these surveys, though, did not appear in the original appraisements. Worse, when McClellan's army departed the region, so did the board officers authorized to amend the original survey appraisements. When Col. Alfred Torbert's brigade broke camp near Bakersville in late October

10 Quint, *The Record of the Second Massachusetts Infantry*, 144-145; Comey, *Legacy of Valor*, 90-91; Claim of the heirs of Samuel Grove (No. 9313). Witnesses deposed that Milroy's command and the 12th Pennsylvania Cavalry encamped on the Grove farm during the winter of 1862–63. Supporting this allegation, Sergeant Aaron E. Burlew of the 12th Pennsylvania Cavalry wrote a letter from Sharpsburg on Feb. 17, 1863. See Burlew letters, Special Collections and College Archives, Musselman Library, Gettysburg College.

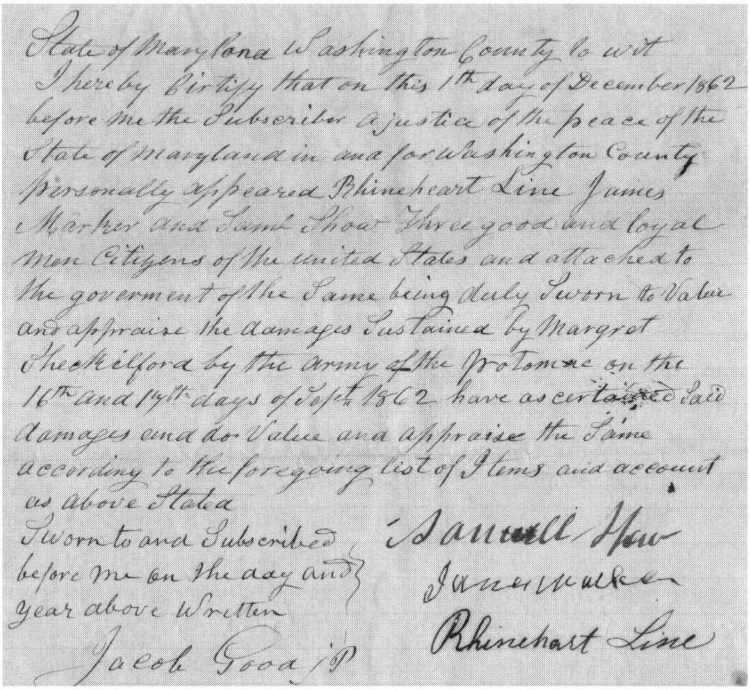

[Handwritten affidavit:]

State of Maryland Washington County to wit

I hereby Certify that on this 1th day of December 1862 before me the Subscriber a justice of the peace of the State of maryland in and for washington County personally appeared Rhineheart Line James Marker and Saml Shaw Three good and loyal men Citizens of the united States and attached to the government of the Same being duly Sworn to Value and appraise the damages Sustained by Margret Sheckilford by the army of the Potomac on the 16th and 17th days of Sept 1862 have ascertained Said damages and do Value and appraise the Same according to the foregoing list of Items and account as above Stated

Sworn to and Subscribed
before me on the day and
year above written

Jacob Good jp

Samuell Shaw
James Walker
Rhinehart Line

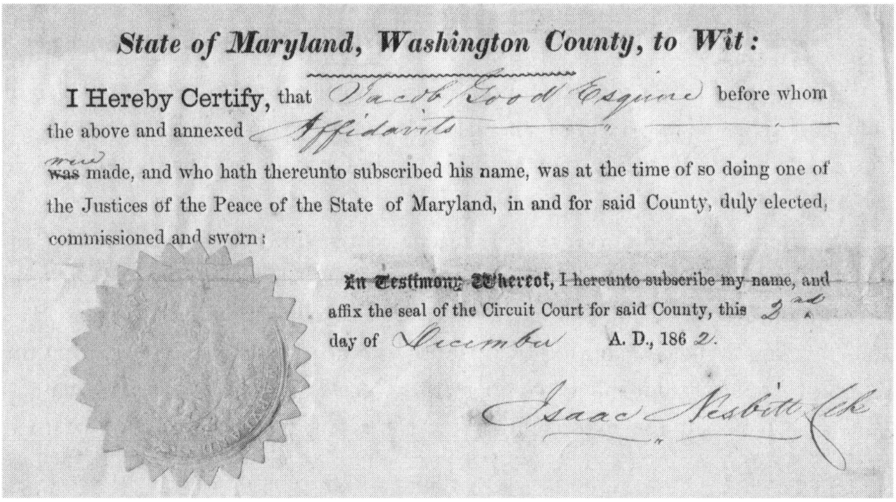

State of Maryland, Washington County, to Wit:

I Hereby Certify, that *Jacob Good Esquire* before whom the above and annexed *Affidavits* was made, and who hath thereunto subscribed his name, was at the time of so doing one of the Justices of the Peace of the State of Maryland, in and for said County, duly elected, commissioned and sworn:

In Testimony Whereof, I hereunto subscribe my name, and affix the seal of the Circuit Court for said County, this 3rd day of *December* A. D., 186 2.

Isaac Nesbitt Clk

1862, African American farmer Thomas Barnum sensed the urgency to document his losses. He tracked down the brigade quartermaster, finding him "settling with several white men." Giving priority to the white claimants, the quartermaster told Barnum to have the commissary officer, B. F. Painter, sign the papers. When Barnum located Painter, he "look[ed] at my paper and said, 'Barnum, I can not do you any good; go to him [the quartermaster] and tell him that he must fix this paper."' Barnum returned to the quartermaster's camp but found that "he was gone; I did not see him after that." Torbert's officers reportedly seized all of Barnum's livestock and crops during their six-week encampment. Still, they failed to furnish a single receipt or a board of survey report to help the tenant farmer recover his losses.

Fortunately for Thomas Barnum and other residents, another option existed: citizens' appraisements. These documents were similar to the board of survey appraisals, in which claimants recruited "three disinterested citizens" in the community "to view and appraise the damages & to estimate the amount" of property taken by Federal forces. After completing this task, the witnesses needed to appear before Sharpsburg's justice of the peace to swear to the veracity of quantities and values claimed. Although citizens' appraisements were time-consuming and labor-intensive, they allowed claimants the opportunity to list all of their AOP-related losses in an official document. Once a justice of the peace certified the appraisements, claimants delivered the documents to their attorneys, who forwarded the papers to Washington. Thence began the waiting game, in which claimants anxiously anticipated further word—and fair settlements—from Uncle Sam.[11]

* * *

As the fall of 1862 progressed, President Lincoln relieved George McClellan of duty and replaced him with General Ambrose Burnside. A few weeks later, Burnside attacked Robert E. Lee at Fredericksburg, Virginia. The resulting battle was a disastrous Union defeat.[12]

When news of the bloody contest reached Sharpsburg, Joshua and Mary Ann Newcomer learned that their son was among those killed. Private John Clinton Newcomer, 20, joined the Confederate army's Purcell (Virginia) Artillery in June 1862, serving alongside another Sharpsburg youth, Joseph McGraw. During the Battle of Fredericksburg in December 1862, Newcomer and McGraw's battery "was engaged near the extreme right of the Confederate line." One of their

---

11 Claim of Thomas Barnum (*RG* 123, No. 333). Citizens' appraisements included AOP-related losses from Sep. 15–Oct. 30, 1862. By contrast, board of survey appraisals typically reflected losses from Sept. 15 until early October.

12 Murfin, *Gleam of Bayonets*, 319; Rafuse, *McClellan's War*, 375-76; "Fredericksburg," web page, American Battlefield Trust, https://www.battlefields.org/learn/civil-war/battles/ fredericks-burg.

comrades observed McGraw "thumbing [the] vent when a shell struck a caisson near by. It exploded with terrific force killing or maiming every man at the gun except Joe and two others."

Newcomer was among those killed on December 13. Compounding his parents' grief, Union troops claimed possession of the young Rebel's body. After three months and through negotiations between Maj. Gen. Joseph Hooker and General Robert E. Lee, the Newcomers finally received their son's remains. It's not known if the family held a service, because army hospital personnel still occupied Sharpsburg's churches and severely ravaged other houses of worship.[13]

Indeed, the long-term use of churches as field hospitals had damaging effects on the buildings—especially those in Sharpsburg village. Surgeons and their staff treated wounded soldiers in the German Reformed Church "up to about the 19th or 20th of January 1863." Afterward, the church's consistory sought reparations for replacing the windows, carpet, and fencing, along with repainting the interior. Lizzie K. Miller, representing the Ladies Aid Society of Sharpsburg, wrote that the Reformed church "was greatly injured during those trying times, and the congregation has never been able to put the building in thorough repair since the war. When vacated little remained but the walls."

Among those hired to repair the 42' x 56' brick structure was Jacob Snyder, described as "the leading builder and contractor in our village." Snyder and Samuel D. Piper "undertook to make the repairs . . . which were rendered necessary by reason of its occupation as a hospital." The congregation invested nearly $400 in renovations but managed to save the building.[14]

13 Fred W. Cross, "Joseph McGraw at Antietam," second installment, in *The Daily Mail*, February 15, 1934, 15; Joseph Hooker to Robert E. Lee, March 7, 1863, *OR*, vol. 25, 2:129. Hooker notified Lee, "I will have an officer ready on Monday, the 9th instant to receive the body of J. C. Newcomer, killed in the engagement at Fredericksburg December 13, 1862, and which I have learned you have authorized to be sent across the river;" Scharf, HWM, 2:1307. Scharf cited the Washington County burial of "J. Clinton Newcomer, aged 20, killed in C.S. army;" *Daily Dispatch* [Richmond, VA], December 16, 1862; WCC, Wilson District 23, 49, WHILBR. Records cite the burial of "J. Clinton Newcomer," age 20, with his parents and siblings. Additional burial records place the grave at St. Paul's Reformed Church Cemetery near Clear Spring. As cited in Chapter Two, *CWSS*, M382, Roll 41, lists J. Clinton Newcomer as a private in Cayce's Company, Virginia Light Artillery (Purcell Artillery).

14 Claim of the Sharpsburg German Reformed Church (*RG* 123, No. 11014); Lizzie K. Miller to veterans of the 16th Connecticut Infantry, 1890, in Christ Reformed United Church of Christ, Pamphlet, November 2, 2014, Sharpsburg, Maryland. Courtesy Reverend Delancy Catlett. Miller's original letter is archived at the Connecticut State Library.

St. Paul's Protestant Episcopal Church sustained horrific damages at the hands of medical workers. According to a claim filed by its rector, wardens, and vestry, St. Paul's "was so used and occupied until on or about the 20th day of December, 1862" and "greatly damaged" by hospital personnel. "This Church was made a complete wreck," the claim alleged, "not by shot and shell, but by the soldiers and for use as a hospital."

Colonel Charles E. Phelps of Brig. Gen. John R. Kenly's brigade saw the damage firsthand. Kenly's command departed Williamsport on December 21, 1862, en route to their winter encampment on Maryland Heights. The brigade halted in Sharpsburg, quartering overnight in the houses of worship. "Of the four churches in the town," Phelps recalled, "Alexander's Battery occupied one . . . the Eighth Maryland Regiment another, our regiment filled the third with five companies, and I went with the balance of the regiment to the remaining one, the Episcopal church." Stepping inside St. Paul's, Phelps "found every sash taken from the windows." In addition, the church was "littered with dirty rags, bloody bandages, old poultices, refuse lint, and all the offal of a hospital." Disgusted by the filth, Phelps slept outside in the church's graveyard.

St. Paul's claim for damages included "25 windows, glass and Sash destroyed," along with the destruction of five doors, a double front door, the pulpit, two stairways, and 46 pews. In addition, the church sought compensation for "Joice, Galley, Panels and floor destroyed." Reflecting the army's need for firewood after the battle, Robert W. Grove recalled that "the whole interior" of St. Paul's "was destroyed or used as fuel." Another witness deposed, "[I]n order to better adapt the building to such purposes of a hospital and to afford more room, the pews were removed and afterwards burned as fuel . . . [and] the pulpit and all the interior woodwork, with the floor, were all torn out and burned."[15]

Members of Sharpsburg's Lutheran Church also sought reparations for hospital-related damages. Medical workers occupied the 33' x 38' log building until "the latter part of February 1863." Jacob McGraw recounted, "When it was vacated it was worthless so far as use was concerned . . . all the church fixtures and furniture were taken away." After AOP personnel left the Lutheran Church, Van S. Brashears remembered the structure "was pretty well tore up—nothing in there but

---

15 Claim of St. Paul's Protestant Episcopal Church (*RG* 123, No. 13674); Mrs. Lincoln Phelps, ed., *Our Country, In Its Relations to the Past, Present and Future* (Baltimore, 1864), 152-154.

Interior view of St. Paul's Protestant Episcopal Church in Sharpsburg, circa 1865. The church's vestry filed this photograph as evidence in their case. *NARA*

the floor; the windows were pretty much broke and smashed out and benches all gone, so was the floor and benches and floor from the gallery."[16]

Interior damages were only part of the problem. Robert W. Grove explained that all churches "in this little town of 1000 people were taken and used as hospitals for the wounded soldiers," preventing congregations from occupying the buildings for worship. After medical forces vacated the area, some churchgoers lacked the funds to repair their ravaged structures. Referring to the Lutheran Church, John P. Smith deposed that it "was never used after it was occupied by the soldiers." The Lutheran congregation decided to raze the church and erect a new building. However, construction stalled because the worshippers, suffering financially from military appropriations, could not help pay for the new project. "We were not able to rebuild until 1867," John P. Smith recalled, "and until that time we were at the mercy of other churches here, using Methodist and Reformed churches."[17]

Members of St. Paul's Church faced a similar dilemma. William F. Blackford, "a baptized member of the Church at that time," declared, "[I]t was entirely ruined for church purposes." Robert W. Grove added that the building "was abused and about ruined . . . so that the church could never be used again for anything." Due to the war's inflation, high rent prices prevented the churchgoers from securing a temporary place to worship. "[T]here was no standard or rate of rent then, in force in Sharpsburg," a member of St. Paul's explained. "It was the result of war, when everything was unusually high. Most of the houses were occupied by their owners and could not be rented, and churches were never rented."

"We were without a church for more than thirteen years," William F. Blackford testified. "The [St. Paul's] Church almost went to pieces. It was hard to keep the members together. Service was held in other churches and in private houses." The damage and disruption were so significant, St. Paul's claim alleged, "that the members became so disheartened and were on the verge of disruption while struggling to raise funds with which to rebuild."

Reverend John A. Adams, the rector of St. Paul's Church, wrote to the Bishop of Maryland in May 1863. "We are without a church building or place of worship in Sharpsburg. We have few opportunities of meeting together for services in public but these I have so far as possible embraced. At our home we have Sabbath services

---

16 Claim of the Lutheran Church of Sharpsburg (RG 123, No. 4058). John P. Smith described the church as 33' x 38', while Jacob McGraw and Van S. Brashears stated its size as 38' x 40,' "with a very high ceiling."

17 Claim of St. Paul's Protestant Episcopal Church (No. 13674); Noyes, *The Bivouac and the Battlefield*, 258-259; Claim of the Lutheran Church of Sharpsburg (No. 4058).

when not engaged elsewhere." Touching on his congregation's financial hardships, Adams explained, "Our members having generally suffered great losses in the Battle of Antietam, without remuneration yet, have neither the means nor the heart for rebuilding until confidence and peace are restored to our suffering country." Continuing, Adams wrote, "We are thus completely destitute of a place of worship. No Sabbath bell invites us to the House of God, and no prayer ascends from thence for the blessings on a dying world. The Rector [Adams], whose health still remains delicate, has to confine his services to his own home."

The disruption continued throughout 1864. "The church is still in ruins," Rev. Adams reported, "and supporters of the congregation are still suffering from their unrequited losses in the war." Adams may not have recovered from the 1862–63 disease outbreak and described his health as "insufficient for the active duties of his ministry." St. Paul's congregation, he concluded, "which in 1860 was in a very encouraging condition, is now sadly changed."

Summing up the claims case for St. Paul's Church, Samuel F. Hebb testified, "[I]t had been my church all my life. My father and mother attended there. I also went to Sunday school there . . . the soldiers ruined this church." After estimating costs to renovate the building, Hebb deposed, "It was decided that a new church could be built cheaper than to repair the old one." He was among those who helped slowly rebuild the structure until its completion in 1875. "I was active all the time in helping to rebuild the new church," Hebb recalled. "I took my six-horse team and hauled lumber from Rev. Adams' farm to Hagerstown and had them made into pews." Reflecting on the trials and tribulations, Hebb deposed, "[I]t has been a great struggle to maintain this Church. It was almost broken up."[18]

*   *   *

As 1863 approached, Union pickets remained in the area, putting Sharpsburg's farmers in a quandary. With nearly all fencing in the community destroyed, farmers could not protect crops or contain new livestock, making farming impossible. Investing in new fencing was the obvious solution. Nevertheless, with armed forces still encamped at Sharpsburg, new fence rails were vulnerable to appropriation, likely ending up, once again, in soldiers' campfires.

18 Claim of St. Paul's Protestant Episcopal Church (No. 13674); John A. Adams to William Rollinson Whittingham, May 26, 1863, *History of St. Paul's Episcopal Church.*

Squire Jacob Miller updated his daughter in early December 1862, "[T]here was still some fencing on the [W]ilson farm," located west of the village, "but now … there are none but a few pannels around the house and barn." Miller added that some rails remained on his other properties "when the main army left," but to his dismay, "the pickets are now burning them, so I think by Spring I will not have any fence left, except an outside fence around my home farm and one field fenced off." Wishfully thinking, Miller wrote, "[I]f the soldiers all go away we will have a fine chance for a large crop of corn next summer if we can get fenses made."[19]

Many landowners, mired in debt by Antietam's hardships, gambled by rebuilding fences. Even though U.S. troops remained at Sharpsburg, civilians bartered, secured loans, or mortgaged properties to acquire wood, which remained in short supply and commanded high prices. As spring approached, farmers and tenants began plowing and seeding the newly fenced fields, hoping that a strong harvest might expedite their financial recovery. Numerous challenges, however, were presented.

Farmers who lost horses to military appropriations lacked the means to drive ploughs through the soil. Even in ordinary times, ploughing was a laborious undertaking. One researcher found that preparing Washington County fields "took a tremendous amount of man hours with the technology of that day." Depending on the size and type of plow used, a "farmer and his team of four or five horses would take an hour and a half to two hours to plow an acre and the farmer would walk around five miles." Plowing a 75-acre field, meanwhile, "would require up to 150 hours." Without horses, none of this was possible.

Civilians who possessed equines encountered other problems. They found their topsoil in some fields so firmly compacted by military encampments, army animals, and wagon traffic, that ploughing was nearly impractible. Also, while breaking apart the hardened ground, farmers and their hands needed to clear fields of horse bones and battle-related debris to minimize damage to plow blades. The dead of Antietam presented yet another obstacle to plowing. Human bones, residents found, were scattered everywhere.

About three weeks after the battle, the *Middletown Valley Register* reported, "The fields over which the battles of the Antietam raged are dotted in every direction with graves. These graves are very shallow, and it will be very difficult hereafter to turn up the soil to any depth without disturbing the bones of those who repose in them." Shortly after the article ran, resident C. M. Keedy visited the battlefield and

---

19 Jacob Miller to Amelia and Christian Houser, December 7, 1862, WMR.

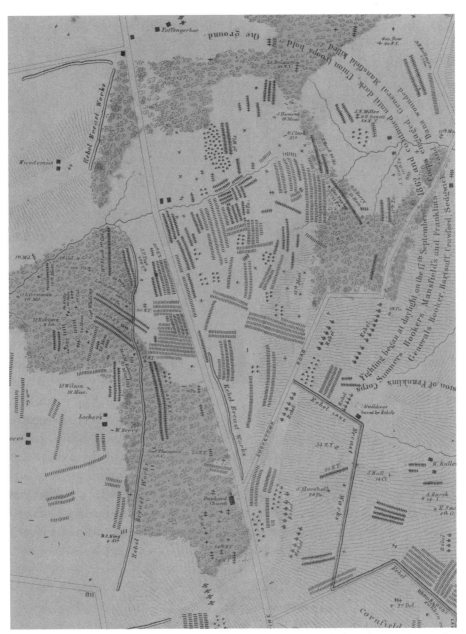

Map of the battlefield of Antietam. Cartographer S. G. Elliott visited Sharpsburg in 1864 and made note of burial trenches (rows of dashes), horse carcasses (comma symbols), and single graves. This detailed view of Elliott's map shows a high concentration of Union and Confederate graves on several properties, including the Miller, Locher, Mumma, and Roulette farms. *New York Public Library Digital Collections*

found that hogs had unearthed some of the graves and fed on corpses. Frequently, Keedy remembered, "hogs would be seen with limbs in their mouths."[20]

Private George K. Harlow of the 23rd Virginia Infantry witnessed the same sight. While visiting the battlefield in 1863, he observed, "[D]ead Yankees in any number just lying on top of the ground with a little dirt throwed over them and the hogs rooting them out of the ground and eating them."[21]

Nearly 6,000 corpses laid in Sharpsburg's fields—soil needed for growing commercial crops to aid in the recovery of Antietam's property losses. Families living on the battlefield, like the Millers, Mummas, Pipers, and Roulettes, faced tremendous challenges in tilling their fields, for graves were ubiquitous. Needing cash crops to avoid losing their farms to bankruptcy, farmers steered ploughs closely to graves and often planted atop the remains. Unfortunately, this fieldwork sometimes unearthed human bones.

Journalist Jonathan Trowbridge toured David R. Miller's farm in 1865, at a time when ploughing was in progress. "We noticed loose head-boards overturned by the plough," Trowbridge wrote, "and lying half imbedded in the furrows. This man was ploughing over graves!" When Trowbridge questioned Miller's farmhand, he learned that hogs had damaged many of the graves. The worker remarked that David R. Miller, having lost so much fencing to soldiers in 1862, penned livestock inside his only enclosed field, which contained burial trenches. "I tol' the old man he oughtn't to turn the hogs in yer," the farmhand told Trowbridge, "but he said he'd no other place to put 'em, and he had to do it." The hogs did not unearth all of the dead, though, for the plowman admittedly did the same. "I always skip a Union grave when I know it," he explained, "but sometimes I don't see 'em, and I plough 'em up."[22]

During the battle, many shells fired by Federal and Confederate batteries missed their marks and embedded into farm fields. These heavy missiles, hidden in the soil, were capable of damaging plough blades. They were also loaded with

---

20 "Thomas Barnum Family Papers," Joseph Davis collection, Kingsport, TN. Davis donated a copy of his papers to the WMR; *Valley Register*, October 3, 1862, 2D; Reilly, *BOA*; Williams, HWC, vol. 1, 2:359-360. As described earlier, the AOP's encampments and wagon traffic caused one family's topsoil to break up "in great clods and lumps which had to be pulverized with axes and mallets" before plowing could commence.

21 John Michael Priest, *Antietam: The Soldier's Battle* (New York, 1989), 316. Priest cited George K. Harlow, letter to family, July 3, 1863, Harlow Family Papers 1858–64, Virginia Historical Society, Richmond, Virginia, microfilm reel C597.

22 Trowbridge, *A Picture of the Desolate States*, 46-49.

gunpowder and primed to detonate. In early October 1862, a local newspaper warned its readers, "Many unexploded shells have also buried themselves beneath the surface, and if these should come into violent contact with the plow-cutter they would certainly explode, and render ploughing very unsafe in such a soil."

To avoid such a catastrophe, farmers and their slaves went to great lengths to locate and remove deadly shells from the topsoil. Philip Pry and his slave, Georgianna Rollins, "collected cannon balls and artillery shells from around the property and buried them near the barn." The farm of Henry B. Rohrback, Martha Ada Mumma Thomas recounted, "was covered with shells, some exploded and some not." The Rohrbacks hauled and dumped the dangerous objects into Antietam Creek. Fortunately, Martha recalled, the shells "were handled without an explosion although many people were killed after the battle . . . while handling shells which were loaded."[23]

Across Antietam Creek from the Rohrbacks, Hilary Watson recalled, "I've ploughed up a many a shell in our fields since the battle. You'd find 'em most anywheres." Often, he explained, "I've broke 'em in two. It's a wonder I wasn't killed. There was balls inside and brimstone and stuff." It may seem puzzling why someone would tamper with a live bomb, but Watson's account is one of many examples.[24]

In Keedysville, George W. Reilly allegedly "put a round shell in some wood and set fire to it, along the creek near the old stone schoolhouse." The resulting explosion nearly killed citizens standing nearby. On January 13, 1863, Dr. A. A. Biggs rushed to an accident in Sharpsburg village, finding two wounded children. He dressed the head of Jacob Hewett's daughter and the leg of Susan Jackson's son. The reason for the injuries, Biggs noted in his daybook, was an "explosion of shell."[25]

On February 27, 1863, Alva Shuford, a son of Rev. Mortimer Shuford, opened a live round, "endeavoring to remove the contents." The shell exploded, killing the teenager. "Great care should be taken in handling these shells," the *Maryland Free*

---

23 *The Valley Register*, October 3, 1862, 2D; Walker and Kirkman, *Antietam Farmsteads*, 136; Hildebrand, "Recollections of Martha Ada Thomas," WMR.

24 Johnson, *BA*, 107.

25 Reilly, *BOA*; Biggs daybook, WMR. Land and census research shows that Jacob Hewett (Lot 122) and Susan Jackson (Lot 121) owned adjoining properties in the southwest part of Sharpsburg village. The 1860 census shows that Hewett had two daughters, ages 10 and 8, while Jackson had two sons, 14 and 12. Biggs did not identify the injured children. Primary sources also list Hewett's surname as Huyett, Heigett, and Hewitt.

Press wrote after Shuford's death. "[M]any of them are easily exploded as is evidenced by the number of accidents which have already occurred in handling them."[26]

Jonathan Keplinger did not heed the warning. The 48-year-old cooper and his wife tenanted a home on Joshua Newcomer's farm, raising nine kids with a tenth child on the way. So it boggles the mind why Keplinger, being the breadwinner of a large family, risked his life dismantling artillery projectiles. He supposedly opened dozens of shells without incident, but in March 1863, his luck ran out. While Keplinger was "trying to remove the screw or cap" of a conical shell, the ordnance exploded, "blowing off two of his fingers and driving the cap through his leg, severing the femoral artery." The blast drew residents to the accident scene. Joshua Newcomer's daughter found Keplinger "terribly torn from the explosion," and Dr. A. A. Biggs treated the wound, extracting a "slug from thigh explosion of shell." *The Valley Register* wrote that Keplinger "died in a few hours after the occurrence" and "leaves a wife and nine children to mourn his untimely end." In announcing the fatal accident, the *Herald and Torch Light* vented, "[S]ome six or eight lives have been lost" from handling shells, "and quite as many persons maimed or crippled for life." Although "warning upon warning of the danger of handling these shells has been given," the advice "seems to be disregarded, and we continue to have such occurrences of the foregoing to record."[27]

While farmers replaced fencing, cleared soil of explosives, and navigated ploughs around skeletal remains, they kept a watchful eye on their horses, which remained in great demand by armies north and south. In March 1863, Confederate guerillas, led by Andrew Leopold, crossed the Potomac at Blackford's Ford. Leopold was a Sharpsburg native and knew the area well. After stealing horses from residents near Smoketown Hospital, Leopold's raiders attempted to return to Virginia via the Sharpsburg-Shepherdstown ferry. However, a confrontation ensued, and gunfire killed one of the ferry operators. The Confederates "seized the ferry boat and made their way over the river with a portion of their booty."

Union authorities arrested Andrew Leopold one month later. A jury found the "guerilla chief" guilty of murder and other crimes, including spying "near Sharpsburgh, on or about the 20th of April, 1863." Leopold wrote a farewell letter

26 *Maryland Free Press*, March 6, 1863; Smith register, WCHS. Smith cited that Shuford was "killed by the explosion of a shell."

27 Smith register, WCHS; Biggs daybook, WMR; *The Examiner*, April 29, 1863; *The Valley Register*, May 1, 1863; *HTL*, May 6, 1863; Reilly, *BOA*.

to his mother in Sharpsburg before hanging to his death. Nevertheless, his execution did little to calm the nerves of Antietam Valley residents, for rogue characters continued to roam the countryside.

On one occasion, "highway robbers" drew guns on women leaving Sharpsburg village. The thieves warned the ladies, "[I]f they made a noise, they would put a ball through them," then plundered the wagon and stole their horse. "[W]e have a full Set of Such devils in and around town," Jacob Miller complained, "I still hope these fellows will be put up to the mark."

In May 1863, Rev. John A. Adams wrote to Bishop William Wittingham, "Everything around us in the public road is unenclosed and desolate. All characters are daily and nightly passing, and it would not be safe, even if my health would permit, to leave home. You cannot, my dear Bishop, realize the suffering of losses we have had in this part of our border state."

Dangers aside, by June 1863, those able to farm began cutting and stacking their hay and wheat. Yields were strong, and with Indian corn growing unmolested in the fields, financial gain for these farmers seemed within reach. Then came Gettysburg.[28]

*   *   *

General Robert E. Lee, determined to take the war north again, marched his Army of Northern Virginia toward Maryland in June 1863. After defeating Union forces at Winchester, Virginia, Lee's command advanced to the Potomac River.

The ANV entered Maryland at two different points. Four of nine divisions crossed the Potomac at Light's Ford in Williamsport. Lee's five other divisions splashed across Blackford's Ford at Sharpsburg. Major General Edward Johnson's division (Ewell's Corps) led the crossing at Blackford's Ford on June 18. Johnson's men "encamped upon the battle-ground of Sharpsburg" for four days, sprawling across riverside farmsteads southwest of town.

28 Scharf, HWM, 1:267. Scharf cited the *Herald and Torch Light*, March 25, 1863; Steve French, "Two Scouts of the Border, Part 2," *Crossfire Magazine: The Magazine of the American Civil War Roundtable (UK)*, No. 122, Spring 2020, 22-27; *New York Times*, May 26, 1864. Leopold was also known as Lapole or Laypole, and his Fort McHenry hanging took place on May 20, 1864; Herrin, *Antietam Rising*, 41-42; Smith register, WCHS. Smith noted that Charles Edward Entler, one of the Ferry operators, was "shot and killed" on March 17, 1863. Leopold's mother was Mary "Polly" Zittle, a Sharpsburg housekeeper who appears in the 1860 census household of Morgan and Andrew Rentch Miller, Dwelling #1342; Jacob Miller to Amelia and Christian Houser, September 6, 1864, WMR; John A. Adams to William Rollinson Wittingham, May 26, 1863, *History of St. Paul's Episcopal Church*.

For civilians desperate to recover from Antietam's hardships, their worst nightmare unfolded. Farmers were aghast to find large bodies of soldiers once again encamping on farms, burning rails, and driving army animals into crop fields to graze. For instance, Brigadier General John M. Jones's brigade bivouacked near the ford on William M. Blackford's farm. For three days, 223 horses in Jones's command grazed in Blackford's fields.[29]

When Gen. Johnson's division rested at Sharpsburg, the Mumma family had just moved into their newly built house on the battlefield. Interestingly, Johnson's command included some of the very troops who set fire to the Mummas' house during the battle. During their 1863 stay at Sharpsburg, men from the 3rd North Carolina Infantry visited the Mumma farm. One of the soldiers spoke with "the old gentleman . . . the owner of the house burned." Mr. Mumma reportedly told the Confederates "that he hoped the next time they fought, they would get out of his cornfields, as he gathered no corn or crops that year."[30]

Before leaving Sharpsburg, Johnson's troops approached civilian Martin Eakle, who "carried on a flouring mill at Antietam Iron Works" during the war. General Johnson, through written orders, instructed Eakle to "at once proceed to grind flour for the Confederate States Army or his Mill will be impressed for that purpose." Eakle reportedly complied, but his monetary losses of wheat and flour are not known.[31]

---

29 Scharf, HWM, 1:271; Grivno, *Historic Resource Study: Ferry Hill*, 62. Per Grivno, "The bulk of General Robert E. Lee's Army of Northern Virginia crossed the Potomac River at Blackford's Ford;" W. G. Loyd, "Second Louisiana at Gettysburg," *Confederate Veteran* (Nashville, TN, 1898), vol. VI, 417; Edward Johnson to A. S. Pendleton, September 30, 1863, OR, vol. 27, 2:503. Johnson wrote, "June 18, we crossed the Potomac at Boteler's [Blackford's] Ford, and encamped upon the battle-ground of Sharpsburg. Thence marched, via Hagerstown and Chambersburg, to within 3 miles of Carlisle;" Claims of William M. Blackford (*RG* 123, No. 1324) and John Kretzer (*RG* 92, 54-1471). Describing the fencing on his out lots, Kretzer testified, "24 panels of worm fence were taken by the rebels under command of Genl. E. Johnson when he moved to Gettysburg."

30 Alexander, "Destruction, Disease, and Death," 167; Mumma, *Antietam: The Aftermath*, 24-26. Samuel Mumma, Jr. described the 1863 visit with North Carolina soldiers in 1906 correspondence with Sergeant Major James F. Clark of the 3rd North Carolina. Clark was not among the soldiers who visited the Mumma farmstead in 1863, but wrote that his brother was present and "thought he talked with the owner of the house burned." Samuel Mumma, Jr. noted that his parents and siblings "rebuilt our house and had just moved in before the Army went to Gettysburg."

31 Claim of John Roulette (L-830). Martin Eakle owned Roulette's tract and testified in the case. Eakle also referred to his Antietam Iron Works mill in the Henry Wade heirs' claims (G-2398 and No. 6585). Eakle operated another mill at Eakles Mills, about seven miles from

Edward Johnson's division remained at Sharpsburg, one of his men remembered, "til the 22d, when we moved in the direction of Harrisburg, Pa., marching through Hagerstown." As Johnson's Confederates departed, Major General Jubal A. Early's division arrived.

Early's forces reportedly took "an old dirt road" from Blackford's Ford to Sharpsburg Pike, then marched through the town of Sharpsburg. Given that Confederates ransacked the village's homes nine months earlier, Sharpsburg's townsfolk may have trembled at the sight of Rebels streaming up Main Street. Fortunately, Early's men continued moving north.[32]

After Early's division left Sharpsburg, three divisions of Lt. Gen. A. P. Hill's corps crossed Blackford's Ford on June 24. Major General Richard H. Anderson's command led the advance, followed by Major General William Dorsey Pender and Major General Henry Heth. Like Jubal Early's division, A. P. Hill's corps didn't linger in Sharpsburg and continued marching north. There was, at least, one exception. Now commanding the Richmond "Purcell" Battery (Pegram's battalion), Captain Joseph McGraw took a short leave to visit his mother in Sharpsburg village.[33]

Future research may reveal how much property Confederates took from the Sharpsburg community in June 1863. Otho Nesbitt noted that Washington County was "trampled down, run over, and eaten up" by the armies in June and July 1863.

Sharpsburg, but the Iron Works mill was considerably closer to Johnson's division at Blackford's Ford; "Confederate Extends Aid To Wounded Union Soldier," *Morning Herald*, August 30, 1962. 21. For more information on Eakle's wartime connection to the Antietam Iron Works mill, see J. Schaaf Stockett, *Reports of Cases Argued and Determined in the Court of Appeals of Maryland* (Baltimore, 1870), vol. XXX, 322-326; Claim of Joshua Newcomer (F-854). Newcomer's claim cites that he "suffered a heavy loss at the hands of the Rebels" during the war, losing a "large quantity of flour, horses, cattle, etc., amounting to about eleven thousand dollars." Newcomer did not identify Edward Johnson's division as a responsible party. Still, given that Johnson's Confederates were the first to arrive in Sharpsburg in 1863, encamped for nearly four days, and took flour from Martin Eakle, they may have been responsible for some of the losses described in Newcomer's claim.

32 Loyd, "Second Louisiana at Gettysburg," 417; Official Report of Major General Jubal A. Early, August 22, 1863, OR, vol. 27, 2:464. Early reported, "I crossed the Potomac at Shepherdstown, and moved through Sharpsburg and Boonsborough, encamping on the road toward Hagerstown, about 3 miles from Boonsborough;" Scott L. Mingus, Sr., *The Louisiana Tigers in the Gettysburg Campaign, June–July 1863* (Baton Rouge, 2009), 61-62.

33 Edwin B. Coddington, *The Gettysburg Campaign: A Study in Command* (New York, 1968), 113-114; James Longstreet, "General James Longstreet's Account of the Campaign and Battle," *Southern Historical Society Papers* (Richmond, VA, 1878), vol. 5, 59. Longstreet recalled, "My corps crossed the Potomac at Williamsport, and General A. P. Hill crossed at Shepherdstown;" Fred W. Cross, scrapbook, ANBL.

During the Gettysburg Campaign, historian Kent Masterson Brown wrote that "foraging parties from every regiment, brigade, division, and corps in Lee's army scoured the countryside for horses, mules, cattle, sheep, hogs, wagons, and quartermaster and subsistence stores." Likewise, historian Stephen W. Sears estimated that the ANV appropriated from Pennsylvanians and Marylanders several hundred horses, 1,000 hogs, 2,400 sheep, 5,200 cattle, 6,700 barrels of flour, 7,900 bushels of wheat, and 51,000 pounds of cured meat. With these figures in mind, Lee's troops in June 1863, as they did from September 15–18, 1862, may have appropriated significant amounts of forage, subsistence, and horses from Sharpsburg-area civilians. While these 1863 losses did not relate to Antietam, they inflicted setbacks to those attempting to recover from the 1862 campaign.[34]

The Battle of Gettysburg took place from July 1–3, 1863, and the Union victory forced the Army of Northern Virginia to retreat toward the Maryland-Virginia border. General Meade's army pursued as torrential rain soaked the contending armies. When the ANV reached the Potomac River at Williamsport, Confederates found that the rainfall deepened Light's Ford, blocking their escape to Virginia. Backed to the impassable Potomac, Robert E. Lee established a battle line in front of Williamsport.

Meade, meanwhile, massed the AOP atop South Mountain on July 9. Then, on July 10, he ordered his men to confront the enemy. Most corps moved through Boonsboro, but XII Corps and II Corps marched from Rohrersville through Keedysville. The columns crossed the Upper Bridge near Pry's Ford and continued north to Tilghmanton. III Corps followed the same route, and after crossing the Upper Bridge, bivouacked for the night on Keedysville-area farmsteads.

Hiram Showman, who lived on the Keedysville-Bakersville road, alleged that U.S. soldiers "were about claimant's place after the battle of Gettysburg," taking wheat, straw, corn, and other items. Abraham Hammond resided near the Upper Bridge along the Keedysville-Bakersville Road. He lost large quantities of hay to the

---

34 Ernst, *TATC*, 210; Kent Masterson Brown, *Retreat From Gettysburg* (Chapel Hill, NC, 2005), 266-267, 274-275, 313. Brown unearthed a trove of Gettysburg-related Confederate quartermaster records at the Museum of the Confederacy's manuscript collection. Of note, however, this manuscript collection, archived at the Virginia Museum of History and Culture, has very few Confederate quartermaster records for the Sharpsburg / Antietam Campaign; Stephen W. Sears, *Gettysburg* (Boston, 2003), 108; Lee's forces may have appropriated most of the described supplies from Southern Pennsylvania civilians. Nonetheless, as shown in the cases of William M. Blackford and Martin Eakle, some Sharpsburg-area farmers and millers suffered ANV-related losses in June 1863, especially during Gen. Edward Johnson's four-day stay near Blackford's Ford.

ambulance corps after Antietam and suffered losses of grains and fence rails in 1863 "after the battle of Gettysburg." The command which took the property, Hammond alleged, was "Genl. Prince of French's Corps [III Corps]."[35]

Reaching the Williamsport area, Meade formed his line, basing the right flank at Funkstown and left near Jones's Crossroads and Tilghmanton. The opposing armies dug into the land and prepared for battle, inflicting damages to numerous farmsteads. One source reported, "[F]arms have been terribly devastated. Fences have been destroyed, timber cut down, embankments thrown up, ditches dug, wheat, corn, and clover fields destroyed . . . a scene of desolation and destruction painful to behold." Some farmers allegedly lost between $6,000–$10,0000 of property, "and renters and others say they are entirely ruined."[36]

During the standoff, military forces on Meade's left flank seized forage from residents near Bakersville and Tilghmanton, many of whom lost property during the Antietam Campaign. Alfred Showman claimed to have lost wheat and hay in July 1863 to "the commands of Genls French and Slocum on their way from Gettysburg." Another resident, Joseph Snively, testified that General William Hays's soldiers took wheat, corn, and cordwood in July 1863. Federal stragglers supposedly ransacked the home of Henry A. Poffenberger "during the month of July 1863 near St. James College." Poffenberger accused the men of taking his wife's silk dresses, shawls, and bonnets, along with silverware, horse tack, and a "large Family Bible."[37]

Thomas Barnum suffered devastating losses after the Battle of Antietam but certainly hoped that his 1863 wheat and hay crops would help him recover. Nonetheless, misfortune again struck the tenant farmer when, "soon after the

---

35 *OR*, vol. 27, 1:118. Meade reported, "[T]he army moved through the South Mountain, and by July 12 was in front of the enemy;" *OR*, vol. 27, 3:616-617. Meade's circular issued on July 9 instructed "The Twelfth Corps, followed by the Second Corps," to "move at daylight, passing through Centreville (Keedysville) and take post near Bakersville." This order routed both corps through Keedysville, across the Upper Bridge, and along the Keedysville-Bakersville Road to Bakersville; *OR*, vol. 27, 1:146-147. On July 10, II Corps marched "from Rohrersville to near Tilghmanton" and XII Corps moved "from Rohrersville to Bakersville;" *OR*, vol. 27, 1:537. On July 10, 1863, Brig. Gen. Henry Prince replaced Brig. Gen. Andrew Humphreys as commander of the 2nd division, III Corps. Upon taking command, Prince led the division "through Keedysville, where it crossed the Little Antietam on a stone bridge and bivouacked a mile from the bridge at 7:15 p.m., on top of the hill;" Coddington, *The Gettysburg Campaign*, 558; Claims of Hiram Showman (No. 1522) and Abraham Hammond (F-1430).

36 Brown, *Retreat From Gettysburg*, 310, 316-318; Scharf, HWM, 1:281.

37 Claims of Alfred Showman (F-1179), Joseph Snively (*RG* 92, Entry 812, Box 96, Claim G-1688), and Henry A. Poffenberger (No. 7178).

battle of Gettysburg, his place was encamped on four or five days by the cavalry command of General Kilpatrick and Averill." According to Barnum's claim, these troops "fed to their horses his hay and wheat" because they were "entirely dependent on the country for such forage as they needed." Before the appropriations, Barnum had "65 or more acres of wheat, two fields of 25 acres each and one of 15 or 18 acres, and that all thereof was cut and in shock." Of this amount, "the entire crop of wheat, except 40 bushels . . . was fed to the animals of the commands aforesaid." The horsemen also seized Barnum's "three ricks of hay—timothy and clover mixed—stacked near his stable, each containing about eight or nine loads or tons." This entire amount, he testified, "was fed to horses of the cavalry, also to some artillery horses."[38]

Barnum's neighbors also suffered property losses during Meade's standoff with Lee. Tenant farmer John E. Knode, who also lost everything during the Antietam Campaign, declared in his claim that "Kilpatrick's & Buford's cavalry were on the place in 1863, just after the battle of Gettysburg," taking large quantities of grain for their horses. These cavalrymen remained on Knode's farm "2 or 3 days."

Eliza Davis, whose farm adjoined Barnum's tenancy, testified "that in July '63 some wheat was taken from two fields and used as bedding for the soldiers, the ground being very wet, and some fed to the horses by the pickets." On the nearby farmstead of Elias Eakle, U.S. forces destroyed three acres of "green corn which they fed to their horses" and "one field of 13 acres of wheat." Eakle identified the command as "Custer's men after they returned from Gettysburg."

David Coffman owned multiple properties in 1862–63, including Thomas Barnum's farm. After suffering losses during Antietam's aftermath, Coffman sold his Home farm near the battlefield and relocated to Jones's Crossroads, perhaps wanting to escape the war-torn Sharpsburg area. In July 1863, Coffman found himself in the center of the Union-Confederate confrontation, as U.S. soldiers occupying his farm destroyed over 100 panels of worm fencing. Coffman deposed that "Genl Mead[e]'s army encamped on his place, and that a line of breastworks was thrown up on his farm, that his fences were torn down and used in the construction of the breastworks" and troops "drove through his place with their wagons." Coffman's neighbor, William James, recalled that Federals "prepared for

---

38 Claim of Thomas Barnum (RG 92, 198-629). Supporting Barnum's allegations, Kent Masterson Brown (*Retreat From Gettysburg*, 293) wrote that Kilpatrick's and Buford's commands "were forced to live off the land" while pursuing Lee's army, and "impressed all the hay and grain they could find on neighboring farms."

an engagement with the enemy" on Coffman's farm and "threw up breastworks on a Sunday evening."

Generals Lee and Meade stared each other down until July 13, when levels of the Potomac waned. Under cover of darkness, Lee withdrew his army across the river.

On July 14, Union cavalry attacked the Confederate rearguard at Falling Waters, but after a sharp skirmish, the last of the Southern army escaped to Virginia. In response, Meade directed his army south to Harpers Ferry and Berlin, in attempt to intersect the enemy while protecting Washington. This route sent most of the Army of the Potomac near the Antietam battlefield.

Less than one month after five Confederate divisions passed through the Sharpsburg neighborhood, five Union army corps did the same. II and XII Corps marched through Sharpsburg village en route to Harpers Ferry. I Corps and V Corps moved through Smoketown, Keedysville, and Rohrersville, while III Corps encamped near the Lower Bridge.[39]

In the town of Sharpsburg, AOP forces again converted the German Reformed Church into a field hospital. Soldiers of the 13th New Jersey (XII Corps) visited the "little Dunker Church" and reflected on their regiment's losses at Antietam ten months earlier. After "passing through Sharpsburg," a member of the 13th recalled, "we halted in that vicinity for the night."

Various Union commands bivouacked at Sharpsburg on July 15 and appropriated food, forage, and fence rails from Antietam Valley farmsteads. According to Kathleen Ernst, farmers "who had lost their apples the previous autumn now found their cherry crops in jeopardy, and dusty harvest crews watched helplessly while entire fields of grain were commandeered."[40]

In July 1863, Adam Michael raised two 10-acre fields of timothy on his tract near the southern limits of Sharpsburg village. He and his sons had recently cut one

---

39 OR, vol. 27, 1:223. Meade's orders on July 15 were as follows: "The Twelfth and Second Corps to move [by the way] of Downsville, Bakersville, Mercersville, Sharpsburg, and the Antietam Iron Works, and encamp in Pleasant Valley . . . the Fifth and First Corps . . . to Keedysville by the road between the Sharpsburg pike and the Antietam to Keedysville; thence through Fox's Gap;" OR, vol. 27, 1:148. III Corps on July 15 marched "from Marsh Creek to near Burnside's bridge, on the Antietam;" OR, vol. 27, 1:572. Colonel George C. Burling, 6th New Jersey (III Corps) reported that, on July 15, 1863, "[W]e resumed the march at daylight, passing through Fair Play and Sharpsburg, crossing the Antietam over Burnside's bridge, marching about half a mile, and bivouacked for the night;" Brown, *Retreat From Gettysburg*, 325-352; Scharf, HWM, 1:280-281.

40 Claim of the Sharpsburg German Reformed Church (RG 123, No. 11014); Toombs, *Reminiscences of the War*, 89; Ernst, *TATC*, 208.

field and prepared to cut the other when elements of Meade's army "halted overnight" near Michael's tract. Unfortunately for the aged farmer, "all of this grass was fed and destroyed."

Nearby landowners suffered similar appropriations. Benjamin F. Rohrback lost 400 bushels of oats and "10 Tons uncut Clover Hay" seized in "July 1863 by a portion of Genl. Mead[e]'s Army." Referring to Henry Piper's farm, Jeremiah Summers testified that U.S. military personnel in July 1863 "pastured a herd of beef cattle on his fields, and that the same forces took wheat from the rick."[41]

Samuel I. Piper stated that "Union cavy" took nine tons of hay "soon after the battle of Gettysburg," and Jacob F. Miller accused Federal soldiers of destroying 1,100 fence rails and 75 bushels of wheat on July 15, 1863. Near Antietam Iron Works, James Marker and the Showman brothers alleged that the AOP took grains, livestock, and rails during the Gettysburg Campaign. The heirs of Henry Wade, who resided next to the Iron Works, testified that General French's command burned 20,000 fence rails while encamped on "the Upper farm . . . in July 1863."[42]

United States cavalry after the Battle of Gettysburg literally ran their horses into the ground, as stormy weather, muddy roads, and relentless work lamed hundreds of mounts. Similar to Antietam, some cavalrymen appropriated horses from Maryland farmers—including those living near Sharpsburg.

In early July, Cerusha and Samuel Reel were relaxing after a day of cutting hay. "We were at dinner and I heard a disturbance at the stable," Cerusha Reel recalled. "I went out and saw the horse going down the lane with the soldier a leading it. It was a Union soldier—we never got the horse back and I have never seen him since."

John Poffenberger, a resident of Smoketown, alleged that one horse valued at $175 was taken from him "on or about July 9, 1863, by Maj. W. Steadman, commanding the 6th Ohio Cavalry." Shortly after Gettysburg, Henry F. Neikirk rode past a Union quartermaster, who stopped the farmer and proposed a trade. Neikirk agreed to the deal and "swapped his horse" in "an Indian trade," acquiring

---

41 Claims of Adam Michael (199-161), Benjamin F. Rohrback (F-617 and F-619), and Henry Piper (No. 445).

42 Claims of Samuel I. Piper (D-2392), Jacob F. Miller (No. 4294), James Marker (No. 1292), Raleigh Showman (F-1183), and the heirs of Henry Wade (G-2398). The Wades Upper farm was located southeast of the Lower Bridge. After the Battle of Antietam, the Wades lost nearly all the fencing on their other three farms near Antietam Iron Works.

a branded army mount in exchange. Eight days later, Neikirk claimed, his "branded horse . . . was stolen away" by a Union soldier.[43]

"Before the battle of Gettysburg," Mayberry Beeler recalled, "I happened to be at Keedysville, Md., where I had gone to sell a fat heifer belonging to my father." Around sundown, Beeler passed Josiah Hill, another Sharpsburg resident, who was returning on horseback from Frederick County. At that time, Beeler recalled, "Some eight to ten Union soldiers surrounded him [Hill] and took from him a nice young mare . . . and took him (Mr. Hill) toward Harpers Ferry."

Explaining the incident, Josiah Hill deposed, "A few days before the battle of Gettysburg a horse belonging to me was taken from me at Keedysville. It was a strawberry mare, just rising five years old." The mare, Hill pointed out, "was taken by a squad of five or six soldiers," who then apprehended Hill because "they were ordered to arrest every body on the road." The troops put him "on a worn out horse & sent him with the others to Maryland Heights, and soon after, they were sent to Baltimore." Colonel William S. Fish, Provost Marshall of Baltimore, eventually released Hill. The tenant farmer returned home, but "his mare saddle and bridle were kept by the soldiers who arrested him."

Confederates also took horses from the Sharpsburg community in 1863. Hilary Watson recounted, "We didn't lose any of our own horses" during the Antietam Campaign, "but the next year some Rebel raiders got 'em all except two blind ones." Federal troops seized three horses from Samuel Swain in 1862, and his seven remaining equines "were taken by rebels in 1863," leaving him without the means to conduct his job boating on the canal.[44]

At Bakersville, Eliza Davis lost three horses to Southern soldiers in 1863. In the same vicinity, Theodore C. Beeler assisted Andrew Rentch in evacuating equines. "I went along with him when he went to hide his horses," Beeler recalled, "so that the rebels could not get them. This was in the year 1863." Similarly, Sharpsburg villager John Grice fled town with his horses to "hide in the hills by the river." He recalled, "I only run away once, and that was from the rebels in 1863. I wanted to save my horses and so I did."[45]

43 Brown, *Retreat From Gettysburg*, 165, 215; Claims of Samuel Reel (No. 3209), John Poffenberger (*RG* 92, Entry 812, Book L, Box 183, Claim L-2096), and Henry F. Neikirk (H-4108 and H-4109).

44 Claims of Josiah Hill (*RG* 92, 212-721 and *RG* 123, No. 8532); Johnson, *BA*, 108; Claim of Samuel Swain (N-2188).

45 Claims of Eliza Davis (F-1536), Andrew Rentch (No. 4235), and John Grice (No. 5872).

General Meade's forces didn't halt long in Sharpsburg and marched south in attempt to cut off Lee's army. In their wake, elements of Maj. Gen. Robert H. Milroy's division arrived on July 16, 1863, including the 1st New York Cavalry and 12th Pennsylvania Cavalry. Milroy's command encamped at Sharpsburg for nearly three weeks, feeding their horses hay and corn from various farms, including properties owned by Squire Jacob Miller. A trooper in the 1st New York Cavalry remembered visiting the Antietam battlefield, then finding "comfortable quarters…in [William M.] Blackford's barn" near Blackford's Ford. Other horsemen camped in the West Woods "near Dunker Church, the little shelter tents pitched in order."

Reflecting on his time at Sharpsburg, William Hewitt of the 12th West Virginia recalled, "For more than two weeks we remained at this old village, which is indeed, a very old one apparently; there being one or more old-style churches in it gone into disuse, and tumbling down." In describing the town, Hewitt was apparently unaware that hospital occupation after the Battle of Antietam, not old age, wrecked the church buildings.[46]

Milroy's forces left Sharpsburg on August 4, but Union pickets from other commands encamped along the Potomac River throughout 1863, and continued taking forage and other items from the community. These post-Antietam appropriations surely frustrated civilians. Not only did the losses add to their debts, but each incident required claimants to amend their citizens' appraisements. "You see," David Otto explained to a quartermaster agent, "there were soldiers stationed here more or less until the war was over, and for a year after the fight of Antietam."

While based near the Potomac River, Northern troops burned newly erected fence rails on Sharpsburg's farms. Solomon Renner testified that "there wasn't a fence left" on Capt. David Smith's property after McClellan's soldiers departed in 1862. "I helped to make the fences after they left," Renner recalled, "so that they could farm some of their fields." According to Angeline Jackson, the Smiths constructed new fencing in hope they "would raise some corn" in 1863. Unfortunately, Jackson stated, "Union soldiers came the second time to take the fence down after they had fenced up one field." Determined to grow corn but devoid of fences, Captain Smith "had to hire an old colored man to keep the people's cows away" from his unfenced field.

---

46 Claims of Jacob Miller (No 4296) and Morgan and Andrew Rentch Miller (H-3252); William H. Beach, *The First New York (Lincoln) Cavalry From April 19, 1861, to July 7, 1865* (New York, 1902), 272-274; Bates, *History of the Pennsylvania Volunteers*, 3:1146; William Hewitt, *History of the Twelfth West Virginia Volunteer Infantry* (Charleston, WV, 1892), 51-52.

James Marker also lost new rails in 1863. His farmhand, William Shackelford, recalled, "[S]ome of these fences had been taken after they had been rebuilt / renewed. I helped to rebuild some of these fences after they were taken, and some were taken again." Susan C. Marker, Marker's daughter-in-law, remembered, "[S]ome would be rebuilt and then taken the second time, that around the front of the house and barn were taken the third time." James Marker reflected on his overall losses by testifying, "I can only say that I lost all or nearly all my fencing during the different years of the war."[47]

* * *

The winter of 1863–64 brought unusually frigid temperatures to Sharpsburg. Squire Miller wrote, "[O]ur apples and potatoes are froze hard in the cellar where nothing froze this winter before." Inside the home, he added, "[T]he water froze in my wash basin and pitcher" and "some pumpkins in the first room as we go up Stairs . . . froze hard." In early 1864, "[A] regiment of cavalry came through this place from the Army of the Potomack," Miller explained, and cold weather "caused them to burn a number of rails." Along with destroying 3,000 rails on David R. Miller's farm, the cavalry "fed a field of corn fodder" on Jacob Nicodemus's property and "burned some of the post and rail fence along the pike next to Henry Pipers field."

Aside from occasional appropriations, the first half of 1864 passed quietly in the Sharpsburg environs. Union military offensives in Virginia pushed the Army of Northern Virginia south, placing Maryland out of harm's way. Although Federal pickets remained in the area, people of the Antietam Valley attempted to recover. Canal commerce resumed and farmers repeated the same steps as 1863, securing loans or mortgaging land to replace stolen horses and fencing. As summer approached, crops of hay, wheat, and corn thrived on many farmsteads. Families hoping for a fruitful, 1864 harvest grew anxious, however, when rumors began swirling of another Confederate invasion.[48]

---

47 Claim of Morgan and Andrew Rentch Miller (No. 4295). David Otto testified in the case; Claims of David Smith (Nos. 1244, 1262, and 10237) and James Marker (No. 1292).

48 WCC, WHILBR; Ditto journal, SHS; HTL, December 3, 1863. The Nicodemus children died on November 26, December 8, and December 11, 1863. Martin Gift died of smallpox on January 6, 1863; Jacob Miller to Amelia and Christian Houser, February 19, 1864, WMR.

By May 1864, the AOP, now commanded by Lieutenant General Ulysses S. Grant, forced the ANV to entrench at Petersburg, Virginia, nearly 200 miles south of Sharpsburg. Despite his predicament, Gen. Robert E. Lee surmised that the enemy left Washington, DC thinly defended. To relieve pressure on his Southern army, Lee ordered Lt. Gen. Jubal Early to move north with 14,000 troops from the ANV's II Corps and clear the enemy from the Shenandoah Valley. From there, if circumstances allowed, Early could then enter Maryland and attempt to capture the Northern capital.[49]

Jubal Early moved quickly and flushed U.S. forces from the Shenandoah Valley. On July 4, 1864, the Confederates reached Harpers Ferry amid a barrage of Union artillery fire from Maryland Heights. Early intended to drive the enemy off the high ground "so as to enable me to move directly from Harper's Ferry for Washington." The heavy Federal bombardment, however, forced Early to approach Maryland Heights from a different direction. This action took the ANV's II Corps straight to Sharpsburg.[50]

On July 5, Early's command—now known as the Army of the Valley—began crossing Blackford's Ford. Brigadier General Bradley T. Johnson's cavalry brigade forded first, followed by Major General John B. Gordon's division (Major General John C. Breckinridge's corps). Gordon's men marched to the mouth of Antietam Creek, halting near the farm of James Marker. As per Marker's claim for damages, "A portion of Gen. Breckinridge's command encamped on the farm several hours in the summer of 1864 when they destroyed 15 acres of wheat and a small lot of cord wood." These Confederates burned no rails during their stay, Marker

49 In March 1864, Lincoln promoted Grant to general-in-chief of all Union armies. Grant based his headquarters with the AOP; "The Battle of Monocacy," web page, National Park Service, https://www.nps.gov/mono/learn/historyculture/the-battle-of-monocacy.htm; Raymond K. Bluhm, Jr., *The Shenandoah Valley Campaign: March–November 1864*, Center of Military History, United States Army, Washington, DC, 2014, 28-31, https:// history.army. mil/html/books/075/75-14/cmhPub_75-14.pdf. Jubal Early was promoted to lieutenant general in May 1864; Claim of Jacob Miller (No 4296). Early's advance drove Major General Franz Sigel's forces from Winchester. Sigel's command crossed Blackford's Ford and then marched to Maryland Heights near Harpers Ferry. A detachment remained at Sharpsburg to watch the ford. While based near the village, Sigel's pickets seized from Squire Jacob Miller ten tons of hay, 135 bushels of wheat, and 400 bushels of oats. They also burned Miller's cordwood reserved for the winter of 1864–65.

50 Jubal A. Early, *A Memoir of the Last Year of the War for Independence* (New Orleans, 1867), 42-55; Dennis E. Frye, "Harpers Ferry Stalls an Invasion," *The Sentinel*, National Park Service, 2014, 12-15, https://www.nps.gov/cebe/learn/news/upload/Washington-Attacked-Sentinel-FINAL.pdf; Joseph Barry, *The Strange Story of Harper's Ferry: With Legends of the Surrounding Country* (Martinsburg, WV, 1903), 129-130.

deposed, because "the fence had been previously taken by U.S. troops." Breckinridge's other division, commanded by Brigadier General John C. Vaughn, crossed Blackford's Ford on July 5 and bivouacked near Sharpsburg village.

Like the Gettysburg Campaign, questions undoubtedly raced through the residents' minds. How long would the Rebels remain? How much would they take? Would there be another battle here? Although portions of Early's army marched to Maryland Heights on July 6 to confront the Federals, other Confederate commands crossed Blackford's Ford and bivouacked at Sharpsburg. These units included Major General Robert E. Rodes's corps and Brigadier General John McCausland's cavalry brigade. Captain Robert E. Park, 12th Alabama Infantry, recalled that Rodes's command "marched through the famous town of Sharpsburg," rested near the battlefield, and bathed in Antietam Creek.

During Gen. Early's stay at Sharpsburg, Confederates seized whatever grains and fence rails they could find and sabotaged the C & O Canal. Levin Benton, canal superintendent, reported that the Rebels had "torn the aqueduct at Antietam very badly." Also, Early's men destroyed four lock gates and 38 canal boats, disrupting canal operations until September 1864.[51]

News of the raid spread throughout lower Washington County, along with reports that Rebels "were taking all the horses that they could lay their hands upon." "When word came that the Confederates were crossing the river," Martha Ada Mumma Thomas remembered, the residents "would round up all the horses and take them to the mountain in order to save as many as possible." Martha's father, Henry C. Mumma, "had a general merchandise store in Sharpsburg which he moved on wagons when the soldiers would come, as this was the only way that supplies for the town could be maintained." After Early's men crossed Blackford's Ford in 1864, Martha recalled, "the town was filled with Confederate soldiers for several days." Squire Jacob Miller remembered that "the rebels came over and Staid a fiew days" in July 1864, frightening pro-Union residents. Among them were Henry Piper's daughters, who "packed up their clothes two or three times to be ready at a moments warning."[52]

---

51 *OR*, vol. 43, 1:1020; Claim of James Marker (No. 1292); Robert E. Park, "The Twelfth Alabama Infantry, Confederate States Army," *Southern Historical Society Papers* (Richmond, VA), vol. 33, Jan.–Dec., 1905, 264-65; Snyder, *Trembling in the Balance*, 200.

52 Stonebraker, *A Rebel of '61*, 60; Hildebrand, "Recollections of Martha Ada Thomas," WMR; Jacob Miller to Amelia and Christian Houser, September 6, 1864, WMR. Miller noted that the Piper girls packed up their clothes during the "great rade about the first of July [1864]."

Confederates seized numerous horses from the community in July 1864. Mary C. Seiss, a resident of Sharpsburg, testified that Rev. John A. Adams had several equines "taken from him by the Rebels in their last raid into Maryland." Also describing Early's 1864 invasion, Squire Miller recounted, "The Rebs took all our horses but one when they made their great rade about the first of July." Josiah Hill recalled that Southern forces "took nine head of horses and mules from me. They did not pay me for them." Likewise, Samuel I. Piper alleged that Confederates "impressed a great deal of stuff from me, including twelve horses. I never got any compensation for these horses. I never got a dollar." His son, Luther Piper, recalled that the thefts occurred "in 1863 & 1864," when "the rebel raiders & Jay Hawkers took eleven head of horses from him."[53]

Some citizens resisted handing over their animals. At "the time of Early's raid through here," Solomon Lumm testified, "they were trying to take Daniel Rohrback's horses; Mr. Rohrback came by my place with his horses." With Rebels in pursuit, Rohrback "jumped off his horse and ran around my house," Lumm recalled. "[M]y wife saw him run through the gate as she came out with a child on her arm." Hearing the commotion, Lumm "came from the mill; one rebel, mounted, stopped above and close to my house with gun cocked; then he called me a S_of B_; my wife called to the rebel, 'don't shoot, that is my husband." The horseman, Lumm stated under oath, "rode up in front of my house and swore that he would shoot in the house as he believed that Rohrback was in the house."

Henry F. Neikirk endured a similar scare. "During a raid made by Confederate scouts," a local historian wrote, "an effort was made to get . . . Neikirk's eleven head of horses which he had hidden away near Antietam Creek, behind some large rock cliffs." When Neikirk refused to divulge the whereabouts of his equines, the soldiers threatened to burn his barn, then hung the farmer "by a leather halter until he was black, trying to force him to tell, but he would not tell." After the men left, Neikirk's son "cut him down just in time to save his life."[54]

---

53 Claim of John A. Adams (G-1933); Jacob Miller to Amelia and Christian Houser, September 6, 1864, WMR; Claims of Josiah Hill (No. 8532) and Samuel I. Piper (No. 1310).

54 Claim of Solomon Lumm (No. 340); Reilly, *BOA*. Reilly wrote that the Neikirk incident occurred "during a raid made by Confederate scouts through this section about the time of the Antietam battle." The account may be valid, but Neikirk testified in his claims (H-4108 and H-4109) that "no rebel cavalry was on the place" during the Antietam Campaign. It is impossible to determine when the incident might have occurred, but the soldiers' violent behavior toward civilians resembles other reports from Jubal Early's 1864 raid. In a similar account, Reilly wrote, "Mr. Aaron Cost was ordered and did lead his five horses out of his stable, at the point of a pistol and handed them over either to Confederate soldiers or

During previous Federal occupations of Sharpsburg, it wasn't uncommon for the town's Unionists to rat out local Secessionists. This snitching often resulted in Yankee officers harassing or arresting the suspected Southern sympathizers. When Jubal Early's command occupied the town in 1864, Sharpsburg's Secessionists settled the score. Squire Miller recalled, "Some of those union Shrekers ware terably alarmed" during Early's raid. Miller wrote that John Benner, a staunch Unionist, "was in considerable danger they threatened to Shoot him if they caught him, they went to his house but did not find him." Convinced Benner was hiding inside the dwelling, Rebels "threatened to burn the house down if he was not Surrendered." The troops soon learned that Benner fled town, but the tense incident caused his wife to be "fritened verry much."

John Benner was not the only pro-Union citizen who feared for his safety. John Kretzer testified that "he was threatened by the rebels to be taken as hostage, if the Federals disturbed the secession population of the place." Confederates also tried to capture Dr. A. A. Biggs because of the doctor's "devotion to the Union . . . but the plan failed."

After the Antietam Campaign, Henry B. Rohrback moved his family to Sharpsburg village, being "greatly grieved by the events of the battle." On July 4, 1864, the night before Jubal Early's arrival, Rohrback answered his door. Three masked men "rushed in saying, 'We are Mosby's men and want your horses. Give us the keys to your stable.'" Unable to find the keys, Rohrback went upstairs to wake his brother, Jacob. When he and the gunmen entered the room, Jacob "raised up in bed to see who it was, and when he did so one of the men shot him killing him instantly." The guerillas grabbed Jacob Rohrback's keys, watch, and money and then stole his horse and fled town.

With so many horses confiscated during Early's raid, burying Jacob Rohrback was difficult. "On the morning of the day on which my uncle was buried," Martha Ada Mumma Thomas recalled, "not a horse could be found in town that could be used by the undertaker." So the pallbearers, she recalled, "were forced to pull the hearse to the cemetery by man power."[55]

---

sympathizers." Some historians have associated the Cost incident with the 1862 Maryland Campaign, but Reilly did not specify a date, noting only that the robbery occurred during a Confederate raid. Like Neikirk's account, Aaron Cost may have lost his horses during Jubal Early's 1864 raid. Regardless of when the thefts occurred, such hostile events certainly caused great stress to local civilians.

55 Jacob Miller to Amelia and Christian Houser, September 6, 1864, WMR; Claim of John Kretzer (RG 92, 54-1471); Williams, HWC, vol. 2, 1:838; Hildebrand, "Recollections of Martha

*   *   *

Elements of Early's army spent July 6 and 7 demonstrating against Maryland Heights and probing for weaknesses, to no avail. Concluding that the Federal position "could not be approached without great difficulty," Jubal Early decided to resume his march toward Washington, DC, taking an alternative route through the gaps of South Mountain.

The remaining Confederates departed Sharpsburg on July 8. As the Southern forces circled toward Washington, they ransomed the towns of Middletown and Frederick, pocketing more than $200,000. South of Frederick, a small but stubborn Federal command clashed with Early's Confederates on July 9. The eight-hour fight, known as the Battle of Monocacy, further delayed Early's advance on Washington. By the time the Southerners reached the outskirts of the U.S. capital, Union reinforcements from Petersburg had arrived. Jubal Early consequently aborted his mission to capture Washington and withdrew to Virginia. Soon after, though, Early sent part of his army, commanded by Brig. Gen. John McCausland, to ransom Chambersburg, Pennsylvania. This new operation indirectly affected Sharpsburg.

On July 29, 1864, McCausland's cavalry slipped across the Potomac River and rode to Chambersburg, where they demanded $100,000 in gold or $500,000 in cash. When city officials failed to pay the sum promptly, McCausland's men set fire to Chambersburg, burning several hundred buildings.[56]

To support McCausland's raid, part of Jubal Early's army recrossed Blackford's Ford at Sharpsburg on August 5. Witnesses observed that "2,000 [Confederate] cavalry and 200 wagons" continued up the Hagerstown Pike, while "about 2,000 infantry and 150 wagons were left near Sharpsburg during the day."

Ada Thomas." Thomas incorrectly dated Rohrback's murder as 1863. WCC and Ditto's journal list a July 1864 death date, and the *Herald and Torch Light*, Aug. 31, 1864, announced claims against Jacob Rohrback's estate.

56 Early, *A Memoir of the Last Year of the War for Independence*, 55-56; *OR*, vol. 43, 1:1020; Scharf, HWM, 1:283-295; Ernst, *TATC*, 214-218; Early's forces also collected a $20,000 ransom from Hagerstown on July 6; "The Battle of Monocacy;" Bluhm, Jr., *The Shenandoah Valley Campaign*, 39-40; Dennis E. Frye, email message to author, February 14, 2022. Frye wrote that Jubal Early's delay at Maryland Heights on July 6-7, 1864 "is as important as the Battle of Monocacy in preventing the capture of Washington."

Union pickets reported that these latter forces "engaged in gathering wheat from farmers near Sharpsburg."[57]

To the civilians' dismay, Southern soldiers, once again, bivouacked near the ford and seized forage from the community. During his second stay at Sharpsburg in 1864, Lt. Gen. Early toured the Antietam battlefield and "took dinner in Sharpsburg." The following day, after loading their wagons with Sharpsburg's grains, Early's command moved to Williamsport.[58]

In response to the Confederate invasions, U.S. reinforcements arrived to monitor the Potomac River. Civilians like Samuel I. Piper weren't surprised to see the Northern forces occupy Sharpsburg. "Every time there was a raid there after the rebels were gone," Piper recalled, "the United States troops would send in there to do picket duty." After Early's raids, Squire Miller wrote, "[E]verything appears quiet except that we have almost everyday [U.S.] Soldiers passing through hear."[59]

On August 7, 1864, Union cavalry routed McCausland's command, capturing hundreds of Rebel cavalrymen and weakening the Confederacy's defense of the Shenandoah Valley. To clear the region of Southern forces, Gen. Grant ordered Major General Philip Sheridan to destroy Early's army. "[F]ollow him to the death," Grant instructed Sheridan. "Wherever the enemy goes, let our troops go also."[60]

In late August 1864, Jubal Early's Army of the Valley once again marched toward Maryland. On August 25, Union cavalry commanded by Brigadier General George Armstrong Custer, reconnoitering near Shepherdstown, was "attacked and nearly surrounded." One of Custer's men recalled that the brigade "had to cut our way through to the river," escaping across the Potomac to Sharpsburg. Custer reported, "My command crossed at Boteler's [Blackford's] Ford in as good order as if marching from parade . . . my loss is quite small, considering the circumstances." Custer's brigade rode south and encamped near Antietam Iron Works.[61]

On August 26, Federal scouts observed Early's "main body" gather on the Virginia side of Blackford's Ford. In response, Maj. Gen. Sheridan ordered Brigadier General James Harrison Wilson, based "three miles north of

57 *OR*, vol. 43, 1:699-700.

58 Ibid., 567, 720.

59 Claim of Samuel I. Piper (*RG* 123, No. 1310); Jacob Miller to Amelia and Christian Houser, September 6, 1864, WMR.

60 Bluhm, Jr., *The Shenandoah Valley Campaign*, 40-43.

61 *OR*, vol. 43, 1:466, 922. Custer rose to the rank of brigadier general in 1863.

Sharpsburg," to "move your command to the Shepherdstown [Blackford's] Ford at once."[62]

Rather than cross the river, Early's Confederates retired toward Winchester. In the meantime, Wilson's command—two cavalry brigades, two batteries, ambulances, and an ammunition train—remained at Sharpsburg to guard the ford. While these troops awaited further orders, their horses and mules devoured crops from nearby farms. Wilson's men crossed into Virginia on August 28, but cavalry detachments remained behind to watch the river.[63]

After the 1864 Confederate raids, U.S. military occupations took their toll on Sharpsburg's farmers. William M. Blackford lost an entire 35-acre cornfield to the horses of "Gen. Torbert's Cavalry" in August and September 1864, along with fodder, timothy hay, one horse, and 1,500 fence rails. Reverend John A. Adams claimed the loss of standing corn and 1,390 fence rails to "quartermasters from the commands of Generals [Alfred N.] Duffie and Custer." Adding to Adams's woes, shortly after Jubal Early's Confederates stole most of his equines, two Federal "Express riders" seized the reverend's remaining horse, described as a "dark bay mare." Mary C. Seiss intervened, but the soldiers explained that "they had important dispatches to carry to Harpers Ferry—that they would return it the next day." Adams never saw his mare after that. The 1864 confiscations by both armies left him "without horses for even putting in a crop."

Squire Jacob Miller shared Adams's pain. After losing all but one equine during the Antietam Campaign and Jubal Early's raid, U.S. forces in 1864 confiscated Miller's only draft horse. "The Yankees took him from the threshing Machine," Miller wrote, "so we have not a horse or anything of the kind but a yearling Colt."[64]

Federal cavalry staged near Blackford's Ford took grains from several farmers during this time. For example, Benjamin F. Cronise lost 450 bushels of corn to officers commanded by "Gen. G. A. Custer . . . on or about the 25th day of August 1864." While these expropriations occurred, "a large body of U.S. cavalry, infantry and artillery" encamped on the Sharpsburg farm of Benjamin Graves "and remained three or four weeks, or may be longer." Graves testified that "General Duffie's command was there, does not remember what others." The farmer dedicated most of his acreage to growing hay, and in 1864 raised 43 tons. "[I]n the

---

62 Bluhm, Jr., *The Shenandoah Valley Campaign*, 40-43; *OR*, vol. 43, 1:925, 928, 935-36.

63 *OR*, vol. 43, 1:936, 946-948.

64 Claims of William M. Blackford (No. 1324) and John A. Adams (G-1933); Jacob Miller to Amelia and Christian Houser, September 6, 1864, WMR.

latter part of July and all of the month of August 1864," Graves attested, "the troops were on his farm and fed to their horses all his hay."[65]

Shortly after the Confederate raids, a Federal wagon train halted near David R. Miller's farm. Teamsters then drove their horses into Miller's standing corn to graze. The concerned farmer approached the commanding officer, Colonel William P. Maulsby of the Potomac Home Brigade. Maulsby explained that he was returning from Hagerstown with subsistence for his "troops at Harpers Ferry, who were entirely destitute of rations—all supplies having been destroyed by the rebel forces under Genl. Early." Maulsby's horses also lacked forage and, consequently, destroyed part of Miller's cornfield.

Several weeks later, "[A] large cavalry force—several thousand of them," encamped on the farm of Stephen P. and Maria Grove. Teamsters seized the couple's corn as forage, and cavalrymen "fed a rick of wheat in the straw" to their horses. In addition, Grove's claim for damages alleged that "[O]ne thousand men were quartered in claimant's barn to shelter them from the severer inclemency of the weather." As a result, the couple's hay "was destroyed by the men laying on it in the barn." Frustrated by his seemingly endless losses, Stephen P. Grove testified, "My farm was used as camping ground until the close of the war."[66]

Philip Sheridan's offensives in the Shenandoah Valley prevented the Confederates from launching further forays across Blackford's Ford. The people of Sharpsburg, though, had to contend with Federal troops encamped nearby. Some soldiers, as well as Unionist civilians, harassed suspected Secessionists during the war's late stages.

When word spread that Peter Beeler harbored sympathies for the South, a pro-Union mob threatened to burn his barn behind Sharpsburg's Methodist Church. A Federal officer, Major Joseph Ashbrook of the 118th Pennsylvania, intervened and saved Beeler's property.

In August 1864, a squad of Federals arrested Squire Jacob Miller and his adult children, then hauled the family to Harpers Ferry. There, the civilians remained under guard for two and one-half weeks. Miller complained, "I had to pay our boarding Six dollars per weak . . . we had a guard at our dore all the time." Compounding his frustration, soldiers refused to explain why they arrested the

---

65 Claim of Benjamin F. Cronise (*RG* 92, Entry 797, Box 113, Claim Number 113-1023). In 1863, Cronise purchased Samuel Beeler's 75-acre farm, located near Capt. David Smith. See land records IN 17 / 202 and WMCKK 3 / 767; Claim of Benjamin Graves (F-713).

66 Claims of David R. Miller (L-594) and Stephen P. Grove (No. 7354).

family. When an officer finally investigated the case, Miller recalled, he "found that there was no charge . . . then the provost Marshal discharged us without asking a word." When Miller returned home, he found that "Some fiendish rascal Set fire to our barn, and burned it to the ground, with all its contents, wheat, rye, oats, timothy & clover Seede, three Sleighs one wheat drill and many other things of value." Miller, approaching the age of 82, lost nearly everything during the Antietam Campaign and had to start from scratch once again.[67]

Philip Sheridan's army eventually decimated Jubal Early's Army of the Valley. In April 1865, Ulysses S. Grant forced Robert E. Lee to surrender at Appomattox Court House. Other Confederate armies followed suit in laying down their arms, and the American Civil War finally ended. Like other ravaged towns throughout the Northern and Southern states, Sharpsburg began the slow process of recovery.

* * *

At the end of the war, Sharpsburg's destitute villagers hadn't yet repaired their damaged buildings. Riding through town in June 1865, a reporter observed that "most of the houses bear marks of the shot and shell." In November 1865, another correspondent reported, "The town of Sharpsburg still bears many marks of the fight, the houses being perforated by shells." Journalist Jonathan Trowbridge in 1865 described Sharpsburg as "lonesome . . . a tossed and broken sort of place." The village's "battle-scars," he wrote, "add to its dilapidated appearance." Most of the homes bore marks of artillery damage, Trowbridge observed, "and indeed I do not know that any altogether escaped." Having seen enough of the forlorn town, he concluded, "Sharpsburg is not a promising place to spend the night in, and I determined to leave it that evening."[68]

Evidence of the Battle of Antietam extended to farmsteads, where human bones lay scattered across the fields of David R. Miller, Henry Piper, David Reel, Alfred Poffenberger, and others. Many properties lacked fencing, and remnants

67 *Hagerstown Mail*, May 6, 1904; Reilly, *BOA*. Major Ashbrook befriended Peter Beeler's family while he recovered from wounds after the Battle of Antietam and trusted they were loyal to the Union. The barn incident occurred later in the war when he passed through town. Ashbrook ranked as sergeant at Antietam and later rose to the rank of major. See Smith, *History of the 118th Pennsylvania Volunteers*, 544; Jacob Miller to Amelia and Christian Houser, September 6, 1864, WMR.

68 *HTL*, June 14, 1865 and November 22, 1865; Trowbridge, *A Picture of the Desolate States*, 50-51, 57.

from the fighting continued to litter fields. When a journalist visited the Lower Bridge in 1866, he found that "if the dead leaves are stirred with a stick, heaps of rotting haversacks, boots, socks, and other relics of the struggle are turned up." Riding to the Sunken Lane, he observed that it was "still covered with broken knapsacks, boots, and pieces of leather."[69]

Early historian Thomas J. C. Williams wrote, "The close of the Civil War found the people of Washington County greatly impoverished. Their losses had been heavy and there was yet a decade before substantial recovery began." For farmers in the Sharpsburg area, the military appropriations of horses, livestock, grains, and fencing in 1863–64 reversed attempts to recover from Antietam's hardships, sinking families deeper into debt. Canal workers faced the same dilemma, as armies throughout the war disrupted commerce, destroyed boats, and confiscated horses and mules. Finally, with inflation hammering the local economy in 1865, scores of Sharpsburg-area families faced the prospect of losing their homes.

There was, however, a glimmer of hope: financial relief in the form of claims settlements. Ever since the Battle of Antietam, claimants anxiously awaited reimbursement from the U.S. government for their property losses. By the war's end, though, cases remained pending, and the vast majority of residents hadn't received a penny. Securing settlements could save some families from bankruptcy, but civilians soon learned that navigating the exhausting, bureaucratic claims process would be their biggest challenge yet.[70]

69 The Bowie List, 23, 25, 35-37; *Timaru Herald*, February 23, 1866.

70 Williams, HWC, vol. 1, 2:367-368.

Chapter 11

The Claimants' Misfortune:
The Act of July 4, 1864

In early October 1862, the *Herald of Freedom and Torch Light* reported, "The claims of those whose farms have been laid waste and buildings destroyed during the battle are referred to the authorities at Washington for settlement." The newspaper's editor recognized the suffering of his Union-loyal readers and declared that "the Government should take the matter in hand, and instantly relieve their wants."

By August 1863, however, Sharpsburg-area claimants had heard nothing from Washington. The *Herald of Freedom and Torch Light* complained, "We have been invaded—our fences burned—our wheat crops obliterated from the face of the earth—our stock driven off—our farms and houses pillaged . . . but if the Government has failed to protect us, ought it not to make some compensation for the failure?" Additionally, the newspaper asked, "If because of our allegiance to it we have lost everything, ought it not to make some return for the sacrifice? Many of us are ruined. We are as naked in property as we were in the flesh when we were born into the world. Cannot the Government make some provision for us?"[1]

Finally, good news arrived. The *Herald of Freedom and Torch Light* reported in July 1864 that Congress passed "an Act to restrict the jurisdiction of the Court of Claims, and to provide for the payment of certain demands for Quartermaster's stores and Subsistence supplies furnished to the army of the United States." This

1 *HFTL*, October 2, 1862, 3A; Ibid., August 5, 1863, 2D.

enactment, known as the Act of July 4, 1864, prohibited the Court of Claims from hearing cases involving war-related damages and losses. Instead, the 1864 act made the offices of the U.S. quartermaster general and commissary general of subsistence "the place for the settlement of the claims." Of note, "[O]nly claims of loyal citizens in States not in rebellion could be passed on by the Quartermaster-General and Commissary-General."[2]

Maryland remained loyal throughout the war, and its residents could hence file claims under the act. Unfortunately, the quartermaster and commissary departments would only consider losses relating to the United States army. Although Confederates took costly amounts of grains, fencing, subsistence, and horses from the Sharpsburg community during the war, petitioners could not recoup these losses under the Act of July 4, 1864.

Adding to the claimants' woes, the Fourth of July act eliminated the possibility of payment for board of survey reports. As a result, all citizens filing claims had to undergo the application, appraisal, and investigation processes from scratch. Also, any settlements awarded would not reflect inflation. Instead, the act required petitioners to base their losses on market prices for the year of the appropriations.[3]

The Act of July 4, 1864 had yet another drawback. Investigations did not begin, in earnest, until the 1870s. The delay partly resulted from the staggering volume of claims filed by citizens, pensioners, churches, and businesses in Northern and border states. Nonetheless, the holdup frustrated Sharpsburg's claimants and their heirs. The children of David Reel and David Spong, for instance, penned letters to the quartermaster general, Montgomery C. Meigs, inquiring about the status of their claims.[4]

---

2 *HTL*, July 27, 1864; *Congressional Record: The Proceedings and Debates of the Fifty-Second Congress, Second Session* (Washington, DC, 1893), vol. XXIV, 607-609; "Fourth of July Claims," *The Reports of Committees of the House of Representatives, Third Session of the Fifty-Third Congress, 1894-1895* (Washington, DC, 1895), vol. 2, Report No. 1783, 4-9; "Charles J. McKinney, Letter From the Secretary of War," *Third Session, Forty-Second Congress, Executive Documents, 1872–73* (Washington, DC, 1873), vol. 8, ex. doc. no. 115, 3.

3 "Fourth of July Claims," 7-8. The Act of July 4, 1864 only considered claims from loyal persons in Northern and border states. In 1871, Congress established the Southern Claims Commission, which accepted claims from Union-loyal citizens in former Confederate states; Claim of Solomon Lumm (No. 340). Lumm testified, "I gave testimony before in support of my loyalty . . . between 12 and 15 years ago, in the office of Mr. Alexander Hagner [in] Hagerstown . . . I paid for it."

4 Claims of Philip Pry (H-3907 and H-3908) and Alfred Poffenberger (95-1685). A review of 127 July Fourth claims related to Sharpsburg / Antietam found that Pry and Poffenberger were the only claimants to receive settlements in the 1860s. The U.S. Treasury recorded Pry's

William Roulette grew anxious over the status of his case. He asked an acquaintance, Chaplain H. S. Stevens of the 14th Connecticut Infantry, to see what information he could glean from the quartermaster general. Likewise, Henry C. Mumma, hoping to secure a settlement in his father's case, wrote to U.S. representative L. E. McComas in Washington, "If you want any other Proof . . . please let me know and we will make the case as plain as we can." Determined to move the case forward, Mumma remarked, "I will come Down at any time I am needed."

David R. Miller and his father, Colonel John Miller, also grew impatient with the slow process. David testified that he "was with his father in Washington several times in relation to this claim." As time passed, David's wife, Margaret Miller, wrote the quartermaster general, "asking a speedy settlement of the claim."[5]

While claimants awaited word regarding their cases, Congress passed a joint resolution in 1866 that further restricted the jurisdiction of the Act of July 4, 1864. One of the changes eliminated settlements "for the occupation of or injury to real estate . . . [and] the consumption, appropriation, or destruction of or damage to

---

settlement in 1865 and Poffenberger's in 1867; Kyle S. Sinisi, *Sacred Debts: State Civil War Claims and American Federalism, 1861–1880* (New York, 2003), xi-xii. Sinisi estimated that the U.S. Government spent more than $3 billion on the war and became inundated by demands for pensions, subsidies, and claims reimbursement. "Always concerned with a depleted Treasury," Sinisi wrote, "Congress and the executive departments resisted . . . attempts to facilitate reimbursement." Additionally, any paid settlements "would have to be pried from the hands of an army of clerks, patronage appointees, and even elected officials, all anxious to defend the treasury." Corroborating Sinisi's estimate, one study found that "the North experienced $3.37 billion in direct costs" during the war. See Claudia D. Goldin and Frank D. Lewis, "The Economic Cost of the American Civil War: Estimates and Implications," *Journal of Economic History*, 35(2), 1975, 321; Claims of David Reel (F-847) and David Spong (54-1462).

5   Claim of William Roulette (L-832). Chaplain Stevens wrote to Brig. Gen. Meigs, explaining, "I was with the company that struck Mr. R's house when the charge was made capturing the sharp-shooters and liberating Mr. Roulette, and the acquaintance so suddenly formed has been continued." Stevens then inquired, "If you can send me any information regarding the present status of the claim to communicate with Mr. Roulette or will write to him directly concerning it I shall feel obliged to you;" Claim of Samuel Mumma, Sr. (No. 334). Louis E. McComas served as U.S. Representative from Maryland at the time of Mumma's letter. See "Louis E. McComas (1846–1907)," Archives of Maryland, web page, https://msa.maryland.gov/msa/speccol/sc3500/sc3520/002000/002074/html/msa02074.html; Claims of John Miller (No. 2227) and David R. Miller (F-1499). David R. Miller had vested interest in his father's war claim, according to Col. John Miller's equity court case (liber 24 / folio 421, Case No. 3318, Maryland State Archives). Being the tenant of Col. Miller's farm, David was not financially responsible for repairing the property's fences. However, David deposed that he invested "large sums of money in refencing the said lands, after the fence had been destroyed during the Battle of Antietam in 1862." See Paula S. Reed, *History Report: The D. R. Miller Farm* (Sharpsburg, MD, 1991), ANBL, 24-25.

personal property." In short, this 1866 clause prohibited claims for war-related damages. Thus, civilians who lost buildings to fire, crop fields to combat, or acreage for burials could not seek reimbursement for such losses.

By denying payment for the occupation of real estate, the July Fourth Act barred claims for rent. Although residents, shopkeepers, and church congregations temporarily relinquished their buildings to the AOP, the government would pay no settlements for said use, regardless of any damages caused during the occupation. Some Sharpsburg petitioners applied for rent regardless. Notwithstanding, the quartermaster department denied their requests because "such cases are not admissible when rent relates to the occupation of a building in the vicinity of a battle field for hospital purposes." Moreso, a quartermaster agent remarked, "it was the misfortune of claimants if they happened to be in such a vicinity."[6]

Another clause added to the Act of July 4, 1864, barred "claims for damages or for losses sustained by thefts or depredations committed by troops." Soldiers from both armies ransacked homes during the Antietam Campaign, stealing valuables, clothing, and other items, but evidence does not support that Sharpsburg's claimants had insurance policies to cover stolen personal property. Thus, victims of theft or vandalism received nothing for their losses.[7]

The July Fourth Act empowered the quartermaster general to appoint special agents and send them into the field to "investigate and report upon all claims filed under said act" and "administer oaths and affirmations and to take depositions of witnesses." These field investigations ensured in-depth examination of claims relating to quartermaster supplies. Unfortunately, the same did not apply to cases involving subsistence.

"As for the Commissary General," claimants learned, "no law was passed to allow him special agents, and consequently he did not investigate the claims by means of such agents. He acted only on such claims as were supported by vouchers or affidavits furnished by officials." The commissary general of subsistence later reported, "It will . . . be impracticable to properly investigate the claims presented under the act of July 4, 1864, unless an appropriation be made for the employment and transportation of officers and agents to investigate the claims."

6 "Fourth of July Claims," 5; Claims of John H. Smith (F-1205), Catherine Showman (F-1176), George Line (F-1186 and 1187), and Henry F. Neikirk (H-4108).

7 "Fourth of July Claims," 8, 11-12, 16; *HTL*, February 15, 1865, 2F. An 1865 advertisement offered war risk insurance for buildings and merchandise. Further research is required to determine whether similar policies existed in 1862. No mention of insurance appears in board of survey appraisals, July Fourth claims, or congressional cases reviewed in this study.

Because the commissary general lacked special agents to interview claimants and their witnesses, he could only consider cases that included receipts or vouchers. Evidence shows that it was difficult, if not impossible, for claimants to obtain receipts from officers and army surgeons after the battle. Consequently, the commissary general rejected every subsistence claim for July Fourth cases reviewed in this study. In other words, Sharpsburg-area claimants received nothing for their valuable losses of livestock, poultry, orchard fruit, potatoes, and other subsistence confiscated by the Union army.[8]

*   *   *

For petitioners in the Sharpsburg environs, most of the quartermaster claims examinations took place between 1874 and 1879. Two agents examined the majority of the cases: Madison Sallade and Jean-Baptise Victor Vifquain. Both men were former Union soldiers. Sallade served as a quartermaster sergeant in the Pennsylvania Militia, 53rd Regiment. Vifquain enlisted in several Federal regiments and earned the Congressional Medal of Honor for capturing a flag at Fort Blakely, Alabama, in 1865. Vifquain is perhaps best known, though, for attempting to kidnap Confederate president Jefferson Davis in 1862.[9]

Compared to military boards of survey, the July Fourth claims process was far more demanding and consisted of two parts: merits and loyalty. The investigation of merits involved facts and evidence of the case, whereas examinations of loyalty determined whether a claimant was a friend or enemy of the United States government during the war.

While scrutinizing the merits of claims, special agents conducted on-site inspections, similar to board of survey appraisements. They also recorded sworn testimonies with applicants, witnesses, and appraisers. During the interviews, agents grilled subjects on their knowledge of property losses. Agent Victor Vifquain explained to the quartermaster general that during sworn interviews, "I do not allow claimants or witnesses to look at any of the [papers], nor do I allow more than one witness before me at one time." Vifquain then quizzed the subjects,

---

8 "Fourth of July Claims," 6, 9. Brigadier General Robert Macfeely served as commissary general of subsistence from 1875–90.

9 Bates, *History of the Pennsylvania Volunteers*, 5:1298; "Victor Vifquain," Congressional Medal of Honor Society, web page, https://www.cmohs.org/recipients/victor-vifquain. For information on the attempted kidnapping, see Victor Vifquain, *The 1862 Plot to Kidnap Jefferson Davis* (Lincoln, NE, 2005).

testing their memories on specific details of property losses more than one decade after the battle. "[I]t is fair to admit," he wrote, "that the figures (which they swear to, agreeing with the appraisement) must be the correct figures." Given the elapsed span since the battle, it wasn't uncommon for claimants and witnesses to forget details.[10]

Furthermore, some applicants died by the 1870s, and others were too ill or aged to testify. David Reel, Agent Vifquain observed in July 1876, "has of late been stricken by apoplexy and I was unable to obtain any evidence from him, his mind being strongly affected." When Agent Madison Sallade attempted to interview Magdalene Jones, he concluded, "She is too old and infirm to give any information regarding the claim." Sallade also delved into the case of Col. John Miller in July 1879 and reported, "I visited that claimant at his residence in Sharpsburg, Md., but was unable to obtain from him anything to the point regarding his claim. He is now ninety two years of age, and by reason of deafness and feebleness unfit to attend to business."

Once agents completed an investigation, they forwarded the report to the depot quartermaster in Washington, along with a recommendation for rejection or settlement. Upon receipt, the depot quartermaster approved, amended, suspended, or rejected the suggestion. In claims reviewed for this study, the depot quartermaster typically approved recommendations for rejection but reduced, disallowed, or suspended suggested settlements. From there, the depot quartermaster sent the claims to Quartermaster General Meigs for final action.

If Meigs rejected a claim filed under the Act of July 4, 1864, it could not be reopened. He could, though, reexamine suspended cases if claimants produced new evidence containing credible merit. If Meigs allowed a claim, he authorized the third auditor of the Treasury to pay the petitioner the allowed amount.[11]

For a claim to reach the quartermaster general's desk, it underwent intense scrutiny in the field. For example, the department did not award settlements for wheat, hay, or straw seized as bedding, as such use fell under the category of damages. To receive reimbursement, claimants had to convince investigators that their property was taken strictly for use as animal forage. If agents suspected that

---

10 Claims of William F. Hebb (F-1417) and Noah Rohrback (H-3874).

11 Claims of David Reel (No. 6619), Magdalene Jones (54-1470), and John Miller (No. 2227); Wiley Britton, *The Aftermath of the Civil War: Based on Investigation of War Claims* (Kansas City, MO, 1924), 52; Three depot quartermasters appear in July Fourth claims reviewed for this study: Captain A. F. Rockwell, Major William Myers, and Major George Bell.

soldiers used any amount of crops as bedding—even so much as an armful—they rejected the entire amount claimed.

As a case in point, AOP soldiers confiscated most of Henry A. Poffenberger's unthreshed wheat for forage but used a small portion as bedding. Agent Victor Vifquain deduced that the "scarcity of forage on hand at the time," along with "the tacit consent of the officers commanding the men encamped upon this farm in the midst of the great excitement succeeding such a battle as the Antietam battle . . . fill all the requirements of a direct order from the proper authority." But because Poffenberger and his witnesses could not substantiate the exact quantity of wheat seized as bedding for soldiers, Vifquain wrote, "My abstension to a recommendation is one solely to the fact that I am unable to say how much was used as forage." Thus, Vifquain recommended that Poffenberger receive nothing for his 1862 wheat crop.[12]

Applicants encountered other difficulties proving the merits of their cases. Evaluators in citizens' appraisements, for instance, needed to have estimated losses objectively, without guidance from the claimants. If the quartermaster general suspected that a claimant assisted appraisers in this process, he disallowed the affected items. Joseph Poffenberger, James Marker, and Jacob Avey, Sr., all suffered the rejection of numerous articles because of suspected assistance with the appraisements.[13]

The locations of farms weighed heavily on the outcome of claims cases. Special agents had a general understanding of where the armies maneuvered and fought during the battle. Therefore, applicants living on or near the battlefield needed to prove their losses were not related to war-related damages. Losses of standing corn, in particular, required proof that the crop served strictly as forage for AOP animals. If agents surmised that soldiers damaged any portion of these fields by marching or fighting, they rejected the entire amount of corn claimed.

In the cases of Joseph Sherrick and Leonard Emmert, combat destroyed part of the farmers' jointly owned cornfield. On September 19, Federals fed the remainder of corn to their horses as forage. The investigating agent found that "a great deal of this corn may have been fed to Government Animals but much was

---

12 Claim of Henry A. Poffenberger (RG 123, Entry 22, Book 784, Case No. 7178). In September 1862, Henry Poffenberger owned the wheat crop on Samuel Poffenberger's tenant farm. Henry made this arrangement upon selling the farm earlier in 1862 to Samuel Doub.

13 Claims of James Marker (No. 1292), Joseph Poffenberger (No. 1300), and Jacob Avey, Sr. (F-602). Subjective appraisals were one of several reasons the quartermaster general disallowed the three claims.

doubtless destroyed during the progress of the battle." Hence, he noted, "[I]t seems impossible to determine how much was actually consumed by animals belonging to the Union Army [and] this item must be held as one of damages."[14]

Petitioners who lived within or behind Confederate lines from September 15–18 faced a similar challenge because ANV-related losses were not allowed under the Act of July 4, 1864. Complicating investigations, after Robert E. Lee's army withdrew on September 18, Federal soldiers encamped upon the same ground. Thus, residents in this sector had to prove that Confederates took no portion of their claimed losses.

The quartermaster general rejected a part of Hezekiah Myers's claim for this reason. Testifying in the case, John Kretzer admitted, "We included in our appraisement the damages by both armies as it was impossible to distinguish or to separate the property taken by each." Another claimant, David Reel, lost all the fencing on his 110-acre farm. His brother and son told Agent Vifquain that Rebels destroyed a few of the rails, but "federals burned the bulk of the fencing after the battle." Because Confederates were partly to blame for the losses, the quartermaster general's office refused to pay David Reel for a single rail.

Evidence in Alfred Poffenberger's case supported that I Corps troops seized large quantities of the farmer's hay, corn, and wheat from September 19–October 26. Victor Vifquain, nonetheless, asked the quartermaster general to disallow the entire claim. "[T]he fact that the rebel forces were for four days on the place," Vifquain declared, "and that for one day severe fighting was done upon it, leaves no room to doubt but what justice is done to the Government by my recommendation."[15]

*   *   *

In proving the merits of their cases, applicants needed to convince the quartermaster general's department that their stores and supplies were taken by "proper military authority, for the use of the United States Army." Requirements under the Act of July 4, 1864 made this no easy feat. "Proof must be furnished," the act mandated, "that the quartermasters' stores or subsistence supplies mentioned

---

14 Claims of Joseph Poffenberger (No. 1300), John C. Middlekauff (F-1587), Michael Miller (F-1437 and F-1438), William Unger (K-516), and Leonard Emmert (F-1577). As tenant, Emmert owned one-half of all crops raised on Sherrick's farm in 1862.

15 Claims of Hezekiah Myers (No. 1301), David Reel (No. 6619), and Alfred Poffenberger (M-917).

have actually been used by the Army of the United States." Said proof had to "consist of the certificate or affidavit of the officer who took the stores, or who ordered them taken." Evidence also needed to show that the supplies "have been accounted for as required by the regulations of the Army; and if accounted for, upon what returns."

Along with listing the articles, quantities, and prices charged, the act instructed petitioners to furnish the "name the brigade, division and corps" responsible for confiscating the property and the "name, rank, regiment, and, when known, the post-office address of each officer who took any portion of the stores."

Predictably, claimants in the 1870s struggled to identify officers who took their property in 1862. Philip Pry's attorney argued that "it was impracticable to obtain a certificate or receipt from the officers at this time, because their places of residence are unknown to claimant." Eli Wade wrote to the quartermaster general in 1876, "As far as naming the particular Regts, Companies or Detachments, which consumed those stores, this is an impossibility." Simply put, Wade explained, "Genl. Burnside's Corps, in part, was encamped on this farm for six weeks in the fall of 1862, and took and used what they wished. No person could follow up and watch the different sections of troops and specify what each took, even if authority was given to do so." Another claimant, Joseph Thomas, petitioned the government for one horse seized by AOP troops. However, during the 1870s claims investigation, Thomas had no receipt for the horse and no way of identifying the authorizing officer. Agent Madison Sallade surmised, after reviewing Thomas's case, "[I]t is more than likely that the horse was taken by some marauding soldiers." Subsequently, Sallade concluded, the property loss was "the claimants misfortune."[16]

If citizens identified persons responsible for the appropriations, the quartermaster's department attempted to contact the named officers and request their sworn statements regarding the matter. The case of Samuel I. Piper illustrates the complexity of this process.

Piper deposed that James Rickett's division encamped for six weeks on his farm and confiscated more than $3,000 in property. Three officers from the 26th New York denied the charges. Captain G. S. Jennings attested, "I believe that the forage was purchased and vouchers given for it by the proper officers. At least it was so understood at the time." Major E. F. Wetmore added, "I do not know of a

---

16 "Fourth of July Claims," 7-8; Claims of Philip Pry (G-1759), Alfred N. Cost (95-1031), John A. Wade (G-2400), and Joseph Thomas (F-611).

single thing taken by our forces from private individuals, as the stores furnished by the Qr Master was suff[icient] . . . and I do not think there was a rail an ear of corn a wisp of hay or straw taken."

Regarding Piper's rails, Capt. Jennings wrote, "As to fences, my belief is, that none were destroyed by our troops." He recounted that "it was very well understood by all . . . that any use of private property such as fences, forage, &c &c except under the direction of the officers of the Q M Dept would be severely punished . . . and fear of consequences prevented it completely." Captain E. R. P. Shurly of the 26th New York agreed with Jennings, writing, "No fences were destroyed . . . I know that the orders of General Ricketts were very strict prohibiting any foraging or destruction of private property in Maryland. Believe most of this account is a swindle."

Did Samuel I. Piper attempt to swindle the government? Let's look at his side of the story. The officers' statements about punishment are valid, as orders forbid unauthorized foraging. However, quartermaster agent Madison Sallade inspected Ricketts's former campsites on the Piper property. He concluded, "The fences were to a great extent burned from the farm, the soldiers using them in lieu of the regular supplies of fuel." Also supporting Piper's case, seven witnesses swore under oath to having observed Ricketts's men take and use large amounts of Piper's grains, fencing, and timber. In addition, William Roulette, who appraised Piper's losses, testified, "We gentlemen exercised due care and made all proper inquiries so as to convince us . . . that these stores were actually taken by the army at that time."

We cannot discount the testimony of the 26th New York officers. Still, if Ricketts's division in September and October 1862 contained thirteen regiments and two batteries, did the quartermaster general's office contact other officers regarding Piper's case? Based on the farmer's claim, only a handful of other Union veterans provided written statements, four of whom remembered little to nothing about Piper's losses. The exception was Lieutenant D. A. Griffith of the 88th Pennsylvania. Griffith sent an affidavit to the quartermaster general deposing that "his Regiment with the rest of the Division was encamped . . . to the best of his knowledge and belief on the farm of Samuel I. Piper." Griffith recalled that the "Wood, Fences and Forage surrounding them was used and consumed by the Division." He noted that "none of these Quartermaster Stores were taken (as alleged) by his orders, but furnished by the Brigade and Division Quartermasters, to his Regiment, with perhaps the exception of the wood, to which the men helped themselves."

Both sides in Samuel I. Piper's claim presented strong arguments. Ultimately, Brig. Gen. Meigs sided with the New York officers. He disallowed payment to

Piper because "there seems to be no means of ascertaining at this late day what portion of the supplies charged for was appropriated to the legitimate uses of the Quartermaster Department."[17]

Countless claimants struggled to identify officers responsible for the appropriations. In some instances, petitioners asked the special agents to consider the AOP's supply shortage after the battle. One resident explained that wagons and depots could not "supply so large an Army . . . and it was necessary to take from the farmers living in the vicinity." John Ecker deposed, "[T]he wagon trains were in the rear and could not move with regularity . . . and in order to comfortably subsist the men and animals of the army, impressments were made from farmers." Catherine Showman's sons stated that McClellan's army "was not near enough to any depot of supplies" and to sustain itself "it was necessary to make impressments of Forage, Stock and such supplies as were needed by the horses and men."[18]

Other petitioners furnished written statements from high-ranking commanders. When Samuel D. Piper failed to identify the officer who seized his livestock, he asked Brig. Gen. Abner Doubleday for help. "At the request of Mr. Samuel D. Piper, a resident of Sharpsburg, Md.," Doubleday wrote to the commissary general of subsistence, "I have a vague recollection that his property was largely taken for the use of the Union Army and I have no doubt whatsoever that his statement as to his losses are accurate and just." The commissary general, nevertheless, insisted on the need for receipts and rejected Piper's case.

After Samuel Pry confused an officer's name in his petition, he wrote to Quartermaster General Meigs. "I have been mistaken only in regard to the name of the officer by who's order my property was taken," Pry explained, "but I have not mistaken the officer himself. The property in question was taken by the Chief Quarter Master of Maj Genl Hookers (1st) Army Corps . . . after the battle of Antietam was over."

Pry's letter made its way to Maj. Gen. Joseph Hooker, who contacted Meigs regarding the matter. "I have no means of determining the precise amount of the

---

17 Claims of Samuel I. Piper (RG 92, D-2392 and RG 123, No. 1310). Ricketts's command also comprised rookie regiments attached to the division after the battle. William D. Piper was one month shy of turning sixteen at the time of the appropriations; Cashin, *War Stuff*, 58-59, 100. Cashin wrote that the Federal army's discipline of unauthorized foragers throughout the war "proved to be lenient and sporadic, and it did little to avert wrongdoing." In regard to fencing, Cashin noted that Union soldiers commonly confiscated rails "without getting an officer's permission or giving out documents to civilians."

18 Claims of Susan Hoffman (No. 1318), John Ecker (F-1523), and Catherine Showman (F-1185).

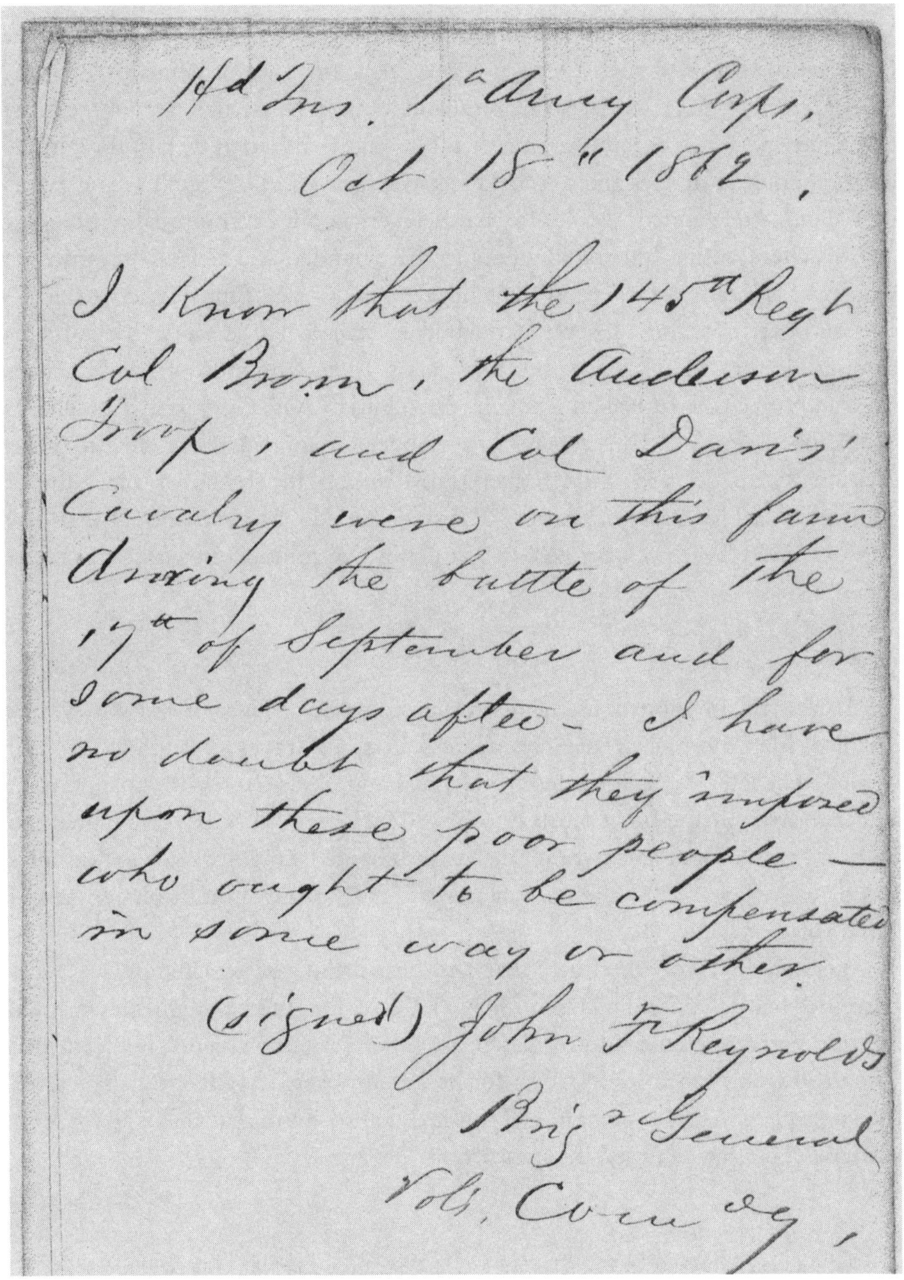

Hd Qrs. 1ᵃ Army Corps,
Oct 18ᵗʰ 1862 .

I know that the 145ᵗʰ Regt
Col Brown, the Anderson
Troop, and Col Davis'
Cavalry were on this farm
during the battle of the
17ᵗʰ of September and for
some days after — I have
no doubt that they imposed
upon these poor people —
who ought to be compensated
in some way or other.

(signed) John F. Reynolds

Brig. General
Vols, Comdg,

Major General John F. Reynolds furnished this note to Joseph Stonebraker after Federal forces appropriated the farmer's property during and after the battle. *NARA.*

loss sustained by Samuel Pry," Hooker wrote, "but from my knowledge of the character of that gentleman I have no doubt that the claim presented is a correct and just one, and I earnestly recommend that it be settled at your earliest convenience." Hooker remembered that "the injury sustained by him [Pry] in the destruction of his fences and out buildings were heavy but of them I see he makes no mention." He added, "Mr. S. Pry has been eminently loyal throughout the war and his attentions and liberal kindness to the wounded and sick of our army are worthy of all praise. Mr. Pry has only mistaken the name of my quartermaster."

Another claimant, Joseph Stonebraker, failed to identify the officers responsible for taking his livestock and grains. In an attempt to prove his losses were authorized, he furnished a note given to him by Maj. Gen. John F. Reynolds on October 18, 1862. The general wrote on the document that elements of his division "were on this [Stonebraker] farm during the battle of the 17th of September and for some days after." Reynolds added, "I have no doubt that they imposed upon these poor people—who ought to be compensated in some way or other."[19]

*   *   *

During the investigations, agents suspected some civilians of dishonesty. For instance, Madison Sallade deemed witness Francis Graves's testimony as "not worthy of belief." He also rejected Abraham Hammond's request for hospital rent, an item barred by the July Fourth Act. In 1862, Hammond could have rented out his property for six dollars per month. Yet, he charged ten dollars due to "troubles and damages" caused by the medical department's occupation of his house and barn. Sallade rejected the item.

Stephen P. Grove testified that the destruction of fencing by V Corps prevented him from farming from 1863–65. Grove admitted, though, that in 1863, "fearing perhaps destruction of his crop by the army movements, he deemed it wise to sow only ten acres of wheat for bread purposes." Agent Vifquain noticed the contradiction and concluded, "I am inclined to think that this is a sign that claimant could have farmed if he wanted to."[20]

---

19 Claims of Samuel D. Piper (D-2392 and D-2393), Samuel Pry (81-1489), and Joseph Stonebraker (Box 771, Claim 173). It is unknown whether Reynolds's note helped secure payment to Stonebraker. The general died in action the following year at Gettysburg.

20 Claims of Benjamin Graves (F-713), Abraham Hammond (F-1430), and Stephen P. Grove (No. 7354).

After examining Hiram Showman's petition, Vifquain observed, "[A]ll through the claim the prices seem to be such exactly double of what the things were really worth." Showman's neighbor, George Line, agreed that Showman exaggerated his losses. Line stated, "I cannot & will not testify in a case where the amount claimed is over $6000 when I believe that $1000 would fully cover all losses." Further damning the case, Vifquain learned that one of Showman's witnesses, Franklin T. Hine, was "a horse thief and a convict," considered as "altogether uncreditable, even under oath." The quartermaster general rejected Showman's claim.

Victor Vifquain found several discrepancies in Henry F. Neikirk's case. He reported, "I will right here state that I have myself heard claimant say that the only way to get fair compensation is to charge well for those things that are allowed, so as to make up the deficiency for those things that have been taken, and which were not allowed." Suppose Neikirk confessed this information to the agent. How should we view him—as a victimized farmer wanting to fully recoup his losses or a dishonest claimant attempting to defraud the government? Agent Vifquain sided with the latter and called for the rejection of Neikirk's claim.[21]

Quartermaster agents needed to be on the lookout for fraud, but primary sources reveal that most of Sharpsburg's claimants and witnesses followed the straight and narrow. Eli Hiatt, for example, corrected an item in his mother-in-law's petition. He told the agent, "The hay taken was not over 4 tons . . . the crop that year was a poor one." Joseph Sherrick's appraisers discovered an error in their citizens' appraisement, and asked the agent to reduce Sherrick's loss of 13,048 fence rails to 5,774. In response, the agent described them as "men of the highest character in this County evidenced by the frank manner in which they met every question put to them." John Roulette's claim included the amount owed to his landlord, Martin Eakle. After reviewing Roulette's petition, Eakle told a quartermaster agent that he "considers the estimate made by his tenant far too high . . . he does not wish to claim from the Government the amount set down."[22]

In another example of honest testimony, George Line pointed out a mistake in his paperwork, testifying, "I will call the attention of the Department to the fact that the report of the Board of Survey contains many Q.M. stores for which

21 Claims of Hiram Showman (No. 1522) and Henry F. Neikirk (H-4108 and H-4109). According to Susan Hoffman's case (No. 1318), Franklin T. Hine lived on Hoffman's farm from 1860–69, working as a laborer. He later served as constable of Rohrersville District.

22 Claims of Joseph Sherrick (F-1433), Magdalene Jones (54-1470), and John Roulette (L-830).

claimant makes no charge." Jacob Nicodemus of Sharpsburg deposed "that he has been careful not to overestimate the quantity [of corn] furnished for the use of the Govt." The special agent found Nicodemus's prices "very reasonable and just" and "somewhat lower" than neighboring claimants.

In another case, Henry Piper clarified to the agent that he "charged in the foregoing bill of items for only such supplies and property as remained on my farm on my return on the 18th." He added, "The amount charged in this bill is but a trifle over one half of the amount of property & supplies actually taken by the army." Piper did not charge for his total losses because "the difficulty of obtaining the necessary proofs as to the taking and use of the property by the army of the United States compelled me to abandon a large portion of my claim." He added, "I make no claim for property taken in my absence."[23]

Despite the applicants' efforts to abide by the rules of the Act of July 4, 1864, their attorneys sometimes committed mistakes that jeopardized or prolonged cases. Attorney Albert Small assured Thomas Barnum that his claims papers "were in Washington on file." But as time passed, the distressed tenant farmer—who suffered compounded losses from the Antietam and Gettysburg campaigns—journeyed to the war department in Washington, DC to confirm that his papers were on file. To his dismay, Barnum "found they were not."[24]

Gregory and Jones, a law firm based in Washington, represented several Sharpsburg claimants. These attorneys "mislaid" a voucher in Stephen P. Grove's claim. The receipt documented Grove's expenses for purchasing hospital supplies in Hagerstown with his own money. Without it, however, Grove could not recoup the amount owed to him.

Gregory and Jones also lost Samuel Mumma Sr.'s citizens' appraisement. Without the important document, Mumma relied on a board of survey appraisement to prove his losses. Major George Bell, the depot quartermaster, found this evidence insufficient. "[T]he report of the Board," Bell informed the quartermaster general, "shows that the claimant suffered severe losses in the destruction by fire of his house, barn, furniture, fencing, hay, &c." Continuing, Bell wrote, "[B]ut there is nothing in the report to show that any of the property described in the list assessed by the Board was used in the public service."

---

23 Claims of George Line (F-1186 and F-1187), Jacob Nicodemus of Sharpsburg (95-1683), Samuel Mumma, Sr. (113-1024), and Henry Piper (No. 445).

24 Claim of Thomas Barnum (No. 333). An advertisement for Albert Small's legal services in the *Herald and Torch Light*, July 27, 1864, 4, cites that his clientele included former slaves, like Barnum.

Mumma's claim, Bell concluded, was "respectfully returned without recommendation for settlement."[25]

Another claim agent, Captain Joseph Addison McCool, misfiled a receipt in John L. Highbarger's claim. This error prevented Highbarger from recouping payment for "three tons of hay . . . [taken] from his stable in the village of Sharpsburg." Interestingly, claims filed by the heirs of Henry Wade disappeared under Attorney McCool's management. When the case came under investigation, Eli Wade explained that he gave the paperwork to "Capt. J. A. McCool, a claim agent, who was a man somewhat of intemperate habits." Worsening matters, Wade explained, "In 1866, he [McCool] visited Harpers Ferry, fell in the Ches. & Ohio Canal and drowned. I have never been able to hear of or repossess those papers since."[26]

The quartermaster department knew that claims attorneys worked on commission and stood to earn considerable sums on high settlements. For instance, Michael Miller's lawyer charged "40 per ct for collecting." One agent remembered, though, that most petitioners "were perfectly willing to pay an attorney fee of one-half of the amount allowed." Thus, if the quartermaster department noticed that a claims attorney edited an original document, they suspected that he tampered with evidence to swell the total amount claimed.[27]

Victor Vifquain noticed that someone edited a document in Stephen P. Grove's claim. In response, the agent notified the depot quartermaster, "I will remark right here, that the pencil note found by me in the margin on one of the claims . . . is not understood by me . . . I am unable to state who made erasures or marks on face of petition."

Vifquain did not accuse Grove's attorney of wrongdoing. But, of note, the same lawyer represented William F. Hebb, whose citizens' appraisement contained a similar alteration. Vifquain's copy of Hebb's document listed "196 acres clover used as pasture," which implied that army animals consumed the clover as forage.

---

25 Claims of Stephen P. Grove (No. 7354) and Samuel Mumma, Sr. (No. 334).

26 Claims of John L. Highbarger (54-1487), William Wade (G-2397), the heirs of Henry Wade (G-2398), and John A. Wade (G-2400). Attorneys representing July Fourth cases were also known as claims agents. By "intemperate," Wade implied that Captain Joseph Addison McCool suffered from a drinking problem. The *United States Army and Navy Journal and Gazette of the Regular and Volunteer Forces,* (New York, 1864) vol. 1, 332, shows that McCool was dismissed from the 3rd U.S. Infantry in 1864 "for drunkenness and absence without authority."

27 Claim of Michael Miller (F-1437 and F-1438). Miller's attorney penciled a note next to Miller's $399.60 award, citing his fee of $159.85; Britton, *The Aftermath of the Civil War,* 65.

But when the agent compared it to Hebb's original appraisement, he discovered that it read, "Damage done to 196 acres clover and land."

"[I]t is seen therein," Vifquain complained to Washington, "that the charge is for damages done to 196 acres of clover land & added to it without my authority are the words by pasturing & c. These last words are in hand-right of Atty." Vifquain accused Hebb's lawyer of "knowing full well that the Govt. made no allowance for damages" caused by the encampment of troops. The quartermaster agent vented to his department, "An Atty. that changes sworn appraisement, of his own author, deserves the severest . . . punishment. The evidence does not allow me to make any recommendation for this item, because our men were encamped in said meadow & that their destruction of the grass cannot be counted as forage."[28]

The attorney in question was George W. Z. Black. He served as a lieutenant in the 107th Pennsylvania Infantry and suffered a wound at Antietam. After the war, Black practiced law in Frederick, Maryland, and represented most of Sharpsburg's claimants in cases filed under the Act of July 4, 1864.

Some clients encountered issues with George W. Z. Black. Hannah Nicodemus, wife of Sharpsburg farmer Jacob Nicodemus, informed Brig. Gen. Meigs that she dropped Black as her attorney because of "serious delays." Another petitioner, Ann Maria Smith, learned that Black filed a claim in her name without requesting permission. She wrote to Quartermaster General Meigs, "I never gave a Q.M. claim to Col. Black of any kind and never intended to do so . . . I gave him no authority to file such claim." Concerned about the outcome of her case, Mrs. Smith declared Black's action "as a fraud on my rights, and I respectfully ask the Department to return the same to me or hold it as I declare it void."[29]

John Kretzer also complained about George W. Z. Black. He informed Victor Vifquain "that there are two items which he wishes to be understood he does not charge to the Government of the U.S." One involved fencing taken by Confederates in 1863, and the other was "4 tons of fodder for which 25 dollars are claimed, he says he does not know what it means." These items, the claimant insisted, "were inserted by his attorney without [Kretzer being] aware of it." Agent Vifquain reported to his superiors, "I do not know if fraud was intended by

---

28 Claims of Stephen P. Grove (No. 7354) and William F. Hebb (F-1417).

29 Hough, *History of Duryee's Brigade*, 154; Brian Downey, "Lieutenant George Washington Ziegler Black," web page, Antietam on the Web, http://antietam.aotw.org/officers.php?officer_id=10313; Claims of Jacob Nicodemus of Sharpsburg (95-1683) and David Smith (F-846). Ann Maria Smith was the wife of Captain David Smith. She became executrix of the claims after Captain Smith's death in 1869.

Attorney G. W. Z. Black of Frederick City, but the absence of the appraisement should lead me to believe that he was anxious to swell the claim; it is not the first time that I decover some irregularities in the action of said attorney."

Attorney fraud proved costly for Philip Pry. The farmer initially placed his multiple claims "in the hands of S. H. Keedy, for collection." Afterward, though, he heard "unfavorable reports in regard to Keedy [and] endeavored to get the papers out of his hands." In 1866, Pry hired Baltimore lawyer William B. Hill, but after "several years delay," grew frustrated and transferred his case to attorney C. E. Rittenhouse. This third lawyer discovered that the government had already settled Pry's claims—years earlier, in fact—and sent a payment of $2,662.50 to the first attorney, S. H. Keedy, in 1865.

Upon learning of the settlement, Pry "was astonished and said that he had neither heard of it before nor has he ever received a cent." Upon reviewing a copy of the settled claims, he found "that the payment of 2,500 bushels of corn ... was a fraud, as he never had but 900 bushels, and that he had no oats, although settlement was made for 600 bushels."

After adjusting Pry's claims, the quartermaster's department determined three things. First, Pry was entitled to $1,000 for wheat. Second, the $2,662.50 settlement "fraudulently paid to S. H. Keedy" contained an overpayment of $1,209.38 for the inflated quantities of corn and oats. Third, Pry could not receive the $1,000 award for wheat until he returned the $1,209.38 overpayment to the United States Treasury. Correspondence in Philip Pry's claim shows that "steps were immediately taken by him to recover the Amt. paid to Keedy." Nevertheless, attorney C. E. Rittenhouse later informed the quartermaster general that Pry "has great difficulty in collecting the amount overpaid & refunded the same to the Govt." It's not known if S. H. Keedy paid Pry any amount of the $2,662.50.[30]

*   *   *

Receipts were the most important evidence for proving the merits of July Fourth claims. Also referred to as vouchers and certificates, these IOUs included the names of the claimant and authorizing officer. The receipts also cited the

---

30 Claims of John Kretzer (54-1471) and Philip Pry (H-3907 and H-3908). Agent Sallade recommended a $1,700 settlement to Pry for wheat, which the depot quartermaster reduced to $1,000.

officer's command, place and date of appropriation, description of supplies taken, and prices charged.

Joshua Newcomer, Thomas Barnum, and Henry Shamel obtained signed vouchers for some of their seized property. The quartermaster department, though, did not immediately approve settlements. Rather, protocol required verification that the officers' signatures were genuine. The adjutant general of the army compared the claimants' receipts to other records on file, such as payrolls and muster rolls. He verified that the handwriting matched, and the quartermaster general awarded the receipted amounts to the three claimants.[31]

Unfortunately, few civilians received certificates after the battle, for various reasons. For instance, chaos prevailed in Antietam's aftermath, making it difficult to identify commands and determine which officers—if any—ordered the appropriations. William Unger blamed the "confusion ensuing after the bloody battle of Antietam," which made it "impossible to find Quartermasters and get vouchers." William Roulette added, "We were all upset so and did not get any [vouchers] and did not know who to get them from." Similarly, Joseph Poffenberger testified, "I did not know what steps to take to get my pay." Agent Sallade reported that Lydia Long, "being an old lady," failed to secure receipts because she was "unacquainted with what would be required to facilitate the collection of her claim."[32]

Some civilians requested certificates, to no avail. William M. Blackford remarked, "I applied for receipts to the officers . . . and was generally promised vouchers when they should move, but they failed in nearly every instance to do so." After the battle, Adam Showman made nine trips to Hagerstown to retrieve supplies for Smoketown Hospital, leaving "every day at 4 o'clock in the morning and got back at 9 o'clock p.m." Afterward, Showman "asked the Surgeon in charge of the Hospital for a receipt for the hauling, and was promised one time and again, but never succeeded in getting it." Another farmer, Jacob Nicodemus of Springvale, hauled supplies with his four-horse team for 20 days from Hagerstown to the Locust Spring hospital. When he requested a voucher for his services, the surgeon's staff "were short and did not want to give me audience; said they didn't

31 Claims of Joshua Newcomer (F-854), Thomas Barnum (131-1078), and Henry Shamel (RG 92, Entry 797, Book 54, Box 15, Claim 54-1461); Britton, *The Aftermath of the Civil War*, 43.

32 Claims of William Unger (K-516), Samuel Mumma, Sr. (No. 334), Joseph Poffenberger (No. 1300), and Lydia Long (RG 92, Entry 812, Book F, Claim F-1289). William Roulette testified in Mumma's case. Lydia Long suffered damages from Slocum's division, VI Corps. Her claim cited that she owned "some sixty acres of land . . . on the Sharpsburg turnpike."

know whether I was loyal or not & c., all of which I offered to prove, but they didn't want to be bothered."[33]

Some AOP officers informed distressed civilians they would eventually be paid—without or without receipts. Susan Hoffman requested paperwork to certify her losses. Still, she dropped the matter "because of the assurance of several officers that the Gov't would pay for the claim without asking for vouchers." An 8th Illinois cavalry quartermaster offered John Kretzer a voucher for appropriated hay. The certificate, nonetheless, did not cover the total amount taken. Kretzer consulted with the regiment's commander, Colonel John Farnsworth, who advised the townsman to decline the receipt and seek full payment from the government in Washington.

Samuel Mumma, Jr. testified that his father suffered from "feebleness in body" after the battle and could not request receipts. As a result, Mumma, Jr. "called upon the officer who took the stores and asked him for proper papers or vouchers." The quartermaster, however, "[R]efused to give it and said the government would pay it."[34]

*   *   *

George McClellan, to remind readers, ordered his quartermasters at the onset of the 1862 Maryland Campaign to "make the purchases of forage, pay for the same in money, or in lieu thereof, will issue to the owners certificates."[35]

If Federal officers received these orders before appropriating copious amounts of private property during the campaign, why did so few claimants receive certificates for their losses? One could argue that Confederates took most of the items listed in Sharpsburg's claims. Indeed, ANV soldiers seized forage, rails, and other articles during their three-day stay in Sharpsburg. By comparison, though, the AOP encamped in the neighborhood for six weeks and occupied scores of properties outside the Confederate lines.

One might also allege that Federal stragglers confiscated most of Sharpsburg's property. This theory would explain the lack of receipts given to civilians, but far

33 Claims of William M. Blackford (No. 1324), Catherine Showman (F-1176), and Jacob Nicodemus of Springvale (G-1854).

34 Claims of Susan Hoffman (No. 1318), John Kretzer (54-1471), and Samuel Mumma, Sr. (113-1024). Kretzer's claim noted that Farnsworth "was sick at Claimant's house" when the 8th Illinois took hay from Kretzer's out lots.

35 Claim of Jeremiah P. Grove (G-1632). Lt. Col. Rufus Ingalls, chief quartermaster of the AOP, issued McClellan's circular. Grove's claim contains a copy of the document.

too many witnesses observed the appropriated forage, rails, livestock, and timber used in AOP camps and hospitals. Thus, if Union quartermasters confiscated private property and issued certificates in exchange, would these transactions not appear in the officers' money accounts and returns?

The United States government searched for this evidence, that much is certain. During investigations of claims filed under the Act of July 4, 1864, the third auditor of the Treasury weeded through volumes of AOP quartermaster returns and money accounts from September–October 1862. Evidence shows that the auditor's staff searched multiple records for each claim in attempt to locate documents citing the alleged transactions. Clerks hunted through the accounts of 14 officers in the claim of Adam Michael, 15 officers for Solomon Lumm, 17 for Joseph Poffenberger, and 19 for Noah Rohrback. The searches found no mention of property taken from the claimants.[36]

Other inquiries made by the Treasury clerks yielded similar results. "The money accounts and property returns on file in this office, for the period stated," the third auditor reported, did not show any property taken from Henry Griffith, Josiah Hill, Rev. John A. Adams, and other Washington County residents.

Treasury staff reviewed the files of eleven officers in Jeremiah P. Grove's case but found no records confirming that U.S. forces took property from the farmer. Notably, all officers listed in the auditor's report belonged to V Corps. Testimony in the claim, though, identified commands from I Corps—not V Corps—as taking Grove's property. The auditor's focus on V Corps may have stemmed from Agent Sallade's report declaring that "a portion of the Union Army under the command of Maj. Gen. F. J. Porter and others" encamped on Jeremiah P. Grove's farm. But, confusion aside, Grove's claim does not show that the auditor's office searched for transactions in the accounts of I Corps officers.[37]

Samuel I. Piper's case contains a similar anomaly. More than one dozen regiments from Ricketts's division encamped on and near Piper's farm from September 19–October 26. During this time, Lt. D. A. Griffith of the 88th

---

36 Claims of Adam Michael (199-161), Solomon Lumm (N-546), Joseph Poffenberger (No. 1300), and Noah Rohrback (H-3874).

37 Claims of Henry Griffith (212-707), Josiah Hill (No. 8532), John A. Adams (G-1933), and Jeremiah P. Grove (G-1632). Grove's petition of losses, along with the testimony of two witnesses, alleged that I Corps forces commanded by Maj. Gen. John F. Reynolds encamped on Grove's farm and confiscated the farmer's property. However, neither the petition nor the witnesses mentioned Porter's V Corps, suggesting that Sallade may have confused the commands when compiling his report.

Pennsylvania recalled that brigade and division quartermasters seized Piper's timber, rails, and grains. According to the farmer's claim, the third auditor's staff searched the accounts of only one quartermaster—Lieutenant Charles Eager of the 136th Pennsylvania. This regiment did not join Ricketts's division until mid-October 1862, possibly explaining why Lt. Eager did "not account for any property as taken or purchased from Sam'l I. Piper in his returns from Sept. 1, '62 to Dec. 31, '62." The Treasury's lack of findings possibly factored into the quartermaster general's decision to reject Piper's claim.[38]

In defense of the third auditor of the Treasury, he and his clerks managed a flood tide of claims. Under different circumstances, with clearer communications from the quartermaster general's special agents, they may have conducted more thorough investigations. Three months after Congress passed the Act of July 4, 1864, Elijah Sells, the third auditor, reported to the secretary of the Treasury, "In view of the steady increase of accounts in this office . . . I respectfully recommend that Congress grant authority to add five clerks of class four, fifteen clerks of class three, thirty clerks of class two, and fifty clerks of class one to the force of this office." This was no small operation—and neither was the task at hand.[39]

The auditor's staff examined the correct accounts in other Sharpsburg claims but still found no evidence proving that McClellan's quartermasters seized private property. David R. Miller testified that "Major Gleason, Q.M. General, Joshua T. Owens Brigade" took 60 tons of hay in September 1862, offering no pay in exchange. However, the third auditor found that "Major James Gleason, A.Q.M. does not account for any property purchased or taken from David R. Miller during the period from September 1st 1862 to November 31st 1862." This discrepancy contributed to the quartermaster general's decision to suspend Miller's claim "until more positive proof is submitted as to what officer and troops took the property."[40]

The heirs of Henry Wade identified several IX Corps officers in their claims, including "Q masters Fitch, Capt. Armor & T. E. Hall." Yet, the third auditor failed to find "any property to have been purchased or taken" from the claimants. One of

---

38 Claim of Samuel I. Piper (No. 1310).

39 *Report of the Secretary of the Treasury on the State of Finances for the Year 1864*, (Washington, DC, 1864), 105.

40 Claim of David R. Miller (RG 92, F-1499). In 1862, Gleason served as quartermaster in the 69th Pennsylvania and "at various times served as division and brigade quartermaster." See James Gleason, *Official Letters and Orders Concerning the Military Career of James Gleason, During the Late Civil War* (Washington, DC, 1870), 7.

the officers, Captain Theron E. Hall, refuted the Wades' allegation, stating, "I know nothing of this case whatever." Hall admitted being "in charge of the Q.M. Dept of Genl Burnsides command after the battle of Antietam." He also recounted, "We moved from Sharpsburg soon after the battle to Pleasant Valley—my recollection is that the troops found it difficult to obtain fuel at the time as the Confederate army occupied the ground before we did and gleaned it pretty effectively."

Hall's statement is subject to debate. First, the Wades lived distant from Confederate lines. Even if Rebel pickets briefly occupied the properties, they could not have "gleaned" the vast amount of fencing described in the claims. Second, IX Corps did not depart Sharpsburg "soon after the battle" but remained in the region for nearly three weeks. For a good portion of this time, more than 15,000 of Burnside's men encamped on and near the Wade heirs' farms.[41]

Captain Hall also appears in Washington C. Snively's claim. After appropriating Snively's property in September 1862, Hall gave the farmer a written statement reading, "Capt. T. E. Hall, A.Q.M. Vols, will pay the above account." The captain, though, neither paid Snively nor accounted for the property. When Treasury clerks searched IX Corps records from September 1–December 31, 1862, they found "that the property returns and money accounts of Capt. T. E. Hall, for the period required, do not show any wood, fencing, lumber and hay to have been taken or purchased from, or payments made to the claimant [Snively]."

Keedysville resident Samuel Doub received several receipts after the Battle of Antietam. When the third auditor's clerks searched for Doub's name in quartermaster accounts, they found a match. Three quartermasters documented the appropriation of corn and hay from Samuel Doub on September 17 and 18, 1862. This finding raises an important question. How often did the office of the third auditor locate evidence proving that Federal officers appropriated private property from Sharpsburg-area civilians from September–October 1862? Of 179 July Fourth claims reviewed in this study, Samuel Doub was the only example located. But if quartermasters logged the appropriations, where were the records?[42]

41 Claims of the heirs of Henry Wade (G-2398), John A. Wade (G-2400), Eli Wade (G-2404), and William Wade (G-2397); *OR*, vol. 19, 2:336, 374. Returns for IX Corps on Sep. 20, 1862, show 10,734 present for duty. By Sep. 30, the number increased to 15,361. As cited in Chapters Five and Ten, most of IX Corps encamped near Sharpsburg village from Sep. 19–26, moved to the Antietam Iron Works area until Oct. 7, and then marched to Pleasant Valley. The Kanawha Division remained near Antietam Iron Works until Oct. 8.

42 Claim of Washington C. Snively (H-3458). Agent Sallade recommended a settlement to Snively, but the depot quartermaster, Major William Myers, denied the request on account of

A possible explanation for the missing evidence is that it never existed in the first place. This argument assumes that McClellan's officers, in most instances, authorized the seizure of private property but neither furnished receipts to residents nor logged the appropriations in their accounts. This practice did not only apply to Sharpsburg; evidence shows that it was common throughout the war. "Even if soldiers had the right forms" for issuing receipts, historian Joan E. Cashin argued, "they didn't always follow policy." Cashin noted that during the summer of 1862, a member of General Pope's army admitted that Federal quartermasters "sometimes gave out documents for confiscated food but more often did not." A Virginia citizen recounted that U.S. army officers initially distributed vouchers for supplies taken, but "those civilians received documents exactly once for those items, and after that the troops issued no more papers."

Cashin's research revealed that some Union officers during the war "refused to keep duplicates of the forms, as regulations stipulated, again, probably because it was too much trouble." In simplest terms, she opined, "They were not good bureaucrats—in fact, they were very bad." Supporting Cashin's argument, a Federal quartermaster, while encamped in Tennessee for three months in 1863, wrote that the Union army cut down "large forests" and destroyed "at least 200 miles of fencing . . . of which no account is kept and for which no payment is made."[43]

Circumstances didn't always allow for proper record keeping. In the chaos following the clash at Antietam, some officers may have lacked time to address bookkeeping. New regiments, like the 16th Maine, rushed to Sharpsburg after the battle to reinforce the AOP. In their haste, the Mainers left behind "the trunks of company officers containing all the company books and papers." This mistake prompted Colonel Charles W. Tilden to complain, "The absence of company books is exceedingly annoying to my officers, as their accounts are necessarily behind."[44]

Several examples show that AOP quartermasters did not document acquisitions of private property. Colonel Fred Myers served as chief quartermaster

---

"the absence of any official evidence on record on the subject;" Claims of Samuel Doub (RG 92, Entry 812, Box 115, G-2935-2937).

43 Cashin, *War Stuff*, 58-59, 70-72; Fitch, *Annals of the Army of the Cumberland*, 269.

44 Small, *The Sixteenth Maine Regiment*, 33, 42-44. The 16th Maine joined Colonel Richard Coulter's brigade, Ricketts's division, on Sep. 20, 1862. The regiment encamped at Sharpsburg for more than five weeks, departing on Oct. 26.

of I Corps until September 16, 1862. He testified, "I know that fences were burned by the soldiers and [am] satisfied that large amounts of corn was taken from the different farmers in the vicinity of Antietam." But Myers admitted, though, "[N]o reports were made to me at that time by any of the officers of the Qr. Mr. Dept. or have been since."

Captain Fielding Lowry replaced Myers as chief quartermaster of I Corps on September 20. Lowry recalled, upon arriving in Sharpsburg, "I gave orders to the different Quarter Masters and Batteries of the Corps to take what forage they could find in the Country that they required, and to give the owner a receipt for it, with instructions to present the receipt to me for settlement." But how accurate was Lowry's statement regarding the issuance of receipts? Civilian Jacob Houser testified that Capt. Lowry seized $1,600 in grains on September 20. Yet, Houser explained, "[I]t being directly after the battle of Antietam, much confusion prevailed and I furnished the above named stores for which no receipts were given." When the third auditor attempted to find records of Houser's losses, he reported that "Capt. Fielding Lowry A.Q.M. & Chf Q.M. 1st A.C. does not account for the within mentioned property on his returns for Sept. & Oct. 1862."[45]

Officers of the 3rd Pennsylvania Cavalry also practiced lax bookkeeping after the battle. Samuel Swain identified Captain S. P. Boyer as the quartermaster who authorized the seizure of his three horses in September 1862. The third auditor could not confirm the appropriation because "Capt. S. P. Boyer, Qr. Mr. 3d Pa. Cav., has no returns on file from August to October 1862."

Another Sharpsburg petitioner, Catherine Tenant, included a memorandum receipt in her claim for wheat taken on September 28, 1862, by "W. P. Dodson Q.M. Segt. 3d Penna V. Cavalry." Dodson, though, failed to record the appropriation in his books. The third auditor's searches revealed, "[T]he money accts and property returns of Lieut. W. P. Dodson Q.M. 3d Penna V. Cavalry . . . do not show any wood or forage to have been purchased paid for or taken from Michael or Catherine Tenant of Washington Co. Md."

Another example relates to Henry Piper. He alleged that 3rd Pennsylvania troopers, commanded by Lieutenant Philip Pollard, slaughtered his livestock after

---

45 Fred Myers to Samuel H. Keedy, July 2, 1866, and Fielding Lowry to M. C. Meigs, April 30, 1866, claim of Samuel Pry (81-1489); Claim of Jacob Houser (F-814). Myers clarified, "I was not the Chief Qr. Mr. of the 1st Army Corps after the 16th I having been placed on duty at Genl. McClellans Head Qrs. and had no means of knowing what was taken by the 1st Army Corps." Houser's claim cites, "Alleged to have been taken during the months of Sept & Oct 1862 . . . by Captain Fielding Lowry, R.Q.M. and Chief Q.M. 1st Army Corps."

the Battle of Antietam without offering payment or receipts. Lieutenant Pollard provided an affidavit explaining the appropriations. "I was encamped on the pike leading from Sharpsburg to Boonsboro on the land of Henry Piper," the cavalryman recalled. "I know we were in great need of subsistence . . . it was customary after a battle or pending a battle to capture and confiscate for the use of the army whatever subsistence stores could be found in this way. I remember that several heads of cattle, sheep and hogs were taken from Mr. Piper."

Continuing, Pollard wrote, "I may add that they were informally taken without direct orders from any competent authority but were used for the subsistence of the army all the same, to supply the pressing necessity of the army." Some of Piper's cattle, the lieutenant added, "were taken under my own direction and observation, and under the direction of other officers; but no receipts were given therefore, probably because none were asked for by Mr. Piper at the time." Of note, Pollard admitted, "I did not take up on my returns stores taken in this irregular way, probably owing to the excitement of the times."[46]

*　*　*

The other half of quartermaster investigations under the Act of July 4, 1864, centered on the claimants' loyalty to the U.S. government during the war. The required paperwork consisted of an oath of allegiance to the U.S. and a certificate signed by a Federal officer. Instead of the latter document, claimants could submit sworn statements "of at least two witnesses" whose own "loyalty and credibility shall be vouched for by the certificate of the officers before mentioned."

These prerequisites did not prevent disloyal persons from filing claims under the 1864 act. To further weed out Southern sympathizers, special agents recorded depositions from petitioners, witnesses, and other community members. Questioning centered on the claimant's voting record, political leanings, and actions taken to aid the Union and Confederate armies during the war. If an agent suspected an applicant of disloyalty, they recommended the rejection of the entire claim.[47]

---

46 Claims of Samuel Swain (N-2188), Catherine Tenant (54-1464), and Henry Piper (No. 445). Pollard noted that Piper's property "was not all taken by my regiment. I remember the 4th Pa. and the 8th N.Y. Calv. were encamped at the same place with my own regiment."

47 "Fourth of July Claims," 7.

Since Sharpsburg was predominantly a pro-Union district, quartermaster agents found that most claimants remained loyal throughout the war. Examples include John E. Knode, who "bore the reputation of being one of the best Union men in his neighborhood." Likewise, David R. Miller was "one of the few men who stood firm during the dark days of the rebellion." Joseph Poffenberger, meanwhile, was "bitterly opposed to secession." Furthermore, David R. Miller testified, "[O]ne instance I remember definitely, he [Poffenberger] told me that when Sheridan was in the Valley of the Shenandoah he ought to have burned it up to stop the war."[48]

Sharpsburg's Democrats faced a stricter challenge proving their loyalty. As Mayberry C. Beeler explained, "[C]ontention between the democrat and republican party was close and sharp during the war; the republicans designated the democrats as copperheads and Southern sympathizers." Although both parties contained "good loyal men," Beeler admitted that "a man's reputation for loyalty depended on which party he belonged to." Thus, in claims cases, Sharpsburg's Democrats endured an uphill battle proving they did not favor the Confederacy.[49]

In Hezekiah Myers's case, John Kretzer deposed, "Mr. Myers was not regarded as a loyal man during the war his sympathies were notoriously with the South." Benjamin F. Rohrback also exposed Myers, stating, "He always expressed himself in my presence against the Union cause and called the Union soldiers nothing but a set of 'd—d blue bellys.'"

Myers defended himself by deposing, "I was a Democrat and never was anything else. I tried to treat both armies alike in order to save my property . . . never aided the rebels in any way and never gave them any information as to the

---

48 Some of Sharpsburg's Unionists included William F. Hebb (F-1417) and Henry B. Rohrback (No. 1323), both described as "old line Whigs." Additionally, George Line (F-1186 and F-1187) and Captain David Smith (F-846) voted for Abraham Lincoln in 1860. Michael Miller recalled that John C. Middlekauff (No. 329) "was a Bell and Everett man at the election in 1860, which of itself is proof of strong attachment to Union principles." John Bell and Edward Everett ran on the Constitutional Union Party ticket in 1860 and were "strongly opposed to secession." See Lauren Jensen, "The Struggle for the Union: The Constitutional Union Party in the Election of 1860," *Constructing the Past* (Bloomington, IL, 2005), vol. 6, issue 1, article 5, https://digitalcommons.iwu.edu/constructing/vol6/iss1/5; Claims of John E. Knode (No. 8587), David R. Miller (F-1499), and Joseph Poffenberger (No. 1300).

49 Claim of Jacob H. Grove (RG 123, No. 1267). Mayberry Beeler testified in the case. Giving full context to Beeler's statement, he added, "[T]he democrats called the republicans black republicans and nigger lovers." Jacob McGraw's wartime sentiments also showcase the complexity of divided loyalties in the Sharpsburg community. At the onset of the war, he recalled, "I felt toward the South because I had a brother in the Confederate army." Later, McGraw "didn't care which side won if only they put a stop to the fightin', though it did seem to me it would be better to have one country" (Johnson, *BA*, 113).

movements of the Union army." Having heard both sides, Agent Sallade concluded, "The claimant's loyalty is exceedingly doubtful." Accordingly, he disallowed Myers's claim.

In other cases, deponents asserted that Eliza Davis "associated with southern sympathizing" and painted John Poffenberger as "an outspoken and bitter sympathizer with the rebellion" who "never expressed a favorable sentiment to the Gov't." Witnesses accused Morgan and Andrew Rentch Miller of boarding Rebel guerilla Andrew Leopold during the Battle of Antietam. They also heard the brothers "curse the Pst. of the U.S. and call the federals S_ of _B." The unfavorable testimonies torpedoed all three cases.[50]

Some citizens were uncomfortable testifying against their neighbors. Martin Line told Agent Sallade in confidence that John Poffenberger was disloyal during the war. Regardless, Line "refused to make a written statement for the reason that he and decedent were good friends and he therefore did not wish his name to appear as testifying against him." One local described James Marker as a "violent and outspoken rebel," who reportedly once stated "that he wished the Confederates would drive the dame Yankees out of Virginia." Benjamin A. Edmonds, testifying in Marker's case, admitted hearing these rumors. Still, he "avoided conversing with him [Marker] on the subject of the war" because "I did not wish to incur his ill will as we had frequent business transactions with each other."

The Showman family's powerful status intimidated witnesses from testifying against them. While investigating the loyalty of Hiram Showman, Agent Vifquain complained, "The family of claimant is one of influence and I have found it difficult to get witnesses to testify in the case." Vifquain remarked that Showman's "nearest neighbor G. Line personally refused to do so, and so also did Adam Hentzel . . . [who] was not willing to be sworn nor sign anything."[51]

---

50 Claims of Hezekiah Myers (G-1796), Eliza Davis (F-1536), John Poffenberger (L-2096), and Morgan and Andrew Rentch Miller (No. 4295). Martin Cramer testified that Leopold boarded with the Millers after suffering a head wound during the battle at Sharpsburg. Cramer described Leopold as "a hard character, a rebel guerilla," and referred to him as "Lapole." The 1860 Federal census for Sharpsburg lists Andrew Leopold's mother, Mary "Polly" Zittle, in the Miller brothers' dwelling, where she worked as a housekeeper. The Millers' claim does not identify who accused them of cursing the president or calling U.S. troops "S_ of _B," but the special agent mentioned the allegation while questioning witness Martin Cramer.

51 Claims of John Poffenberger (L-2096), James Marker (No. 1292), and Hiram Showman (No. 1522). "G. Line" and "Adam Hentzel" were George Line and Adam Hutzell, Showman's adjoining neighbors.

Throughout the Civil War, Sharpsburg's Democrats could not vote unless they presented a certified oath of loyalty to the judge of elections, or took the oath before election officials. In 1863, Squire Jacob Miller complained about a new clause inserted into the sworn statement. This revision "for-bid the person takeing the oath from holding any conversation with any person living in any one of the rebellious states." Miller asked Sharpsburg's election judges "if they would leave out that clause" because he "had many reletives" in Virginia. The officials refused. Consequently, Miller wrote, "[T]here was verry fiew if any took the oath . . . [and] the democrats generally took no interest in the Election."

Refusing to take a loyalty oath during the war, for any reason, backfired on claimants during the July Fourth claims examinations. Although no persons testified against Hiram Showman, Agent Vifquain found that the claimant did not take the oath of allegiance until 1864. He used this evidence to declare Showman a "rebel sympathizer."

Vifquain added, "To my many investigations of claims here, I have found that those Democrats who were truly loyal to the Government never hesitated from the start to take the oath of allegiance, and in fact there was no reason for any Democrat who was loyal to refuse doing so." One example, the agent noted, was John Snyder, who lived near Antietam Iron Works. Vifquain described Snyder as "an old line Democrat . . . held by all to have been loyal to the Government of the U.S." Vifquain reported that Snyder "was turned out from office by the exertions of the ring Democracy, or what is called the 'rebel' Democracy. I have no reasons to doubt the sincerity of claimant."[52]

Regardless of how much favorable evidence a claimant presented to the quartermaster general's office, the 1864 act allowed special agents to use a single, incriminating statement—truthful or not—as a basis for rejecting a claim. Wiley Britton remembered that many agents who investigated quartermaster claims did not take the "care and trouble in finding and examining witnesses who would testify in favor of the claimant that they had displayed in finding witnesses to testify against him." Also, Britton wrote, "[I]f any agent entertained any bias in the investigation of a claim, a claim would not likely get justice."

Wiley Britton knew this firsthand, for he himself was a quartermaster agent who examined claims filed under the Act of July 4, 1864. He wrote that his fellow

---

52 Jacob Miller to Amelia and Christian Houser, November 16, 1863, WMR; Claims of Hiram Showman (No. 1522) and John Snyder (F-859). Ring Democrats were associated with William "Boss" Tweed and Tammany Hall.

agents were given the same authority as a United States Commissioner, which made them a "traveling court," or the "Judge, Jury, and Prosecutor, for they could ask a claimant or witness any question they desired relating to the claim." Possessing such authority, a special agent "could, if he allowed his prejudices to influence him for or against a claim, make his investigation conform to his prejudices." A biased investigator, Britton wrote, could selectively "fail to examine witnesses whose testimony would weaken or strengthen a case." This type of agent "considered it his duty to defeat as many claims as possible [and] he could easily direct his investigations to that end."

Additionally, the Act of July 4, 1864 limited the claimants' ability to defend themselves against wrongful accusations. In this respect, one U.S. Representative argued, the July Fourth Act was unfair because it was not "until the act of June 13, 1880 . . . that claimants or their attorneys were allowed to be present and cross-examine witnesses before special agents." Petitioners and their lawyers were also "denied access to the reports of the agents of the Quartermaster-General." Consequently, the one-sided investigations prevented petitioners, like Sharpsburg's Democrats, from responding to incriminating or erroneous allegations. Not only was this unjust, the U.S. Representative declared, but "this practice continued for sixteen years."[53]

Indeed, bias presented in Sharpsburg's investigations, affecting Republicans and Democrats alike. For example, Benjamin F. Rohrback, a Republican, confessed to Agent Vifquain that Rebels confiscated some of his corn in September 1862. In other claims, agents usually awarded no settlements if Confederates took a portion of the property. In Rohrback's case, Vifquain reported, "[I]t is evident that the rebels did not do much damage: yet to be safe I shall only recommend an allowance for one half of the field, or 100 bushels."

Claimants were not allowed to assist appraisers in estimating losses. Yet, when Victor Vifquain learned that Noah Rohrback's claim for old corn was "appraised upon representations of the claimant & not upon the knowledge of the appraisers," he made an exception. "[I]t is fair to presume that a farmer knows how much he has in his crib, and I believe to be safe in accepting his figures at one hundred bushels."

---

53 Britton, *The Aftermath of the Civil War*, 47-49, 56-57, 81; "Fourth of July Claims," 9. The U.S. Representative was Frank Beltzhoover of Pennsylvania, who served on the Committee on War Claims.

Besides, Vifquain wrote, "[T]he loyalty of the whole Rohrback family is well known in this community and they are all staunch Republicans."[54]

Vifquain's tone differed while investigating Democrats. One resident described David Reel as "a strict Union man" who "wished he could blow the rebels to the devil with a keg of powder." But another witness stated that Reel, a Democrat, "kept on with both sides as they came on so as to get along," in effort to save his property. Based on the latter testimony, Agent Vifquain reported David Reel as disloyal and recommended the rejection of his entire petition.

John H. Snavely's sentiments also shifted during the war, but unlike David Reel, he recruited Republicans as witnesses. Samuel Show testified that Snavely "always was a Union man although he is a Democrat." Benjamin F. Rohrback, though, told Agent Vifquain that Snavely's sympathies "were with the south until Pres. Lincoln offered to pay the south for their slaves in case the rebels laid down their arms." Vifquain found that "the two witnesses of the claimant are staunch republicans and their evidence is somewhat contradictory," but "[I] am compelled to recommend him as loyal."

Like Snavely, Jacob C. Grove professed that "his feelings were in favor of the South" at the war's onset. But after Lincoln issued the Emancipation Proclamation, Grove, a slave owner, "relinquished all his sympathies for the south." This confession spelled doom for the Democrat, who had no Republican witnesses to vouch for his loyalty. Agent Vifquain asked his department to disallow Grove's claim "on account of his rebel proclivities."

Vifquain's bias against Grove carried into another claim. Testifying in the case of his late father, Jacob C. Grove deposed that "[R]ebels did not encamp on his place prior to the battle of Antietam; encamped there only during the battle." Grove's witnesses concurred, but Agent Vifquain bristled at the testimony. "[T]here is undoubtedly fraud attached to the getting up of such claims," he wrote, "perhaps more ignorance than fraud, for it is evident that the people did lose large amounts of timber and fencing; charging the Federal government extraordinary amounts, so as to cover such losses as they evidently incurred by the rebels when

---

54 Claims of Jacob Snyder (F-1537), John J. Keedy (No. 2157), Benjamin F. Rohrback (F-617 and F-619), and Noah Rohrback (H-3874). The depot quartermaster found the evidence insufficient and denied Vifquain's requests to grant settlements to the four pro-Union claimants.

they were encamped right here." Vifquain informed the depot quartermaster, "I am carefully set to recommend it be disallowed as to quantities demanded."[55]

A quartermaster agent's conduct, Wiley Britton explained, "should have been in every case absolutely impartial as between the claimant and the Government, and then the provisions of the Act would have had their intended effect." Unfortunately, Britton noted, "The conceptions of duty in this respect were not uniform among the agents of the department" because "there was no developed procedure or definite instructions to agents when they were sent into the field."

Using Missouri as an example, Britton recalled that agents "seemed to consider it their mission to defeat as many of the claims sent to them as practicable, and it was their duty to prevent claimants from presenting all the evidence available to support the justness of their claims." Special agents selected witnesses to testify against claimants, and many facts supporting a given case "were invariably ignored and the claimant not informed of his rights." Consequently, agents recommended the rejection of countless cases, which Britton described as the "slaughtering of the claims."

Special agents may have operated similarly while examining the July Fourth claims at Sharpsburg. Before his investigation began, Stephen P. Grove learned "that a malicious private person had declared that he would keep me out of payment of my claims if possible." Anticipating the malcontent's attempt to sabotage his case, Grove recruited reputable witnesses to verify his Union loyalty. Federal officers, prominent citizens, and a former Maryland senator all went on record to avow Grove as loyal. Only one witness, Martin L. Fry, spoke negatively. He declared Grove "a southern sympathizer during the war and is yet—never was loyal."

Grove did not identify Martin L. Fry as the "malicious private person," but the incriminating testimony gave agent Victor Vifquain reason to doubt Grove's loyalty. The agent asked the claimant, "When the battle of Antietam was being fought, what side do you hope would be victorious?" Grove purportedly replied, "I do not know that I hoped either; I looked upon it as if I had nothing to do with it . . . [I was] a neutral to the war that was being waged." This testimony did not sit well

---

55 Claims of David Reel (F-847), John H. Snavely (F-1441), Jacob C. Grove (G-1649), and the heirs of Samuel Grove (G-1632). In the Grove heirs' case, witness testimony conflicted as to whether Confederates encamped on the property. One of the heirs, Jacob C. Grove, admitted seeing Rebels on the farm during the battle. This statement may have given Vifquain reason to call for the rejection of the Grove heirs' fencing and trees, which amounted to 20,000–30,000 rails and several acres of timber.

with Vifquain. He notified Washington "that claimants own confessions prove that he did not care a straw which side won our great battles . . . and therefore claimant must not expect us to care for him."

Quartermaster General Meigs accepted Vifquain's recommendation to declare Stephen P. Grove disloyal and reject the farmer's multiple claims. Later, Grove read Vifquain's report. He discovered that the agent rewrote his testimony to make him appear neutral—a position that he insisted never taking. Trying to make sense of the accusation, Grove presumed that Vifquain "misunderstood me or tortured my language in to a different meaning than I intended."[56]

A similar accusation arose in Andrew Rentch's claim. All but one witness testified that the wealthy farmer was loyal to the Union, but Theodore C. Beeler reportedly dissented. He stated that Rentch "was regarded as a disloyal man; knows that he had a son shot at Williamsport for being a rebel and aiding rebels." This statement contributed to the dismissal of Rentch's claim on the grounds of disloyalty.

After reading the final report, Theodore C. Beeler declared that he never said such a thing. "I did not make a written statement to Agent Clark of the Quartermaster General's office," Beeler asserted under oath, "to the effect that Andrew Rentch was disloyal during the war, and that his son was a rebel spy and he had been killed by the soldiers. I always regarded Mr. Rentch a loyal man." Rentch's attorney, George W. Z. Black, accused Agent Clark of fabricating Beeler's testimony. "The absolutely unreliable character of this agent's report," Black argued, "is apparent on its face. That he falsely reported the evidence of witness Beeler will not be disputed, and that he concealed some important facts connected with the killing of claimant's son is also beyond question . . . in this case he committed a gross outrage on a citizen who was entitled to fair treatment."

Another claimant, William M. Blackford, remembered that agent Victor Vifquain questioned him about his wartime loyalty. Thereafter, he "read the affidavit over to me" to ensure the farmer's answers were correct. Blackford approved the agent's transcription but later learned that the quartermaster general rejected his claim due to suspected disloyalty. In reviewing a copy of the agent's report, Blackford found that Vifquain inserted a sentence in which "I am made to say that my sentiments and feelings [were] with the South." Blackford swore that he

---

56 Britton, *The Aftermath of the Civil War*, 47-49, 52-57; Claims of Stephen P. Grove (No. 7354) and Elias S. Grove (No. 7356). Elias S. Grove's case file includes evidence relating to his brother, Stephen P. Grove.

never made such a statement. Furthermore, he insisted that this portion of the testimony "was not read to me" when Blackford approved the affidavit.[57]

During Squire Jacob Miller's claim investigation, most witnesses described the Democrat as Union-loyal throughout the war. There was one exception. Henry F. Neikirk told the special agent that Squire Miller "was notoriously disloyal"—a remark that led to the case's rejection. But did Neikirk make this statement? After learning of the outcome, Neikirk stated, "I don't consider that the agent reported me correctly in regard to the loyalty in this matter. I did not know or don't know of my own knowledge, any disloyal acts on the part of these parties interested."

When Victor Vifquain interviewed Henry A. Poffenberger, he asked the farmer to sign a document to facilitate the settlement of his two claims. "He was an agent of the United States," Poffenberger recalled, "and I supposed he would treat me fairly and justly and I signed the paper on his statement that it was right for me to do so." Afterward, Poffenberger learned, the document he signed was a relinquishment of claim.

Poffenberger protested the agent's report. "I have never relinquished either of these claims to the United States," he insisted. "I find my signature to such a paper prepared by Mr. Vifquain the Quartermasters agent . . . if he got me to sign it by any trick or by any promise held out to me it don't look right that I should lose it as it is as just as the other." Agent Vifquain stood his ground, stating, "In justice to myself I will say that I have only followed my instructions as regards [to] investigations, and that I have never, in no case, attempted to intimidate either the claimants or their witnesses." The agent added that the "relinquishment was made by the claimants free will."

Poffenberger's attorney, George W. Z. Black, attacked Vifquain's explanation. "[T]his paper was procured when no attorney or counsel was present to advise claimant as to his rights and would and should be held worthless in any court of justice." Moreover, Black argued, "When the Quartermaster's agent was investigating these two claims, he endeavored to take advantage of the claimant by getting him to sign the relinquishment of one claim by the assurance that by doing so it would facilitate or secure the settlement of the other claim." Black's argument

---

57 Claims of Andrew Rentch (No. 4235) and William M. Blackford (No. 1324). If Blackford's allegation is true, Vifquain may have sabotaged the claim because of Blackford's relation to Rev. Robert Douglas. The reverend, a suspected Secessionist, married Blackford's sister and lived on the adjoining farm. The couple had two sons in the Confederate army.

fell on deaf ears, for once the quartermaster general closed a case, he could not reopen it.[58]

*   *   *

When we consider the number of Fourth of July claims rejected by the quartermaster and commissary departments, along with countless other cases barred by the rules and jurisdiction of the act, it comes as no surprise that Antietam Valley claimants received little for their losses. One resident remembered, "When my father presented his bill to the Government for supplies . . . he received just one-half the sum he had actually expended." The context of "just one-half" suggests a disappointing award, but the fifty-percent settlement is significantly larger than what the government paid other civilians.[59]

In 1880, the U.S. Secretary of War released a summary of July Fourth claims filed from 1864–80. During the sixteen years, applicants in Northern and border states filed 53,505 cases with the quartermaster general's office, totaling $38,084,867. Of this amount, Brig. Gen. Meigs approved 10,499 claims and awarded $4,301,584. Viewing this from another angle, of all claims filed from 1864–80, Meigs only approved 20 percent of the cases and awarded 11 percent of the total amount claimed.

Taking a closer look at Maryland, the secretary of war's 1880 report shows that petitioners from the Old Line State filed $3,808,407 in claims from 1864–80, of which the quartermaster general awarded $430,158. These statistics mirror the 11 percent settlement rate for claimants in border and Northern states.[60]

In quartermaster cases reviewed for this study, all related to the Battle of Antietam, 127 Sharpsburg-area petitioners filed 179 claims under the Act of July 4, 1864, totaling $260,117.19. Of this amount, Meigs approved 77 claims filed by 71 claimants, to whom he awarded $40,409.84. This translates to a 43 percent approval rate and a 15.5 percent settlement average. Both figures are substantially higher than the rates for applicants in Northern and border states.

The total quartermaster supplies claimed by 127 Sharpsburg-area claimants, $260,117.19, converts to $7.3 million in 2022 U.S. real prices. If we combine other losses not included in this figure—commissary items, household possessions,

---

58 Claims of Jacob Miller (No. 4296) and Henry A. Poffenberger (No. 7178).

59 Williams, HWC, vol. 1, 2:362.

60 *Annual Report of the Secretary of War for the Year 1880,* (Washington, DC, 1880), vol. 1, 473-474.

The U.S. quartermaster general rejected the July Fourth claims of several dozen Sharpsburg-area claimants, including James Marker, featured in this photograph. *Sharpsburgh Museum of History*

property damages, and Confederate-related appropriations—it's no wonder that Antietam and its aftermath thrust so many families to the brink of bankruptcy.[61]

Along with receiving diminutive awards, the July Fourth claims process negatively affected claimants in several ways. First, the Treasury paid most of Sharpsburg's settlements from 1876–79, and some petitioners did not receive awards until the 1880s. For families teetering on financial ruin at the close of the war, such payment was too little, too late. Second, by accepting settlements, claimants agreed to close their cases against the U.S. government. By doing so, they permanently relinquished the unpaid portion of their losses, which comprised, on average, 67 percent of the total bill. Last, rejections due to insufficient evidence or suspected disloyalty prevented 56 claimants from receiving a penny for their losses.[62]

Not surprisingly, the denial of payment outraged many civilians, including the heirs of Henry Wade. The family filed claims for property taken by IX Corps from four different farms. After agent Madison Sallade spent several days investigating the Wades' cases and confirming the family's loyalty to Union, he recommended a

---

61 The totals are based on 179 Sharpsburg / Antietam claims archived in *RG* 92 at the National Archives; Williamson, *PPT*; Sharpsburg-area claimants listed $22,045.83 in commissary supplies and $7,850 for buildings destroyed by artillery fire. These combined losses convert to almost $840,000 in 2022 U.S. real prices. It's difficult to quantify Sharpsburg's property losses to the ANV in Sep. 1862. As mentioned in Chapter Ten, the Museum of the Confederacy's manuscript collection, archived at the Virginia Museum of History and Culture, has few quartermaster materials relating to Antietam. Further research may reveal such records at the *NA*.

62 At least ten applicants, including Raleigh Domer, did not receive July Fourth claims payments until the 1880s. Domer filed claim 92-551 in 1867, seeking $484.50. The government finally paid him in 1886, reducing his settlement to $62. Examination of the 77 settlements awarded by Meigs found that 71 Sharpsburg-area claimants received, on average, 33 percent of their original amount claimed.

settlement of $3,738.30 ($105,000 in 2022 money). But, to the Wades' dismay, Quartermaster General Meigs overturned Sallade's suggestion and rejected all four claims. Meigs did not elaborate on his final action, but the decision centered on the claimants' inability to name specific officers who confiscated the property.

Eli Wade, the administrator of the claims, responded to the findings with marked indignation. The Union-loyal farmer believed he had furnished solid evidence to the department, derived from "good and reliable sources," which included testimonies from former Union soldiers, neighbors, and farmhands, who knew "all about the quantity" of property taken by Burnside's men. Any evidence beyond this, Wade argued, "would be merely cumulative," given that Agent Sallade "visited our farm twice and examined thoroughly into our losses."

Wade implied that Meigs's ruling defied common sense. "Almost the whole community was cognizant of those losses," the farmer vented, "and no one knows better than Gen. Burnside himself, now a Senator in Washington, of the thorough consumption of all stores, and the burning of fencing, the six weeks occupation of that section." Wade wrote that "the whole sale destruction and use of our property" threw the heirs into catastrophic circumstances, and "in consequence we did not undertake to enclose our farms again until 1866." Major General Burnside could not have been ignorant to such facts, Wade argued, because "his headquarters was at Raleigh Showman's, within 300 yards of our land; a large part of his corps occupied our farm." Not only was Burnside aware of it, the claimant insisted, but "while these forces were here President Lincoln reviewed the troops." Moreso, "Genl. Ingalls, the Q.M. General of the army, also knows well that the whole country was left almost a bare commons." Salt of the earth farmers like Eli Wade saw their losses in simple terms: if evidence proved that the U.S. army took property from Sharpsburg's farmers, the U.S. government should pay.[63]

Empathizing with Wade was Stephen P. Grove, who also felt victimized by the quartermaster general's decision to reject his claims. Grove sent a letter of protest to Brig. Gen. Meigs, underlining for emphasis, "I can conscientiously say I never wished during the whole war for the success of the rebel cause; my associations and my acts were all against such an influence." Grove reminded Meigs that his losses were "verified by Boards of Surveys and private appraisements." Although the Union army stripped his farm bare, Grove noted, "I saw all this done and never raised a finger against the union cause nor did I ever give 'aid and comfort to the enemy.' What in the world would then make me disloyal?"

---

63 Claim of the heirs of Henry Wade (*RG* 123, No. 6585); Williamson, *PPT*.

Grove insisted that false statements by Agent Vifquain and a "malicious private person" wrongfully smeared him as disloyal. He added, "[M]y loyalty was endorsed by a number of Union officers, who knew me well during the war . . . ought not the evidence of such men have weight?" Closing, Grove made a final plea: "Mine is a very hard case and if I am debarred of Compensation for such a large amount of property furnished [to] our armies <u>cheerfully</u> upon such a false and Slanderous charge, I will think there is justice to be found no where." Grove's allies piled on the protests. Dr. Henry B. Wilson, a Boonsboro physician, wrote to Washington, "[W]hen Mr. G. had 1300 wounded in his house and on his beautiful lawn, he and his wife gave up all of their fine and large residence, cut up their Brussels carpet for the sick and wounded, and fed and attended them for three months. Does not such a man deserve payment?"

Grove's attorney, C. E. Rittenhouse, implored Meigs to reopen the case. "[Y]our adverse action on these several claims of Mr. Grove resulted from a most unjust report by your agent, who reported him disloyal upon the most frivolous ground." The attorney cautioned Meigs, "[I]f Mr. Grove's services rendered by him at a critical time to the Union cause are to be ignored upon such unfounded reports, there will not be much encouragement for any citizen to uphold his Government in any future emergency." Rittenhouse understood that Meigs "declined to reopen claims once disallowed," but requested an exception. He wrote, "I hope it may be a general rule and not like 'the laws of the Medes and Persians' who were comparatively a benighted people and ruled by an Arbitary Government—'fiat justitia ruat calum.'"[64]

The complaints lodged by Eli Wade and Stephen P. Grove failed to reopen their cases. Still, hundreds of other claimants in Northern and border states also felt cheated by the rules and investigations of the Act of July 4, 1864. "The unfairness of many of the agents," Wiley Britton wrote, "was so manifest that in the course of time claimants commenced sending in protests to the Quartermaster General about the methods of extorting adverse testimony against their claims." As time passed, the outpouring of complaints inundated the quartermaster general's office and pressured state representatives to take action. In response, on March 3, 1883, Congress expanded the jurisdiction of the U.S. Court of Claims. It passed "An act to afford assistance and relief to Congress and the Executive Departments in the

---

64 Claim of Elias S. Grove (*RG* 123, No. 7356). Grove's case file contains letters relating to Stephen P. Grove. The law of the Medes and Persians is a biblical phrase referring to an unalterable law. Merriam-Webster dictionary translates *Fiat justitia, ruat caelum* as "Let justice be done, though the heavens fall."

investigation of claims and demands against the Government." This new measure, known as the Bowman Act, gave Sharpsburg's claimants one more chance to settle their score with the United States government.[65]

65 Britton, *The Aftermath of the Civil War*, 57; "The Bowman Act," *The Reports of Committees of the House of Representatives for the Third Session of the Fifty-Third Congress, 1894–95* (Washington, DC, 1895), vol. 2, report no. 1792, 2-3.

Chapter 12

Sharpsburg vs. the United States:
The Struggle to Recover

"**Look at** this book," bellowed U.S. Representative Selwyn Z. Bowman of Massachusetts, "the Calendar of the House, a veritable tomb of the Capulets, a grave of dead hopes. There are more tragedies bound up within the covers of this book than in any novel or set of novels ever written." The book referred to, Bowman proclaimed to the House of Representatives in 1882, "represents hopes that have been abandoned. It represents claimants who have come here, year after year, praying the United States to pay its honest debts." Moreso, propounded Bowman, "[I]t represents the disgrace of the United States in not paying its just dues to honest men, women, and children, and to soldiers and sailors, and to many a one who deserved better treatment at his country's hands."

This problem was not new, Bowman complained. "[C]laimants come to us and their heirs and descendants for all the years from the beginning of the Government to the present time. And do they get their pay? Not one out of ten. The cases serve as footballs between the two Houses of Congress."

Bowman's argument held merit in the wake of the war department's controversial claims rejections. Something had to give—and it did.

Referring to petitions filed under the July Fourth Act and Southern Claims Commission, U.S. Representative Benjamin A. Enloe of Tennessee stated, "On account of the arbitrary and secret methods pursued by the War Department in taking proof, and the manifest injustice of many of the decisions in the War Department, Congress passed the Bowman Act." Also known as the Act of March

3, 1883, the Bowman Act authorized Congress "to send to the Court of Claims for a new trial disallowed claims filed before the War Department or the Southern Claims Commission which had not been barred by the statute of limitations."[1]

For claims involving military appropriations, the United States Court of Claims only considered previously presented petitions, which the quartermaster general or commissary general of subsistence rejected in full. Like the July Fourth Act, petitioners could not seek reimbursement for losses relating to war damages, depredations, or Confederate appropriations.

A key difference between the 1864 and 1883 acts was that the latter was "a remedial statute intending to give redress to the claimant," whereas the July Fourth Act was penal. Also, the Bowman Act directed the U.S. Court of Claims, rather than the war department, to consider cases. To initiate the process, Sharpsburg applicants forwarded their claims to a Maryland representative or senator. From there, politicians introduced the cases as individual relief bills to one of the houses of Congress or the Committee on War Claims. After considering the cases, legislators transmitted the pending bills to the Court of Claims.

For previous claims filed under the Act of July 4, 1864, the quartermaster general and commissary general of subsistence had the final say to reject or allow settlements. In Bowman Act cases, the Court of Claims only determined the facts of each case. Their decisions usually involved barring or dismissing claims for want of jurisdiction or estimating monetary amounts of property losses. Thereafter, the Court referred its findings of facts "to the House or to the committee from which the case was transmitted for its consideration." If Congress agreed with the Court's findings, they grouped approved cases into bills, passed them as acts, and authorized the third auditor of the Treasury to pay claimants the allowed amounts. The process, as readers can imagine, was dreadfully slow.[2]

---

1 *Congressional Record: The Proceedings and Debates of the Forty-Seventh Congress, First Session* (Washington, DC, 1882), vol. 13, pt. 4, 3153; Charles E. Schamel, "Untapped Resources: Private Claims and Private Legislation in the Records of the U.S. Congress," *Prologue 27, no. 1* (Spring 1995), *NA*, https://www.archives.gov/publications/prologue/1995/spring/private-claims-1.html; *Congressional Record: The Proceedings and Debates of the Fifty-Second Congress, Second Session*, vol. XXIV, 608.

2 *Statutes at Large of the United States of America*, 47th Congress, Session 2 (Washington, DC, 1883), Chapter 116, 485-486; *The Reports of Committees of the House of Representatives for the Third Session of the Fifty-Third Congress, 1894–1895* (Washington, DC, 1895), vol. 2, No. 1792, 2; William M. McKinney, *Federal Statutes Annotated: Containing All the Laws of the United States of a General and Permanent Nature in Force on the First Day of January 1903* (Long Island, NY, 1903), vol. 2, 75-76; "Reference of Claims to the Court of Claims," *Congressional Record: Proceedings of Congress and General Congressional Publications* (Washington, DC, 1882), House of Representatives, vol. 13,

The Bowman Act authorized the attorney general or his assistants "to appear for the defense and protection of the interests of the United States in all cases which may be transmitted to the Court of Claims." In cases reviewed for this study, the U.S. Attorney General dispatched attorneys to the Sharpsburg environs. There, counsel for the United States met in law offices with petitioners, witnesses, and claimants' attorneys to record lengthy depositions. Unlike investigations under the Act of July 4, 1864, the Bowman Act's testimony briefs allowed claimants and their lawyers to cross-examine witnesses. Next, the opposing attorneys recorded their briefs on merits and loyalty and then transmitted the cases to the Court of Claims. Judges determined many claims based on the reports, but some cases were "argued orally before the Court."

Attorney George W. Z. Black represented most of Sharpsburg's Bowman Act cases. Although the lawyer had a questionable track record managing some of the July Fourth claims, many petitioners entrusted him to represent their cases and go head-to-head against the experienced attorneys of the U.S. Department of Justice.[3]

Despite the differences between the 1864 and 1883 acts, the process from the claimant's perspective was equally demanding. After seeing their claims rejected under the Act of July 4, 1864, petitioners knew they needed strong evidence to support their Bowman Act cases. Accordingly, they re-calculated losses, secured affidavits, and obtained professional surveys of haymows, fence lines, and timber tracts.

In *Estate of David Smith v. the United States*, a Federal attorney asked surveyor Moses Poffenberger, "I desire to know if you have measured the barn . . . so that you can give the dimensions thereof, including the mows or the apartments for storing the hay?" Poffenberger swore that Captain Smith's barn "is the same barn that was there in Sept. 1862. I find it to be 65 feet long and 43 feet wide. The mows are 20 x 36 feet each by 15 ½ from bottom to the square. These mows, if full, will hold about 53 ½ tons of hay." The Smith heirs may have paid a pretty penny for the surveyor's services, but his title and testimony were precisely the types of stuff needed to satisfy the Court of Claims.[4]

---

pt. 4, 3147; "Payment of Claims in Accordance with Findings of the Court of Claims, Reported Under the Bowman and Tucker Acts, and Section No. 151 of the Judicial Code," *63rd Congress, 2nd Session, House Reports, Vol. A* (Washington, DC, 1914), Report No. 97, 4-9.

3 "Payment of Claims in Accordance with Findings of the Court of Claims," 6.

4 Claims of David Smith (*RG* 123, Nos. 1244, 1262, and 10237).

Facing page: Plat of the Home and Antietam farms owned by the heirs of Henry Wade. The map depicts fencing and timber allegedly destroyed by Union forces after the battle. NARA

Claimants also introduced property plats as evidence. Thomas R. Blackford attested in *William M. Blackford v. the United States*, "[L]ast Wednesday Van S. Brashears, A. D. Grove and myself went over and measured the lines on that day. I could see the old fence rows and was familiar with the fence lines . . . I made a rough plat, or map, and marked the lengths and distances on it." Likewise, the heirs of Henry Wade, to bolster their case, furnished "a plat of the several farms," which "exhibits the various lines of fencing, timber &c."[5]

The Wades went to other extremes to prove their losses to the Court of Claims. By 1888, the family had finally re-fenced their farms, but Eli Wade emphasized that "these fences were replaced by us at very great expense." To ensure accuracy of the rails claimed, Wade in December 1888 "went over the lines of fences taken from the heirs of Henry Wade . . . in company with Martin L. Miller and James Freeze." Wade deposed that "these two men carried a chain and measured the lines of fences taken," and found the fence lines to be "exactly the same now as they were when taken by the Federal army."

Defending the heirs, attorney George W. Z. Black informed the Court that the Wades' losses were supported by "the evidence of some ten, eleven, twelve witnesses." Black also referred to special agent Madison Sallade's report confirming that "67,860 rails were burned from these farms; that 1500 cords of wood were cut and used by the army, and the contents of two houses taken for army use." Continuing, Black expounded, "If human testimony is worth anything at all it establishes with certainty the number of rails, and the quantity of timber and materials taken, so the Court is not left in doubt as to the actual quantity taken from these claimants, and used by the Federal army." The amount claimed by the Heirs, Black noted, was "about half of the amount set forth in claimants original petition."

An attorney defending the U.S. disagreed, protesting, "The evidence in regard to the taking of the property is vague, indefinite and uncertain . . . statements are made of gross quantities of property taken, and no facts are given in support of the statements—except those based on information." Also, counsel retorted, "The

5 Claims of William M. Blackford (No. 1324), David Smith (Nos. 1244, 1262, and 10237), and the heirs of Henry Wade (No. 6585).

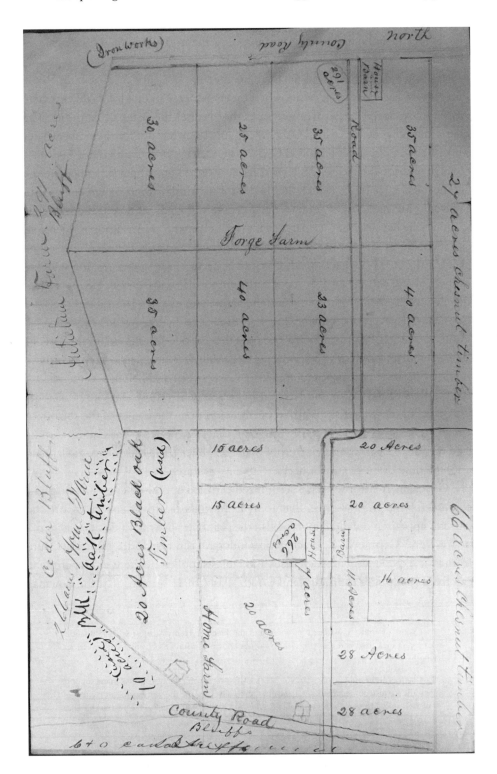

whole direct examination is objected to . . . as the measurement and calculations should have been made by a county surveyor."[6]

In other cases, landlord-tenant agreements came under attack. In 1862, Lafayette Miller tenanted a farm owned by his father, Colonel John Miller, where AOP forces allegedly destroyed 475 trees shortly after the Battle of Antietam. The quartermaster general rejected Col. Miller's July Fourth claim for the timber. After Miller's death, his sons petitioned Congress under the Bowman Act.

To support their case, Miller's sons introduced an affidavit penned by the colonel before his death, which outlined the 1862 landlord-tenant agreement with Lafayette Miller. U.S. attorney Henry Foote, though, declared the evidence inadmissible because the "ex-parte affidavit of claimant . . . was not considered of sufficient importance by the Quartermaster General to warrant an allowance of the claim." Moreso, Foote reasoned, "[W]hen a party seeks to recover for standing timber cut and carried away, it is not sufficient to show possession. He must show that he was the owner of the land and the nature and extent of his estate." Because Colonel Miller "has not shown what kind of interest he had in the timber taken," Foote concluded, "[W]e respectfully submit that the petition should be dismissed."

George W. Z. Black, representing Col. Miller's heirs, needed few words to refute Foote's statement. "Standing timber is a part of and belongs to the realty," Black informed the Court, "and it needs no argument to show that John Miller was the owner of the timber since he has been shown to be the owner of the soil out of which the trees grew." Cementing his point, Black introduced Washington County land record SS / 67-68, showing proof that Col. Miller "held the title to said land up until the time of his death about the 27th day of March 1882."[7]

Government attorneys also scrutinized certified appraisements. For example, counsel for the U.S. asserted that John L. Mayer's board of survey report and citizens' appraisement did "not establish the claim because the value of each item is not proven." George W. Z. Black, representing Mayer, responded that "the Court, from long experience with such cases and tables supplied by the War Department, can fix proper prices for forage and wood." Also, Black argued, "[I]f the Bowman

---

6　Claims of John A. Wade (No. 6586) and the heirs of Henry Wade (No. 6585). Early surveyors measured acreage with chains—often known as Gunter's chains—cut to various lengths.

7　Claim of John Miller (RG 123, No. 2227). Claims testimonies and historical maps support that the farmstead tenanted by Lafayette Miller in 1862 is the same property cited in "WA-II-1142 Morgan Property, Ruin (Colonel John Miller House)," which Lafayette later purchased.

Act were a penal statute the objections raised by counsel might be entitled to some consideration, but it is a remedial statute and as such should receive fair and reasonable construction by the Court and its purposes not defeated by captious objections which counsel submits."[8]

If Federal lawyers doubted the values and quantities listed in Bowman Act petitions, Sharpsburg farmer George Line put things in commonsensical terms, explaining that the estimations were not as complicated as they seemed. Testifying in *Joseph Poffenberger v. the United States*, Line deposed, '[W]e were all farmers and neighbors, and one farmer who lives near another and knows the size of his neighbor's farm, and his method of farming, can always tell about what his crop is." He added, "The yield of wheat and corn averages up pretty even in a series of years … we could see the ground from which the wheat had been cut, and also the mow from which it had been taken . . . we could easily fix the quantity of corn taken, as the ground from which it had been taken showed that very plainly." When questioned about the number of bovines claimed by Poffenberger, Line replied, "[E]veryone about there knew that seven cattle had been taken . . . a farmer generally knows what stock his neighbor has." Besides, said Line, "I know they got my farm supplies at the same time, of about the same character as those embraced in this appraisement. I was paid for my losses several years ago by the Quartermaster General."

To George Line, testifying in 1891, it wasn't fair that the government had not yet paid Joseph Poffenberger's estate. "The claimant was cleaned out of about everything on his farm, as well as in his house, and he was probably one of the heaviest loosers around," Line testified. "I gave this matter rather more care than I would to an ordinary business matter, and wished to see just what was right done between the claimant and the United States."[9]

If petitioners failed to identify officers responsible for the appropriation of supplies, Federal attorneys in Bowman Act cases often blamed the losses on marauding troops. In *Jacob F. Miller v. the United States*, U.S. lawyer James H. Nixon conjectured that depredating soldiers took Miller's property because, in September and October 1862, "The army was near Washington and could not have been in need of supplies. It had been near there for several weeks, and all of its lines of

---

8 Claim of John L. Mayer (No. 8586). U.S. attorneys also objected to board of survey reports in the cases of Captain David Smith and Stephen P. Grove.

9 Claim of Joseph Poffenberger (RG 123, No. 1300). Joseph Poffenberger died in 1888. Thereafter his nephew, Lawson Poffenberger, became executor of Joseph's estate.

communication were open. There was no need to subsist off the country." Nixon blamed "lawless raids" on the confiscation of 250 bushels of apples from Miller's orchard. Even if the seizures were authorized, he alleged, the government should not be held accountable because "green apples are not furnished to the army as commissary supplies."

Nixon also referred to Miller's testimony in which he stated, "Col. Ewing had his head-quarters there in the orchard, and he came and told me, if we couldn't keep the soldiers out of here to shoot them." Using Miller's words against him, Nixon argued that Colonel Ewing "not only deprecated this seizure of supplies, but authorized the claimant to shoot the marauding and disobedient soldiers who persisted in doing it contrary to orders." Hence, Nixon asserted, the appropriations were "unlawful and irregular, and in no sense such a taking as will render the Government liable under the Bowman Act."[10]

The elapsed span since the 1862 battle proved disadvantageous for some Bowman Act claimants. By the time cases were brought to hearings in the 1880s, Henry Piper was "too old and feeble" to leave his house and testify. Samuel Poffenberger failed to recruit witnesses, he explained, because "one of my appraisers is dead, and one, Mr. Thomas, is eighty two years old and unwell and unable to be present." Other litigants died before the Bowman Act passed, including Col. John Miller, Capt. David Smith, James Marker, Samuel Mumma, Sr., and Benjamin F. Rohrback. With claimants and their original appraisers deceased or debilitated, the cases relied on the memories of secondary witnesses.[11]

Not unlike July Fourth claims, civilians testifying in congressional cases struggled to recount details of property taken by military forces. Maria Grove testified in the case of her late husband in 1893. She admitted to U.S. attorney James D. Butt, "I can't now remember any officers who were present when the timber was cut, as it is a long time ago, and I am an old woman now." In *Josiah Hill v. the United States*, Hill initially attested that troops seized some of his wheat as bedding but later deposed that they used it only as forage. Whether the tenant farmer erred by intention or poor memory is open to debate. Nonetheless, Henry Foote, Federal attorney, suspected the former. "Claimant has made a very bad showing in his testimony," Foote grumbled, "and I am afraid in his last evidence he has entirely forgotten what he formerly testified to." Continuing, he vented, "One

---

10 Claim of Jacob F. Miller (No. 4294).

11 Claims of Samuel Mumma, Sr. (No. 334) and Samuel Poffenberger (No. 4298). Mumma's son testified about Henry Piper's infirm condition.

turns from a case like this with anything but pleasant reflections. Claimant ought to be satisfied if he gets off with simply a disallowance of his claim. Such reckless swearing as this is simply terrible."

Hill's attorney, George W. Z. Black, countered Foote's remark. "I indignantly protest against the use of this language as being unwarranted by the facts," Black complained, "and totally uncalled for by anything in the record. I simply ask the Court to read the counsel's brief to show how utterly it disproves his own conclusions." Reminding the Court of Claims that the Bowman Act was a remedial statute, Black softened his tone. "The claimant in this case is a poor man, a tenant farmer, and asks payment for a small quantity of wheat and a horse . . . it would seem that under the circumstances the Court should lean to the side of liberality in such a case."[12]

After Benjamin F. Rohrback died, his case hinged on the memories of two neighbors, John and Mary Grice, who answered interrogatories in August 1891. Counsel for the U.S., John Q. Thompson, attested that "Mary A. Grice and John Grice, the main witnesses, do not agree entirely on their estimates . . . [which] might be reasonably expected, when it is considered that the witnesses are 72 and 78 years old, respectively, and are testifying to matters happening twenty-nine years before." Furthermore, Thompson reasoned, "[O]ne of them is a woman, who probably had not the same ability to make an accurate estimate as had her husband."

Not all witnesses had hazy memories, for the battle and its aftermath made lasting impressions on many residents. Answering "interrogatories and cross-interrogatories" related to his father's claim in 1900, Ezra Marker professed, "[T]he war and proceeding at that time was so unusual that it impressed my mind to such an extent that I could never forget it." Ezra's sister-in-law, Susan C. Marker, also testified in the case. An attorney asked her, "How do you happen to remember so explicitly the taking of this property?" She replied, "I was there all the time and I was perfectly familiar with the farm. My husband consulted with me in many things and I knew a great deal about farming. These things were in our care, and I felt the responsibility with my husband."

When counsel continued to question her memory of the appropriations, Susan retorted, "In every way it was serious, and I could not forget it. The Confederates did not take any of this property. All of this that I have stated was taken by the Union army. I know the difference." Additionally, she deposed, "[N]either James Marker or my husband ever received pay or compensation for this property—to

---

12 Claims of Stephen P. Grove (No. 7354) and Josiah Hill (No. 8532).

my knowledge—and I feel confident if they had I would have known it. Matters of such importance would never have been kept from me."

In September 1900, a lawyer asked domestic servant Angeline Jackson, "Do you remember the battle of Antietam?" She replied, "I do, very well; it was fought on the 17th day of Sept., 1862; the line of battle was about two and one half miles east of the farm of Capt. David Smith at whose house I was stopping and living at the time." When pressed to recount Smith's losses of corn, horses, rails, and other items, Jackson provided explicit details, emphasizing to the attorneys present, "I remember all these things distinctly; it seems to have been burned into my mind, as it were and I shall remember it as long as I can remember anything."[13]

*   *   *

Petitioners passing the merits tests, as they did in Fourth of July claims, had to prove their wartime allegiance to the United States government. After conducting preliminary inquiries on loyalty, U.S. attorneys recorded testimony briefs of claimants and witnesses. This approach differed from July Fourth claims, in which special agents asked anything they desired. Instead, it resembled Southern Claims Commission cases, which required subjects to answer a series of standing interrogatories on loyalty.[14]

Asked if he ever left Maryland from 1861–65, Henry Piper made clear that his sole visit to the Confederate state of Virginia was not for business or pleasure. "[T]hat was in September 1862 for a short time during the progress of the battle of Antietam," Piper testified. "For a few hours I passed with my family over the

---

13 Claims of Benjamin F. Rohrback (No. 4234), Henry Piper (No. 445), James Marker (No. 1292), and David Smith (Nos. 1244, 1262, and 10237).

14 "About the Southern Claims Commission Papers," *The Valley of the Shadow: Two Communities in the American Civil War*, digital archive, Virginia Center for Digital History, University of Virginia, https://valley.lib.virginia.edu/VoS/claims/aboutSCC.html. Standing interrogatories reviewed for this study varied. Some questions sought the claimants' political sentiments on various topics, such as slavery and the Baltimore Riots. Petitioners sometimes showed their true colors in responding to the questions. For example, when a U.S. attorney asked Philip Beck how he felt about the Emancipation Proclamation, the wealthy Leitersburg farmer replied, "I wanted the Union to stay together—I thought the 'nigger' was like a horse, he ought to be paid for. I did not want any war at all." Assailing Beck's statement, U.S. attorney Henry M. Foote urged the Court to dismiss the case because Beck "considered his slaves only as cattle, [and] didn't believe in their emancipation without compensation . . . there can be no doubt about claimant's disloyalty." Based on Beck's slim case file (*RG* 123, Entry 22, Box 232, Case No. 1290), the Court of Claims promptly dismissed his claim.

Potomac River into the [Virginia] cliffs to be out of the danger of the battle. A number of my neighbors with their families crossed a ford with us. We did not remain in the cliffs more than two or three hours when we all returned and were within Union lines. I was never out of the state of Maryland at any other time."

In Samuel Reel's case, counsel asked Reel's wife if her late husband ever aided Confederate troops. "No sir," Cerusha Reel replied, "because he would fuss with me if I would give them something to eat." The lawyer then inquired if Reel, a former slave owner, "questioned the right or authority of Mr. Lincoln issuing the emancipation proclamation." Again, Cerusha responded, "No, sir. I never knew him to do anything of the kind."[15]

Attorneys asked deponents to provide general examples of loyalty. Jane Sinclair, a former slave owned by Stephen P. Grove during the war, testified, "I saw Mr. Grove several times a day during this time, as I was living in his house. I heard him talk about the war many times. He was very much opposed to it." Grove fretted that the conflict "would ruin the country," Ms. Sinclair recalled. "He said the South was wrong, and should have settled their troubles inside the Union . . . he was glad when the war was over."

Under cross-examination, Mary A. Grove told an attorney that her late husband, Elias S. Grove, "never broke his oath" of allegiance. Elias, she deposed, "was always glad & rejoiced when the Union forces were victorious. We were Union people." Referring to her deceased husband, John E. Knode—who devoutly supported the U.S.—Esther Knode testified, "I differed in politics with my husband, I was raised a southern woman. [M]y husband was a thorough straightforward Union Man he voted for Mr. Lincoln. I did not object to him voting for Mr. Lincoln, I am glad the slaves are all free I think it is right."

Testifying in the case of Sharpsburg's Lutheran Church, Van S. Brashears recalled that "some of the members were in favor of the confederacy but the church never aided the rebels and then a good many of the members were in the Union army." Another Lutheran, John P. Smith, stated, "The church never in any way aided the rebellion. We had a minister at that time (Rev. Christian Startzman, now dead) who said that Jeff Davis and his cabinet ought to be in hell, and I think his congregation agreed with him. He said this in his pulpit."[16]

---

15 Claim of Henry Piper (No. 445). The ford lay near the farm of Samuel I. Piper, where Henry and his family sheltered during the battle; Claim of Samuel Reel (No. 3209).

16 Claims of Stephen P. Grove (No. 7354), Elias S. Grove (No. 7356), John E. Knode (G-1647), and the Lutheran Church of Sharpsburg (No. 4058).

Attorneys sought to ascertain if claimants were actively or passively loyal from 1861–65. Joshua Newcomer swore that he was faithful to the U.S. and testified that he "told some Confederate soldiers that if they gained the ascendancy he would not remain in the State two hours if he could get away." But a Federal lawyer argued that if Newcomer "had been a loyalist he could have shown affirmative acts of fidelity." A loyalist, the attorney remarked, "is defined by Webster to be 'a person who adheres to his sovereign or to the lawful authority; especially one who maintains his allegiance to his price or government and defends his cause in times of revolt or revolution.'" Closing, the attorney stated, "Loyalty is an active not a passive quality. Is the evidence sufficient to convince the Court that the claimant was a true Union man?"[17]

Resembling the third auditor's search for matching records in July Fourth claims, the attorney general's office reviewed files in the Confederate Archives to determine if petitioners sold supplies to the Rebel army. If U.S. attorneys suspected that a claimant signed a Confederate voucher, they urged the Court of Claims to declare the person disloyal and dismiss the case.

Justice department clerks found that Southern officers issued receipts to Stephen P. Grove, John Grice, and Andrew Rentch. Regarding Jacob C. Grove, the attorney general's office reported, "There are on file in the Confederate archives of this office four vouchers signed [by] J. C. Grove . . . dated at Sharpsburg, Maryland, Sept. 15, 1862 and June 23, 1863." David Coffman's autograph on five Confederate receipts could not be disputed, a U.S. attorney affirmed, because "the signatures upon the vouchers bear a very striking resemblance to the signature on file in this case . . . there can be but little doubt but that he is the one who signed the vouchers."[18]

Litigants admitted signing the receipts but insisted that they had no say in the transactions. When asked if he sold anything to the Southern army, Alfred Poffenberger replied, "No, only what they took by force." John E. Knode's attorney confessed that a voucher was "undoubtably signed by decedent." Still, at the time Knode signed it, "Confederate money was entirely worthless in Maryland," making it "incredible that a farmer in Maryland would have voluntarily sold cattle to the Confederates."

17 Claims of Henry A. Poffenberger (No. 7178) and Joshua Newcomer (No. 272).

18 Claims of Stephen P. Grove (No. 7354), John Grice (No. 5872), Andrew Rentch (No. 4235), the heirs of Samuel Grove (No. 9313), and David Coffman (No. 1268).

William M. Blackford recounted that it was "the custom of the Confederates" to issue certificates for "property or supplies when they came north of the Potomac river . . . they took supplies from some persons in the locality, and we people were powerless to prevent it." Solomon Lumm's attorney, addressing a Confederate voucher bearing Lumm's signature, told the Court that Rebels "would have taken the corn whether or not" Lumm accepted the receipt. Moreso, "[I]f the Confederates had taken the corn without paying and the claimant had refused to accept pay for it he would have been in the position of practically making a gift of it."[19]

Attorneys defending the U.S. inquired if claimants had relatives who served in the Rebel army. Colonel John Miller had one son and two sons-in-law who fought for the Confederacy. Sharpsburg's Republicans, though, vouched for Miller's Union loyalty. When counsel inquired if John C. Middlekauff ever spoke to his father about enlisting in the Northern or Southern armies, the tenant farmer responded, "No, sir, after the battle of Antietam they would not have gotten me to enlist in either one." Asked to explain why, he answered, "I saw too much of it."[20]

Describing the complex case of the heirs of Samuel Grove, lawyer George W. Z. Black avowed, "It might be stated here that this family was divided on the question of war. Two brothers went into the Confederate army and one brother into the United States navy." Jeremiah P. Grove, the oldest sibling, enlisted in the U.S. Navy in 1864, but after showing "occasional evidences of insanity" in January 1865, shot himself while stationed in North Carolina. A coroner's inquest ruled Grove's death as suicide, determining that he "had pulled off his right boot, and, placing the muzzle of the gun under his chin, discharged the piece with his toe. His head was completely shattered."

When the Grove heirs' case came to a hearing, William H. Grove, who served in Captain James Breathed's battery, C.S.A., had died. Franklin L. Grove was denied any interest in the case because of his Confederate enlistment in the 1st Maryland Cavalry. Consequently, Franklin "relinquished his right unto this claim to his brother and sister." The forfeiture left Laura L. Grove Mumma and her brother, Jacob C. Grove, as the case's remaining heirs.

Testifying in 1907, Robert W. Grove, the petitioners' cousin, recalled, "Laura and Jacob C. Grove did not share in the sentiments of their brother Franklin L.

---

19 Claims of Alfred Poffenberger (No. 1308), John E. Knode (No. 8587), William M. Blackford (No. 1324), and Solomon Lumm (No. 340).

20 Claims of John Miller (No. 2227) and John J. Middlekauff (No. 1261).

Grove; they objected to him going into the army—the Confederate army." Also, Robert deposed, "They did not share in the sentiments of their brother William. I heard Jake swearing at Will for going in the Confederate army." Alex Davis testified, "I did on one occasion hear Jacob complain that his brothers Franklin and William were serving in the Confederate army, and he said if those boys had stayed at home and minded their own business the [U.S.] soldiers would not have been so hard on him."

After grilling Jacob C. Grove on his loyalty, Federal attorneys set their sights on Laura L. Grove Mumma. When the attorney general's office interviewed Ms. Mumma in 1910, they found "that she was too young to have an opinion during the war upon issues of secession or the war." Yet, "[S]he had two brothers, William and Franklin Grove in the Confederate army and three cousins, Dr. Phil Grove, Tom Grove and Frank Grove who lived near her home in the Confederate army." Ms. Mumma's relation to five Confederate soldiers led U.S. attorney George E. Borne to argue that her testimony "over-turns any presumption of loyalty indulged by a fiction of law in her favor when it is shown that . . . she herself says that she gave no aid or comfort to the Union cause throughout the civil war."[21]

The case of Jacob H. Grove, uncle to the heirs of Samuel Grove, faced similar scrutiny. Felix Brannigan, counsel for the U.S., suggested that the Court dismiss the case because Grove "was a prominent Democrat, and hence was classed by some Republicans as a 'Copperhead.'" More damning to Jacob H. Grove's case, Brannigan added, "He had two sons in the Confederate Army." Grove's youngest son, Robert W. Grove, testified that his brother, Dr. Philip D. Grove, "was a doctor [who] resided at home, and was practicing medicine in Sharpsburg until

---

21 Claims of the heirs of Samuel Grove (Claim G-1633 and Case No. 9313); Claim of Laura L. Grove Mumma (*RG* 123, Entry 22, Box 1007, Case No. 9502); *Brooklyn News*, January 9, 1865. The article identified Jeremiah P. Grove as a 33-year-old Marylander. Witnesses in the Grove heirs' case testified that Jeremiah P. Grove served in the U.S. Navy and died during the war. Among them, Martin L. Hines (also known as Martin L. Himes) deposed that Grove "died in the navy on a U.S. gunboat," and Martin L. Fry stated that Grove "died from an accidental shot." William H. Grove's service appears in Daniel D. Hartzler, *Marylanders in the Confederacy* (Westminster, MD, 1986), 161, and Keller, *Roster of Civil War Soldiers from Washington County*, 93; The Grove heirs' case may have misidentified the middle initial of Franklin L. Grove. Robert J. Driver, Jr. in *First and Second Maryland Cavalry, C.S.A.* (Charlottesville, VA, 1999), 234, wrote that Franklin Samuel Grove of Sharpsburg served in the 1st Maryland Cavalry, Co. C. The 1870 Federal census for Sharpsburg, Dwelling #160, lists Franklin S. Grove, 24, with siblings Jacob C. Grove and Laura L. Grove; The cousins mentioned in the case were Dr. Philip D. Grove and Thomas H. Grove, sons of Jacob H. Grove, and Franklin T. Grove, a son of Joseph Grove. During the Grove heirs' July Fourth claim investigation, special agent Victor Vifquain concluded, "Laura L. Grove being a child at the time of the war cannot be treated as a rebel."

Thomas H. Grove, a son of Jacob H. Grove, served in the 1st Regiment, Maryland Cavalry, Co. C., C.S.A. *Joseph R. Stonebraker, A Rebel of '61*

September 1862." Soon after the ANV's occupation of Sharpsburg, Philip "went away from home and some six weeks afterwards we learned he was in the Confederate army." Robert deposed that another brother, Thomas H. Grove, "was at college—St. James College—near Hagerstown; he ran away from school with one John Hager another student and went into the confederate army; we didn't learn of this for several weeks." The family feared that Thomas enlisted when "college authorities sent word that he had left and asked if he was at home."

Robert W. Grove confessed that his late father "was in sympathy for the Southern people," and believed that the South "had been drawn into the war by a few hot-headed fire-eaters who merited nothing but contempt, but that the great majority of the people were in no way responsible for the misery and suffering they had to endure." Despite these sentiments, Robert emphasized that his father "was opposed to his sons going into the confederate army; that he didn't know anything about it until they had gone; he sent word to Thos. H. that if he would leave the army and come home he would give him a deed to one of the farms."[22]

In cases heard under the Bowman Act, claimants had to start from scratch proving their wartime allegiance, regardless of whether they were found loyal in July Fourth claims. The quartermaster general rejected Solomon Lumm's claim "on merits alone." Nevertheless, when Lumm petitioned Congress under the 1883

22 Claims of Jacob H. Grove (*RG* 123, No. 1267 and *RG* 92, Entry 820, Box M, Claim Number 905); Stonebraker, *A Rebel of '61*, 112. Stonebraker wrote that Thomas H. Grove served in "Co. C, Maryland Battalion." *CWSS*, M379, Roll 1, lists Thomas H. Grove in the 1st Regiment, Maryland Cavalry, Co. C., C.S.A. Regarding Dr. Philip D. Grove, *CWSS*, M818, Roll 10, cites "P. D. Grove" as an acting assistant surgeon in "General and Staff Officers, Non-Regimental Enlisted Men, C.S.A." Heros von Borcke in *Memoirs*, 1:225-227, referred to a Sharpsburg civilian named "Dr. G.," who was likely Dr. Philip D. Grove. Julia D. Grove, a daughter of Jacob H. Grove, testified that her father "was opposed to their going into that army; he threatened to disinherit Tom if he did not return to college."

act, the attorney general's office "produced four witnesses to attempt to rebut the claimant's prima facie case of loyalty." Jacob Lakin described Lumm's reputation regarding Union loyalty as "not so good." Also, Adolphus R. Renner attested that Lumm's associates "were all termed southern sympathizers, and they boarded at Hebb's store. They called that the 'rebel hole.'"

Lumm swore that he was loyal, avowing that he "participated in [Union] meetings." One such event, he recalled, took place "in the square of the town, addressed by Mr. Alex Boteler, before the battle of Antietam." He also attended a Unionist meeting "at the building occupied now by the Red Men, on the public square of the town." In addition, Lumm professed, "I regarded the result of the battle of Antietam as a union victory and was glad."

The attorney general's office centered its questions on Lumm's arrest after the battle. As described in Chapter Three, testimony alleged that Lumm was "detained over night" at General Burnside's headquarters "because it was found that port holes had been made in the roof of his house, and from them Union soldiers were fired upon and killed during the battle, as a result of which arrest the soldiers talked of hanging him." Based on this evidence, George Walker, assistant attorney, declared, "it is respectfully submitted that claimant should be found disloyal." Lumm's attorney, George W. Z. Black, informed the Court that Federal authorities never charged his client, and "the fact that the claimant was only detained one day … is to our mind the best sort of proof that the claimant was not guilty."[23]

Personal enemies possessed the power to sabotage Fourth of July claims but faced pushback in cases filed under the Bowman Act. For example, attorney George W. Z. Black, representing Squire Jacob Miller, argued that his client's suspected disloyalty was "founded upon no evidence, but upon insinuations of personal or political enemies," and dismissing the case on such feckless grounds "would be an act of great injustice and one unworthy of the standing and dignity of the national government."

In John Grice's July Fourth claim, witness Samuel Show testified that "when Gen. Custer was coming up the street in 1863, with a band playing, I was telling John Grice how nice it looked." Grice, according to Show, replied that "he hoped the time would soon come that every Union man would be banished from the face of the earth … that it was his firmest hope." Show relayed this statement to local

23 Claim of Solomon Lumm (*RG* 123, No. 340). In reference to "Alex Boteler," Lumm may have described a prewar rally featuring Alexander R. Boteler of Shepherdstown. See *HFTL*, Sep. 24, 1856, and Aug. 29, 1860. After Virginia seceded in 1861, Boteler sided with the Confederacy.

election judges, "and on the strength of it, he [Grice] was not allowed to vote." Because the Act of July 4, 1864, did not allow claimants to cross-examine witnesses, Show's damaging testimony went uncontested and contributed to the rejection of Grice's claim.

Telling his side of the story in *John Grice v. The United States*, Grice remembered seeing "Genl. Custers Cavalry command pass through the streets in 1863," but did not recall conversing with Samuel Show at the time or making a negative comment about Union men. Grice admitted that election judges prevented him from voting. He clarified, though, that the matter had nothing to do with Samuel Show's story. "[A] soldier of Reynolds Dvn. had insulted my wife," Grice explained, "and I took his gun away from him and throwed it away, and knocked him down with my fists. I did no doubt use some hard language and it was heard and reported against me."[24]

Witnesses in *Daniel Poffenberger v. the United States* disagreed about the petitioner's loyalty. David R. Miller, a Republican, and Charles W. Adams, a veteran of the U.S. army, recollected that Daniel Poffenberger was Union-loyal, despite being a Democrat. Conversely, John Benner and Judge David Smith accused the claimant of being a "sympathizer with the Confederacy." U.S. attorney Felix Brannigan sided with the latter two claimants and launched into a tirade against Poffenberger and the community of Sharpsburg. "[I]n claimant's neighborhood," Brannigan asserted, "a charge of loyalty to the United States, during the late rebellion, would probably have been considered a severe impeachment." Brannigan hypothesized that "the people of that locality were so virulently disloyal during the war" and alleged that Poffenberger's witnesses "naturally desired to avoid doing anything in the matter in such a way as might injure their business in that community." He labeled Poffenberger as "one of that cowardly tribe of Confederate sympathizers known during the rebellion as 'copperheads,' for whom all honorable men, North and South, had unqualified contempt." Brannigan asked the Court of Claims to "require strong and conclusive proof of loyalty in the case of some claims coming from such a community . . . better to make a mistake in the

---

24 Claims of Jacob Miller (No. 4296) and John Grice (Claim 131-1330 and Case No. 5872). Custer's ride through Sharpsburg may have occurred after the Battle of Gettysburg or during the summer of 1864. Grice's reference to "Reynolds Dvn" could relate to Antietam, where Brigadier General John F. Reynolds led a division before taking command of I Corps in the battle's aftermath. However, after Reynolds's death at Gettysburg in 1863, his corps passed near Sharpsburg.

cases of a score of claimants from States which were in rebellion, than to pay one dollar to a claimant who had no excuse whatever for his disloyalty."[25]

*   *   *

While many cases awaited hearings in the Court of Claims, Congress passed the Tucker Act on March 3, 1887. Similar to the Bowman Act, the Tucker Act expanded the jurisdiction of the Court of Claims "to include all claims founded on the Constitution including claims that had already been presented and disallowed." Thus, the 1887 act gave applicants of dismissed Bowman Act cases another opportunity to petition Congress.[26]

Once the Court of Claims heard a given case filed under the Bowman or Tucker Act, its judges convened to determine the findings of facts. If the Court found that the U.S. army took supplies from a petitioner, they decided upon a fair valuation of the amount taken and transmitted the findings to Congress. The House and Senate, notwithstanding, were mired in claims cases. To save "precious floor time" processing "large numbers of private bills," archivist Charles E. Schamel wrote, Congress passed omnibus claims bills, which "combined into a single bill large numbers of claims that had been referred to one committee."

The House and Senate passed several bills from 1891 to 1915 authorizing the Treasury to pay Sharpsburg-area claimants. Of the 59 Bowman and Tucker Act cases reviewed for this study, the Court recommended allowances to 34 petitioners. The settlements constituted, on average, 51.7 percent of the total amount claimed. Although these persons failed to recover their total losses, they may have been

---

25 Claim of Daniel Poffenberger (*RG* 123, No. 1505).

26 "Payment of Claims in Accordance with Findings of the Court of Claims," 4-9. The Tucker Act was formally called "An Act to Provide for the Bringing of Suits Against the Government of the United States." Like the 1883 act, claims presented under the 1887 Tucker Act needed to pass as bills before being transmitted to the Court for findings of facts. The Tucker Act's jurisdiction was wider than the Bowman Act, and considered "every claim, legal or equitable, presented by a bill except a pension." This included hospital rent claims for the occupation of or injury to real estate; James T. Clark, "The United States Court of Claims With a Special Consideration of 'Congressional Reference' Cases," Ph.D. dissertation, Georgetown University Graduate School of Law, 1934–35, 22-24; *Antietam National Battlefield Historic Resource Study*, 48-50; "Court of Claims to Investigate Certain Bills, Etc., by Authority of the Tucker Act," *House of Representatives, 58th Congress, 2nd Session* (Washington DC, 1904), Report No. 2729, 2-4.

content to have received anything, given that their claims suffered outright rejection under the Act of July 4, 1864.[27]

Congress did not approve the first Bowman Act payments to Sharpsburg-area citizens until 1891. Litigants listed in this bill included Henry Piper, Samuel Reel, Henry B. Rohrback, Alfred Poffenberger, Samuel D. Piper, Samuel I. Piper, and "Hezekiah Myers, of Sharpsburgh, Maryland." There was, however, a catch.

Before authorizing the Treasury to pay parties in the 1891 bill, Congress stipulated "that no one of the claims hereinafter mentioned . . . shall be paid until the Attorney-General shall have certified to the Secretary of the Treasury that he has caused to be examined the evidence heretofore presented." This proviso empowered the attorney general to certify that there were "no grounds sufficient, in his opinion, to support a motion for a new trial." Unfortunately for Sharpsburg's suppliants, the U.S. Department of Justice motioned for new trials in all nine cases listed in the 1891 bill. This action suspended the Court of Claims' previous findings along with the pending payments.[28]

Another omnibus claims bill passed on March 3, 1899 and authorized the Treasury to pay nearly two-dozen Antietam battlefield-area claimants. The act granted $1,918 to the estate of Joseph Poffenberger. It also awarded two claims to the heirs of Henry Wade, amounting to $4,658. The 1899 bill paid three people who were declared disloyal in their July Fourth claims: John Grice, Stephen P. Grove, and William M. Blackford. Grove and Blackford received large awards of $3,292 and $6,206, respectively.

Referring to the case of Samuel Mumma, Sr., the Court of Claims found that most of the farmer's property was "taken or destroyed during the battle as due to the ravages of war and the depredations of individuals." But after the battle, the Court determined, the United States army took grains, livestock, and fencing valued at $853. Congress authorized the U.S. Department of the Treasury to pay this amount to Mumma's estate in the 1899 bill.[29]

In 1902, Congress passed another omnibus bill that granted $491 to Henry A. Poffenberger, who suffered the controversial relinquishment of his July Fourth

---

27 Schamel, "Untapped Resources," 45-57; Clark, "The United States Court of Claims," 22.

28 *The Miscellaneous Documents of the Senate of the United States for the Second Session of the Fifty-First Congress, 1890–1891* (Washington, DC, 1891), vol. 7, 411, 416-417. The quartermaster general rejected Hezekiah Myers's July Fourth claim on the grounds of disloyalty, but the Court of Claims found that Myers was loyal to the Union.

29 *Statutes at Large of the United States of America*, 55th Congress, Session 3 (Washington, DC, 1899), Chapter 426, 1170-1172.

claims. The 1902 bill also awarded the estates of Benjamin F. Rohrback and David R. Miller for their previously rejected supplies and paid the administrator of Jacob H. Grove $1,891. This settlement also exonerated Grove, who was reported disloyal in his July Fourth claim.

In February 1905, the House and Senate passed a Miscellaneous Claims Appropriation Act, directing the secretary of the Treasury to pay the administrators and executors of Jacob Avey, Sr., Susan Hoffman, John C. Middlekauff, James Marker, and Capt. David Smith. They also approved settlements to Sharpsburg's German Reformed Church and Lutheran Church.[30]

The bills passed from 1891–1905 excluded at least 25 Sharpsburg-area claimants. Also, the nine petitioners listed in the 1891 omnibus bill do not appear in subsequent acts authorizing claims payments. This likely suggests that the attorney general motioned for new trials and the Court ultimately dismissed all nine cases.

Samuel I. Piper was one of the litigants listed in the 1891 bill. Initially, the Court recommended a large settlement to Piper, which Congress approved. But before the Treasury drafted the payment, Acting Attorney General William Howard Taft, future president of the United States, motioned for "a new trial on loyalty" for Piper. Taft deemed it necessary to retry Piper, he explained, because "evidence has been discovered in the Confederate Archives since the former trial, that said claimant sold to the army of the Confederate States Aug. 5 1864 corn and fodder for the value of $31.75." Referring to the Rebels, Piper insisted in September 1891, "I never sold them anything in my life." Nonetheless, the discovery of the Confederate voucher—reflecting losses Piper may have been helpless to prevent—effectively suspended the farmer's $1,625.25 settlement. Evidence does not support that Congress ever paid it.[31]

The Court of Claims dismissed other cases for various reasons. It found the evidence unsatisfactory in Samuel Poffenberger's and William Roulette's claims. [32]

---

30 *Statutes at Large of the United States of America*, 57th Congress, Session 1 (Washington, DC, 1902), Chapter 887, 210-211; *Statutes at Large of the United States of America*, 58th Congress, Session 3 (Washington, DC, 1905), Chapter 777, 751-753.

31 Claim of Samuel I. Piper (*RG* 123, No. 1310). Taft's signature in Piper's case file matches handwriting samples of the 27th U.S. president. Taft's father, Alphonso Taft, served as U.S. attorney general from 1867 to 1877. The claims bills passed in 1899, 1902, 1905, and 1915 do not contain the clause in the 1891 bill empowering the attorney general to reopen approved cases.

32 Claim of Samuel Poffenberger (*RG* 123, No. 4298); *The Miscellaneous Documents of the House of Representatives for the First Session of the Fifty-Second Congress*, (Washington, DC, 1892), vol. 1, doc. no. 294, 1-2; Claim of William Roulette (No. 4299); *The Miscellaneous Documents of the House of*

After examining Thomas Barnum's case, the attorney general's office discovered that the farmer failed to petition the commissary general of subsistence under the Act of July 4, 1864, for nine cattle, 16 sheep, and 18 hogs. "Following these precedents," the Court of Claims found, "the court decides that it has no jurisdiction of the case at bar, and the same is therefore dismissed."[33]

Federal judges rejected the claims of Andrew Rentch and Daniel Poffenberger on the grounds of disloyalty. Likewise, the Court found that "upon the evidence it does not appear that Solomon S. Lumm . . . was loyal to the Government of the United States throughout the war, and the case is dismissed for want of further jurisdiction."[34]

The case of the heirs of Samuel Grove came to a hearing in February 1913. After a lengthy examination, the Court determined that Jacob C. Grove and his sister, Laura L. Grove Mumma, were loyal to the U.S. government during the war. However, the attorney general's office found that the heirs had previously accepted a small July Fourth claim settlement for Jeremiah P. Grove's individual losses. Thus, the Court declared the case settled and "no additional amount is stated." This ruling barred Jacob C. Grove and Laura L. Grove Mumma from receiving any portion of their $6,586.50 claim.

Squire Jacob Miller's $11,692 claim dragged into the year 1912, when the Court of Claims declared, "It is ORDERED that the submission of this case be vacated and set aside because of non-compliance with Rule 89." One of the heirs, Francis M. Miller, complained to the *Shepherdstown Register* in 1915 that "the Millers have a claim for $12,000 before the government for the property taken or damaged, but have never been able to get it settled." Squire Miller's congressional case file

---

Representatives for the Second Session of the Fifty-First Congress (Washington, DC, 1891), vol. 1, doc. no. 68, 1-2; *House of Representatives Documents, 59th Congress,* 2nd Session, Vol. 52 (Washington, DC, 1907), doc. no. 602, 4. David Reel's claim (No. 6619) appears in a "list of sundry cases . . . dismissed for want of prosecution."

33 Claim of Thomas Barnum (No. 333). As discussed in Chapter Eleven, Barnum traveled to Washington to check on the status of his claim, only to learn that his papers were not on file. Hence, Barnum's attorney or government clerks may have lost or misfiled the commissary claim.

34 Claims of Andrew Rentch (No. 4235) and Daniel Poffenberger (No. 1505). The Court found, "[I]t does not appear that Andrew Rentch . . . was loyal to the Government of the United States throughout said war; and the case is dismissed for want of further jurisdiction." Daniel Poffenberger's case file cites, "The claimant in this case was not found loyal by this Honorable Court." Poffenberger's attorney filed a motion for a rehearing, but evidence does not show that the Court granted the motion; Claim of Solomon Lumm (No. 340); *House Documents, 59th Congress, 2nd Session,* Vol. 48 (Washington, DC, 1907), doc. no. 159, 2.

contains no mention of a Tucker Act filing or a Treasury settlement. In all likelihood, the Court dismissed the case.[35]

Congress authorized the final payments to Sharpsburg-area claimants in 1915. Grant Wyand, a son of Frederick Wyand, received a settlement for his father's Antietam-related losses. Likewise, the 1915 bill paid the trustees and consistory of the Mount Vernon Reformed Church of Keedysville for the AOP's use of their house of worship in 1862. Additionally, Congress awarded $1,350 to Sharpsburg's St. Paul's Protestant Episcopal Church for hospital rent and damages. The settlements to Grant Wyand and the two churches, all related to Antietam, came 53 years after the battle—a testament to the painfully slow claims process and the persistence of Sharpsburg-area petitioners.

New legislation closed the lid on Civil War claims. The seemingly never-ending submission of war-related cases to the Court of Claims became too much, historian Stephen C. Neff wrote, and "eventually, the Federal government's patience was exhausted." Neff reported that, in 1915, "a little-remarked piece of legislation called the 'Crawford Amendment' finally removed from the jurisdiction of the Court of Claims all cases of this kind. Piece by piece, the great conflict was winding down."[36]

*   *   *

Losses suffered during the 1862 Maryland Campaign, combined with the decades-long claims process, had lasting effects on the Sharpsburg community. Many citizens teetered on economic insolvency following the Battle of Antietam, and their conditions did not improve when the war ended.

Historians Judkin Browning and Timothy Silver wrote that Sharpsburg's residents "faced ruin" after the battle. "Farms went bankrupt and some families depended on charity to survive. Such was the aftermath of nearly every major battle of the war." Jonathan Trowbridge saw this devastation firsthand when he traveled

---

35 Claim of the heirs of Samuel Grove (No. 9313). The heirs' $6,586.50 claim converts to $175,000 in 2022 currency; *House Documents, 64th Congress, 1st Session*, Vol. 147 (Washington, DC, 1916), doc. 214, 1-2; Claim of Jacob Miller (No. 4296). Savilla S. Miller, a daughter of Squire Miller, became administratrix of the $11,692 claim after the deaths of her father and older brother, Samuel H. Miller. Further research may reveal the specifics of "Rule 89;" *Shepherdstown Register*, January 14, 1915.

36 *The Statutes at Large of the United States of America from March 1913 to March 1915, Vol. XXXVIII* (Washington, DC, 1915), pt. 1, 975; Claim of St. Paul's Protestant Episcopal Church (No. 13674); Stephen C. Neff, *Justice in Blue and Gray: A Legal History of the Civil War* (Cambridge, MA, 2010), 241.

to Sharpsburg in 1865. A woman living on the farm of Jacob Avey, Sr. told Trowbridge, "It was a right hard time, stranger . . . I haven't got well over it yet . . . we are jist getting things a little to rights again now, but the place a'n't what it was, and never will be again, in my day."

Author Kathleen Ernst found that compounded property losses throughout the war ruined many families in Western Maryland. "More than one woman looked at once-again empty shelves and knew with certainty that this time the catastrophe could not be met," Ernst wrote. "More than one man threw up his hands, sold his land for whatever he could get, and moved his family on."

Those who remained struggled to get by. As late as 1890, Sharpsburg inhabitant Lizzie K. Miller noted that the recovery process "was no little tax on the people over whose farms and homes had swept the raking destructive shot and shell from friend and foe, and what was still worse, the presence of two armies had depleted garner and cupboard." Indeed, Miller wrote, "the community has never fully recovered from the effects of the war."[37]

Testimony briefs in claims cases imply that some petitioners of little means lost all of their belongings to military forces during and after the battle at Sharpsburg. Ezra Nalley recalled, "[T]he Union soldiers camped right where I lived. They took everything I had." After troops ransacked the tenant home of Jacob Myers, he submitted an $82.47 petition for three beds, cookware, food, a rocking cradle, and "family clothing." This small list, the poor farmer testified, "was nearly all the property belonging to me." When Martha Schlosser met with a special agent regarding her claim, the elderly widow explained that in "Sept. 1862 everything she had was taken."

Likewise, tenant farmer Otho B. Smith and his wife "lost heavily" during the medical department's occupation of their property. Consequently, "The farm was finally sold, and the Smith family removed to Boonsboro." Civilians struggled through impoverishment long after the war. After Victor Vifquain interrogated John Snyder in the 1870s, the agent informed Washington that the Sharpsburg claimant—who sustained extensive losses after the Battle of Antietam—is "an old man and . . . in poor circumstances now."

Unfortunately, evidence does not shed light on how military appropriations affected enslaved persons living near the Sharpsburg battlefield in 1862. Given that

---

37 Browning and Silver, *An Environmental History of the Civil War*, 78-79; Trowbridge, *The South*, 52; Ernst, *TATC*, 210; Lizzie K. Miller to Connecticut Civil War veterans, 1890.

soldiers plundered farmhouses, village homes, and tenant shacks during the Antietam Campaign, troops undoubtedly ransacked slave quarters, as well.[38]

On account of their war-related debts, many civilians struggled to pay property taxes, which subjected their homes to lawful seizure. In one example, the *Herald and Torch Light* in 1867 announced a collector's sale for eighteen houses and lots in Sharpsburg village. Due to taxes owed from 1865, state officials seized the properties and placed them for sale at public auction.[39]

Battlefield farmers also struggled to recover. William Roulette was unable "to raise grain sufficient to support his family" in 1864 and, out of desperation, applied for a job as a cemetery agent. Describing Joseph Poffenberger's postwar struggles, one study examined the farmer's tax records, finding that "the stress from the battle and its aftermath must have been a terrible ordeal." Before Antietam, Poffenberger's annual income placed him in the three-percent tax bracket for earnings between $600 and $10,000. After the 1862 battle, the study found, tax records show that Poffenberger's income "never surpassed $600.00 again."[40]

Henry Piper deposed that his neighbor, Joshua Newcomer, "was one of the heaviest lossers by the war." Newcomer alleged that McClellan's troops took $3,097.15 worth of supplies in September and October 1862. Making matters worse, the miller-farmer "also suffered a heavy loss at the hands of the Rebels, including a large quantity of flour, horses, cattle, etc., amounting to about eleven thousand dollars." The Court of Claims awarded Newcomer $880 for his Bowman Act case but did not pay the settlement until 1899. In the interim, Newcomer's claim cites that financial difficulties from the war "obliged the claimant to sell his farm and mill and has thus deprived him of a house of his own."[41]

---

38 Claims of John J. Middlekauff (No. 1261), Jacob Myers (*RG* 92, Entry 843, Box 772, Book 304, Claim 323), and Martha Schlosser (Box 771, Claim 170); Williams, HWC, vol. 2, 1:753-754; Claim of John Snyder (No. 6617).

39 *HTL*, June 12, 1867. Among the affected homeowners were Mrs. James Early, Mrs. James Clayton, Squire Jacob Miller, Adam Michael, and Jacob H. Grove. The legal notice also announced the seizure of six vacant lots in Sharpsburg village.

40 Trail, "Remembering Antietam," 73; "WA-II-279 Joseph R. Poffenberger Farm," sec. 8, p. 3-4; "The First Income Tax," American Battlefield Trust, web page, https://www. battlefields.org/learn/articles/first-income-tax.

41 Claims of Joshua Newcomer (Claim F-854 and Case No. 272). Newcomer did not specify what amount of his $11,000 in Confederate-related losses related to Antietam. General Edward Johnson's command possibly seized some of Newcomer's crops and mill products during the Gettysburg Campaign, given that the same troops impressed flour from miller Martin Eakle in June 1863.

Samuel Mumma, Sr., was one of the few farmers who recovered quickly. Historian Dean Herrin wrote that the Mumma farm in 1870 was "more prosperous than it had been before the war." Comparing agricultural schedules for Sharpsburg, Herrin found that the amount of Mumma's acreage, livestock, wheat, and corn increased from 1860 to 1870. The farmer's real and personal estate values improved during this span, as well.

Eight years after the battle, a census enumerator traveled to the Antietam Valley and briefly quartered with the Mumma family. He observed that a new house and barn "sprung up over the ashes of the old ones; and where death's harvest of slaughtered men lay thick as sheaves in grain fields, now was to be seen the green, wavy corn in all its luxuriance of growth." The enumerator searched for signs of the bloody contest, to no avail. "[N]ature has kindly covered over every trace of the fearful conflict that raged here between brothers," he wrote. "[N]o one would dream that there ever had been a battle here."[42]

Some of the physical evidence of Antietam's damage and destruction may have faded by 1870, but the financial suffering of local inhabitants did not. A major cause of the slow recovery was postwar inflation.

As mentioned earlier by historian Thomas J. C. Williams, the end of the Civil War found the people of Washington County "greatly impoverished" by military-related property losses, "and there was yet a decade before substantial recovery began." Several factors were to blame, Williams wrote. First, the county from 1861–65 "had lost the wealth producing energies of one or two thousand able-bodied men" who enlisted in the Northern and Southern armies and were subsequently "withdrawn from industrial work." Also impacting the economy, "Fifteen hundred slaves had been set free. Crops had been destroyed, horses and all farm animals carried off and fencing burned by marching armies."

A larger problem loomed, "caused by the fluctuating currency." Williams—who moved to Washington County shortly after the war—recalled that gold prices remained steady, "but the depreciated greenback was the measure of values. As the greenback became less valuable the price, or rather the nominal price, of lands and wheat and corn advanced." This tempted persons "to buy lands at inflated values, giving mortgages to secure deferred payments." Other farmers had to "mortgage their lands to pay for horses and cattle which they had to buy in

42 Herrin, *Antietam Rising*, ANBL, 66-68. Herrin cited the *Boonsboro* [MD] *Odd Fellow*, August 19, 1870; The 1860 and 1870 Federal censuses for Sharpsburg, Dwellings #1544 and #211, cite Mumma's values of real estate and personal property; Johnson, *BA*, 124.

place of those taken by the soldiers, and upon these mortgages the interest charged was at the rate of from 8 to 10 per cent." Farmers struggled to afford the rising costs of machinery and labor. Once they paid wages for fertilizing, seeding, harvesting, and threshing, little profit remained.

To the misfortune of Washington County farmers, land values decreased and acreage "bought in the flush times at $100 or more per acre . . . sold under the hammer at mortgagee's or trustee's or sheriff's sales for less than half that sum." Consequently, landowners "made deeds of trust of their property for the benefit of creditors and the columns of the County were filled with advertisements." Unable to recover, Williams wrote, "Many farmers sold their property and emigrated to the West. For years each spring two or more special trains left Hagerstown each Tuesday carrying emigrants away from their old homes." In this manner, Williams observed, "Washington County lost several thousand of valuable and industrious citizens."[43]

*   *   *

Sharpsburg's poor postwar economy, combined with new opportunities in western states, drove many families to leave the region. One source observed that Sharpsburg's population "dropped slightly after the war . . . reflecting the post war losses and the post war depression." Later, "[F]our and five families a month left town . . . they headed west for a better chance to make a living." Two decades after the battle, the *Sharpsburg Enterprise* announced, "The western fever is prevailing to a considerable extent among our people. Every week we have to record the departure of families toward the setting sun, and, judging from the tone of many others, the exodus has scarcely attained its height."[44]

Westward migration was not a new trend for Antietam Valley inhabitants. Several dozen Washington County families moved to Ogle and Carroll Counties, Illinois, from the 1830s to the 1850s. These settlements—rife with extended family members—made the Prairie State a welcome destination for Sharpsburg civilians

---

43 Williams, HWC, vol. 1, 2:367-368. For other discussions on Washington County's postwar economy, see John Sanderson, "The Decline of the Agricultural Economy of Washington County as a Result of the Ravages Caused by the Civil War," Piper Farm historical report, 1973, ANBL. See also James R. Johnson, "A Community Caught in the Cross-Fire: The Citizens of Sharpsburg, Maryland Before, During, and After the Battle of Antietam," thesis, Wayne State University, 2007, WMR.

44 Herrin, *Antietam Rising*, ANBL, 68-69. Herrin cited the *Sharpsburg Enterprise*, March 31, 1882; Barron and Barron, *The History of Sharpsburg*, 64.

after the Civil War. Following Henry Reel's death, his wife and children moved to Illinois, as did Elijah Avey and his sister, Catherine Avey Highbarger. Squire Jacob Miller's daughter and son-in-law also emigrated to Illinois, and many others followed.[45]

Joshua Newcomer, staggered by wartime debt, sold his real estate and moved his family to Ogle County. In 1868, a Washington County citizen traveling through Illinois bumped into Newcomer and other "former residents of our county." So many familiar faces called Ogle County home, the traveler found, that "it made us feel as if we were in Hagerstown on a Tuesday."[46]

Wartime losses bankrupt Esther Knode. She testified that, after the Battle of Antietam, "[T]he Union troops came on the farm and took everything we had and ruined us, the farm was black with people . . . I know we lost all we had." She and her husband, John E. Knode, struggled to recover after the war. Between 1871 and 1873, the tenant couple mortgaged the few assets they owned after becoming indebted to private parties and the National Bank of Hagerstown. John eventually had to borrow money from Esther, and the distress from debt and multiple mortgages may have factored into his death at the age of 60 in 1875.

When a quartermaster agent investigated the Knodes' July Fourth claim in 1876, he informed Washington, "The widow is now in very strained circumstances and needs an allowance from the Govt. if it can be consistently made." The depot

---

45 Harry G. Kable, *Mount Morris: Past and Present: An Illustrated History of the Village of Mount Morris, Ogle County, Illinois* (Salem, MA, 1938), 16-17; Piper, *Piper Family History*; "History of Carroll County," web page, Carroll County, Illinois, https://www.carroll-county.net/history; Barbara Reel and her children appear in the 1880 Federal census, Panola Township, Woodford County, Illinois, Dwelling #64. The enumerator misidentified Barbara as "Bradly." Samuel Mumma, Jr., in a 1906 letter to James F. Clark, wrote, "[T]he rest of the [Henry Reel] family have moved west." See Mumma, *Antietam: The Aftermath*, 26; The 1870 census for Polo, Ogle County, Illinois, lists Elijah Avey in Dwelling #273. Catherine Avey Highbarger appears in the 1880 Federal census for Polo, Ogle County, Dwelling #319, as a widowed, 55-year-old seamstress from Maryland; Jacob Miller to Amelia and Christian Houser, November 16, 1863, WMR. Miller referred to his son-in-law, Jacob Mumma; James M. Guinn, *History of the State of California and Biographical Record of the Sacramento Valley, California: A Historical Study of the State's Marvelous Growth From Its Earliest Settlement to the Present Time* (Chicago, IL, 1906), 440-443. Guinn noted the emigration of Jacob and Ann Mary Mumma from Sharpsburg to Mount Morris, Illinois. He also mentioned that two other sons of Samuel Mumma, Sr. moved west after the war.

46 "Editorial Correspondence," *HTL*, September 23, 1868. The 1870 Federal census for Haldane Township, Ogle County, Illinois, lists Newcomer, his wife, and children in Dwelling #10. He claimed no amount of real or personal estate in 1870. Newcomer retired by 1880 and returned to Maryland. He and his family appear in the 1880 Federal census for Clear Spring, Washington County, Dwelling #122.

quartermaster rejected the request, being unable to certify "that the stores were actually received or taken for the use of and used by the Army." Ruined by the war, Esther Knode moved her children to Illinois.[47]

Many other civilians left Western Maryland. "A number of our young men," the *Boonsboro Odd Fellow* reported in 1876, "have taken Horace Greeley's advice and started, or are about to start for the West." Among these residents, the *Odd Fellow* announced, "Alfred Poffenberger, from near Sharpsburg left last week for Iowa; Peter H. Gigous, from Keedysville, left last week for Illinois. Both Poffenberger and Gigous took their families with them, and intend making their homes in the West."[48]

All ten children of David R. and Margaret Miller left Sharpsburg. Sons Robert, Marion, and Frederick Miller emigrated to California, while others relocated to Ohio, Pennsylvania, and Washington, DC. One of the daughters, Mary "Mollie" Miller, married Reverend Arthur Jewson and moved to Calcutta, India, where the couple ran a Christian orphanage. By separating in different directions, the Millers, like many other families who relocated, went great lengths of time without seeing one another. In 1929, Charles P. Miller traveled to California to visit his brothers, Marion and Frederick. It marked the first time he had seen his siblings in several decades.[49]

Dozens of residents moved to Kansas after the war, including sons of John J. Keedy and James Marker and the families of Samuel Beeler and Barney Houser. Referring to Lincoln County, Kansas, the *Hagerstown Mail* noted in 1878, "In that

---

47 Claim of John E. Knode (*RG* 92, G-1647); Washington County land records (WMCKK 3 / 449, WMCKK 4 / 680, WMCKK 4 / 715, WMCKK 5 / 241, and WMCKK 5 / 807); Esther Knode appears in the 1880 Federal census, LaSalle County, Illinois, Dwelling #35.

48 *New York Daily Tribune*, July 13, 1865; *Boonsboro Odd Fellow*, March 17, 1876.

49 The Miller children and their residences appear in the obituaries of Margaret Miller (*HTL*, November 15, 1888) and David R. Miller (*HTL*, September 14, 1893). Regarding Mary Miller's move to India, see Daniel Long Miller, *Girdling the Globe: From the Land of the Midnight Sun to the Golden Gate* (Elgin, IL, 1898), 435. The author visited Calcutta and boarded with "Mrs. Jewson (nee Miller)," who "formerly resided at Sharpsburg, Md." Also referring to Mary Miller, Wilbur B. Stover in "The Missionary Visitor," Vol. XXVIII, January 1926, 3, spoke with "Sister Allie Moomaw [Mumma], of Sharpsburg, Md." who "had a friend, an American Methodist girl, who had gone to India and married an English Baptist missionary. His name was Arthur Jewson." *The Herald and Torch Light*, June 7, 1894, reported, "A few days ago John P. Smith, Sharpsburg, received from Rev. and Mrs. Jewson, of Calcutta, Hindostan, a large box of brass idols, potter's ware, fans, shells, coins and a praying machine, with numerous other articles characteristic of that country;" *Woodland Daily Democrat*, August 21, 1929, 1. The article noted that Charles P. Miller visited his brother Marion 25 years earlier but had not seen Frederick in 42 years. The *Daily Democrat* incorrectly listed the brothers' birthplace as Baltimore.

county there are now eighteen families from our county residing." Antietam Valley civilians also emigrated to Nebraska, including tenant farmer Jacob Snyder and several descendants of Jacob Avey, Sr.[50]

Jacob Bowers, a grandson of Jacob Avey, Sr., moved to Auburn, Nebraska. Leaving Sharpsburg was not an easy decision for the young man, *The Lincoln Sunday Star* observed, "but it could scarcely offer less than he was receiving in Maryland, which still suffered from the Civil War." Several decades later, in 1925, Jacob reunited with his brother, John Bowers. The brothers, ages 80 and 88, barely recognized one another, *The Lincoln Sunday Star* reported, and "tears, unashamed, streamed down their faces when they met at last."[51]

After the Battle of Antietam, Samuel I. Piper's losses "were so numerous . . . including valuables, timber and hardwood rail fences," that the financial burden "brought him to bankruptcy and the farm was lost." Seeing opportunity elsewhere, all seven of Piper's sons left Maryland and settled in Ohio and Pennsylvania. Described as "easily depressed," one can imagine Samuel I. Piper's feelings upon losing his farm and watching his boys leave home. William D. Piper recalled that when he left Maryland, "[H]is father was nearly heart-broken."[52]

After suffering heavy losses to the AOP in 1862, Philip Pry struggled to refund an overpaid claims settlement to the U.S. Treasury. Facing ruin, Pry and his wife,

---

50 *HTL*, October 20, 1892. Jacob Marker's obituary listed a surviving brother, "Mr. Ezra Marker, of Kansas;" The 1880 Federal census for Matfield Green, Chase County, Kansas, shows Barney Houser and his family in Dwelling #67. See also "Barney Houser," Find a Grave, database, https://www.findagrave.com/memorial/128498406/barney-houser; Claim of Samuel Beeler (201-56). The claim cites, "Case of Samuel Beeler, dec'd. Mrs. Amanda Beeler, Adm. Franklin County, Kas.," for supplies taken "in Washington Co. Md." Amanda Beeler's obituary in the *Ottawa Daily Republic* (Ottawa, KS), November 1, 1882, notes her postwar move to Kansas. See "Amanda Kalb Beeler," Find a Grave, database, https://www.findagrave.com/memorial/46751280/amanda-beeler; *Hagerstown Mail*, October 18, 1878, 2; Claim of Adam Hutzell (*RG* 123, No. 4292). Hutzell deposed that "Jacob Snyder, a subscribing witness, was a near neighbor . . . he now lives in Nebraska;" The Lewis Publishing Company, *A Biographical and Genealogical History of Southeastern Nebraska* (Chicago, IL, 1904), vol. 1, 57-59. A sketch on Thomas J. Keedy cites his marriage "to Miss Sarah Snyder, a native of Maryland;" Jacob Snyder's burial in Auburn, Nebraska appears in "Jacob Snyder," Find a Grave, database, https://www.findagrave.com/memorial/59942617/jacob-snyder.

51 Michael Garland Avey, *Cultural Resources of the Avey Family: Phase 1, Inventory of Archeological Sites* (Fort Steilacoom, WA, 1986), 40-41; *The Lincoln* [NE] *Sunday Star*, Sunday, July 10, 1925.

52 Piper, *Piper Family History*. Luther, Elias, Charles, and Otho Piper settled in Pennsylvania. William D. Piper and his brothers, Joseph and Benjamin, moved to Ohio. The boys' departures certainly devastated their mother, Mary Sophia (Baker) Piper, as well. Sisters Anna and Laughty Piper remained in the Sharpsburg area. Luther Piper moved back to Sharpsburg years later after he retired.

Elizabeth, sold their real estate. Describing Philip Pry in 1874, Senator William T. Hamilton wrote, "Before the war he was a prosperous man, owning one of the finest farms in the county lying in the vicinity of the battlefield of Antietam. He is now in serious circumstances." One year later, when special agent Madison Sallade compiled his report for Pry's July Fourth claim, he wrote that Pry "lost heavily" after the Antietam battle. "All his fencing was burned, his corn and wheat fed, together with a large quantity of hay . . . the war made him poor and he emigrated to Tenn to begin life anew."[53]

Before the Prys left Maryland for Tennessee, friends and family members presented Elizabeth Pry with a personalized "memory quilt" containing handwritten farewell notes. Thirty-eight members of the Keedysville-Sharpsburg community signed the quilt, including Rowena Nicodemus, Annie Neikirk, Alice M. Mumma, and "Aunt Catherine Cost." The loved ones penned heartwarming messages. Widow Susan Hoffman, perhaps realizing that she and Elizabeth Pry would never meet again, wrote, "Remember me when this you see though many miles apart we be. Your friend Susie Hoffman."[54]

The postwar emigrations took an emotional toll on Antietam Valley civilians, but many people bettered their finances by moving to western states—California, especially. When Sharpsburg citizen Charles W. Adams visited the Upper Sacramento Valley in 1891, he "met a great many Washington county people, who have emigrated to that state within the past fifteen or twenty years." The large concentration of former Antietam Valley residents impressed the Hagerstown *Herald and Torch Light*, which described the settlement as the "Maryland Colony."

Adams interviewed many former Sharpsburg residents during his California visit. Among them were two sons of John H. Snavely, two sons of David R. Miller, and three sons of Samuel Mumma, Sr. Other Californians included three children of Elizabeth Miller Blackford, two sons of Susan Kennedy, and sons of Morgan

---

53 "About the Pry House," web page, National Museum of Civil War Medicine," https://www.civilwarmed.org/pry/about-the-pry-house/; Claims of Philip Pry (H-3907 and H-3908); Washington County land records (LBN 2 / 42, LBN 2 / 178-179, LBN 2 / 156, LBN 2 / 419, LBN 2 / 604, WMCKK 5 / 646, and WMCKK 6 / 278); Reilly, *BOA*. Reilly wrote that the Prys "moved by wagon to Johnson City, E. Tenn." Alfred L. Pry, one of the Prys' sons, may have relocated elsewhere. The 1880 Federal census for Toulon, Illinois, lists Alfred Pry of Maryland, age 29, in Dwelling #54 with his wife and children. Death certificate no. 31950 for Butler, Missouri, accessed at Ancestry.com, documents Alfred Pry's death in 1922. It lists his birthplace as Keedysville, Maryland, and cites his parents as Philip Pry and Elizabeth Cost.

54 Sue Gemeny, Keedysville Historical Society, email message to author, June 5, 2020. The Keedysville Historical Society possesses Elizabeth Pry's quilt. Many of the persons who signed the quilt's squares belonged to the Mount Vernon Reformed Church of Keedysville.

Miller and Stephen P. Grove—to name a few. Adams closed his 1891 letter, writing, "You will readily see that I was among friends who, I am proud to say, have bettered their condition since leaving Maryland, and among them are a number who have become wealthy and are to-day looking for investments for their surplus cash."[55]

*   *   *

Those who stayed in Sharpsburg sloughed through the slow process of recovery. When the war ended, farmers on the battlefield still lacked full access to their acreage on account of the ubiquitous graves. Thousands of Northern and Southern soldiers remained buried on private properties. As previously described, most graves were shallow, allowing plows, storms, and animals to scatter bones across the landscape. This presented gross disrespect to the deceased and a macabre spectacle to residents. C. M. Keedy, son of John J. Keedy, remembered that "it was a common thing to see human bones lying loose in gutters and fence corners for several years." Jonathan Trowbridge found the sight repulsive when he visited Sharpsburg in 1865. He wrote, "Skeletons, rooted up by hogs, and blanching in the open fields, are a sight not becoming a country that calls itself Christian."[56]

Concerned over the desecration of military graves, the Maryland General Assembly pushed for creating a national cemetery dedicated to Antietam's Union dead. Once the state purchased part of Susan Kennedy's land on Sharpsburg Heights, Quartermaster General Meigs arranged the shipment of 6,000 coffins to

---

55 *HTL*, April 2, 1891, 2. The wives of Zachary and William Mumma also emigrated to Woodland. They were, respectively, Emma Rohrback, daughter of Benjamin F. Rohrback, and Laura L. Grove, one of the heirs of Samuel Grove; Guinn, *History of the State of California*, 1906, 878, 1058. The 1860 Federal census for Sharpsburg, Dwelling #1455, lists Hezekiah Miller in his parents' household; Tom Gregory, *History of Yolo County, California: With Biographical Sketches of the Leading Men and Women of the County, Who Have Been Identified with Its Growth and Development from the Early Days to the Present* (Los Angeles, CA, 1913), 794-796; John Hart appears in his parents' Sharpsburg household in the 1860 Federal census, Dwelling #1662. Sources described Hart as "one of the best known citizens of Yolo County" and "a self-made man in the truest acceptation of the term." See the *Woodland Daily Democrat*, April 1, 1926, and Guinn, *History of the State of California*, 1175; Widow Susan Kennedy's two sons, Thomas and John Kennedy, are buried in Capay Cemetery in Yolo County. John Kennedy moved to California with his wife, Jeanette Blackford, daughter of Elizabeth Miller Blackford.

56 Reilly, *BOA*; Trowbridge, *The South*, 55.

the battlefield environs. In October 1866, laborers began transferring the remains of U.S. troops to the new burial ground.[57]

The interment crews worked for ten months, locating graves with lists provided by two Sharpsburg men. Finally, they completed the reburial process in 1867, transferring 4,695 Union soldiers to the new graveyard on Sharpsburg Heights. The State of Maryland appointed Dr. A. A. Biggs as president and superintendent of the national cemetery. Also, Col. John Miller donated the "sodding off one of his fields" for the burial ground. The dedication of the Antietam National Cemetery took place on the fifth anniversary of the battle, on September 17, 1867.[58]

As the new Federal cemetery developed, hundreds of Confederates remained buried on Sharpsburg's farmsteads. In 1868, Thomas Boullt, an Antietam National Cemetery trustee, submitted a report "describing the deplorable condition of the Confederate dead on Antietam battlefield." Eventually, workers moved some of the remains to Shepherdstown, West Virginia. Finally, from 1872–1875, a burial crew supervised by civilian Henry C. Mumma transferred the remaining 1,721 Southern dead to a plot within Rose Hill Cemetery in Hagerstown. Trustees dedicated this ground, known as the Washington Confederate Cemetery, in 1877.[59]

---

57 Charles W. Snell and Sharon A. Brown, *Antietam National Battlefield and National Cemetery: An Administrative History*, U.S. Department of the Interior, National Park Service (Washington, DC, 1986), 14-15; Trail, "Remembering Antietam," 68-69, 73-74, 86-88; 108.

58 "Antietam National Cemetery," web page, ANB, https://www.nps.gov/anti/learn/historyculture/antietam-national-cemetery.htm. Many remains "were identified by letters, receipts, diaries, photographs, marks on belts or cartridge boxes, headstones and by interviewing relatives and survivors." Soldiers transferred some of the remains from Frederick and Allegany Counties, and other parts of Washington County. Of the 4,695 U.S. soldiers initially buried in the Antietam cemetery, more than 1,700 were unknown. Over the years, "more than 200 non-Civil War dead" were interred in the cemetery; Board of Trustees of the Antietam National Cemetery, Maryland. *History of the Antietam National Cemetery: Including a Descriptive List of the Loyal Soldiers Buried Therein, Together with the Ceremonies and Address on the Occasion of the Dedication of the Grounds, September 17, 1867* (Baltimore, MD, 1869), 10, WHILBR. Two Sharpsburg men, Aaron Good and Joseph A. Gill, devoted their time to record the names and burial locations of Union dead. Their lists helped the burial corps locate hundreds of graves; "History of the Antietam National Cemetery," web page, WHILBR, http://www.whilbr.org/antietamNationalCemetery/index.aspx; Claim of John Miller (No. 2227). Miller's sodding may have come from his stone mill property near the cemetery. For a discussion on postwar tensions between Sharpsburg civilians and the war department's management of the Antietam National Cemetery, see Snell and Brown, *Antietam National Battlefield and National Cemetery*, 25, 48-49, and Trail, "Remembering Antietam," 131-147.

59 Trail, "Remembering Antietam," 108-114; "A History of Elmwood Cemetery," web page, Elmwood Cemetery, http://elmwoodcemeteryshepwv.org/html/history.html. Per the

Given the magnitude of Antietam's casualties, burial crews responsible for relocating the remains overlooked many graves. Months later, roadwork near the Dunker Church unearthed the bones of six Confederates. Also, a Sharpsburg man unexpectedly "dug out the remains of a Union soldier supposed to be a member of the 12th or 13th Massachusetts Regiment." Another grave, according to Oliver T. Reilly, "was dug up when the Massachusetts State Monument was put up, besides many others in different places since, which is proof that many others of the unaccounted for lie buried in the fields, some never to be found." In 1907, laborers on Capt. David Smith's former farm "came across the remains of six soldiers," which initially appeared intact, "but a few moments after the air reached them they crumbled into dust."[60]

With most farmsteads finally free of human bones, Sharpsburg moved one step closer to recovery. Properties on the battlefield, however, would never be the same. After establishing the national cemetery, the U.S. war department gradually transformed the battleground into a military park. First, it marked the agrarian landscape with tablets to educate visitors about the armies' positions during the battle. Next, it purchased land to create avenues across farms. These byways

---

website, 114 Confederates killed at Antietam lie at Elmwood Cemetery, along with 125 Southern soldiers unassociated with the 1862 campaign; Greg Stiverson, "Washington Confederate Cemetery, Hagerstown," *The Archivist's Bulldog,* Maryland State Archives, Annapolis, MD, vol. 7, no. 2, January 25, 1993, https://msa.maryland.gov/msa/ refserv/ bulldog/bull93/html/bull93.html; "History of Rose Hill," web page, Rose Hill Cemetery, https://rosehillcemeteryofmd.org/rich-in-history/history-of-rose-hill/. 726 Confederate dead from South Mountain were also moved to Rose Hill Cemetery; Burial crews transferred some of Sharpsburg's Confederate remains to Mount Olivet Cemetery in Frederick. See "The American Civil War," web page, Mount Olivet Cemetery, http://www. mountolivetcemeteryinc.com/the-civil-war.html. Most of the Confederates buried at Mount Olivet are unidentified casualties of the Battle of Monocacy in 1864; "Antietam National Cemetery," ANB; "Washington Confederate Cemetery, Hagerstown, Maryland," WHILBR, http://www.whilbr.org/WashingtonConfederateCemetery/index. aspx; Prior to the transfer of dead, the State of Maryland hired Sharpsburg residents Aaron Good and Moses Poffenberger to log the locations of 3,300 Confederates buried in Washington and Frederick Counties. The men undertook this task in early 1869.

60 *The Evening Star,* September 17, 1896; Reilly, *BOA; Shepherdstown Register,* May 23, 1907. A headboard at the burial site identified one of the Confederates as Lieutenant Arthur W. Speight of the 3rd North Carolina. Additional remains of soldiers surfaced on the battlefield in 1988 and 2009. See B. Drummand Ayres, Jr., "Clues From Antietam Grave Offer Hope Soldier May Regain Identity," *New York Times,* August 19, 1988. See also Jameel Moses, "Remains of Civil War Soldier Return Home on Anniversary," online article, U.S. Army, September 18, 2009, https://www.army.mil/article/27510/remains_of_civil_war_soldier_return_home_on_anni versary.

"facilitate[d] movements about the fields . . . without trampling upon and injuring growing crops, gardens, orchards, etc."

While the war department began work on the avenues, veterans' groups and state representatives approached landowners about buying parcels to erect monuments. As noted by author Susan C. Hall, "Sharpsburg residents again faced an 'invasion' of the Federal Government and Civil War soldiers . . . as they sought to preserve a portion of the Antietam Battlefield for posterity." Many farmers may have needed the money, but parceling off their land was likely a difficult decision. Hannah Nicodemus, Michael Tenant, Urias Gross, and the heirs of Mary Locher were among the real estate owners who agreed to the initial sales offers.[61]

Some landowners, including Samuel D. Piper and William Roulette, demanded steep prices for their acreage, perhaps bitter at the government's rejection of their July Fourth and Bowman Act claims. Other farmers disrespected the Federal development by driving machinery and livestock along the new avenues. Historian Susan W. Trail wrote that the Sharpsburg community's "perceived ill-treatment at the hands of the Federal occupiers following the battle left a bad taste." This created a "lack of interest on the part of the local people regarding the Antietam battlefield. They worked to erase the effects of the battle as quickly as possible and, unlike their neighbors to the north at Gettysburg, did not move to capitalize upon it."[62]

*   *   *

Political tensions in Sharpsburg, like socioeconomic hardships, continued after the war. Strained relations existed within families, as well. In August 1865, Samuel

---

61 Trail, "Remembering Antietam," 185-188; Snell and Brown, *Antietam National Battlefield and National Cemetery*, 94-95; Herrin, Antietam Rising, 80; Washington County land records of Hannah Nicodemus (105 / 366; 105 / 379; 106 / 40; 118 / 493), Catherine and Michael Tenant (104 / 56), Urias and Sarah Gross (104 / 57), and the heirs of Mary Locher (103 / 606); Susan C. Hall, *Antietam National Battlefield, Observation Tower*, Historic American Buildings Survey, National Park Service, U.S. Department of the Interior (Washington, DC, 2009), 6.

62 Trail, "Remembering Antietam," 69-70, 195-196, 202-213; Herrin, *Antietam Rising*, 80-81. After the war, Samuel D. Piper acquired his parents' farm on the battlefield near Bloody Lane. It is not within the scope of this study to detail the development of the battleground. Of note, however, the war department transferred management of the battlefield to the National Park Service in 1933. Over time, the government purchased around 3,000 acres from Sharpsburg's landowners in establishing the Antietam National Battlefield. See "Basic Information," web page, ANB, https://www.nps.gov/anti/planyourvisit/basicinfo.htm. See also "Short History of the Park," web page, ANB, https://www.nps.gov/anti/learn/historyculture/short-history -of-the-park.htm.

Michael, a pro-slavery Democrat, penned a bitter letter to his brother David, a Federal soldier who served in the 42nd Indiana Infantry. As Samuel Michael saw it, the Union army stole his father's property, spread fatal diseases to his mother and sister, and fought to destroy slavery. "I suppose you are satisfied with the Nigger war," Samuel complained. "I suppose you are satisfied that you helped whip Jeff Davis and company out . . . the South lost no honor, only property. They fought all the combined powers of Europe and the damned Abolotionists of the North and the Nigger to boot and come very near whipping out after all." Furthermore, Samuel griped, "The Yankee Abolotionists have destroyed the property of the people better than they dare be for the purpose of freeing the negroe and establishing Negro equality, a race that never ought to be free, but to be held as servants from generation to generation." He finished his intolerant rant by writing, "You cannot pick and meaner set in hell to compete with the Yankee Abolitionist, that as many as Old Abe has already sent in yonder who are now quarreling with Old Abe there about Negroes equality. I must stop. Theres no more room to write."[63]

In the war's aftermath, many Union-loyal Marylanders disdained the notion of welcoming home neighbors who served in the Confederate army. Shortly after President Lincoln's assassination, Washington County Unionists voted to form a Vigilance Committee to prohibit the return of residents "who left the County and entered the Rebel service . . . and united with the outcast Jeff. Davis."[64]

A few Confederate veterans returned, regardless. Henry Kyd Douglas took residence in Hagerstown, where he practiced law and helped establish the Washington Confederate Cemetery. John Mutius Gaines, an ANV surgeon, moved to Boonsboro and married Helen Jeanette Smith, a daughter of Dr. Otho J. Smith.[65]

---

63 Samuel Michael to David Michael, August 7, 1865, WMR.

64 *HTL*, May 10 and May 24, 1865; Donald B. Jenkins, *The Lost Civil War Diary of John Rigdon King* (Mount Pleasant, SC, 2018), 231-32. Jenkins wrote that Unionists "not only wanted to discourage Confederates from coming home to Washington County. They also did not want them to have any power as officeholders."

65 After Rev. Robert Douglas died in 1867, Henry Kyd Douglas's mother sold the Ferry Hill farm at Sharpsburg and joined her son in Hagerstown. The 1870 Federal census for Hagerstown lists Douglas in the Washington House hotel, Dwelling #1024. In 1880, Henry, his mother, sister, and two children appear in Dwelling #141; Williams, HWC, vol. 2, 1:913-914; "Historic Walking Tour: Stop #18," Town of Boonsboro, Maryland, web page, https:// www.town.boonsboro.md.us/historicboonsborowalkingtour; Dr. John Mutius Gaines, vertical file, ANBL. Gaines met Helen Smith while he treated the wounded in Boonsboro

Most of Sharpsburg's Confederates relocated to other states. Two sons of Jacob H. Grove—Philip D. Grove and Thomas H. Grove—did not return to Maryland, and Col. John Miller's son, William M. Miller of the 2nd Virginia, moved to Texas. Captain Joseph McGraw moved to New York, "where he became a traveling salesman for a large willow and woodenware wholesale house." He married Charlotte Fowler and had two children, "a little boy who died infancy, and a daughter, Amelia." After making a sojourn to Sharpsburg to visit his mother and siblings, "Joe dropped out of sight and was never heard from or seen by his friends again."[66]

In Sharpsburg, former slaves adjusted to life after the war while toiling to establish financial independence. George W. Fisher returned to the Antietam Valley after serving in the United States Colored Troops. He resided with Samuel I. Piper as a farm laborer and later married and raised a family near Keedysville.[67]

---

during the 1862 Maryland Campaign. After Helen died in 1868, Gaines remarried to Susan Rentch, a daughter of Andrew Rentch, and practiced medicine in Washington County until 1893.

66 Claim of Jacob H. Grove (*RG* 123, No. 1267). Dr. Philip D. Grove lived in Virginia and West Virginia after serving as a Confederate surgeon. The 1870 Federal census for Craig County, Virginia, lists P. D. Grove and his wife in Dwelling #10; *The Shepherdstown Register*, April 13, 1905. Thomas H. Grove moved to Iowa after serving in the 1st Regiment, Maryland Cavalry. He lost touch with his family for several decades. Just before his death in 1905, Thomas resurfaced, sending word to his sisters that he was in Grand Junction, Colorado, "in feeble health and alone;" Details of William M. Miller's Confederate service are explained in Chapter Ten; Cross, "Joseph McGraw at Sharpsburg," second installment, *The Daily Mail*, February 15, 1934, 14. Colonel William Gordon McCabe, who served with McGraw in Pegram's Battery, believed that McGraw committed suicide after the death of his infant son. Jacob McGraw disagreed, opining that his brother was "killed by someone who imagined that he had a large sum of money . . . or that he fell an unknown victim to one of the yellow fever epidemics which about that time swept over the Gulf states." The 1875 Federal census for Brooklyn Ward 25, Kings County, New York, lists Joseph and Charlotte McGraw in Dwelling #652. Joseph disappeared by 1880, and Charlotte lived with her mother in Dwelling #93 in Brooklyn.

67 In 1863, the U.S. war department issued General Order No. 329, which aided the recruitment of slaves and free blacks in border states. A section of the order stipulated that slaveowners who enlisted their male servants into the U.S. army were "entitled to compensation for the service or labor of said slave, not exceeding the sum of three hundred dollars, upon filing a valid deed of manumission and of release, and making satisfactory proof of title." Consequently, Washington C. Snively manumitted his slaves, including George W. Fisher, into the United States Colored Troops in 1863. The 1870 Federal census for Sharpsburg, Dwelling #163, lists George W. Fisher in Samuel I. Piper's household. The census for Keedysville lists Fisher in Dwellings #35 (1880) and #208 (1900). For further reading on Sharpsburg's African American soldiers in the Civil War, see Herrin, *Antietam Rising*, ANBL, 18-27.

Jane Sinclair, enslaved to Stephen P. and Maria Grove during the war, continued living with the couple as a domestic servant. Then, in 1877, she purchased a residential parcel near Sharpsburg village. Jeremiah Summers, a slave owned by Henry Piper in 1862, remained in the Piper family's household as a farm laborer until settling into a cabin near Bloody Lane.[68]

Freed from slavery, Christina and Hilary Watson moved into a dwelling near William Roulette and David R. Miller. Over time, the couple saved enough money to buy Lot 102 in Sharpsburg village, where they resided in a log home. Surviving slavery, the inseparable couple embraced freedom, raised a family, and lived until the 1900s, dying two years apart in 1915 and 1917. Author Clifton Johnson interviewed Christina Watson shortly before her death. As she shared her memories of the Antietam battle, Johnson observed that Mrs. Watson's "tiny sitting-room" was furnished with family photographs and individual images of the crucifixion, Abraham Lincoln, and "[John] Wilkes Booth with the devil looking over his shoulder."[69]

Domestic servant Georgianna Rollins, a free African American in 1862, remained in the household of Philip and Elizabeth Pry until the family moved to Tennessee. Georgianna stayed in the Keedysville area, married John Rose, and had ten children, seven of whom lived to adulthood. Later in life, Georgianna relocated to Columbus, Ohio, with her son, Jesse.[70]

Another free domestic servant, Nancy Campbell, stayed with William Roulette's family for the rest of her life. Before her death in 1892, Nancy

---

68 The 1870 Federal census lists "Jane St. Clair" in Stephen P. Grove's household, Dwelling #143. In 1880, the Federal census for Sharpsburg shows Jane Sinclair as head of household in Dwelling #131; Washington County land record 75 / 115. Sinclair's lot was northwest of the town limits; "WA-II-702 Tolson's Chapel, Black A.M.E. Church," architectural survey file, MHT, https://mht.maryland.gov/secure/medusa/PDF/Washington/WA-II-702.pdf. The 1870 Federal census for Sharpsburg shows Jeremiah Summers in the household of Samuel D. Piper, Dwelling #209. In 1880, Jeremiah, his wife, and children occupied dwelling #264 on the battlefield. Summers's brother, Emory Summers, another former slave, lived in Henry Piper's household in 1870, Dwelling #159. By 1900, Emory settled into his own home on Chapline Street in Sharpsburg village, Dwelling #348.

69 "WA-II-702 Tolson's Chapel, Black A.M.E. Church;" The 1870 census for Sharpsburg lists the Watsons in Dwelling #213. In 1880, the couple resided in Dwelling #208 on Antietam Street; Washington County land records (WMCKK 5 / 124-125, 88 / 153, and 147 / 757). The 1877 Sharpsburg village map depicts "H. Watson" on Lot 102; Johnson, *BA*, 104, 109.

70 Federal census listings from 1870–1930 show Georgianna Rollins Rose in dwellings #185 (1870 household of Philip Pry), #341 (1880, Sharpsburg), #182 (1900, Keedysville), and #237 (1930, Columbus, Ohio).

Jeremiah "Jerry" Summers, photographed at his home by Fred Wilder Cross in 1924.
Boonsborough Museum of History

bequeathed the majority of her estate—$100, along with a bed, clothing, and personal effects—to Susan Roulette Santee, the daughter of William Roulette.[71]

Thomas Barnum, a free African American, continued farming as a tenant in postbellum Washington County, despite suffering from rheumatism and a lame ankle. Through hard work, the former slave overcame his wartime losses and purchased a farm of his own, where he resided with his wife and children until dying in 1895. One source noted that Barnum "played the role of banker" to help African Americans in the area. His obituary reported that "if he knew of an instance where an injustice was done to a man of his own race he was always willing to assist in bringing his case to court." Upon his death, the value of Thomas Barnum's farm was an impressive $10,000–$12,000. "Considering his success in life and the obstacles which he overcame," the *Herald and Torch Light* informed its readers, "Mr. Barnum was a remarkable man."[72]

In 1865, African American residents organized a congregation in Sharpsburg, led by Methodist preacher John R. Tolson. The following year, they erected a chapel on Lot 104 in the village. Members of the new house of worship included John Francis, who lived with Samuel D. Piper in 1862, and David B. Simons, who testified in the case of the heirs of Samuel Grove. In addition, Nancy Campbell and Jeremiah Summers belonged to the congregation, as did Hilary and Christina

---

71 The Federal census for Sharpsburg lists Nancy Campbell with the Roulette family in 1870 (Dwelling #212) and 1880 (Dwelling #247); *HTL*, January 14, 1892; Will liber H / folios 404-405. Some sources identify her as Nancy Camel and Nannie Campbell.

72 "Thomas Barnum Family Papers," Joseph Davis collection; *HTL*, April 18, 1895.

Watson. Parishioners utilized the building as a school for their children and dedicated part of the ground as a cemetery. Known as Tolson's Chapel, the house of worship "became the spiritual and educational center of a vibrant community of African American families in Sharpsburg after the Civil War, and a symbol of their struggles and triumphs." Tolson's Chapel, its website cites, is a "tangible reminder of what the Civil War was about for many Americans, particularly for the four million enslaved on the eve of the war—freedom."[73]

*   *   *

Kathleen Ernst described the wartime residents of Western Maryland as "ordinary people facing extraordinary challenges." Most civilians, Ernst wrote, survived the war and its grueling aftermath, "somehow finding the courage to face a new day." Many who stayed in the area struggled to earn a living but made ends meet through grit and resilience. Sharpsburg's "cooper's shop, tannery and four shoe shops . . . did not survive after the war," local historians Lee and Barbara Barron wrote, but "many businesses did survive and prosper."

Commerce on the C & O Canal helped some people recover. "[A]s time went on into the 1860s and 1870s," the Barrons wrote, canal jobs "increased so much that by 1870–1890 two thirds of all men of Sharpsburg worked on the canal either as boatmen or maintenance workers, boat builders or carpenters." Tourism also helped revitalize the local economy. Private Alexander Hunter of the 17th Virginia Infantry described Sharpsburg, before the Battle of Antietam, as "a little village nestling at the bottom of the hills, a simple country hamlet, that none outside, save perhaps a postmaster, ever heard of before, and yet which in one day awoke to find itself famous." As Hunter noted, whether it liked it or not, the community would never return to its quiet, unassuming, prewar state. Susan W. Trail observed that the United States government transformed Sharpsburg after the war "into a highly Union and nationalistic military landscape." Beginning in 1868, Decoration Day,

73 "Tolson's Chapel," web page, National Park Service, https://www.nps.gov/places/tolson-s-chapel.htm; "WA-II-702 Tolson's Chapel, Black A.M.E. Church;" Washington County land records (LBN 1 / 712 and WMCKK 4 / 30); Michael Trinkley and Debi Hacker, *Preservation Assessment of Tolson's Chapel Cemetery, Sharpsburg, Maryland* (Columbia, SC, 2013); "A Significant Place in American History," web page, Tolson's Chapel, https://tolsonschapel.org/history/.

later known as Memorial Day, attracted hundreds of visitors each May to the Antietam National Cemetery.[74]

In 1883, the Shenandoah Valley Railroad established Sharpsburg Station near the town's western limits. The depot provided convenient transportation for the area's citizenry and facilitated the export of agricultural products and other goods. More importantly, the direct rail access allowed tourism to flourish. A report in 1888 noted that Sharpsburg was "visited by 15 or 20,000 people, and during six months of the year, the number of visitors is very large." When the war department officially established the Antietam battlefield site in 1890, the numbers spiked all the more. Dean Herrin wrote that Decoration Day in May and the battle's anniversary in September attracted thousands of visitors to the area each year—veterans, especially—"and they all needed transportation, food, and lodging."

Despite feeling scorned by wartime depredations and rejected claims, some locals saw the opportunity presented. They cast aside bitter feelings to accommodate the Antietam veterans. Church congregations sold meals to the visitors, and other citizens charged for rides in their hacks (horse-drawn carriages). For one reunion, Pennsylvania veterans hired "50 local wagons . . . to drive them around the various sites." During the battle's anniversary in 1891, a newspaper announced, "Our hackmen reaped a rich harvest . . . they were kept busy all the time." With few hotels in the area, residents cashed in, charging guests for food and lodging. Once again, years after the battle, civilians and soldiers slept under the same roofs.[75]

---

74 Ernst, *TATC*, 241; Barron and Barron, *The History of Sharpsburg*, 64, 75-76. Railroad competition and flooding of the Potomac River eventually forced the canal to close; Hunter, "A High Private's Sketch of Sharpsburg," 10; Trail, "Remembering Antietam," 146; "Memorial Day Order," web page, National Cemetery Administration, U.S. Department of Veterans Affairs, https://www.cem.va.gov/history/memdayorder.asp.

75 "History of Antietam Station," website, Hagerstown Model Railroad Museum, http://www.antietamstation.com/hHistory.htm; Blair Williamson, "Reminiscing the Rails: Rail Collision Forces Name Change From Sharpsburg to Antietam Station," *Maryland Cracker Barrel*, February/March 2005, 32-34. Known initially as Sharpsburg Station, the depot later became Antietam Station. Fire destroyed the structure in 1910. The current depot was built in 1912 and operated until 1962; Snell and Brown, *Antietam National Battlefield and National Cemetery*, 41-44. To improve travel between the depot and national cemetery in the late 1800s, Congress appropriated funds to macadamize Main Street, install sidewalks, and plant 300 Norway maple trees along the road to shade the visitors; Herrin, *Antietam Rising*, ANBL, 75-80; Trail, "Remembering Antietam," 160-64; Like Oliver T. Reilly, Martin L. Burgan, and Martin E. Snavely, some residents profited from the out-of-towners' visits by giving guided tours of the

The reunions at Sharpsburg allowed bonds to form between residents and veterans. Virginia Mumma Hildebrand recounted, "[M]y grandmother's home was always open to these soldiers and it was always exciting to talk with these men and hear their experiences." Thirty-one years after the Battle of Antietam, Private John Van Horn of the 133rd Pennsylvania visited Sharpsburg and tracked down villager Sarah Smith, extending "his gratitude for her kindness to him" while he battled typhoid fever inside the Lutheran Church hospital. Decades after the war, Major Joseph Ashbrook of the 118th Pennsylvania sought out Mayberry Beeler, whom he befriended while recovering from wounds received in September 1862. Ashbrook "called on Mr. Beeler at his home" near Sharpsburg, "and the two were glad to see each other again."[76]

Major John Meade Gould of the 10th Maine wrote that he was "most hospitably entertained" by Samuel Poffenberger during two Antietam reunions in 1891 and 1894. Poffenberger and his wife also hosted Caroline Helen Jemison Plane. Her husband, Captain William Fisher Plane of the 6th Georgia Infantry, died of wounds inside the Poffenbergers' parlor after the battle. During her postwar stay with the Sharpsburg couple, the Georgia widow "painted pictures of the house in which her soldier husband died."[77]

Veterans paid respect to Sharpsburg's churches. For example, members of the 107th New York returned a Bible to the Dunker Church. One of their comrades, the New Yorkers explained, stole the book as a souvenir in September 1862. Forty-one years later, "the old Bible was restored to its former place in the church,"

battlefield and local area. See Doyle and Doyle, *Sharpsburg*, 23, Barron and Barron, *The History of Sharpsburg*, 74, Trail, "Remembering Antietam," 168-169, and Recker, "O. T. Reilly."

76 *Morning Herald*, August 27, 1962; *HTL*, October 5, 1893; *Hagerstown Mail*, May 6, 1904.

77 John Meade Gould, *Joseph K. F. Mansfield, Brigadier General of the U.S. Army: A Narrative of Events Connected with His Mortal Wounding at Antietam, Sharpsburg, Maryland, September 17, 1862* (Portland, ME, 1895), 19, 21. Gould ranked as a lieutenant in 1862; Gloria Dahlhamer, "Area Around Keedysville Rich in Historical Lore of Battle," *The Daily Mail* [Hagerstown, MD], September 10, 1962, 11; Schildt, *Drums Along the Antietam*, 195; Williams, HWC, vol. 2, 1:928. Dahlhamer, Schildt, and Williams referred to the fallen captain as "Tayne" and "Payne;" Brian Downey, "Captain William Fisher Plane," web page, Antietam on the Web, http://antietam.aotw.org/officers.php?officer_id=4825. The website cites that Capt. Plane "died of wounds in the Stone House Hospital on Samuel Poffenberger's farm near Sharpsburg in 1862;" Caroline Helen Jemison Plane organized the Atlanta chapter of the United Daughters of the Confederacy. For further reading, see "Helen Plane," web page, Stone Mountain Guide, https://www.stonemountainguide.com/Helen-Plane.html. See also Lorraine Boissoneault, "What Will Happen to Stone Mountain, America's Largest Confederate Memorial?" *Smithsonian Magazine*, August 22, 2017, https://www.smithsonianmag.com/history/what-will-happen-stone-mountain-americas-largest-confederate-memorial-180964588/.

and "again its sacred pages were opened to the eyes of ministering elders." When parishioners later rebuilt and rededicated the Dunker Church, Maryland's governor orated, "May it stand, as it did in war, as a beacon to guide men searching their way through the darkness. May it stand throughout all ages as a symbol of mercy, peace, and understanding."

In 1890, Lizzie K. Miller, representing the Ladies Aid Society of Sharpsburg's German Reformed Church, wrote to Connecticut veterans, "The members of the congregation gave all the assistance in their power in aid of the wounded after the battle." She added, "[S]ome of the ladies of the Aid Society may have ministered to you as you languished in your bed of pain within the walls of this sanctuary." Miller asked the veterans to help restore the house of worship, explaining that "the church was greatly injured during those trying times, and the congregation has never been able to put the building in thorough repair since the war."

Responding to Miller's inquiry, veterans of the 16th Connecticut donated cash and stained glass windows "as a memorial to those brave comrades that gave their ultimate sacrifice" at Antietam. One window contained an inscription reading, "Peace on Earth, Good Will to Men." Images in another window depicted weapons of war transformed into implements of farming, symbolizing a passage of Isaiah 2:2-4, which reads, "[T]hey shall beat their swords into ploughshares, and their spears into pruning-hooks; nation shall not lift up sword against nation, neither shall they learn war any more."[78]

When the 9th Regiment, New York State Militia, marched through Sharpsburg on July 6, 1861, it marked the first time that military forces entered the village during the Civil War. Patriotic residents cheered the troops, gave them food, and gifted them American flags. After the Battle of Antietam, the same regiment encamped near town and "had an opportunity to renew many of the pleasant acquaintances they had formed" with the community.

In September 1886, veterans of the 9th New York State Militia again visited Sharpsburg. "Citizens of the town and a number of ladies" welcomed the guests

---

78 Ankrum, *Sidelights on Brethren History*, 117-122; Schmidt and Barkley, *September Mourn*, 53-55, 114. The New York veterans gave the Bible to John T. Lewis, an African American Marylander, who returned it to the Sharpsburg congregation. A storm destroyed the original Dunker Church in 1921; Lizzie K. Miller to veterans of the 16th Connecticut Infantry, 1890; Reverend Delancy Catlett, pastor, Christ Reformed United Church of Christ, Sharpsburg, MD, phone communications with author, November 18, 2020. Reverend Catlett shared information about the 16th Connecticut's windows and mentioned that veterans of the 11th Connecticut donated a smaller, stained glass window to the church, as did members of Grand Army of the Republic posts in Pennsylvania.

"in the parlor of the Shay House," located on the public square. Charles G. Biggs, a son of Dr. A. A. Biggs, addressed the visitors, recalling, "I remember how you marched from town under a cloud of red, white and blue bunting, presented by our citizens. This was your first visit. Your second was far different." Referring to Antietam, Biggs informed the veterans that "some of our loyal houses yet bear marks of your leaden messengers." Nevertheless, he acknowledged that Union shells fired toward the town of Sharpsburg were "not, however, directed against us, but against those who, at that time, were, unhappily, our mutual enemies."[79]

Veterans throughout the 1880s and 1890s made pilgrimages to the battlefield. On September 17, 1891, the 29th anniversary of the battle, 330 survivors of the 14th Connecticut visited the battleground and "lodged at various farm houses in Sharpsburg." Some of them boarded with William Roulette's family and planted their regimental flag outside the farmhouse. Describing the 1891 visit, one veteran remembered, "[A]s darkness approached a huge camp-fire was kindled near the bank of Bloody Lane where by speech and song hours sped on till midnight." He recalled that "fervent and patriotic addresses were made" and "the occasion attracted a large gathering of neighboring people who were impressed with the weirdly fascinating scene." Chaplain H. S. Stevens of the 14th Connecticut described the same event. He remembered that the Roulettes donated their old fence rails for the fire, the roaring flames of which attracted "hosts of people from the town and vicinity." The gathering civilians, Stevens recalled, found the scene "weird, novel, and exciting—entrancing."

Younger residents may have found the moment novel, but Sharpsburg's older folks were well acquainted with the sight of soldiers burning fence rails. Still, on September 17, 1891, the nighttime gathering peacefully united civilians and soldiers around a crackling bonfire near Bloody Lane, perhaps bringing some of Antietam's witnesses full circle to attain closure.[80]

Dr. Bushrod Washington James, a surgeon with the U.S. Christian Commission, traveled to Sharpsburg for the battle's 33rd anniversary. He toured Stephen P. Grove's Mount Airy farm and reflected upon his time treating the wounded of both armies. Comparing memories from 1862 to his visit in 1895, Dr. James waxed poetic. "I turned and took a long survey of the peaceful scene," he

79 *HTL*, September 23, 1886.

80 Charles D. Page, *History of the Fourteenth Regiment Connecticut Vol. Infantry* (Meriden, CT, 1906), 358; Stevens, *Souvenir of Excursion to Battlefields*, 46, 63-68. Union and Confederate veterans of the battle continued reuniting at Sharpsburg until the 1930s, culminating with the battle's 75th anniversary in 1937.

wrote. "No bloodstains, no tortured human beings crying for water, for release from pain, for the dear ones at home. Instead, the velvet greensward, the waving branches of fruit-laden trees, and near by a great cider-press with barrels standing round, telling in silent language of the expectation of an abundant harvest." Dr. James could "not soon forget the contrast between my first and last visit to that spot. Then I beheld the harvest of strife between fiercely contending armies—and it was only blood and pain and misery and death. To-day I am gazing upon the rich harvest of peace and its happiness and prosperity. Well may we pray and trust that our beautiful land shall never again be marred by contention and bloodshed."

Farmhand Alex Davis, giving an interview in his golden years, harkened back to the Battle of Antietam, its aftermath, and its long-lasting impact on the Sharpsburg community. He stated something along the same lines as Dr. Bushrod Washington James, but in fewer words. "I never want to see no war no more," Davis remarked. "I'd sooner see a fire."[81]

81 James, *Echoes of Battle*, 82-84; Johnson, *BA*, 100-101.

Bibliography

Primary Sources

Manuscript Collections

Antietam National Battlefield Library, Sharpsburg, MD

    Antietam National Battlefield Historic Resource Study: Sharpsburg and the Battle of Antietam Washington, DC: National Park Service, 2008

    Antietam National Battlefield: Building Survey of Sharpsburg, Maryland. National Capital Region history files. 1934

    Beltemacchi, Margaret to Goodloe Byron. Letter. June 3, 1971

    "Civilian Reports." 1934 interviews with local people. Folder

        Mrs. A. D. Grove [Julia Mumma]

        Henry Marion Johnson

        Stella Biggs Lyne

        Joe Marrow

        J. A. Miller

        William "Bud" Shackelford

    Cross, Fred W. Personal scrapbook

    Gaines, Dr. John Mutius. Vertical file

    Herrin, Dean. *Antietam Rising: The Civil War and Its Legacy in Sharpsburg, Maryland, 1860–1900.* Sharpsburg, MD: Antietam National Battlefield, 2002

    Nelson, John. Research materials from *As Grain Falls Before the Reaper: The Federal Hospital Sites and Identified Federal Casualties at Antietam.* Vertical file

    Nesbitt, Otho. Diary

    Reed, Paula S. *History Report: The D. R. Miller Farm.* Sharpsburg, MD: Antietam National Battlefield, 1991

    Smith, John P. "History of the Antietam Fight." Typescript

    Smith, John P. "Recollections of John P. Smith: The Battle of Antietam, the History of Antietam and the Hospitals of Antietam, 1895." Typescript

Bentley Historical Library, University of Michigan, Ann Arbor, MI
  Whiteside, John C. Letter, October 4, 1862

Harris-Elmore Public Library, Grace Luebke Local History Room, Elmore, OH
  Pearce, Philo Stevens. "Civil War Memories of Mr. Philo Stevens Pearce." Typescript

John Clinton Frye Western Maryland Room, Hagerstown, MD
  Biggs, Dr. Augustin A. Daybooks and Ledgers, Vol. 2, 2/23/1862 – 8/7/1863. Medical ledger
  Biggs, Dr. Augustin A. *The Obstetrical Records of Dr. Augustin A. Biggs, of Sharpsburg, Washington County, Maryland, 1836–1888*. Medical ledger
  Biggs, Dr. Augustin A. to Elijah Kalb. Letter. *Weekly Lancaster Gazette* (Lancaster, Ohio), October 16, 1862. Published in Masters, Daniel A. "A Sharpsburg Resident's View of the Battle of Antietam, Maryland, September 17, 1862." *Maryland Historical Magazine*, Volume 110, No. 4 (Winter 2015). 489-494
  Davis, Angela Kirkham. W*ar Reminiscences*. Letter
  Hildebrand, Virginia Mumma. *Antietam Remembered*. New York: Book Craftsmen Association, Inc., 1959
  Grove, Stephen P. *Ledger of Stephen P. Grove of Mt. Airy, Sharpsburg, Washington County, Maryland*. Business ledger
  [Adam] Michael Family Letters Collection. Unpublished correspondence, 1859–1865
  Mumma, Wilmer. *Out of the Past: A Collection of Creative Writings of a Human Interest Nature, Spotlighting the Historic Sharpsburg, Maryland Area*. Two volumes. Sharpsburg, MD: self-published, 1993
  Reilly, Oliver T. "Fifty Years Ago at Sharpsburg." *Shepherdstown* [WV] *Register*, November 21, 1912. "Newspaper Articles," vertical file
  Reilly, Oliver T. "Sharpsburg Letter." *Shepherdstown* [WV] *Register*, March 15, 1934. "Newspaper Articles," vertical file
  Smith, John Philemon. "Reminiscences of Sharpsburg, Washington County, Maryland, From the Date of its Laying Out July 9, 1763 to the Present Time, July 9th, 1899." Typescript, 1912
  "The Letters of the Jacob Miller Family of Sharpsburg, Washington County, Maryland." Unpublished correspondence, 1851–1865

Maryland State Archives, Annapolis, MD
  1860 United States Federal Census, Agricultural Schedule, Sharpsburg District
  Active Land Record Indices, 1776-1977. Washington County Circuit Court Land Records. MDLANDREC.net
  Maryland Register of Wills Records, 1629-1999. Washington County, Register of Wills Office, Hagerstown, MD
  Wilmer, L. Allison, Jarrett, J. H., and Vernon, Geo. W. F. *History and Roster of Maryland Volunteers, War of 1861–65*. 2 vols. Baltimore: Guggenheimer, Weil & Co., 1898-99

National Archives and Records Administration, Washington DC
  Record Group 92: Office of the Claims of the Quartermaster General, Claims Branch 1861–1889, Quartermaster Stores (Act of July 4, 1864)
  Record Group 123: Records of the U.S. Court of Claims, Congressional Jurisdiction Case Files, 1884–1943
  Adams, Rev. John, RG 92, Book G, Box 99, Claim G-1933
  Avey, Elijah, RG 92, Entry 843, Box 772, Book 304, Claim 242

Avey, Jacob Jr., RG 92, Entry 843, Box 772, Book 304, Claim 245

Avey, Jacob, Sr., RG 92, Entry 843, Box 772, Book 304, Claim 243; RG 92, Entry 812, Book F, Box 77, Claim F-602; RG 123, Entry 22, Box No. 1049, Case No. 9908

Barnum, Thomas, RG 92, Entry 817, Book 198, Box 455, Claim 629; RG 92, Entry 797, Book 131, Box 434, Claim 131-1078; RG 123, Entry 22, Box 83, Case No. 333

Beck, Philip, RG 123, Entry 22, Box 232, Case No. 1290

Beeler, Peter, RG 92, Entry 797, Box 87, Claim 729; RG 92, Entry 812, Box F, Claim 1326; RG 92, Entry 812, Box G, Claim 1771

Beeler, Samuel, RG 92, Entry 843, Box 772, Book 304, Claim 401

Biggs, Augustin A., RG 92, Entry 843, Box 771, Claim 178

Blackford, Henry V. S., RG 92, Box 95, Book G, Claims G-1630, G-1648, and G-1654

Blackford, William M., RG 92, Entry 843, Box 772, Book 304, Claim 400; RG 123, Entry 22, Box 236, Case No. 1324

Church, Sharpsburg Lutheran; RG 123, Entry 22, Box 522, Case No. 4058

Church, Sharpsburg German Reformed, RG 123, Entry 22, Box 1208, Case No. 11014

Church, Keedysville Mount Vernon Reformed, RG 123, Entry 22, Case No. 14133

Church, Sharpsburg St. Paul's Protestant Episcopal, RG 123, Entry 22, Box 1557, Case No. 13674

Coffman, David, RG 92, Entry 812, Book F, Box 91, Claim F-1514; RG 123, Entry 22, Box 229, Case No. 1268

Coin, Timothy, RG 92, Entry 817, Book 212, Box 578, Claim 212-719

Clopper, Josephus, RG 92, Book G, Claim G-1916

Cost, Aaron, RG 92, Entry 843, Box 771, Claim 180; RG 92, Entry 797, Book 95, Box 230, Claim 95-1029

Cost, Alfred, RG 92, Entry 843, Box 771, Claim 171; RG 92, Entry 797, Book 95, Box 231, Claim 95-1031

Cost, Jacob H., RG 92, Entry 797, Book 95, Box 230, Claim 95-1028

Cox, John U. & William I., RG 92, Entry 812, Box 208, Book M, Claim M-901

Cox, Moses, RG 92, Entry 812, Book G, Box 95, Claim G-1657

Cronise, Benjamin F., RG 92, Entry 797, Box 113, Claim 113-1023

Davis, Eliza, RG 92, Entry 812, Book F, Box 92, Claim F-1536

Domer, Raleigh, RG 92, Entry 797, Book 92, Box 211, Claim 92-551

Doub, Samuel, RG 92, Entry 812, Box 115, Claims G-2935-2937

Douglas, Robert (Reverend), RG 92, Entry 843, Box 772, Book 304, Claim 398; RG 123, Entry 22, Box 539, Case No. 4271; Robert Douglas to Fitz John Porter. Letter. October 24, 1862. RG 109, M-345. Union Provost Marshals' File of Papers Relating to Individual Civilians. Microfilm Roll 0076

Eakle, Elias, RG 123, Entry 22, Box 232, Case No. 1291

Ecker, John, RG 92, Entry 812, Box 91, Claim F-1523

Emmert, Leonard, RG 92, Entry 812, Book F, Box 93, Claim F-1577; RG 123, Entry 22, Box 538, Case. No. 4257

Fisher, Thomas, RG 92, Book H, Claims H-4113 and H-4114

Graves, Benjamin, RG 92, Entry 843, Box 772, Book 304, Claim 397; RG 92, Book F, Box 78, Claim F-713; RG 92, Book H, Box 126, Claim H-3825

Grice, John, RG 92, Entry 843, Box 772, Book 304, Claim 313; RG 92, Entry 797, Book 131, Box 439, Claim 131-1330; RG 123, Entry 22, Box 692, Case No. 5872

Griffith, Henry, RG 92, Entry 812, Box 576, Claim 212-707

Grove, Elias S., RG 92, Entry 843, Box 772, Book 304, Claim 396; RG 92, Entry 817, Book 212, Box 578, Claim 212-721; RG 123, Entry 22, Box 804, Case No. 7356

Grove, Jacob C., RG 92, Book G, Box 95, Claim G-1649

Grove, Jacob H., RG 92, Entry 820, Box M, Claim 905; Book O, Claim 1169; RG 123, Entry 22, Box No. 228, Case No. 1267

Grove, Jeremiah P., RG 92, Book G, Box 94, Claim G-1632

Grove, Joseph (Heirs), RG 123, Entry 22, Box 957, Case No. 9057

Grove, Samuel (Heirs), RG 92, Entry 843, Box 772, Book 304, Claim 315; RG 92, Entry 812, Book G, Box 94, Claim G-1633; RG 123, Entry 22, Box 985, Case No. 9313

Grove, Stephen P., RG 92, Entry 843, Box 772, Book 304, Claim 314; RG 92, Entry 843, Box 772, Book 304, Claim 395; RG 123, Entry 22, Box 804, Case No. 7354

Hammond, Abraham, RG 92, Book F, Box 89, Claim F-1430

Hebb, William F., RG 92, Entry 843, Box 772, Book 304, Claim 256; RG 92, Book F, Box 89, Claim F-1417

Highbarger, Catherine Avey, RG 92, Entry 843, Box 772, Book 304, Claim 254

Highbarger, John L., RG 92, Book 54, Box 15, Claim 54-1476 (filed as 54-1487)

Hill, Josiah, RG 92, Entry 817, Book 212, Box 578, Claim 212-721; RG 123, Entry 22, Box 913, Case No. 8532

Himes, Sarah, RG 92, Entry 843, Box 772, Book 304, Claim 229

Hoffman, Susan, RG 123, Entry 22, Box 235, Case No. 1318

Houser, Jacob, RG 92, Entry 843, Box 772, Book 304, Claim 318; RG 92, Book F, Box 80, Claim F-814

Hutzell, Adam, RG 92, Entry 812, Book F, Box 92, Claim F-1538, RG 123, Box 540, Entry 22, Case No. 4292

Jones, Magdalene, RG 92, Entry 797, Book 54, Claim 54-1470

Keedy, John J., RG 92, Entry 843, Box 772, Book 304, Claim 402; RG 92, Entry 797, Book 54, Box 15, Claim 54-1488; RG 123, Entry 22, Box 348, Case No. 2157

Kennedy, Susan, RG 92, Entry 812, Book F, Box 81, Claim F-865

Kidwiler, Joanna, RG 92, Entry 843, Box 772, Book 304, Claim 252

Knode, Elias U., RG 92, Entry 812, Claim L-2074

Knode, John E., RG 92, Entry 812, Book G, Box 95, Claim G-1647; RG 123, Entry 22, Box 917, Case No. 8587

Kretzer, John, RG 92, Entry 817, Box 212, Claim 212-759; RG 92, Entry 797, Box 54, Claim 54-1471

Line, George, RG 92, Entry 843, Box 772, Book 304, Claim 316; RG 92, Book F, Box 86, Claims F-1186 and F-1187; RG 123, Entry 22, Box 957, Case No. 9058

Long, Lydia; RG 92, Entry 812, Book F, Claim F-1289

Lumm, Solomon; RG 92, Entry 812, Book N, Box 223, Claim N-546; RG 123, Entry 22, Box 83, Case No. 340

Marker, James, RG 123, Entry 22, Box 232, Case No. 1292

Mayer, John L., RG 92, Entry 843, Box 772, Book 304, Claim 389; RG 123, Entry 22, Box 917, Case No. 8586

Michael, Adam, RG 92, Entry 820, Box 199, Claim 199-161

Middlekauff, John C., RG 92, Entry 812, Book F, Box 93, Claim F-1587; RG 123, Entry 22, Case No. 321

Middlekauff, John J., RG 123, Entry 22, Box 228, Case No. 1261

Miller, David R., RG 92, Entry 843, Box 772, Book 304, Claim 322; RG 92, Entry 812, Book F, Box 91, Claim F-1499; RG 92, Entry 812, Box 166, Claim L-594; RG 123, Entry 22, Book 228, Case No. 1266

Miller, Jacob F., RG 92, Entry 843, Box 772, Book 304, Claim 261; RG 123, Entry 22, Box 530, Case No. 4294

Miller, Jacob (Squire), RG 92, Entry 843, Box 772, Book 304, Claim 391; RG 123, Entry 22, Box 541, Case No. 4296

Miller, John (Colonel), RG 92, Entry 843, Box 772, Book 304, Claim 319; RG 123, Entry 22, Box 358, Case No. 2227

Miller, Michael & Daniel, RG 92, Entry 843, Box 772, Book 304, Claim 321; RG 92, Book F, Box 89, Claims F-1437 and F-1438

Miller, Morgan & Andrew Rentch, RG 92, Entry 843, Box 772, Book 304, Claim 390; RG 92, Entry 812, Book H, Box 119, Claim H-3252; RG 123, Entry 22, Box 541, Case No. 4295

Miller, Nancy, RG 92, Entry 843, Box 772, Book 304, Claim 233

Mose, Daniel, RG 92, Entry 843, Box 772, Book 304, Claim 263

Mumma, Laura L. (Grove), RG 123, Entry 22, Box 1007, Case No. 9502

Mumma, Samuel, RG 92, Entry 797, Book 113, Box 329, Claim 113-1024; RG 92, Entry 812, Book D, Box 54, Claims D-1927 and D-1928; RG 123, Entry 22, Box 82, Case No. 334

Myers, Hezekiah, RG 92, Entry 812, Book G, Box 98, Claim G-1796; RG 123, Entry 22, Box 234, Case No. 1301

Myers, Jacob A., RG 92, Box 242, Book N, Claim F-2190

Myers, Jacob, RG 92, Entry 843, Box 772, Book 304, Claim 323

Myers, John Henry, RG 92, Book G, Box 94, Claim G-1622

Neikirk, Henry, RG 92, Entry 812, Book H, Box 131, Claims H-4108 and H-4109

Newcomer, Joshua, RG 92, Entry 812, Book F, Box 81, Claim F-854; RG 92, Entry 812, Book H, Box 124, Claim H-3618; RG 123, Entry 22, Box 70, Case No. 272

Nicodemus, Jacob (of Sharpsburg, son of Conrad), RG 92, Book 95, Box 238, Claim 95-1683

Nicodemus, Jacob (of Springvale, son of Valentine), RG 92, Entry 797, Book G, Box 98, Claims G-1854, G-1855, and F-613

Otto, David, RG 92, Entry 843, Box 772, Book 304, Claim 403; RG 92, Book G, Box 101, Claim G-2077

Otto, John, RG 92, Book G, Box 98, Claim G-1857

Pennel, David, RG 92, Entry 843, Box 772, Book 304, Claim 248

Piper, Henry, RG 92, Entry 843, Box 772, Book 304, Claim 244; RG 92, Entry 812, Book D, Box 61, Claim D-2395; RG 123, Entry 22, Box 100, Case No. 445

Piper, Samuel D., RG 92, Entry 812, Book D, Box 61, Claim D-2392 and D-2393; RG 123, Entry 22, Box 100, Case 440

Piper, Samuel I., RG 92, Entry 812, Book D, Box 61, Claim D-2392; RG 123, Entry 22, Box 234, Case No. 1310

Poffenberger, Alfred, RG 92, Entry 812, Book M, Box 208, Claim M-917; RG 92, Book 95, Box 238, Claim 95-1685; RG 123, Entry 22, Box 234, Case No. 1308

Poffenberger, Daniel, RG 92, Entry 843, Box 771, Claim 175; RG 92, Entry 843, Box 771, Claim 333; RG 123, Entry 22, Case No 1505

Poffenberger, Henry A., RG 123, Entry 22, Book 784, Case No. 7178

Poffenberger, John, RG 92, Entry 812, Book L, Box 183, Claim L-2096

Poffenberger, Joseph, RG 123, Entry 22, Box 233, Case No. 1300

Poffenberger, Samuel, RG 92, Entry 812, Book F, Box 89, Claim F-1434; RG 123, Entry 22, Case No. 4298

Pry, Philip, RG 92, Book H, Box 127, Claims H-3907, H-3908, G-2696, G-2697, and 95-1030; RG 92, Book G, Box 92, Claim G-1759

Pry, Samuel, RG 92, Entry 843, Box 771, Claim 182; RG 92, Entry 797, Book 95, Box 238, Claim 95-1691; RG 92, Entry 797, Box 145, Claim 81-1489

Reel, David, RG 92, Entry 843, Box 772, Book 304, Claim 331; RG 92, Entry 812, Book F, Box 81, Claim F-847; RG 123, Entry 22, Box 744, Case No. 6619

Reel, Henry, RG 92, Entry 843, Box 772, Book 304, Claim 328

Reel, Samuel, RG 92, Entry 843, Box 772, Book 304, Claim 330; RG 92, Entry 812, Book G, Box 99, Claim G-1923; RG 123, Entry 22, Box 437, Case No. 3209 (includes Case No. 4346)

Rentch, Andrew, RG 123, Entry 22, Box 537, Case No. 4235

Roderick, George, RG 92, Entry 843, Box 772, Book 304, Claim 232

Rohrback, Benjamin F., RG 92, Entry 812, Box 76, Book F, Claims F-617 and F-619; RG 123, Entry 22, Box 537, Case No. 4234.

Rohrback, Catherine, RG 92, Entry 843, Box 772, Book 304, Claim 234, RG 92, Book H, Box 127, Claim H-3902

Rohrback, Daniel, RG 92, Entry 843, Box 772, Book 304, Claim 231; RG 92, Entry 797, Book 113, Box 329, Claim 113-1021

Rohrback, Henry B., RG 92, Entry 843, Box 772, Book 304, Claim 235; RG 123, Entry 22, Box 231, Case No. 1323

Rohrback, Noah, RG 92, Book H, Box 126, Claim H-3874

Roulette, John, RG 92, Entry 812, Box 169, Claim L-830

Roulette, William, RG 92, Entry 812, Book F, Box 76, Claim F-618; RG 92, Entry 812, Book L, Box 169, Claim L-832; RG 92, Entry 843, Box 772, Claim 230; RG 123, Entry 22, Box 541, Case No. 4299

Rowe, James A., RG 92, Book 92, Box 211, Claim 92-553; RG 92, Entry 797, Book 113, Claim 113-76; RG 123, Entry 22, Box 234, Case No. 1303

Schlosser, Martha, RG 92, Entry 843, Box 771, Claim 170

Shackelford, Margaret, RG 92, Entry 843, Box 772, Book 304

Shamel, Henry, RG 92, Entry 797, Book 54, Box 15, Claim 54-1461

Sherrick, Joseph, RG 92, Book F, Box 89, Claim F-1433

Showman, Alfred, RG 92, Book F, Box 85, Claim F-1179

Showman, Catherine, RG 92, Entry 812, Book F, Box 86, Claim F-1185; RG 92, Entry 812, Book F, Box 85, Claim F-1176; RG 123, Entry 22, Box 744, Case No. 6622

Showman, Hiram, RG 123, Entry 22, Box 268, Case No. 1522

Showman, Kesia, RG 92, Entry 843, Book 50, Box 772, L-304, Claim 268

Showman, Raleigh, RG 92, Book F, Box 85, Claims F-1180, F-1181, F-1182, and F-1183

Smith, David (Captain), RG 92, Entry 843, Box 772, Book 304, Claim 393; RG 92, Entry 812, Book F, Box 92, Claim F-1532; RG 92, Entry 812, Book F, Box 81, Claim F-846; RG 123, Entry 22, Box 1097, Cases 1244, 1262, and 10237

Smith, Israel, RG 92, Entry 843, Box 772, Book 304, Claim 392

Smith, John H., RG 92, Book F, Box 86, Claim F-1205

Smith, Otho B., RG 92, Book F, Box 89, Claim F-1432

Smith, Otho J., RG 92, Book K, Box 157A, Claim K-1565

Snavely, John H., RG 92, Entry 820, Claim F-1441; RG 123, Entry 22, Box 1049, Case No. 9910

Snively, Joseph, RG 92, Entry 843, Box 772, Book 304, Claim 332; RG 92, Entry 812, Box 96, Claim G-1688

Snively, Washington C., RG 92, Book H, Box 121, Claim H-3458 and Claim L-3128

Snyder, Jacob, RG 92, Book F, Box 92, Claim F-1537

Snyder, John, RG 92, Book F, Box 81, Claim F-859; RG 123, Entry 22, Box 744, Case No. 6617

Spong, David, RG 92, Entry 843, Box 772, Book 304, Claim 394; RG 92, Entry 797, Book 54, Box 15, Claim 54-1462

Spong, John L., RG 92, Book D, Box 46, Claim D-946

Stonebraker, Joseph, RG 92, Entry 843, Box 771, Claim 173

Swain, Samuel, RG 92, Book N, Box 242, Claim N-2188

Tenant, Catherine, RG 92, Entry 797, Book 54, Box 15, Claim 54-1464

Thomas, Joseph, RG 92, Book F, Box 76, Claim F-611

Unger, William, RG 92, Entry 843, Box 771, Claim 181; RG 92, Entry 812, Box 151, Claim K-516

Wade, Eli, RG 92, Book G, Box 106, Claim G-2404

Wade, Henry (Heirs), RG 92, Entry 812, Book G, Box 106, Claim G-2398; RG 92, Entry 812, Book G, Box 106, Claim G-2394; RG 123, Entry 22, Box 741, Case No. 6585

Wade, John A., RG 92, Entry 812, Book G, Box 106, Claim G-2400; RG 123, Entry 22, Box 741, Case No. 6586

Wade, William, RG 92, Entry 812, Book G, Box 106, Claim G-2397; RG 123, Entry 22, Box 985, Case No. 9314

Wyand, Frederick, RG 92, Entry 812, Book G, Box 94, Claim G-1624; RG 123, Entry 22, Box 1625, Case No. 14112

Wyand, Simon, RG 92, Entry 843, Box 771, Claim 174

Private Collections

Barnum, Thomas. Family Papers. Joseph Davis collection

Davis, Eliza. Citizens' appraisement, "1862 Damage". Joseph Davis collection

Houser, Barney. Inventory of Antietam losses. Robert Eschbach collection

Piper, Samuel Webster. *Piper Family History*. Unpaginated binders. Regina and Lou Clark collection

Rauner Special Collections Library, Dartmouth College, Hanover, NH

Gould, John M. Papers relating to the Battle of Antietam

Ruth Scarborough Library, Archives and Special Collections, Shepherd University, Shepherdstown, WV

Hoffman, Lloyd K. "The Hoffman Family: Two Hundred Years in America." Unpublished manuscript

Sharpsburg Historical Society, Sharpsburg, MD

"Deed Chains and House Histories" http://david.hackley.googlepages.com/sharpsburghistory

Ditto, Lucy C. Grayson. "Journal of Deaths in Sharpsburg." Loose-leaf notebook

"Sharpsburg Lot Sales Through 1899." Spreadsheet

Upper Midwest Literary Archives, Elmer L. Andersen Library, University of Minnesota, Minneapolis, MN

Geeting, Ephraim and J. Russell, 1862-1863. Record of accounts against the U.S. Government for supplies furnished to Locust Spring Hospital during and after the Battle of Antietam

U.S. Army Military History Institute, Brake Collection, Carlisle PA

Nickerson, Mark S. "Recollections of the Civil War by a High Private in the Front Ranks." Unpublished manuscript

Washington County Historical Society, Hagerstown, MD
Smith, John P. "Register of Persons Who Have Died in Sharpsburg, Washington County Maryland and Surrounding Neighborhood From the Year 1831." Loose-leaf notebook, 1904

Online Collections

Auburn University, Civil War Diaries Collection, Auburn, AL
Bancroft, John Milton. Diary / Scrapbook, http://content.lib.auburn.edu/cdm/ compoundobject/ collection/civil/id/26093/rec/3

Digital Maine Repository, Maine State Library, Augusta, ME
Fogg, Isabella. Letters, https://digitalmaine.com/cw_misc_doc/10/

Houghton Library, Harvard University, Cambridge, MA
Shaw, Robert Gould. Robert Gould Shaw Letters to His Family, https://hollisarchives.lib.harvard.edu/ repositories/24/resources/1892

Johns Hopkins Sheridan Libraries, Baltimore, MD
Lake, Griffing & Stevenson. *An Illustrated Atlas of Washington County, Maryland*, sheet 32. Philadelphia: Lake, Griffing & Stevenson, 1877. Johns Hopkins Sheridan Libraries. Sheets 32-33. "Sharpsburg & 5th Ward of Hagerstown," https://jscholarship.library.jhu.edu/handle/1774.2/32766

Library of Congress, Washington, DC
Maps
United States War Department. Atlas of the battlefield of Antietam, prepared under the direction of the Antietam Battlefield Board, Lieut. Col. Geo. W. Davis, U.S.A., president, Gen. E.A. Carman, U.S.V., Gen. H Heth, C.S.A. Surveyed by Lieut. Col. E.B. Cope, engineer, H.W. Mattern, assistant engineer, of the Gettysburg National Park. Drawn by Charles H. Ourand, . Position of troops by Gen. E. A. Carman.Published by authority of the Secretary of War, under the direction of the Chief of Engineers, U.S. Army, 1908. [Washington, Govt. print. off, 1908] Map. https:// www. loc.gov/item/2008621532/
Photographs and Illustrations
Forbes, Edwin, Artist. *The Battle of Antietam—Charge of Burnside 9th Corps on the right flank of the Confederate Army / E. Forbes.* Antietam Maryland United States, 1862. Sept. 17. Sketch. https:// www. loc.gov/ item/2004661896/
Gardner, Alexander. *Antietam, Maryland. Antietam Bridge, eastern view.* Photograph, 1862. https:// www.loc.gov/item/2018671864/
Gardner, Alexander. *Antietam, Maryland. Bodies of dead, Louisiana Regiment.* Photograph, 1862. https://www.loc.gov/item/2018671466/
Gardner, Alexander. *Antietam, Maryland. Sherrick's house, near Burnside bridge.* Photograph, 1862. https://www.loc.gov/item/2018671858/
Gardner, Alexander. *Antietam, Maryland. View on Antietam creek.* Photograph, 1862. https://www.loc.gov/item/2018671478/
Gardner, Alexander. *Keedysville, Md., vicinity. Smith's barn, used as a hospital after the battle of Antietam.* Keedysville Maryland United States, 1862. September. Photograph. https://www. loc.gov/item/ 2018666244/

Gardner, Alexander. *Keedysville, Maryland vicinity. Straw huts erected on Smith's farm used as a hospital after the battle of Antietam.* United States, 1862. Sept. Photograph. https://www.loc.gov/item/2018671857/

Gardner, Alexander. *Sharpsburg, Md. Lutheran church.* Photograph, 1862. https://www.loc.gov/item/2018666247/

Gibson, James F. *Antietam, Maryland. Bridge across the Antietam. Northeast view.* United States, 1862. Sept. Photograph. https://www.loc.gov/item/2018671863

Schell, Frank H., Artist. *Maryland and Pennsylvania farmers visiting the battle-field of Antietam while the National troops were burying the dead and carrying off the wounded Brick house on the Potomac, near Williamsport, after a rebel cannonade / / From a sketch by our special artist, Mr. F. H. Schell.* United States Maryland Williamsport Antietam, 1862. [New York: Frank Leslie] Photograph. https://www.loc.gov/item/2017650942/.

Waud, Alfred R., Artist. *Sharpsburg citizens leaving for fear of the Rebels.* 1862. Sketch. https://www.loc.gov/item/2004660777/

New York Historical Society Museum & Library, Digital Collections, New York, NY

Strong, George Templeton. Diary, http://digitalcollections.nyhistory.org/islandora/object/ nyhs%3A54776

New York Public Library Digital Collections, New York, NY

Lionel Pincus and Princess Firyal Map Division. "Map of the Battlefield of Antietam." New York Public Library Digital Collections, http://digitalcollections.nypl.org/items/185f8270-0834-0136-3daa-6d29ad33124f

New York State Military Museum, Division of Military and Naval Affairs, Saratoga Springs, NY

Ferguson, John V. Letters. Transcribed by Leith Regan, http://dmna.ny.gov/historic/reghist/civil/infantry/97thInf/97thInfFergusonLetters.pdf

Western Maryland Historical Library, Hagerstown, MD

Board of Trustees of the Antietam National Cemetery, Maryland. (Oden Bowie). *A descriptive list of the burial places of the remains of Confederate soldiers: who fell in the battles of Antietam, South Mountain, Monocacy, and other points in Washington and Frederick counties, in the state of Maryland.* Hagerstown, MD: "Free press" print, 1868

Board of Trustees of the Antietam National Cemetery, Maryland. *History of the Antietam National Cemetery: Including a Descriptive List of the Loyal Soldiers Buried Therein, Together with the Ceremonies and Address on the Occasion of the Dedication of the Grounds, September 17, 1867.* Baltimore: John W. Woods, 1869

"Confederate Soldiers Killed at Antietam" http://www.whilbr.org/confederateSoldiers/index.aspx

"History of the Antietam National Cemetery" http://www.whilbr.org/antietam National Cemetery/index.aspx

Piper, Samuel Webster. *Washington County Cemeteries—Samuel Piper and the DAR.* Volume 1, 1936 https://digital.whilbr.org/digital/collection/p16715coll31

"Washington Confederate Cemetery, Hagerstown, Maryland" http://www.whilbr.org/WashingtonConfederateCemetery/index.aspx

Books

Aldrich, Thomas M. *The History of Battery A, First Regiment Rhode Island Light Artillery.* Providence, RI: Snow & Farnham, 1904.

Alexander, Edward Porter. *Military Memoirs of a Confederate: A Critical Narrative.* New York: Charles Scribner's Sons, 1907.

Allen, E. Livingston. *Descriptive Lecture: Both Sides of Army Life, the Grave and the Gay.* NY, Poughkeepsie, NY, n.p., 1885.

Andrews, W. H. *Footprints of a Regiment: A Recollection of the 1st Georgia Regulars, 1861–1865.* Atlanta: Longstreet Press, 1992.

Baquet, Camille. *History of the First Brigade, New Jersey Volunteers from 1861–1865.* Trenton, NJ: MacCrellish & Quigley, 1910.

Bartlett, Napier. *A Story of the War Including the Marches and Battles of the Washington Artillery.* New Orleans: Clark and Hofeline, 1874.

Bates, Samuel P. *History of the Pennsylvania Volunteers, 1861-65; Prepared in Compliance with Acts of the Legislature.* 5 vols. Harrisburg, PA: B. Singerly, 1870.

Beach, William H. *The First New York (Lincoln) Cavalry from April 19, 1861, to July 7, 1865.* New York: The Lincoln Cavalry Association, 1902.

Beale, George. *A Lieutenant of Cavalry in Lee's Army.* Boston: The Gorham Press, 1918.

Beasley, Henry. *The Book of Prescriptions: Containing 2900 Prescriptions Collected from the Practice of the Most Eminent Physicians and Surgeons.* Philadelphia: Lindsay & Blakiston, 1855.

Bidwell, Frederick David. *History of the 49th New York Volunteers.* Albany: NY: J. B. Lyon Company, 1916.

Blackford, William W. *War Years with Jeb Stuart.* New York: Charles Scribner's Sons, 1945.

Blakeslee, Bernard F. *History of the Sixteenth Connecticut Volunteers.* Hartford, CT: The Case, Lockwood and Brainard Company, 1875.

Bogardus, Stephen H. *Dear Eagle: The Civil War Correspondence of Stephen H. Bogardus, Jr. to the Poughkeepsie Daily Eagle.* Edited by Joel Craig. Wake Forest: Scuppernong Press, 2004.

Bosbyshell, Oliver Christian. *Pennsylvania at Antietam: Report of the Antietam Battlefield Memorial Commission of Pennsylvania and Ceremonies at the Dedication of the Monuments Erected by the Commonwealth of Pennsylvania to Mark the Position of Thirteen of the Pennsylvania Commands Engaged in the Battle.* Harrisburg, PA: Harrisburg Publishing, 1906.

Britton, Wiley. *The Aftermath of the Civil War: Based on Investigation of War Claims.* Kansas City, MO: Smith-Grieves, 1924.

Brockett, Linus P., and Mary C. Vaughn. *Woman's Work in the Civil War: A Record of Heroism, Patriotism and Patience.* Boston: Zeigler, McCurdy & Co., 1867.

Bryant, Edwin E. *History of the Third Regiment of Wisconsin Veteran Volunteer Infantry 1861–1865.* Madison, WI: Higginson Book Company, 1891.

Burrage, Henry S., *History of the Thirty-Sixth Regiment Massachusetts Volunteers 1862–1865.* Boston: Rockwell & Churchill, 1884.

Butterfield, Daniel. *Camp and Outpost Duty for Infantry.* New York: Harper & Brothers, 1862.

Carman, Ezra, A. *The Maryland Campaign of September 1862. Vol. 1: South Mountain.* Edited by Thomas G. Clemens. El Dorado Hills, CA: Savas Beatie, 2010.

———. *The Maryland Campaign of September 1862. Vol. 2: Antietam.* Edited by Thomas G. Clemens. El Dorado Hills, CA: Savas Beatie, 2012.

Castleman, Alfred L. *The Army of the Potomac: Behind the Scenes.* Milwaukee, WI: Strickland, 1863.

Child, William. *History of the Fifth Regiment, New Hampshire Volunteers.* Bristol, NH: R.W. Musgrove, 1893.

Child, William. *Letters from a Civil War Surgeon: The Letters of Dr. William Child of the Fifth New Hampshire Volunteers.* Transcribed by Timothy C. Sawyer, Betty Sawyer, and Merrill C. Sawyer. Solon, ME: Polar Bear, 2001.

Coffin, Charles Carleton. *The Boys of '61; or, Four Years of Fighting.* Boston: Estes & Lauriat, 1896.

———. *Following the Flag.* Boston: Estes & Lauriat, 1886.

Colby, Newton T. *The Civil War Papers of Lt. Colonel Newton T. Colby, New York Infantry.* Jefferson, NC: McFarland, 2003.

Comey, Lyman Richard. *A Legacy of Valor: The Memoirs and Letters of Captain Henry Newton Comey, 2nd Massachusetts Infantry.* Knoxville: University of Tennessee Press, 2004.

Cook, Benjamin F. *History of the Twelfth Massachusetts Volunteers (Webster Regiment).* Boston: Twelfth (Webster) Regiment Association, 1882.

Corby, William. *Memoirs of Chaplain Life: Three Years with the Irish Brigade in the Army of the Potomac.* Edited by Lawrence Frederick Kohl. New York: Fordham University Press, 1992.

Cox, Jacob D. *Military Reminiscences of the Civil War.* 2 vols. New York: Charles Scribner's Sons, 1900.

Crowninshield, Benjamin W. *A History of the First Regiment of Massachusetts Cavalry Volunteers.* Boston: Houghton Mifflin, 1891.

Curtis, George Ticknor. *McClellan's Last Service to the Republic.* New York: D. Appleton, 1885.

Cutcheon, Byron M. *The Story of the Twentieth Michigan Infantry, July 15th, 1862, to May 30th, 1865.* Lansing, MI: Robert Smith, 1904.

Davis, Charles E., Jr. *Three Years in the Army: The Story of the Thirteenth Massachusetts Volunteers.* Boston: Estes & Lauriat, 1894.

Douglas, Henry Kyd. *I Rode with Stonewall, Being Chiefly the War Experiences of the Youngest Member of Jackson's Staff from the John Brown Raid to the Hanging of Mrs. Surratt.* Chapel Hill: University of North Carolina Press, 1940.

Dyer, Jonah Franklin. *The Journal of a Civil War Surgeon.* Edited by Michael B. Chesson. Lincoln: University of Nebraska Press, 2003.

Early, Jubal A. *A Memoir of the Last Year of the War for Independence.* New Orleans: Blelock, 1867.

Edwards, Todd S. *The Young Farmers' Manual.* New York: C. M. Saxton, Barker, 1860.

Ellis, Thomas T. *Leaves from the Diary of an Army Surgeon; or, Incidents of Field, Camp, and Hospital Life.* New York: John Bradburn, 1863.

Erving, Annie Priscilla. *Reminiscences of the Life of a Nurse in Field, Hospital and Camp during the Civil War.* Newburgh, NY: Daily News, 1904.

Favill, Josiah M. *The Diary of a Young Officer: Serving with the Armies of the United States during the War of the Rebellion.* Chicago: R. R. Donnelley & Sons, 1909.

Fay, Franklin Brigham. *War Papers of Franklin Brigham Fay. With Reminiscences of Service in the Camps and Hospitals of the Army of the Potomac, 1861–1865*. Boston: George H. Ellis, 1911.

Figg, Royal W. *Where Men Only Dare to Go! Or, The Story of a Boy Company (C.S.A.)*. Richmond: Whittet & Shepperson, 1885.

Fiske, Samuel. *Mr. Dunn Browne's Experiences in the Army: The Civil War Letters of Samuel W. Fiske*. Edited by Stephen W. Sears. New York: Fordham University Press, 1998.

Fitch, John. *Annals of the Army of the Cumberland*. Philadelphia: J.B. Lippincott, 1864.

Fuller, Edward H. B*attles of the Seventy-Seventh New York State Foot Volunteers*. Gloversville, NY, 1901.

Gage, M. D. *From Vicksburg to Raleigh; or, A Complete History of the Twelfth Regiment Indiana Volunteer Infantry and the Campaigns of Grant and Sherman, with an Outline of the Great Rebellion*. Chicago: Clarke, 1865.

Galwey, Thomas Francis. *The Valiant Hours: Narrative of "Captain Brevet," an Irish-American in the Army of the Potomac*. Edited by W. S. Nye. Harrisburg, PA: Stackpole, 1961.

Goss, Warren Lee. *Recollections of a Private. A Story of the Army of the Potomac*. New York: Thomas Y. Crowell, 1890.

Gould, John Meade. *Joseph K. F. Mansfield, Brigadier General of the U.S. Army: A Narrative of Events Connected with His Mortal Wounding at Antietam, Sharpsburg, Maryland, September 17, 1862*. Portland: Stephen Berry, 1895.

Graham, Matthew John. *The Ninth Regiment, New York Volunteers (Hawkins' Zouaves): Being a History of the Regiment and Veteran Association from 1860 to 1900*. New York: E. P. Coby, 1900.

Green, Robert M. *History of the One Hundred and Twenty-Fourth Regiment Pennsylvania Volunteers*. Philadelphia: Ware Bros., 1907.

Hallowell, Norwood P. *Reminiscences Written for My Children by Request of Their Mother*. West Medford, MA: Self-published, 1897.

Hard, Abner. *History of the Eighth Cavalry Regiment*. Aurora: Illinois Volunteers, 1868.

Hewitt, William. *History of the Twelfth West Virginia Volunteer Infantry*. Charleston, WV: Twelfth West Virginia Infantry Association, 1892.

Holmes, Oliver Wendell, Sr. *Pages from an Old Volume of Life. A Collection of Essays 1857–1881*, vol. VIII. Boston: Houghton Mifflin, 1863.

Holstein, Anna. *Three Years in Field Hospitals of the Army of the Potomac*. Philadelphia: J.B. Lippincott, 1867.

Holt, Daniel. *A Surgeon's Civil War: The Letters and Diary of Daniel M. Holt, M.D.* Edited by James M. Greiner, Janet L. Coryell, and James R. Smither. Kent, OH: Kent State University Press, 1991.

Hosmer, George W. *Report of the Delegates from the General Aid Society for the Army at Buffalo, New York*. Buffalo, NY: Franklin Steam Printing House, 1862.

Hough, Franklin B. *History of Duryée's Brigade, during the Campaign in Virginia under Gen. Pope, and in Maryland under Gen. McClellan, in the Summer and Autumn of 1862*. Albany, NY: J. Munsell, 1864.

Hunter, Alexander. *Johnny Reb and Billy Yank*. New York: Neale, 1905.

Hussey, George A. *History of the Ninth Regiment N.Y.S.M.—N.G.S.N.Y. (Eighty-Third N.Y. Volunteers) 1845–1888*. New York: Veterans of the Regiment, 1889.

Huyette, Miles Clayton. *The Maryland Campaign and the Battle of Antietam*. Buffalo, NY: Hammond Press, 1915.

James, Bushrod Washington. *Echoes of Battle*. Philadelphia: Henry T. Coates, 1895.

Jenkins, Donald B. *The Lost Civil War Diary of John Rigdon King*. Mount Pleasant, SC: Arcadia Publishing, 2018.

Johnson, Charles B. *Muskets and Medicine*, Philadelphia: F. A. Davis Company, 1917.

Johnson, Charles F. *The Long Roll: Being a Journal of the Civil War, as Set Down During the Years 1861–1863*. East Aurora, NY: The Roycrofters, 1911.

Johnson, Clifton. *Battleground Adventures: The Stories of Dwellers on the Scenes of Conflict in Some of the Most Notable Battles of the Civil War*. New York: Houghton Mifflin, 1915.

Lamon, Ward Hill. *Recollections of Abraham Lincoln*. Edited by Dorothy Lamon Teillard. Washington, DC: Dorothy Teillard and Cambridge University Press, 1911.

Lord, Edward O. *History of the Ninth Regiment, New Hampshire Volunteers*. Concord, NH: Republican Press, 1895.

Macnamara, Daniel George. *The History of the Ninth Regiment, Massachusetts Volunteer Infantry, Second Brigade, First Division, Fifth Army Corps, Army of the Potomac, June, 1861–June, 1864*. Boston: E. B. Stillings, 1899.

Maine Artillery. *History of the Fourth Maine Battery Light Artillery in the Civil War, 1861–1865*. Augusta, ME: Burleigh & Flynt, 1905.

McClellan, George B. *McClellan's Own Story*. New York: Charles L. Webster, 1887.

McMaster, F. W. *Proceedings of a General Court Martial, in the Trial of Col. F. W. McMaster, 17th Regiment, S.C.V., Held at Wilmington, N.C., March 30th, 1863*. Columbia, SC: South Carolina Steam Press, 1863.

Meade, George. *The Life and Letters of George Gordon Meade*. 2 vols. New York: Charles Scribner's Sons, 1913.

Members of the Regiment. *A History of the Eleventh Regiment, Ohio Volunteer Infantry*. Dayton, OH: Horton & Teverbaugh, 1866.

Monroe, Albert J. *Battery D, First Rhode Island Light Artillery at the Battle of Antietam*. Providence, Rhode Island: The Society, 1886.

Moore, Edward A. *The Story of a Cannoneer Under Stonewall Jackson*. New York: Neale, 1907.

Neese, George M. *Three Years in the Confederate Horse Artillery*. New York: Neale, 1911.

Newell, Joseph Keith. *Ours. Annals of 10th Regiment, Massachusetts Volunteers in the Rebellion*. Springfield, MA: C. A. Nichols, 1875.

Noyes, George F. Noyes. *The Bivouac and the Battle-Field; or, Campaign Sketches in Virginia and Maryland*. New York: Harper & Brothers, 1863.

Oliver, James. *Ancestry, Early Life and War Record of James Oliver, M.D.* Athol, MA: Athol Transcript, 1916.

Owen, William Miller. *In Camp and Battle with the Washington Artillery of New Orleans*. Boston: Ticknor and Company, 1885.

Page, Charles D. *History of the Fourteenth Regiment Connecticut Vol. Infantry*. Meriden, CT: Horton Printing Co., 1906.

Parker, Francis J. *The Story of the Thirty-Second Regiment Massachusetts, Infantry.* Boston: C. W. Calkins, 1880.

Parker, John Lord. *Henry Wilson's Regiment: History of the Twenty-Second Massachusetts Infantry.* Boston: Regimental Association, 1887.

Phelps, Mrs. Lincoln, ed., *Our Country, In Its Relations to the Past, Present and Future.* Baltimore: John D. Toy, 1864.

Pollard, Edward A. *Southern History of the War: The Second Year of the War.* New York: Charles B. Richardson, 1864.

Quint, Alonzo H. *The Record of the Second Massachusetts Infantry, 1861-1865.* Boston: James P. Walker Publishing, 1867.

Racine, J. Polk. *Recollections of a Veteran of Four Years in Dixie.* Elkton, MD: Appeal Printing Office, 1894. Reprinted by the Cecil County Bicentennial Committee, 1987.

Raymer, Jacob Nathaniel. *Confederate Correspondent: The Civil War Reports of Jacob Nathaniel Raymer.* Edited by E. B. Munson. Jefferson, NC: McFarland, 2009.

Regan, Timothy J. *The Lost Civil War Diaries: The Diaries of Corporal Timothy J. Regan.* Edited by David C. Newton and Thomas Pluskat. Victoria, Canada: Trafford, 2003.

Reilly, Oliver T. *The Battlefield of Antietam.* Hagerstown, MD: Hagerstown Bookbinding & Printing, 1906. https://catalog.hathitrust.org/Record/102359684.

Remmel, William. *Like Grass Before the Scythe— the Life and Death of Sgt. William Remmel, 121st New York Infantry.* Edited by Robert Patrick Bender. Tuscaloosa, AL: The University of Alabama Press, 2007.

Richardson, Albert Deane. *The Secret Service, the Field, the Dungeon, and the Escape.* Hartford, CT: American, 1865.

Scott, Henry Lee. *Military Dictionary: Comprising Technical Definitions; Information on Raising and Keeping Troops; Actual Service, Including Makeshifts and Improved Matériel; and Law, Government, Regulation, and Administration Relating to Land Forces.* New York: D. Van Nostrand, 1864.

Sherman, William T. *Memoirs.* 2 vols. New York: D. Appleton & Company, 1891.

Shotwell, Randolph A. *The Papers of Randolph Abbott Shotwell.* 3 vols. Raleigh, NC: The North Carolina Historical Commission, 1929.

Slocum, Charles Elihu. *The Life and Services of Major-General Henry Warner Slocum.* Toledo, OH: Slocum, 1913.

Small, Abner R. *The Sixteenth Maine Regiment in the War of the Rebellion, 1861–1865.* Portland, ME: B. Thurston, 1886.

Smith, Edward P. *Incidents of the United States Christian Commission.* Philadelphia: J. B. Lippincott, 1869.

Smith, J. L. *History of the Corn Exchange Regiment: 118th Pennsylvania.* Philadelphia, 1888.

Spooner, Henry J. *The Maryland Campaign with the Fourth Rhode Island, Personal Narratives of Events in the War of the Rebellion: Being Papers Read Before the Rhode Island Soldiers and Sailors Historical Society.* Providence, RI: Snow & Parnham, 1903.

Stearns, Austin C. *Three Years with Company K.* Edited by Arthur A. Kent. Cranbury, NJ: Farleigh Dickinson University Press, 1976.

Steiner, Lewis H. *Report of Lewis H. Steiner, M.D., Inspector of the Sanitary Commission: Containing a Diary Kept During the Rebel Occupation of Frederick, Md. and an Account of the Operations of the U.S. Sanitary Commission During the Campaign in Maryland, September, 1862.* New York: Anson D. F. Randolph, 1862.

Stevens, George Thomas. *Three Years in the Sixth Corps.* New York: D. Van Norstrand, 1870.

Stevens, Henry S. *Souvenir of Excursion to Battlefields by the Society of the Fourteenth Connecticut Regiment and Reunion at Antietam, September 1891.* Washington, DC: Gibson Brothers Printers & Bookbinders, 1893.

Stille, Charles J. *History of the United States Sanitary Commission: Being the General Report of its Work during the War of the Rebellion.* New York: Hurd & Houghton, 1868.

Stonebraker, Joseph R. *A Rebel of '61.* New York: Wynkoop Hallenbeck Crawford Co., 1899.

Strother, David Hunter. *A Virginia Yankee in the Civil War: The Diaries of David Hunter Strother.* Edited by Cecil D. Eby, Jr. Chapel Hill: University of North Carolina Press, 1961.

Taylor, William H. *De Quibus: Discourses and Essays.* Richmond, VA: The Bell Book and Stationery Company, 1908.

Thayer, George A. *History of the Second Massachusetts Regiment of Infantry: Chancellorsville.* Boston: George H. Ellis, 1882.

Thayer, William Roscoe. *The Life and Letters of John Hay.* 2 vols. Boston: Houghton Mifflin Company, 1908.

Third Pennsylvania Cavalry Regimental History Committee. *History of the Third Pennsylvania Cavalry, Sixtieth Regiment Pennsylvania Volunteers, in the American Civil War, 1861–1865.* Philadelphia: Franklin Printing Company, 1905.

Toombs, Samuel. *Reminiscences of the War: Comprising a Detailed Account of the Experiences of the Thirteenth Regiment New Jersey Volunteers.* Orange, NJ: Journal Office, 1878.

Trowbridge, Jonathan T. *The South: A Tour of Its Battlefields and Ruined Cities, a Journey through the Desolated States, and Talks with the People.* Hartford, CT: L. Stebbins, 1866.

United States Army, *13th New Jersey Regiment. Historical Sketch of Co. "D," 13th Regiment, N. J. Vols: Part of the 3d Brigade, 1st Division, 12th Army Corps, U.S.A. with the Muster Roll of the Company.* Newark, NJ: D. H. Gildersleeve, 1895.

United States Christian Commission, *United States Christian Commission for the Army and Navy: First Annual Report, Volume 1.* Philadelphia: U.S. Christian Commission, 1863.

Von Borcke, Heros. *Memoirs of the Confederate War for Independence.* 3 vols. Philadelphia: J. B. Lippincott, 1867.

Wainwright, Charles S. *A Diary of Battle: The Personal Journals of Colonel Charles S. Wainwright, 1861–1865.* Edited by Allan Nevins. New York: Harcourt, Brace & World, 1962.

Washburn, George H. *A Complete Military History and Record of the 108th Regiment N.Y. Vols., From 1862 to 1894.* Rochester, New York: E. R. Andrews, 1894.

Westbrook, Robert S. *History of the 49th Pennsylvania Volunteers.* Atoona, PA: Altoona Times Print, 1897.

Westervelt, William B. *Lights and Shadows of Army Life: As Seen by a Private Soldier.* Marlboro, New York: C. H. Cochrane, 1886.

Williams, Alpheus. *From the Cannon's Mouth: The Civil War Letters of General Alpheus S. Williams.* Edited by Milo M. Quaife. Detroit, MI: Wayne State University Press, 1959.

Woodward, Evan Morrison. *Our Campaigns: or, The marches, bivouacs, battles, incidents of camp life and history of our regiment during its three years term of service.* Philadelphia: J. E. Potter, 1865.

Woodward, Joseph. *Outlines of the Chief Camp Diseases of the United States Armies.* Philadelphia: J. B. Lippincott, 1863.

Government Sources

Annual Report of the Secretary of War for the Year 1880, vol. 1. Washington, DC: U.S. Government Printing Office, 1880.

Catalogue of the Surgical Section of the United States Army Medical Museum. Washington, DC: U.S. Government Printing Office, 1866.

"Charles J. McKinney, Letter from the Secretary of War." *Third Session, Forty-Second Congress, Executive Documents, 1872–73.* Washington, DC: U.S. Government Printing Office, 1873.

Congressional Record: The Proceedings and Debates of the Forty-Seventh Congress, First Session. Washington, DC: U.S. Government Printing Office, 1882.

Congressional Record: The Proceedings and Debates of the Fifty-Second Congress, Second Session. Washington, DC: U.S. Government Printing Office, 1893.

"Court of Claims to Investigate Certain Bills, Etc., by Authority of the Tucker Act." *House of Representatives, 58th Congress, 2nd Session.* Washington DC: U.S. Government Printing Office, 1904.

"Forestry in Germany," *Consular Reports: Commerce, Manufactures, Etc.*, 71 (January–April 1903): 81. Washington, DC: U.S. Government Printing Office.

"Fourth of July Claims." *The Reports of Committees of the House of Representatives, Third Session of the Fifty-Third Congress, 1894–1895.* Washington, DC: U.S. Government Printing Office, 1895.

Fradin, Morris. "The Story of Clara Barton." United States Senate. *Hearing Before the Subcommittee on Parks and Recreation of the Committee on Interior and Insular Affairs. S.3700. A Bill to Provide for the Establishment of the Clara Barton House National Historic Site.* Washington, DC: U.S. Government Printing Office, 1974.

Frye, Susan W., and Dennis E. Frye. *Maryland Heights: Archeological & Historical Resources Study.* Washington, DC: National Park Service, 1989.

Grivno, Max L. *Historic Resource Study: Ferry Hill Plantation.* U.S. Department of the Interior, National Park Service, Chesapeake & Ohio National Historical Park. Hagerstown, MD, August 2007.

Hall, Susan C. *Antietam National Battlefield, Observation Tower.* Historic American Buildings Survey, U.S. Department of the Interior. Washington, DC: National Park Service, 2009.

House of Representatives Documents, 59th Congress, 2nd Session, Vol. 48. Washington, DC: U.S. Government Printing Office, 1907.

———. 59th Congress, 2nd Session, Vol. 52. Washington, DC: U.S. Government Printing Office, 1907.

———. 64th Congress, 1st Session, Vol. 147. Washington, DC: Government Printing Office, 1916.

Lackey, Rodney C. *Notes on Civil War Logistics: Facts & Stories*, United States Army Transportation Corps. https://transportation.army.mil/History/PDF/Peninsula%20Campaign/Rodney%20 Lackey%20Article_1.pdf.

Parker, Horatio N., Bailey Willis, R. H. Bolster, W. W. Ashe, and M. C. Marsh. *The Potomac River Basin*. Department of the Interior, United States Geological Survey. Washington, DC: U.S. Government Printing Office, 1907.

"Payment of Claims in Accordance with Findings of the Court of Claims, Reported Under the Bowman and Tucker Acts, and Section No. 151 of the Judicial Code." *63rd Congress, 2nd Session, House Reports, Vol. A*. Washington, DC: U.S. Government Printing Office, 1914.

"Proceedings of a Board of Survey Convened in Conformity with Special Order No. 36," October 22, 1862. Record Group 92: Office of the Claims of the Quartermaster General, Claims Branch 1861–1889, Quartermaster Stores (Act of July 4, 1864), Entry 843, Box 771. Washington, DC: National Archives and Records Administration.

"Reference of Claims to the Court of Claims." *Congressional Record: Proceedings of Congress and General Congressional Publications*. House of Representatives, vol. 13, pt. 4. Washington, DC: U.S. Government Printing Office, 1882.

Report of the Secretary of the Treasury on the State of Finances for the Year 1864. Washington, DC: U.S. Government Printing Office, 1864.

Snell, Charles W. and Sharon A. Brown. *Antietam National Battlefield and National Cemetery: An Administrative History*. U.S. Department of the Interior, National Park Service, Washington, DC, 1986.

Statutes at Large of the United States of America, 47th Congress, Session 2. Washington, DC: U.S. Government Printing Office, 1883.

Statutes at Large of the United States of America, 55th Congress, Session 3. Washington, DC: U.S. Government Printing Office, 1899.

Statutes at Large of the United States of America, 57th Congress, Session 1. Washington, DC: U.S. Government Printing Office, 1902.

Statutes at Large of the United States of America, 58th Congress, Session 3. Washington, DC: U.S. Government Printing Office, 1905.

Statutes at Large of the United States of America from March 1913 to March 1915, Vol. XXXVIII. Washington, DC: U.S. Government Printing Office, 1915.

"The Bowman Act." *The Reports of Committees of the House of Representatives for the Third Session of the Fifty-Third Congress, 1894–95*, vol. 2, report no. 1792. Washington, DC: U.S. Government Printing Office, 1895.

The Miscellaneous Documents of the House of Representatives for the First Session of the Fifty-Second Congress, vol. 1. Washington, DC: U.S. Government Printing Office, 1892.

The Miscellaneous Documents of the House of Representatives for the Second Session of the Fifty-First Congress, vol. 1. Washington, DC: U.S. Government Printing Office, 1891.

The Miscellaneous Documents of the Senate of the United States for the Second Session of the Fifty-First Congress, 1890-1891, vol. 7. Washington, DC: U.S. Government Printing Office, 1891.

The Reports of Committees of the House of Representatives for the Third Session of the Fifty-Third Congress, 1894-1895. Washington, DC: U.S. Government Printing Office, 1895.

United States Department of Agriculture, Economic Research Service. "Weights, Measures, and Conversion Factors for Agricultural Commodities and Their Products." Washington, DC, June 1992.

United States Department of Agriculture. *Soil Survey of Washington County, Maryland.* Washington, DC: U.S. Government Printing Office, 1919.

United States Department of Transportation. *Mass Casualties, A Lessons Learned Approach: Accidents, Civil Unrest, Natural Disasters, Terrorism.* Washington, DC: National Highway Traffic Safety Administration, 1982.

United States Sanitary Commission. "Appeal to the Public, with Letters Concerning Army Operations in the Relief Work of the Commission in Maryland (September 24, 1862)." *Documents of the U.S. Sanitary Commission.* New York, 1866.

United States War Department. *Revised United States Army Regulations of 1861, with an Appendix Containing the Changes and Laws Affecting Army Regulations and Articles of War to June 25, 1863.* Washington, DC: U.S. Government Printing Office, 1863.

United States War Department. *The War of the Rebellion: A Compilation of the Official Records of the Union and Confederate Armies.* 128 vols. Washington, DC: U.S. Government Printing Office, 1880–1901.

Unrau, Harland D. *Historic Resource Study: Chesapeake & Ohio Canal.* U.S. Department of the Interior, National Park Service. Hagerstown, MD, 2007. https://www.nps.gov/parkhistory/online_books/choh/unrau_hrs.pdf.

Wheelock, Perry Carpenter. *Farming Along the Chesapeake and Ohio Canal, 1828–1971.* Washington, DC: U.S. Department of the Interior, National Park Service, Chesapeake & Ohio Canal National Historical Park, August 2007.

Newspapers

Altoona [PA] *Tribune*, October 2, 1862

Antietam Valley Record [Keedysville, MD], March–October 1895

Brooklyn News, January 9, 1865

Daily Dispatch [Richmond, VA], December 16, 1862

Daily Intelligencer [Wheeling, WV], September 22, 1862

Elmira [NY] *Telegram*, May 21, 1893

Frank Leslie's Illustrated Newspaper [NY], October 18, 1862

Hagerstown [MD] Mail, 1875–1904

Herald of Freedom and Torchlight [Hagerstown, MD], 1856–1862

Herald and Torch Light [Hagerstown, MD], 1863–1895

Holmes County Farmer [Millersburg, OH], October 9, 1862

Maryland Free Press [Hagerstown, MD], October 1862–March 1863

Mobile [AL] *Daily Advertiser and Register*, October 2, 1862

Morning Herald [Hagerstown, MD], 1931–1962

New York Daily Tribune, July 13, 1865

New York Tribune, September 15 and 18, 1862

Philadelphia Inquirer, September 25 and October 27, 1862

Pittsburgh Press, December 4, 1927

Rochester [NY] *Daily Union and Advertiser*, September 26, 1862

Shepherdstown [WV] *Register*, 1905–1934

The Athens [OH] *Messenger*, December 4, 1862

The Boonsboro [MD] *Odd Fellow*, 1870–76

The Daily Mail [Hagerstown, MD], 1891–1997

The Evening Star [Washington, DC], October 3–4, 1862 and September 17, 1896

The Evening Times [Cumberland, MD], April 30, 1906

The Examiner [Frederick, MD], September 24, 1862 and April 29, 1863

The Hartford [CT] *Courant*, June 1, 2009

The Lincoln [NE] *Sunday Star*, July 10, 1925

The Nashville [TN] *Daily Union*, October 3, 1862

The New York Times, 1862–1988

The Plymouth [MA] *Rock*, November 27, 1862

The Valley Register [Middletown, MD], 1859–1912

The Washington [DC] *Post*, May 21, 1909

Timaru [New Zealand] *Herald*, February 23, 1866

Valley Spirit [Chambersburg, PA], September 24, 1862

Woodland [CA] *Daily Democrat*, 1926–29

Secondary Sources

Books

Alexander, Ted. *The Battle of Antietam: The Bloodiest Day*. Charleston, SC: The History Press, 2011.

Avey, Michael Garland. *Cultural Resources of the Avey Family: Phase 1, Inventory of Archeological Sites*. Fort Steilacoom, Washington: Pierce College, 1986.

Barron, Lee, and Barbara Barron. *The History of Sharpsburg, Maryland*. Self-published, 1972.

Barry, Joseph. *The Strange Story of Harper's Ferry: With Legends of the Surrounding Country*. Martinsburg, WV: Thompson Brothers, 1903.

Barton, William E. *The Life of Clara Barton in Two Volumes*. Boston: Houghton Mifflin Company, 1922.

Bluhm, Raymond K., Jr. *The Shenandoah Valley Campaign: March–November 1864*. Washington, DC: Center of Military History, United States Army, 2014. https://history.army.mil/html/books/075/75-14/cmhPub_75-14.pdf.

Bollet, Alfred Jay. *Civil War Medicine: Challenges and Triumphs*. Tucson, AZ: Galen Press, 2002.

Bowen, Roland. *From Ball's Bluff to Gettysburg ... and Beyond: The Civil War Letters of Private Roland E. Bowen, 15th Massachusetts Infantry 1861–1864*. Edited by Gregory A. Coco. Gettysburg, PA: Thomas Publications, 1994.

Brockett, Linus P. *Lights and Shadows of the Great Rebellion: Or, The Camp, the Battle Field and Hospital, Including Thrilling Adventures, Daring Deeds, Heroic Exploits, and Wonderful Escape of Spies and Scouts, Together With the Songs, Ballads, Anecdotes, and Humorous Incidents of the War.* Philadelphia: William Flint, 1866.

Brown, Kent Masterson. *Retreat from Gettysburg.* Chapel Hill, NC: University of North Carolina Press, 2005.

Browning, Judkin, and Timothy Silver. *An Environmental History of the Civil War.* Chapel Hill: University of North Carolina Press, 2020.

Cashin, Joan E. *War Stuff: The Struggle for Human and Environmental Resources in the American Civil War.* Cambridge, UK: Cambridge University Press, 2018.

Chapman Publishing Company. *Portrait and Biographical Record of the Sixth Congressional District, Maryland.* New York: Chapman, 1898.

Coddington, Edwin B. *The Gettysburg Campaign: A Study in Command.* New York: Simon and Schuster, 1968.

Cordell, Eugene Fauntleroy, *The Medical Annals of Maryland, 1799–1899.* Baltimore: Williams & Wilkins, 1903.

Doyle, Vernell, and Tim Doyle. *Sharpsburg. Images of America Series.* Charleston, SC: Arcadia, 2009.

Ernst, Kathleen A. *Too Afraid to Cry: Maryland Civilians in the Antietam Campaign.* Mechanicsburg, PA: Stackpole Books, 2007.

Faust, Drew Gilpin. *This Republic of Suffering: Death and the American Civil War.* New York: Alfred A. Knopf, 2008.

Flannery, Michael A. *Civil War Pharmacy: A History of Drugs, Drug Supply and Provision, and Therapeutics for the Union and Confederacy.* Carbondale: Southern Illinois University Press, 2017.

Frassanito, William A. *Antietam: The Photographic Legacy of America's Bloodiest Day.* Toronto: Mills & Boon, 1979.

Freemon, F. R. *Gangrene and Glory: Medical Care during the American Civil War.* Chicago: University of Illinois, 2001.

Frye, Dennis E. *Antietam Revealed: The Battle of Antietam and the Maryland Campaign as You Have Never Seen It Before.* Collingswood, NJ: C. W. Historicals, 2004.

———. *Antietam Shadows: Mystery, Myth & Machination.* Sharpsburg, MD: Antietam Rest, 2018.

———. *Harpers Ferry Under Fire: A Border Town in the American Civil War.* Harpers Ferry, WV: Harpers Ferry Park Association, 2012.

———. *The Battle of Harpers Ferry: History and Battlefield Guide.* Harpers Ferry, WV: Harpers Ferry Park Association, 2011.

Fusonie, Alan E., and Leila Moran, eds. *Heritage of Agriculture in Maryland, 1776–1976.* Beltsville, MD: Associates of the National Agricultural Library, 1976.

Gerrish, Theodore, and John S. Hutchinson. *The Blue and the Gray: A Graphic History of the Army of the Potomac and that of Northern Virginia, Including the Brilliant Engagements of These Forces from 1861 to 1865.* Portland: Hoyt, Fogg & Donham, 1883.

Gregory, Tom. *History of Yolo County, California: With Biographical Sketches of the Leading Men and Women of the County, Who Have Been Identified with Its Growth and Development from the Early Days to the Present.* Los Angeles: Historic Record Company, 1913.

Guinn, James M. *History of the State of California and Biographical Record of the Sacramento Valley, California: A Historical Study of the State's Marvelous Growth From Its Earliest Settlement to the Present Time.* Chicago: Chapman Publishing Company, 1906.

Hall, W. W. *Health at Home; or, Hall's Family Doctor.* Hartford, CT: James Betts, 1879.

Harsh, Joseph L. *Sounding the Shallows: A Confederate Companion for the Maryland Campaign of 1862.* Kent, OH: Kent State University Press, 2000.

———. *Taken at the Flood: Robert E. Lee and the Confederate Strategy in the Maryland Campaign of 1862.* Kent, OH: Kent State University Press, 1999.

Hartshorne, Henry. *Essentials of the Principles and Practice of Medicine: A Handbook for Students and Practitioners.* Philadelphia: Henry C. Lea, 1874.

Hartwig, D. Scott. *To Antietam Creek: The Maryland Campaign of September 1862.* Baltimore: John Hopkins University Press, 2012.

Henry, J. Maurice. *History of the Brethren Church in Maryland.* Elgin, IL: Brethren, 1936.

Johnson, Curt, and Richard C. Anderson, Jr. *Artillery Hell: The Employment of Artillery at Antietam.* College Station: Texas A & M University Press, 1995.

Kable, Harry G. *Mount Morris: Past and Present: An Illustrated History of the Village of Mount Morris, Ogle County, Illinois.* Salem, Massachusetts: Higginson Book Company, 1938.

Keller, Roger. *Roster of Civil War Soldiers from Washington County, Maryland.* Baltimore: Clearfield / Genealogical, 1998.

Kenamond, A. D. *Prominent Men of Shepherdstown During Its First 200 Years.* Charles Town, WV: Jefferson County Historical Society, 1963.

Kunhardt, Philip B., Jr., Philip B. Kunhardt III, and Peter W. Kunhardt. *Lincoln: An Illustrated Biography.* New York: Alfred A. Knopf, 1992.

Magner, Blake A. *Traveller & Company: The Horses of Gettysburg.* Gettysburg, PA: Farnsworth House Military Impressions, 1995.

Marshall, John A. *American Bastile: A History of the Illegal Arrests and Imprisonment of American Citizens during the Late Civil War.* Philadelphia: Thomas W. Hartley, 1869.

Mason, F. R., and Kathryn Garst. *The Michael Miller and Susanna Bechtol Family Record.* Bridgewater, VA: Beacon Printing, 1993.

McGaugh, Scott. *Surgeon in Blue: Jonathan Letterman, the Civil War Doctor Who Pioneered Battlefield Care.* New York: Arcade, 2013.

McGrath, Thomas A. *Shepherdstown: Last Clash of the Antietam Campaign, September 19–20, 1862.* Lynchburg, VA: Schroeder, 2012.

McKinney, William M. *Federal Statutes Annotated: Containing All the Laws of the United States of a General and Permanent Nature in Force on the First Day of January 1903.* Long Island, New York: Edward Thompson Company, 1903.

McPherson, James M. *Crossroads of Freedom: Antietam.* New York: Oxford University Press, 2002.

Miller, Sally M., A. J. H. Latham, and Dennis O. Flynn. *Studies in the Economic History of the Pacific Rim*. New York: Routledge, 2003.

Mingus, Scott L., Sr. *The Louisiana Tigers in the Gettysburg Campaign, June–July 1863*. Baton Rouge: Louisiana State University Press, 2009.

Mumma, Wilmer. *Antietam: The Aftermath*. Self-published, 1993.

Murfin, James V. *The Gleam of Bayonets: The Battle of Antietam and the Maryland Campaign of 1862*. Baton Rouge: Louisiana State University Press, 1965.

Neff, Stephen C. *Justice in Blue and Gray: A Legal History of the Civil War*. Cambridge, MA: Harvard University Press, 2010.

Nelson, John H. *As Grain Falls Before the Reaper: The Federal Hospital Sites and Identified Federal Casualties at Antietam*. Self-published, 2004.

Ouchley, Kelby. F*lora and Fauna of the Civil War: An Environmental Reference Guide*. Baton Rouge: Louisiana State University Press, 2010.

Pawlak, Kevin R. *Shepherdstown in the Civil War: One Vast Hospital*. Charleston, SC: The History Press, 2015.

Peterson, Don. *Native American Fish Traps in the Potomac River, Brunswick, Maryland*. Brunswick, MD: Brunswick Heritage Museum, 2018.

Powell, William H. *The Fifth Army Corps (Army of the Potomac): A Record of Operations during the Civil War in the United States of American, 1861–1865*. New York: G. P. Putnam's Sons, 1896.

Priest, John Michael. *Antietam: The Soldier's Battle*. New York: Oxford University Press, 1989.

Rafuse, Ethan S. *McClellan's War: The Failure of Moderation in the Struggle for the Union*. Indianapolis: Indiana University Press, 2005.

Reed, William Howell. *The Heroic Story of the United States Sanitary Commission, 1861–1865*. Boston: G. H. Ellis, 1910.

Reese, Timothy J. *Sealed with Their Lives: The Battle for Crampton's Gap*. Baltimore: Butternut and Blue, 1998.

Rossino, Alexander B. *Their Maryland: The Army of Northern Virginia from the Potomac Crossing to Sharpsburg in September 1862*. El Dorado Hills, CA: Savas Beatie, 2021.

Rutkow, Ira K. *Bleeding Blue and Gray: Civil War Surgery and the Evolution of American Medicine*. New York: Random House, 2005.

Scharf, J. Thomas. *History of Western Maryland: Being a History of Frederick, Montgomery, Carroll, Washington, Allegany, and Garrett Counties from the Earliest Period to the Present Day; Including Biographical Sketches of their Representative Men*. 2 vols. Philadelphia: Louis H. Everts, 1882.

Schildt, John W. *Antietam Hospitals*. Chewsville, MD: Antietam, 1996.

———. *Drums Along the Antietam*. Parsons, WV: McClain, 2004 (reprint of 1972 edition).

Schmidt, Allan and Terry Barkley. S*eptember Mourn: The Dunker Church of Antietam Battlefield*. El Dorado Hills, CA: Savas Beatie, 2018.

Schulz, B. W., and Rachel de Vienne. *A Separate Identity: Organizational Identity Among Readers of Zion's Watch Tower, 1870–1887*. 2 vols. Self-published, 2014.

Sears, Stephen W. *Gettysburg*. Boston: Houghton Mifflin, 2003.

———. *Landscape Turned Red*. Boston: Houghton Mifflin, 2003.

Shuford, Julius H. *A Historical Sketch of the Shuford Family.* Hickory, NC: A. L. Crouse & Son, 1902.

Sinisi, Kyle S. *Sacred Debts: State Civil War Claims and American Federalism, 1861–1880.* New York: Fordham University Press, 2003.

Snyder, Timothy R. *Trembling in the Balance: The Chesapeake and Ohio Canal During the Civil War.* Boston: Blue Mustang Press, 2011.

The Lewis Publishing Company. *A Biographical and Genealogical History of Southeastern Nebraska.* Chicago: The Lewis Publishing Company, 1904.

Trimble, David Churchman. *History of St. Paul's Episcopal Church.* n.p., 1998.

Walker, Kevin M., and K. C. Kirkman. *Antietam Farmsteads: A Guide to the Battlefield Landscape.* Sharpsburg, MD: Western Maryland Interpretive Association, 2010.

Wallace, Lew, et al. *The Story of American Heroism: Thrilling Narratives of Personal Adventures During the Great Civil War as Told by the Medal Winners and Roll of Honor Men.* Springfield, Ohio: J. W. Jones, 1897.

Warner, Beers & Co. *History of Cumberland County, Pennsylvania. History of Cumberland and Adams Counties, Pennsylvania.* Chicago: Warner, Beers & Co., 1886.

Welsh, Jack D. *Medical Histories of Confederate Generals.* Kent, Ohio: Kent State University Press, 1999.

Wiley, Bell Irvin. *The Life of Billy Yank.* Baton Rouge: Louisiana State University Press, 1952.

Williams, Thomas J. C. *A History of Washington County, Maryland: From the Earliest Settlements to the Present Time, Including a History of Hagerstown.* 2 vols. Hagerstown, MD: John M. Runk and L. R. Titsworth, 1906.

Wilson, Arabella M. *Disaster, Struggle, Triumph: The Adventures of 1000 "Boys in Blue."* Albany, NY: Argus, 1870.

Articles and Essays

"About the Southern Claims Commission Papers." *The Valley of the Shadow: Two Communities in the American Civil War.* Virginia Center for Digital History, University of Virginia. https://valley.lib.virginia.edu/VoS/claims/aboutSCC.html.

Aftermath. "The Stages of Human Decomposition." https://www.aftermath.com/content/human-decomposition/.

Aikens, Charlotte A. "Protection Against Typhoid." *The Trained Nurse and Hospital Review* 49 (July 1912). New York: Lakeside Publishing, 99.

Aines, Don. "Many Sharpsburg Homes Have Civil War History." *Herald Mail* [Hagerstown, MD], September 13, 2013.

Alexander, Ted. "Destruction, Disease and Death: The Battle of Antietam and the Sharpsburg Civilians." *Civil War Regiments, a Journal of the American Civil War* 6, no. 2 (1998), 143-73.

American Battlefield Trust. "Fredericksburg." https://www.battlefields.org/learn/civil-war/battles/fredericksburg.

Banks, John. "Antietam: A Rare Piece of History from Roulette Farm?" *John Banks' Civil War Blog* (blog). October 24, 2013. http://john-banks.blogspot.com/2013/10/antietam-rare-piece-of-history-from.html.

———. "Antietam: Two Rural Graves, Two Tragedies" *John Banks' Civil War Blog* (blog). August 18, 2013. http://john-banks.blogspot.com/2013/08/antietam-two-rural-graves-two-tragedies.html.

———. "Our Hearts Ached with Pity: A Journey with an Antietam Nurse" *John Banks' Civil War Blog* (blog). May 30, 2017. http://john-banks.blogspot.com/2017/05/our-hearts-ached-with-pity-journey-with.html.

Barton, Clara. "Antietam: Clara Barton and the International Red Cross Association." Transcribed from Clara Barton Papers, Library of Congress, reel #109, beginning at frame #409. Antietam National Battlefield website. https://www.nps.gov/clba/learn/historyculture/antietam.htm.

Basden, Thomas J., A. O. Abaye, and Richard W. Taylor. "Chapter 5: Crop Production." Abstract, University of Maryland Extension, 94-126. https://extension.umd.edu/sites/extension.umd.edu/files/_docs/programs/anmp/MANMChapter5.pdf.

Boccadoro, Paul A. "Examination of Original Tools Excavated from Federal Camps." Online article, The Liberty Rifles. https://www.libertyrifles.org/research/uniforms-equipment/original-tools.

———. and John C. Holman. "U.S. Army Tool Contracts, 1863–1865." Online article, The Liberty Rifles. https://www.libertyrifles.org/research/uniforms-equipment/tool-contracts.

Briggs, Vernon M., Jr. "Rail Fences." *Railroad Brotherhoods*. Abstract, Cornell University, ILR School, 1976, 19. http://digitalcommons.ilr.cornell.edu/articles/142/.

Carr, Richard. "Excreta-Related Infections and the Role of Sanitation in the Control of Transmission." Online article, World Health Organization, 2001. https://www.who.int/water_sanitation_health/dwq/iwachap5.pdf.

Carroll County, Illinois. "History of Carroll County." Carroll County website. https://www.carroll-county.net/history.

Cirillo, Vincent J. "'Winged Sponges': Houseflies as Carriers of Typhoid Fever in 19th- and Early 20th-Century Military Camps." *Perspectives in Biology and Medicine* 49, no. 1 (2006): 52-63. doi:10.1353/pbm.2006.0005.

Carter, Robert Goldthwaite. "Four Brothers in Blue." *The Maine Bugle* (October 1897): 313–33.

Catton, Bruce. "Gallant Men in Deeds of Glory." *Life.* January 6, 1961, 48-76.

Caughley, Donald C. "The Cavalry Escape from Harpers Ferry, Part III," *Crossed Sabers* (blog). September 15, 2007. http://crossedsabers.blogspot.com/2007/09/.

Centers for Disease Control and Prevention. "Typhoid Fever and Paratyphoid Fever." https://www.cdc.gov/typhoid-fever/sources.html.

Centers for Disease Control and Prevention. "Water-Related Diseases and Contaminants in Public Water Systems." https://www.cdc.gov/healthywater/drinking/public/water_diseases.html.

Christ Reformed United Church of Christ. Pamphlet. Sharpsburg, MD, November 2, 2014.

Civil War Digest. "Civil War Cornfields—Like Antietam—Vol. II, Episode 19." YouTube video. September 14, 2016. https://www.youtube.com/watch?v=3LoBGQ-docQ.

Clem, Richard. "Civilians Fall Victim at Bloody Antietam." *Washington* [DC] *Times*, January 2, 2004. https://m.washingtontimes.com/news/2004/jan/02/20040102-091328-1739r/.

———. "Farmer Cheers Federals at Antietam." *Washington* [DC] *Times*, February 5, 2009. https://www.washingtontimes.com/news/2009/feb/5/witness-to-americas-bloodiest-day/.

———. "Misery Lasts Long after Antietam Battle." *Washington* [DC] *Times*, September 22, 2007. https://www.washingtontimes.com/news/2007/sep/22/misery-lasts-long-after-antietam-battle/.

Clemens, Thomas G. "Antietam Rebirth." HistoryNet.com, September 2017. https://www.historynet.com/antietam-rebirth.htm.

———. "Antietam Remembered." HistoryNet.com, August 25, 2010. https://www.historynet.com/antietam-remembered.htm.

———. In Search of McClellan's Headquarters." *Civil War Times*, June 2016, 26-33.

———. *The History of Keedysville*. Keedysville, Maryland. YouTube video, October 1, 2018. https://www.youtube.com/watch?v=AxYX0vtUWhU.

Coffin, Charles Carleton. "Antietam Scenes." *Battles and Leaders of the Civil War*. 4 vols. Vol. 2, pt. 2, pp. 682-5. Robert Underwood Johnson and Clarence Clough Buel (Eds.). New York: Century, 1887.

Congressional Medal of Honor Society. "Victor Vifquain." https://www.cmohs.org/recipients/victor-vifquain.

Connor, L. G. "A Brief History of the Sheep Industry in the United States," *Agricultural History Society Papers* 1. Washington, DC: Government Printing Office, 1921, 93-197.

"Corn Harvesting Machinery." *The American Thresherman* 10, no. 4 (August 1907): 10. Clarke Publishing Co., 1910.

"Correspondence: Albany Military Hospital." *Medical and Surgical Reporter* 6, no. 19 (August 10, 1861): 432-4.

Cross, Fred W. "Alexander W. Davis, of Sharpsburg." *The Daily Mail* [Hagerstown, MD], March 13, 1934. 3.

———. "A Sharpsburg Boy at Antietam." *The Daily Mail* [Hagerstown, MD], January 16, 1934. 10.

———. "Gallant Officers at Antietam." *Morning Herald* [Hagerstown, MD], February 13, 1934. 8.

———. "Joseph McGraw at Antietam," *Morning Herald* [Hagerstown, MD]. Two installments: February 1, 1934, and February 15, 1934.

———. "Recollections of Another Sharpsburg Boy." *The Daily Mail* [Hagerstown, MD], March 12, 1934, 4.

———. "Story of Flag at Antietam." *The Daily Mail* [Hagerstown, MD], January 30, 1934.

———. "Story of Flag Woman Saved at Antietam." *The Daily Mail* [Hagerstown, MD], April 9, 1931. 2.

———. "The Strong Stone House." *The Daily Mail* [Hagerstown, MD], March 22, 1934, 2.

Dalhamer, Gloria. "Area Around Keedysville Rich in Historical Lore of Battle." *The Daily Mail* [Hagerstown, MD], September 10, 1962, 11.

The Daily Mail [Hagerstown, MD]. "Sharpsburg Citizen Tells Own Story of Taking Refuge During Battle of Antietam." September 10, 1962, 12.

Dowart, Bonnie Brice. "Disease in the Civil War." Essential Civil War Curriculum. https://www.essentialcivilwarcurriculum.com/disease-in-the-civil-war.html.

Downey, Brian. "Lieutenant George Washington Ziegler Black." Antietam on the Web. http://antietam.aotw.org/officers.php?officer_id=10313.

———. "Captain William Fisher Plane."Antietam on the Web. http://antietam. aotw.org officers. php?officer_id=4825.

Duncan, Louis C. "The Bloodiest Day in American History: Antietam." *Military Surgeon* 32, no. 5 (May 1913): 427-71.

Ed Arey & Sons, Inc. "Hand Split & Snake Rail Fence." http://edareyandsons. com/products/ hand-split-snake-rail-fence/.

Elmwood Cemetery. "A History of Elmwood Cemetery." http://elmwoodcemeteryshepwv. org/html/history.html.

Evans, Thomas H. "The Enemy Sullenly Held on to the City." *Civil War Times Illustrated*, April 1968, 32-40.

Evening Times [Cumberland, MD]. "A Forgotten Hero—Why Is No Mention Ever Made of Brave Major Magraw?" April 30, 1906, 5.

"Farming in Maryland." *The Cultivator: A Monthly Journal for the Farm and Garden* 10 (April 1862). 115.

Freedman, Rachel, and Ron Fleming. "Water Quality Impacts of Burying Livestock Mortalities." Ridgetown College, University of Guelph, Ontario, August 2013. https://www.ridgetownc.com/ research/documents/fleming_carcassburial.pdf.

French, Steve. "Two Scouts of the Border, Part 2," *Crossfire Magazine: The Magazine of the American Civil War Roundtable* (UK) 122 (Spring 2020). 22-27.

Frye, Dennis E. "Harpers Ferry Stalls an Invasion." *The Sentinel*. National Park Service, 2014. https://www.nps.gov/cebe/learn/news/upload/Washington-Attacked-Sentinel-FINAL.pdf.

Gallagher, Gary W. "Season of Opportunity." *Antietam: Essays on the 1862 Maryland Campaign*. Edited by Gary W. Gallagher. Kent, OH: Kent State University Press, 1989. 1-13.

Goodrich, Calvin. "Rural Fences of Michigan." *Michigan Alumnus Quarterly Review* 49 (December 19, 1942): 250-52.

"Greasy Heel." *EquiMed*. July 22, 2014. http://equimed.com/diseases-and-conditions/ reference/greasy-heel.

Hagerstown Model Railroad Museum. "History of Antietam Station." http://www.antietamstation. com/hHistory.htm.

Heim, Janet. "Unsung Heroines Offered Care, Compassion after Battle of Antietam," *Herald Mail* [Hagerstown, MD], September 12, 2012.

Hennessy, John. "Civilians Endure the Battle of Fredericksburg." American Battlefield Trust. https: //www.battlefields.org/learn/articles/voices-storm-0.

Hicks, E. Russell. "The Church and the Battlefield." *Church of the Brethren Gospel Messenger* (Elgin, IL) 101, no. 6 (February 9, 1952). 12-15.

"Hints and Observations on Military Hygiene, Relating to Diet, Dress, Exercise, Exposure, and the Best Means of Preventing and Curing Medical and Surgical Diseases in the Army." *Medical and Surgical Reporter* 6, no. 12 (June 22, 1861): 263-68.

Historical Marker Database. "Antietam Station: Railroad to Reunion." https://www.hmdb.org/m. asp?m=1968.

"History of Sharpsburg." Sharpsburg, Maryland website. http://sharpsburgmd.com/history/.

Holmes, Oliver Wendell, Sr. "My Hunt After 'The Captain.'" *Atlantic Monthly* 10 (December 1862): 738–62.

Hunter, Alexander. "A High Private's Sketch of Sharpsburg." *Southern Historical Society Papers* 11 (1883). Richmond, VA: Rev. J. Wm. Jones. 10-21.

Hyde, Embriette R., Daniel P. Haarmann, Aaron M. Lynne, Sibyl R. Bucheli, and Joseph F. Petrosino. "The Living Dead: Bacterial Community Structure of a Cadaver at the Onset and End of the Bloat Stage of Decomposition." *PloS One* (October 30, 2013). https://www.ncbi.nlm.nih.gov/pmc/articles/PMC3813760.

International Committee of the Red Cross. "Why Dead Bodies Do Not Cause Epidemics." November 13, 2013. https://www.icrc.org/en/doc/resources/documents/faq/health- bodies-140110.htm.

Israel, David K. "The Origins of 10 Nicknames." *Mental Floss*, December 16, 2015. https://www.mentalfloss.com/article/24761/origins-10-nicknames.

Jack, Jeff. "Environmental Problems in Karst Lands." *Regional Updates*. Prentice-Hall. https://wps.prenhall.com/wps/media/objects/2894/2963555/update13.html.

Kalhor, Koosha, Reza Ghasemizadeh, Ljiljana Rajic, and Akram Alshawabkeh. "Assessment of Groundwater Quality and Remediation in Karst Aquifers: A Review." *Groundwater for Sustainable Development* 8 (April 2019): 104-21. https://doi.org/10.1016/j.gsd.2018.10.004.

Kratochvil, Bob. "10 Steps to Profitable Wheat Production." *Maryland Agronomy News* (blog). University of Maryland, August 2, 2017. http://blog.umd.edu/agronomynews/2017/08/02/10 -steps-to-profitable-wheat-production/.

Krick, Robert E. L. "Defending Lee's Flank." *The Antietam Campaign*. Edited by Gary Gallagher. Chapel Hill: University of North Carolina Press, 1999. 192-222.

Leavenworth, Jesse. "Civil War Stress." *The Hartford* [CT] *Courant*, June 1, 2009. https://www.courant.com/news/connecticut/hc-xpm-2009-06-01-civilwar-ptsd-0601-art-story.html.

"Life as a Lock Keeper on the C & O Canal." C & O Canal Trust. February 29, 2016. https://www.canaltrust.org/2016/02/life-as-a-lock-keeper-on-the-co-canal/.

Longstreet, James. "General James Longstreet's Account of the Campaign and Battle." *Southern Historical Society Papers* 5 (1878). Richmond, VA: Rev. J. Wm. Jones. 54-86.

———. "The Invasion of Maryland." *The Century Illustrated Monthly Magazine*, May 1886 to October 1886. 307-15.

Loyd, W. G. "Second Louisiana at Gettysburg." *Confederate Veteran* 6 (1898): 417. Nashville, TN: S. A. Cunningham.

McElfresh, Earl. "Only Take the Top Rail." *Civil War Times*, April 2008. https://www.historynet.com/take-top-rail.htm.

Marineli, F., G. Tsoucalas, M. Karamanou, and G. Androutsos. "Mary Mallon (1869–1938) and the History of Typhoid Fever." *Annals of Gastroenterology* 26 no. 2 (2013): 132-34. https://pubmed.ncbi.nlm.nih.gov/24714738/.

Masters, Daniel A. "Elizabeth Piper and the Battle of Antietam." *Dan Masters' Civil War Chronicles* (blog). September 29, 2017. https://dan-masters-civil-war.blogspot.com/2017/09/elizabeth-piper-and-battle-of-antietam.html.

Mitchell, Mary B. "A Woman's Recollections of Antietam." *Battles and Leaders of the Civil War*, vol. 2, pt. 2, 686-95. Edited by Robert Underwood Johnson and Clarence Clough Buel. New York: Century, 1887.

Moore, J. B. "Sharpsburg: Graphic Description of the Battle and Its Results." *Southern Historical Society Papers* 27 (1899). Richmond, VA: Rev. J. Wm. Jones. 210-219.

Morning Herald [Hagerstown, MD]. "Aged Woman Tells of Giving Food to Antietam Soldiers." July 10, 1937, 10C.

―――. "Confederate Extends Aid to Wounded Union Soldier." August 30, 1962, 20-21.

―――. "Miller Recalls Antietam Battle." September 17, 1948, 19.

―――. "Widow of Civil War Veteran Here for Commemoration." August 13, 1937, 20.

Mukhtar, Saquib. "Routine and Emergency Burial of Animal Carcasses." Texas A & M AgriLife Extension. https://agrilifeextension.tamu.edu/library/ranching/routine-and-emergency-burial-of-animal-carcasses/.

Mumma, Douglas M. "The Mumma Graveyard, Antietam National Battlefield, Sharpsburg, Maryland." Mumma.org, July 2014. https://www.mumma.org/archives/MummaCemetery.pdf.

Nair, R. K., S. R. Mehta, and S. Kumaravelu. "Typhoid Fever Presenting as Acute Psychosis." *Armed Forces India* 59, no. 3 (2003): 252-53. https://doi.org/10.1016/S0377-1237(03)80023-0.

National Cemetery Administration. "Memorial Day Order." U.S. Department of Veterans Affairs. https://www.cem.va.gov/history/memdayorder.asp.

National Museum of Civil War Medicine. "About the Pry House." https://www.civil warmed.org/pry/about-the-pry-house.

―――. "How Parasites Changed the American Civil War." June 1, 2018. https://www.civilwarmed.org/parasites/.

National Park Service. "Antietam National Cemetery." Antietam National Battlefield website. https://www.nps.gov/anti/learn/historyculture/antietam-national-cemetery.htm.

―――. "The Battle of Monocacy." Monocacy National Battlefield website. https://www.nps.gov/mono/learn/historyculture/the-battle-of-monocacy.htm.

―――. "Casualties of Battle." Antietam National Battlefield website. https://www.nps.gov/anti/learn/historyculture/casualties.htm.

―――. "Cave/Karst Systems." Antietam National Battlefield website. April 10, 2015. https://www.nps.gov/anti/learn/nature/cave-karst-systems.htm.

―――. "Clara Barton at Antietam." Antietam National Battlefield website. https://www.nps.gov/anti/learn/historyculture/clarabarton.htm.

―――. "The Dunker Church at Antietam." Antietam National Battlefield website. April 10, 2015. https://www.nps.gov/anti/learn/historyculture/dunkerchurch.htm.

―――. "Henry Kyd Douglas." https://www.nps.gov/people/henry-kyd-douglas.htm.

―――. "Lesson Two: 'One Vast Hospital.'" Educational brochure. Antietam National Battlefield. https://www.nps.gov/museum/tmc/Antietam/Lesson2/Lesson2_attachments.pdf.

―――. "Tour Stop 8: The Sunken Road." Antietam National Battlefield website. https://www.nps.gov/anti/learn/photosmultimedia/tour-stop-8.htm.

————. "Tour Stop 10: The Final Attack." Antietam National Battlefield website. https://www.nps.gov/anti/learn/photosmultimedia/tour-stop-10.htm.

————. "War at Your Doorstep: The Story of the Mumma Family at the Battle of Antietam." Educational document. https://www.nps.gov/common/uploads/teachers/lessonplans/CURRENT%20twhp%20mumma%20farm(508).pdf.

Nazari, Mansour, Tahereh Mehrabi, Seyed Mostafa Hosseini, and Mohammed Yousef Alikhani. "Bacterial Contamination of Adult House Flies (*Musca domestica*) and Sensitivity of These Bacteria to Various Antibiotics, Captured from Hamadan City, Iran." *Journal of Clinical and Diagnostic Research* 11, no. 4 (2017): DC04–7. https://doi.org/10.7860/JCDR/2017/23939.9720.

Nelson, John H. "Antietam Hospital." WHILBR. http://www.whilbr.org/itemdetail.aspx?idEntry=2345&dtPointer=0.

————. "Battle of Antietam: Union Surgeons and Civilian Volunteers Help the Wounded." HistoryNet.com.https://www.historynet.com/battle-of-antietam-union-surgeons-and-civilian-volunteers-help-the-wounded.htm.

Obituaries. *Gospel Visitor* (Columbiana, OH) 13, no. 1–12 (January 1863): 63. https://archive.org/details/gospel3112kurt/page/n69/mode/2up.

Orr, Timothy. "This is Not the Way We Bury Folks at Home: Killed in the West Woods, Part 3." *Tales from the Army of the Potomac* (blog). June 10, 2015. http://talesfromaop.blogspot.com/2015/06/this-is-not-way-we-bury-folks-at-home.html?m=1.

Park, Robert E. "The Twelfth Alabama Infantry, Confederate States Army," *Southern Historical Society Papers* 33 (January/December 1905). Richmond, VA: Rev. J. Wm. Jones. 193-296.

Pawlak, Kevin. "Railroads—Tracks to the Antietam: The Railroad Supplies the Army of the Potomac, September 18, 1862." Emerging Civil War website, October 27, 2018. https://emergingcivilwar.com/2018/10/27/railroads-tracks-to-the-antietam-the-railroad-supplies-the-army-of-the-potomac-september-18-1862/.

————. "What Did Antietam's Cornfield Look Like in September 1862?" *Antietam Brigades* (blog). March 1, 2020. http://antietambrigades.blogspot.com/2020/03/what-did-antietams-cornfield-look-like.html.

Penn State Extension. "Horse Stable Manure Management." September 25, 2019. https://extension.psu.edu/horse-stable-manure-management.

Perry, Kristina. "Contamination and Collapse: Human Settlement and Karst." Abstract, San Francisco State University, May 21, 1999. http://online.sfsu.edu/jerry/geog810/1999/Perry.html.

Pittsburgh Press. "Wedded 65 Years." December 4, 1927, 101.

Powell, Michael. "Civil Liberties in Crisis." Online article, Crossroads of War. http://www.crossroadsofwar.org/discover-the-story/civil-liberties-in-crisis/civil-liberties-in-crisis-full-story/.

Recker, Stephen J. "O. T. Reilly—Relic Collector and Early Antietam Tour Guide." HistoryNet. https://www.historynet.com/o-t-reilly-relic-collector-and-early-antietam-tour-guide.htm.

Reimer, Terry. "Wounds, Ammunition, and Amputation." National Museum of Civil War Medicine, November 9, 2007. http://www.civilwarmed.org/surgeons-call/amputation1/.

Rose Hill Cemetery. "History of Rose Hill." Rose Hill Cemetery website. https://rosehillcemeteryofmd.org/rich-in-history/history-of-rose-hill/.

Ruby, Thomas, Laura McLaughlin, Smita Gopinath, and Denise Monack. "Salmonella's Long-Term Relationship with its Host." *FEMS Microbiology Reviews* 36, no. 3 (May 2012): 600-615, https://doi.org/10.1111/j.1574-6976.2012.00332.x.

Schell, Frank H. "Sketching Under Fire at Antietam: A War Correspondent's Personal Account of His Experience During the Battle." *McClure's Magazine* 22 (November 1903–April 1904): 418-29.

Schamel, Charles E. "Untapped Resources: Private Claims and Private Legislation in the Records of the U.S. Congress." *Prologue* 27, no. 1 (Spring 1995). https://www.archives.gov/publications/prologue/1995/spring/private-claims-1.html.

Schmidt, Alann. "Battlefield Burials After Antietam: A Most Disagreeable Duty." *Antietam Journal* (blog). October 22, 2013. http://antietamjournal.blogspot.com/2013/10/v-behaviorurldefault vmlo.html.

Schooley, Pat. "Kef-Poff Farm: Early 1800s farmhouse served as a hospital after Antietam." *The Daily Mail* [Hagerstown, MD], September 5, 1997.

Shipe, J. Scott. "Sharpsburg Maryland—Typhoid Waterborne Outbreak—1862–63. Historical Analysis." YouTube video. *Water Advocacy*, February 20, 2019. https://www.youtube.com/watch?v=XgqCIvo5lJ0.

Skelly, Christine. "One Horse or a Hundred: Manure and Water Don't Mix." Michigan State University, October 23, 2015. https://www.canr.msu.edu/resources/one_horse_or_a_hundred_manure_and_water_dont_mix_wo1020.

Slawson, Robert G. "The Story of the Pile of Limbs." National Museum of Civil War Medicine, December 6, 2018. http://www.civilwarmed.org/surgeons-call/limbs/.

Smith, Crystal. "Horse Manure Management." *VCE Publications*, May 1, 2009. https://www.pubs.ext.vt.edu/406/406-208/406-208.html.

Smith, John P. "No Civilian Died in the Great Battle of Antietam in '62." *Morning Herald* [Hagerstown, MD], January 25, 1951, 2.

Snyder, Keith. Televised C-SPAN interview, September 16, 2012. https://www.c-span.org/video/?307917-103/keith-snyder-battle-antietam.

Snyder, Timothy R., and Jim Surkamp. "Destroy the C & O Canal—Fall, 1862." *Civil War Scholars* (blog). April 4, 2014. http://civilwarscholars.com/2014/04/destroy-the-co-canal-fall-1862-by-t-r-snyder-and-jim-surkamp/.

"Sore Tongue in Horses." *American Turf Register and Sporting Magazine* 2, no. 4 (December 1830), 169.

Stickley, Ezra E. "The Battle of Sharpsburg," *Confederate Veteran* 22, no. 2 (1914): 66-67.

Stiverson, Greg. "Washington Confederate Cemetery, Hagerstown." *The Archivist's Bulldog*, Maryland State Archives, Annapolis, MD, vol. 7, no. 2, January 25, 1993. https://msa.maryland.gov/msa/refserv/bulldog/bull93/html/bull93.html.

Sundman, Jim. "Disease: A Tale of Two Regiments (Part 2)." *Emerging Civil War* (blog). January 16, 2012. https://emergingcivilwar.com/2012/01/16/disease-a-tale-of-two-regiments-part-2/.

Swine Health Information Center. "Vesicular Stomatitis Virus." Center for Food Security & Public Health, College of Veterinary Medicine, Iowa State University, November 2015. https://www.swinehealth.org/wp-content/uploads/2016/03/Vesicular-stomatitis-virus-VSV.pdf.

Thomas, William G. III. "Nothing Ought to Astonish Us: Confederate Civilians in the 1864 Shenandoah Valley Campaign." *The Shenandoah Valley Campaign of 1864.* Edited by Gary W. Gallagher. Chapel Hill: University of North Carolina Press, 2006, 222-56.

Town of Boonsboro, Maryland. "Historic Walking Tour." https://www.town.boonsboro.md.us/historicboonsborowalkingtour.

U.S. Army Medical Department, Office of Medical History. "Louis Caspar Duncan, M.D." https://history.amedd.army.mil/booksdocs/rev/MedMen/LouisCDuncan.html.

Walsh, Michael. "Typhoid Fever." Infection Landscapes, November 10, 2011. http://www.infectionlandscapes.org/2011/11/typhoid-fever.html.

Warner, Harry. "Battle of Sharpsburg's Effect on Civilians." *The Daily Mail* [Hagerstown, MD], September 21, 1976, 4.

Washington County Health Department, Environmental Health Division. "Source Water Assessment Report: Washington County, Maryland." April 2006.

Washington County Historical Trust. "198—Burnside's Headquarters, Circa 1840. South of Sharpsburg, MD." http://washingtoncountyhistoricaltrust.org/198-burnside-headquarters-circa-1840-south-of-sharpsburg-md/.

Weidman, Budge. "Black Soldiers in the Civil War." National Archives. https://www.archives.gov/education/lessons/blacks-civil-war/article.html.

Whatley, Theodore R., George W. Comstock, Howard J. Garber, and Fernando S. Sanchez, Jr. "A Waterborne Outbreak of Infectious Hepatitis in a Small Maryland Town." *American Journal of Epidemiology* 87, no. 1 (January 1968): 138-47. https://doi.org/10.1093/oxfordjournals.aje.a120794.

Williamson, Blair. "Reminiscing the Rails: Rail Collision Forces Name Change From Sharpsburg to Antietam Station." *Maryland Cracker Barrel* (February/March 2005), 32-34.

Williamson, Samuel H. "Purchasing Power Today of a U.S. Dollar Transaction in the Past." MeasuringWorth, 2020. https://www.measuringworth.com/calculators/ppowerus/index2.php.

Woodring, Frank. "Window to Yesterday." *Maryland Cracker Barrel* (August/September 1992), 14-17.

World Health Organization. "Diarrhoeal Disease." May 2, 2017. https://www.who.int/en/news-room/fact-sheets/detail/diarrhoeal-disease.

———. "Management of Dead Bodies: Frequently Asked Questions." November 2, 2016. https://www.who.int/hac/techguidance/management-of-dead-bodies-qanda/en/.

———. "Water Sanitation Hygiene: Are There Disease Risks from Dead Bodies and What Should Be Done for Safe Disposal?" https://www.who.int/water_sanitation_health/emergencies/qa/emergencies_qa8/en/.

Wright, Cynthia. "*Arctostaphylos uva-ursi*, Bearberry." National Park Service, NPS History Electronic Library. http://npshistory.com/publications/lewi/bearberry.pdf.

Zychowski, Józef, and Tomasz Bryndal. "Impact of Cemeteries on Groundwater Contamination by Bacteria and Viruses—a Review." *Journal of Water and Health* 13, no. 2 (June 1, 2015): 285-301. doi: https://doi.org/10.2166/wh.2014.119.

Online Databases

Ancestry, https://www.ancestry.com/

  Civil War Draft Registrations Records, 1863–1865

  Death, Cemetery, and Obituary Records

  Newspaper Articles

  United States Federal Census, Slave Schedules, Sharpsburg, Maryland, 1850–1860

  United States Federal Census, Population Schedules, Subdivision 2, Washington County, Maryland, 1850

  United States Federal Census, Population Schedules, 1860–1880, 1900–1930

    Districts of Bakersville, Boonsboro, Keedysville, Sharpsburg, Rohrersville, and Tilghmanton

Antietam on the Web, http://antietam.aotw.org/

Crossroads of War (Civil War database for Western Maryland), https://www.crossroadsofwar.org/

Fairview Cemetery Records. Town of Keedysville, https://keedysvillemd.com/portfolio/fairview-cemetery-records/

Find a Grave (Burial records), https://www.findagrave.com/

Hathitrust Digital Library (Archival materials), https://www.hathitrust.org/

Internet Archive Digital Library (Archival materials), https://archive.org/

Maryland Historic Trust, Crownsville, MD, https://mht.maryland.gov/

Maryland Inventory of Historic Properties. Architectural Survey Reports and National Register of Historic Places forms, https://mht.maryland.gov/research_mihp.shtml

    F-7-140 "Frederick Junction (Monocacy Junction, Araby)"

    WA-II-034 "Blackford's Ford (Boteler's Ford, Packhorse Ford)"

    WA-II-108 "Showman Farm"

    WA-II-110 "Mt. Pleasant Secondary Dwelling"

    WA-II-151 "Avey-Stransky House"

    WA-II-255 "Snyder-Thomas Farmstead"

    WA-II-279 "Joseph R. Poffenberger Farm"

    WA-II-281 "Middlekauff-Poffenberger Farm"

    WA-II-297 "Aluminum Sided Farmhouse"

    WA-II-298 "Ruins of Log House (Locher-Poffenberger Farm)"

    WA-II-331 "Joseph Parks Farm (Log Farmhouse, Antietam Creek, Cunningham Farm)"

    WA-II-332 "Wilson-Miller Farm"

    WA-II-368 "Conococheague Sportman's Club (Blackford Cement Company)"

    WA-II-381 "Miller's Sawmill Vicinity"

    WA-II-397 "Log and Frame Farmstead"

    WA-II-398 "Frame Farmstead"

    WA-II-407 "Late 19th Century Farmhouse"

    WA-II-408 "Mid 19th Century Brick Farmstead"

    WA-II-461 "Part of Mt. Pleasant"

    WA-II-541 "Grove-Delauney House"

    WA-II-702 "Tolson's Chapel; Black A.M.E. Church"

WA-II-702 "Tolson's Chapel." National Register of Historic Places Registration Form

WA-II-703 "Piper House"

WA-II-723 "Sharpsburg Historic District"

WA-II-1112 "Keedysville Survey District"

WA-II-1141 "Pat Holland Property (D. Reel House)"

WA-II-1142 "Morgan Property, Ruin (Colonel John Miller House)"

WA-II-1143 "Morgan Property (Portion of the Mt. Pleasant Estate of Captain Joseph Chapline)"

WA-II-1145 "Keedysville Historic District." National Register of Historic Places Registration Form

Medusa (Database of Maryland's architectural and archaeological sites and standing structures) https://mht.maryland.gov/secure/medusa/

Maryland Tombstone Transcription Project (Washington County burial records) http://www.usgwtombstones.org/maryland/maryland.html

National Park Service. Civil War Soldiers and Sailors System (Military service records) https://www.nps.gov/civilwar/soldiers-and-sailors-database.htm

Washington County Free Library (Genealogy resources) https://www.washcolibrary.org/
Cemetery and Death Records
Historic Newspaper Index Project (1790-1890)
Marriage Records (1861-1919)
Obituaries (1790-2020)

Dissertations and Theses

Clark, James T. "The United States Court of Claims With a Special Consideration of 'Congressional Reference' Cases." Ph.D. dissertation, Georgetown University Graduate School of Law, 1934–1935.

Husky, Nancy. "Coffman Farm: From Deer Path to Tourism—How a Transportation Network Shaped a Homestead." Thesis, University of Leicester, 2004.

Trail, Susan W. "Remembering Antietam: Commemoration and Preservation of a Civil War Battlefield." Ph.D. dissertation, University of Maryland, 2005. https://drum.lib.umd.edu/handle/1903/2353.

Index

Steven Cowie earned a degree from California State University, Long Beach. As part of the Los Angeles film industry, he penned spec screenplays and sold his award-winning short film to the Sundance Channel. A lifelong student of the Civil War, Cowie dedicated fifteen years to exclusively researching the Battle of Antietam. *When Hell Came to Sharpsburg* is his first book.